Connected Mathematics™

Bits and Pieces I

Understanding Rational Numbers

Teacher's Edition

Glenda Lappan
James T. Fey
William M. Fitzgerald
Susan N. Friel
Elizabeth Difanis Phillips

Developed at Michigan State University

DALE SEYMOUR PUBLICATIONS®
MENLO PARK, CALIFORNIA

Connected Mathematics™ was developed at Michigan State University with financial support from the Michigan State University Office of the Provost, Computing and Technology, and the College of Natural Science.

This material is based upon work supported by the National Science Foundation under Grant No. MDR 9150217.

This project was supported, in part,
by the
National Science Foundation
Opinions expressed are those of the authors
and not necessarily those of the Foundation

The Michigan State University authors and administration have agreed that all MSU royalties arising from this publication will be devoted to purposes supported by the Department of Mathematics and the MSU Mathematics Education Enrichment Fund.

This book is published by Dale Seymour Publications®, an imprint of Addison Wesley Longman, Inc.

Dale Seymour Publications
2725 Sand Hill Road
Menlo Park, CA 94025
Customer Service: 800 872-1100

Managing Editor: Catherine Anderson
Project Editor: Stacey Miceli
Book Editor: Mali Apple
Revision Editor: James P. McAuliffe
ESL Consultant: Nancy Sokol Green
Production/Manufacturing Director: Janet Yearian
Production/Manufacturing Coordinators: Claire Flaherty, Alan Noyes
Design Manager: John F. Kelly
Photo Editor: Roberta Spieckerman
Design: Don Taka
Composition: London Road Design, Palo Alto, CA
Electronic Prepress Revision: A. W. Kingston Publishing Services, Chandler, AZ
Illustrations: Pauline Phung, Margaret Copeland, James Larson, Scott Baldridge, and Ray Godfrey
Cover: Ray Godfrey

Photo Acknowledgements: 31 © Paul Mozell/Stock, Boston; 39 © James R. Holland/Stock, Boston; 51 © Charles Orrico/SuperStock, Inc.; 57 © Bob Daemmrich/The Image Works; 58 © George Bellerose/Stock, Boston; 68 © Gary Neil Corbett/SuperStock, Inc.; 77 © Gary Walts/The Image Works

DALE
SEYMOUR
PUBLICATIONS®

Order number 45810
ISBN 1-57232-615-8

3 4 5 6 7 8 9 10-ML-01 00 99 98

The Connected Mathematics Project Staff

Project Directors

James T. Fey
University of Maryland

William M. Fitzgerald
Michigan State University

Susan N. Friel
University of North Carolina at Chapel Hill

Glenda Lappan
Michigan State University

Elizabeth Difanis Phillips
Michigan State University

Project Manager

Kathy Burgis
Michigan State University

Technical Coordinator

Judith Martus Miller
Michigan State University

Collaborating Teachers/Writers

Mary K. Bouck
Portland, Michigan

Jacqueline Stewart
Okemos, Michigan

Curriculum Development Consultants

David Ben-Chaim
Weizmann Institute

Alex Friedlander
Weizmann Institute

Eleanor Geiger
University of Maryland

Jane Mitchell
University of North Carolina at Chapel Hill

Anthony D. Rickard
Alma College

Evaluation Team

Mark Hoover
Michigan State University

Diane V. Lambdin
Indiana University

Sandra K. Wilcox
Michigan State University

Judith S. Zawojewski
National-Louis University

Graduate Assistants

Scott J. Baldridge
Michigan State University

Angie S. Eshelman
Michigan State University

M. Faaiz Gierdien
Michigan State University

Jane M. Keiser
Indiana University

Angela S. Krebs
Michigan State University

James M. Larson
Michigan State University

Ronald Preston
Indiana University

Tat Ming Sze
Michigan State University

Sarah Theule-Lubienski
Michigan State University

Jeffrey J. Wanko
Michigan State University

Field Test Production Team

Katherine Oesterle
Michigan State University

Stacey L. Otto
University of North Carolina at Chapel Hill

Teacher/Assessment Team

Kathy Booth
Waverly, Michigan

Anita Clark
Marshall, Michigan

Theodore Gardella
Bloomfield Hills, Michigan

Yvonne Grant
Portland, Michigan

Linda R. Lobue
Vista, California

Suzanne McGrath
Chula Vista, California

Nancy McIntyre
Troy, Michigan

Linda Walker
Tallahassee, Florida

Software Developer

Richard Burgis
East Lansing, Michigan

Development Center Directors

Nicholas Branca
San Diego State University

Dianne Briars
Pittsburgh Public Schools

Frances R. Curcio
New York University

Perry Lanier
Michigan State University

J. Michael Shaughnessy
Portland State University

Charles Vonder Embse
Central Michigan University

Field Test Coordinators

Michelle Bohan
Queens, New York

Melanie Branca
San Diego, California

Alecia Devantier
Shepherd, Michigan

Jenny Jorgensen
Flint, Michigan

Sandra Kralovec
Portland, Oregon

Sonia Marsalis
Flint, Michigan

William Schaeffer
Pittsburgh, Pennsylvania

Karma Vince
Toledo, Ohio

Virginia Wolf
Pittsburgh, Pennsylvania

Shirel Yaloz
Queens, New York

Student Assistants

Laura Hammond
David Roche
Courtney Stoner
Jovan Trpovski
Julie Valicenti
Michigan State University

Patricia Wagner
Holmes Middle School

Greg Williams
Gundry Elementary School

Lansing
Susan Bissonette
Waverly Middle School

Kathy Booth
Waverly East Intermediate School

Carole Campbell
Waverly East Intermediate School

Gary Gillespie
Waverly East Intermediate School

Denise Kehren
Waverly Middle School

Virginia Larson
Waverly East Intermediate School

Kelly Martin
Waverly Middle School

Laurie Metevier
Waverly East Intermediate School

Craig Paksi
Waverly East Intermediate School

Tony Pecoraro
Waverly Middle School

Helene Rewa
Waverly East Intermediate School

Arnold Stiefel
Waverly Middle School

Portland
Bill Carlton
Portland Middle School

Kathy Dole
Portland Middle School

Debby Flate
Portland Middle School

Yvonne Grant
Portland Middle School

Terry Keusch
Portland Middle School

John Manzini
Portland Middle School

Mary Parker
Portland Middle School

Scott Sandborn
Portland Middle School

Shepherd
Steve Brant
Shepherd Middle School

Marty Brock
Shepherd Middle School

Cathy Church
Shepherd Middle School

Ginny Crandall
Shepherd Middle School

Craig Ericksen
Shepherd Middle School

Natalie Hackney
Shepherd Middle School

Bill Hamilton
Shepherd Middle School

Julie Salisbury
Shepherd Middle School

Sturgis
Sandra Allen
Eastwood Elementary School

Margaret Baker
Eastwood Elementary School

Steven Baker
Eastwood Elementary School

Keith Barnes
Sturgis Middle School

Wilodean Beckwith
Eastwood Elementary School

Darcy Bird
Eastwood Elementary School

Bill Dickey
Sturgis Middle School

Ellen Eisele
Sturgis Middle School

James Hoelscher
Sturgis Middle School

Richard Nolan
Sturgis Middle School

J. Hunter Raiford
Sturgis Middle School

Cindy Sprowl
Eastwood Elementary School

Leslie Stewart
Eastwood Elementary School

Connie Sutton
Eastwood Elementary School

Traverse City
Maureen Bauer
Interlochen Elementary School

Ivanka Berskshire
East Junior High School

Sarah Boehm
Courtade Elementary School

Marilyn Conklin
Interlochen Elementary School

Nancy Crandall
Blair Elementary School

Fran Cullen
Courtade Elementary School

Eric Dreier
Old Mission Elementary School

Lisa Dzierwa
Cherry Knoll Elementary School

Ray Fouch
West Junior High School

Ed Hargis
Willow Hill Elementary School

Richard Henry
West Junior High School

Dessie Hughes
Cherry Knoll Elementary School

Ruthanne Kladder
Oak Park Elementary School

Bonnie Knapp
West Junior High School

Sue Laisure
Sabin Elementary School

Stan Malaski
Oak Park Elementary School

Jody Meyers
Sabin Elementary School

Marsha Myles
East Junior High School

Mary Beth O'Neil
Traverse Heights Elementary School

Jan Palkowski
East Junior High School

Karen Richardson
Old Mission Elementary School

Kristin Sak
Bertha Vos Elementary School

Mary Beth Schmitt
East Junior High School

Mike Schrotenboer
Norris Elementary School

Gail Smith
Willow Hill Elementary School

Karrie Tufts
Eastern Elementary School

Mike Wilson
East Junior High School

Tom Wilson
West Junior High School

Minnesota

Minneapolis

Betsy Ford
Northeast Middle School

New York

East Elmhurst

Allison Clark
Louis Armstrong Middle School

Dorothy Hershey
Louis Armstrong Middle School

J. Lewis McNeece
Louis Armstrong Middle School

Rossana Perez
Louis Armstrong Middle School

Merna Porter
Louis Armstrong Middle School

Marie Turini
Louis Armstrong Middle School

North Carolina

Durham

Everly Broadway
Durham Public Schools

Thomas Carson
Duke School for Children

Mary Hebrank
Duke School for Children

Bill O'Connor
Duke School for Children

Ruth Pershing
Duke School for Children

Peter Reichert
Duke School for Children

Elizabeth City

Rita Banks
Elizabeth City Middle School

Beth Chaundry
Elizabeth City Middle School

Amy Cuthbertson
Elizabeth City Middle School

Deni Dennison
Elizabeth City Middle School

Jean Gray
Elizabeth City Middle School

John McMenamin
Elizabeth City Middle School

Nicollette Nixon
Elizabeth City Middle School

Malinda Norfleet
Elizabeth City Middle School

Joyce O'Neal
Elizabeth City Middle School

Clevie Sawyer
Elizabeth City Middle School

Juanita Shannon
Elizabeth City Middle School

Terry Thorne
Elizabeth City Middle School

Rebecca Wardour
Elizabeth City Middle School

Leora Winslow
Elizabeth City Middle School

Franklinton

Susan Haywood
Franklinton Elementary School

Clyde Melton
Franklinton Elementary School

Louisburg

Lisa Anderson
Terrell Lane Middle School

Jackie Frazier
Terrell Lane Middle School

Pam Harris
Terrell Lane Middle School

Ohio

Toledo

Bonnie Bias
Hawkins Elementary School

Marsha Jackish
Hawkins Elementary School

Lee Jagodzinski
DeVeaux Junior High School

Norma J. King
Old Orchard Elementary School

Margaret McCready
Old Orchard Elementary School

Carmella Morton
DeVeaux Junior High School

Karen C. Rohrs
Hawkins Elementary School

Marie Sahloff
DeVeaux Junior High School

L. Michael Vince
McTigue Junior High School

Brenda D. Watkins
Old Orchard Elementary School

Oregon

Portland

Roberta Cohen
Catlin Gabel School

David Ellenberg
Catlin Gabel School

Sara Normington
Catlin Gabel School

Karen Scholte-Arce
Catlin Gabel School

West Linn

Marge Burack
Wood Middle School

Tracy Wygant
Athey Creek Middle School

Canby

Sandra Kralovec
Ackerman Middle School

Pennsylvania

Pittsburgh

Sheryl Adams
Reizenstein Middle School

Sue Barie
Frick International Studies Academy

Suzie Berry
Frick International Studies Academy

Richard Delgrosso
Frick International Studies Academy

Janet Falkowski
Frick International Studies Academy

Joanne George
Reizenstein Middle School

Harriet Hopper
Reizenstein Middle School

Chuck Jessen
Reizenstein Middle School

Ken Labuskes
Reizenstein Middle School

Barbara Lewis
Reizenstein Middle School

Sharon Mihalich
Reizenstein Middle School

Marianne O'Connor
Frick International Studies Academy

Mark Sammartino
Reizenstein Middle School

Washington

Seattle

Chris Johnson
University Preparatory Academy

Rick Purn
University Preparatory Academy

Contents

Rational numbers are at the heart of the middle-grades experience with number concepts. The concepts of fractions, decimals, and percents are often difficult for students. Research tells us that part of the reason for students' confusion about rational numbers is a consequence of the rush to symbol manipulation with fractions and decimals. Students need time to develop a deep understanding of fractions and decimals. The investigations in *Bits and Pieces I* ask students to make sense of fractions, decimals, and percents in different contexts.

The many different and powerful interpretations of and models for rational numbers can make grasping ideas about such numbers difficult. To gain a mature knowledge of rational numbers, students must be able to handle these various interpretations. We have carefully chosen the interpretations and models used in the unit. Some models are more powerful than others, as they contribute to developing the meaning of rational numbers and to understanding operations on rational numbers.

This unit does not teach specific algorithms for work with rational numbers. Instead, it helps the teacher create a supportive environment for students to grapple with interesting problems in which ideas of fractions, decimals, and percents are imbedded. As students work—individually, in groups, and as a class—they will develop ways of thinking about rational numbers. The teacher's role is to help students make explicit their growing ideas about this world of rational numbers. The intent of this unit is to provide a rich set of experiences that focus on developing meaning.

In this unit, students will meet several interpretations and models of fractions. These have been carefully chosen so that the move between problems will add to a deepening knowledge and comfort with fractions.

Interpretations of Fractions

The major interpretations on which this unit focuses are

- fractions as parts of a whole

- fractions as measures or quantities

- fractions as indicated division

- fractions as decimals

- fractions as percents

Other interpretations—such as fractions as operators ("stretchers" or "shrinkers") and fractions as rates, ratios, or parts of a proportion—are postponed until later grades.

Fractions as Parts of a Whole

This interpretation of rational numbers is applied in situations that are continuous and in situations that consider discrete objects. The important characteristic is that this interpretation depends on partitioning an object or a set into equal-size parts and making a comparison of some of the parts to the whole object or set. For example, if there are 27 students in the class and 13 are girls, the part of the whole that is girls can be represented as $\frac{13}{27}$.

In the following diagram, two parts are shaded.

The shaded portion can be represented as $\frac{2}{3}$. The 3 tells into how many equal-size parts the whole has been divided, and the 2 tells how many of the equal-size parts have been shaded.

In the part-whole interpretation of fractions, the difficulties for students center on the following:

- determining what the whole is

- subdividing the whole into equal-size parts—not equal *shape,* but equal *size*

- recognizing how many parts are needed to represent the situation

- forming the fraction by placing the parts needed over the number of parts into which the whole has been divided

Fractions as Measures or Quantities

In this interpretation, a fraction is thought of as a number. For example, a fraction can be a measurement that is "in between" two whole measures. Students meet this every day in such references as $2\frac{1}{2}$ feet or 11.5 million people. Understanding this interpretation is important for students' mathematical development, and it leads to comparison of fractions and operations on fractions.

Fractions as Indicated Divisions

To move with flexibility between fraction and decimal representations of rational numbers, students need to understand how fractions can be thought of as indicated divisions. Sharing is a natural context in which to help students see how this interpretation is related to whole-number division. If students see that sharing 36 apples among 6 people calls for division (36 ÷ 6 = 6 apples each), then they can move to an understanding that sharing 3 apples among 8 people calls for dividing 3 by 8 to find out how many each person receives.

Fractions as Decimals

A byproduct of the division interpretation of fractions is the relationship between a fraction and decimal representation of the same quantity. For the fraction $\frac{2}{5}$, for example, we can find the decimal representation by dividing 2 by 5. Given the modern tools of calculators and computers, decimal representations are even more important today than in the past. Students need time to develop comfort and ease in moving between fractions and decimals, and they need to understand decimals in two ways:

- as special fractions with denominators of 10 and powers of 10

- as a natural extension of the place-value system for representing quantities less than 1

Fractions as Percents

Rather than treating fractions, decimals, and percents as separate topics, this unit seeks to build the connections between them. Students will see that the ideas and concepts are related and that the differences are in the symbols used to represent those ideas. Ten percent, 10%, is simply another way to represent 0.10 or 0.1, which is another way to represent $\frac{10}{100}$ or $\frac{1}{10}$. Percents are introduced as special names for parts of 100.

Models of Fractions

The models of rational numbers used throughout this unit were chosen because they connect directly to the interpretations of rational numbers that the unit raises. The models on which this unit focuses are

- fractions-strip models

- number-line models

- grid-area models

- partition models

Fraction-Strip Models

Students are introduced to fractions in a situation that uses a *fraction strip* as a model. Fraction strips can be created by dividing a strip of paper into equal-size parts by folding. This is a fraction strip for halves:

Number-Line Models

The collection of fraction strips are used to move to a number-line model of rational numbers. The *number-line model* helps make the connection to fractions as numbers or quantities. This is a number line for 0 to 2 with a few fractional quantities marked:

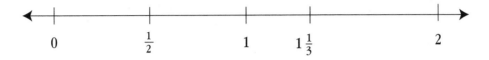

Grid-Area Models

Because 100 and powers of 10 are so useful in understanding decimals and percents, *grid-area models* are introduced and developed in this unit. This grid shows a shaded area of 12%.

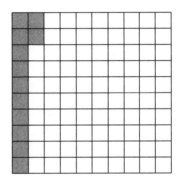

Partition Models

Students also use a more general model of fraction situations that is based on *partitioning an area,* such as a circle, into equal-size parts. The circle shows a shaded portion of $\frac{3}{10}$.

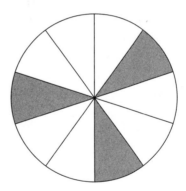

B*its and Pieces I* **was created to help students**

- Build an understanding of fractions, decimals, and percents and the relationships between and among these concepts and their representations

- Develop ways to model situations involving fractions, decimals, and percents

- Understand and use equivalent fractions to reason about situations

- Compare and order fractions

- Move flexibly between fraction, decimal, and percent representations

- Use 0, $\frac{1}{2}$, 1, and $1\frac{1}{2}$ as benchmarks to help estimate the size of a number or sum

- Develop and use benchmarks that relate different forms of representations of rational numbers (for example, 50% is the same as $\frac{1}{2}$ and 0.5)

- Use physical models and drawings to help reason about a situation

- Look for patterns and describe how to continue the pattern

- Use context to help reason about a situation

- Use estimation to understand a situation

The overall goal of Connected Mathematics is to help students develop sound mathematical habits. Through their work in this and other number units, students learn important questions to ask themselves about any situation that can be represented and modeled mathematically, such as: *When do we need to consider amounts that do not represent whole numbers? How can we represent concepts such as parts of a whole? Why can there be different fraction names for the same quantity? How can we tell when two names refer to the same quantity? How can we tell which of two fractions is greater or smaller? What are some situations in which fractions are commonly used? What value is there in having decimal names for fractional quantities? How can one change a fractional name to the equivalent decimal name? Why are fractions with a denominator of 100 useful? How is a percent like a fraction? What techniques can be used to find fractional, decimal, or percent names for the same quantity?*

Investigation 1: Fund-Raising Fractions

Students explore three components of understanding fractions: the visual model (fraction strips), word names for fractions, and symbols for fractions. The part-whole interpretation of fractions is developed. Students make fraction strips to study the progress toward a fund-raising goal. The aim is to focus on the meaning of such phrases as, "two thirds of the goal has been reached."

Investigation 2: Comparing Fractions

The most important concept in understanding and using rational numbers is equivalence of fractions. This concept underlies operations with fractions, changing representations of fractions, and reasoning proportionally. The context of comparing fraction strips is used to motivate an investigation of equivalence and the creation of a number line that contains all of the information of the individual fraction strips. The idea of using benchmarks to estimate the size of fractions and to make comparisons is introduced.

Investigation 3: Cooking with Fractions

The context of cooking—parts of cups or other measures often called for in recipes, and the need to make multiples of a recipe, sets the stage for introducing students to different kinds of area models for fractions. The square and the rectangle are particularly useful areas because they are easy to subdivide and to shade. The circle is explored because of its use in data analysis and probability.

Investigation 4: From Fractions to Decimals

Students are introduced to decimal representations of fractions and explore the place-value interpretation of decimals. They investigate a 100-square grid and explore how it could continue to be subdivided to show 1000 parts or 10,000 parts. This process of subdividing and naming the new parts is very important mathematically; the underpinnings of the infinite process are met in this problem. The process will continue to help students understand equivalence of fraction and equivalence of decimals as well as to see the connections between fractions and decimals.

Investigation 5: Moving Between Fractions and Decimals

This investigation proposes a situation in which fractions with denominators larger than students' fraction strips show must be compared. Students find decimal estimates for fractions using the visual model. They are asked to consider whether fractions or decimals are easier to compare. Sharing is used as a context to motivate the division interpretation of fractions, leading to a strategy for changing a fraction into a decimal. Calculators are used to do the computation, providing additional evidence that the division interpretation as a way to find decimal equivalents makes sense.

Investigation 6: Out of One Hundred

By this time, students should feel comfortable with the meaning of fractions and decimals and be able to move back and forth between the two. Percents are now introduced as another form of representation. A database of information about cats is used as a context for understanding percent. Students are engaged in activities requiring them to move among fractions, decimals, and percents.

The ideas in *Bits and Pieces I* build on and connect to several big ideas in other Connected Mathematics units.

Big Idea	Prior Work	Future Work
understanding, comparing, and applying fractions	comparing whole numbers and finding least common multiples (*Prime Time*); studying 2-D shapes to understand better their use as area models (*Shapes and Designs*)	developing algorithms for performing calculations (*Bits and Pieces II*); using scale factors (*Stretching and Shrinking*); applying rational numbers (*Comparing and Scaling*); interpreting slope (*Moving Straight Ahead*); interpreting fractions as probabilities (*What Do You Expect?*); identifying and finding equivalent expressions (*Say It With Symbols*)
understanding, comparing, and applying decimals	comparing whole numbers; exploring multiples of 10 (*Prime Time*); studying 2-D shapes to understand better their use as area models (*Shapes and Designs*)	interpreting decimals as probabilities (*How Likely Is It?, What Do You Expect?*); applying rational numbers (*Bits and Pieces II, Comparing and Scaling, Samples and Populations*)
understanding, comparing, and applying percents	comparing whole numbers; finding the greatest common factor or least common multiple of two numbers (*Prime Time*); using area models to better understand percent as a comparison to 100 (*Shapes and Designs*)	applying rational numbers (*Bits and Pieces II, Comparing and Scaling, Samples and Populations*); interpreting percents as probabilities (*How Likely Is It?, What Do You Expect?*); working with statistics and data reported as percents (*Data Around Us*)
connecting fractions, decimals, and percents	studying multiples and exponents (*Prime Time*); studying 2-D shapes to better compare area models of fractions, decimals, and percents (*Shapes and Designs*); dividing whole numbers (*elementary school*)	using fractions, decimals, and percents as expressions of probabilities (*How Likely Is It?, What Do You Expect?, Samples and Populations*); using fractions and decimals as slopes or variable coefficients in equations (*Variables and Patterns; Moving Straight Ahead; Thinking with Mathematical Models; Growing, Growing, Growing; Frogs, Fleas, and Painted Cubes; Say It With Symbols*); connecting fractions, decimals, and percents by interpreting percentages and decimals as fractions (*Bits and Pieces II, Comparing and Scaling*)

Technology

Connected Mathematics was developed with the belief that calculators should always be available and that students should decide when to use them. For this reason, we do not designate specific problems as "calculator problems." Fraction calculators are *not* required. However, if fraction calculators are available, your students can use them as an additional tool for exploring the ideas of this unit.

Materials

For students

- Labsheets
- Calculators
- $8\frac{1}{2}$" strips of paper for making fraction strips
- Distinguishing Digits puzzle cards (provided as blackline masters)
- Scissors
- Rulers or other straightedges
- Colored cubes or tiles (optional)
- Blank transparency film (optional)
- Large sheets of blank paper (optional)
- Index cards (optional)
- Grid paper (optional; provided as a blackline master)

For the teacher

- Transparencies and transparency markers (optional)
- $8\frac{1}{2}$" fraction strips for the overhead projector
- 16 cm fraction strips for the overhead projector (optional; copy Labsheet 1.5 onto blank transparency film)
- $5\frac{2}{3}$" strips of paper (optional)
- A transparent centimeter ruler (optional)
- Transparency of newspaper advertisement (optional)

Pacing Chart

This pacing chart gives estimates of the class time required for each investigation and assessment piece. Shaded rows indicate opportunities for assessment.

Investigations and Assessments	Class Time
1 Fund-Raising Fractions	5 days
2 Comparing Fractions	5 days
Check-Up 1	$\frac{1}{2}$ day
3 Cooking with Fractions	2 days
Quiz	1 day
4 From Fractions to Decimals	3 days
5 Moving Between Fractions and Decimals	4 days
Check-Up 2	$\frac{1}{2}$ day
6 Out of One Hundred	4 days
Self-Assessment	Take home
Unit Test	1 day

Vocabulary

The following words and concepts are introduced and used in *Bits and Pieces I*. Concepts in the left column are those that are essential for student understanding of this and future units. The Descriptive Glossary gives descriptions of these and other words used in *Bits and Pieces I*.

Essential	Nonessential
decimal	base ten number system
denominator	benchmark
equivalent fraction	unit fraction
fraction	
numerator	
percent	

Assessment Summary

Embedded Assessment

Opportunities for informal assessment of student progress are embedded throughout *Bits and Pieces I* in the problems, the ACE questions, and the Mathematical Reflections. Suggestions for observing as students discover and explore mathematical ideas, for probing to guide their progress in developing concepts and skills, and for questioning to determine their level of understanding can be found in the *Launch, Explore,* or *Summarize* sections of all investigation problems. Some examples:

- Investigation 4, Problem 4.2 *Launch* (page 52b) suggests ways to assess your students's understanding of decimals.
- Investigation 2, Problem 2.5 *Explore* (page 30h) suggests questions you might ask to help your students think about how to label points on the number line with improper fractions.
- Investigation 1, Problem 1.4 *Summarize* (page 18h) suggests questions you might ask to assess your students' understanding of fractions of different wholes.

ACE Assignments

An ACE (Applications—Connections—Extensions) section appears at the end of each investigation. To help you assign ACE questions, a list of assignment choices is given in the margin next to the reduced student page for each problem. Each list indicates the ACE questions that students should be able to answer after they complete the problem.

Partner Quiz

One quiz, which may be given after Investigation 3, is provided with *Bits and Pieces I*. This quiz is designed to be completed by pairs of students with the opportunity for revision based on teacher feedback. You will find the quiz and its answer key in the Assessment Resources section. As an alternative to the quiz provided, you can construct your own quizzes by combining questions from the Question Bank, the quiz, and unassigned ACE questions.

Check-Ups

Two check-ups, which may be given after Investigations 2 and 5, are provided for use as quick quizzes or warm-up activities. Check-ups are designed for students to complete individually. You will find the check-ups, their answer keys, and a guide for assessing the check-ups in the Assessment Resources section.

Question Bank

A Question Bank provides questions you can use for homework, reviews, or quizzes. You will find the Question Bank and its answer key in the Assessment Resources section.

Notebook/Journal

Students should have notebooks to record and organize their work. In the notebooks will be their journals along with sections for vocabulary, homework, and quizzes and check-ups. In their journals, students can take notes, solve investigation problems, and record their mathematical reflections. You should assess student journals for completeness rather than correctness; journals should be seen as "safe" places where students can try out their thinking. A Notebook Checklist and a Self-Assessment are provided in the Assessment Resources section. The Notebook Checklist helps students organize their notebooks. The Self-Assessment guides students as they review their notebooks to determine which ideas they have mastered and which ideas they still need to work on.

The Unit Test

The final assessment for *Bits and Pieces I* is a two-part test. The first part is an individual, in-class unit test. The second part is a short individual research and writing assignment and is meant to be treated as a take-home portion to the test.

For the research and writing piece, students are to find two different articles that contain fractions, decimals, and/or percents. They are to write a one- to two-paragraph summary of each article, explaining how the rational numbers are used in the articles and what they represent.

Blackline masters for the in-class and take-home portions of the unit test, as well as an answer key for the in-class test, are provided in the Assessment Resources section.

Introducing Your Students to *Bits and Pieces I*

Several days before starting this unit, ask your students to find examples of how fractions, decimals, or percents are used in everyday life. Encourage them to look at advertisements, magazines, or newspapers or to interview an adult. On the day you start the unit, let your students present the examples they found. Ask students to explain what they think the fractions, decimals, or percents in their examples mean. Don't worry about getting correct explanations at this time; this excercise is meant to get students interested in this unit and to start them thinking about fractions. If you think an example is especially interesting, you may want to return to it later in the unit, when students can apply what they have learned to make sense of it.

When everyone has had a chance to share his or her example, discuss the three questions posed on the opening pages of the student edition. It is not necessary to come up with correct answers at this time. These questions are raised later in the unit when students have the skills necessary to answer them.

Bits and Pieces I

In a survey of 200 cat owners, 59% said they fed their pet only pet food, not human food. How many people is this?

Samuel is getting a snack for himself and his little brother. There are two candy bars in the refrigerator. Samuel takes half of one candy bar for himself and half of the other candy bar for his little brother. His little brother complains that Samuel got more. Samuel says that he got half and his brother got half. What might be the problem?

Tisia made 19 out of 30 free throws; Clarise made 8 out of 13; and Dorothea made 14 out of 21. Who is the best free-throw shooter?

Tips for the Linguistically Diverse Classroom

Enactment The Enactment technique is described in detail in *Getting to Know Connected Mathematics*. Students act out mini-scenes, using props, to make information comprehensible. Example: For the question about the pet food survey, one student could survey other students about what type of food they feed their pets. A survey, a can of pet food, and a sample of human food could be used as props.

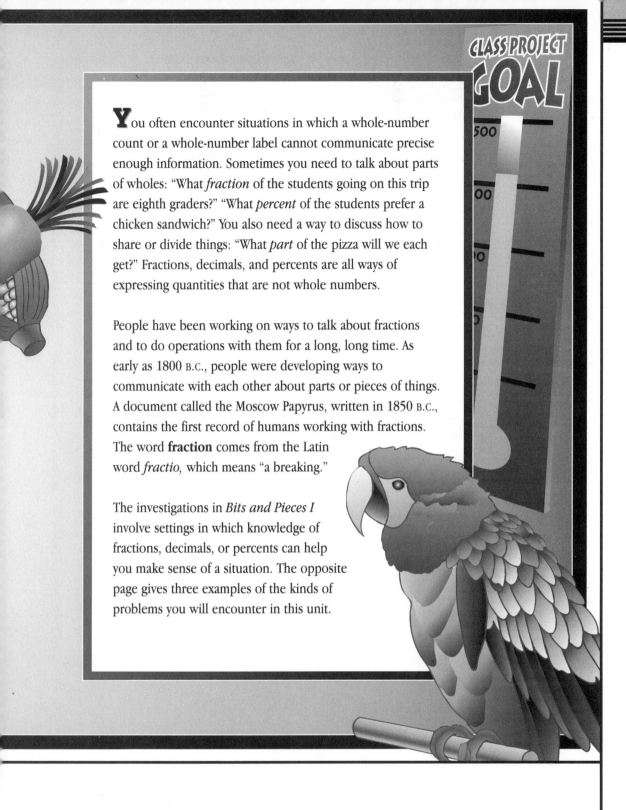

You often encounter situations in which a whole-number count or a whole-number label cannot communicate precise enough information. Sometimes you need to talk about parts of wholes: "What *fraction* of the students going on this trip are eighth graders?" "What *percent* of the students prefer a chicken sandwich?" You also need a way to discuss how to share or divide things: "What *part* of the pizza will we each get?" Fractions, decimals, and percents are all ways of expressing quantities that are not whole numbers.

People have been working on ways to talk about fractions and to do operations with them for a long, long time. As early as 1800 B.C., people were developing ways to communicate with each other about parts or pieces of things. A document called the Moscow Papyrus, written in 1850 B.C., contains the first record of humans working with fractions. The word **fraction** comes from the Latin word *fractio,* which means "a breaking."

The investigations in *Bits and Pieces I* involve settings in which knowledge of fractions, decimals, or percents can help you make sense of a situation. The opposite page gives three examples of the kinds of problems you will encounter in this unit.

Mathematical Highlights

The Mathematical Highlights page provides information to students and to parents and other family members. It gives students a preview of the activities and problems in *Bits and Pieces I*. As they work through the unit, students can refer back to the Mathematical Highlights page to review what they have learned and to preview what is still to come. This page also tells parents and other family members what mathematical ideas and activities will be covered as the class works through *Bits and Pieces I*.

Mathematical Highlights

In *Bits and Pieces I*, you will learn to represent and talk about fractions.

- Interpreting a thermometer display, which shows the progress of a sixth-grade fund-raising campaign, helps you understand fractions as parts of wholes.

- Fraction strips, which you fold and label yourself, give you a concrete model for visualizing fractions.

- Transferring the fractions from all of your strips onto a single number line lets you compare fractions with different denominators, find equivalent fractions, and locate benchmarks.

- Finding the possible ways to cut a pan of brownies into equal pieces shows you that fractions can be thought of as parts of regions. Planning a vegetable garden helps you think about expressing fractions as decimals.

- Finding equivalent fractions allows you to choose the best shooter to attempt a game-winning free throw.

- Using a new fraction strip, the hundredths strip, helps you find decimal estimates for all the marks on your other fraction strips.

- Distributing food items among care packages leads you to discover that a fraction is a way to indicate a division.

- A database of information about 100 cats introduces you to percents as a way to represent fractions.

- Rewriting sale signs for a pet store lets you apply what you have learned about moving between fractions, decimals, and percents.

Using a Calculator

In this unit, you will be able to use your calculator as you develop strategies for finding and checking equivalent fractions. A calculator is also useful for working with fractions in their decimal forms. As you work on the Connected Mathematics units, you decide whether to use a calculator to help you solve a problem.

The Investigations

The teaching materials for each investigation consist of three parts: an overview, the student pages with teaching outlines, and the detailed notes for teaching the investigation.

The overview of each investigation includes brief descriptions of the problems, the mathematical and problem-solving goals of the investigation, and a list of necessary materials.

Essential information for teaching the investigation is provided in the margins around the student pages. The "At a Glance" overviews are brief outlines of the Launch, Explore, and Summarize phases of each problem for reference as you work with the class. To help you assign homework, a list of "Assignment Choices" is provided next to each problem. Wherever space permits, answers to problems, follow-ups, ACE questions, and Mathematical Reflections appear next to the appropriate student pages.

The Teaching the Investigation section follows the student pages and is the heart of the Connected Mathematics curriculum. This section describes in detail the Launch, Explore, and Summarize phases for each problem. It includes all the information needed for teaching, along with suggestions for what you might say at key points in the teaching. Use this section to prepare lessons and as a guide for teaching an investigation.

Assessment Resources

The Assessment Resources section contains blackline masters and answer keys for the quiz, check-ups, the Question Bank, and the Unit Test. Blackline masters for the Notebook Checklist and the Self-Assessment are also given. These instruments support student self-evaluation, an important aspect of assessment in the Connected Mathematics curriculum. This section also includes a guide to assessing the check-ups and a discussion about altering assessment pieces for inclusion students.

Blackline Masters

The Blackline Masters section includes masters for all labsheets and transparencies. Blackline masters of grid paper and Distinguishing Digits puzzle cards are also provided.

Additional Practice

Practice pages for each investigation offer additional problems for students who need more practice with the basic concepts developed in the investigations as well as some continual review of earlier concepts.

Descriptive Glossary

The Descriptive Glossary provides descriptions and examples of the key concepts in *Bits and Pieces I*. These descriptions are not intended to be formal definitions, but are meant to give you an idea of how students might make sense of these important concepts.

Fund-Raising Fractions

In this lengthy but important investigation, students use fractions to describe the progress of various fund-raising activities at a typical school. This investigation develops the part-whole interpretation of fractions, explores the fraction-strip model for representing fractions, and shows how the symbolic representation of fractions relates to a physical model (the fraction strips).

In Problem 1.1, Reporting Our Progress, students write short reports describing the progress the sixth graders at Thurgood Marshall School have made toward their fund-raising goal. This activity lets you quickly assess your students' understanding of fractions as parts of wholes. In Problem 1.2, Using Fraction Strips, students are challenged to make fraction strips by folding paper and then to use these strips to investigate the progress of the sixth-grade fund-raiser at various stages. In Problem 1.3, Comparing Classes, students explore comparing fractions with different wholes. Problem 1.4, Exceeding the Goal, involves a fund-raiser in which the amount of money raised surpassed the goal; students must describe situations involving fractions greater than 1. Problem 1.5, Using Symbolic Form, begins to develop the number-line model of fractions. Students label parts of their fraction strips and begin to think about the meaning of the symbolic representation of fractions.

Mathematical and Problem-Solving Goals

- **To use the part-whole interpretation of fractions to create a set of fraction strips**

- **To relate the fraction-strip model to the part-whole interpretation of fractions and to the symbolic representation of fractions**

- **To understand the meaning of fractions larger than a whole**

- **To use fraction strips and symbolic representations of fractions to describe real-world situations**

Materials		
Problem	**For students**	**For the teacher**
All	Calculators	Transparencies 1.1 to 1.5 (optional)
1.2	$8\frac{1}{2}$" strips of paper (9 per student)	$8\frac{1}{2}$" fraction strips for the overhead projector
1.3	Fraction strips from Problem 1.2	$8\frac{1}{2}$" fraction strips for the overhead projector
1.4		$8\frac{1}{2}$" fraction strips for the overhead projector
1.5	Labsheet 1.5 (1 per student)	$8\frac{1}{2}$" fraction strips for the overhead projector, transparent centimeter ruler (optional), 16 cm fraction strips for the overhead projector (optional; copy Labsheet 1.5 onto blank transparency film)

Student Pages 5–18   Teaching the Investigation 18a–18k

Goal — $300

Fund-Raising Fractions

ast year students at Thurgood Marshall School organized three fund-raising projects to raise money for sports and band equipment. The eighth-grade class held a calendar sale in October, the seventh-grade class sold popcorn in January, and the sixth-grade class sold art, music, and sports posters in March. The three grades competed to raise the most money.

1.1 Reporting Our Progress

The sixth-grade class set a goal of raising $300 during its ten-day poster sale. On each day of the sale, the class's progress was marked on a large "thermometer" near the school office.

The thermometer at right shows the progress of the sixth-grade fund-raiser after two days of sales. The goal of $300 is marked near the top of the thermometer. Every day during the fund-raising campaign, the sixth-grade class officers gave a public-address announcement reporting their progress.

Problem 1.1

Write a short—but clever and informative—announcement to report the progress of the sixth-grade poster sale after two days. Be sure to mention what part of the sales goal of $300 had been reached and what part remained to be raised.

▪ Problem 1.1 Follow-Up

Describe the strategies you used to decide what part of the sales goal of $300 had been reached and what part remained to be raised.

Day 2

Sixth-Grade Poster Sale

Reporting Our Progress

At a Glance

Grouping: Small Groups

Launch

- Discuss the thermometer model often used to track the progress of fund-raisers.

- Introduce the story problem presented in the student edition.

Explore

- Circulate while students write public-address announcements, helping them to clarify their messages.

Summarize

- Have a few groups present and explain their announcements.

- As a class, analyze the strategies and information in the different announcements.

Answer to Problem 1.1

Answers will vary depending on how comfortable your students are with fractions, decimals, and percents. Your students may not be able to respond in a precise mathematical way. The thermometer is registering 25%, or one fourth ($\frac{1}{4}$), of the goal, so students have raised $75 of the $300 needed. The students still need to meet 75%, or three fourths ($\frac{3}{4}$), of their goal; they must still raise $225 of the $300. Some students may comment on the fact that the sixth-grade class has raised one fourth ($\frac{1}{4}$) of the goal in only one fifth ($\frac{1}{5}$) of the time allotted for the campaign.

Answers to Problem 1.1 Follow-Up

See page 18j.

Assignment Choices

Challenge students to look for examples of fractions and decimals used outside of school.

1.2

Using Fraction Strips

Launch

- Discuss the thermometers showing the progress of the sixth-grade fund-raisers.

- Demonstrate how to make fraction strips for halves and thirds.

Explore

- Circulate while students explore techniques for making fraction strips.

- As a class, discuss the various folding techniques students found, focusing on the concepts of part and whole.

- Have students continue their work on the problem.

Summarize

- Have students share their estimates and strategies.

- Focus students on how fraction strips allow us to estimate parts of wholes.

Assignment Choices

ACE question 26

1.2 Using Fraction Strips

The thermometers on the next page show the progress of the sixth-grade poster sale after two, four, six, eight, and ten days. One way to determine the progress of the fund-raiser is to use strips of paper the same length as the distance from the bottom of the thermometer to the goal. By folding the strips into fractional parts, you can determine what part of the goal has been reached.

Problem 1.2

Start with nine $8\frac{1}{2}$-inch strips. Fold the strips to show halves, thirds, fourths, fifths, sixths, eighths, ninths, tenths, and twelfths. Mark the folds in the strips with a pencil so you can see them more easily.

Use your strips to estimate the sixth-grade class's progress after two, four, six, eight, and ten days.

■ Problem 1.2 Follow-Up

1. Which fraction strips were easy to fold? Why?
2. Which fraction strips were difficult to fold? Why?

Answer to Problem 1.2

On day 2, the students had reached one fourth, two eighths, or three twelfths of their goal. On day 4, they had reached one third, two sixths, three ninths, or four twelfths of their goal. On day 6, they had reached three fifths or six tenths of their goal. On day 8, they had reached three fourths, six eighths, or nine twelfths of their goal. On day 10, they had reached five sixths or ten twelfths of their goal.

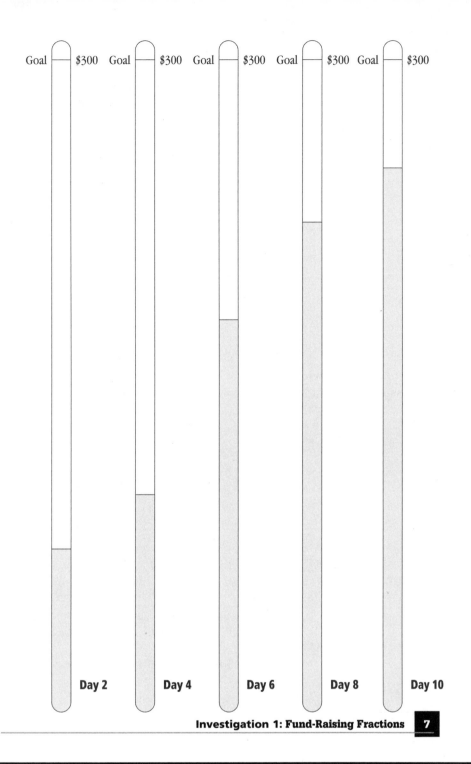

Goal $300 Goal $300 Goal $300 Goal $300 Goal $300

Day 2   Day 4   Day 6   Day 8   Day 10

Investigation 1: Fund-Raising Fractions **7**

Answers to Problem 1.2 Follow-Up

1. Answers will vary. Students may indicate that the halves, fourths, and eighths strips were easy to fold because they simply required repeatedly folding in half.

2. Answers will vary. Students may indicate that the thirds, fifths, and ninths strips (and perhaps the sixths, tenths, and twelfths strips) were hard to fold because they could not be made by simply folding strips in half.

1.3

Comparing Classes

Grouping:
Small Groups

Launch

- Talk about the thermometers showing the results of the three grades' fund-raisers.

- Discuss how to determine from the thermometer the amount of money the sixth graders raised.

Explore

- Circulate while students explore strategies for evaluating the seventh and eighth graders' claims.

- Look for students who are using effective strategies and for students who are having difficulty.

Summarize

- As a class, compare the various arguments proposed by the groups.

- Have groups present arguments for each grade level.

- Ask students to predict how long the fund-raisers would need to continue for each grade to reach its goal.

Assignment Choices

ACE questions 13–25 and unassigned choices from earlier problems

---

1.3 **Comparing Classes**

In Thurgood Marshall School, the seventh-grade class is larger than the sixth-grade class, and the eighth-grade class is smaller than the sixth-grade class. Because they are different sizes, each class set a different goal for its fund-raiser. The sixth grade set a goal of $300 for its poster sale, the seventh grade set a goal of $400 for its popcorn sale, and the eighth grade set a goal of $240 for its calendar sale.

The thermometers on the next page show the results of the sixth-grade, seventh-grade, and eighth-grade fund-raisers. Both the seventh graders and the eighth graders claimed to do better than the sixth graders.

Problem 1.3

Use the fraction strips you made in Problem 1.2 to investigate the seventh and eighth graders' claims.

A. How much money did each grade raise?

B. What fraction of the goal did each grade reach?

C. What argument could the eighth graders use to claim that their class did better than the sixth grade?

D. What argument could the seventh graders use to claim that their class did better than the sixth grade?

■ Problem 1.3 Follow-Up

Which of the three classes do you think did the best job? Explain your reasoning.

Answers to Problem 1.3

A. The seventh-grade class raised about $300. The eighth-grade class raised about $220. The sixth-grade class raised $250.

B. The seventh-grade class is about three fourths ($\frac{3}{4}$) of the way to its goal. The eighth-grade class is about eleven twelfths ($\frac{11}{12}$) of the way to its goal. The sixth grade is about five-sixths ($\frac{5}{6}$) of the way.

C. The eighth graders can say they are closer to their goal.

D. The seventh graders can say they have raised more money.

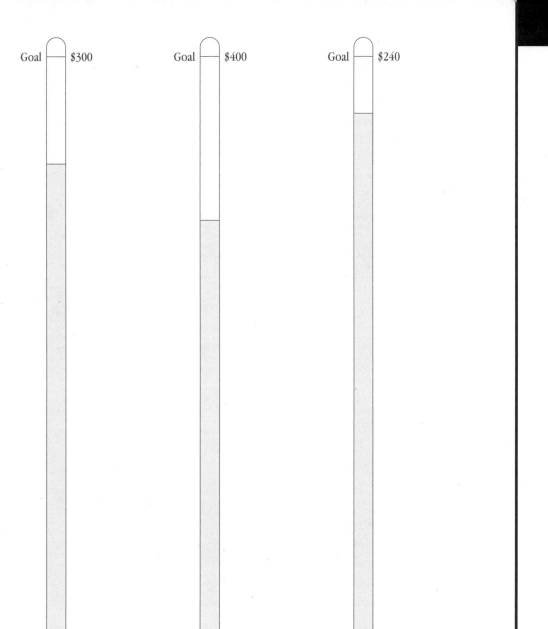

Goal $300   Goal $400   Goal $240

Day 10   **Day 10**   **Day 10**

Sixth-Grade   Seventh-Grade   Eighth-Grade
Poster Sale   Popcorn Sale   Calendar Sale

Investigation 1: Fund-Raising Fractions   9

Answer to Problem 1.3 Follow-Up

Answers will vary. Some students may say that the eighth grade is closer to their goal even though they have raised less money than the other grades. Other students may pick the seventh grade because, although they have reached a smaller fraction of their goal, they have raised more money.

Exceeding the Goal

At a Glance

Grouping:
Small Groups

Launch

- As a class, examine the teachers' thermometers, focusing on the facts that the teachers' thermometer is shorter than the students' and that the teachers exceeded their goal.

Explore

- Circulate while students explore strategies for analyzing the teachers' thermometers.

- Note any creative strategies students use.

Summarize

- Have students share their strategies for working with the new whole.

- Ask questions to extend the class's thinking about the part-whole meaning of fractions.

In April, the Thurgood Marshall School needed money to put on the annual Year's End Festival. Since the students had worked hard on the earlier fund-raising campaigns, the teachers volunteered to raise the money. They decided to sell paperback books for summer reading, and they set a goal of $360.

The thermometers on the next page show the teachers' progress at the end of the second, sixth, and tenth days.

Problem 1.4

A. Notice that the teachers used a shorter thermometer than the students did to report their progress. Can you use your fraction strips to measure these thermometers? Explain.

B. What fraction of their goal did the teachers reach at the end of each of the days shown? Explain how you determined your answers.

C. How many dollars did the teachers raise by the end of each of these days?

■ Problem 1.4 Follow-Up
What school announcement might the teachers make at the end of the tenth day?

Assignment Choices

ACE questions 8–11 and unassigned choices from earlier problems

Answers to Problem 1.4

A. Since the distance to the goal for the teachers' thermometer is not the length of the fraction strips used to measure the students' thermometers, these strips cannot be used *in the same way* to reason about the teachers' thermometers. Some students may come up with other ways to use these strips (see the discussion in the "Explore" section on page 18h).

B. At the end of day 2, the teachers were one fourth ($\frac{1}{4}$) of the way to their goal. At the end of day 6, the teachers had reached their goal. At the end of day 10, the teachers had reached five fourths ($\frac{5}{4}$), or one and one fourth ($1\frac{1}{4}$), of their goal. Explanations of strategies will vary.

C. Teachers raised $90 at the end of day 2, $360 at the end of day 6, and $450 at the end of day 10.

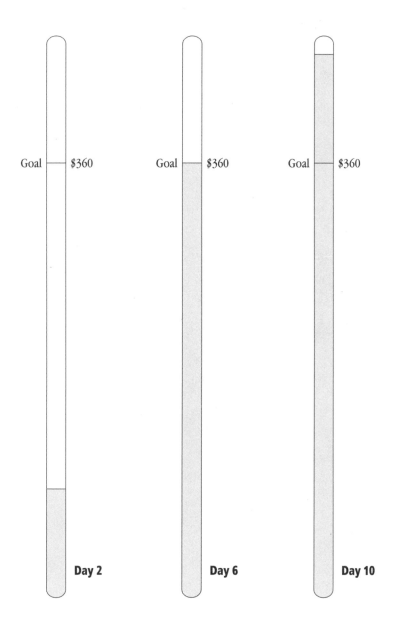

Teachers' Book Sale

Answer to Problem 1.4 Follow-Up

Answers will vary. The announcement should mention that the teachers exceeded their goal; they have raised about $450, which is $1\frac{1}{4}$ of their goal.

1.5

Using Symbolic Form

Fractions can be written in *symbolic form,* using two whole numbers separated by a bar. For example, one half is written $\frac{1}{2}$ and two thirds is written $\frac{2}{3}$.

The number above the bar is called the **numerator,** and the number below the bar is called the **denominator.**

> ## Think about this!
>
> **W**hat do the numerator and the denominator tell you in the fractions $\frac{1}{2}$, $\frac{1}{3}$, $\frac{2}{3}$, and $\frac{4}{5}$?

Problem 1.5

The next page shows nine fraction strips of the same length. Each strip is divided into a different number of equal-length parts. On your copy of Labsheet 1.5, label each of the marks on the strips with fraction names in symbolic form. The label for a mark should represent the fraction of the strip to the left of the mark.

■ Problem 1.5 Follow-Up

Compare these fraction strips with the strips you made in Problem 1.2. Does $\frac{1}{4}$ represent the same length on both strips? Why or why not?

Save your labeled strips so you can use them for the ACE questions and for your work in the next investigation.

At a Glance

Grouping:
Pairs

Launch

- Discuss the accuracy of the students' fraction strips.

- Talk about the meaning of the numerator and the denominator in a fraction.

Explore

- Circulate while pairs label the fraction strips on Labsheet 1.5.

- Ask questions to focus students on the meaning of the symbols they are writing.

Summarize

- As a class, compare the printed fraction strips with the strips the students folded and with a centimeter ruler.

Assignment Choices

ACE questions 1–7, 12, and unassigned choices from earlier problems

Answer to Problem 1.5

See page 18k.

Answer to Problem 1.5 Follow-Up

No, $\frac{1}{4}$ does not represent the same length on both strips because the strips are different lengths.

halves

thirds

fourths

fifths

sixths

eighths

ninths

tenths

twelfths

Investigation 1: Fund-Raising Fractions 13

Answers

Applications

1a. The Heron has completed two thirds ($\frac{2}{3}$) of the race and has one third ($\frac{1}{3}$) left to complete. The Palomino has completed one half ($\frac{1}{2}$) of the race and has one half ($\frac{1}{2}$) left to complete. The Flamebird has completed five sixths ($\frac{5}{6}$) of the race and has one sixth ($\frac{1}{6}$) left to complete.

1b. The Heron has completed 400 meters and has 200 meters left to complete. The Palomino has covered 300 meters and has 300 meters left to complete. The Flamebird has covered 500 meters and has 100 meters left to complete.

2.–7. Answers will vary.

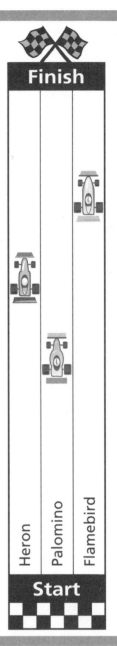

As you work on these ACE questions, use your calculator whenever you need it.

Applications

1. At right is a snapshot of three cars drag racing.

    a. For each car, measure from the front of the car to estimate the fraction of the race course completed and the fraction of the race course yet to be covered. You may want to use your fraction strips from Labsheet 1.5.

    b. The drag race course is 600 meters long. For each car, estimate the distance already covered and the distance yet to be covered.

In 2–5, use your fraction strips from Labsheet 1.5 to find something in your home with the given length. Record the name of each object.

2. half ($\frac{1}{2}$) the length of a fraction strip

3. two thirds ($\frac{2}{3}$) the length of a fraction strip

4. one and one half ($1\frac{1}{2}$) times the length of a fraction strip

5. twice the length of a fraction strip

6. Use your fraction strips from Labsheet 1.5 to measure three things in your home that are shorter than a fraction strip. Record the name of each object and its length in terms of a fraction strip.

7. Use your fraction strips from Labsheet 1.5 to measure three things in your home that are longer than a fraction strip. Record the name of each object and its length in terms of a fraction strip.

In 8–11, use this drawing of a restaurant drink container. The gauge on the side of the container shows how much of the liquid remains in the container.

8. A full container holds 120 cups.

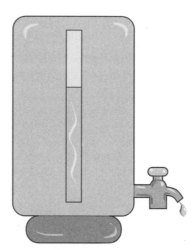

a. About what fraction of the container is filled with liquid?

b. About how many cups of liquid are in the container?

c. About what fraction of the container is empty?

d. About how many cups of liquid would it take to fill the container?

9. Tell whether each amount is closer to a full container, a half-full container, or an empty container.

a. five sixths ($\frac{5}{6}$) of a full container

b. three twelfths ($\frac{3}{12}$) of a full container

c. five eighths ($\frac{5}{8}$) of a full container

10. About what fraction of the drink container is each of the following amounts?

a. 37 cups

b. 10 cups

c. 55 cups

11. How many pitchers of liquid would it take to fill an empty drink container if a pitcher holds the given amount?

a. one fourth ($\frac{1}{4}$) of a full container

b. one third ($\frac{1}{3}$) of a full container

c. two thirds ($\frac{2}{3}$) of a full container

8a. about two thirds ($\frac{2}{3}$)

8b. about 80 cups

8c. about one third ($\frac{1}{3}$)

8d. about 40 cups

9a. a full container

9b. exactly halfway between empty and half full

9c. one half of a full container

10a. about one third ($\frac{1}{3}$)

10b. one twelfth ($\frac{1}{12}$)

10c. about half ($\frac{1}{2}$)

11a. 4 pitchers

11b. 3 pitchers

11c. one and one half ($1\frac{1}{2}$) pitchers

12a. 4 beetles

12b. 12 beetles

12c. three and one fourth ($3\frac{1}{4}$) fraction strips

Connections

13. six twelfths ($\frac{6}{12}$) or one half ($\frac{1}{2}$)

14. four twelfths ($\frac{4}{12}$) or one third ($\frac{1}{3}$)

15. three twelfths ($\frac{3}{12}$) or one fourth ($\frac{1}{4}$)

16. two twelfths ($\frac{2}{12}$) or one sixth ($\frac{1}{6}$)

17. one twelfth ($\frac{1}{12}$)

18. eight twelfths ($\frac{8}{12}$) or two thirds ($\frac{2}{3}$)

19. nine twelfths ($\frac{9}{12}$) or three fourths ($\frac{3}{4}$)

20. fifteen twelfths ($\frac{15}{12}$), five fourths ($\frac{5}{4}$), or one and one fourth ($1\frac{1}{4}$)

21. eighteen twelfths ($\frac{18}{12}$), three halves ($\frac{3}{2}$), or one and one half ($1\frac{1}{2}$)

22.–25. Answers will vary.

---

12. Ricky found a beetle that was one fourth ($\frac{1}{4}$) the length of a fraction strip from Labsheet 1.5.

    a. How many beetles, placed end to end, would have a total length equal to the length of a fraction strip?

    b. How many beetles, placed end to end, would have a total length equal to three times the length of a fraction strip?

    c. Ricky lined up 13 paper beetles, end to end, each the same length as the one he found. How many times the length of a fraction strip is the length of Ricky's line of beetles?

Connections

In 13–21, tell what fraction of a foot (12 inches) the given length is.

13. 6 inches   **14.** 4 inches   **15.** 3 inches

16. 2 inches   **17.** 1 inch   **18.** 8 inches

19. 9 inches   **20.** 15 inches   **21.** 18 inches

In 22–25, estimate each length as a fraction of a foot.

22. the width of your hand

23. the length of your hand from wrist to fingertip

24. the distance from your wrist to your elbow

25. the distance from your fingertip to your elbow

Extensions

26. Look back at the thermometers on page 7, which show the sixth graders' progress toward their goal.

    a. Make a coordinate graph that shows the sixth-grade fund-raising progress.

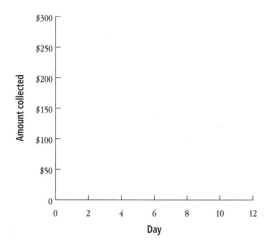

    b. Predict from your graph when the sixth graders would reach their goal if the fund-raiser continued.

    c. Describe the strategy you used to make your prediction.

26a. See below left.

26b. Possible answers: day 12, day 13

26c. Possible answer: After 10 days, $250 has been raised, so the students have averaged approximately $25 per day. At this rate, the remaining $50 would be raised in the next two days. However, the graph shows that the amount of money raised per day is declining, so it may take 13 or more days.

26a.

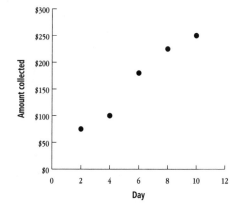

Possible Answers

1. The denominator tells you into how many equal parts the whole has been divided. For example, in the fraction $\frac{2}{3}$, the 3 tells you that the whole has been divided into three equal parts. The numerator tells you how many of those equal parts are being referred to. The 2 in $\frac{2}{3}$ refers to two of the three equal parts.

2. The whole in Problem 1.4 is shorter than the whole in earlier problems, so the fraction strips from Problems 1.2 and 1.3 could not be used *in the same way* they were used for Problems 1.2 and 1.3. Some students may have made new fraction strips; some may have found a different way to use their fraction strips from Problems 1.2 and 1.3; and others may have done Problem 1.4 without fraction strips.

3. The two classes collected the same amount of money only if their dollar goals were the same. If their goals differed, the two classes did not collect the same amount of money. For example, if Ramón's class set a goal of $200 and Melissa's class set a goal of $300, then Ramón's class raised $\frac{3}{5}$ of $200, or $120, and Melissa's class raised $\frac{3}{5}$ of $300, or $180.

Mathematical Reflections

In this investigation, you made fraction strips to help you identify fractional parts of a whole. These questions will help you summarize what you have learned:

1 What do the numerator and the denominator of a fraction tell you?

2 When you worked on Problem 1.4, did you make new fraction strips? Explain why or why not.

3 Both Ramón's class and Melissa's class reached $\frac{3}{5}$ of their fund-raising goals. Did the two classes raise the same amount of money? Explain your answer.

Think about your answers to these questions, discuss your ideas with other students and your teacher, and then write a summary of your findings in your journal.

Tips for the Linguistically Diverse Classroom

Original Rebus The Original Rebus technique is described in detail in *Getting to Know Connected Mathematics*. Students make a copy of the text before it is discussed. During discussion, they generate their own rebuses for words they do not understand as the words are made comprehensible through pictures, objects, or demonstrations. Example: Question 1—key words for which students are *numerator* ($\frac{1}{2}$ with the 1 circled), *denominator* ($\frac{1}{2}$ with the 1 circled), *fraction* ($\frac{1}{2}$).

1.1 • Reporting Our Progress

In this problem, your students will write announcements describing the progress that a sixth-grade class has made toward their fund-raising goal. This activity lets you quickly assess where your students are in their understanding of fractions as parts of wholes. This problem raises issues about fractions that will be explored in a more systematic way in later problems in the investigation. You should not expect your students to be able to respond in precise mathematical ways to the challenge in this problem.

Launch

Your students need to understand the context of this problem. You could begin by asking whether anyone has ever seen a thermometer display showing the progress of a fund-raising effort. Have a student draw an example of such a thermometer on the board, or draw one yourself. Ask questions about the example, focusing attention on the whole. Emphasize that the whole is the distance from the bottom of the thermometer to the goal; it is not necessarily the entire length of the thermometer.

When the class understands the thermometer model, tell them the story of the fund-raising campaigns at Thurgood Marshall School. Have students look at the thermometer on page 5 of the student edition (or display Transparency 1.1). Explain that this thermometer shows the progress of the sixth graders after the second day of their sale.

> Work with your group to write an interesting and informative message describing how the sixth-grade campaign is going. Make sure your announcement tells what part of the $300 goal has been reached and what part remains to be raised.

Explore

Have students work on this problem in pairs or small groups. As groups work, ask questions to help them clarify their messages. Ask them how they drew their conclusions, and encourage them to find other mathematical ways to describe the situation. Be on the lookout for clever ideas and for problems that should be discussed in the summary. You want to keep students focused and to get an idea of who understands the situation and who is confused. You may want to have groups write their results on large sheets of paper or blank transparencies so that they can be shared.

Here are some questions students may ask as they work:

> Do we use fractions or money?

Encourage students to explore both so they understand how the two relate.

> What do you mean by "clever and informative"?

Ask students to think about what they would find interesting to know in such a situation and what they want their announcement to accomplish.

Can I just say a "little bit"?

Explain that one of the nice things about mathematics is that it helps us to convey precise information. A "little bit" is hard to interpret. Encourage the group to be more precise.

How long does the message have to be?

Emphasize that the amount of information the message provides is more important than its length.

Summarize

From your observations of the students, you will have ideas about questions that must arise during the summary and about which groups should be called upon to ensure that important ideas are discussed.

> I am going to choose a few groups to share their messages. After you present your message, explain how you came up with the numbers you used. Those of you listening, note similarities and differences in the strategies and information that the groups report.

Have some or all of the groups read their announcements. After each presentation ask the class some questions.

> Does this announcement make sense?
>
> Do you agree or disagree? Why or why not?
>
> What strategy did your group use to reason about the problem?

In one class, a group said that five twelfths of the goal had been reached. The rest of the class agreed that this was an acceptable answer, even though they had all concluded that one fourth, or $75, of the goal had been reached. The teacher did not take the time to correct the students, but instead asked them to continue to think about this as they worked on the next problem.

1.2 • Using Fraction Strips

In this problem, students make fraction strips by folding strips of paper. Then they use the strips to estimate the fund-raising progress displayed on several thermometers. In Problem 1.5, students will be provided with a set of preprinted fraction strips to ensure accuracy. However, it is essential that they make their own strips first to explore the concept of fractions as parts of wholes.

Launch

Provide each student with a set of nine $8\frac{1}{2}$-inch paper strips. Students will make strips to show halves, thirds, fourths, fifths, sixths, eighths, ninths, tenths, and twelfths. The length of each strip is the distance to the goal on the thermometer. If you make the strips 1-inch wide, you can make 11 strips from an $8\frac{1}{2}$-by-11-inch sheet of paper. You will want to have extra strips available for students who make mistakes.

Refer students to page 7 in the student edition, or display Transparency 1.2A. Explain that the thermometers indicate the progress of the sixth-grade fund-raiser after two, four, six, eight, and ten days.

> We can devise a measuring device to help us estimate the progress of the fund-raiser for each of these days.

> I have cut some strips that are the same length as the distance from the bottom of the thermometer to the goal. (*Hold up a strip.*) I can make a strip to show halves by folding it into two equal pieces. (*Demonstrate this.*) This fold mark shows me how high the "mercury" must be to indicate one half. I'm going to draw over this fold mark with my pencil so that it is easy to see. (*Demonstrate.*) I can now use this strip to see if any of the thermometers are halfway to the goal.

> (*Hold up a new, unfolded strip.*) How can I fold this strip to show thirds?

Fold a strip by following a student's instructions. Ask the class whether they agree that the method results in a strip that is divided into thirds.

> Now, I want you to make your own fraction strips. When everyone is finished, we will discuss what we have found before we move on to the rest of the problem.

Explore

Each student should make a set of fraction strips. Encourage students to label the strips "halves," "thirds," and so on, so that the meaning of each label can be discussed before moving to symbols. It is not necessary for students to label each mark with a fraction, although some of your students may be comfortable enough with symbols to do this.

If students are having difficulty, suggest that they ask another student for help. You may want to establish a rule that students can help each other by giving oral directions, but no student may fold another student's strips.

As students work, circulate and ask questions about what they are doing.

> How can you use the strategy for making the halves strip to help you make the fourths strip?

> Did you compare your strips to someone else's to check for accuracy?

> Can you explain your folding strategy to another student or to me, so you can see if it makes sense?

Here are some strategies students have used to make their strips.

Halves   Fold a strip in half.

Thirds   Fold a strip into three parts so that the sections are the same length. Or, make an S with a strip and "squish" it together, keeping all three pieces the same size.

Fourths   Fold a strip in half and then in half again.

Fifths   Roll a strip around two fingers two and a half times. Take the strip off your fingers still rolled, and carefully flatten the roll, making the five sections as close as possible to the same length. Or, fold the ends of the strip in toward the middle so that the two sections with overlap and the section in the middle are about the same length. Then make a fold on each side where the overlapping part ends.

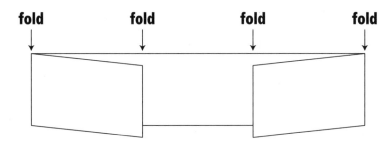

Sixths   Make a thirds strip, then fold each section in half.

Eighths   Make a fourths strip, then fold each section in half.

Ninths   Make a thirds strip, then divide each section into three equal parts.

Tenths   Make a fifths strip, then fold each section in half.

Twelfths   Make a sixths strip, then fold each section in half. Or, make a fourths strip, then fold each section into three equal parts.

When most students are finished making their strips, begin a class discussion in which students share their folding strategies. It is important that students spend time connecting fraction words to the fraction-strip model before moving to symbols. Focus on characteristics of the fraction strips that indicate important ideas about fractions. For example, emphasize that the parts into which a strip is folded must be the same size. Point out that you can make strips for both fourths and eighths by starting with a halves strips, and that two fourths and four eighths are the same as one half.

A student may suggest estimating the size of the parts and then tearing off the end of the strip so that the folded pieces are the same length. Here you can emphasize that a set of strips used to compare fractions must represent the *same* whole. In this case, each strip must be exactly $8\frac{1}{2}$ inches long, the distance from the bottom of the thermometer to the goal.

After this discussion, have students work on the rest of the problem, using their strips to describe the progress the sixth graders have made on days 2, 4, 6, 8, and 10 of their fund-raiser.

Summarize

Allow students to share their estimates and strategies. You may want to have them use Transparency 1.2A and a set of fraction strips made from transparency film to explain their answers. It is possible that students will get different estimates; it is hard to be precise with folded fraction strips. Accept estimates that are reasonable.

Focus on word descriptions of fractions. Some students will be able to use symbols from the start. Do not discourage this, but ask them to explain in words so you can assess their understanding.

For the Teacher: Modeling Fractions

Throughout the early problems in this investigation, we encourage you to focus on two ways of representing fractions: visual models (for example, fraction strips) and word names. Since your students may be at a variety of developmental levels in their understanding of fractions, we encourage you to move back and forth between these two representations repeatedly. Research has shown that understanding of fractions is stronger if the use of symbols is delayed until the use of word names is firmly in place. In Problem 1.5 symbols are introduced. At this point, you should begin asking questions that focus on all three representations of fractions—visual models, word names, and symbols. Here are examples of the types of questions you can ask your students to help their understanding:

> What is the whole for this situation?
>
> Into how many equal-size parts do you need to divide the whole so that you can model the problem?
>
> What does the denominator of the fraction mean? What does the numerator of the fraction mean?
>
> If two classes reach half their goal, have they raised the same amount of money? Why or why not?
>
> If we make the denominator bigger, what does that say about the size of the parts into which the whole has been divided?
>
> If we make denominator smaller, what does that say about the size of the parts into which the whole has been divided?
>
> If we make the numerator bigger, what does that mean?
>
> If we make the numerator smaller, what does that mean?

You may want to raise the idea of equivalent fractions:

> Gloria said she thought the sixth-graders had reached $\frac{1}{4}$ of the goal on day two. Is there another way to name the progress on day two? Is there another fraction strip that has a fold that matches the progress?

You don't need to spend a lot of time discussing equivalent fractions, since we will return to this idea in several investigations, but you don't want to miss the opportunity to have your students begin to search for equivalent fractions.

Continually encourage students to explain and to use more precise language so that everyone can understand what they are sharing. As a result of this discussion, you want your students to be able to describe how to use fraction strips to estimate parts of wholes.

1.3 • Comparing Classes

In this problem, students compare fractions for which the wholes vary. The sixth-, seventh-, and eighth-grade classes at Thurgood Marshall School have each set a different number of dollars as their fund-raising goal. The problem involves estimating both the fraction of the goal that has been reached and the amount of money that has been raised. This situation is effective because the students easily understand that half of $300 is not as much money as half of $360.

Launch

Although the goal amounts for the three classes differ, the lengths of the thermometers are the same. Students use their fraction strips from Problem 1.2 to reason about the part of each whole being shown and then use the goal amounts to determine how much money has been raised. This problem gives students a good sense of the importance of knowing what the whole is when making comparisons.

Refer students to page 9 in the student edition, or show Transparency 1.3A.

> Remember that three classes held fund-raisers. These thermometers show the final results of the fund-raisers for the sixth, seventh, and eighth grades.
>
> At the end of ten days, the seventh graders claimed their class was the most successful. But so did the eighth graders!
>
> Take a minute to examine these thermometers. How are the thermometers alike? How are they different?

You want students to observe that the distance to the goal is the same on all the thermometers. This means that the same fraction strips can be used to measure the progress on each thermometer. However, the dollar amount of the goal is different for each thermometer. This means that the same fraction describes different amounts on each thermometer. So, for example, half of the seventh-grade goal is $200, while half of the eighth-grade goal is only $120. This problem focuses students on the concepts of models and wholes.

> Each grade has a different goal. Look at the sixth-grade thermometer for day 2. We agreed that the class had reached one fourth of its goal by the end of day 2. How much money had been collected?

This conversation may have come up during the summary of Problem 1.1, but you will want to raise it again. Be sure students give a complete explanation for how they determined the amount of money represented. You may have to model a way to think about this:

> If we separate the goal amount of money into four equal parts, how much is each part? Would this amount represent one fourth of the goal? Why or why not?
>
> In your groups, work on Problem 1.3 and the follow-up. You will need to decide what argument the seventh graders could use to support their claim. Then decide what argument the eighth graders could use. These will probably be different arguments.

Explore

Look for students who are using effective strategies and for students who are having difficulty. Make sure both the strategies and the difficulties are discussed in the summary.

Summarize

Discuss the answers to parts A and B to see whether students have found reasonable answers. Then move to parts C and D. Have each group present its arguments for the seventh and eighth grades. Discuss what is alike and what is different about the arguments presented. This is a good time to focus on the attributes of a convincing argument.

You may want to have students present arguments for all three grade levels. You could also ask them to predict how much longer each fund-raiser would need to continue for each class to reach its goal.

1.4 • Exceeding the Goal

In Problems 1.2 and 1.3, students were asked to think of the whole both as an amount of money and as the height of the goal mark on a thermometer. Using thermometers that were the same length but which represented different money goals focused students' attention on the importance of considering the whole when interpreting fractions.

Problem 1.4 extends students' thinking in two ways. First, the distance to the goal for the teachers' thermometer is shorter than the distance to the goal for the students' thermometers, so the same fraction strips cannot be used to reason about the teachers' progress. Students will have to create new strips, invent ways to use parts of the strips they already have, or invent a strategy for reasoning without fraction strips. Second, the teachers have exceeded their fund-raising goal, so students must consider fractions that represent more than a whole—that is, fractions greater than 1.

Launch

Describe the situation to your students. Refer them to page 11 in the student edition or display Transparency 1.4A. Students should notice that the teachers' thermometer is shorter and that the mercury eventually goes beyond the goal mark, indicating that the teachers have exceeded their goal. You may want them to compare the students' thermometers with the teachers' thermometer to observe what is alike and different about them.

Tell students that during the summary you will expect them to tell about the strategies they used to solve the problem and to explain why they think their announcement is an accurate portrayal of the teachers' progress.

Explore

Have students work in groups on Problem 1.4 and the follow-up. Circulate as they work, noting creative or interesting strategies that should be shared with the class.

Although the $8\frac{1}{2}$-inch strips are difficult to use for this problem, some students may make use of them in some way. Question these students about how they are reasoning. In one class, a student said the sixths strip could be used because four sixths of it equaled the distance to the teachers' goal. He explained that the thermometer for day 2 represented one fourth of the teachers' goal, because the mercury was the length of one of the four sixths sections needed to make the whole thermometer. He reasoned that the thermometer for day 6 represented 100% of the goal because the mercury went up to the goal mark, and that the thermometer for day 10 represented one and one fourth of the goal because it was five sixths of his strip—four sixths represented a whole, and the other sixth represented one fourth of the way to another goal.

Some students will want to make new strips. Have some strips cut to the length of the distance to the teachers' goal in case a group decides they need to fold new strips to represent the problem. The students do not need to make new strips if they find other strategies to solve the problem.

Summarize

Have students share strategies for working with the new whole and present the announcements they wrote for the follow-up. Make sure they explain why they think their strategy is reasonable. This will tell you much about their understanding of the part-whole meaning of fractions. You may want to give groups a few minutes to revise their announcements after the class discussion of strategies.

Following are additional questions to stretch the class's thinking:

> The sixth graders' goal was $300. Where would $300 be on the teachers' thermometer?

Students will need to determine what part $300 is of $360. Some might see that if $360 is thought of as six groups of $60, then $300 is five of these groups. So $300 would be represented by a mark five sixths of the way to the goal mark. You might remind students that they know how to analyze whole numbers to see what they have in common. Knowing the greatest common factor is helpful in reasoning about this problem.

> Why is $300 at a different height on the teachers' thermometer than on the sixth graders' thermometer?

How high would one half be on the seventh graders' thermometer? On the teachers' thermometer? Why are the lengths different?

If fractions tell parts of a whole, how do we talk about more than a whole?

Fractions tell us how to talk about any number of wholes and parts of wholes. The teachers' thermometer for day 10 shows one complete whole plus one fourth of another whole. (That is what $1\frac{1}{4}$, or $\frac{5}{4}$, means.)

1.5 • Using Symbolic Form

Up to this point, your students have worked with fraction strips they folded themselves. The intent has been to develop a secure sense of meaning for parts of the strips. In this problem, students are asked to make the connection between parts of fraction strips and the symbols that represent them, helping them to understand what the numerator and denominator stand for in the symbolic representation of fractions.

Launch

After they complete this problem, students will know three ways to represent fractions: concrete models, word names, and symbols. It is important for you to cycle through these three representations repeatedly so that your students make strong connections among them and develop the ability to move flexibly between representations.

Discuss with your students the precision of their folded strips.

> The fraction strips you folded gave you a pretty good way to measure the fund-raising progress, but most are not accurate enough for work that requires more precision—such as accurately comparing fractions or finding fractions that represent the same quantity.

> I will give each of you a labsheet with printed fraction strips. These strips were created with a computer and will allow you to measure more accurately.

Pass out a copy of Labsheet 1.5 to each student. Note that these strips are 16 cm long, not $8\frac{1}{2}$ inches long like the hand-folded strips.

Talk about what the numerator and denominator of a fraction are, focusing on the part-whole interpretation. The *denominator* tells us into how many *equal-size* parts the whole has been divided, and the *numerator* tells us how many of these *equal-size* parts represent the quantity to which we are referring.

Explore

Circulate as students work in pairs to label their page of fraction strips, asking questions about what the symbols mean. Have students refer to their strips to show you what some of the fractions they wrote mean. As you look at a student's fractions strips, you can ask which of two fractions on a strip represents the greater amount. You can also begin to pose questions about different symbol names for a particular length. These ideas of *comparing* fractions and finding *equivalent* fractions will be central themes in many of the remaining investigations.

Summarize

Ask students to compare the fraction strips they folded to the preprinted strips.

> Is one half the same in both sets of strips? Why or why not?

Students should understand that one half does not represent the same length on both strips because the strips are different lengths. However, in each case the symbol notation $\frac{1}{2}$ represents one of two equal-size parts of a whole.

You may want to show a transparent fraction strip and a transparent centimeter ruler on the overhead projector.

> How do our new fraction strips compare to a centimeter ruler? How are they alike? How are they different?

The centimeter ruler has marks that align with marks on many of the fraction strips. For example, on the fourths strip, the first mark is at 4 cm, the second is at 8 cm, the third is at 12 cm, and the whole is at 16 cm. However, the marks on the ninths strip do not align with centimeter marks on the ruler.

Students should save these fractions strips. These strips will be used in the ACE questions and in future investigations. You may want to have students destroy their folded strips to prevent confusion about which fraction strips the investigations that follow involve.

Additional Answers

Answer to Problem 1.1 Follow-Up

Answers will vary. Students may have used a ruler to measure the length of the "mercury" and then compared this length to the total distance to the goal (the distance to the goal is $8\frac{1}{2}$ inches, and the thermometer registers $2\frac{1}{8}$ inches). The distance to the goal is the width of a sheet of paper, so students may have folded a sheet of notebook paper to determine their answers.

Answer to Problem 1.5

halves

| $\frac{1}{2}$ |

thirds

| $\frac{1}{3}$ | $\frac{2}{3}$ |

fourths

| $\frac{1}{4}$ | $\frac{2}{4}$ | $\frac{3}{4}$ |

fifths

| $\frac{1}{5}$ | $\frac{2}{5}$ | $\frac{3}{5}$ | $\frac{4}{5}$ |

sixths

| $\frac{1}{6}$ | $\frac{2}{6}$ | $\frac{3}{6}$ | $\frac{4}{6}$ | $\frac{5}{6}$ |

eighths

| $\frac{1}{8}$ | $\frac{2}{8}$ | $\frac{3}{8}$ | $\frac{4}{8}$ | $\frac{5}{8}$ | $\frac{6}{8}$ | $\frac{7}{8}$ |

ninths

| $\frac{1}{9}$ | $\frac{2}{9}$ | $\frac{3}{9}$ | $\frac{4}{9}$ | $\frac{5}{9}$ | $\frac{6}{9}$ | $\frac{7}{9}$ | $\frac{8}{9}$ |

tenths

| $\frac{1}{10}$ | $\frac{2}{10}$ | $\frac{3}{10}$ | $\frac{4}{10}$ | $\frac{5}{10}$ | $\frac{6}{10}$ | $\frac{7}{10}$ | $\frac{8}{10}$ | $\frac{9}{10}$ |

twelfths

| $\frac{1}{12}$ | $\frac{2}{12}$ | $\frac{3}{12}$ | $\frac{4}{12}$ | $\frac{5}{12}$ | $\frac{6}{12}$ | $\frac{7}{12}$ | $\frac{8}{12}$ | $\frac{9}{12}$ | $\frac{10}{12}$ | $\frac{11}{12}$ |

Comparing Fractions

In this investigation, students continue to use fraction strips as tools for understanding fractions. The problems in this investigation were designed to develop an understanding of equivalence and comparison of fractions.

Problem 2.1, Comparing Notes, asks students to investigate competing claims of three teachers about their fund-raising progress. Two of the teachers' claims turn out to be the same, raising the issue of equivalent fractions. In Problem 2.2, Finding Equivalent Fractions, students are asked to find other names for $\frac{2}{3}$ and $\frac{3}{4}$ by comparing fraction strips. They use the patterns they discover to find equivalent fractions for $\frac{1}{8}$, $\frac{2}{5}$, and $\frac{5}{6}$. In Problem 2.3, Making a Number Line, students transfer the fractions from all of their fraction strips onto a single number line. This helps them make sense of the number line and the numbers—fractions—used to label the points between whole numbers. In Problem 2.4, Comparing Fractions to Benchmarks, students use the benchmark values of 0, $\frac{1}{2}$, and 1 to estimate the size of fractions and to compare fractions. Problem 2.5, Fractions Greater Than One, asks students to consider fractions greater than 1 on the number line. As students label points between 1 and 2, they should begin to think about the notion of density: between any two fractions, there is another fraction.

Mathematical and Problem-Solving Goals

- **To continue to use fraction strips as tools for understanding fraction concepts**

- **To investigate the concepts of comparison and equivalence of fractions**

- **To use fractions that are less than, equal to, and greater than 1**

- **To apply knowledge gained by using fraction strips to name, estimate, and compare fractions and to find equivalent fractions**

- **To build a number line and label points between whole numbers**

Materials		
Problem	**For students**	**For the teacher**
All	Calculators	Transparencies 2.1 to 2.5 (optional), fraction strips for the overhead projector (optional; copy Labsheet 1.5 onto blank transparency film)
2.2		
2.3	Labeled fraction strips from Labsheet 1.5	
2.4		Index cards (optional)
2.5	Labeled fraction strips from Labsheet 1.5	A large number line to display in the classroom (see Problem 2.5)

Comparing Fractions

In Investigation 1, you made fraction strips to help you determine what fraction of the fund-raising goal students had reached. You learned to interpret fractions as parts of a whole. In this investigation, you will look at situations in which you need to compare fractions. Your fraction strips will be a useful model to help you make comparisons.

2.1 Comparing Notes

At the end of the fourth day of their fund-raising campaign, the teachers at Thurgood Marshall School had raised $270 of the $360 they needed to reach their goal. Three of the teachers got into a debate about how they would report their progress.

- Ms. Mendoza wanted to announce that the teachers had made it three fourths of the way to their goal.

- Mr. Park said that six eighths was a better description.

- Ms. Christos suggested that two thirds was really the simplest way to describe the teachers' progress.

Problem 2.1

A. Which of the three teachers do you agree with? Why?

B. How could the teacher you agreed with in part A prove his or her case?

■ **Problem 2.1 Follow-Up**

Name another fraction that describes the teachers' progress.

Goal $360

Day 4

Teachers'
Book Sale

Answers to Problem 2.1

A. Ms. Mendoza and Mr. Park are correct, since three fourths of $360 and six eighths of $360 are both equal to $270. Ms. Christos is incorrect, since two thirds of $360 is $240.

B. Ms. Mendoza could say that if you divide $360 into four equal parts, each part would be $90 and three of these parts would be $270; three fourths of $360 is $270. Mr. Park could say that if you divide $360 into eight equal parts, each part would be $45 and six of these parts would be $270; six eighths of $360 is $270.

Answer to Problem 2.1 Follow-Up

Possible answer: The teachers could say they had reached $\frac{9}{12}$ of their goal.

At a Glance

Grouping:
Pairs

Launch

- Review with students the story of the teachers' debate.

Explore

- Using a think-pair-share strategy, have students explore the problem.

- Watch for students with particularly creative reasoning or with ideas that need further development.

Summarize

- Have several pairs share their results.

Assignment Choices

Unassigned choices from earlier problems

Finding Equivalent Fractions

At a Glance

Grouping:
Small Groups

Launch

- Review what students discovered about $\frac{3}{4}$ and $\frac{6}{8}$ in Problem 2.1.

- Help students understand Problem 2.2.

Explore

- Visit groups as they work, asking questions to guide them in exploring equivalent fractions.

Summarize

- Have several groups share the patterns they discovered for finding equivalent fractions.

- Ask questions to help students discover the pattern: multiply the numerator and denominator by the same number.

- Use visual tools to help students understand that when they multiply the numerator and denominator by the same number they are cutting each of the pieces into which the whole has been divided into smaller pieces.

As you worked with your fraction strips, you found that some quantities can be described by several different fractions. In fact, *any* quantity can be described by an infinite number of different fractions!

Did you know?

Hieroglyphic inscriptions from more than 4000 years ago indicate that, with the exception of $\frac{2}{3}$, Egyptian mathematicians used only fractions with 1 in the numerator. Such fractions are known as *unit fractions.* Other fractions were expressed as sums of these unit fractions. The fraction $\frac{2}{7}$, for example, was expressed as $\frac{1}{4} + \frac{1}{28}$.

Two fractions that name the same quantity are called **equivalent fractions.** For example, you probably know several names for the quantity $\frac{1}{2}$. As long as the whole is the same, $\frac{1}{2}$ means the same as $\frac{2}{4}, \frac{3}{6}, \frac{4}{8}, \frac{5}{10}$, and so on. You can show this with fraction strips.

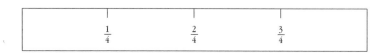

Assignment Choices

ACE questions 1–7, 19, 38–40, and unassigned choices from earlier problems

Answers to Problem 2.2

A. The fractions shown on the strips are $\frac{4}{6}, \frac{6}{9}$, and $\frac{8}{12}$. Additional equivalent fractions include $\frac{10}{15}, \frac{12}{18}$, and $\frac{14}{21}$.

B. The fractions shown on the strips are $\frac{6}{8}, \frac{9}{12}$, and $\frac{12}{16}$. Additional equivalent fractions include $\frac{15}{20}, \frac{18}{24}$, and $\frac{21}{28}$.

C. Answers will vary. Students may realize that you can find equivalent fractions by multiplying the numerator and the denominator by the same number.

Problem 2.2

The fraction strips on the left below show $\frac{2}{3}$ and three fractions equivalent to $\frac{2}{3}$. The strips on the right show $\frac{3}{4}$ and three fractions equivalent to $\frac{3}{4}$. Study the two sets of strips. Look for patterns that will help you find other equivalent fractions.

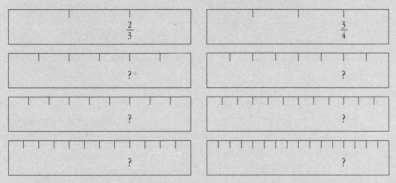

A. What are the three fractions shown that are equivalent to $\frac{2}{3}$? Name three more fractions that are equivalent to $\frac{2}{3}$.

B. What are the three fractions shown that are equivalent to $\frac{3}{4}$? Name three more fractions that are equivalent to $\frac{3}{4}$.

C. What pattern do you see that can help you find equivalent fractions?

■ Problem 2.2 Follow-Up

Test your ideas by naming at least five fractions equivalent to each given fraction.

1. $\frac{1}{8}$

2. $\frac{2}{5}$

3. $\frac{5}{6}$

Answers to Problem 2.2 Follow-Up

1. Possible answers: $\frac{2}{16}, \frac{3}{24}, \frac{4}{32}, \frac{5}{40}, \frac{6}{48}, \frac{7}{56}$

2. Possible answers: $\frac{4}{10}, \frac{6}{15}, \frac{8}{20}, \frac{10}{25}, \frac{12}{30}, \frac{14}{35}$

3. Possible answers: $\frac{10}{12}, \frac{15}{18}, \frac{20}{24}, \frac{25}{30}, \frac{30}{36}, \frac{35}{42}$

Making a Number Line

At a Glance

Grouping: Individuals

Launch

- Demonstrate how to transfer marks from fraction strips to a number line.

Explore

- Have students create their own number lines.

- Have students work on the follow-up to add numbers that are not represented on their fraction strips to their number lines.

Summarize

- Display several students' number lines.

- Focus students on using their number lines to compare two fractions by finding equivalent fractions with the same denominator.

It would be helpful to have one strip that shows all of the fractions in your set of fraction strips. That way, you could measure fractional lengths using only one strip.

To make this master strip, you can copy the fractions from all of your fraction strips onto a single number line. The result will be a number line from 0 to 1 with marks for $\frac{1}{4}, \frac{1}{3}, \frac{1}{2}, \frac{2}{4}$, $\frac{2}{3}, \frac{3}{4}$, and all the other fractions on your strips.

Here's one way to transfer all of the fractions from your fraction strips onto one number line.

1. Draw a line at the top of a sheet of paper. This will be your number line. Label the left end of the number line with the numeral 0. Line up one end of a fraction strip with this 0 point, and make a mark where the other end crosses the number line. Label this mark with the numeral 1.

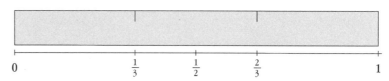

2. Align the end of your halves fraction strip (from Labsheet 1.5) with the 0 mark. Make a mark where the $\frac{1}{2}$ mark crosses the number line. Label this mark with the fraction $\frac{1}{2}$.

3. Align the end of your thirds fraction strip with the 0 mark. Make and label marks where the $\frac{1}{3}$ and $\frac{2}{3}$ marks cross the number line.

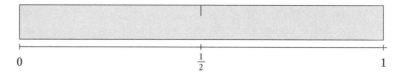

4. Continue this process with the rest of your strips.

Assignment Choices

ACE questions 20–27, 37, and unassigned choices from earlier problems

Answers to Problem 2.3

A. See page 30j.

B. Answers will vary.

Answers to Problem 2.3 Follow-Up

Answers will vary.

Problem 2.3

A. Make a number line as described above. When you find another name for a mark you have already labeled, record the new name below the first name.

B. Look for patterns in your finished number line. Record your findings.

■ Problem 2.3 Follow-Up

Mark and label three fractions on your number line that are not represented on your set of fraction strips.

2.4 Comparing Fractions to Benchmarks

When you solve problems involving fractions, you may find it useful to estimate the size of fractions quickly. One strategy is to compare each fraction to 0, $\frac{1}{2}$, and 1. These values serve as **benchmarks**—or reference points. First, you can decide whether a fraction is between 0 and $\frac{1}{2}$, between $\frac{1}{2}$ and 1, or greater than 1. Then you can decide whether the fraction is closest to 0, $\frac{1}{2}$, or 1.

Problem 2.4

A. Decide whether each fraction below is between 0 and $\frac{1}{2}$ or between $\frac{1}{2}$ and 1.

$$\frac{1}{5} \quad \frac{2}{3} \quad \frac{8}{10} \quad \frac{3}{12} \quad \frac{3}{5} \quad \frac{5}{6} \quad \frac{5}{8} \quad \frac{4}{5} \quad \frac{3}{8} \quad \frac{3}{4} \quad \frac{2}{9} \quad \frac{7}{12} \quad \frac{1}{3}$$

B. Decide whether each fraction from part A is closest to 0, $\frac{1}{2}$, or 1. Record your information in a table.

C. Explain your strategies for comparing fractions to 0, $\frac{1}{2}$, and 1.

D. Use benchmarks and other strategies to help you write the fractions from part A in order from smallest to largest.

■ Problem 2.4 Follow-Up

1. In a–d, decide which fraction is larger by using benchmarks or another strategy that makes sense to you. Then write each pair of fractions, inserting a less-than symbol (<), a greater-than symbol (>), or an equals symbol (=) between the fractions to make a true statement. Describe your reasoning.

a. $\frac{3}{12}$ $\quad$ $\frac{7}{12}$ **b.** $\frac{5}{6}$ $\quad$ $\frac{5}{8}$

c. $\frac{2}{3}$ $\quad$ $\frac{3}{9}$ **d.** $\frac{13}{12}$ $\quad$ $\frac{6}{5}$

At a Glance

Grouping:
Small Groups

Launch

■ Demonstrate how to determine whether a fraction is closest to 0, $\frac{1}{2}$, or 1.

Explore

■ Circulate as groups work, asking students to explain their strategies for determining which benchmark each fraction is near and for ordering the fractions.

Summarize

■ Have students share their strategies for categorizing and ordering the fractions.

■ As a class, further develop the concepts raised in each part of the problem.

■ Discuss the exercises in the follow-up.

Answers to Problem 2.4

A. See the lists in the "Summarize" section on page 30e.

B. See the table in the "Summarize" section on page 30f.

C. Answers will vary.

D. $\frac{1}{5}$, $\frac{2}{9}$, $\frac{3}{12}$, $\frac{1}{3}$, $\frac{3}{8}$, $\frac{7}{12}$, $\frac{3}{5}$, $\frac{5}{8}$, $\frac{2}{3}$, $\frac{3}{4}$, $\frac{8}{10} = \frac{4}{5}$, $\frac{5}{6}$

Answers to Problem 2.4 Follow-Up

See page 30j.

Assignment Choices

ACE questions 8–15, 41, 42, and unassigned choices from earlier problems

Fractions Greater Than One

Grouping:
Pairs

Launch

- With the class, explore the section of the number line between 1 and 2.

- Discuss how to label points with both mixed numbers and improper fractions.

Explore

- Circulate as pairs label the lettered points on the number line, asking questions to help them understand improper fractions.

- Have pairs locate points fitting the constraints in part B.

Summarize

- Have students share their strategies for labeling points.

- If students are ready, discuss an efficient strategy for converting between mixed numbers and improper fractions.

---

2. In a–f, use your fraction strips or another method to compare the fractions in each pair. Then write each pair of fractions, inserting <, >, or = between the fractions to make a true statement. Describe your reasoning.

a. $\frac{4}{7}$ $\frac{6}{7}$ b. $\frac{7}{10}$ $\frac{8}{12}$

c. $\frac{5}{8}$ $\frac{6}{9}$ d. $\frac{10}{12}$ $\frac{5}{6}$

e. $\frac{2}{4}$ $\frac{5}{9}$ f. $\frac{3}{9}$ $\frac{3}{10}$

2.5   Fractions Greater Than One

The whole-number points on a number line follow one another in a simple, regular pattern. But, as you saw in Problem 2.3, between every pair of whole numbers are many other points that may be labeled with fractions.

The portion of the number line shown below has marks for halves, thirds, fourths, fifths, sixths, eighths, ninths, tenths, and twelfths. These marks are different from the marks you identified in Problem 2.3, because they indicate fractions that are between 1 and 2 instead of between of 0 and 1.

Problem 2.5

A. Use the fraction strips from Labsheet 1.5 to find as many labels as you can for each of the lettered points. For each point, record the letter and the fraction labels.

B. Copy the number line onto a sheet of paper. Mark and label a point fitting each description below. Do not use points that are already marked.

1. a point close to, but larger than, 1

2. a point close to, but smaller than, $1\frac{1}{2}$

3. a point close to, but larger than, $1\frac{1}{2}$

4. a point close to, but smaller than, 2

Assignment Choices

ACE questions 16–18, 28–36, and unassigned choices from earlier problems

Assessment

It is appropriate to use Check-Up 1 after this problem.

Answers to Problem 2.5

A.

a. $1\frac{1}{8}$ and $\frac{9}{8}$

b. $1\frac{1}{4}$, $1\frac{2}{8}$, $1\frac{3}{12}$, $\frac{5}{4}$, $\frac{10}{8}$, and $\frac{15}{12}$

c. $1\frac{5}{12}$ and $\frac{17}{12}$

d. $1\frac{3}{5}$, $1\frac{6}{10}$, $\frac{8}{5}$, and $\frac{16}{10}$

e. $1\frac{3}{4}$, $1\frac{6}{8}$, $1\frac{9}{12}$, $\frac{7}{4}$, $\frac{14}{8}$, and $\frac{21}{12}$

f. $1\frac{9}{10}$ and $\frac{19}{10}$

g. $1\frac{1}{12}$ and $\frac{13}{12}$

h. $1\frac{1}{5}$, $1\frac{2}{10}$, $\frac{6}{5}$, and $\frac{12}{10}$

i. $1\frac{1}{3}$, $1\frac{2}{6}$, $1\frac{3}{9}$, $1\frac{4}{12}$, $\frac{4}{3}$, $\frac{8}{6}$, $\frac{12}{9}$, and $\frac{16}{12}$

j. $1\frac{1}{2}$, $1\frac{2}{4}$, $1\frac{3}{6}$, $1\frac{4}{8}$, $1\frac{5}{10}$, $1\frac{6}{12}$, $\frac{3}{2}$, $\frac{6}{4}$, $\frac{12}{8}$, $\frac{15}{10}$, and $\frac{18}{12}$

k. $1\frac{2}{3}$, $1\frac{4}{6}$, $1\frac{6}{9}$, $1\frac{8}{12}$, $\frac{5}{3}$, $\frac{10}{6}$, $\frac{15}{9}$, and $\frac{20}{12}$

l. $1\frac{4}{5}$, $1\frac{8}{10}$, $\frac{9}{5}$, and $\frac{18}{10}$

(continued on next page)

■ Problem 2.5 Follow-Up

Find an equivalent fraction, with a denominator greater than 12, for one of the lettered points. Explain how you arrived at your answer.

B. 1. Possible answer: $1\frac{1}{16}$ 2. Possible answer: $1\frac{7}{16}$

3. Possible answer: $1\frac{9}{16}$ 4. Possible answer: $1\frac{15}{16}$

Answers to Problem 2.5 Follow-Up

Answers will vary.

Applications

1.–4. See below right.

5. $\frac{3}{4}$, $\frac{6}{8}$, $\frac{9}{12}$

6. See page 30j.

7. See page 30j.

8. $\frac{8}{10} > \frac{3}{8}$

9. $\frac{2}{3} > \frac{4}{9}$

10. $\frac{3}{5} > \frac{5}{12}$

11. $\frac{1}{3} < \frac{2}{3}$

Applications • Connections • Extensions

As you work on these ACE questions, use your calculator whenever you need it.

Applications

In 1–4, decide whether the statement is true or false. Explain your reasoning in words or by drawing pictures.

1. $\frac{1}{3} = \frac{4}{12}$ **2.** $\frac{4}{6} = \frac{2}{3}$ **3.** $\frac{2}{5} = \frac{1}{3}$ **4.** $\frac{2}{4} = \frac{5}{10}$

5. The drawing below shows the volume indicator on a stereo receiver. Use the fraction strips shown to find three fractions that describe the part of the maximum volume shown by the indicator.

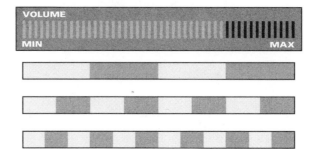

In 6 and 7, draw fraction strips to show that the two fractions are equivalent.

6. $\frac{2}{5}$ and $\frac{6}{15}$ **7.** $\frac{1}{9}$ and $\frac{2}{18}$

In 8–15, use benchmarks or another strategy that makes sense to you to decide which fraction is larger. Then write each pair of fractions, inserting a less-than symbol (<), a greater-than symbol (>), or an equals symbol (=) between the fractions to make a true statement. Describe your reasoning.

8. $\frac{8}{10}$ $\frac{3}{8}$ **9.** $\frac{2}{3}$ $\frac{4}{9}$

10. $\frac{3}{5}$ $\frac{5}{12}$ **11.** $\frac{1}{3}$ $\frac{2}{3}$

---

1. true;

 equals

2. true;

 equals

3. false;

 does not equal

4. true;

 equals

12. $\frac{3}{4}$ $\frac{3}{5}$ **13.** $\frac{3}{2}$ $\frac{7}{6}$

14. $\frac{8}{12}$ $\frac{6}{9}$ **15.** $\frac{9}{10}$ $\frac{10}{11}$

16. Describe, in writing or with pictures, how $\frac{7}{3}$ compares with $2\frac{1}{3}$.

17. Which is larger, $\frac{7}{6}$ or $\frac{13}{12}$? Explain your reasoning.

18. On the number line from 0 to 10, where is $\frac{13}{3}$ located? Explain your reasoning.

19. Write an explanation to a friend of how to find a fraction that is equivalent to $\frac{3}{5}$. You can use words and pictures to help explain.

Connections

In 20–25, copy each number line, and then estimate and mark where the numeral 1 would be.

20.

21.
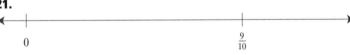

22.

23.
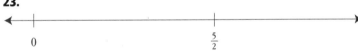

12. $\frac{3}{4} > \frac{3}{5}$

13. $\frac{3}{2} > \frac{7}{6}$

14. $\frac{8}{12} = \frac{6}{9}$

15. $\frac{9}{10} < \frac{10}{11}$

16. $\frac{7}{3}$ and $2\frac{1}{3}$ are equivalent. Since 3 thirds is equal to 1 whole, 7 thirds equals 2 wholes plus a third, or $2\frac{1}{3}$.

17. $\frac{7}{6} > \frac{13}{12}$; $\frac{7}{6}$ is equal to $\frac{14}{12}$, and $\frac{14}{12}$ is greater than $\frac{13}{12}$.

18. $\frac{13}{3}$ falls one third of the way from 4 to 5 on the number line. Since 3 thirds is one whole, 13 thirds is 4 wholes plus a third, or $4\frac{1}{3}$.

19. Possible answer: You could draw a fraction strip and divide it into five equal parts. Shade three of these parts to represent $\frac{3}{5}$. Then divide each of the five parts into two equal parts. You would then have ten equal parts, and six of the parts would be shaded. Therefore, $\frac{3}{5}$ is the same as $\frac{6}{10}$, so $\frac{6}{10}$ is equivalent to $\frac{3}{5}$.

Connections

20. See below left.

21. See below left.

22. See page 30k.

23. See page 30k.

20.

21.

24. See below right.

25. See below right.

26. $\frac{1}{3}$

27. $\frac{5}{6}$

24.

25.

In 26 and 27, write a fraction to describe the part of the length of a new pencil represented by the old pencil.

26.

27.

In 28–36, compare each fraction to the benchmarks $0, \frac{1}{2}, 1, 1\frac{1}{2}$, and 2. Determine between which two benchmarks the fraction falls, and then determine to which benchmark the fraction is nearest. Organize your answers in a table. The columns of your table should be labeled as shown here:

Number	Lower benchmark	Upper benchmark	Nearest benchmark

24.

25.

28. $\frac{3}{5}$　　　　**29.** $1\frac{2}{6}$　　　　**30.** $\frac{12}{10}$

31. $\frac{2}{18}$　　　　**32.** $1\frac{8}{10}$　　　　**33.** $1\frac{1}{10}$

34. $\frac{12}{24}$　　　　**35.** $\frac{9}{6}$　　　　**36.** $1\frac{12}{15}$

37. These bars represent trips that Ms. Axler took in her job this week.

300 km

180 km

240 km

a. On a copy of each bar, shade in the distance Ms. Axler had traveled when she had gone one third of the total distance for the trip.

b. How many kilometers had Ms. Axler traveled when she was at the one-third point in each trip? Explain your reasoning.

Extensions

In 38–40, find every fraction with a denominator less than 50 that is equivalent to the given fraction.

38. $\frac{3}{15}$　　　　**39.** $\frac{8}{3}$　　　　**40.** $1\frac{4}{6}$

41. Find five fractions between $\frac{1}{4}$ and $\frac{1}{2}$.

42. Which of the fractions below represents the largest part of a whole? Explain your reasoning.

$$\frac{4}{5} \qquad \frac{17}{23} \qquad \frac{51}{68}$$

28.–36. See below left.

37a. See page 30k.

37b. 100 km, 60 km, 80 km; Explanations will vary.

Extensions

38. $\frac{1}{5}, \frac{2}{10}, \frac{6}{30}, \frac{9}{45}$

39. $\frac{16}{6}, \frac{24}{9}, \frac{32}{12}, \frac{40}{15}, \frac{48}{18}, \frac{56}{21}, \frac{64}{24}, \frac{72}{27}, \frac{80}{30}, \frac{88}{33}, \frac{96}{36}, \frac{104}{39}, \frac{112}{42}, \frac{120}{45}, \frac{128}{48}$

40. $\frac{5}{3}, \frac{10}{6}, \frac{15}{9}, \frac{20}{12}, \frac{25}{15}, \frac{30}{18}, \frac{40}{24}, \frac{50}{30}, \frac{60}{36}, \frac{70}{42}, \frac{80}{48}$, or the equivalent mixed number

41. Possible answer: $\frac{5}{16}, \frac{3}{8}, \frac{13}{32}, \frac{7}{16}, \frac{31}{64}$

42. $\frac{4}{5}$; To compare $\frac{4}{5}$ to $\frac{17}{23}$, you can write equivalent fractions with 5×23, or 115, as the denominator. This gives $\frac{4}{5} = \frac{92}{115}$ and $\frac{17}{23} = \frac{85}{115}$. So $\frac{4}{5}$ is larger. To compare $\frac{4}{5}$ and $\frac{51}{68}$, you can use 5×68, or 340, as the common denominator to get $\frac{4}{5} = \frac{272}{340}$ and $\frac{51}{68} = \frac{255}{340}$. So $\frac{4}{5}$ is larger.

	Number	Lower benchmark	Upper benchmark	Nearest benchmark
28.	$\frac{3}{5}$	$\frac{1}{2}$	1	$\frac{1}{2}$
29.	$1\frac{2}{6}$	1	$1\frac{1}{2}$	$1\frac{1}{2}$
30.	$\frac{12}{10}$	1	$1\frac{1}{2}$	1
31.	$\frac{2}{18}$	0	$\frac{1}{2}$	0
32.	$1\frac{8}{10}$	$1\frac{1}{2}$	2	2
33.	$1\frac{1}{10}$	1	$1\frac{1}{2}$	1
34.	$\frac{12}{24}$	$\frac{1}{2}$	$\frac{1}{2}$	equal to $\frac{1}{2}$
35.	$\frac{9}{6}$	$1\frac{1}{2}$	$1\frac{1}{2}$	equal to $1\frac{1}{2}$
36.	$1\frac{12}{15}$	$1\frac{1}{2}$	2	2

Possible Answers

1. $\frac{6}{10}$, $\frac{9}{15}$, $\frac{12}{20}$, $\frac{15}{25}$, $\frac{18}{30}$, and $\frac{21}{35}$; These fractions can be found by multiplying the numerator and denominator of $\frac{3}{5}$ by the whole numbers 2, 3, 4, 5, 6, and 7.

2. Start by deciding whether the fraction is in the interval from 0 to $\frac{1}{2}$ or the interval from $\frac{1}{2}$ to 1. Then decide to which endpoint of the interval the fraction is closest. You can think of dividing the number line into the number of equal parts indicated by the denominator, and use the numerator to determine approximately where the fraction would be on the number line. This will give you an idea of which endpoint the fraction is closest to.

3. If the denominators are the same, the fraction with the greater numerator is larger. If the numerators are the same, the fraction with the smaller denominator is larger. If the denominators are different, check to see if one fraction is between 0 and $\frac{1}{2}$ and the other is between $\frac{1}{2}$ and 1. If this is true, the fraction between $\frac{1}{2}$ and 1 is larger. If both the numerators and the denominators are different, try to change one of the fractions to an equivalent fraction with the same denominator as the other fraction or find an equivalent fraction for each fraction so that the denominators are the same. Then, compare the numerators.

Mathematical Reflections

In this investigation, you explored equivalent fractions and compared fractions to benchmarks and other fractions. These questions will help you summarize what you have learned:

1 Find six fractions that are equivalent to $\frac{3}{5}$. Explain how you found the fractions.

2 How can you decide whether a given fraction is closest to 0, $\frac{1}{2}$, or 1?

3 How can you compare any two fractions to decide which is largest?

Think about your answers to these questions, discuss your ideas with other students and your teacher, and then write a summary of your findings in your journal.

TEACHING THE INVESTIGATION

2.1 • Comparing Notes

In this problem, students examine competing claims of three teachers about their fund-raising progress. Two of the teachers' claims turn out to be the same, raising the issue of equivalent fractions.

Launch

Tell the class the story of the teachers' debate about how best to report their fund-raising progress.

Explore

Problem 2.1 can be done rather quickly using a think-pair-share strategy. First, have students *think* about the problem on their own for 3 to 5 minutes. Then put the students in *pairs,* and have them *share* their ideas and try to reach consensus. If the students in a pair disagree, have each student listen to the other explain his or her argument. If, after hearing each other's arguments, the students still do not agree, have them write separate arguments to support their positions.

Take note of students who are reasoning in creative or interesting ways and call on them during the summary. Also, watch for naive reasoning that should be explored during the summary.

Summarize

Have several pairs present their answers. If possible, make sure there is at least one presentation supporting each teacher. It is possible that no pair will think Ms. Christos is correct. If so, ask your students to explain why Ms. Christos is incorrect. Students should see that both Mr. Park and Ms. Mendoza are correct and should be able to begin an explanation of why three fourths and six eighths describe the same part of the whole. If students understand the issues in the problem, move quickly to Problem 2.2.

2.2 • Finding Equivalent Fractions

In this problem, students compare fraction strips to find other names for $\frac{2}{3}$ and $\frac{3}{4}$. They use the patterns they discover to find fractions that are equivalent to $\frac{1}{8}$, $\frac{2}{5}$, and $\frac{5}{6}$.

Launch

Remind students what they discovered in Problem 2.1.

> In Problem 2.1, we found that $\frac{3}{4}$ and $\frac{6}{8}$ represent the same quantity. Can you think of another name for $\frac{3}{4}$?

> What about $\frac{2}{3}$? Do you know a different name for this fraction? Can you find another name by using your fraction strips?

Help students to understand the question posed in Problem 2.2. Point out that strips shown are a different length than those used in previous problems. Students need to develop flexibility in thinking about fractions modeled with strips of different lengths. At the same time, they need to recognize that comparing and interpreting fractions depend on the whole. For example, to use fraction strips to find different names for $\frac{3}{4}$, we need to look at a set of strips of a *single* length.

When you feel students understand what is being asked, have them work in small groups to explore the problem and the follow-up.

Explore

This problem is designed to encourage students to notice a pattern in finding equivalent fractions. This pattern can be generalized by the observation that you "multiply the numerator and denominator of the fraction by the same number" to produce an equivalent fraction. The *why* behind this observation is essential. *Do not give them the rule;* allow them to discover the pattern for themselves. If they do not see the pattern, wait until the summary to ask questions that will focus them and help them to see the pattern.

Circulate as students work, asking questions about why they think they are correct and how they are finding equivalent fractions. Students should use both mathematical and informal language to explain their thinking. They need to discuss their reasoning. Try not to assist them by filling in the missing parts of their explanations; just continue to guide them through your questions.

Summarize

Have a few students report on the patterns they discovered that were helpful for finding equivalent fractions. Many students will see that they can generate equivalent fractions by multiplying the numerator and the denominator by the same number. Some students may see the pattern as multiplying by 2 repeatedly, which is actually only part of the pattern. For example, in generating fractions equivalent to $\frac{3}{4}$, they would find $\frac{3}{4}, \frac{6}{8}, \frac{12}{16}$, and so on, skipping the other equivalent fractions. Ask questions to expose other possibilities, such as $\frac{9}{12}$ and $\frac{15}{20}$. You want students to propose the idea that you can multiply the numerator and the denominator of the original representation of the fraction by the same number—any whole number—to obtain an equivalent fraction. Once this idea comes up, be sure to ask:

> Why do you you think this works?

It is easy to get students to routinely multiply the numerator and denominator of a fraction by the same number to produce an equivalent fraction. However, it is important for them to build visual images and language to help them understand why this method works. They will need to spend time drawing pictures and comparing strips to really understand the concept. Use the following example to help explain the idea.

> Let's use fraction strips to explore what happens when we multiply the numerator and the denominator of a fraction by the same number.
>
> I can represent the fraction $\frac{1}{3}$ using a fraction strip. The denominator tells me to divide the whole strip into three equal parts. The numerator tells me that I am concerned with one of these three parts. (*Draw the following picture on the board, or show the first diagram on Transparency 2.2B.*)

What does it mean when I multiply the denominator of a fraction by a number? For example, what happens if I multiply the denominator of $\frac{1}{3}$ by 5?

Multiplying the denominator by 5 gives a new denominator of 15, so the strip is now divided into 15 equal parts. This means that each of the 3 parts of the original strip is now divided into 5 equal parts. Divide each section of your drawing into 5 equal parts, or show the second diagram on the transparency.

What does it mean when I multiply the numerator by the same number I multiplied the denominator by? For example, what happens when I multiply the numerator of $\frac{1}{3}$ by 5?

The new numerator, 5, tells you that you are concerned with 5 of these 15 parts. This make sense because, since each part of the original fraction strip has been divided into five pieces, it takes five times as many pieces to represent the same quantity. You can see from the drawing that 5 of these 15 smaller parts is exactly the same as 1 of the 3 original parts. That is, $\frac{5}{15}$ is equivalent to $\frac{1}{3}$.

$$\frac{1}{3} = \frac{5}{15}$$

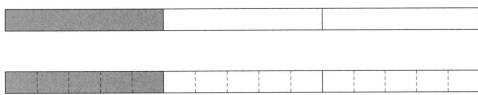

Help students understand that when they multiply the numerator and the denominator by the same number, they are actually multiplying by 1.

When I multiply the numerator and the denominator by the same number—for example, by 3—it is the same as multiplying by $\frac{3}{3}$. What is another name for this fraction?

Some students may suggest $\frac{4}{4}$ or $\frac{6}{6}$, but help them see that all of these fractions are equivalent to 1. Since the fraction is being multiplied by 1, the resulting fraction must have the same value as the original fraction.

2.3 • Making a Number Line

In this problem, students build a number line from 0 to 1, using information from all of their fraction strips. This problem enhances their understanding of equivalent fractions.

Launch

Launch the problem by demonstrating how to transfer the marks and labels from the halves and the thirds fraction strips to a number line. This process is described in the student edition.

You may want to demonstrate using the fourths strip as well, so that the issue of how to label numbers with more than one name arises.

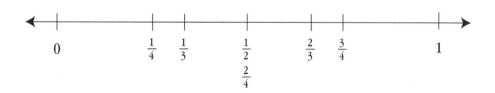

Explore

Circulate as students work individually, asking questions to keep them focused on why fractions they used to label the same mark are equivalent. As students finish, have them work on the follow-up, which asks them to add labels for fractions not included on their fraction strips.

Summarize

Display a few examples of student work, and talk about the equivalent fractions that are visible on the number lines.

This is a good time to revisit the meaning of fractions and to point toward finding equivalent fractions. Here are some questions you might ask:

> Which fraction strip shows a fraction equivalent to $\frac{2}{3}$ and a fraction equivalent to $\frac{3}{4}$?

Students can find this answer by inspecting $\frac{2}{3}$ and $\frac{3}{4}$ on their number lines. The marks for both of these numbers are also named by fractions with denominators of 12. The mark for $\frac{2}{3}$ is also labeled $\frac{8}{12}$, and the mark for $\frac{3}{4}$ is also labeled $\frac{9}{12}$. This indicates that the twelfths fraction strip shows fractions equivalent to both $\frac{2}{3}$ and $\frac{3}{4}$.

> What fraction strip could we add to our set that would also show a fraction equivalent to $\frac{2}{3}$ and a fraction equivalent to $\frac{3}{4}$?

Here you hope students begin to make the connection to multiples by observing, for example, that a twenty-fourths strip would show a name for both fractions.

> How can finding fractions equivalent to $\frac{2}{3}$ and $\frac{3}{4}$ that have the same denominator help you to compare $\frac{2}{3}$ and $\frac{3}{4}$?

When two fractions have the same denominator, you can compare their numerators; the fraction with the greater numerator is larger. Since $\frac{9}{12}$ is larger than $\frac{8}{12}$, $\frac{3}{4}$ is larger than $\frac{2}{3}$.

> Which is larger, $\frac{4}{6}$ or $\frac{7}{10}$? How do you know?

Students can find these fractions on their strips or on the number line and make visual comparisons. They can, but are not likely to, find equivalent fractions and compare them. Since 30 is a common multiple of 6 and 10, $\frac{4}{6}$ can be written $\frac{20}{30}$ and $\frac{7}{10}$ can be written $\frac{21}{30}$. Now it is clear that $\frac{7}{10}$ is larger—in fact, exactly $\frac{1}{30}$ larger.

2.4 • Comparing Fractions to Benchmarks

In this problem, students compare fractions to benchmarks. Benchmarks are numbers that are easy referents. For work with fractions, good benchmarks are 0, $\frac{1}{2}$, and 1.

Launch

Discuss the material on page 23 of the student edition. The text suggests that one way to estimate the size of a fraction is to compare it to 0, $\frac{1}{2}$, and 1. An example can help to make the method clear. You might use $\frac{2}{5}$, which is not in the list given in the problem.

> Which two benchmarks is $\frac{2}{5}$ between? Which benchmark is it closest to?

Some students may reason that if you divide a number line from 0 to 1 into fifths, it takes two and a half of these fifths to make one half. So, $\frac{2}{5}$ must be between 0 and $\frac{1}{2}$. Since two fifths is closer to two and a half fifths than it is to zero fifths, $\frac{2}{5}$ is closer to $\frac{1}{2}$ than to 0.

When you feel students understand this kind of reasoning, let them work in small groups on the problem.

Explore

Circulate as the groups work, asking students to explain their strategies for determining which benchmark each fraction is near and for ordering the fractions.

Summarize

Have students share strategies for making comparisons to benchmarks and for ordering fractions. Collect students' answers to part A and record the results in two lists on the board.

Between 0 and $\frac{1}{2}$ **Between $\frac{1}{2}$ and 1**

$\frac{1}{5}$ $\frac{2}{3}$

$\frac{3}{12}$ $\frac{8}{10}$

$\frac{3}{8}$ $\frac{3}{5}$

$\frac{2}{9}$ $\frac{5}{6}$

$\frac{1}{3}$ $\frac{5}{8}$

                $\frac{4}{5}$

                $\frac{3}{4}$

                $\frac{7}{12}$

> Look at the information displayed in the two lists. What do you notice about all the fractions in the interval from 0 to $\frac{1}{2}$?

Students usually notice that all the fractions have a numerator that is less than half its denominator.

What do you notice about all the fractions in the interval from $\frac{1}{2}$ to 1?

The numerator is more than half of the denominator for each of these fractions.

You may want to continue by collecting students' answers to part B and displaying the results in a table.

Closest to 0	Halfway between 0 and $\frac{1}{2}$	Closest to $\frac{1}{2}$	Halfway between $\frac{1}{2}$ and 1	Closest to 1
$\frac{1}{5}$	$\frac{3}{12}$	$\frac{3}{8}$	$\frac{3}{4}$	$\frac{8}{10}$
$\frac{2}{9}$		$\frac{1}{3}$		$\frac{5}{6}$
		$\frac{2}{3}$		$\frac{4}{5}$
		$\frac{3}{5}$		
		$\frac{5}{8}$		
		$\frac{7}{12}$		

Ask students to explain why $\frac{3}{8}$ is closer to $\frac{1}{2}$ than to 0 and why $\frac{3}{5}$ is closer to $\frac{1}{2}$ than to 1. Spend some time discussing where $\frac{3}{12}$ and $\frac{3}{4}$ belong. Students often want to "round up" and say that these numbers are closer to the right-hand benchmark. Take some time to discuss why rounding is not the issue in this problem. The question is concerned with the benchmarks these numbers are closest to in terms of *distance,* and these numbers are located exactly between two benchmarks.

To summarize part D, you may want to have students place the fractions on a large number line marked with 0, $\frac{1}{2}$, and 1. Ask students how their work with benchmarks in parts A and B helped them to order the fractions and what additional work they had to do to complete part D.

Work as a class on the follow-up. These questions provide an opportunity to review the methods the class has developed so far for comparing two fractions. Discussing these questions will help students review and synthesize what they know *right now.* We suggest that you work as a class to build a list of strategies for comparing fractions. Make sure students can explain why each strategy works. Here are some ideas the list might include:

- If the denominators are the same, compare the numerators. The fraction with the greater numerator is larger.

- If the numerators are the same, compare the denominators. The fraction with the smaller denominator is larger.

- If the denominators are different, check whether one fraction is between 0 and $\frac{1}{2}$ and the other is between $\frac{1}{2}$ and 1. If this is true, the fraction between $\frac{1}{2}$ and 1 is larger.

- If both the numerators and the denominators are different, try to change one of the fractions to an equivalent fraction with the same denominator as the other fraction. Then, compare the numerators.

- If both the numerators and the denominators are different, find equivalent fractions for both fractions so that the denominators are the same. Then, compare the numerators.

Discuss the fact that the fewer "rules" students must remember, the better off they will be. Ask students for ideas about how they could have fewer rules and still be able to make the necessary comparisons. Don't insist on formalizing the algorithm (that is, to find equivalent fractions with like denominators). Rather, help students go as far as they can in generalizing a strategy for finding equivalent fractions.

Continue working with your students, offering examples of fractions to compare or having them make up examples for each other. You may want to create a deck of index cards showing a variety of possible fractions, such as:

$$\frac{1}{2} \quad \frac{2}{2} \quad \frac{3}{2} \quad \frac{4}{2} \quad \frac{5}{2} \quad \frac{6}{2}$$

$$\frac{1}{3} \quad \frac{2}{3} \quad \frac{3}{3} \quad \frac{4}{3} \quad \frac{5}{3} \quad \frac{6}{3}$$

$$\frac{1}{4} \quad \frac{2}{4} \quad \frac{3}{4} \quad \frac{4}{4} \quad \frac{5}{4} \quad \frac{6}{4} \quad \frac{7}{4} \quad \frac{8}{4}$$

$$\frac{1}{5} \quad \frac{2}{5} \quad \frac{3}{5} \quad \frac{4}{5} \quad \frac{5}{5} \quad \frac{6}{5} \quad \frac{7}{5} \quad \frac{8}{5} \quad \frac{9}{5} \quad \frac{10}{5}$$

$$\frac{1}{6} \quad \frac{2}{6} \quad \frac{3}{6} \quad \frac{4}{6} \quad \frac{5}{6} \quad \frac{6}{6} \quad \frac{7}{6} \quad \frac{8}{6} \quad \frac{9}{6} \quad \frac{10}{6}$$

$$\frac{1}{8} \quad \frac{2}{8} \quad \frac{3}{8} \quad \frac{4}{8} \quad \frac{5}{8} \quad \frac{6}{8} \quad \frac{7}{8} \quad \frac{8}{8} \quad \frac{9}{8} \quad \frac{10}{8}$$

$$\frac{1}{10} \quad \frac{2}{10} \quad \frac{3}{10} \quad \frac{4}{10} \quad \frac{5}{10} \quad \frac{6}{10} \quad \frac{7}{10} \quad \frac{8}{10} \quad \frac{9}{10} \quad \frac{10}{10} \quad \frac{11}{10}$$

$$\frac{1}{12} \quad \frac{2}{12} \quad \frac{3}{12} \quad \frac{4}{12} \quad \frac{5}{12} \quad \frac{6}{12} \quad \frac{7}{12} \quad \frac{8}{12} \quad \frac{9}{12} \quad \frac{10}{12} \quad \frac{11}{12} \quad \frac{12}{12}$$

Students can turn two index cards face up and compare the two fractions, recording the fractions and the result of their comparison. You might challenge them to arrange all the cards in pairs so that the first fraction in each pair is larger than the second fraction.

Periodically, you can return to the class list of strategies to see whether students have found better ways to make comparisons.

2.5 • Fractions Greater Than One

Making the transition from fractions between 0 and 1 to fractions greater than 1 is often difficult for students. This problem is designed to help them see that they can reason about fractions within the interval between any two consecutive whole numbers in the same way they reason about fractions between 0 and 1. To write a fraction greater than 1 as a mixed number, students can find the fraction portion the same way they find fractions between 0 and 1; the whole number portion is simply the whole number on the number line immediately to the left of the fraction.

Launch

This is a good time to begin making a class number line that extends from 0 to 10 (or beyond) with consecutive whole numbers exactly 16 cm apart (so that the class can use their fraction strips to fill in the in-between points).

> So far, we have worked with the part of the number line between 0 and 1. In this problem, we will look at the part of the number line between 1 and 2.

Show a 16 cm number line from 1 to 2 on the overhead projector, or demonstrate using the section of the class number line from 1 to 2.

> How can we use our strips to find fractions between these two whole numbers? (*Ask a student who has an idea to demonstrate.*)
>
> How would we label this amount? (*Point to the halfway mark.*) How about this amount? (*Point to the mark that is one fourth of the way from 1 to 2.*)

Discuss how to label the point halfway between 1 and 2 as both a mixed number ($1\frac{1}{2}$) and an improper fraction ($\frac{3}{2}$). You may need to ask how many halves are in $1\frac{1}{2}$ to get students to think about labeling points with improper fractions. Then, ask them to help you label the point one fourth of the way between 1 and 2 with both an improper fraction and a mixed number. This point can be labeled $1\frac{1}{4}$. Since there are four fourths in 1, plus another fourth after the 1, it can also be labeled $\frac{5}{4}$.

> What are some ways we can reason about how to label marks on this number line without using our fraction strips?

Students may suggest making a copy of the number line and folding it. Others might want to measure the line and find what part of the length each mark represents. Since the number line is 16 cm in length, this strategy can be used to label some of the points quite easily. For instance, the fourths marks will be 4 cm apart.

> With your partner, look at the number line on page 24. Use your strips, or other strategies that make sense to you, to label all of the lettered points. Add to your answers any equivalent labels for the flagged points that have denominators of 12 or smaller. Label the points with both mixed numbers and improper fractions.

Explore

Some pairs will need help labeling the points with improper fractions. Help these pairs by asking them questions.

> How many parts of this size would be in the whole? We have this many more parts of this size. How many does that make in all?

When students seem ready, explain part B of Problem 2.5.

> The second part of the problem asks you to add and label some points. The problem has requirements on where the points are to be added. Read these carefully, and work with your partner to find good answers that you can defend.

If pairs finish early, ask them to think about the follow-up.

Summarize

Have students share their answers and strategies for labeling the lettered points. You could choose a pair of students to label the marks representing the lettered points on the class number line. Challenge other pairs to fill other intervals on the number line. You might assign a pair of students to each whole number interval. Leave this number line on display; adding to it is a good way for students to continue to build an understanding of fractions as numbers that measure lengths in between whole numbers.

If you think your students are ready, pose the following questions to encourage them to think about an efficient way to convert a mixed number to an improper fraction and vice versa.

> I noticed an interesting pattern when you were presenting your evidence on this problem. Look at this mixed number. (*Write* $4\frac{3}{5}$ *on the board.*) How can we write this number as an improper fraction—that is, as a fraction whose numerator is larger than its denominator?

Students should be able to reason that since there are 20 fifths in 4, plus 3 more fifths in $\frac{3}{5}$, the improper fraction representation is $\frac{23}{5}$.

> (*Point to the appropriate numbers in the* $4\frac{3}{5}$ *you have written on the board as you explain the following.*) If I multiply 4 by 5 and add 3, I get 20 + 3, or 23. (*Write 20 + 3 = 23 on the board.*) This is the *numerator* of the improper fraction representation. Do you suppose this will always work? Why?

This always works. When we multiply the whole number, 4, by the denominator, 5, the result tells us how many fifths there are in the whole number. When we add 3, we are finding the total number of fifths in the mixed number. The result, 23, becomes the numerator, and 5 becomes the denominator.

> I wonder whether we can go the other way. How would we write a number like $\frac{11}{3}$ as a number with a whole number part and a fraction less than 1?

Ask students to share their ideas. Hopefully they will see that they need to make as many wholes as possible and write the parts left over as a fraction. In this example, we have 11 parts. It takes 3 parts to make one whole. There are 3 groups of 3 parts in 11, with 2 parts left over. This gives us 3 wholes and 2 thirds, or $3\frac{2}{3}$. If your students do not come up with this, just continue to ask questions as opportunities arise during the remainder of the unit. The terms *improper fraction* and *mixed number* are not important; they are just convenient ways to be more precise. Your students may do just fine using their own informal words to describe these two kinds of representation.

Additional Answers

Answers to Problem 2.3

A.

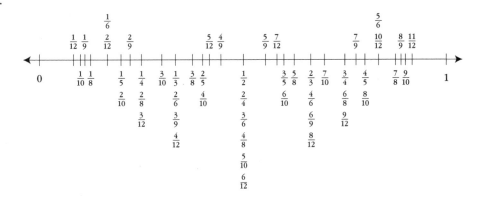

Answers to Problem 2.4 Follow-Up

1. Explanations will vary.

   a. $\frac{3}{12} < \frac{7}{12}$

   b. $\frac{5}{6} > \frac{5}{8}$

   c. $\frac{2}{3} > \frac{3}{9}$

   d. $\frac{13}{12} < \frac{6}{5}$

2. Explanations will vary.

   a. $\frac{4}{7} < \frac{6}{7}$

   b. $\frac{7}{10} > \frac{8}{12}$

   c. $\frac{5}{8} < \frac{6}{9}$

   d. $\frac{10}{12} = \frac{5}{6}$

   e. $\frac{2}{4} < \frac{5}{9}$

   f. $\frac{3}{9} > \frac{3}{10}$

ACE Answers

Applications

6.

7.

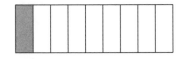

Connections

22.

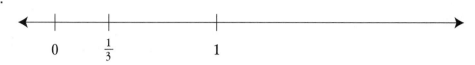

23.

37a. 300 km [bar graph]

180 km [bar graph]

240 km [bar graph]

Cooking with Fractions

So far in this unit, we have been using fractions to express parts of a whole. Our visual model for representing fractions has been the fraction strip, which is related to a number line and a ruler. In this investigation, students are introduced to another powerful visual representation of fractions: representations that model fractions as subdivisions of areas of figures.

In one sense, the fraction strip is an area model. However, we have ignored width and focused on length as the salient feature of the model. In this investigation, we focus on ways to subdivide the area of a figure to model fractions. While rectangles and squares are nice figures to work with because they are easy to subdivide, we include some nonrectangles in the ACE questions to help students see that, theoretically, we can use any area as long as we can divide it into equal-size parts.

In Problem 3.1, Area Models for Fractions, students explore the possible ways to cut a square pan of brownies into 15 equal-size large brownies, 20 equal-size medium brownies, and 30 equal-size small brownies. Problem 3.2, Baking Brownies, challenges students to adjust a recipe to make enough brownies to serve a given number of students.

Mathematical and Problem-Solving Goals

- *To continue building an understanding of equivalent fractions*

- *To explore the use of squares and other areas as a way to build visual models of fractional parts of a whole*

- *To explore real-life problems that require operations on fractions in a context that invites the use of informal strategies rather than formal rules and algorithms*

Materials		
Problem	**For students**	**For the teacher**
All	Calculators	Transparencies 3.1 to 3.2B (optional)
3.1	Labsheet 3.1 (1 per student)	Transparencies of Labsheet 3.1 (optional)
3.2	Rulers or other straightedges	

Student Pages 31–38   **Teaching the Investigation 38a–38g**

INVESTIGATION 3

Cooking with Fractions

$\mathbf{Y}$ou have made and used fraction strips to help you think about fractions as parts of wholes. You have used your strips to name fractional amounts, to compare fractions, to find equivalent fractions, and to make a number line showing fractions between whole numbers.

3.1 Area Models for Fractions

You can also think about fractions as parts of a region. For example, if a pizza is cut into eight slices of the same size, and you eat two of the slices, you have eaten two eighths of the pizza. If you eat five of the slices, you have eaten five eighths of the pizza.

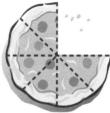 

$\frac{2}{8}$ has been eaten $\frac{5}{8}$ has been eaten

If you divide a square pan of brownies into equal-size brownies and then eat two brownies, what part of the batch have you eaten? To answer this question, you need to know the total number of brownies in the batch.

Problem 3.1

Use the squares on Labsheet 3.1 as models for pans of brownies. Show the cuts you would make to divide a pan of brownies into
A. 15 equal-size large brownies
B. 20 equal-size medium brownies
C. 30 equal-size small brownies

Answers to Problem 3.1

See page 38d.

Answers to Problem 3.1 Follow-Up

1. $\frac{1}{30}$, $\frac{1}{20}$, $\frac{1}{15}$; If a pan of brownies is divided into 30 equal-size pieces, then one of these pieces is $\frac{1}{30}$ of the whole pan. Explanations for the medium and large brownies are similar.

2. a. There are two ways; see answer to Problem 3.1, part A.
    b. There are three ways; see answer to Problem 3.1, part B.
    c. There are four ways; see answer to Problem 3.1, part C.

- - - - - - - - - - - - - -
At a Glance

Grouping:
Small Groups

Launch

■ Elicit ideas about how a pan of brownies could be cut into equal-size pieces.

Explore

■ As students work, remind them of things they already know that may help.

■ Encourage students to connect the brownie-cutting problem to factors of numbers.

■ Have groups that are thinking in creative ways record their answers on transparencies of Labsheet 3.1.

Summarize

■ Have students explain their results.

■ Ask questions to help students think more deeply about the problem.

■ Have students create their own brownie-cutting problems. (*optional*)
- - - - - - - - - - - - - -

Assignment Choices

ACE questions 13, 18–23, 24–32, and unassigned choices from earlier problems

Baking Brownies

■ **Problem 3.1 Follow-Up**

1. What fraction of a whole pan is one small brownie? One medium brownie? One large brownie? Explain.

2. **a.** Is there more than one way to cut a pan of brownies into 15 equal-size large brownies? If so, show the other ways. If not, explain why it cannot be done.

    b. Is there more than one way to cut a pan of brownies into 20 equal-size medium brownies? If so, show the other ways. If not, explain why it cannot be done.

    c. Is there more than one way to cut a pan of brownies into 30 equal-size small brownies? If so, show the other ways. If not, explain why it cannot be done.

3.2 Baking Brownies

Next week, the eighth graders from Sturgis Middle School are attending school camp. Samantha, Romero, and Harold have the job of making brownies for an afternoon snack for the entire camp—all 240 people!

Chunky Brownies with a Crust

$1\frac{1}{4}$ cups flour

$\frac{1}{4}$ cup sugar

$\frac{1}{2}$ cup cold butter or margarine

1 14-ounce can sweetened condensed milk

$\frac{1}{4}$ cup unsweetened cocoa

1 egg

1 teaspoon vanilla

$\frac{1}{2}$ teaspoon baking powder

1 7-ounce bar milk chocolate, broken into small chunks

$\frac{3}{4}$ cup chopped nuts (optional)

Preheat the oven to 350 degrees. In a medium bowl, combine 1 cup of flour and the sugar. Cut in the margarine or butter until crumbly. Press the mixture firmly into the bottom of a 10-by-10-inch baking pan. Bake 15 minutes. Meanwhile, in a large mixing bowl, beat the sweetened condensed milk, the cocoa, the egg, the remaining flour, the vanilla, and the baking powder. Stir in the nuts and chocolate chunks. Spread over the prepared crust. Bake 20 minutes. Cool. Sprinkle with confectioner's sugar if desired. Store tightly covered at room temperature. Makes 15 large, 20 medium, or 30 small brownies.

Problem 3.2

A. Do you think Samantha, Romero, and Harold should make small, medium, or large brownies?

B. If they make brownies of the size you chose in part A, how much of each ingredient will they need to make enough to serve a brownie to each person at camp?

C. Describe the strategy you used to get your answer to part B.

■ Problem 3.2 Follow-Up

Compare your answers for part B to the answers of classmates who did calculations for the other two sizes.

Suppose you get to decide which size brownies will be served to the campers. Tell which size you would choose in each situation below. Explain your answer.

1. You are in charge of buying the ingredients, and you have a limited budget.

2. You have to help make the brownies.

3. You don't have to do any work, you just get to eat the brownies.

Answers to Problem 3.2

A. Answers will vary.

B. See the table on page 38c.

C. Answers will vary.

Answers to Problem 3.2 Follow-Up

1. Most students will choose the small brownies because they would cost the least to make.

2. Answers will vary.

3. Answers will vary.

Answers

Applications

1. Possible answer:

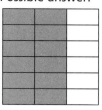

2. Possible answer:

3. Possible answer:

4. Possible answer:

5. Possible answer:

6. See right.

7. See right.

8. See page 38d.

9. See page 38e.

10. $\frac{1}{8}$

11. $\frac{5}{16}$

12. $\frac{9}{28}$

13. $\frac{10}{64} = \frac{5}{32}$

Applications • Connections • Extensions

As you work on these ACE questions, use your calculator whenever you need it.

Applications

In 1–4, illustrate each fraction by drawing a square, subdividing it into equal-size regions, and shading the fractional part indicated.

1. $\frac{7}{20}$ **2.** $\frac{3}{15}$ **3.** $\frac{12}{18}$ **4.** $\frac{3}{7}$

In 5–8, illustrate each fraction by drawing a square and subdividing it in a different way than you did for questions 1–4.

5. $\frac{7}{20}$ **6.** $\frac{3}{15}$ **7.** $\frac{12}{18}$ **8.** $\frac{3}{7}$

9. Show $\frac{3}{12}$ in three different ways by subdividing and shading a square.

In 10–13, tell what fractional part of the whole figure is shaded.

10. 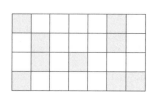   **11.**

12.    **13.**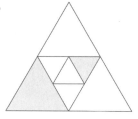

---

6. Possible answer:

7. Possible answer:

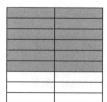

14. Gerhard wants to make Tahini Granola Cookies to bring on a hiking trip.

Tahini Granola Cookies

These cookies are an excellent high-energy snack
to take on camping trips or hikes.

$\frac{1}{2}$ cup tahini	$\frac{1}{2}$ cup melted butter
$\frac{2}{3}$ cups honey	2 cups of your favorite granola
2 teaspoons vanilla	$\frac{1}{4}$ cup chopped nuts

Preheat the oven to 350°. Blend the tahini and honey together. Add the vanilla
and butter and mix well. Add the granola and nuts and mix well. Drop by
tablespoon, $1\frac{1}{2}$ to 2 inches apart, on the cookie sheet and bake 10–15 minutes
or until golden brown. Transfer to a dry surface to cool. Makes about 3 dozen
cookies.

---

a. How much of each ingredient will Gerhard need to make five batches of
granola cookies?

b. Instead of dropping spoonfuls of dough onto the pans, Gerhard pressed the
dough evenly into square pans. When the granola cookie mix had baked, he
cut it into bars. Show several ways Gerhard can cut a pan of granola cookies
to get three dozen bars.

Connections

15. **a.** How many fourths are in $4\frac{1}{4}$? (A number like $4\frac{1}{4}$ is called a *mixed number*—it
is a mix of a whole number and a fraction.)

b. Use your answer to part a to write $4\frac{1}{4}$ as a fraction with a denominator of 4.
(This is sometimes called changing the form of a number from a mixed
number to an *improper fraction.*)

Investigation 3: Cooking with Fractions 35

14a. tahini: $\frac{5}{2}$ or $2\frac{1}{2}$ cups

honey: $\frac{10}{3}$ or $3\frac{1}{3}$ cups

vanilla: 10 teaspoons

butter: $\frac{5}{2}$ or $2\frac{1}{2}$ cups

granola: 10 cups

nuts: $\frac{5}{4}$ or $1\frac{1}{4}$ cups

14b. See page 38e.

15a. There are 17 fourths in $4\frac{1}{4}$.

15b. $\frac{17}{4}$

Connections

16a. There are 8 fifths in $1\frac{3}{5}$.

16b. $\frac{8}{5}$

17a. There are 23 sixths in $3\frac{5}{6}$.

17b. $\frac{23}{6}$

18. See below right.

19. See page 38e.

20. See page 38e.

21. See page 38f.

22. See page 38f.

23. See page 38f.

24. $\frac{2}{5}$

25. $\frac{1}{9}$

26. Possible answer:

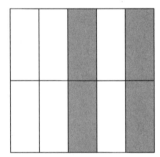

27. Possible answer:

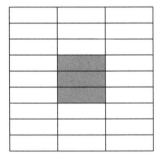

---

16. a. How many fifths are in $1\frac{3}{5}$?

    b. Use your answer to part a to write $1\frac{3}{5}$ as a fraction with a denominator of 5.

17. a. How many sixths are in $3\frac{5}{6}$?

    b. Use your answer to part a write $3\frac{5}{6}$ as a fraction with a denominator of 6.

In 18–23, draw, subdivide, and shade square regions to illustrate and complete each statement. For example, the statement $\frac{?}{10} = \frac{3}{5}$ can be illustrated like this:

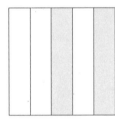
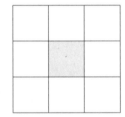

The illustration shows that $\frac{6}{10} = \frac{3}{5}$.

18. $\frac{3}{15} = \frac{?}{30}$ **19.** $\frac{18}{30} = \frac{?}{15}$ **20.** $\frac{1}{2} = \frac{?}{20}$

21. $\frac{?}{15} = \frac{3}{5}$ **22.** $\frac{?}{20} = \frac{3}{5}$ **23.** $\frac{9}{15} = \frac{?}{30}$

In 24 and 25, tell what fraction of each square is shaded.

24. 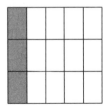   **25.**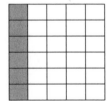

26. Draw a picture to illustrate a fraction with a denominator of 10 that is equivalent to the fraction shown in question 24.

27. Draw a picture to illustrate a fraction with a denominator of 27 that is equivalent to the fraction illustrated in question 25.

36   **Bits and Pieces I**

---

18. $\frac{3}{15} = \frac{6}{30}$. Possible illustrations:

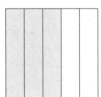

28. Order the following fractions from smallest to largest:

$$1\frac{7}{10} \qquad \frac{5}{3} \qquad 1\frac{12}{18} \qquad \frac{25}{15}$$

In 29–31, use this drawing of a portion of a ruler. The numbers indicate inches.

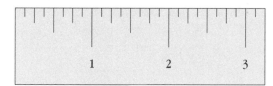

29. What fraction does each mark between the left end of the ruler and the 1-inch mark represent?

30. If the smallest sections of the ruler were each divided into two equal parts, how should the new parts between 0 and 1 be labeled?

31. What fractions do the marks between 1 inch and 2 inches represent?

Extensions

32. If a 13-by-9-inch brownie pan is divided into 20 equal-size brownies, what are the dimensions of one brownie?

28. $\frac{5}{3} = \frac{25}{15} = 1\frac{12}{18}$, $1\frac{7}{10}$ ($\frac{5}{3}$, $\frac{25}{15}$, and $1\frac{12}{18}$ are equivalent, and all are less than $1\frac{7}{10}$)

29. See below left.

30. See below left.

31. See page 38f.

Extensions

32. See page 38g.

29.

30.

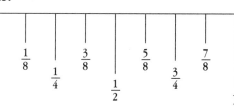

38

Possible Answers

1. You look at the denominator of the fraction to see how many equal parts to divide the square into. Then you shade the number of parts given by the numerator of the fraction.

2. You can compare the square models to determine which has a larger shaded area; this model represents the larger fraction.

3. You count the total number of equal parts; this is the denominator of the fraction. Then you count the number of shaded parts; this is the numerator of the fraction.

In this investigation, you divided squares and rectangles into regions to help you model fractions. These questions will help you summarize what you have learned:

1 Describe your strategy for dividing a square to represent a fraction.

2 How can square models help you decide which of two fractions is larger?

3 How do you find the fraction name for a shaded part of a square? Use a specific example if it helps you to think about the process.

Think about your answers to these questions, discuss your ideas with other students and your teacher, and then write a summary of your findings in your journal.

Tips for the Linguistically Diverse Classroom

Original Rebus The Original Rebus technique is described in detail in *Getting to Know Connected Mathematics*. Students make a copy of the text before it is discussed. During discussion, they generate their own rebuses for words they do not understand as the words are made comprehensible through pictures, objects, or demonstrations. Example: Question 3—key words for which students may make rebuses are *fraction name* ($\frac{a}{b}$), *shaded* (a shaded square), *square* (a square), *example* (a square with $\frac{1}{4}$ shaded).

3.1 • Area Models for Fractions

In this problem, a pan of brownies is used as an area model for fractions.

Launch

Make sure students understand the context of the problem.

> How many of you have made a pan of brownies and cut it into pieces?

Draw a square on the board or at the overhead projector.

> Suppose this square represents a pan of brownies hot out of the oven. If you wanted to cut brownies that are all the same size, how many brownies would you cut? How would you make the cuts?

Try to elicit more than one suggestion. You or students can demonstrate the ideas as they are raised.

> In this problem, you will explore the ways you can cut a pan of brownies to get 30 small brownies, 20 medium brownies, or 15 large brownies.

Give each person a copy of Labsheet 3.1, which has several squares for modeling brownie pans.

Explore

Have students work in small groups or pairs to explore the problem and the follow-up. There are several ways for students to cut the brownies to get 15 large, 20 medium, or 30 small brownies. Some groups will have a hard time finding one or two ways; others will quickly find several.

You may be surprised at how hard it is for students to draw reasonable representations of their cutting strategies. Remind them that they know folding strategies that may help. They can fold strips of paper with the same length as a square side into fractional parts and use the folded strips as guides. Some students will try to measure with a ruler. This can be difficult if the divisions of the measured length do not align with marks on the ruler.

Be on the lookout for students who are connecting this problem to factors of numbers as explored in the *Prime Time* unit. You might encourage this connection by asking questions about the factors of 15, 20, and 30. The rectangles students made for these numbers in *Prime Time* can help them here. Note that in this problem the factor pairs do not represent the dimensions of rectangles, but the number of strips cut in each direction to produce the given number of pieces.

Look for groups that are thinking about the problem in an organized, interesting, or creative way. Give these groups transparencies of Labsheet 3.1 on which to record their answers. They can use these transparencies to present their strategies during the summary.

Summarize

Have students share their answers and strategies. Ask them to explain why the cuts they made will work.

> What part of the whole pan would a small brownie be? ($\frac{1}{30}$) What part of the whole pan would a medium brownie be? ($\frac{1}{20}$) A large brownie? ($\frac{1}{15}$).
>
> How would you describe the shape of a small brownie cut in each of the ways we have found? (*They range from long and very skinny to almost square.*)
>
> Are all the small brownies the same size (area) even though they have different shapes? (*yes; They are all $\frac{1}{30}$ of a pan.*)
>
> If I ate three small brownies, two medium brownies, and one large brownie, how much of a pan of brownies would I have eaten? ($\frac{4}{15}$, or $\frac{8}{30}$, or $\frac{16}{60}$) How would I feel?

Here students must add $\frac{3}{30} + \frac{2}{20} + \frac{1}{15}$. Let them try to devise strategies for tackling the problem. If the strategy of finding a common multiple and renaming the fractions does not come up, suggest it yourself.

> Would it be easier to find the total amount if we renamed the fractions so they all had the same denominator? Why would this be a helpful strategy? What denominator could we use?

Don't compel students to consider an algorithm for adding fractions at this time. There will be many opportunities for them to think about how to combine fractions. They will have a deeper understanding if you let them make sense of these ideas. Just continue to ask questions whenever the opportunity arises.

Always try to ask questions that reverse the information students know and the information they must figure out. In this problem, students started out knowing the number of brownies, and they determined what fraction of the whole that number of brownies represented. Here is a problem that begins with fractions.

> Rodrigo ate the equivalent of a fourth of a pan of brownies before he turned green. He ate at least one brownie of each size. What are some possibilities for the number of brownies of each size that Rodrigo ate? (*The possibilities are three medium, one large, and one small brownie; or two large, one medium, and two small brownies.*)

At this point, you may want to have students make up some problems of their own about brownies of different sizes.

3.2 • Baking Brownies

Since the students do not have any formal way to add or multiply fractions, this problem is designed to encourage them to construct their own ways of combining fractions. Some of your students will exhibit some very good thinking; some will struggle. Since the fractions are simple, involving halves and fourths, most students should be able to reason through the problem.

Launch

Read the story about the students making brownies aloud to your class. Then have students read the problem. Make sure they understand what is being asked.

As it is written, the problem asks students to choose which size brownies to serve and then to figure out how much of each ingredient is needed. To make checking the answers more manageable, you may wish instead to have all the groups do calculations for small brownies.

Explore

If students are having trouble, you can get them started by asking questions.

> What size brownie did you choose? How many brownies of that size are in one batch? How many batches would you need to make 240 brownies?

One batch is 15 large, 20 medium, or 30 small brownies. Since the brownies must feed 240 people, 16 batches are needed to make large brownies, 12 batches are needed to make medium brownies, and 8 batches are needed to make small brownies.

Once they have determined the number of batches needed, students must find the amount of each ingredient required. For example, the quantity of chopped nuts required to make the large brownies is $16 \times \frac{3}{4}$. One group found this quantity by first combining $\frac{3}{4} + \frac{3}{4} + \frac{3}{4} + \frac{3}{4}$ to get $\frac{12}{4}$. They recognized this as 3 cups and then reasoned that they needed 4×3 cups or 12 cups of nuts.

Summarize

Have students share their ideas about the solutions. Here is a summary chart for each brownie size (this chart appears on Transparency 3.2B).

	Small brownie (30)	Medium brownie (20)	Large brownie (15)
Batches for 240	8 batches	12 batches	16 batches
Cups flour	10	15	20
Cups sugar	2	3	4
Cups butter	4	6	8
Cans milk	8	12	16
Cups cocoa	2	3	4
Eggs	8	12	16
Tsp. vanilla	8	12	16
Tsp. baking powder	4	6	8
No. 7-oz choc. bars	8	12	16
Cups nuts	6	9	12

Some of your students will probably see that they can obtain the values for the "Medium brownie" column by taking one and a half of the corresponding ingredient in the "Small brownie" column. Also, large brownies will take twice as many pans and twice as much of each ingredient as small brownies.

Additional Answers

Answers to Problem 3.1

A.   Possible answers:

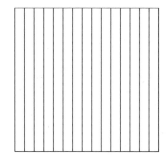   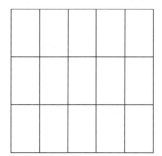

B.   Possible answers:

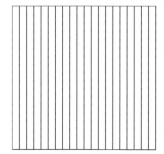   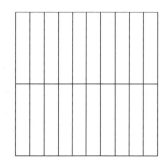   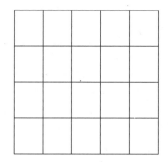

C.   Possible answers:

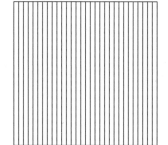   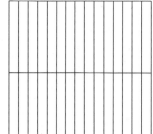   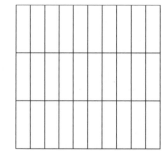

ACE Answers

Applications

8. Possible answer:

9. Possible answer:

 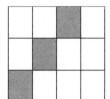 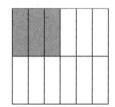

14b. Possible answers:

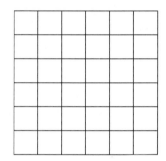 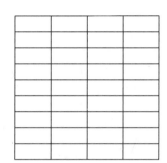 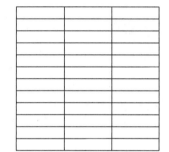

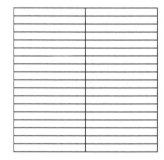 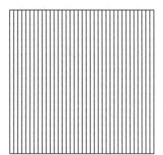

Connections

19. $\frac{18}{30} = \frac{6}{10}$ Possible illustrations:

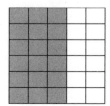 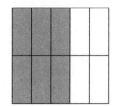

20. $\frac{1}{2} = \frac{10}{20}$. Possible illustrations:

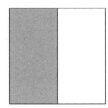 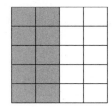

21. $\frac{9}{15} = \frac{3}{5}$. Possible illustrations:

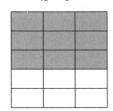 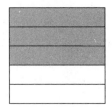

22. $\frac{12}{20} = \frac{3}{5}$. Possible illustrations:

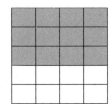 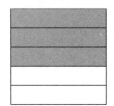

23. $\frac{9}{15} = \frac{18}{30}$. Possible illustrations:

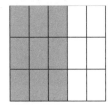 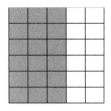

31.

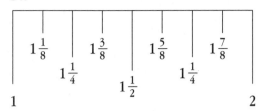

Extensions

32. There are two possible ways to cut the brownies. For the first pan, each brownie has dimensions $2\frac{1}{4}'' \times 2\frac{3}{5}''$ (or $\frac{9}{4}'' \times \frac{13}{5}''$). For the second pan, each brownie has dimensions $1\frac{4}{5}'' \times 3\frac{1}{4}''$ (or $\frac{9}{5}'' \times \frac{13}{4}''$).

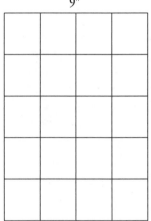

9"

13"

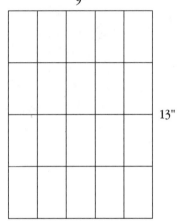

9"

13"

From Fractions to Decimals

This investigation uses square grids as a context for introducing decimal numbers. It is assumed that students have dealt with decimals in previous grades.

In Problem 4.1, Designing a Garden, students plan a 100-square-meter garden plot, arranging it to accommodate specified vegetables. In doing so, they explore representing fractional parts of a whole. In Problem 4.2, Making Smaller Parts, students are encouraged to visualize what happens as a tenths grid is partitioned into increasingly smaller subdivisions, resulting in first a hundredths grid, then a thousandths grid, and finally a ten-thousandths grid. This promotes a sense of pattern as students think about what would be the next decimal place and how this decimal place can be represented graphically. In Problem 4.3, Using Decimal Benchmarks, benchmarks are revisited to relate fractions and decimals. In Problem 4.4, Playing Distinguishing Digits, students solve puzzles that help further their understanding of place value. The puzzles also provide opportunities for students to reason about digits using clues that connect to their work in *Prime Time*.

Mathematical and Problem-Solving Goals

- **To extend knowledge of place value of whole numbers to decimal numbers**

- **To represent fractions with denominators of ten and powers of 10 as decimal numbers**

- **To visualize the representation of decimal numbers using a 10-by-10-grid area model**

- **To relate fraction benchmarks to decimal benchmarks**

- **To write, compare, and order decimals with place values to ten thousandths**

	Materials	
Problem	**For students**	**For the teacher**
All	Calculators, grid paper (provided as a blackline master)	Transparencies 4.1 to 4.4 (optional)
4.1	Labsheet 4.1 (1 per student), colored cubes or tiles (optional; 100 per group), Transparency 4.2D and transparency markers (optional; for sharing answers with class)	
4.2	Labsheet 4.2 (1 per student)	
4.3	Distinguishing Digits cards. (Provided as blackline masters. Copy the cards, cut them out, and put them in envelopes marked with the puzzle number.)	
ACE	Labsheet 4.ACE (1 per student)	

Student Pages 39–52   Teaching the Investigation 52a–52k

INVESTIGATION

From Fractions to Decimals

So far in this unit, you have expressed numbers as fractions. In the elementary grades, you studied another way to represent numbers—as *decimals*. Decimals are a convenient way to express fractions with denominators such as 10, 100, 1000, or 10,000. In this investigation, you will have a chance to review decimals and to connect the decimal representation of a number to the fraction representation of the same number.

4.1 Designing a Garden

In Dayton, Ohio, the town council and the Benjamin Wegerzyn Garden Center created the largest community garden in the world. A community garden is a garden that is shared by several people. The community garden in Dayton has 1173 square plots of land that can be used by that many individual people or families to make gardens. Each plot of land has an area of 100 square meters.

Justin's family has a plot in the community garden. His father wants Justin to design the vegetable garden for his family. Justin may decide how much of the land to allocate for each type of vegetable his family wants to grow, but he must satisfy a set of conditions they put on the garden. Justin has to present the plan to his family with a drawing of the garden that specifies what fraction of the plot will be planted with each kind of vegetable.

Tips for the Linguistically Diverse Classroom

Rebus Scenario The Rebus Scenario technique is described in detail in *Getting to Know Connected Mathematics*. This technique involves sketching rebuses on the chalkboard that correspond to key words in the story or information you present orally. Example: some key words and phrases for which you may need to draw rebuses while discussing the material on this page: *Dayton, Ohio* (an outline of the U.S. with an X approximately where Ohio is), *garden* (a vegetable patch), *type of vegetable* (carrots, string beans, corn, and so on), *plan* (a grid with some squares dotted and some squares striped and a key that says dots = carrots, stripes = corn).

4.1

Designing a Garden

Grouping: Individuals or Pairs

Launch

- Introduce the story of the family garden plot, making sure students understand how the hundredths grid relates to the problem.

Explore

- Circulate while students work, asking questions to refocus students who are struggling and to further challenge groups that finish early.

Summarize

- Have a few groups present and explain their plans.

- Challenge the class to make designs that extend the ideas in the follow-up.

Assignment Choices

ACE questions 38–41 and unassigned choices from earlier problems

To help plan, Justin first draws a grid with 100 squares, each representing 1 square meter of the 100-square-meter plot.

Problem 4.1

Here are the family's requirements for the garden.
- Justin's father wants to be sure potatoes, beans, corn, and tomatoes are planted. He wants twice as much of the garden to be planted in corn as potatoes. He wants three times as much land planted in potatoes as tomatoes.
- Justin's sister wants cucumbers in the garden.
- Justin's brother wants carrots in the garden.
- Justin's mother wants eggplant in the garden.
- Justin wants radishes in the garden.

Use Labsheet 4.1 to make a suitable plan for the garden. Write a description of the garden you plan. Name the fraction of the garden space that will be allotted to each kind of vegetable as part of your description. Explain how your garden will satisfy each member of Justin's family.

■ Problem 4.1 Follow-Up

1. Justin's father says that he will not plant less than a square meter of any vegetable. Design a garden with the largest possible amount of land planted in potatoes that fits the conditions of the problem and has at least one square meter allotted for each vegetable.
2. Design a garden with the smallest possible amount of land planted in potatoes that fits the conditions of the problem and has at least one square meter allotted for each vegetable.

Answer to Problem 4.1

Even though the relationship of square meters for vegetables chosen by Justin's father will be the same for all groups, the way the vegetables are arranged on the grid and the number of square meters given to corn, potatoes, and tomatoes will vary, as will the choices for the other vegetables. Students should have included an explanation for their design and labeled the fractional parts.

Answers to Problem 4.1 Follow-Up

1. Potatoes should make up $\frac{27}{100}$ of the garden, tomatoes $\frac{9}{100}$, and corn $\frac{54}{100}$. The remaining vegetables should make up a total of $\frac{10}{100}$ of the garden.

2. Potatoes should make up $\frac{3}{100}$ of the garden, tomatoes $\frac{1}{100}$, and corn $\frac{6}{100}$. The remaining vegetable should make up a total of $\frac{90}{100}$ of the garden.

Making Smaller Parts

Decimals give us a way to write special fractions that have denominators like 10, 100, 1000, and 10,000. A tenths grid can help you to understand decimals.

A *tenths grid* is divided into ten equal parts. It resembles the tenths fraction strip you have been using, only it is square.

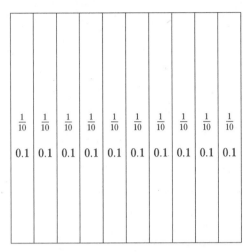

Here are some examples of fractions represented on tenths grids. Fraction names and decimal names for the shaded part are given below each drawing.

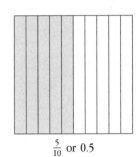

$\frac{3}{10}$ or 0.3

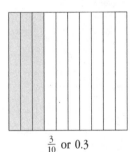

$\frac{5}{10}$ or 0.5

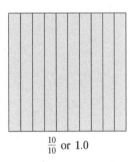

$\frac{10}{10}$ or 1.0

Making Smaller Parts

At a Glance

Grouping:
Individuals or Pairs

Launch

- Review decimal notation with your students.

- Discuss how decimals can be represented on tenths and hundredths grids.

Explore

- As students translate the fractions on their garden plans to decimals, ask questions to guide them into seeing that all the decimal parts must add to 1.

Summarize

- Have a few groups present and explain their solutions.

- As a class, talk about the follow-up questions, and explore thousandths and ten-thousandths grids in greater depth.

- Discuss the base ten number system using the place-value chart. (*optional*)

Assignment Choices

ACE questions 1–9 (9 requires Labsheet 4.ACE) and unassigned choices from earlier problems

We can further divide a tenths grid by drawing horizontal lines to make ten rows. Now we have 100 parts. This *hundredths grid* is what Justin used to plan his garden.

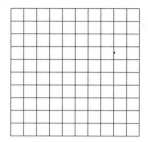

Fractions can also be represented on a hundredths grid. We can write fractional parts of 100 as decimal numbers.

Fraction	Decimal	Meaning	Representation on a hundredths grid
$\frac{7}{100}$	0.07	7 out of 100	
$\frac{27}{100}$	0.27	27 out of 100	
$\frac{51}{100}$	0.51	51 out of 100	

Answer to Problem 4.2

Answers will vary.

Problem 4.2

Look back at the original plan you drew for Justin's garden. Write each of the fractional parts for the vegetables in your plan as a decimal.

■ **Problem 4.2 Follow-Up**

1. a. What would a hundredths grid look like if each square of the grid were divided into ten equal parts? How many parts would the new grid have?
   b. What is a fraction name for the smallest part of this new grid? A decimal name?
   c. How would you shade an area of this new grid to show $\frac{1}{10}$?
   d. What fraction or decimal names could you call this shaded area?
   e. What would you call this new grid, which has every square of a hundredths grid divided into ten equal parts?

2. a. You can write $\frac{9}{100}$ as the decimal 0.09. How could you write $\frac{9}{1000}$ as a decimal?
   b. How could you write $\frac{469}{1000}$ as a decimal?

3. a. What would you need to do to the new grid you discovered in question 1 to make a grid that shows *ten thousandths?*
   b. How could you write $\frac{9}{10,000}$ as a decimal?
   c. How could you write $\frac{469}{10,000}$ as a decimal?

4.3 Using Decimal Benchmarks

In Investigation 2, we developed benchmarks to help us estimate fractions. Benchmarks can also help us estimate and compare decimals. You can use what you already know about fractions to make estimating and comparing decimals easier.

Did you know?

Throughout history mathematicians have used many different notations to represent decimal numbers. For example, in 1585, Simon Stevinus would have written 2.57 as either 2, 5' 7" or 2 ⓪ 5 ①7 ②. In 1617, John Napier would have written 2/57. Other commonly-used notations included an underscore, 2<u>57</u>, and a combination of a vertical line and an underscore, 2|<u>57</u>. Even today, the notation varies from country to country. For example, in England, 2.57 is written as 2•57, and, in Germany, it is written as 2,57.

Answers to Problem 4.2 Follow-Up

1. a. 1000 parts **b.** $\frac{1}{1000}$; 0.001
   c. You would still shade $\frac{1}{10}$ of the grid, but now the tenth would be subdivided into 100 parts.
   d. Possible answers: $\frac{100}{1000}$, 0.100, 0.10, 0.1
   e. A thousandths grid

2. a. 0.009 **b.** 0.469

3. a. Subdivide each of the thousand sections into 10 parts, which would give 10,000 squares.
   b. 0.0009 **c.** 0.0469

At a Glance

Grouping: Small Groups

Launch

■ As a class, develop the set of five decimal benchmarks, and use them to compare pairs of decimals.

Explore

■ Circulate, asking questions to help students apply what they learned about fractions to the decimals they are now considering.

Summarize

■ Discuss the answers to the problem and the follow-up.

■ Extend the discussion, posing more difficult ordering problems for students and focusing on the meaning of decimal place values.

Assignment Choices

ACE questions 10–36, 43, 44, and unassigned choices from earlier problems

Problem 4.3

A. Rename each of these fraction benchmarks as a decimal.

1. 0 **2.** $\frac{1}{4}$ **3.** $\frac{1}{2}$ **4.** $\frac{3}{4}$ **5.** 1

B. Now use the decimal benchmarks and other strategies that make sense to you to help you order each set of numbers from smallest to largest.

1. 0.23   0.28   0.25

2. 2.054   20.54   2.54

3. 0.78   0.708   0.078

C. For each of the three decimals in parts 1 and 3 of question B, give the name of the decimal in words, and tell which benchmark the number is nearest. Give the benchmark as a fraction and as a decimal. For each decimal benchmark chosen, explain your reasoning. Organize your work in a table like the one below.

Number	Name in words	Nearest decimal benchmark	Nearest fraction benchmark	Reasoning
0.23				
0.28				
0.25				
0.78				
0.708				
0.078				

■ Problem 4.3 Follow-Up

1. Write, as a decimal, a fraction with a denominator of 10,000 that is near, but less than, $\frac{3}{4}$.

2. Write, as a decimal, a fraction with a denominator of 1000 that is near, but less than, 1.

Answers to Problem 4.3

A. 1. 0   2. 0.25   3. 0.5   4. 0.75   5. 1

B. 1. 0.23   0.25   0.28
      2. 2.054   2.54   20.54
      3. 0.078   0.708   0.78

C. See page 52h.

Answers to Problem 4.3 Follow-Up

1. Answers will vary. Possible answers: $\frac{7398}{10,000}$, $\frac{7450}{10,000}$, $\frac{7499}{10,000}$

2. Answers will vary. Possible answers: $\frac{999}{1000}$, $\frac{987}{1000}$, $\frac{970}{1000}$

 Playing Distinguishing Digits

Distinguishing Digits is a collection of number puzzles. In each puzzle, you use clues to help find a Mystery Number.

For each puzzle, a Mystery Number Card is presented for everyone on the team to see. It shows blank spaces for the digits of a Mystery Number. Then the team inspects several Clue Cards for clues to help them decode the Mystery Number.

Look at the following example. As a class, decide what the Mystery Number must be.

Mystery Number

1 ___ . ___ ___ ___

Clue 1 The digit in the thousandths place is double the digit in the ones place.

Clue 2 The digit in the tenths place is odd, and it represents the sum of the digits in the tens place and the thousandths place.

Clue 3 There are exactly two odd digits in the Mystery Number.

Clue 4 The digit in the hundredths place is three times the digit in the ones place.

Problem 4.4

Play the Distinguishing Digits puzzles with your group. Record the strategies you use to solve the puzzles.

■ **Problem 4.4 Follow-Up**

With your group, create a new Distinguishing Digits puzzle. Try out the puzzle on another group. If the other group finds a problem with your puzzle, rework the clues until your puzzle works.

Playing Distinguishing Digits

At a Glance

Grouping: Small Groups

Launch

■ As a class, investigate the sample Distinguishing Digits puzzle.

■ Talk about how the clues relate to place value.

Explore

■ Circulate while students solve the puzzles, focusing them on the importance of place value in working with the clues.

Summarize

■ As a class, check answers and share puzzle-solving strategies.

■ Have groups share the puzzles they created and discuss the strategies they used for developing their puzzles. (*optional*)

Answers to Problem 4.4

Note that some of the puzzles have more than one answer.

Puzzle 1: 842

Puzzle 2: 513

Puzzle 3: 826,413 and 862, 431

Puzzle 4: 0.248

Puzzle 5: 0.132 and 0.396

Puzzle 6: 0.468 and 0.486

Puzzle 7: 0.3609 and 0.1203

Puzzle 8: 216.12

Puzzle 9: 5612.034

Puzzle 10: 44,527.42986

Assignment Choices

Unassigned choices from earlier problems

Answers

Applications

1. $\frac{30}{100}$, $\frac{3}{10}$, 0.30, 0.3
2. $\frac{32}{100}$, $\frac{16}{50}$, $\frac{8}{25}$, 0.32
3. $\frac{53}{100}$, 0.53
4. $\frac{60}{100}$, $\frac{30}{50}$, $\frac{15}{25}$, $\frac{3}{5}$, 0.60, 0.6
5. $\frac{90}{100}$, $\frac{45}{50}$, $\frac{9}{10}$, 0.90, 0.9
6. $\frac{75}{100}$, $\frac{15}{20}$, $\frac{3}{4}$, 0.75

Applications • Connections • Extensions

As you work on these ACE questions, use your calculator whenever you need it.

Applications

In 1–6, the hundredths grid is partially shaded. Write fraction and decimal names to describe the shaded part.

1.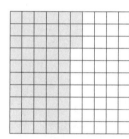

2.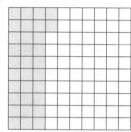

3.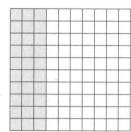

4.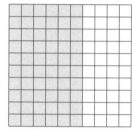

5.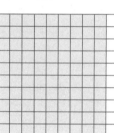

6.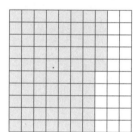

46   Bits and Pieces I

46   Investigation 4

In 7–8, the whole is one hundredths grid. Write fraction and decimal names to describe the shaded part.

7.

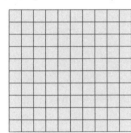

8.

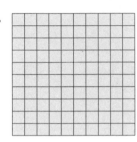 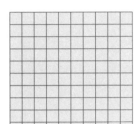 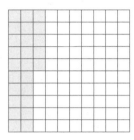

9. In a–f, use the blank hundredths grids on Labsheet 4.ACE to shade the given fractional part. Write the fraction as an equivalent decimal.

a. $\frac{1}{2}$ of the hundredths grid

b. $\frac{3}{4}$ of the hundredths grid

c. $\frac{99}{100}$ of the hundredths grid

d. $1\frac{3}{10}$ of the hundredths grids

e. $2\frac{7}{10}$ of the hundredths grids

f. $1\frac{3}{5}$ of the hundredths grids

In 10–13, rewrite each pair of numbers, inserting a less-than symbol (<), a greater-than symbol (>), or an equals symbol (=) between the numbers to make a true statement.

10. $\frac{3}{5}$ 0.3

11. 0.205 0.21

12. 0.1 0.1000

13. $\frac{37}{50}$ 0.74

7. $1\frac{6}{100}$, $1\frac{3}{50}$, 1.06

8. $2\frac{25}{100}$, $2\frac{5}{20}$, $2\frac{1}{4}$, 2.25

9a. See below left.

9b. See below left.

9c. See page 52i.

9d. See page 52i.

9e. See page 52i.

9f. See page 52j.

10. $\frac{3}{5}$ > 0.3

11. 0.205 < 0.21

12. 0.1 = 0.1000

13. $\frac{37}{50}$ = 0.74

9a. 0.50 or 0.5; Possible answer:

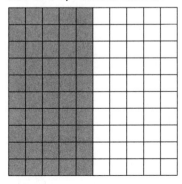

9b. 0.75; Possible answer:

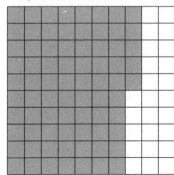

14. 0.12, 0.127, 0.2, 0.33, $\frac{45}{10}$

15. $\frac{3}{1000}$, 0.005, $\frac{3}{100}$, 0.34

16. 0.827, $\frac{987}{1000}$, 1.23, $\frac{987}{100}$

17.–20. See below right.

21. 0.3 < 0.6

22. 0.4 < $\frac{3}{5}$

23. 0.7 > $\frac{1}{2}$

In 14–16, rewrite the numbers in order from smallest to largest.

14. 0.33   0.12   0.127   0.2 $\frac{45}{10}$

15. $\frac{3}{100}$ 0.005 $\frac{3}{1000}$ 0.34

16. 0.827   1.23 $\frac{987}{100}$ $\frac{987}{1000}$

In 17–20, copy the part of the number line given. Then, find the "step" by determining the difference from one mark to another. Label the unlabeled marks with decimal numbers. The first step is given for you.

17. (number line: 0.2 ... 0.8) The step is 0.2.

18. (number line: 0.15 ... 0.17) The step is _____.

19. (number line: 0.028 ... 0.029) The step is _____.

20. (number line: 1.8 ... 1.9) The step is _____.

In 21–35, rewrite each pair of numbers, inserting a less-than symbol (<), a greater-than symbol (>), or an equals symbol (=) between the numbers to make a true statement.

21. 0.3   0.6

22. 0.4 $\frac{3}{5}$

23. 0.7 $\frac{1}{2}$

17. The step is 0.2.

18. The step is 0.01.

19. The step is 0.001.

20. The step is 0.1.

24.   0.34   0.23

25.   0.60   0.6

26.   0.52 $\frac{2}{4}$

27.   0.34   0.4

28.   0.08   0.8

29.   0.92   0.9

30.   2.45   2.3

31.   0.56   0.056

32.   0.037   0.029

33.   0.7   0.725

34.   0.41   0.405

35.   0.10   0.108

Connections

36. Su computed her free-throw average on her calculator and got 0.6019. Ahmed computed his free-throw average and got 0.602. Solange's free-throw average was 0.62. Who is the best free-throw shooter? Explain your answer.

37. Chad, Roman, and Kari wanted to know who was the best free-throw shooter among them. Chad's free-throw average was about 0.588. Roman's average was close to 0.611. Kari consistently made 6 out of 10. Who is the best free-throw shooter? Explain your answer.

In 38–40, show the fraction by drawing and shading squares. Then, write each improper fraction as an equivalent mixed number.

38. $\frac{7}{5}$ **39.** $\frac{7}{3}$ **40.** $\frac{11}{6}$

Investigation 4: From Fractions to Decimals   **49**

---

38. $\frac{7}{5} = 1\frac{2}{5}$. Possible illustration:

 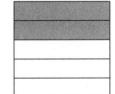

---

24.   0.34 > 0.23

25.   0.60 = 0.6

26.   0.52 > $\frac{2}{4}$

27.   0.34 < 0.4

28.   0.08 < 0.8

29.   0.92 > 0.9

30.   2.45 > 2.3

31.   0.56 > 0.056

32.   0.037 > 0.029

33.   0.7 < 0.725

34.   0.41 > 0.405

35.   0.10 < 0.108

Connections

36. Solange is the best free-throw shooter. Possible explanation: 0.62 is the same as 0.6200, and 0.602 is the same as 0.6020. Now that all three decimals have the same number of decimal places, you can just compare the digits. Since 6200 > 6020 > 6019, 0.62 is the largest decimal.

37. Roman is the best free-throw shooter. Possible explanation: Kari's average can be written as 0.600. Since 611 > 600 > 588, 0.611 is the largest decimal.

38. See below left.

39. See page 52j.

40. See page 52j.

Investigation 4   **49**

41a. $\frac{9}{16}$

41b. $\frac{8}{25}$

41c. $\frac{9}{16}$

41. Determine what part of each figure is shaded.

a.

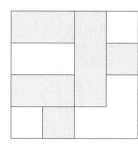

b.

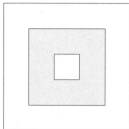

c.

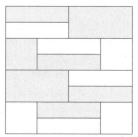

Extensions

Problems 42–43 involve the Dewey Decimal system, which is used in many libraries to catalog books. The Dewey Decimal system is based on the decimal number system.

42. Serita looked up *elephant* in the library's computer. She saw that there were several books about elephants, with these call numbers: 599.55, 599.504, 599.5, and 599.5044. The librarian showed Serita the guide numbers on the ends of the shelves and explained that the books were arranged in numerical order from smallest to largest and from left to right. In what order will the books about elephants be arranged on the shelf? Explain your reasoning.

43. Huang wanted to reshelve two books he had been reading about the history of rock and roll music. The books' call numbers were 782.42 and 781.66. Huang located the shelf where his book belonged, but the other books he found there were completely out of order: 781.5, 782.005, 781.053, 781.035, and 782.409. He rearranged the books already on the shelf and then placed his books among them. In what order did Huang put the books that were already on the shelf? Where did he put his books?

44. Microchips can process information in as little as one billionth of a second, which is called a *nanosecond*. Write the decimal representation of a nanosecond.

1. You could divide it into two strips in one direction and five strips in the other. Or, you could divide it into ten vertical or horizontal strips.

To represent hundredths, you could divide each section of the square representing tenths into ten equal parts.

To represent thousandths, you could divide each section of the square representing hundredths into ten equal parts. That would give you 1000 equal parts.

2. First, see whether the whole numbers to the left of the decimal point are different. If they are, then the larger whole number will determine which decimal number is larger. If they are the same, rewrite each decimal so there are the same number of digits after the decimal. Then, the digits can be compared, starting with the tenths place, until one is found to have a larger place value.

3. Reading from left to right, the 2 represents two ten thousands, the 5 represents five thousands, the 7 represents seven hundreds, the 0 represents zero tens, the 8 represents eight ones, the 2 represents two tenths, the 0 represents zero hundredths, and the 1 represents one thousandth.

4. See page 52j.

Mathematical Reflections

In this investigation, you used square grids to help you model decimals. You found that decimals are special kinds of fractions. These questions will help you summarize what you have learned:

1 Describe the process of dividing a square to represent tenths; to represent hundredths; to represent thousandths.

2 When comparing two decimals, how can you decide which decimal represents a larger number?

3 Decimals are an extension of the place-value system you studied for whole numbers in elementary school. Tell what each digit in 25,708.201 represents.

4 Express each of the following decimal numbers in words.

0.16   1.069   33.109   431.0115

Think about your answers to these questions, discuss your ideas with other students and your teacher, and then write a summary of your findings in your journal.

Tips for the Linguistically Diverse Classroom

Diagram Code The Diagram Code technique is described in detail in *Getting to Know Connected Mathematics*. Students use a minimal number of words and drawings, diagrams, or symbols to respond to questions that require writing. Example: Question 2—A student might answer this question by writing 2.21 < 3.99, Why? 2.21, 3.99, 2 < 3; 3.3 > 3.20, Why? 3.30, 3. 20, 30 > 20.

TEACHING THE INVESTIGATION

4.1 • Designing a Garden

In this problem, students plan a 100-square-meter garden by using a 10 by 10 grid. Students express the area of the garden allotted to each vegetable as a fraction of the total area. In the next problem, students will express these fractions in decimal form.

Launch

This is a good problem for students to work on individually or in pairs. Each student or pair of students will need one or more copies of Labsheet 4.1. Each square on the grid represents 1 square meter of the 100-square-meter plot.

Introduce the problem by telling the story of the family garden plot.

> You must determine how many square meters of the garden area need to be planted with each vegetable. Justin's father wants twice as much of the garden to be planted with corn as potatoes (that is, for every 1 square meter planted with potatoes, there will be 2 square meters planted with corn). He also wants three times as much land planted with potatoes as tomatoes (that is, for every 1 square meter planted with tomatoes, there will be 3 square meters planted with potatoes). This means that the numbers of square meters planted in corn, potatoes, and tomatoes are linked.

Students will have to determine relationships that work; for example, for 1 square meter of tomatoes, there will be 3 square meters of potatoes and 6 square meters of corn.

> The remaining square meters can be used for the other vegetables that the family wants planted.

Be sure students understand that their designs must satisfy all of the requirements of Justin's family. Beginning with the grid may be too abstract for many students. Consequently, you may want to give each team of students 100 colored tiles or cubes, which will help them distinguish different sections of the plot they are to make. They can translate their finished plan to the grid.

Explore

Circulate and ask questions, refocusing students who are off-task. Encourage students who are struggling. Each group should be able to show how their garden design satisfies the conditions.

You may want to have a few groups translate their plan to copies of Transparency 4.2D to make sharing with the class easier. If some groups finish early, ask them to work on the follow-up questions.

Summarize

Let a few groups show their garden plans. Ask each group for proof that their design fits the necessary conditions.

Raise the follow-up questions of the largest possible amount of land planted in potatoes and the smallest possible amount planted in potatoes. Have groups share the largest and the smallest they found, and challenge the class to see whether they can make a design that fits the conditions with fewer or more square meters in potatoes than any found so far.

4.2 • Making Smaller Parts

In this problem, students are introduced to tenths and hundredths using grid models. In moving from the tenths grid to the hundredths grid, encourage students to focus on the fact that they are moving from a grid of 10 columns to one on which horizontal lines have been added to make 10 rows, resulting in 100 squares.

Launch

We assume students have met decimals before, but you will want to review them. If your students have trouble reading decimals, remind them that decimals are just easy ways to write fractions with denominators of 10, 100, 1000, 10,000, and other powers of ten. The chart in the "For the Teacher" box on page 52e will be helpful.

The grids on Transparencies 4.2C and 4.2D can make the class discussion of tenths and hundredths easier. Use shading to highlight equal amounts on the tenths grid and hundredths grid. In particular, note that 0.5 and 0.50 represent the same area of the grid.

> Can you show 0.3 and 0.4 on a hundredths grid? Why or why not? (*Yes, because tenths can be rewritten as hundredths.*) Can you show 0.63 and 0.36 on a tenths grid? Why or why not? (*No, because while 0.30 and 0.40 can be rewritten as tenths, 0.63 and 0.36 cannot. We need smaller divisions of the grid to show these amounts.*)

Now, read the problem with the students.

> The problem asks what decimal amount you planned for each vegetable in Justin's garden. You need to represent the fractional amount for each area as a decimal.

Let students work on Problem 4.2 individually or in their groups from Problem 4.1.

Explore

As you circulate, ask what the fractions for each type of vegetable should add to. Many students will need several opportunities to see that the sum of all the fractional parts must equal the whole, which is 1. You may want a couple of groups to add their decimal amounts to the copy of Transparency 4.2D that they prepared for Problem 4.1 for sharing with the class.

Summarize

Have a few groups share their answers with the class. Discuss the follow-up questions, which encourage students to visualize further dividing the hundredths grid to create thousandths and ten-thousandths grids, and to name parts of these grids with decimals and fractions.

Give each student a copy of Labsheet 4.2, which contains a large hundredths grid. Have students do some initial brainstorming and sketching in their groups about how to create a thousandths grid from the hundredths grid. Then, as a class, discuss what it would mean to show each square divided into ten parts.

Each square on the grid would be a replica of the tenths grid, only much smaller. You may want to demonstrate dividing one of the hundredth squares on Transparency 4.2D into ten equal parts.

What would happen if each of the hundred squares were divided in this way? How many divisions would there be? (*1000*) What would we call this grid? (*a thousandths grid*)

In one classroom, the following discussion occurred.

Teacher In your book on page 41, you see a square that is divided into ten parts to show tenths. Could someone tell me how I could take this square and divide it into tenths like what is shown in the book? (*The teacher displayed Transparency 4.2B.*)

Ted You could divide the square in half by drawing a line down the middle, and then divide each half into five equal parts by drawing more lines from the top to the bottom.

Teacher How do I know where to draw the lines to divide each half into five equal parts?

Ted You could measure each half and divide that by 5 to see how wide to make each part.

Teacher Is that reasonable? Do others think that will give me a square divided into ten equal parts? (*The teacher and class determined where to place the lines.*)

In your book on page 42 is a square that has been divided into hundredths. Could someone tell me how I could take our square, which is now divided into tenths, and further divide it to make a square showing hundredths?

Latisia Turn the square so that the lines are going across, and then do the same thing Ted told you to do before.

Teacher Is that reasonable? Do others think that will give me a square divided into 100 equal pieces? (*The teacher followed Latisia's directions.*)

Suppose you wanted to show each of these hundredth squares divided into ten equal parts. How many parts would the new grid have? How would you divide each of the squares into ten equal parts?

I will give each of you a hundredths grid that looks similar to what I have on the overhead. I want you to divide a couple of the hundredths squares into ten equal parts and then share what you have done with the person next to you. See if you both agree that you have done what was asked, and then discuss how many parts the grid would have if you continued this process. (*The teacher noticed that several students were struggling to divided a hundredths square into ten parts. Many divided squares into fourths and then didn't know how to proceed.*) Think about the strategy Ted used to divide the large original square. Can you use that strategy here?

Having students begin to divide the hundredths grid to get thousandths was worthwhile, because several misconceptions became clear and the teacher was able to address them in the class discussion. Also, students got a better feel for how thousandths relate to hundredths and to tenths.

Ask questions to assess what your students are understanding about representing quantities as decimals, and have students discuss how to write numbers involving thousandths as decimals.

Can you show 0.3 on a tenths grid? On a hundredths grid? A thousandths grid? Why or why not?

Can you show 0.34 on a tenths grid? On a hundredths grid? A thousandths grid? Why or why not?

Can you show 0.345 on a tenths grid? On a hundredths grid? A thousandths grid? Why or why not?

In follow-up question 3, students think about a ten-thousandths grid. You can use Transparencies 4.2E and 4.2F to help students visualize moving from the thousandths to the ten-thousandths grid.

What would you need to do to the thousandths grid to make a grid with 10,000 squares? Can you see that this is like creating 100 squares in each of the squares on a hundredths grid?

When students understand the ten-thousandths grid, you may want to extend the ideas in the follow-up. Shade in decimal amounts on the grids as you consider various fractions, using copies of Transparencies 4.2C, 4.2D, 4.2E, and 4.2F.

Can we show 0.3 and 0.8 on a ten-thousandths grid? Can we show 0.34 and 0.89 on a ten-thousandths grid? Can we show 0.345 and 0.897 on a ten-thousandths grid? Can we show 0.3452 and 0.8974 on a ten-thousandths grid? On a thousandths grid? A hundredths grid? A tenths grid? Why or why not?

For the Teacher: Using the Place Value Chart

You may want to make a wall display or a bulletin board of the place-value chart on the next page and work with students to think about what it means to extend the chart in either direction. This chart is also shown on Transparency 4.2G.

The system we use for writing numbers is called the *base ten number system.* It uses groups of ones, tens, hundreds, thousands, ten thousands, and so on. For example, 69 represents 6 groups of ten and 9 groups of one; 28,590 represents 2 groups of ten thousand, 8 groups of one thousand, 5 groups of one hundred, 9 groups of ten, and 0 groups of one.

Over time, people realized they needed to extend the number system to represent numbers smaller than 1. A decimal point separates these digits so that the numbers to the right of the decimal point represent fractions whose denominators are ten (tenths), one hundred (hundredths), one thousand (thousandths), ten thousand (ten thousandths), and so on. For example, 5.8 represents 5 groups of one and 8 groups of one tenth; 36.420 represents 3 groups of ten, 6 groups of one, 4 groups of one tenth, 2 groups of one hundredth, and 0 groups of one thousandth.

(continued)

Ask questions to help students interpret the chart.

> Do you see the symmetry of the names of the place values about the 1? What are your predictions for the next few lines of the chart if you were to extend it both to the left and to the right?

> Choose a number from the chart. What relationships do you see between it and the numbers directly to its right and left?

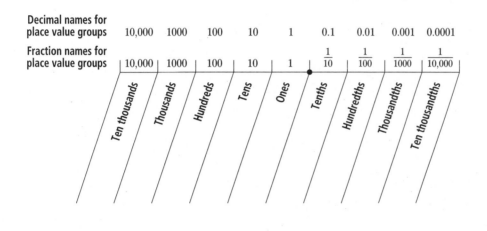

Decimal names for place value groups	10,000	1000	100	10	1	0.1	0.01	0.001	0.0001
Fraction names for place value groups	10,000	1000	100	10	1	$\frac{1}{10}$	$\frac{1}{100}$	$\frac{1}{1000}$	$\frac{1}{10,000}$

Ten thousands | Thousands | Hundreds | Tens | Ones | Tenths | Hundredths | Thousandths | Ten thousandths

4.3 • Using Decimal Benchmarks

This problem gives students an opportunity to connect the fraction benchmarks $0, \frac{1}{4}, \frac{1}{2}, \frac{3}{4}$, and 1 to decimal benchmarks.

Launch

Launch the problem by exploring an example.

> For decimals to be useful to us, we need to be able to estimate how large a number is and to make comparisons between numbers. Remember that we did this for fractions, so we can build on what we know about fractions. Here are two decimal numbers: 0.05 and 0.3. (*Write these on the board.*) Which of these represents the greater quantity? How do you know?

Some students have a hard time giving up on their whole-numbers idea that 5 is larger than 3. Having someone shade grids at the overhead, perhaps using Transparency 4.2D, to show the two values can be helpful, and gives you a chance to reinforce the meaning of decimals and how to read them.

> Who can give me a fraction name for each of these numbers? $(\frac{5}{100}, \frac{3}{10})$ Tell me how you found the fraction equivalents.

When we looked at benchmarks with fractions, we used 0, $\frac{1}{2}$, and 1. Using these benchmarks, which number is $\frac{5}{100}$ closest to? (*0*) Which number is $\frac{3}{10}$ closest to? ($\frac{1}{2}$) Explain your answers.

Let's add more benchmarks to our set: $\frac{1}{4}$ and $\frac{3}{4}$.

The problem asks students to find decimal representations for these new benchmarks. You may want to help your students to convert the new fraction benchmark set of 0, $\frac{1}{4}$, $\frac{1}{2}$, $\frac{3}{4}$, and 1 into decimal benchmarks: 0, 0.25, 0.5, 0.75, and 1. Then write the fraction benchmarks 0, $\frac{1}{4}$, $\frac{1}{2}$, $\frac{3}{4}$, and 1 on the board with their decimal equivalents underneath.

With this new benchmark set, is $\frac{5}{100}$ closer to 0 or $\frac{1}{4}$? (*0*) Is $\frac{3}{10}$ closer to $\frac{1}{4}$ or $\frac{1}{2}$? ($\frac{1}{4}$) How do you know? What is the decimal representation for $\frac{1}{4}$? (*0.25*) How do you know? If we say that $\frac{5}{100}$ is closer to 0 than $\frac{1}{4}$, then 0.05 must be closer to 0 than 0.25. If $\frac{3}{10}$ is closer to $\frac{1}{4}$ than $\frac{1}{2}$, then 0.3 must be closer to 0.25 than 0.5.

If your students are struggling, you might do another example together. You could choose decimals on either side of $\frac{1}{2}$, such as 0.52 and 0.499. This pair again raises the issue of whether we are comparing 52 and 499 or the fractions $\frac{52}{100}$ and $\frac{499}{1000}$.

When your students seem to understand the task, let them work in pairs or groups on Problem 4.3.

Explore

As you visit the groups, ask questions that encourage students to use the reasoning they developed for fractions to help estimate the size of the numbers they are now investigating. As students look for ways to compare decimals directly, don't let the process proceed to an algorithm too soon. Students will be better served if the focus stays on, Why is this true? rather than on, How do I do this?

Summarize

A quick check of answers and a discussion of strategies will make a good beginning to the summary. Then you can pose a harder ordering problem for students using a think-pair-share strategy. Have students think individually about the problem you pose, then share their ideas in pairs and try to reach consensus. For example, have students order these numbers from smallest to largest:

$$0.827 \qquad \frac{827}{100} \qquad 1.827 \qquad \frac{1827}{10,000} \qquad 0.087$$

One way to tackle the problem is to rewrite the numbers as decimals:

$$0.827 \qquad 8.27 \qquad 1.827 \qquad 0.1827 \qquad 0.087$$

When pairs have considered the problem, discuss it as a class.

Which two of these numbers are greater than a whole? (*8.27 and 1.827*) Which of these is larger, and how do you know? (*Here the whole number part tells the story: 8.27 is larger.*) The three remaining numbers are 0.827, 0.1827, and 0.087. Which of these is the largest?

0.827, 0.1827, and 0.087. Which of these is the largest?

You want the conversation to center on the meaning of the *places* in the numbers.

> Where is the tenths place? (*to the right of the decimal point*) The hundredths place? (*two places to the right of the decimal point*) Which place has the larger value? (*the tenths place*) Which of the three remaining numbers has the greatest number of tenths? (*0.827, with 8 tenths, then 0.1827, then 0.087*) This gives us our ordering:
>
> 0.087   0.1827   0.827   1.827   8.27
>
> Who can tell me a decimal number between each of these pairs of numbers?

From this summary, your students should have a good set of strategies for making sense of and comparing decimals.

4.4 •

Playing Distinguishing Digits

In this problem, students use a set of clues to fill in the digits of a mystery number. As they work with the clues, students review what they know about place value.

Launch

The best way to launch the Distinguishing Digits puzzle is to investigate the sample puzzle given in the student edition. From the beginning, stress that proving the solution is part of successfully solving the puzzle.

> Look at the Distinguishing Digits puzzle in your books. You will see a Mystery Number, with blanks for the missing digits, and a set of clues about the number. Your challenge is to use the clues to figure out what numerals go in the blanks to make a number that satisfies all of the clues.
>
> First, look at the skeleton for the Mystery Number. What can you tell me about the number? (*It is between 10 and 20. It has three decimal places, so it is a whole number plus some number of thousandths.*)
>
> Look at the first clue. What can you tell me from this information? (*The digit in the thousandths place is 2, 4, 6, or 8 and the digit in the ones place is 1, 2, 3, or 4*)

Be sure students specifically locate the place values to which the clue relates.

> Look at all the clues, and tell me what you know. It is not necessary to use the clues in the order they are given. In fact, it is often helpful to start somewhere else. Look over the clues to decide which convey the

Students will have different beginning ideas. For instance, Clue 3 indicates that we can use only one other odd digit, since one odd digit is already given (the 1 in the tens place). The first part of the second clue tells us where the second odd digit will go.

Next, knowing that all of the remaining digits must be even, the last clue is easier to decipher. Make a list of pairs of even numbers in which the second number is three times the first; the only set of single-digit numbers that works is 2 and 6. This gives us part of our answer:

12. odd 6

Now consider the unused clues. Since the ones place is filled, we can employ Clue 1: the digit in the thousandths place is 4, which leads us to complete the last part of Clue 2. The sum of the digits in the tens place and the thousandths place is 5, giving the solution of 12.564.

Divide students into groups. In solving puzzles, students are sometimes more fully engaged if all students in the group are near the same level of understanding. However, students should have an opportunity to hear different strategies and ways of reasoning, so you may want to begin with a mixture of levels of understanding and have a second round pairing students of more similar understanding. Pass out the envelopes of Mystery Numbers cards and Clue cards to the groups. You may want to have every group try every puzzle, or give every group a few puzzles to solve.

Explore

As you circulate, ask questions about place value. Monitor whether every student is having an opportunity to contribute. When students have finished solving the puzzles, have them work on the follow-up.

Summarize

Give the class a chance to check answers and to share strategies.

You might have students share some of the problems they developed for the follow-up. Ask what they had to think about to develop a set of clues that would work. Developing the puzzles and talking about their strategies will enhance students' understanding of place value.

Additional Answers

Answers to Problem 4.3

C.

Number	Name in words	Nearest decimal benchmark	Nearest fraction benchmark	Reasoning
0.23	twenty-three hundredths	0.25	$\frac{1}{4}$	$\frac{23}{100}$ is very close to $\frac{25}{100}$ or $\frac{1}{4}$.
0.25	twenty-five hundredths	0.25	$\frac{1}{4}$	$\frac{25}{100}$ equals $\frac{1}{4}$.
0.28	twenty-eight hundredths	0.25	$\frac{1}{4}$	$\frac{28}{100}$ is close to $\frac{25}{100}$, or $\frac{1}{4}$.
0.78	seventy-eight hundredths	0.75	$\frac{3}{4}$	$\frac{78}{100}$ is close to $\frac{75}{100}$, or $\frac{3}{4}$. $\frac{708}{1000}$ is close to $\frac{700}{1000}$ or $\frac{70}{100}$.
0.708	seven hundred and eight thousandths	0.75	$\frac{3}{4}$	$\frac{70}{100}$ is close to $\frac{75}{100}$. $\frac{78}{1000}$ is close to $\frac{80}{1000}$, or $\frac{8}{100}$.
0.078	seventy-eight thousandths	0	0	$\frac{8}{100}$ is close to zero.

ACE Answers

Applications

9c. 0.99; Possible answer:

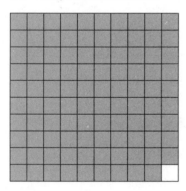

9d. 1.30 or 1.3; Possible answer:

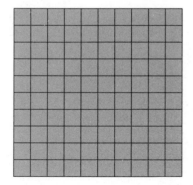 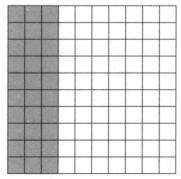

9e. 2.70 or 2.7; Possible answer:

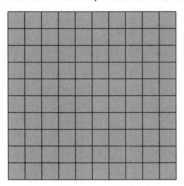 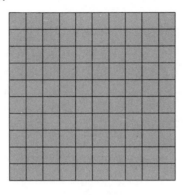 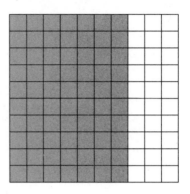

9f. 1.60 or 1.6; Possible answer:

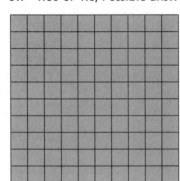 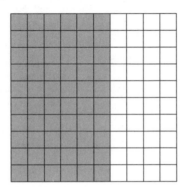

Connections

39. $\frac{7}{3} = 2\frac{1}{3}$. Possible illustration:

40. $\frac{11}{6} = 1\frac{5}{6}$. Possible illustration:

 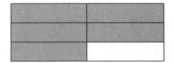

Mathematical Reflections

4. 0.16 is sixteen hundreths; 1.069 is one and sixty-nine thousandths; 33.109 is thirty-three and one hundred nine thousandths; 431.0115 is four hundred thirty-one and one hundred fifteen ten thousandths.

Moving Between Fractions and Decimals

Fractions are especially difficult for students because there are several ways to interpret them. In Investigations 1 and 2, students focused on the part-whole interpretation using fraction strips and number lines as models. In Investigation 3, this model was expanded to include areas of figures, especially rectangles. In Investigation 4, this area model was applied to help students make sense of decimal fractions. In this investigation we develop the meaning of fractions as implied division, an interpretation that allows students to use a calculator to change fractions to decimals, facilitating comparisons and computations.

Problem 5.1, Choosing the Best, focuses on making comparisons among three quantities that can be represented with fractions. In Problem 5.2, Writing Fractions as Decimals, students use fraction strips, including a hundredths strip, to estimate fraction and decimal equivalents. The goal is to help students focus on fractions and decimals as quantities that can be represented in more than one form. In Problem 5.3, Moving From Fractions to Decimals, whole number division helps extend the meaning of fractions as implied divisions. This problem helps students to understand why a fraction can be interpreted as an implied division and to use implied division to change fractions to decimal representations.

Mathematical and Problem-Solving Goals

- *To understand that the decimal representation of a fraction shows the same proportion but is based on a power of 10 as the denominator*

- *To use the concept of equivalence to change the form of simple fractions to fractions with 100 in the denominator*

- *To understand the division interpretation of fractions and use it to change fractions to decimals*

- *To use fraction strips to estimate fractions as decimals and decimals as fractions*

- *To find equivalent forms of fraction quantities*

- *To use hundredths grids to model fractions*

- *To use knowledge of operations, fractions, and decimals to understand real-world situations*

Materials		
Problem	**For students**	**For the teacher**
All	Calculators	Transparencies 5.1 to 5.3 (optional)
5.1	Labsheet 5.1 (1 per student), colored tiles or other manipulatives (optional)	Transparency of Labsheet 4.2D
5.2	Labsheet 5.2 (1 per student), straightedges, chart paper, or a transparency of Labsheet 5.2 and transparency markers (optional; for recording answers to share with the class)	Transparency of Labsheet 5.2 (optional)

Student Pages 53–66   **Teaching the Investigation 66a–66k**

INVESTIGATION 5

Moving Between Fractions and Decimals

In your daily life, you often need to choose among options. You might have to decide which option is the best buy, gives the best outcome, or yields the most money. In these situations, mathematics can help you make comparisons so you can make a good decision.

5.1 Choosing the Best

The Portland Middle School basketball team is playing the Coldwater Colts. The game is tied 58 to 58. In her excitement the Coldwater coach steps onto the court just as the buzzer sounds, and a technical foul is called.

The Portland coach has to choose one of her players to shoot the free throw. If the player makes the free throw, Portland will win.

Did you know?

Basketball was invented in 1891 by James Naismith, a physical education teacher who wanted to create a team sport that could be played indoors during the winter. The game was originally played with a soccer ball, and peach baskets were used as goals.

5.1

Choosing the Best

At a Glance

**Grouping:
Small Groups or Pairs**

Launch

- Tell the story of the coach's choice.

- Make sure students understand that they need to compare the players' scores in a way that accounts for the varying numbers of trials.

Explore

- If some groups are having difficulty, suggest visual models they may use.

- Pose extension questions for groups that finish early.

Summarize

- Allow groups to present their arguments.

- Make sure both the fraction-strip method and the equivalent-fraction method for solving the problem are discussed.

Assignment Choices

ACE questions 17–24, 39, and unassigned choices from earlier problems

5.2

Writing Fractions as Decimals

Launch

- Present the problem, and work through an example or two with the class.

- Make sure both ways of working with Labsheet 5.2—using a straightedge and maneuvering the hundredths strip—are discussed.

Explore

- As you observe, have students find equivalents in the opposite direction as well: converting decimals to fractions.

Summarize

- Have groups present their findings and explain their reasoning.

- As a class, analyze the strategies and the answers.

- Ask questions to focus students on the decimal-to-fraction change.

Assignment Choices

ACE questions 1–16, 35–38, and unassigned choices from earlier problems

---

> ### Problem 5.1
>
> The coach has three players to choose from to shoot the free throw. In their pregame warm-ups:
> - Angela made 17 out of 25 free throws
> - Emily made 15 out of 20 free throws
> - Carma made 7 out of 10 free throws
>
> Which player should the Portland coach select to shoot the free throw? Explain your reasoning.

 Problem 5.1 Follow-Up

Of the top four free-throw shooters on the Coldwater Colts:
- Naomi averages 19 out of 25 free throws
- Bobbie averages 8 out of 10 free throws
- Kate averages 36 out of 50 free throws
- Olympia averages 16 out of 20 free throws

If you were the coach of the Colts, which player would you choose to take the free-throw on a technical foul? Explain your reasoning.

5.2 Writing Fractions as Decimals

The Portland coach chose Emily to take the shot. Emily missed the free throw, but the team won in overtime.

The next day, the players asked their math teacher, Mr. Martinez, what he thought about the problem of whom to choose to take the free throw. He said he always tries to find a decimal name for fractions whose values he needs to compare.

Mr. Martinez explained, "Our fraction strips can help us find decimal names that are good approximations for some fractions. Decimals are ways to express fractions with denominators of 10 or 100. We can use our tenths strip to help us find decimal approximations. We could find even closer approximations if we had a fraction strip divided into hundredths."

Answer to Problem 5.1

Angela's success rate is $\frac{68}{100}$, Emily's is $\frac{75}{100}$, and Carma's is $\frac{70}{100}$. Emily is the most successful shooter and should be chosen to attempt the free throw.

Answer to Problem 5.1 Follow-Up

Naomi averages 76 out of 100 free throws, Bobbie averages about 80 out of 100, Kate averages 72 out of 100, and Olympia averages 80 out of 100 free throws. Most students will probably choose either Bobbie or Olympia to shoot the free throw. They both have the same success rate.

Problem 5.2

On the next page are the fraction strips with which you are already familiar. Below these strips is a hundredths strip, which is a tenths strip that has each segment divided into ten parts. Work with your group to find a way to use the fraction strips to help you estimate each of the fractions represented on the halves, thirds, fourths, fifths, sixths, eighths, ninths, tenths, and twelfths fraction strips as decimals.

You might think about doing this by comparing the marks on each fraction strip to marks on the hundredths strip. For example, to find a decimal name for $\frac{5}{12}$, you can find the mark on the hundredths strip that is nearest to the length $\frac{5}{12}$, since hundredths can easily be written as decimals. Since the mark at $\frac{42}{100}$ on the hundredths strip is the closest mark to $\frac{5}{12}$ on the twelfths strip, $\frac{5}{12}$ is approximately equal to 0.42. Sometimes it is easier to look at the tenths strip. For example, $\frac{1}{2}$ on the fraction strip is at the same mark as $\frac{5}{10}$ on the tenths strip, so $\frac{1}{2}$ is equivalent to 0.5.

On Labsheet 5.2, label each mark on the halves, thirds, fourths, fifths, sixths, eighths, ninths, tenths, and twelfths fraction strips with an approximate decimal representation. Be prepared to explain your answers.

■ Problem 5.2 Follow-Up

1. Did you find any patterns that helped you to predict what some of the fractions would be as decimals?

2. How did your knowledge of equivalent fractions help you to find decimal names for some of your fractions?

3. In a–d, find an approximate fraction for the decimal.
   a. 0.17
   b. 0.29
   c. 0.609
   d. 0.92

Answer to Problem 5.2

See page 66h.

Answers to Problem 5.2 Follow-Up

1. Possible answer: The halves, fifths, and tenths strips are easy because the marks on these strips match exactly with marks on the hundredths strip.

2. Possible answer: It is easy to find equivalent fractions with denominators of 100 for halves, fourths, and tenths. This allows you to quickly find decimal forms for these fractions. Since $\frac{1}{2}, \frac{2}{4}, \frac{3}{6}, \frac{4}{8}, \frac{5}{10}$, and $\frac{6}{12}$ are all equivalent to $\frac{1}{2}$, they all have decimal form 0.5.

3. a. $\frac{1}{6}$ or $\frac{2}{12}$ b. $\frac{3}{10}$ c. $\frac{3}{5}$ or $\frac{6}{10}$ d. $\frac{11}{12}$

halves	

thirds		

fourths			

fifths				

sixths					

eighths

ninths

tenths

twelfths

hundredths

$\frac{10}{100}$ $\frac{20}{100}$ $\frac{30}{100}$ $\frac{40}{100}$ $\frac{50}{100}$ $\frac{60}{100}$ $\frac{70}{100}$ $\frac{80}{100}$ $\frac{90}{100}$ $\frac{100}{100}$

56 Bits and Pieces I

5.3 Moving from Fractions to Decimals

Moving From Fractions to Decimals

In 1992, a hurricane swept through the Bahamas, Florida, and Louisiana, destroying many homes and causing lots of damage to land and buildings. The storm was named Hurricane Andrew. Many people lost everything, and had no place to live and very little clothing and food. In response to the disaster, people from all over collected clothing, household items, and food in a relief effort to send to the victims of the hurricane.

One group of students decided to collect food to distribute to some of the families whose homes were destroyed. They would pack what they collected in boxes to send it to the families. The students had to solve some problems while they were packing the boxes.

Problem 5.3

The students had 24 boxes for packing the food they collected. They wanted to share the supplies equally among the families who would receive the boxes. They had small bags and plastic containers to use to repack items for the individual boxes.

The students collected the following items:

48	tins of cocoa mix	6	pounds of Swiss cheese
72	boxes of powdered milk	3	pounds of hot pepper cheese
264	boxes of juice	7	pounds of peanuts
120	boxes of granola bars	5	pounds of popcorn kernels
36	pounds of wheat crackers	475	apples
18	pounds of peanut butter	195	oranges
12	pounds of cheddar cheese		

A. How much of each item should the students include in each box? Explain your reasoning.

B. What operation $(+, -, \times, \div)$ did you use to find your answers? Why did this operation work?

C. How can your calculator help you decide how to distribute the food items?

■ Problem 5.3 Follow-Up

One student calculated the amount of Swiss cheese to include in each box by entering 6 into her calculator and dividing by 24. Is this a good method? Why or why not?

Launch

- Tell the story of the students' relief effort.

- Remind students that explaining their answers is part of solving the problem.

Explore

- Ask students questions that help them focus on meaning.

Summarize

- As a class, discuss strategies for determining how to distribute the food items.

- Talk about how the idea of sharing relates to the division interpretation of fractions.

Answers to Problem 5.3

A. See page 66h.

B. $\div$; You are *dividing* the total quantity for each item among the 24 boxes.

C. You can use a calculator to divide the total quantity for each item by 24.

Answer to Problem 5.3 Follow-Up

Possible answer: Yes, because you get 0.25, which is equal to $\frac{1}{4}$, which means each box gets a quarter pound of Swiss cheese. Division is a good way to figure out how to share things equally.

Assignment Choices

ACE questions 25–31 (26–28 require Labsheet 5.2), 33, 34, 40–50, and unassigned choices from earlier problems

Assessment

It is appropriate to use Check-Up 2 after this problem.

Answers

Applications

1. Possible answers: $\frac{25}{100}$, $\frac{1}{4}$, $\frac{2}{8}$, $\frac{4}{16}$, $\frac{100}{400}$. The decimal value 0.25 *means* $\frac{25}{100}$. Since 25 is $\frac{1}{4}$ of a 100, $\frac{25}{100}$ is equal to $\frac{1}{4}$.

2. Possible answers: $\frac{40}{100}$ and $\frac{2}{5}$. The decimal value 0.40 *means* $\frac{40}{100}$. If you divide 100 into five equal parts, each part would be 20. Two of the five parts would be 40, so $\frac{40}{100}$ equals $\frac{2}{5}$.

3. Possible answer: $\frac{1}{10}$

4. Possible answer: $\frac{4}{10}$

5. Possible answers: $\frac{1}{20}$ or $\frac{1}{25}$

6. Possible answer: $\frac{8}{10}$ or $\frac{4}{5}$

7. $\frac{7}{2}$ or $3\frac{1}{2}$ or 3.5 pounds of pretzels; 4 melons; $\frac{2}{3}$ or about 0.67 pounds of pecans; $\frac{4}{3}$ or $1\frac{1}{3}$ or about 1.33 pounds of peanut butter; $\frac{10}{3}$ or $3\frac{1}{3}$ or about 3.33 pounds of mozzarella cheese; $\frac{2}{9}$ or about 0.22 pounds of grated parmesan cheese; 9 pizza crusts; 6 cans of pizza sauce.

8a. Antonio's fish; Possible explanation: $\frac{2}{3}$ is equivalent to $\frac{16}{24}$, and $\frac{5}{8}$ is equivalent to $\frac{15}{24}$. Antonio's fish is longer because $\frac{16}{24}$ is greater than $\frac{15}{24}$.

8b. Possible answer: $\frac{2}{3}$ is about 0.67, and $\frac{5}{8}$ is about 0.63. It is easy to see that 0.67 is larger than 0.63 since each decimal has the same number of places. Using decimals, it may have been easier for them to tell which fish was longer.

As you work on these ACE questions, use your calculator whenever you need it.

Applications

1. Name three fractions whose decimal equivalent is 0.25. Explain your answer. Draw a picture if it helps explain your thinking.

2. Name two fractions whose decimal equivalent is 0.40. Explain your answer. Draw a picture if it helps explain your thinking.

In 3–6, give a good fraction estimate for the decimal.

3. 0.08   4. 0.4   5. 0.04   6. 0.84

7. Mr. Paul's class wants to send 18 identical food boxes to victims of a hurricane. The class has collected the following items:

63 pounds of pretzels   60 pounds of mozzarella cheese
72 melons   4 pounds of grated parmesan cheese
12 pounds of pecans   162 pizza crusts
24 pounds of peanut butter   108 cans of pizza sauce

How much of each kind of food will go into each box?

8. **a.** Sarah and Antonio went fishing in the Grand River, and each caught one fish. Sarah's fish was $\frac{5}{8}$ of a foot long and Antonio's was $\frac{2}{3}$ of a foot long. Which fish was longer? Explain.

   b. If Sarah and Antonio had measured their fish in decimals, would it have been easier for them to tell which fish was longer? Explain.

9. Each small square represents $\frac{1}{100}$. What decimal is represented by this set of grids?

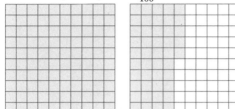

10. Each small square represents $\frac{1}{100}$. What decimal is represented by this set of grids?

In 11–13, use the fraction strips on Labsheet 5.2 to help you estimate a good decimal equivalent for the fraction.

11. $\frac{3}{4}$ **12.** $\frac{2}{3}$ **13.** $\frac{5}{12}$

In 14–16, find a fraction with a denominator of 10 or less that is a good estimate for the decimal.

14. 0.6   **15.** 0.91   **16.** 0.33

In 17–20, compare the two numbers. Then rewrite the numbers, inserting <, >, or = between them to make a true statement.

17. $\frac{4}{6}$ $\frac{2}{3}$ **18.** 0.34   4

19. $\frac{2}{5}$ $\frac{1}{3}$ **20.** 0.08   0.3

21. Which are easier to compare, fractions or decimals? Why?

---

9. 1.45

10. 2.80 or 2.8

11. 0.75

12. 0.67

13. 0.42

14. $\frac{3}{5}$

15. $\frac{9}{10}$

16. $\frac{1}{3}$

17. $\frac{4}{6} = \frac{2}{3}$

18. 0.34 < 4

19. $\frac{2}{5} > \frac{1}{3}$

20. 0.08 < 0.3

21. Possible answer: Decimals are usually easier to compare. When fractions have different denominators, it is often difficult to compare them without first finding equivalent fractions.

22. 0.9 > 0.45; Possible explanation: Since 0.9 is the same as 0.90, you can look at the digits after the decimal point—90 and 45—to find which is larger.

23. 0.75 > 0.6; Possible explanation: Since 0.6 is the same as 0.60, you can look at the digits after the decimal point—75 and 60—to find which is larger.

24. 0.6 = 0.60; Possible explanation: Six tenths and sixty hundredths are the same.

25. 0.375; By looking at the fraction strips, the mark for $\frac{3}{8}$ lines up between the marks for 0.37 and 0.38 on the hundredths strip.

26. $\frac{3}{4}$ = 0.75

27. $\frac{5}{8}$ = 0.625

28. $\frac{13}{25}$ = 0.52

29. $\frac{17}{25}$ = 0.68

30. $\frac{1}{20}$ = 0.05

31. $\frac{7}{10}$ = 0.7

32. See page 66i.

33a. $\frac{8}{10}$ or 0.8 of a pizza

33b. See page 66i.

34. Possible answer: When you divide one number by another, you are distributing equal parts of the first number to the number of groups given by the second number. So, you are *sharing* equal parts of the first number to the number of groups given by the second number.

---

22. Which is greater, 0.45 or 0.9? Explain your reasoning. Draw a picture if it helps explain your thinking.

23. Which is greater, seventy-five hundredths or six tenths? Explain your reasoning. Draw a picture if it helps explain your thinking.

24. Which is greater, 0.6 or 0.60? Explain your reasoning. Draw a picture if it helps you explain.

25. James says a fraction is another way to represent a division problem. For example, he says $\frac{3}{8}$ means the same thing as $3 \div 8$. What do you get when you do this division on your calculator? Compare your decimal answer with your fraction strips to see if this is reasonable. Describe your findings.

In 26–31, use your calculator to find a decimal form for the fraction. Then use the hundredths strip or other fraction strips on Labsheet 5.2 to check whether your answer is reasonable.

26. $\frac{3}{4}$

27. $\frac{5}{8}$

28. $\frac{13}{25}$

29. $\frac{17}{25}$

30. $\frac{1}{20}$

31. $\frac{7}{10}$

32. Suppose a new student starts school today and your teacher asks you to teach her how to find decimal representations for fractions. What would you tell her? How would you convince the student that your method works?

Connections

33. Ten students went to a pizza parlor together. They ordered eight small pizzas.

   a. How much will each student receive if they share the pizzas equally? Express your answer as a fraction and as a decimal.

   b. Explain how you thought about the problem. Draw a picture that would convince someone that your answer is correct.

34. Zachary says division should be called a "sharing operation." Why might he say this?

35. If we look through a microscope that makes objects appear ten times larger, 1 centimeter on a metric ruler looks like this:

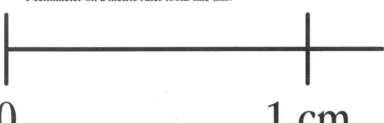

0   1 cm

a. Copy this microscope's view of 1 centimeter. Subdivide the length for 1 centimeter into ten equal parts. What fraction of a centimeter does each of these parts represent?

b. Now think of subdividing one of these smaller parts into ten equal parts. What part of a centimeter does each of the new segments represent?

c. If you were to subdivide one of these new small parts into ten parts again, what part of a centimeter would each of the new small parts represent?

36. Here is what one of the fleas that live on the dog at Mr. Valicenti's fishing camp looks like through the microscope that makes objects appear ten times larger.

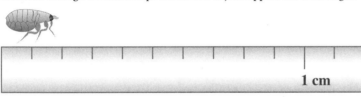

1 cm

a. About how long is the flea in centimeters?

b. How long would a line of 10 fleas be?

c. How many fleas would it take to equal 1 centimeter?

Connections

35a. See below left.

35b. Each part represents $\frac{1}{100}$ or 0.01 of a cm.

35c. Each part represents $\frac{1}{1000}$ or 0.001 of a cm.

36a. about $\frac{2}{10}$ or 0.2 cm long

36b. about 2 cm long

36c. 5 fleas

35a. Each part represents $\frac{1}{10}$ or 0.1 of a cm.

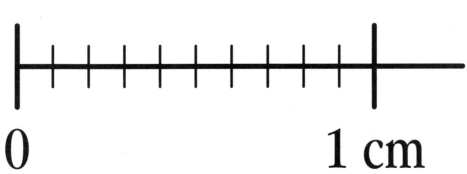

0   1 cm

37a. about 1.3 cm long

37b. about 13 cm long

37c. about 65 fleas

37. There are also ferocious flies at Mr. Valicenti's camp.

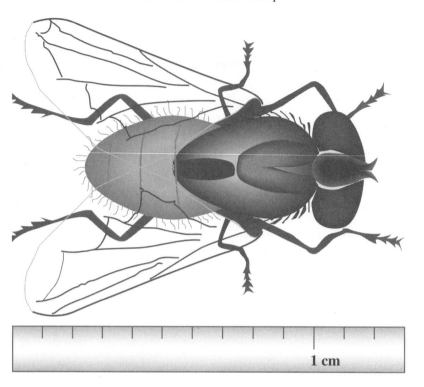

1 cm

   a. About how long is the fly in centimeters?

   b. If we line up ten of these flies end to end, how long would the line of flies be?

   c. About how many fleas lined up end to end (see question 36) would equal the length of a line of ten flies?

38. a. Copy the number line below. Show 0.4 and 0.5 on your number line. Can you place five numbers between 0.4 and 0.5? If yes, place them on your number line with labels. If no, explain why not.

0   1

b. Now, enlarge the line segment from 0.4 to 0.5. Make your new line segment approximately the length of the original number line. Place 0.45 and 0.50 on your new number line. Can you find five numbers that belong between 0.45 and 0.50? If yes, place them on your number line with labels. If no, explain why not.

39. Using the fraction benchmarks $0, \frac{1}{4}, \frac{1}{2}, \frac{3}{4}$, and 1 and the number line below, copy and complete the table to show what two fraction benchmarks each decimal is between. Also, tell which benchmark each decimal is nearest.

Decimal	Lower benchmark	Upper benchmark	Nearest benchmark
0.17	0	$\frac{1}{4}$	$\frac{1}{4}$
0.034			
0.789			
0.092			
0.9			
0.491			
0.627			
0.36			

Investigation 5: Moving Between Fractions and Decimals   **63**

38a. See page 66i.
38b. See page 66i.
39. See page 66j.

Extensions

40. See below right.

41. See below right.

42. See page 66j.

43. See page 66j.

44. See page 66j.

Extensions

In 40–44, copy the segment of the number line given. Then, find the "step" by determining the difference from one mark to another. Label the unlabeled marks with decimals. Here is an example:

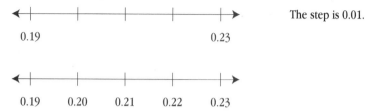

The step is 0.01.

40.

0.003   0.403   The step is _____.

41.

0.198   0.200   0.202   The step is _____.

42.

0.7634   0.7834   0.8034   The step is _____.

43.

0.512   0.520   The step is _____.

44.

0.3   0.4   The step is _____.

40. The step is 0.1.

0.003   0.103   0.203   0.303   0.403

41. The step is 0.001.

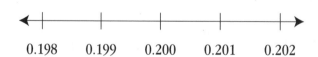

0.198   0.199   0.200   0.201   0.202

In 45–50, find an estimate if you cannot find an exact answer. You may find that making a number line or a diagram is useful in solving the problem. Explain how you reasoned about each problem.

45. What is $\frac{1}{4}$ of 12?

46. What is $\frac{3}{4}$ of 8?

47. What is $\frac{2}{9}$ of 18?

48. What is $\frac{2}{9}$ of 3?

49. What is $\frac{1}{4}$ of 3?

50. What is $\frac{3}{4}$ of 3?

45. See below left.
46. See below left.
47. See page 66j.
48. See page 66j.
49. See page 66k.
50. See page 66k.

45. 3; Possible explanation: 3 of 12 equal parts is $\frac{1}{4}$ of the whole.

46. 6; Possible explanation: 6 of 8 equal parts is $\frac{3}{4}$ of the whole.

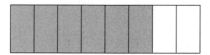

Possible Answers

1. Dividing the numerator of a fraction by the denominator gives you the decimal equivalent. You can check this by writing the decimal as a fraction with a denominator of 10, 100, 1000, or some other power of ten and then observing that the original fraction and the decimal fraction are equivalent (or close to equivalent).

2. To find a fraction equivalent to a given decimal, use the digits of the decimal as the numerator, and use the place value of the last digit to determine the denominator. For example, the numerator for 0.589 is 589. Since the 9 is in the thousandths place, the denominator is 1000. So 0.589 is equal to $\frac{589}{1000}$.

3. When comparing two decimals, it helps if the decimals are expressed with the same number of decimal places. For example, you can express 0.57 as 0.570 and then easily compare the digits to the right of the decimal point. You can compare digit by digit from the largest place value to the smallest until you find one number larger than the other. Since 570 is greater than 559, 0.57 is larger than 0.559.

Mathematical Reflections

In this investigation, you developed ways to represent fractions as decimals. You used your fraction strips to find fractions and decimals that are close to each other. These questions will help you summarize what you have learned:

1 Describe how to find a decimal equivalent to a given fraction. How can you check your strategy to see that it works?

2 Describe how to find a fraction equivalent to a given decimal. Explain why your strategy works.

3 When comparing two decimals—such as 0.57 and 0.559—how can you decide which decimal represents the larger number?

Think about your answers to these questions, discuss your ideas with other students and your teacher, and then write a summary of your findings in your journal.

Tips for the Linguistically Diverse Classroom

Original Rebus The Original Rebus technique is described in detail in *Getting to Know Connected Mathematics*. Students make a copy of the text before it is discussed. During discussion, they generate their own rebuses for words they do not understand as the words are made comprehensible through pictures, objects, or demonstrations. Example: Question 3—key words for which students may make rebuses are *comparing* (> or <?), *decimal* (.), *larger* (>).

TEACHING THE INVESTIGATION

5.1 • Choosing the Best

Problem 5.1 requires students to compare fractions with different denominators. Some of the denominators are larger than those represented on the fraction strips students have used, so they must find new ways to think about equivalent fractions.

Launch

There are two ways to pose this problem. You can present it in its current open form and allow students to generate reasonable ways to make comparisons and to decide who should go to the free-throw line. A less open way to pose the problem is to suggest that students consider finding equivalent representations for the three fractions if they think that would be useful for making comparisons.

Tell students the story of the coach's decision. Whichever way you pose the problem, be sure they are thinking about how to compare the girls' performance when each player took and made a different number of free throws in the warm-ups. Students will gain a lot from working in pairs or small groups, as there are different ways to argue for which player should be chosen.

Explore

In earlier investigations, students learned that the numerator and denominator of a fraction can be multiplied by the same number to obtain an equivalent fraction. Some students will quickly convert all three fractions for easy comparison. Other students will need to use concrete representations to help make sense of the problem.

One way to model the problem is by using a hundredths grid, as on Labsheet 5.1, to show each player's performance. This makes converting to a common number of shots (100) easier to visualize.

For the Teacher: Explaining Problem 5.1

If some students are having difficulty dealing with this problem, consider giving them tiles or other manipulatives to represent each player's performance. Tiles of two colors could be used to show each player's data; for example, red tiles could represent making the shot, and yellow tiles could represent missing the shot. Students could build multiple sets of tiles to make 100 trials. For Angela, they would make four sets of her 25 shots—a total of $4 \times 17 = 68$ red tiles and $4 \times 8 = 32$ yellow tiles, which would visually show her average as 68 out of 100.

If some groups finish early, ask them to work on the follow-up questions.

Summarize

A major point that should arise from the summary is that comparisons of situations with different numbers of trials is difficult unless we find equivalent fraction or decimal representations that allow us to make comparisons.

Let students present their arguments. Try to help them distinguish between making decisions based on mathematical evidence and decisions based on irrelevant details such as the names of the players.

Ask questions to help make students' reasoning more precise.

> Angela said she should be chosen because she shot more free throws than the other two players. Carma said she should be chosen because she missed the fewest shots. Emily said that if the coach looked at their trials closely, she would be chosen because although Angela had attempted more shots, she made only two more than Emily, and Carma missed three shots out of ten. What do you think?

Some of your students will probably support each of these positions. Asking them to clarify their assumptions can help the discussion. Are they assuming that the data they have been given will represent performance in the long run for each player? Are they assuming that the conditions of the game will not affect one player more than another?

Make sure that the two main ways of thinking about the problem—by using a hundredths grid to represent the free throws made by each player, and by converting the fractions to equivalent fractions with denominators of 100—are explored in the summary discussion.

You might want to display Transparency 4.2D while the class discusses the hundredths-grid method.

> Can we use a hundredths grids to show the fraction of free throws made by each player? Explain your reasoning.

Reasoning with a hundredths grid will involve shading 68 out of 100 squares for Angela, 75 out of 100 for Emily, and 70 out of 100 for Carma.

> Can we compare the three fractions by first converting them to equivalent fractions with the same denominator?

These fractions can easily be written with 100 as the denominator. Some students might see this quickly, since 100 is 4×25, 5×20, and 10×10.

In one classroom, the teacher gave groups sheets of chart paper on which to record their decisions and their reasoning. Groups displayed their work at the front of the room.

Teacher Looking at the displays, we can see that not only have you attacked the problem in different ways, but you have reached different conclusions. Which group would like to explain their answer first?

Jordan We think Angela should shoot the free throw because she made the most. Emily shot almost as many times but made two less.

Mirabel I disagree. You need to think about what happens in the long run to compare their free-throw attempts. Our group did this by saying, What would happen if each girl shot 100 times and always shot the same way? If each girl shoots 100 times, Angela will make about 68, because it would be like shooting 25 four times and each time she would make 17. Emily will make about 75, because it would be like shooting 5 groups of 20 and for each group she would make about 15. Carma will make about 70, because it will be like 10 groups of 10 and each time she would make about 7. If we look at the players like this—where they have taken the same number of shots—it is obvious Emily should shoot the free throw.

Hearing this argument, several groups decided that they agreed with Mirabel's answer.

Teacher Based on Mirabel's reasoning, several of you now think Emily should go to the free-throw line. Mirabel's group is saying that it is easier to think about this problem by finding a way to compare $\frac{17}{25}$, $\frac{15}{20}$, and $\frac{7}{10}$. They found equivalent fractions with denominators of 100. Why would you choose 100 as denominator to rename the fractions?

Chuck Because they all can be changed to so many 100s.

Teacher How do you know that?

Chuck Because Mirabel showed that 100 was a common multiple for 25, 20, and 10.

5.2 • Writing Fractions as Decimals

In this problem, students are challenged to find decimal estimates for fractions on the fraction strips with which they are already familiar. The intent is not to build proficiency at using fraction strips to find decimal equivalents, but to use the visual representations to help understand that the same quantity can be represented with two different symbol systems, fractions and decimals. Building this basic visual understanding is important, since the technique of dividing on a calculator—which will be explored shortly—is so efficient that it tends to mask the meaning of fraction-decimal equivalence.

Launch

Read the problem to the class. Display a transparency of Labsheet 5.2, and ask the class how they could use the fraction strips to find a good decimal name for $\frac{1}{5}$. This should lead to a visual check between the hundredths strip and the fifths strip or between the tenths strip and the fifths strip.

If students do not suggest it, you might want to demonstrate two methods of finding equivalent decimals. Students can either cut the hundredths strip from the bottom of Labsheet 5.2 so they can position it alongside the other fraction strips, or they can use a straightedge to help sight along the marks on the fraction strips and read off decimal approximations.

Rather than having all groups find decimal equivalents for every fraction strip, you might want to assign two or three strips to each group and have them report their results during the class discussion. You might, for example, divide the task by having two groups responsible for finding the decimal names for the fourths, sixths, and twelfths strips; two responsible for the thirds, eighths, and tenths strips; two responsible for the fifths, sixths, and ninths strips; and two responsible for the thirds, eighths, and twelfths strips.

Groups might write their answers on chart paper or on Transparencies of Labsheet 5.2 for easy sharing with the class. Explain that by the end of the problem, each student should have written the decimal equivalents for all the fraction strips on his or her labsheet. Ask students to keep these labsheets; they will need them for the ACE questions.

Explore

Even though the problem focuses on changing fractions to decimals, visual comparison also allows us to convert from decimals to fractions. As you circulate, ask groups to move both directions using the fraction strips. For example, ask students to find a fraction that is a good estimate for 0.66. They should see that $\frac{8}{12}$, $\frac{6}{9}$, $\frac{4}{6}$, and $\frac{2}{3}$ are all good answers.

Summarize

In the summary, remember that the intent is to build an appreciation that fractions and decimals are different representations of equivalent quantities.

One teacher summarized the problem in the following way. The groups had displayed their findings for the strips for which they were responsible.

Teacher   We all know $\frac{1}{2}$ can be renamed as the decimal 0.5 or 0.50. (*On the board, she wrote* $\frac{1}{2} = 0.5$ *or* 0.50.) We can demonstrate this by using the halves and hundredths strips, because $\frac{1}{2}$ easily matches up with one of the lines on the hundredths strip.

What other strips were easy to find decimal names for? (*The class suggested fourths, fifths, tenths, and some of the sixths, eighths, and twelfths fractions.*) Let's start with the easy ones. Which group would like to explain their display for fourths?

One group shared their results. Everyone agreed with their findings, so the class moved on to fifths and tenths. Agreement was again reached. The teacher displayed a transparency of Labsheet 5.2.

Teacher   I want to take a moment to record our results so far. (*She wrote the fraction and decimal name for halves, fourths, fifths, and tenths.*) Could someone explain why $\frac{2}{5}$ and $\frac{4}{10}$ have the same decimal name?

Cheryl   They are equivalent fractions, so they must be the same decimal because decimals are just another way to write fractions.

Teacher   We still have thirds, sixths, eighths, ninths, and twelfths. For which of these was it easiest to find decimal names? (*One student suggested eighths.*) Would the eighths group explain your thinking?

The teacher chose the group who had made this display:

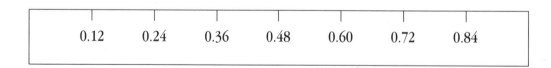

Lauren   We started with the $\frac{1}{8}$ mark and lined it up with the 0.12 mark on the hundredths strip. That made a pattern, because $\frac{2}{8}$ is equal to two $\frac{1}{8}$s. We just doubled what we had for $\frac{1}{8}$ and then we just continued in the same way, adding 0.12 each time.

Teacher   What about when you go from $\frac{7}{8}$ to $\frac{8}{8}$? For $\frac{7}{8}$ you have 0.84. If you add 0.12, you would get 0.96, but you know that $\frac{8}{8}$ is 1, not 0.96.

Lauren   Well, that is our one exception, because $\frac{8}{8}$ has to be 1, so it can't be 0.96.

Denis   Your list doesn't make sense to me. I know $\frac{4}{8}$ is the same as $\frac{1}{2}$ and that $\frac{1}{2}$ is the same as 0.5, but your answer says it's 0.48.

Heidi   I agree with Denis. The decimals don't make sense because you have $\frac{2}{8}$ equal to 0.24, and we know $\frac{1}{4}$ and $\frac{2}{8}$ are equivalent fractions and that $\frac{1}{4}$ equals 0.25.

Teacher   Lauren, do you agree that $\frac{2}{8}$ is equal to $\frac{1}{4}$ and that $\frac{1}{4}$ is equal to 0.25? (*Lauren agreed.*) If that is true, what would $\frac{1}{8}$ have to be?

Lauren   It would have to be $0.12\frac{1}{2}$, but you can't have that.

Teacher   I think you could have that amount.

Lauren   Then I want to change some of our others.

Jabe   My group labeled the thirds strip. We want to change our labels now based on what we learned from the eighths group.

Because of this discussion, the class decided to determine very exact decimals for their fractions. The teacher went along with this precision because of level of understanding about what was being communicated.

For the Teacher: Comparing Hundredths and Thousandths

The number halfway between 0.12 and 0.13 is actually 0.125. You can help your students to understand this by asking them to picture a thousandths strip. On a thousandths strip, 0.12 would be located at the $\frac{120}{1000}$ mark and 0.13 would be located at the $\frac{130}{1000}$ mark. The number halfway between $\frac{120}{1000}$ and $\frac{130}{1000}$ is $\frac{125}{1000}$, so the number halfway between 0.12 and 0.13 is 0.125.

Ask a few questions that focus on the decimal-to-fraction change.

Use the fraction strips to figure out which fraction is equal to or closest to 0.6? ($\frac{3}{5}$ or $\frac{6}{10}$) How about 0.91? ($\frac{11}{12}$ or $\frac{9}{10}$) 0.33? ($\frac{4}{12}$, $\frac{2}{6}$, or $\frac{1}{3}$) 0.04? (*This lies between 0 and $\frac{1}{12}$, but some students may want to be more precise by making fraction strips with smaller parts, such as halving the twelfths strip to get a twenty-fourths strip.*) 0.84? ($\frac{10}{12}$ or $\frac{5}{6}$)

Students should come away from the summary understanding that they have a visual way to find good estimates in both directions—fractions to decimals and decimals to fractions.

This problem is designed to build from students' understanding of the meaning of division to the division interpretation of fractions. It is easy to show students *how* to find a decimal equivalent of a fraction, but it is much harder to help them to understand *why* division is an appropriate interpretation of a fraction.

Launch

Tell students the story context, and challenge them to figure out how much of each food item to put into each box. Remind them that explaining how they decided to distribute the goods among the boxes is part of doing the problem.

This problem could be done by first having students work alone and then in pairs to share their thinking. Or, students could work in groups or pairs from the beginning.

Explore

As you circulate, ask questions that focus on meaning.

> How many 24s are in 48? What does that tell you about how many tins of cocoa must go in each box?

> Which items can be split into fractional parts and which must be in whole units? How does this affect your distribution of supplies?

Summarize

Sharing is a good word to use in discussing the problem, since whole-number division can be used to answer sharing problems and is often used as a context for understanding fractions. Emphasize the connection between sharing a number of items that is evenly divisible by the number of people sharing the items and sharing a number of items that is not evenly divisible by the number of people sharing.

Ask questions that focus on the meaning of division as *equal sharing* to help students understand the division interpretation of fractions. This is a necessary connection for students to understand why dividing with a calculator will change the form of a fraction to a decimal. Have them share their thinking about the problem and the follow-up questions to assess how well they are understanding the relationship between fractions and decimals.

The following discussion took place in one classroom:

Teacher Which food items were easy to share among the 24 boxes, and why?

Angela The first four items: 48 tins of cocoa mix, 72 boxes of powdered milk, 264 boxes of juice, and 120 boxes of granola bars. When you divide each of these by 24, you get a whole number.

Teacher For the cocoa, we can divide 48 by 24 to get 2. What does the 2 mean?

Angela   The 2 means that each box will get two tins of cocoa mix.

Teacher   What made working with some of the other items more difficult?

Ricardo   Some of them didn't turn out to be good amounts, so I didn't know what to do. For the 18 pounds of peanut butter, you can't give every box a pound because there isn't enough.

Frank   Yeah, when I tried to divide with my calculator like I did with the others, I pushed $18 \div 24$ and got 0.75.

Teacher   What do you think the 0.75 means? What is a fraction name for 0.75?

Frank   Well, 0.75 means 75 out of 100. A fraction name for that is $\frac{3}{4}$. I guess I could give $\frac{3}{4}$ of a pound of peanut butter to each box.

Teacher   What do you get when you press $3 \div 4$ on your calculator? Why does that make sense?

The students at first had a hard time talking about why it made sense to take $3 \div 4$ and get 0.75, but the more they worked with the numbers and tried to explain what they thought was happening, the more sense they made of the situation.

Ask additional questions to stimulate discussion during the summary.

> While packing the boxes, Lenora said that division should be called a "sharing operation." What could she have meant?

> Look at the apples and oranges. Since we don't get a whole number when we divide 475 by 24 or 195 by 24, how will we divide the pieces of fruit among the boxes?

Pull Investigation 5 together by returning to Problem 5.1, which involved comparing fractions with different denominators. That problem can be reworked using a calculator to find decimal representations of the proportion of shots each player made. Ask students to explain how to interpret the decimals. They should recognize that the decimal representation shows the same proportion or fraction, but in an equivalent form based on a power of 10 as the denominator. This is the major objective of this investigation.

Additional Answers

Answers to Problem 5.2

Answers will vary, depending on how carefully students aligned their fraction strips. The answers shown are those obtained by estimating to the nearest tenth and then to the nearest hundredth.

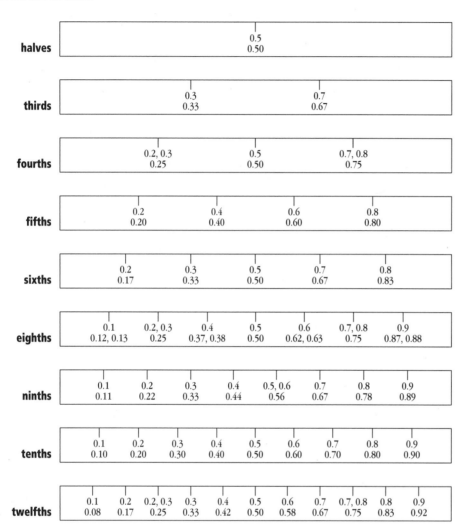

Answers to Problem 5.3

A. tins of cocoa mix: $48 \div 24 = 2$ tins per box
    boxes of powdered milk: $72 \div 24 = 3$ boxes per box
    boxes of juice: $264 \div 24 = 11$ boxes per box
    boxes of granola bars: $120 \div 24 = 5$ boxes per box
    pounds of wheat crackers: $36 \div 24 = 1\frac{1}{2}$ or 1.5 pounds per box
    pounds of peanut butter: $18 \div 24 = \frac{3}{4}$ or 0.75 pound per box
    pounds of cheddar cheese: $12 \div 24 = 0.5$ or $\frac{1}{2}$ pound per box
    pounds of Swiss cheese: $6 \div 24 = 0.25$ or $\frac{1}{4}$ pound per box
    pounds of hot pepper cheese: $3 \div 24 = \frac{1}{8}$ or 0.125 pound per box
    pounds of peanuts: $7 \div 24 = \frac{7}{24}$ or about 0.29 pound per box
    pounds of popcorn kernels: $5 \div 24 = \frac{5}{24}$ or about 0.21 pound per box
    apples: $475 \div 24 = 19$ apples per box, with 19 apples left over
    oranges: $195 \div 24 = 8$ oranges per box, with 3 oranges left over

ACE Answers

32. This question is very hard for students at this stage. We expect students to talk about how they can check to see if the division answer makes sense, but not to give a mathematical proof. Possible answer: I would tell the new student to divide the numerator by the denominator on the calculator. I would then tell her to round to the nearest hundredth. To show her that this makes sense, I would write this decimal as a fraction with 100 in the denominator and show her that the original fraction and this fraction are nearly the same amount. I could do this by finding a number to multiply the numerator and the denominator of the original fraction by that gives a denominator close to 100.

Connections

33b. Possible answer: If every student were to receive one piece of every pizza, each pizza would have to be divided into ten equal pieces, with each piece being $\frac{1}{10}$ of a pizza. Each student would receive eight pieces, giving each $\frac{8}{10}$ of a pizza.

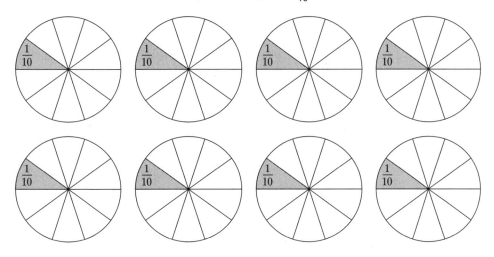

38a. Possible answer:

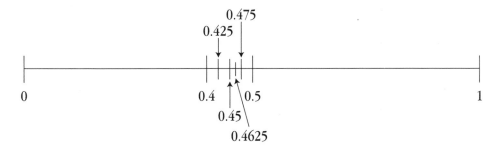

38b. Possible answer:

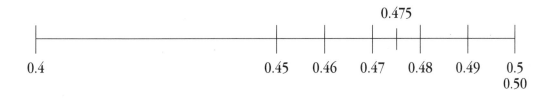

39.

Decimal number	Lower benchmark	Upper benchmark	Nearest benchmark
0.17	0	$\frac{1}{4}$	$\frac{1}{4}$
0.034	0	$\frac{1}{4}$	0
0.789	$\frac{3}{4}$	1	$\frac{3}{4}$
0.092	0	$\frac{1}{4}$	0
0.9	$\frac{3}{4}$	1	1
0.491	$\frac{1}{4}$	$\frac{1}{2}$	$\frac{1}{2}$
0.627	$\frac{1}{2}$	$\frac{3}{4}$	$\frac{3}{4}$
0.36	$\frac{1}{4}$	$\frac{1}{2}$	$\frac{1}{4}$

Extensions

42. The step is 0.01.

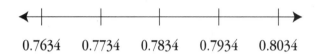

0.7634   0.7734   0.7834   0.7934   0.8034

43. The step is 0.002.

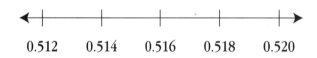

0.512   0.514   0.516   0.518   0.520

44. The step is 0.025.

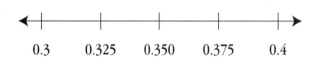

0.3   0.325   0.350   0.375   0.4

47. 4; Possible explanation: 4 of 18 equal parts is $\frac{2}{9}$ of the whole.

48. $\frac{2}{3}$; Possible explanation: $\frac{2}{9}$ of each of 3 wholes is $\frac{6}{9}$ or $\frac{2}{3}$ of a whole.

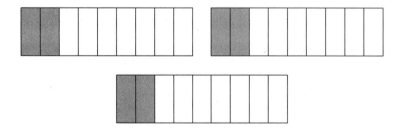

49. $\frac{3}{4}$; Possible explanation: $\frac{1}{4}$ of each of 3 wholes is $\frac{3}{4}$ of a whole.

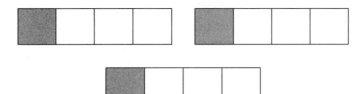

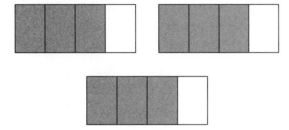

50. $\frac{9}{4}$; $\frac{3}{4}$ of each of 3 wholes is $\frac{9}{4}$ or $2\frac{1}{4}$ wholes.

Out of One Hundred

The context for this investigation is information gathered through surveys. Survey data are most often presented as percents. When we can express data as percents, we can compare different sets of data even when the sample sizes are different.

During students' work in this investigation, we encourage you to focus on two ways to conceptualize percents: using the extension of the visual model of the hundredths grid and the notion of "out of 100." The more readily your students can move among representations of fractions, decimals, and percents, the greater will be their number sense with regard to percent.

In Problem 6.1, It's Raining Cats, students use a database of information about cats to describe the portion of cats who possess some value of an attribute (for example, blue for eye color) as a fraction, a decimal, and a percent. In Problem 6.2, Dealing With Discounts, students consider different ways to express discounts. The goal is to highlight the informal language in daily use and connect it to different representations of quantities. In Problem 6.3, Changing Forms, students move among different forms of representation—sometimes starting with fractions, sometimes decimals, sometimes percents. In Problem 6.4, It's Raining Cats and Dogs, students consider what it means to talk about a percent of a data set involving more than 100 items.

Mathematical and Problem-Solving Goals

- **To use the "out of 100" interpretation of fractions and decimals to develop an understanding of percent**

- **To use the hundredths grid to visualize the concept of percent as meaning "out of 100"**

- **To investigate the relationships among fractions, decimals, and percents and to move flexibly among representations**

- **To understand how to use percent as an expression of frequency, in terms of "out of 100," when a set of data has more or fewer than 100 items**

Materials		
Problem	For students	For the teacher
All	Calculators	Transparencies 6.1 to 6.4B (optional)
6.1	Labsheet 6.1	
6.2	Hundredths (from Labsheet 5.2), fraction strips (optional), hundredths grids (from Labsheet 5.2)	Transparency of newspaper advertisements (optional)
6.3	Labsheet 6.3, hundredths strips (from Labsheet 5.2)	
6.4	Hundredths grids (from Labsheet 5.1)	
ACE	Labsheet 6.ACE	

Student Pages 67–83   **Teaching the Investigation 83a–84**

Out of One Hundred

Because fractions that have 100 as their denominator are so useful, there are many ways to represent them. Two ways you have already studied are with decimals and with hundredths grids.

Another useful way to express a fraction with a denominator of 100 is to use a special symbol: the percent symbol, %. **Percent** means "out of 100."

For example, suppose 78 out of 100 middle-school students say they like to swim. You already know how to represent the portion who like to swim with a fraction ($\frac{78}{100}$), a decimal (0.78), and a hundredths grid:

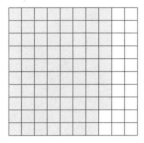

You can also write the fraction of students who like to swim as a percent: 78%.

Look at this grid. How can the shaded part be written as a fraction, a decimal, and a percent?

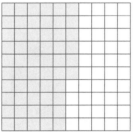

It's Raining Cats

At a Glance

Grouping:
Pairs

Launch

- Have the class share some of their thoughts about cats.

- With students, examine the cat database and the grid of cat names.

Explore

- Circulate while pairs work with the database, helping them to use logical marking strategies.

- Ask extension questions of pairs that finish early.

Summarize

- Have students share their answers, strategies, and questions they wrote.

- Introduce students to the idea of having more or fewer than 100 items in a database.

Assignment Choices

ACE questions 1–8 (1–7 might require Labsheet 6.1), 12, and unassigned choices from earlier problems

---

An advertisement in a local newspaper says that a clothing store is having a 30% off sale. This means that all prices have been reduced by $30 for every $100. If a jacket regularly costs $100, it will cost $70 during the sale. You can represent this situation with a hundredths grid:

30% off

You can write the discount on the jacket in other ways as well.
- 30% of the $100 cost = $30 off
- $100 cost − $30 off = $70 sale price

Think about this!

Think of several situations where you have seen or heard percents used. How was percent used in each case?

6.1 It's Raining Cats

A middle-school class has assembled a database of 100 cats owned by students in the school. The database information about each cat is shown on the next three pages.

Cat Database

Cat	Gender	Age (yrs)	Weight (lbs)	Eye color	Pad color
Alex	m	18	11	green	black
Amanda	f	4.5	9.75	blue	gray
Augustus	m	2	10	yellow/green/blue	pink/black
Baguera	m	0.17	13	yellow	brown
Black Foot	m	0.33	1.5	yellow	gray
Blacky	f	1	5	yellow	gray/black
Blue	f	0.25	2	green	gray
Bob	f	4	12	green	black
Boggie	m	3	10	green	pink
Boo	m	3.5	10.75	yellow/green	brown
Boots	m	0.25	3	brown	black
Bosley	m	0.33	1.5	yellow/brown	pink
Bradley	m	0.6	11	yellow	pink/gray
Buffy	m	0.75	8	blue/green	pink
Charcoal	m	11	12	yellow	black
Chelsea	f	2	9	yellow	black
Chessis	f	1.5	6	green	brown
Chubbs	m	1	7	green	pink
Cookie	f	4	9	gold	black
Dana	f	10	8	green	black
Diva	f	3.5	11	green	pink
Duffy	m	1	9	yellow/green	black
Ebony Kahlua	m	1.5	15	blue	brown
Elizabeth	f	10	9	green	pink
Emma	f	4	9.25	gold	pink
Emmie	f	4	7	green	black
Ethel	f	5	8	green	black
Feather	m	2.5	13	green	pink
Fire Smoke	f	0.25	2.5	green/brown	pink
Fluffy	f	5	10	green	pink
Fuzzy	f	1.25	2	green	pink
Gabriel	m	1	7	blue	white
George	m	12	14.5	green	black
Ginger	f	0.2	2	yellow/green	pink
Gizmo	m	4	10	yellow	black
Gracie	f	8	12	green	pink
Gray Kitty	f	3	9	green	gray

Cat	Gender	Age (yrs)	Weight (lbs)	Eye color	Pad color
Grey Boy	m	13	12	yellow	pink
Grey Girl	f	0.2	1.5	gold	pink/black
Grey Poupon	f	5	16	green	pink/black
Hanna	f	3.5	5	yellow	black
Harmony	m	3	12	yellow/green	black
Jinglebob	m	2	18.5	blue	pink
Kali	m	5	16	yellow	black
Kiki	f	1.5	6	green	black
Kitty	m	1.6	10	green	pink
Lady	f	10	8.5	yellow	black
Libby	f	4	8.5	yellow	gray
Lucky	m	4	5	green	pink
Lucy	f	5	10	green	pink
Matilda	f	4.5	9	yellow	pink
Melissa	f	8	11	yellow	pink
Mercedes	f	10	14	green	pink
Midnight	f	10	18	green	pink
Millie	f	10.5	5	blue	black
Miss Muppet	f	11	12	green	pink/black
Mittens	f	14	10.5	yellow	pink
Molly	f	15.5	10	amber	gray
Momma Kat	f	10	6	chartreuse	gray/white
Nancy Blue	f	0.6	5	blue	gray
Newton	m	5	18	yellow	pink
Peanut	f	15	7	green	pink
Peebles	f	5	9	green	black
Pepper	m	2	12	yellow	pink
Pink Lady	f	1.5	6.5	yellow	pink
Pip	m	1	9	yellow	pink
Precious	f	2	12	green	pink
Priscilla	f	3	8.5	green	pink/black
Prissy	f	4	9	green	pink
Ralph	m	3	9	yellow	black
Ravena	f	6	14	yellow	pink/black
Reebo	m	4	12	green	black
Samantha	f	0.2	2	yellow/green	pink
Sassy	f	3	8	yellow/green	gray
Scooter	m	7	16	gold	black
Sebastian	f	3	8	blue	black

Cat	Gender	Age (yrs)	Weight (lbs)	Eye color	Pad color
Seymour	m	0.25	1.5	gold	pink/black
Shiver	m	3	12	yellow/green	pink
Simon	m	0.25	2	green/brown	peach/gray
Skeeter	m	6	13	green	black
Smokey	f	2.5	8	green	black
Smudge	m	8	10	green	gray
Snowy	m	0.5	1.5	gray	gray
Sparky	m	7	12	green	pink
Speedy	m	3	12	blue	pink
Stinky	m	0.17	3.5	yellow	pink
Sweet Pea	f	16	14.5	green	black
Tabby	f	1.5	7	green	black
Tabby Burton	m	1	10	green	black
Terra	m	3	11	green	pink
Thomas	m	4	8	green	pink
Tiger	f	5	13	green	pink
Tigger	f	4	8	yellow	brown
Ting	f	0.25	2.5	green	pink/black
Tom	m	0.25	3	green	gray
Tomadachi	m	1	6.5	gold	pink
Treasure	f	4	8	green	pink
Wally	m	5	10	green	pink/black
Weary	m	8	15	green	pink
Ziggy	f	7	10	gold	pink/black

Did you know?

Ancient Egyptians considered cats to be sacred. Bastet, the Egyptian goddess of love and fertility, was represented as having the head of a cat and the body of a woman. Punishment for harming a cat was severe, and the sentence for killing a cat was usually death. When a cat died, Egyptians shaved their eyebrows as a sign of mourning. Dead cats were often mummified and buried in cat cemeteries.

Tips for the Linguistically Diverse Classroom

Rebus Scenario The Rebus Scenario technique is described in detail in *Getting to Know Connected Mathematics*. This technique involves sketching rebuses on the chalkboard that correspond to key words in the story or information you present orally. Example: some key words and phrases for which you may need to draw rebuses while discussing the Did you know? feature: *Ancient Egyptian* (a stick figure of an ancient Egyptian), *Baset, the Egyptian goddess* (a figure with the head of a cat and the body of a woman), *sentence for killing a cat* (a stick person next to gallows and a dead cat), *shaved* (razor), *eyebrows* (a face with eyebrows next to the same face without eyebrows), *mourning* (the face without eyebrows crying), *mummified* (a cat wrapped as a mummy), *cat cemeteries* (a tombstone with cat picture).

To help them visualize the different characteristics of the cats in the database, the students made a hundredths grid with each cat's name in one of the squares.

Alex	Boots	Diva	Fuzzy	Hanna	Matilda	Newton	Ravena	Smokey	Thomas
Amanda	Bosley	Duffy	Gabriel	Harmony	Melissa	Peanut	Reebo	Smudge	Tiger
Augustus	Bradley	Ebony Kahlua	George	Jinglebob	Mercedes	Peebles	Samantha	Snowy	Tigger
Baguera	Buffy	Elizabeth	Ginger	Kali	Midnight	Pepper	Sassy	Sparky	Ting
Black Foot	Charcoal	Emma	Gizmo	Kiki	Millie	Pink Lady	Scooter	Speedy	Tom
Blacky	Chelsea	Emmie	Gracie	Kitty	Miss Muppet	Pip	Sebastian	Stinky	Tomadachi
Blue	Chessis	Ethel	Gray Kitty	Lady	Mittens	Precious	Seymour	Sweet Pea	Treasure
Bob	Chubbs	Feather	Grey Boy	Libby	Molly	Priscilla	Shiver	Tabby	Wally
Boggie	Cookie	Fire Smoke	Grey Girl	Lucky	Momma Kat	Prissy	Simon	Tabby Burton	Weary
Boo	Dana	Fluffy	Grey Poupon	Lucy	Nancy Blue	Ralph	Skeeter	Terra	Ziggy

Jane wondered what percent of the cats were female. To answer her question, she used the information in the database and shaded each square in the grid that represented a female cat.

Tang is interested in kittens. He wants to know what percent of the cats in the database are kittens (8 months old or younger) and what percent are adults (over 8 months old).

Answers to Problem 6.1

A. $\frac{54}{100}$, 0.54, 54%

B $\frac{46}{100}$, 0.46, 46%

C. 54% and 46% add to 100%. Since no cat can be both male and female, the percents must add to a whole.

D. $\frac{17}{100}$, 0.17, 17%

E $\frac{83}{100}$, 0.83, 83%

F. 17% and 83% add to 100%. No cat can be both a kitten and an adult, so the percents must add to the whole.

Problem 6.1

Using the database and Labsheet 6.1, mark all the cats that are female on one chart and all the cats that are kittens on another chart. When you are finished, answer the following questions.

A. What fraction of the cats are female? Write the fraction as a decimal and a percent.

B. What fraction of the cats are male? Write the fraction as a decimal and a percent.

C. What do you notice about the combined percentage of female and male cats?

D. What fraction of the cats are kittens? Write the fraction as a decimal and a percent.

E. What fraction of the cats are adults? Write the fraction as a decimal and a percent.

F. What do you notice about the combined percentage of kittens and adult cats?

■ **Problem 6.1 Follow-Up**

Make up another question that could be answered by looking at the database. Find the answer to your question.

6.2 Dealing with Discounts

Sometimes it is easier to think about a number in one representation than in another. For example, you would probably say that one computer screen is 34% larger than another, rather than saying it is $\frac{17}{50}$ larger than the other.

You will often find it helpful to be able to move among percents, decimals, and fractions. To do this you need to remember that percent means "out of 100," because this can help you to change a percent to a decimal. One way to think about changing representations is to write the percent as a fraction with 100 as its denominator.

When a store offers a discount, such as 20% off, it means that for every $100 an item costs, you get $20 off the price. It also means that for every dollar (100¢) an item costs, you get 20¢ off the price. In other words, you pay $80 for each $100 of the original cost, or, equivalently, 80¢ for each dollar of the original cost.

Answer to Problem 6.1 Follow-Up

Possible question: How many cats have a name that starts with the letter B? The answer to this question is $\frac{9}{100}$, 0.09, or 9%.

Dealing with Discounts

At a Glance

Grouping:
Small Groups

Launch

- With the class, explore an example of a store discount.

- Have groups work on the advertisements in the student edition.

Explore

- As you visit the groups, help students to reason about the problem.

Summarize

- Have a few groups present their answers and explain their strategies.

- Expand the students' work by discussing discounts on items costing more or less than $10.

Assignment Choices

ACE questions 9–11, 14–15, and unassigned choices from earlier problems

A pet store is having a big sale.

Problem 6.2

You may want to use fraction strips or hundredths squares to help you to think about these questions.

A. 1. Rewrite the text on the sign for leashes so that the discount is shown as a *fraction off* the original price of the leashes.

   2. What will a $10.00 leash cost after the discount?

B. 1. Rewrite the text on the sign for pet carriers so that the discount is shown as a *percent off* the original price of the carriers.

   2. What will a $10.00 pet carrier cost after the discount?

C. 1. Rewrite the text on the pet food sign so that the discount is shown as a *percent off* the original price of pet food.

   2. Now, write the discount as a *percent* of the original price customers will pay.

   3. Rewrite the discount as a *fraction* of the original price customers will pay.

   4. Rewrite the discount as a *fraction off* the original price customers will pay.

   5. What will $10.00 worth of pet food cost after the discount?

D. 1. Rewrite the text on the pet treats sign so that the discount is shown as a *decimal.*

   2. What will $10.00 worth of pet treats cost after the discount?

Answers to Problem 6.2

A. 1. Possible answer: Leashes: $\frac{3}{10}$ off the marked price on the ticket.
  2. $7.00

B. 1. Possible answer: Take 25% off the list price for pet carriers.
  2. $7.50

C. 1. Possible answer: Take 40% off the original price of pet food!
  2. Possible answer: Pay only 60% of the original price for pet food!
  3. Possible answer: Pay only $\frac{3}{5}$ of the original price for pet food!
  4. Possible answer: Take $\frac{2}{5}$ off the original price of pet food!
  5. $6.00

Problem 6.2 Follow-Up

1. How can you change a percent to a fraction?
2. How can you change a percent to a decimal?
3. How can you change a decimal to a fraction?
4. How can you change a decimal to a percent?
5. How can you change a fraction to a decimal?
6. How can you change a fraction to a percent?

6.3 Changing Forms

There are many different ways to talk about number relationships. When you are telling a story with data, you have choices about how you express the relationships. Fractions or decimals or percents may be more suitable in certain situations. In this problem you will practice using what you know about changing between fractions, decimals, and percents.

A group of cat owners were asked this question: How much ransom would you be willing to pay if your pet was kidnapped? The table shows how the cat owners responded.

	Percent	Decimal	Fraction
$2000 and up	18%		
From $1500 to $1999		0.03	
From $1000 to $1499			$\frac{3}{100}$
From $500 to $999	25%		
From $1 to $499		0.31	
Nothing			$\frac{1}{5}$

Problem 6.3

Labsheet 6.3 contains the table above and a hundredths grid.

A. Fill in the missing information in your table.

B. Shade in the hundredths grid with different colors or shading styles to show the percent responding to each of the six choices. Add a key to your grid to show what each color or type of shading represents. When you finish, the grid should be completely shaded. Explain why.

Problem 6.3 Follow-Up

1. What percent of cat owners would pay less than $1000 ransom to get their pets back?
2. What percent of cat owners would pay less than $2000 ransom to get their pets back?

D. 1. Possible answer: All year long you can count on a 0.125 discount on pet treats.
   2. $8.75

Answers to Problem 6.2 Follow-Up

See page 83g.

Answers to Problem 6.3

See page 83h.

Answers to Problem 6.3 Follow-Up

1. 76%   2. 82%

6.3

Changing Forms

At a Glance

Grouping: Small Groups

Launch

- Talk about the survey and the partially complete table.

Explore

- As you visit the groups, ask them questions about how they are determining their answers.

- Pose extra challenges for groups who finish quickly.

Summarize

- Have a few groups explain their strategies for completing the table.

Assignment Choices

ACE questions 13, 17–20 (17–19 require Labsheet 6.ACE), 22–28, and unassigned choices from earlier problems

It's Raining Cats and Dogs

At a Glance

Grouping:
Small Groups

Launch

- Work through an example survey with the class, calculating percentages and shading grids.

- Make sure students understand that the surveys in the problem do not involve groups of 100 responses.

Explore

- Circulate among the groups, helping students who are confused about how to reason about the problem.

Summarize

- Have a few groups present their answers and explain their strategies.

- Pose additional questions involving surveys with other than 100 respondents.

6.4 It's Raining Cats and Dogs

In a recent survey, 150 dog owners and 200 cat owners were asked what type of food their pets liked. Here are the results of the survey:

Preference	Out of 150 dog owners	Out of 200 cat owners
Human food only	75	36
Pet food only	45	116
Human and pet food	30	48

Problem 6.4

Consider the results of the survey.

A. What kind of food is favored by the greatest number of dogs, according to their owners? Write this number as a fraction, a decimal, and a percent of the 150 dog owners surveyed.

B. What choice is favored by the greatest number of cats, according to their owners? Write this number as a fraction, a decimal, and a percent of the 200 cat owners surveyed.

C. What percent of dog owners reported that their dogs liked either human food only or pet food only? Write this percent as a fraction and a decimal.

D. What percent of cat owners reported that their cats liked either human food only or pet food only? Write this percent as a decimal and a fraction.

Problem 6.4 Follow-Up

1. Suppose only 100 dog owners were surveyed, with similar results. Estimate how many would have answered in each of the three categories.
2. Suppose 400 cat owners were surveyed, with similar results. Estimate how many would have answered in each of the three categories.
3. Suppose 50 cat owners were surveyed, with similar results. Estimate how many would have answered in each of the three categories.

Assignment Choices

ACE question 21 and unassigned choices from earlier problems

Assessment

It is appropriate to use the Unit Test after this problem.

Answers to Problem 6.4

A. Human food only; $\frac{75}{150} = \frac{1}{2}$, 0.5, 50%

B. Pet food only; $\frac{116}{200} = \frac{58}{100} = \frac{29}{50}$, 0.58, 58%

C. 80%, 0.8, $\frac{120}{150} = \frac{4}{5}$

D. 76%, 0.76, $\frac{152}{200} = \frac{76}{100} = \frac{19}{25}$

Answers to Problem 6.4 Follow-Up

See page 83h.

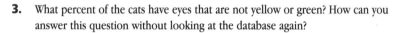

Applications • Connections • Extensions

As you work on these ACE questions, use your calculator whenever you need it.

Applications

In 1–7, use the cat database on pages 69–71 to answer each question. You may want to use the grids on Labsheet 6.1 to help you.

1. What percent of the cats have green eyes (not mixed with green)?

2. What percent of the cats have yellow eyes (not mixed with yellow)?

3. What percent of the cats have eyes that are not yellow or green? How can you answer this question without looking at the database again?

4. What percent of the cats have only pink foot pads?

5. What percent of the cats have only black foot pads?

6. What percent of the cats have only pink/black foot pads?

7. What percent of the cats have foot pads that are not pink, black, or pink/black? How can you answer this question without looking at the database again?

8. 78% of pet owners surveyed say they live in a town where there is a pooper-scooper law in effect.

    a. How would you express this as a decimal?

    b. How would you express this as a fraction?

    c. What percent of people surveyed said they do not live in a town with a pooper-scooper law? Explain your reasoning. Express this percent as a decimal and a fraction.

    d. Can you determine how many people were surveyed? Why or why not?

Investigation 6: Out of One Hundred 77

Answers

Applications

1. 46%

2. 23%

3. 31%; Possible explanation: The percent of cats that have only green eyes or only yellow eyes is 46% + 23% = 69%. So, the percent of cats with eyes that are not only yellow or only green is 100% − 69% = 31%.

4. 41%

5. 28%

6. 10%

7. 21%; Possible explanation: The percent of cats with the three types of foot pads is 41% + 28% + 10% = 79%. So, the percent of cats who have other color foot pads is 100% − 79% = 21%.

8a. 0.78

8b. $\frac{78}{100}$, or $\frac{39}{50}$

8c. 22%, 0.22, $\frac{22}{100} = \frac{11}{50}$; Possible explanation: 100% of the people surveyed represents all the people surveyed, and 78% of those surveyed live in a town with a pooper-scooper law, so 100% − 78% = 22% do not live in a town with a pooper-scooper law.

8d. no; Possible explanation: 78% only tells you *what percentage* of the people surveyed live in a town with a pooper-scooper law; it does not tell you anything about *how many* people were surveyed.

9. 75%; Possible explanation: 100% minus the 25% of the cats weighing less than 7 pounds is 75%. This difference is the percent of cats weighing 7 pounds or more.

10. 28%; Possible explanation: 100% minus the 72% of the cats weighing less than 12 pounds is 28%. This difference is the percent of cats weighing 12 pounds or more.

11. 47%; Possible explanation: The difference between 72% and 25% represents the cats weighing 7 pounds or more and less than 12 pounds.

12. 34%; Possible explanation: 100% represents all the dogs that went to obedience school. The difference between 100% and 66% is the percent of dogs not performing up to par.

13. See below right.

In 9–11, use the following information to answer the questions. Jill noticed that 25% of all the cats in the database on pages 69–71 weigh less than 7 pounds. She also noticed that 72% of all the cats weigh less than 12 pounds.

9. What percent of the cats weigh 7 pounds or more? Explain your reasoning.

10. What percent of the cats weigh 12 pounds or more? Explain your reasoning.

11. What percent of the cats weigh 7 pounds or more and less than 12 pounds? Explain your reasoning.

12. When surveyed, 66% of dog owners who took their dog to obedience school said their dog passed with flying colors. What percent of dog owners said their dogs *didn't* perform up to par? Write an explanation for a friend about how to solve the problem and why your solution works.

13. Copy the table and fill in the missing information.

Percent	Decimal	Fraction
62%		
		$\frac{4}{9}$
	1.23	
		$\frac{12}{15}$

13.

Percent	Decimal	Fraction
62%	0.62	$\frac{62}{100} = \frac{31}{50}$
about 44%	about 0.44	$\frac{4}{9}$
123%	1.23	$\frac{123}{100} = 1\frac{23}{100}$
80%	0.8	$\frac{12}{15}$

In 14 and 15, the large square represents one whole. Represent the shaded area as a fraction, a decimal, and a percent.

14.

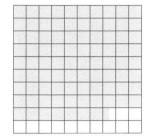

15.

16. Trace the outline of your hand on a hundredths grid. (You can use a copy of Labsheet 4.2.) Estimate what percent of the grid is covered by the area of your hand. Explain how you made your estimate.

In 17–19, use Labsheet 6.ACE to *estimate* what portion of the square is shaded. Explain your reasoning.

17. What percent of this square is shaded? Explain your reasoning.

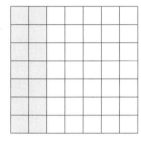

14. $\frac{875}{1000}$, 0.875, 87.5%

15. $\frac{14}{49} = \frac{2}{7}$, about 0.286, about 28.6%

16. Answers will vary. Possible explanation: I counted all the squares completely inside the outline and then added parts of the squares inside the outline to make wholes and then added the wholes to my count.

17. about 50%; Possible explanation: If you draw a horizontal line through the center of the square, you can match up the shaded part on the bottom with the unshaded part on the top, and the unshaded part on the bottom with the shaded part on the top, so about half the square is shaded.

18. about $\frac{3}{8}$ or $\frac{2}{5}$; Possible explanations: I covered the square with a grid and counted the shaded part, and the answer was between $\frac{1}{3}$ and $\frac{1}{2}$. I divided the square into four equal squares, and each of the smaller squares had a little less than half shaded.

19. 0.375; Possible explanation: If you divide the figure into four squares of equal size, you can move two of the shaded parts into the upper left square to fill it. Then you have $1\frac{1}{2}$ of the four squares filled, which is 3 half-squares out of 8 half-squares, or $\frac{3}{8}$.

Connections

20. See below right.

---

18. What fraction of this square is shaded? Explain your reasoning.

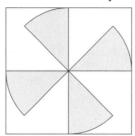

19. What part, in decimal form, of this square is shaded? Explain your reasoning.

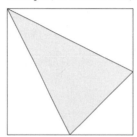

Connections

20. The following percents are a good set of benchmarks to know, because they have nice fraction equivalents and some nice decimal equivalents. The percents are spread out between 0 and 1. Copy the table, and enter the fraction and decimal equivalents for each percent. Use your table until you have learned these relationships.

Percent	10%	$12\frac{1}{2}$%	20%	25%	30%	$33\frac{1}{3}$%	50%	$66\frac{2}{3}$%	75%
Fraction									
Decimal									

20.

Percent	10%	$12\frac{1}{2}$%	20%	25%	30%	$33\frac{1}{3}$%	50%	$66\frac{2}{3}$%	75%
Fraction	$\frac{1}{10}$	$\frac{1}{8}$	$\frac{1}{5}$	$\frac{1}{4}$	$\frac{3}{10}$	$\frac{1}{3}$	$\frac{1}{2}$	$\frac{2}{3}$	$\frac{3}{4}$
Decimal	0.1	0.125	0.2	0.25	0.3	about 0.33	0.5	about 0.67	0.75

Extensions

21. Below are the results when pet owners were asked what kinds of clothing or accessories their pets wear.

	Dogs	Cats
Ribbons	88%	90%
Sweater	65%	20%
Nail Polish	23%	6%
Jeweled Leash	17%	30%
Jewelry	12%	12%

 a. Add the percents in the Dogs column. Write the total as a percent, a decimal, and a fraction.

 b. Add the percents in the Cats column. Write the total as a percent, a decimal, and a fraction.

 c. Why do the columns add to more than 100%?

In 22–25, make a copy of the number line below. Mark and label an approximate point on the number line for each fraction, decimal, and percent given. Use a different number line for each problem.

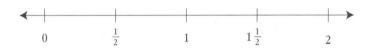

22. $\frac{3}{8}$, 72%, 1.9, $\frac{4}{3}$

23. 175%, $\frac{7}{9}$, 0.5, 120%

24. 1.35, 0.625, $\frac{8}{5}$, 25%

25. 34%, 0.049, 98%, 1.75

Extensions

21a. 205%; 2.05; $2\frac{5}{100}$

21b. 158%; 1.58; $1\frac{58}{100}$

21c. The columns add to more than 100% because some pets wear more than one item.

22.–25. See page 84.

26. $\frac{1}{2}$, 0.50, 50%

27. $\frac{5}{8}$, 0.625, 62.5%

28. $\frac{11}{60}$, about 0.183, about 18%

In 26–28, determine what fraction is the correct label for the mark halfway between the endpoints of the line segment. Write the fraction as a percent and a decimal.

26.

$\frac{1}{3}$? $\frac{2}{3}$

27.

$\frac{1}{2}$? $\frac{3}{4}$

28.

$\frac{1}{6}$? $\frac{1}{5}$

Mathematical Reflections

In this investigation, you explored the relationships among fractions, decimals, and percents. These questions will help you summarize what you have learned:

1. What does *percent* mean?

2. How can you show a percent by using a drawing?

3. **a.** Describe how you can change a percent to a decimal and to a fraction.

   b. Describe how you can change a fraction to a percent.

   c. Describe how you can change a decimal to a percent.

4. Suppose 12% of students surveyed said they had tried rock climbing. If 100 students were surveyed, how many had tried rock climbing? If 200 students were surveyed? If 150 students were surveyed?

5. A store offers a discount of 30% on all reference books. If a dictionary costs $12.00, what is the amount of the discount? If a book on insect identification costs $15.00, how much will you have to pay for it?

Think about your answers to these questions, discuss your ideas with other students and your teacher, and then write a summary of your findings in your journal.

Possible Answers

1. "out of 100"

2. You can shade part of a hundredths grid to show what part of 100 you want to represent.

3a. For a whole number percent, you make the digits of the percent the numerator of the fraction and 100 the denominator. You find the decimal by dividing 100 into the digits of the percent. For example: $78\% = \frac{78}{100} = 0.78$. If the percent is a fraction, such as 12.5%, this means 12.5 out of 100 or 125 out of 1000. This would give $\frac{125}{1000}$ or 0.125.

3b. If you can change the fraction to an equivalent fraction with 100 as the denominator, the numerator would be the digits of the percent. For example, $\frac{3}{20} = \frac{15}{100} = 15\%$. Or, you can divide the numerator by the denominator to change the fraction to a decimal. Then you write the decimal as a percent. For example, $\frac{3}{4} = 0.75 = 75\%$.

3c. If the decimal is given to the nearest hundredth, the digits of the decimal become the numerator of a fraction with 100 as the denominator. The numerator of the fraction is then the digits of the percent. For example, $0.59 = \frac{59}{100} = 59\%$. If the decimal is something like 0.146, you can write it as 14.6%.

4. 12 of 100; 24 of 200; and 18 of 150

5. The discount is 30% of $12.00, or $3.60. You will pay 70% of $15, or $10.50.

TEACHING THE INVESTIGATION

6.1 • It's Raining Cats

In this problem, students work with a database of information about cats. They express the portion of cats with a particular attribute as a fraction, a decimal, and a percent.

Launch

Have a conversation with your class about percents. Ask them what they know about percents and where they have seen or heard percents used. After a few ideas are presented, read and discuss the ideas about the meaning of percent that are presented on page 67 of the student edition.

Begin a class discussion about cats, allowing students to share thoughts about pets they have. Then introduce students to the cat database, perhaps displaying the portion of the database shown on Transparency 6.1B. Ask students what kinds of information are given in the database, and focus their attention on specific information.

> What can you tell me about Fire Smoke? Is Fire Smoke a big cat, a medium-size cat, or a small cat? (*small*) How do you know? (*She is only 0.25 years old and weighs only 2.5 pounds.*)

> The table says that Fire Smoke is 0.25 years old. How old is this in months? (*3*) How did you figure this out? (*0.25 years is $\frac{1}{4}$ of a year. A year is 12 months, so $\frac{1}{4}$ of a year is 3 months.*)

> A kitten is a cat that is 8 months old or younger. Is Fire Smoke a kitten or an adult cat? (*a kitten.*)

Focus students' attention on Labsheet 6.1. Have students work in pairs on this problem.

> Use the grid to keep track of your counting. One person in your pair can shade, color, or label one copy of the grid for sex of the cats, and the other person can mark another grid for adult or kitten. Use any marking scheme that makes sense to you. Express your answers as fractions, decimals, and percents.

Explore

If you notice students having trouble keeping track of what they are marking, you may want to have them compare their charts with another pair's chart before they compute the fractions, decimals, and percents. The notion of checking their data is an important habit for students to develop.

Groups that finish quickly can move on to the follow-up, which asks them to use the database to write another question about the cats. For example, writing questions about weight would require making decisions about what intervals to use to categorize the data set.

Summarize

Allow students to share the fractions, decimals, and percents they found and how they found their answers. One concept you want conveyed is that the fractions, decimals, and percents that describe nonoverlapping categories and that cover the full range of possibilities must add to 1 or 100%. For example, the sum of adult cats and kittens must be 100%, because all cats are in one of these two categories and no cat is in both.

If any pairs have written and explored an additional interesting question, let them share what they found. They should explain their question, what data they needed to tally, and how they found the answer.

Ask questions to better focus students on what they are learning.

> **Why is it easy to move among fractions, decimals, and percents in this database?**

Moving among different representations is easy because the number of cats is 100, and a simple count will give the fraction of cats having the characteristic being considered. Since this fraction will have a denominator of 100, changing to decimal form is easy. Moving from a decimal in hundredths to a percent is also simple because percent means "out of 100."

> **Suppose we had 150 cats in a database and the same fraction of cats were female. How many would be female?**

Students may see different ways to reason about this. In their work, they found that 54% of the 100 cats are female. They might think of the 150 as being 100 plus half of 100. This means that 54 plus half of 54 cats would be female, or 81 out of 150.

> **Suppose we had only 50 cats, but the percent of females was still 54%. How many are female?**

Here we have half of 100 cats, so half of 54 are female, which is 27.

While this strategy is not as efficient as multiplying 0.54×150 or 0.54×50, students need to reason with informal strategies before they move to formal, more efficient strategies. We return to the theme of greater than 100 in a later problem; students need not fully understand the concept now. Just raise questions to get students thinking from the start about what "out of 100" means when the base is not 100. How can we think about scaling up or down from 100 to fit a particular situation?

6.2 • Dealing with Discounts

This problem looks at different forms of advertising to help students become skillful at interpreting what the information in an ad means in terms of fractions, decimals, and percents.

Launch

A good way to launch the activity is to put the following advertisement (or a similar one from your local paper) on the overhead.

Here is a typical advertisement you might see in a store or in the newspaper.

Turtleneck Shirts!

An extra 20% discount will be taken off the ticket price at the register

---

What would the sign say if the store decided to give the discount as a fraction off the ticket price?

Students will have to find a fraction representation for 20%. One way to reason about this is to first find a decimal representation, 0.20, and then a fraction, $\frac{20}{100}$. Others may write $\frac{20}{100}$ right away and explain that since percent means "out of 100," if you have 20% you must have 20 out of 100.

Is the store likely to use the fraction $\frac{20}{100}$, or will it use an equivalent fraction with a smaller denominator? (*The store would be more likely to use $\frac{1}{5}$.*)

When you feel students are ready, explain that they are to rewrite the signs in the problem in the ways specified. In each problem, they will also figure out the price of $10.00 worth of merchandise after the discount.

Explore

As you visit the groups, listen to how students are thinking about the problem. Look for good strategies that should be shared with the class during the summary. Ask questions to help students tie their reasoning to what they already know about fractions, decimals, and percents. Remind them to revisit pages 67 and 68 to look again at what *percent* and *percent off* mean. Encourage students to make drawings if they would find them helpful.

Students may struggle with changing $12\frac{1}{2}\%$ to a decimal in question D. Ask them how they would write 12% as a decimal and how they would write 13% as a decimal, which exposes the fact that $12\frac{1}{2}\%$ is between 12% and 13% and means the decimal is between 0.12 and 0.13. On each dollar, the discount will be 12.5 cents. This means that for $10.00, the discount will be $1.25. Students may need to shade a grid to understand $12\frac{1}{2}\%$.

Summarize

Have students present their answers and carefully explain how they thought about the problems. You may want to expand the conversation by asking students to find discounts on prices other than $10.00. You might want to revisit the problem you used in the launch.

The first ad we talked about offered 20% off turtleneck shirts. Suppose you visit this store and look at the ticket on a turtleneck, and this is what you see:

```
┌─────────────────────────────────┐
│                       ┊         │
│    Style Number 60275 ┊    $19.00│
│  ○ Dept. 27           ┊         │
│    Size M             ┊         │
│                       ┊         │
└─────────────────────────────────┘
```

What would the price be after the discount is taken at the register?

Students will find several ways to reason about this. They may realize that this means 20¢ off each dollar; for $19, this is 19×20 which gives 380 cents or $3.80 off the $19.00. So the price is $15.20. Other students might see that this will be 80¢ for each of the 19 dollars and multiply 80×19 to get 1520 cents or $15.20.

Discuss the conversions in the follow-up questions.

6.3 • Changing Forms

In this problem, students think further about the relationships among percents, decimals, and fractions. We are not looking for the emergence of established algorithms; students will be best served by having time to make sense of the questions and to devise their own ways of thinking about them.

Launch

Tell students about the survey data that was gathered. Pass out a copy of Labsheet 6.3 to each student. You may want to display Transparency 6.3.

Pet owners were asked what ransom they would be willing to pay to get a pet back from a kidnapper. This table shows the data organized in a slightly strange way. We have to fill in the missing parts to be able to compare responses across the money categories.

You have already changed some percents to decimals and fractions, and some decimals to fractions and percents. Use what you already know to complete the table. Notice that you are asked to shade the grid to represent the situation and to make observations about your grid when you are finished.

Explore

As you circulate, help students troubleshoot. You can do this by asking questions:

How do you find an equivalent fraction?

What benchmark is the number near?

Is your answer reasonable?

Pose further challenges for groups who finish early.

Estimate how many people would respond with "$2000 and up" if a total of 1000 people had been surveyed. What if only 300 people had been surveyed?

Summarize

Have students talk about their answers and their strategies for finding solutions. Here are some strategies students have used:

- To change a percent to a fraction, make the number in front of the percent sign the numerator, and make the denominator 100.

- To change a percent to a decimal, first check whether the percent is a one- or two-digit number. If the percent is a two-digit number, drop the percent sign and put a decimal point in front of the first digit. If the percent is a one-digit number, like 5%, drop the percent sign but make sure you write your number so that as a decimal it means "out of 100"—here you would have to write 0.05.

- To change a decimal to a fraction, make the decimal number the numerator of the fraction, and make the denominator whatever place value the last digit of the decimal is in. For 0.32, the numerator would be 32, and the denominator would be 100 because the 2 is in the hundredths place.

- To change a two-digit decimal to a percent, just get rid of the decimal point and write the number and a percent sign. For 0.31, you just write 31%. For a decimal like 0.2, write an equivalent decimal with a denominator of 100—0.20—then write it as a percent, 20%.

- If the denominator of a fraction is a factor of 10 or 100, just write an equivalent fraction with a denominator of 10 or 100. Whatever the new numerator is will be the decimal preceded by a decimal point. If the fraction has a denominator like 8 or 3, you either memorize the relationships or use a calculator to divide the denominator into the numerator, which will give you the decimal equivalent.

- Changing a fraction to a percent is easier if you can first change it to a decimal, as it's easy to change decimals to percents. You might also be able to use benchmarks to estimate the percent a fraction is near.

6.4 • It's Raining Cats and Dogs

This problem focuses on percents of numbers greater than 100.

Launch

A good way to launch the problem is to work through an example with 100 first as a way to help students understand what they need to think about to solve the problem. You might want to use the example on Transparency 6.4A.

> In a recent survey, 100 dog owners and 100 cat owners were asked what type of food their pets liked. Here are the results of the survey.

Preference	Out of 100 dog owners	Out of 100 cat owners
Human food only	50	27
Pet food only	30	58
Human and pet food	20	15

> How do the preferences for dogs compare with the preferences for cats?

You want students to recognize that percents are good ways to make comparisons. They could, for example, easily compare the dogs' preference for human food to the cats' (50%, 0.50, $\frac{50}{100}$ for dogs; 27%, 0.27, $\frac{27}{100}$ for cats) and their preferences for pet food (30%, 0.30, $\frac{30}{100}$ for dogs; 58%, 0.58, $\frac{58}{100}$ for cats).

> What percent of dog owners report that their dogs either liked human food only or dog food only? *(50% + 30% = 80%)* Can you write your answer in a different form? *(0.80, $\frac{80}{100}$)*

Shading a hundredths grid can reinforce how a pictorial representation helps to visualize comparisons. Here are possible ways to shade the two grids for each of the three categories.

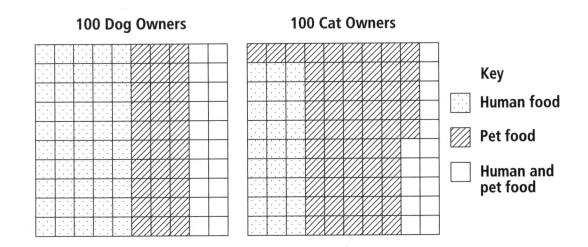

100 Dog Owners   **100 Cat Owners**

Key

Human food

Pet food

Human and pet food

If your students are struggling, make up another problem with a data set of 200 and work through it as a class.

When your students are ready, read the survey results on page 76 of the student edition. Make sure students realize that this time the results are not based on samples of 100. Put students into pairs or small groups, and encourage them to record the ways they are thinking about the problem.

Explore

Pay attention to students' strategies as you visit the groups. Some students will see that 75 out of 150 is the same as 150 out of 300, which they recognize as $\frac{1}{2}$. Others will divide 75 by 150 on their calculators and get 0.5. For students who say that 75 out of 150 means 75%, talk with them about what *percent* means and refer them to page 67 in the student edition.

Some students will look at 45 out of 150 and reason that we should look at 150 in three batches of 50 and look at 45 in three batches of 15. This means that we have $\frac{15}{50}$, which is $\frac{30}{100}$ or 30%.

For the 200 cat owners surveyed, students may reason in hundreds by splitting the 200 into two groups and splitting the amount in each category into two groups. Some students may need to shade two hundredths grids to help think about this. Allow students to stay at this concrete level of thinking if they need to; don't rush to show them that division will immediately give the related decimal.

Summarize

Have groups report their answers and share their strategies. Use this opportunity to help them build flexible ways to think about finding percents when the total is not 100.

> Suppose the person conducting such a survey in your neighborhood only surveyed 75 dog owners. If, of the 75 people who responded, 24 reported that their dogs preferred human food, what percent is this?

Though the total is less than 100, students can scale up to 100. Students might reason that 75 is 3 of 4 equal parts of 100, and if we divide 24 into 3 equal parts we get 8 in each part. Therefore, if we scale up to four parts, we have 32 people reporting that their dogs prefer human food, which is 32%.

Additional Answers

Answers to Problem 6.2 Follow Up

The following answers have been given by students.

1. Possible answer: Make the number in front of the percent sign the numerator, and make the denominator 100.

2. Possible answer: If the percent is a two-digit number, drop the percent sign and put a decimal point in front of the first digit. If the percent is a one-digit number, like 5%, drop the percent sign but make sure you write your number so that as a decimal it means "5 out of 100"—here you would have to write 0.05.

3. Possible answer: Make the decimal number the numerator of the fraction, and make the denominator whatever place value the last digit of the decimal is in. For 0.32, the numerator would be 32, and the denominator would be 100 because the 2 is in the hundredths place.

4. Possible answer: With a two-digit decimal, just write the number and a percent sign. For 0.31, you just write 31%. For a decimal like 0.2, write an equivalent decimal with a denominator of 100—0.20—then write it as a percent, 20%.

5. Possible answer: If the denominator is a factor of 10 or 100, just write an equivalent fraction with a denominator of 10 or 100. Whatever the new numerator is will be the decimal preceded by a decimal point. If the fraction has a denominator like 8 or 3, you either memorize the relationships or use a calculator to divide the denominator into the numerator, which will give you the decimal equivalent.

6. Possible answer: Changing a fraction to a percent is easier if you can first change it to a decimal, as it's easy to change decimals to percents. You might also be able to use benchmarks to estimate the percent a fraction is near.

Answers to Problem 6.3

A.

	Percent	Decimal	Fraction
$2000 and up	18%	0.18	$\frac{18}{100}$ or $\frac{9}{50}$
From $1500 to $1999	3%	0.03	$\frac{3}{100}$
From $1000 to $1499	3%	0.03	$\frac{3}{100}$
From $500 to $999	25%	0.25	$\frac{25}{100}$ or $\frac{1}{4}$
From $1 to $499	31%	0.31	$\frac{31}{100}$
Nothing	20%	0.20	$\frac{20}{100}$ or $\frac{1}{5}$

B. The total percentage is 100% because the results of the survey are reported for all the people who responded; that is, 100%. We don't know the number of people who responded, but we do know that the "whole" is 100%.

Answers to Problem 6.4 Follow-Up

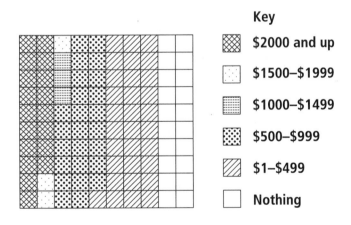

Key

▨	$2000 and up
▢	$1500–$1999
▤	$1000–$1499
▨	$500–$999
▨	$1–$499
☐	Nothing

1. | Preference | Out of 100 dog owners |
   |---|---|
   | Human food only | 50 |
   | Pet food only | 30 |
   | Human and pet food | 20 |

2. | Preference | Out of 400 cat owners |
   |---|---|
   | Human food only | 72 |
   | Pet food only | 232 |
   | Human and pet food | 96 |

3.

Preference	Out of 50 cat owners
Human food only	9
Pet food only	29
Human and pet food	12

ACE Answers

Extensions

22.

23.

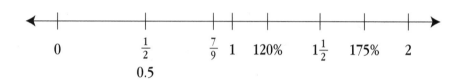

24.

25.

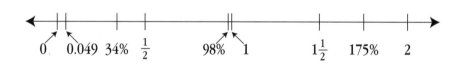

Assessment Resources

Check-Up 1

1. This sketch shows part of a ruler. The main marks indicate inches.

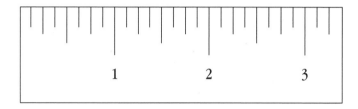

   How do you think each of the marks between the inches should be labeled? Explain your answer.

2. Use your fraction strips or another method to compare the two fractions in each pair. Insert the correct sign: $<$, $>$, or $=$.

   a. $\dfrac{8}{12}$ $\dfrac{3}{4}$ b. $\dfrac{5}{8}$ $\dfrac{6}{10}$ c. $\dfrac{2}{3}$ $\dfrac{5}{6}$ d. $\dfrac{2}{4}$ $\dfrac{7}{12}$ e. $\dfrac{3}{8}$ $\dfrac{3}{12}$

3. Find three different fractions between the benchmarks $\dfrac{1}{2}$ and $\dfrac{3}{4}$.

Check-Up 1

4. Julie's math class and Dave's math class are selling sub sandwiches as a fund-raiser. Each class has a goal of $150. Julie said her class was closer to the goal than Dave's class because her class had earned $\frac{2}{3}$ of their goal, and Dave's class had earned $\frac{5}{8}$ of their goal. Was Julie right? Explain your answer.

5. Estimate and mark where the number 1 will be on each number line. The length that represents the whole may be different on each number line.

   a.

   0        $\frac{1}{6}$

   b.

   0                $\frac{3}{4}$

   c.

   0                        $\frac{3}{2}$

6. Order these numbers from smallest to largest:

   $1\frac{7}{10}$ $1\frac{15}{18}$ $\frac{24}{15}$

Quiz

1. Give a fraction name for the shaded part of the figure below. Explain how you figured out what fractional part of the whole was shaded.

    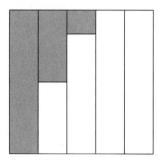

2. Lynette found a worm that is $\frac{2}{3}$ of the length of your fraction strip. How many worms exactly like hers would you need to put end to end to equal two times the length of your fraction strip? Explain your answer.

3. Decide whether each of the following statements is true or false, and explain why:

    a. If you compare two fractions with the same denominator, the fraction with the greater numerator is greater.

    b. If you compare two fractions with the same numerator, the fraction with the greater denominator is greater.

Quiz

4. Antonio's father agreed to help with an Events Night at camp by setting up a pizza stand to sell pizza to visiting family and friends. Antonio's father has only one size of pizza pan, a circular pan with a 16-inch diameter. The class committee decided they wanted him to sell pizza by the slice and to sell small slices and large slices. Antonio's father has a cutting form that can cut a pizza into 12 slices and another form that can cut a pizza into 8 slices.

    a. If a family bought three small slices and three large slices, what fraction of a pizza did they buy? (You might want to draw a picture to help you.)

    b. How much more pizza (what fraction) would they need to buy to purchase a whole pizza?

    c. How many different ways can you combine small slices and large slices to make a whole pizza? Write each of your responses as number sentences. For example: $\frac{2}{8} + \frac{9}{12} = 1$ means that two large slices and nine small slices will make one whole pizza.

5. In each pair of pencils, the length of the new pencil is about what fraction of the length of the old pencil?

    a.

    b.

Check-Up 2

1. For each figure below, give a fraction name and a decimal name for the shaded part.

   a.
   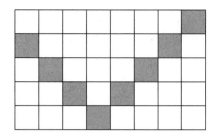

   b.
   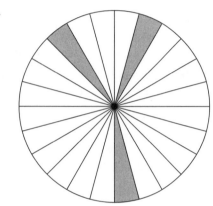

2. Arrange these decimals in order from smallest to largest:

   6.00   0.6   0.006   0.60   0.06   0.00006

Check-Up 2

3. On each figure below, shade the indicated decimal amount.

   a. 0.375

   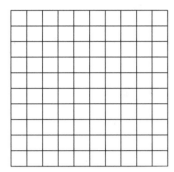

   b. 0.6

   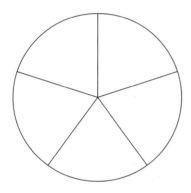

   c. 0.05

   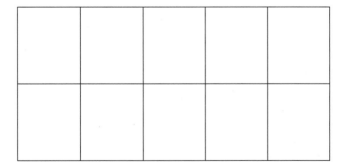

4. Rename each of the decimal amounts in question 3 with fraction names.

   a. _____   b. _____   c. _____

Check-Up 2

5. On the strip below, mark and label where each of these decimals is: 0.09, 0.9, 0.19, 0.190, 0.019.

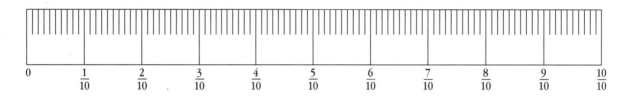

6. For each number line, fill in the missing decimal numbers. For example, filling in the missing decimal numbers on this number line:

would give you this:

a.

b.

c.

Assign these questions as additional homework, or use them as review, quiz, or test questions.

1. This is a carnival game that tests strength. The player hits the block with a mallet and the force of the blow sends a metal ringer up the pole. If the player uses enough force, the ringer rings the bell at the top of the pole and the player receives the top prize of 100 points. The player receives fewer points for hits that only send the metal ringer partway up the pole. The points can be traded for tickets to rides at the carnival.

   a. Where should marks be made on the pole for each of the game point amounts? Mark them on the pole.

10 points	25 points	35 points
70 points	85 points	100 points

   b. What fraction of the pole would each of the marks in part a represent?

   c. What payoff, in game points, should be given for sending the metal ringer $\frac{1}{3}$ of the way up the pole?

   d. What payoff, in game points, should be given for sending the ringer $\frac{3}{5}$ of the way up the pole?

   e. What payoff, in game points, should be given for sending the ringer $\frac{2}{8}$ of the way up the pole?

   f. What payoff, in game points, should be given for sending the ringer $\frac{3}{4}$ of the way up the pole?

   g. Miki's hit sent the metal ringer $\frac{5}{8}$ of the way up the pole. Taylor's hit went $\frac{6}{9}$ of the way to the top. Who received the most game points? Why?

2. You are invited to go out for pizza with several friends. When you get there, your friends are sitting in two separate groups. You can join either group. If you join the first group, there will be a total of 4 people in the group and you will be sharing 6 small pizzas. If you join the second group, there will be a total of 6 people in the group and you will be sharing 8 small pizzas. If pizza will be shared equally in each group—and you are *very* hungry—which would you rather join? Explain your choice.

3. a. Three is what fractional part of 12?

   b. Five is what fractional part of 20?

   c. Two is what fractional part of 9?

   d. Seven is what fractional part of 17?

4. Samuel is getting a snack for himself and his little brother. There are two muffins in the refrigerator. Samuel takes half of one muffin for himself and half of the other muffin for his little brother. His little brother complains that Samuel got more. Samuel says that he got $\frac{1}{2}$ and his brother got $\frac{1}{2}$. What might be the problem?

5. Your best friend was absent when your class learned how to compare decimal numbers. Write a set of directions that would help your friend understand how to compare decimal numbers.

6. The following prices were posted at a local store.

Bananas .39¢ a pound

Notebook Paper 1.02¢

What is wrong with these signs?

7. Use these numbers to fill in the blanks so that the story makes numerical sense:

   645      $\frac{3}{4}$ 65   215   75   161.25   35 $\frac{1}{4}$ 330.65

   ### Events Night a Huge Success!

   The Events Night held by Mr. Martinez's and Ms. Swanson's middle-school classes was a success, raising a total of $_____. The teachers estimated the large turnout of middle-school students included over_____ of the building's student population. Over half of the money, $_____ , was earned by the food booths. _____ game tickets were sold, raising $_____ , which represented_____ of the money. The tickets were_____ cents each. Most of the money that was raised, _____ %, will go toward paying for the class camping trip, and the other _____ % will be used to pay expenses.

8. In each of the sets of numbers below, one number is not equivalent to the others. Tell which one is not like the others and explain why.

   a. 0.60   0.6   6%

   b. $\frac{1}{25}$ 25%   0.25

   c. 0.75   34% $\frac{3}{4}$

9. Write a benchmark fraction that is close to each of these percentages:

   a. 23.6%   b. 45.4545%

Name _____ Date _____

1. In each figure, express the area shaded and the area not shaded as percents.

   a. 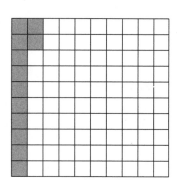 **b.** 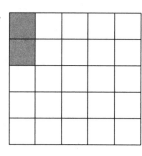 **c.**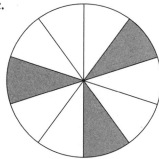

   % shaded _____   % shaded _____   % shaded _____

   % not shaded _____   % not shaded _____   % not shaded _____

2. Write each of the following as a fraction, decimal, and percent.

   a. 30 days out of 100 days   **b.** 55¢ compared to 100¢

   c. 20 correct out of 25 problems   **d.** 3 out of 4 games won

   e. 21 mountain bikes out of 40 bikes   **f.** 5 misspelled words out of 30 words

3. At the pizza shop, 16-inch-diameter pizzas sell for $9.85. The shop has decided to sell pizza by the slice. One cutting form can cut a pizza into 12 slices, and another form can cut a pizza into 8 slices.

   a. To make at least $9.85 on each whole pizza sold, how much should the shop charge for a large slice? (Try to come as close to $9.85 as you can, but make your price easy to handle in terms of making change.)

Unit Test: In-Class Portion

b. To make at least $9.85 on each whole pizza sold, how much should the shop charge for a small slice? (Try to come as close to $9.85 as you can, but make your price easy to handle.)

c. Explain why you think your answers for parts a and b are appropriate.

4. In a recent survey of 600 people, 20% said chocolate chip cookie was their favorite ice cream. How many people in the survey favored chocolate chip cookie ice cream? Explain your answer.

5. Of the people in your math class today (including your teacher), what percent are male? _____

What percent are female? _____

Unit Test: Individual Research

Find two different articles in newspapers or magazines that contain fractions, decimals, or percents. If one article uses mainly one of these forms, the other article must contain at least one of the other two forms.

Write a one- to two-paragraph summary of each article. In your explanation, tell how rational numbers were used in the article and what they represent. Turn in each article with your explanation attached.

Name _____   Date _____

Notebook Checklist

Journal Organization

_____   Problems and Mathematical Reflections are labeled and dated.

_____   Work is neat and easy to find and follow.

Vocabulary

_____   All words are listed.   _____   All words are defined and described.

Quizzes and Check-Ups

_____   Quiz   _____   Check-Up 1

                                         _____   Check-Up 2

Homework Assignments

_____   _____

_____   _____

_____   _____

_____   _____

_____   _____

_____   _____

_____   _____

_____   _____

_____   _____

_____   _____

_____   _____

_____   _____

_____   _____

_____   _____

_____   _____

Name _____ Date _____

Vocabulary

Of the vocabulary words I defined or described in my journal, the word _____ best demonstrates my ability to give a clear definition or description.

Of the vocabulary words I defined or described in my journal, the word _____ best demonstrates my ability to use an example to help explain or describe an idea.

Mathematical Ideas

1. **a.** I learned these things about fractions, decimals, and percents in *Bits and Pieces I:*

    b. Here are page numbers of journal entries that give evidence of what I have learned, along with descriptions of what each entry shows:

2. **a.** These are the mathematical ideas I am still struggling with:

    b. This is why I think these ideas are difficult for me:

    c. Here are page numbers of journal entries that give evidence of what I am struggling with, along with descriptions of what each entry shows:

Class Participation

I contributed to the classroom discussion and understanding of *Bits and Pieces I* when I . . . (Give examples.)

Answer Keys

Answers to Check-Up 1

1. Possible answer: Each space represents an eighth, because there are eight spaces between each number. Each mark would increase by an eighth: $\frac{1}{8}, \frac{2}{8}, \frac{3}{8}, \frac{4}{8}, \frac{5}{8}, \frac{6}{8}, \frac{7}{8}$. If the fractions are reduced, the marks would be $\frac{1}{8}, \frac{1}{4}, \frac{3}{8}, \frac{1}{2}, \frac{5}{8}, \frac{3}{4}, \frac{7}{8}$.

2. **a.** $\frac{8}{12} < \frac{3}{4}$ **b.** $\frac{5}{8} > \frac{6}{10}$ **c.** $\frac{2}{3} < \frac{5}{6}$ **d.** $\frac{2}{4} < \frac{7}{12}$ **e.** $\frac{3}{8} > \frac{3}{12}$

3. Possible answers: $\frac{2}{3}, \frac{53}{100}, \frac{6}{10}, \frac{712}{1000}$

4. Yes, Julie was right. Possible explanations: Dave's class had earned $\frac{5}{8}$ ($150) = $93.75, and Julie's class had earned $\frac{2}{3}$ ($150) = $100. Also, $\frac{5}{8} = \frac{15}{24}$ and $\frac{2}{3} = \frac{16}{24}$, so $\frac{5}{8} < \frac{2}{3}$.

5. **a.**

   b.

   c.

6. $\frac{24}{15}$ $1\frac{7}{10}$ $1\frac{15}{18}$

Answers to Quiz

1. The portion of the figure that is shaded is $\frac{10}{30}$ or $\frac{1}{3}$. If you divide the rectangle into 30 equal pieces, 10 of them are shaded, and $\frac{10}{30}$ equals $\frac{1}{3}$.

2. 3 worms; $3(\frac{2}{3}) = 2$. Students will probably draw a picture to show this, which is quite acceptable at this time.

3. **a.** true; Possible explanation: If the denominators are the same, each piece is the same size. The fraction with the larger numerator is the larger fraction because numerators tell how many pieces you have.

   b. false; Possible explanation: If the numerators are the same, the number of pieces is the same. As the denominator increases, the size of the pieces decreases, so the fraction with the smaller denominator is the larger fraction.

4. **a.** Small slices are $\frac{1}{12}$ of a pizza, and large slices are $\frac{1}{8}$ of a pizza; $\frac{3}{12} + \frac{3}{8} = \frac{15}{24} = \frac{5}{8}$ of a pizza.

   b. $1 - \frac{15}{24} = \frac{9}{24}$ of a pizza

   c. $\frac{2}{8} + \frac{9}{12} = 1$; $\frac{4}{8} + \frac{6}{12} = 1$; $\frac{6}{8} + \frac{3}{12} = 1$

5. **a.** $1\frac{1}{3}$ **b.** $2\frac{1}{2}$

Answer Keys

Answers to Check-Up 2

1. **a.** $\frac{8}{40}$ or $\frac{1}{5}$; 0.2 or 0.20   **b.** $\frac{3}{24}$ or $\frac{1}{8}$; 0.125

2. 0.00006, 0.006, 0.06, 0.60 = 0.6, 6.00

3. Possible answers:

    a. 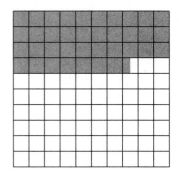   **b.**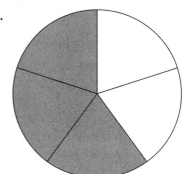

    c.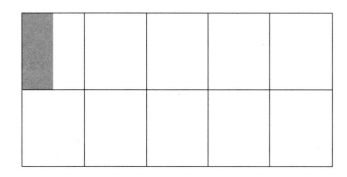

4. **a.** $\frac{375}{1000}$ or $\frac{3}{8}$ **b.** $\frac{6}{10}$ or $\frac{3}{5}$ **c.** $\frac{5}{100}$ or $\frac{1}{20}$

5.

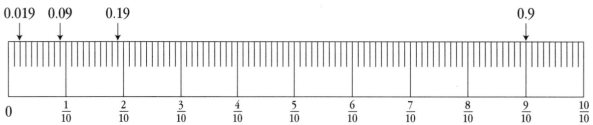

6. **a.**

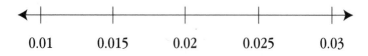

b.

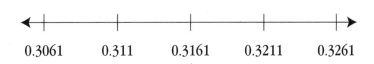

c.

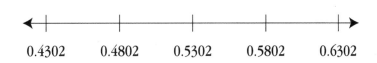

Answers to Question Bank

1. **a.**

b. 10 is $\frac{10}{100}$ or $\frac{1}{10}$; 25 is $\frac{25}{100}$ or $\frac{1}{4}$; 35 is $\frac{35}{100}$ or $\frac{7}{20}$; 70 is $\frac{70}{100}$ or $\frac{7}{10}$; 85 is $\frac{85}{100}$ or $\frac{17}{20}$

c. 33 or 34 points

d. 60 points

e. 25 points

f. 75 points

g. Taylor should receive a few more points than Miki because $\frac{6}{9}$ of the way up the pole is more than $\frac{5}{8}$ of the way.

2. If you want the most pizza possible, join the first group. In the first group, you would share 6 pizzas among 4 people, so you would receive $1\frac{1}{2}$ pizzas. In the second group, you would share 8 pizzas among 6 people, so you would receive $1\frac{1}{3}$ pizzas.

3. a. $\frac{3}{12}$ or $\frac{1}{4}$
   b. $\frac{5}{20}$ or $\frac{1}{4}$
   c. $\frac{2}{9}$
   d. $\frac{7}{17}$

4. The muffins may not have been the same size to start with.

5. When comparing two decimal numbers that are both less than 1, you need compare place-value amounts. For example, 0.37 is less than 0.6. This is because 0.37 means 37 hundredths or 3 tenths and 7 hundredths, and 0.6 means 6 tenths. Tenths are greater than hundredths, so 0.6 is more than 0.37.

6. The decimal point should not be in these signs. The way the prices are written, bananas cost less than a penny a pound, and the price of the paper is between one and two cents.

7. The Events Night held by Mr. Martinez's and Ms. Swanson's middle-school classes was a success, raising a total of $645. The teachers estimated the large turnout of middle-school students included over $\frac{3}{4}$ of the building's student population. Over half of the money, $330.65, was earned by the food booths. 215 game tickets were sold, raising $161.25, which represented $\frac{1}{4}$ of the money. The tickets were 75 cents each. Most of the money that was raised, 65%, will go toward paying for the class camping trip, and the other 35% will be used to pay expenses.

8. a. 6%; In decimal form, 6% is 0.06.
   b. $\frac{1}{25}$; In decimal form, $\frac{1}{25}$ is 0.04; as a percent, it is 4%.
   c. 34%; In decimal form, 34% is 0.34; as a fraction, it is $\frac{34}{100}$ or $\frac{17}{50}$.

9. a. $\frac{1}{4}$ b. $\frac{1}{2}$

Answers to the Unit Test: In-Class Portion

1. a. % shaded: 12%

   % not shaded: 88%

   b. % shaded: 8%

   % not shaded: 92%

   c. % shaded: 30%

   % not shaded: 70%

2. a. $\frac{30}{100}$ or $\frac{3}{10}$; 0.30 or 0.3; 30%
   b. $\frac{55}{100}$ or $\frac{11}{20}$; 0.55; 55%
   c. $\frac{20}{25}$ or $\frac{4}{5}$; 0.80 or 0.8; 80%
   d. $\frac{3}{4}$; 0.75; 75%
   e. $\frac{21}{40}$; 0.525; 52.5% or $52\frac{1}{2}$%
   f. $\frac{5}{30}$ or $\frac{1}{6}$; about 0.167; $16\frac{2}{3}$% or about 16.7%

3. a. The shop should charge around $1.25 (1.23125 is $\frac{1}{8}$ of the price of a pizza).

    b. The shop should charge around $0.85 (about 0.82083 is $\frac{1}{12}$ of the price of a pizza).

    c. Answers will vary depending on answers for parts a and b.

4. 120 people; Possible explanations: 20% means 20 out of every 100. You have 6 hundreds, so $6 \times 20 = 120$. Or, 20% can be written as $\frac{1}{5}$, and a fifth of 600 is 120.

5. Answers will vary.

Check-Up 1 is the first assessment piece for this unit. The blackline master for Check-Up 1 is on pages 86 and 87. Below are the scoring rubric one teacher used to assess the check-up and two examples of student work. After each example, the teacher comments about how she assessed the work.

Suggested Scoring Rubric

Question	Possible score	Scoring breakdown
1	5 points	3 points for labeling the marks 2 points for explaining how the labels were determined
2	10 points	2 points for each pair of numbers—1 point for the correct comparison and 1 point for a reasonable explanation of how the numbers were compared
3	3 points	1 point for each correct answer
4	3 points	1 point for recognizing that Julie is correct 2 points for explaining why Julie is correct
5	6 points	2 points for each correct answer—1 point for placing the number 1 in a reasonable location and 1 point for a explaining (in words or with a drawing) how this location was determined
6	5 points	3 points for the correct order 2 points for an explanation in words or with a drawing

Total Possible Score: 32 points

Grading Scale:
  A: 29–32
  B: 25–28
  C: 21–24
  D: 17–20

Samples 1 and 2

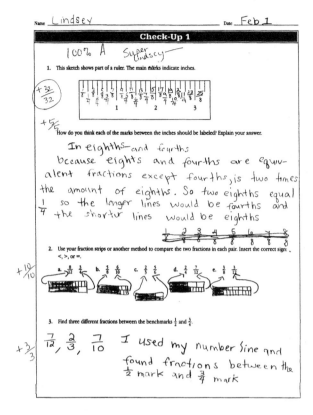

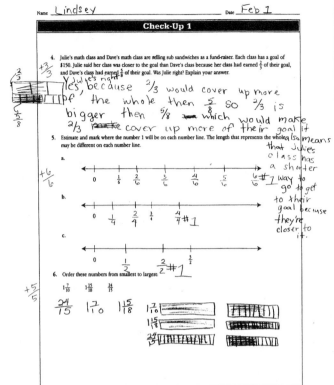

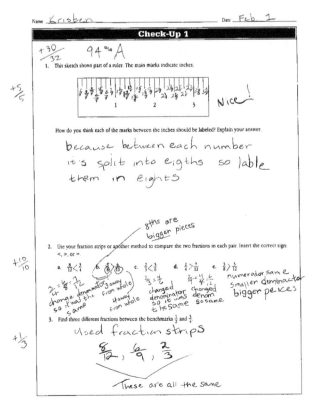

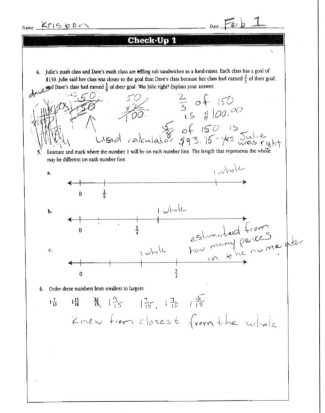

A Teacher's Comments on Sample 1

Lindsey earned all 32 points on her check-up. For question 1, she correctly labeled all of the marks, explained why she labeled the marks as she did, and explained the relationship between fourths and eighths. For question 2, she used the correct symbols to compare the fractions and proved each answer using fraction strips. In questions 3 and 4, she answers the questions correctly and used fraction strips to reason and to justify her answers. Her answers for questions 5 and 6 are also correct. The additional markings she included in questions 5 and her drawings of the strips for question 6 show her reasoning.

The fact that Lindsey used fraction strips as her primary means to solve the problems is fine at this stage in the unit. It is most important that she has a means to solve these types of problems even if her strategy is not what has been traditionally thought of as "sophisticated." As the class continues with this unit, I will continue to encourage Lindsey, and others like her, to think about more sophisticated methods of dealing with fractional relationships.

A Teacher's Comments on Sample 2

Kristen earned 30 of the 32 possible points for her check-up. She earned all of the possible points for questions 1 and 2. Her reasons for question 2 were interesting because she used more than one strategy. For some parts, she found common denominators, and for others, she reasoned about the sizes of the numerators and denominators. She earned only 1 of the three possible points for question 3 because she did not name three *different* fractions. For question 4, I think that Kristen used the strategies we used in class to solve the fund-raiser problems in Investigation 1. Even though she scribbled out some of her work, I can see that she divided 3 into 150 to get 50, and then multiplied 50 by 2 to find that $\frac{2}{3}$ of 150 is 100. Her work for $\frac{5}{8}$ is less clear. She struggled with doing calculations by hand and made some calculation errors. I watched her do the work on her calculator, and then write that $\frac{5}{8}$ would be $93.75, which is correct. Kristen's answers for questions 5 and 6 are correct, and her work makes her statement reasonable.

Kristen incorporated several strategies when reasoning about the problems on the quiz. I need to remind her to be careful and to check over her work before handing it in.

The blackline master for Check-Up 2 is on pages 90–92. Below are the scoring rubric one teacher used to assess the check-up and two examples of student work. After each example, the teacher comments about how she assessed the work.

Suggested Scoring Rubric

Question	Possible score	Scoring breakdown
1	4 points	2 points for each part—1 part for the fraction answer and 1 point for the decimal answer
2	4 points	1 point for stating that 0.6 and 0.60 were equal 3 points for the correct order A point is lost for each number excluded from the list
3	3 points	1 point for each part
4	3 points	1 point for each part
5	5 points	1 point for correctly locating each number
6	3 points	1 point for the correct label in part a Note: I made parts b and c extra credit, awarding a *total* of 1 point for each part. These were very difficult for my students, especially part c.

Total Possible Score: 22 points

Grading Scale: A: 20–22
                 B: 18–19
                 C: 15–17
                 D: 12–14

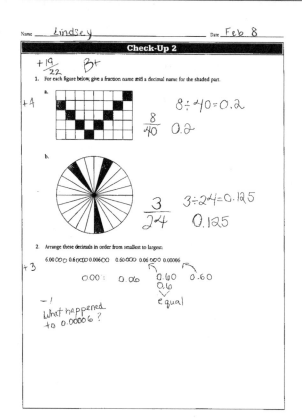

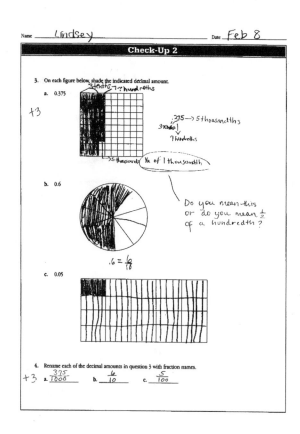

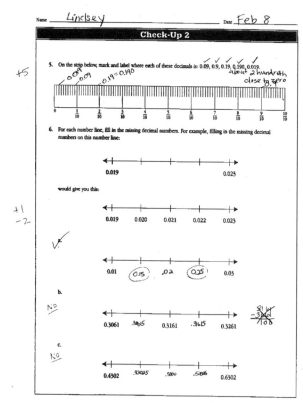

A Teacher's Comments

Lindsey earned 19 of the possible 22 points on this check-up. For question 1, she correctly named the shaded areas with both a fraction name and a decimal name. She lost 1 point for question 2 because she failed to include one of the numbers in her ordered list. For questions 3 and 4, she correctly shades and labels each drawing. She gives hints about her thinking by attempting to explain how she reasoned about part a. She made a small mistake when she wrote that 5 thousandths was $\frac{1}{2}$ of 1 thousandth instead of $\frac{1}{2}$ of 1 hundredth. Because the rest of her work is correct, I did not take off any points for this mistake. She correctly placed each label in question 5, and her added explanations make it clear that she understood the size of the decimals and their locations. She had some trouble with part a of question 6. She had the idea that the marks were 5 units apart but she struggled with the place values of the digits. I gave her 1 out of 3 points for this part; I felt that she could have reasoned through her mistakes, since she was able to label the middle mark correctly. She received no extra credit for parts b and c.

I am a little concerned about Lindsey's struggle with question 6. Because this question was difficult for many of my students, I will take time in class to discuss it. I might make up some questions like this and give them as opening questions for a future lesson.

Name Kristen   Date Feb 8

Check-Up 2

+20/22   A Great!

+A

1. For each figure below, give a fraction name and a decimal name for the shaded part.

a.

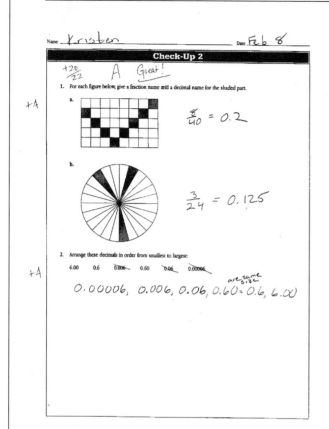

$\frac{8}{40} = 0.2$

b.

$\frac{3}{24} = 0.125$

2. Arrange these decimals in order from smallest to largest:

+A

6.00   0.6   0.006   0.60   0.06   0.00006

are same size

$0.00006, \ 0.006, \ 0.06, \ 0.60 = 0.6, \ 6.00$

Name Kristen   Date Feb 8

Check-Up 2

3. On each figure below, shade the indicated decimal amount.

a.   0.375

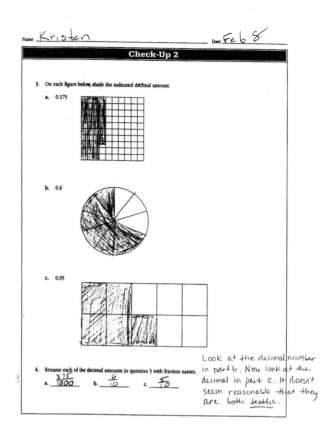

b.   0.6

c.   0.05

4. Rename each of the decimal amounts in question 3 with fraction names.

a. $\frac{375}{1000}$ b. $\frac{6}{10}$ c. $\frac{5}{10}$

Look at the decimal number in part b. Now look at the decimal in part c. It doesn't seem reasonable that they are both tenths.

Name Kristen   Date Feb 8

Check-Up 2

5. On the strip below, mark and label where each of these decimals is: 0.09, 0.9, 0.19, 0.190, 0.019.

+5

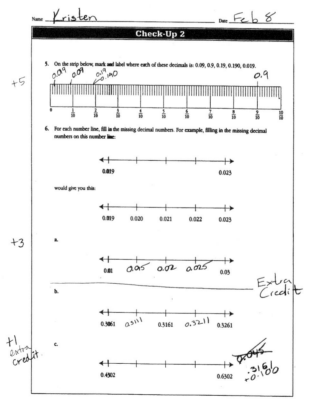

0.09   0.09   0.19, 0.190   0.9

0   1/10   2/10   3/10   4/10   5/10   6/10   7/10   8/10   9/10   10/10

6. For each number line, fill in the missing decimal numbers. For example, filling in the missing decimal numbers on this number line:

0.019   0.023

would give you this:

0.019   0.020   0.021   0.022   0.023

+3   a.

0.01   0.05   0.02   0.025   0.03

b.   Extra Credit

0.3061   0.3111   0.3161   0.3211   0.3261

+1
extra
credit   c.

0.4302   0.6302   0.045   .3161 +0.100

A Teacher's Comments

Kristen earned 21 points (including an extra credit point for question 6). She earned all the possible points for questions 1 and 2. For question 3, she earned 2 of the 3 possible points because she shaded five tenths, rather than five hundredths, for part c. She received 2 of the 3 possible points for question 4. Since the fraction she wrote for part c corresponded with her drawing, I considered not subtracting a point. However, I decided to take off a point, because she could have looked at the decimal names for parts b and c and realized that the fractions could not both be tenths. She earned all the possible points for part a of question 6 and received 1 extra credit point for part b.

This check-up shows me that Kristen has made enough sense of the skills in this unit to move on. I would ask her what she was thinking when she shaded part c of question 3, but I am not too concerned about his because of her ACE work and her work in class.

Several teachers have taught the Connected Mathematics program to special education students who are part of an inclusion program. In one school district, special education students study mathematics in a regular classroom with both a mathematics teacher and a special education teacher present. The teachers work together to teach the curriculum. The mathematics teacher leads the lesson, and the special education teacher joins the discourse and works with the students during the Explore phase.

In this school, the teachers have decided to include the special education students in the classroom for everything, including assessment lessons. For formal assessment, the teachers work together to create special assessment pieces that are similar to the assessments the other students are doing. The teachers' goals are to offer challenging, yet realistic, problems that allow them to assess what their students know and what they are struggling with. Below is an example of a special education student's work on an altered check-up. After the sample, we include the teachers' comments about why they changed each question and how they assessed the student's work.

Sample

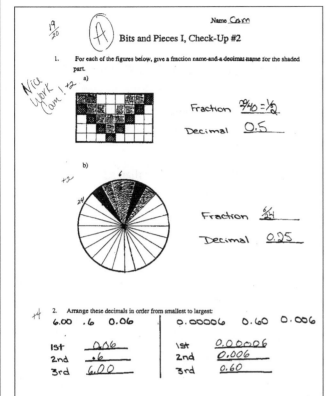

19/20

(A)

Name Cam

Bits and Pieces I, Check-Up #2

1. For each of the figures below, give a fraction name and a decimal name for the shaded part.

Nice work Cam! +2

a)

Fraction 20/40 = 1/2

Decimal 0.5

b)

Fraction 6/24

Decimal 0.25

#4

2. Arrange these decimals in order from smallest to largest:

6.00   .6   0.06   0.00006   0.60   0.006

1st ___0.06___   1st ___0.00006___
2nd ___.6___   2nd ___0.006___
3rd ___6.00___   3rd ___0.60___

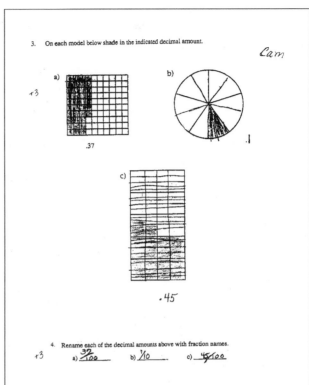

3. On each model below shade in the indicated decimal amount.

Cam

+3

a)

.37

b)

.1

c)

.45

4. Rename each of the decimal amounts above with fraction names.

+3   a) 32/100   b) 1/10   c) 45/100

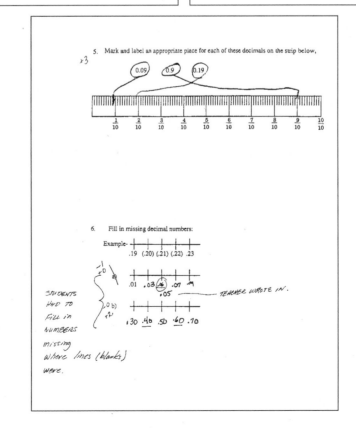

5. Mark and label an appropriate place for each of these decimals on the strip below.

+3

0.09   0.9   0.19

1/10 2/10 3/10 4/10 5/10 6/10 7/10 8/10 9/10 10/10

6. Fill in missing decimal numbers:

Example- .19 (.20) (.21) (.22) .23

a) .01 .03 .04 .07
        .05   TEACHER WROTE IN.

STUDENTS HAD TO FILL IN NUMBERS missing where lines (blanks) were.

b) .30 .40 .50 .60 .70

The Teachers' Comments

Question 1

We altered the drawings to represent friendlier fractions ($\frac{1}{2}$ instead of $\frac{1}{5}$ and $\frac{1}{4}$ instead of $\frac{1}{8}$). We also provided labeled answer blanks to remind students that there are two parts to the question.

Cam answered both questions correctly. He demonstrated that he knows that $\frac{20}{40}$ is equal to $\frac{1}{2}$, but we wonder if he also knows that $\frac{6}{24}$ is equal to $\frac{1}{4}$. One of us will ask him when we hand back the papers.

Question 2

We simplified this question by asking students to work with three numbers at a time, rather than six. The sheer number of items in a question can be so overwhelming for special needs students that they cannot even begin the problem.

Cam answered this question correctly. If we ask a similar question in the future, we might increase the number of items to four.

Questions 3 and 4

From the work in class, we knew that our special education students would not be able to deal with the thousandths in part a (0.375). By changing the question, we could see whether students could make sense of hundredths in both situations where a grid is given (part a) and in situations where it is not (part c).

Cam answered these questions correctly. We found it interesting that, in part c, he divided the rectangle into 100 pieces and then shaded.

Question 5

Once again, we decreased the number of items. We deleted 0.019 because of the difficulty students have in dealing with thousandths. We deleted 0.190, one of the two equivalent decimals, because dealing with equivalent decimals in situations like this has proven very confusing for students. We believe that we need to help our special education students make sense of this idea but do not feel that an assessment situation is the best way to deal with this problem.

Question 6

As it was originally written, this question is very difficult for students. We altered the problem by using only tenths and hundredths, numbers we knew our special needs students could handle. We also simplified the problem by writing in some of the numbers.

Cam struggled with part a, in which the marks increased by 0.02. Many of the other special education students struggled with both part a and part b.

Overall, Cam did well on the check-up. Not all of the special education students were as successful as he. We included his work to show how well special education students can do when they are given some scaffolding. Each time we alter an assessment piece, we must consider whether we are asking enough of our special students or whether we should expect more. For Cam and others, the success they are having gives them encouragement to try harder. Many of these students have had little previous success learning mathematics because of the focus on memorization. With a focus on understanding and making sense of ideas, these students are realizing that they can learn mathematics.

Blackline Masters

Fraction Strips

halves	

thirds	

fourths	

fifths	

sixths	

eighths	

ninths	

tenths	

twelfths	

Brownie Pans

Justin's Garden

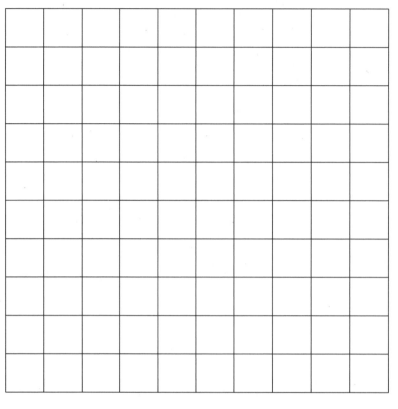

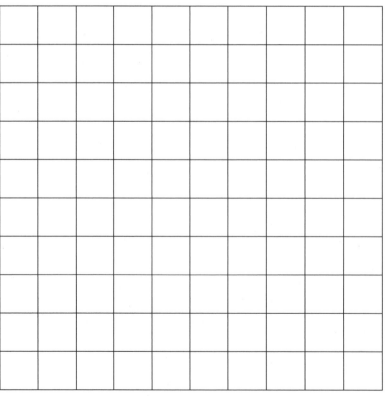

Hundredths Grid

ACE Question 9

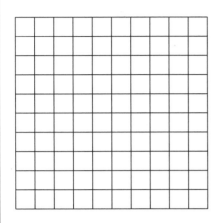
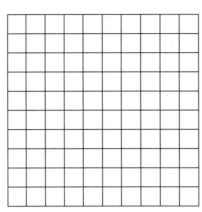
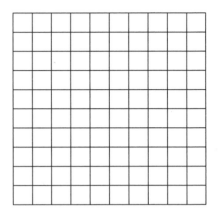

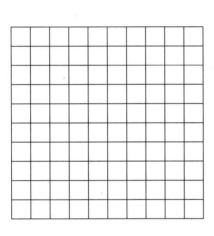
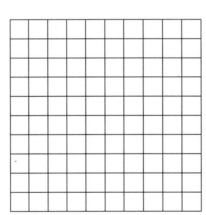
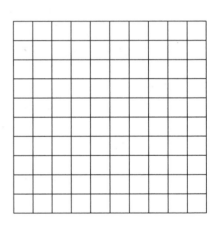

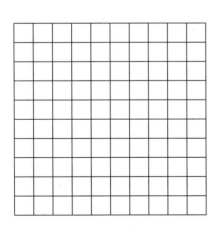
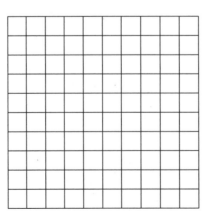
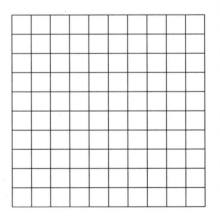

Twelve Hundredths Grids

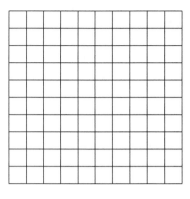
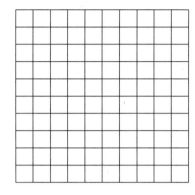
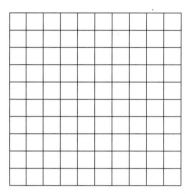

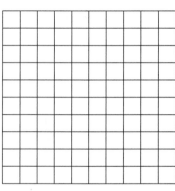
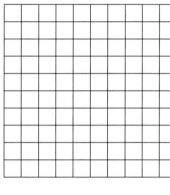
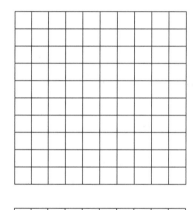

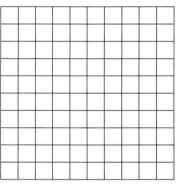
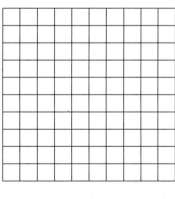
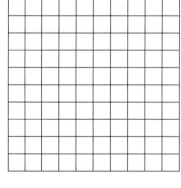

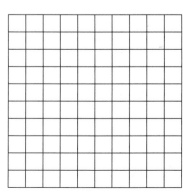
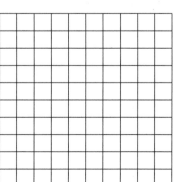
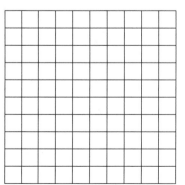

Fraction Strips with Hundredths Strip

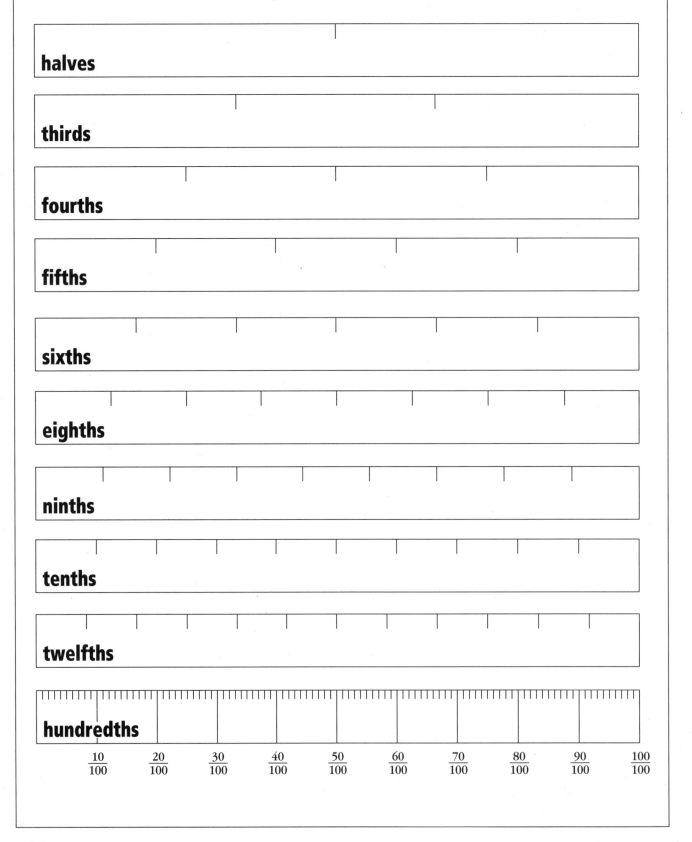

halves

thirds

fourths

fifths

sixths

eighths

ninths

tenths

twelfths

hundredths

$\frac{10}{100}$ $\frac{20}{100}$ $\frac{30}{100}$ $\frac{40}{100}$ $\frac{50}{100}$ $\frac{60}{100}$ $\frac{70}{100}$ $\frac{80}{100}$ $\frac{90}{100}$ $\frac{100}{100}$

100 Cats

Alex	Boots	Diva	Fuzzy	Hanna	Matilda	Newton	Ravena	Smokey	Thomas
Amanda	Bosley	Duffy	Gabriel	Harmony	Melissa	Peanut	Reebo	Smudge	Tiger
Augustus	Bradley	Ebony Kahlua	George	Jinglebob	Mercedes	Peebles	Samantha	Snowy	Tigger
Baguera	Buffy	Elizabeth	Ginger	Kali	Midnight	Pepper	Sassy	Sparky	Ting
Black Foot	Charcoal	Emma	Gizmo	Kiki	Millie	Pink Lady	Scooter	Speedy	Tom
Blacky	Chelsea	Emmie	Gracie	Kitty	Miss Muppet	Pip	Sebastian	Stinky	Tomadachi
Blue	Chessis	Ethel	Gray Kitty	Lady	Mittens	Precious	Seymour	Sweet Pea	Treasure
Bob	Chubbs	Feather	Grey Boy	Libby	Molly	Priscilla	Shiver	Tabby	Wally
Boggie	Cookie	Fire Smoke	Grey Girl	Lucky	Momma Kat	Prissy	Simon	Tabby Burton	Weary
Boo	Dana	Fluffy	Grey Poupon	Lucy	Nancy Blue	Ralph	Skeeter	Terra	Ziggy

Pet Ransom	Percent	Decimal	Fraction
$2000 and up	18%		
From $1500 to $1999		0.03	
From $1000 to $1499			$\frac{3}{100}$
From $500 to $999	25%		
From $1 to $499		0.31	
Nothing			$\frac{1}{5}$

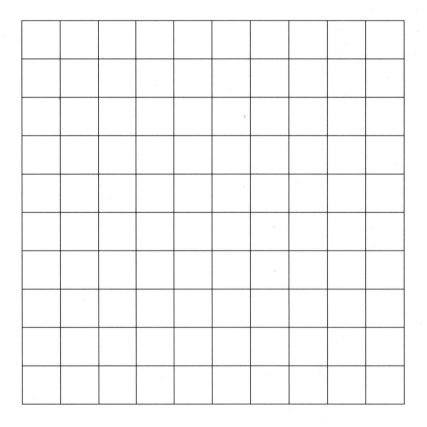

ACE Questions 17–19

17.

18.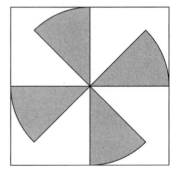

19.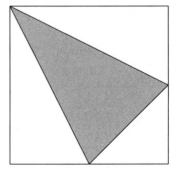

Goal $300

Write a short—but clever and informative—announcement to report the progress of the sixth-grade poster sale after two days. Be sure to mention what part of the sales goal of $300 had been reached and what part remained to be raised.

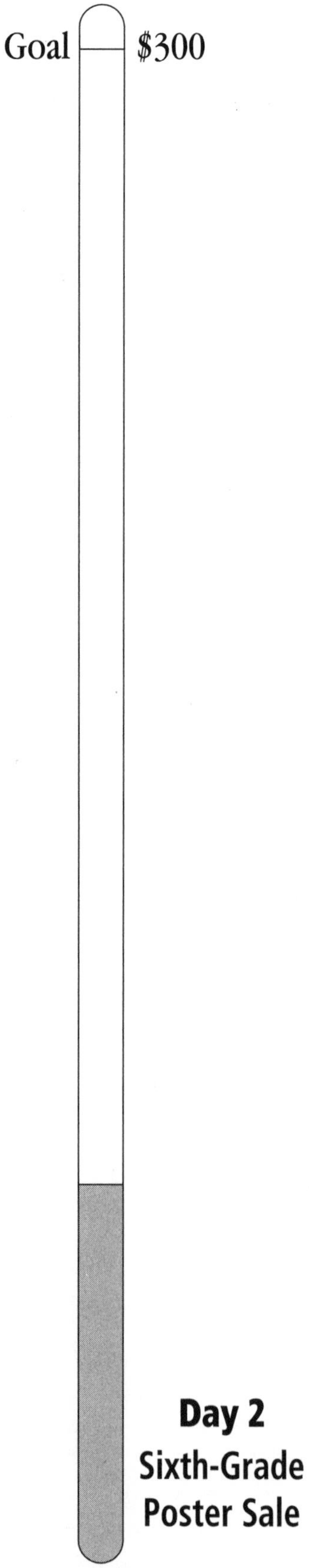

Day 2
Sixth-Grade
Poster Sale

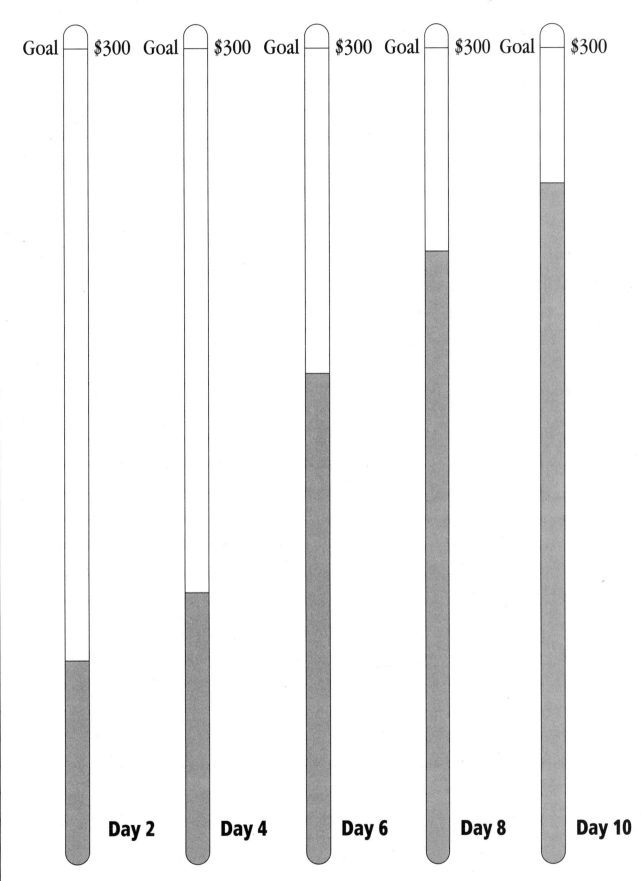

Goal ☐ $300 Goal ☐ $300 Goal ☐ $300 Goal ☐ $300 Goal ☐ $300

Day 2   **Day 4**   **Day 6**   **Day 8**   **Day 10**

Start with nine $8\frac{1}{2}$-inch strips. Fold the strips to show halves, thirds, fourths, fifths, sixths, eighths, ninths, tenths, and twelfths. Mark the folds in the strips with a pencil so you can see them more easily.

Use your strips to estimate the sixth-grade class's progress after two, four, six, eight, and ten days.

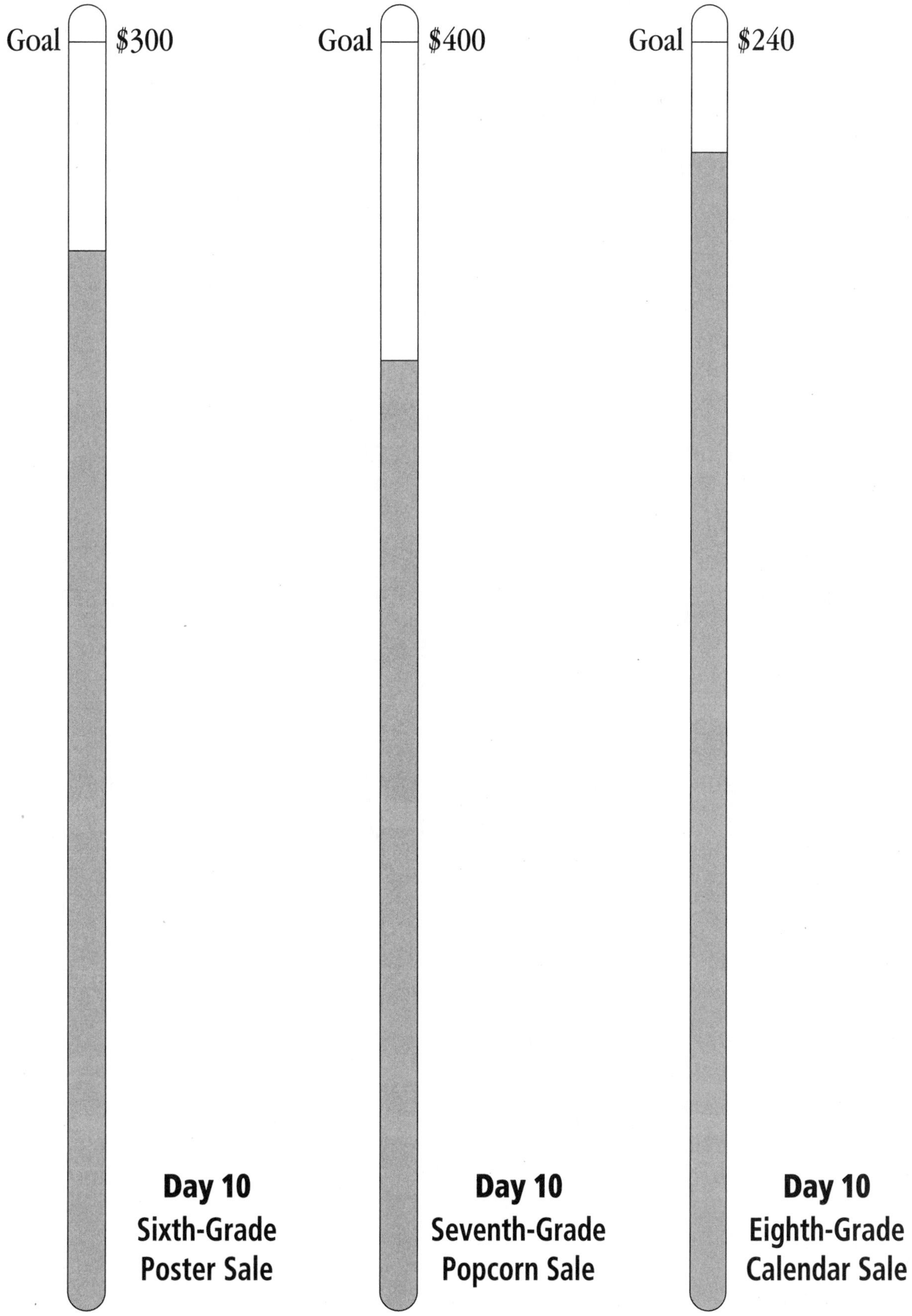

Goal $300

Goal $400

Goal $240

Day 10
Sixth-Grade
Poster Sale

Day 10
Seventh-Grade
Popcorn Sale

Day 10
Eighth-Grade
Calendar Sale

Use the fraction strips you made in Problem 1.2 to investigate the seventh and eighth graders' claims.

A. How much money did each grade raise?

B. What fraction of the goal did each grade reach?

C. What argument could the eighth graders use to claim that their class did better than the sixth grade?

D. What argument could the seventh graders use to claim that their class did better than the sixth grade?

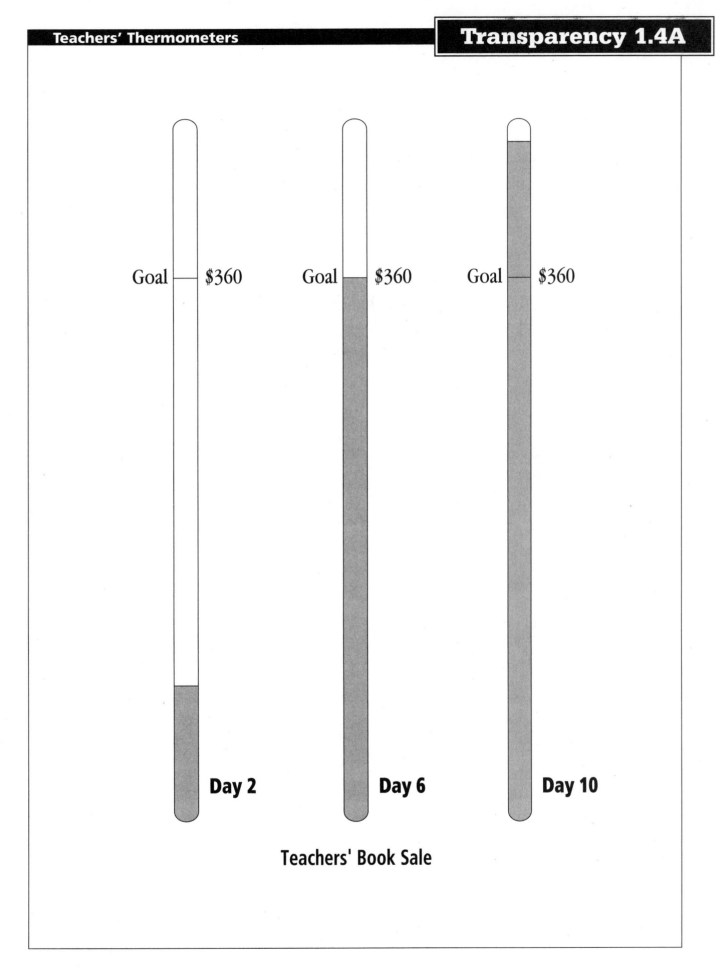

Goal —— $360   Goal —— $360   Goal —— $360

Day 2   **Day 6**   **Day 10**

Teachers' Book Sale

A. Notice that the teachers used a shorter thermometer than the students did to report their progress. Can you use your fraction strips to measure these thermometers? Explain.

B. What fraction of their goal did the teachers reach at the end of each of the days shown? Explain how you determined your answers.

C. How many dollars did the teachers raise by the end of each of these days?

Each strip below is divided into a different number of equal-length parts. On your copy of Labsheet 1.5, label each of the marks on the strips with fraction names in symbolic form. The label for a mark should represent the fraction of the strip to the left of the mark.

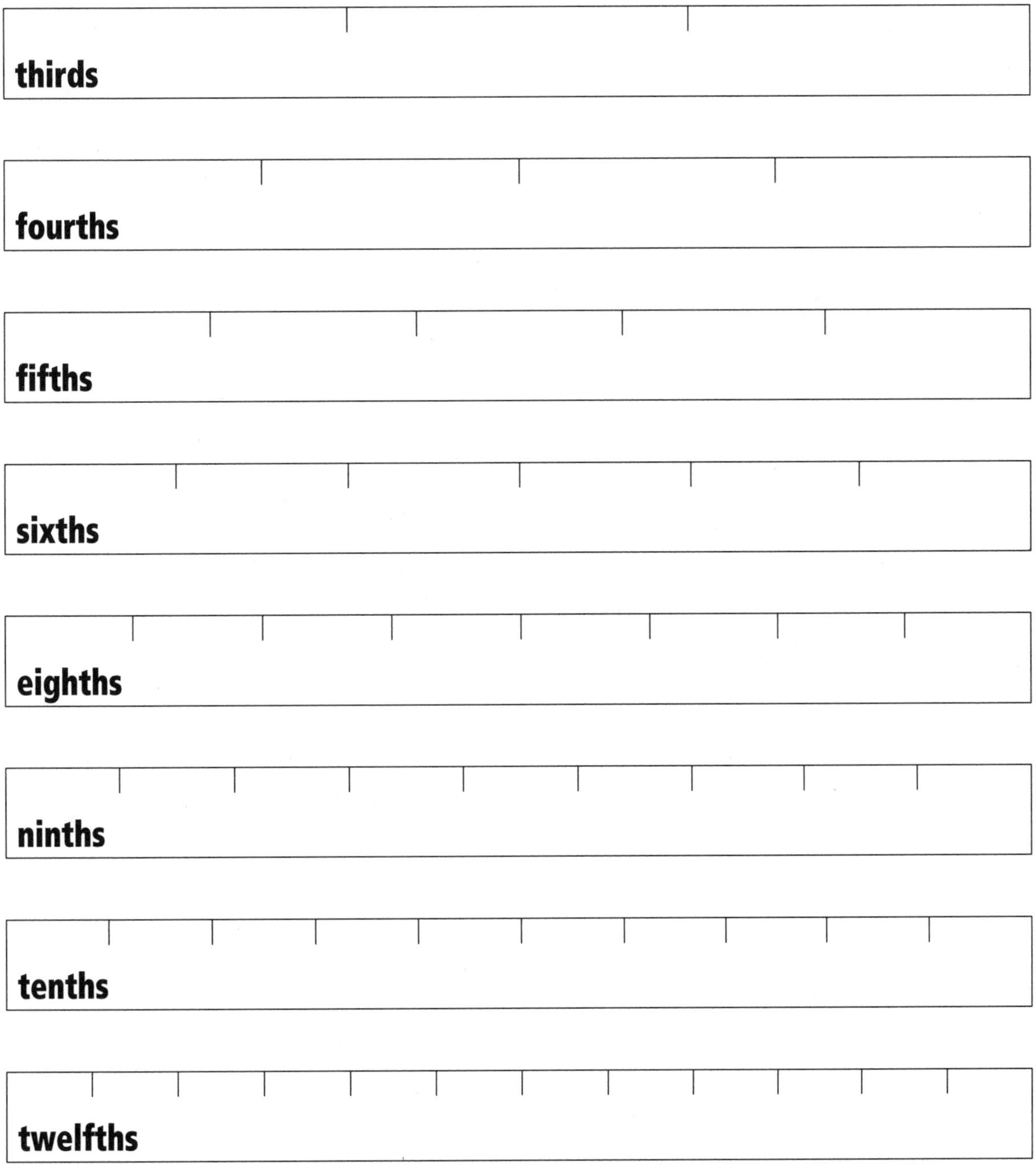

thirds

fourths

fifths

sixths

eighths

ninths

tenths

twelfths

A. Which of the three teachers do you agree with? Why?

B. How could the teacher you agreed with in part A prove his or her case?

Goal — $360

Day 4
Teachers'
Book Sale

The fraction strips on the left below show $\frac{2}{3}$ and three fractions equivalent to $\frac{2}{3}$. The strips on the right show $\frac{3}{4}$ and three fractions equivalent to $\frac{3}{4}$. Look for patterns that will help you find other equivalent fractions.

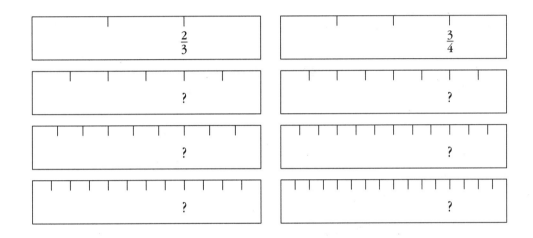

A. What are the three fractions shown that are equivalent to $\frac{2}{3}$? Name three more fractions that are equivalent to $\frac{2}{3}$.

B. What are the three fractions shown that are equivalent to $\frac{3}{4}$? Name three more fractions that are equivalent to $\frac{3}{4}$.

C. What pattern do you see that can help you find equivalent fractions?

$$\frac{1}{3} = \frac{5}{15}$$

A. Make a number line as illustrated below. When you find another name for a mark you have already labeled, record the new name below the first name.

B. Look for patterns in your finished number line. Record your findings.

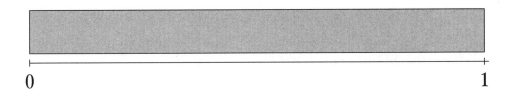

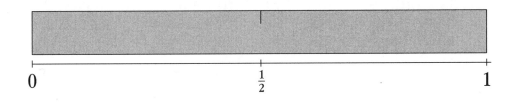

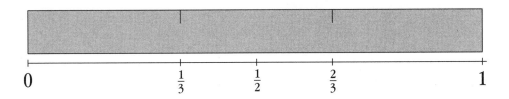

A. Decide whether each fraction below is between 0 and $\frac{1}{2}$ or between $\frac{1}{2}$ and 1.

$$\frac{1}{5} \quad \frac{2}{3} \quad \frac{8}{10} \quad \frac{3}{12} \quad \frac{3}{5} \quad \frac{5}{6} \quad \frac{5}{8} \quad \frac{4}{5} \quad \frac{3}{8} \quad \frac{3}{4} \quad \frac{2}{9} \quad \frac{7}{12} \quad \frac{1}{3}$$

B. Decide whether each fraction from part A is closest to 0, $\frac{1}{2}$, or 1. Record your information in a table.

C. Explain your strategies for comparing fractions to 0, $\frac{1}{2}$, and 1.

D. Use benchmarks and other strategies to help you write the fractions from part A in order from smallest to largest.

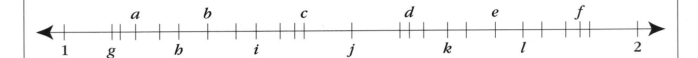

A. Use the fraction strips from Labsheet 1.5 to find as many labels as you can for each of the lettered points. For each point, record the letter and the fraction labels.

B. Copy the number line onto a sheet of paper. Mark and label a point fitting each description below. Do not use points that are already marked.

1. a point close to, but larger than, 1

2. a point close to, but smaller than, $1\frac{1}{2}$

3. a point close to, but larger than, $1\frac{1}{2}$

4. a point close to, but smaller than, 2

Use the squares on Labsheet 3.1 as models for pans of brownies. Show the cuts you would make to divide a pan of brownies into

A. 15 equal-size large brownies

B. 20 equal-size medium brownies

C. 30 equal-size small brownies

A. Do you think Samantha, Romero, and Harold should make small, medium, or large brownies?

B. If they make brownies of the size you chose in part A, how much of each ingredient will they need to make enough to serve a brownie to each person at camp?

C. Describe the strategy you used to get your answer to part B.

Chunky Brownies with a Crust

$1\frac{1}{4}$ cups flour	$\frac{1}{2}$ cup cold butter or margarine
$\frac{1}{4}$ cup sugar	$\frac{1}{4}$ cup unsweetened cocoa
1 egg	1 14-ounce can sweetened condensed milk
1 teaspoon vanilla	$\frac{1}{2}$ teaspoon baking powder

1 7-ounce bar milk chocolate, broken into small chunks

$\frac{3}{4}$ cup chopped nuts (optional)

Preheat the oven to 350 degrees. In medium bowl, combine 1 cup of flour and the sugar. Cut in the margarine or butter until crumbly. Press the mixture firmly into the bottom of a 10-by-10-inch baking pan. Bake 15 minutes. Meanwhile, in a large mixing bowl, beat the sweetened condensed milk, the cocoa, the egg, the remaining flour, the vanilla, and the baking powder. Stir in the nuts and chocolate chunks. Spread over the prepared crust. Bake 20 minutes or until the center is set. Cool. Sprinkle with confectioner's sugar, if desired. Store tightly covered at room temperature. Makes 15 large, 20 medium, or 30 small brownies.

Brownie Table

	Small (30)	Medium (20)	Large (15)
Batches for 240	8 batches	12 batches	16 batches
Cups flour	10	15	20
Cups sugar	2	3	4
Cups butter	4	6	8
Cans milk	8	12	16
Cups cocoa	2	3	4
Eggs	8	12	16
Tsp. vanilla	8	12	16
Tsp. baking powder	4	6	8
No. 7-oz choc. bars	8	12	16
Cups nuts	6	9	12

Here are the family's requirements for the garden.

• Justin's father wants to be sure potatoes, beans, corn, and tomatoes are planted. He wants twice as much of the garden to be planted in corn as potatoes. He wants three times as much land planted in potatoes as tomatoes.

• Justin's sister wants cucumbers in the garden

• Justin's brother wants carrots in the garden.

• Justin's mother wants eggplant in the garden.

• Justin wants radishes in the garden.

Use Labsheet 4.1 to make a suitable plan for the garden. Write a description of the garden you plan. Name the fraction of the garden space that will be allotted to each kind of vegetable as part of your description. Explain how your garden will satisfy each member of Justin's family.

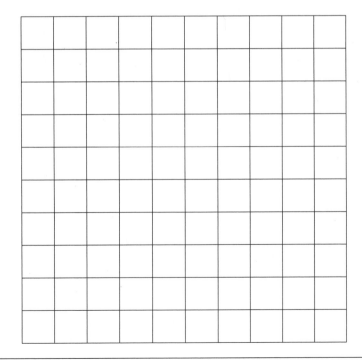

© Dale Seymour Publications®

Look back at the original plan you drew for Justin's garden. Write each of the fractional parts for the vegetables in your plan as a decimal.

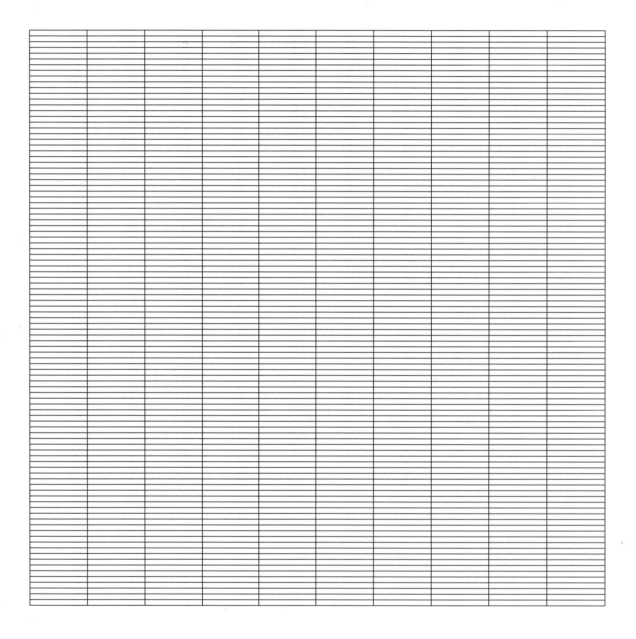

Fraction names for place-value groups	Decimal names for place-value groups		
Ten thousands	10,000	10,000	
Thousands	1000	1000	
Hundreds	100	100	
Tens	10	10	
Ones	1	1	
Tenths	$\frac{1}{10}$	0.1	
Hundredths	$\frac{1}{100}$	0.01	
Thousandths	$\frac{1}{1000}$	0.001	
Ten thousandths	$\frac{1}{10,000}$	0.0001	

A. Rename each of these fraction benchmarks as a decimal.

1. 0   **2.** $\frac{1}{4}$ **3.** $\frac{1}{2}$ **4.** $\frac{3}{4}$ **5.** 1

B. Now use the decimal benchmarks or other strategies to order each set of numbers from smallest to largest.

1. 0.23   0.28   0.25

2. 2.054   20.54   2.54

3. 0.78   0.708   0.078

C. For each of the six decimals below, give the name of the decimal in words, and tell which benchmark the number is nearest as a fraction and as a decimal. For each decimal, explain your reasoning.

Number	Name in words	Nearest decimal benchmark	Nearest fraction benchmark	Reasoning
0.23				
0.28				
0.25				
0.78				
0.708				
0.078				

Play the Distinguishing Digits puzzles with your group. Record the strategies you use to solve the puzzles.

Mystery Number

1 ___ . ___ ___ ___

Clue 1   The digit in the thousandths place is double the digit in the ones place.

Clue 2   The digit in the tenths place is odd, and it represents the sum of the digits in the tens place and the thousandths place.

Clue 3   There are exactly two odd digits in the Mystery Number.

Clue 4   The digit in the hundredths place is three times the digit in the ones place.

The coach has three players to choose from to shoot the free throw. In their pregame warm-ups:

- Angela made 17 out of 25 free throws

- Emily made 15 out of 20 free throws

- Carma made 7 out of 10 free throws

Which player should the Portland coach select to shoot the free throw? Explain your reasoning.

Work with your group to find a way to use the fraction strips to help you estimate each of the fractions represented on the halves, thirds, fourths, fifths, sixths, eighths, ninths, tenths, and twelfths fraction strips as decimals. You might think about doing this by comparing the marks on each fraction strip to marks on the hundredths strip.

For example, to find a decimal name for $\frac{5}{12}$, you can find the mark on the hundredths strip that is nearest to the length $\frac{5}{12}$, since hundredths can easily be written as decimals. Since the mark at $\frac{42}{100}$ on the hundredths strip is the closest mark to $\frac{5}{12}$ on the twelfths strip, $\frac{5}{12}$ is approximately equal to 0.42.

Sometimes it is easier to look at the tenths strip. For example, $\frac{1}{2}$ on the fraction strip is at the same mark as $\frac{5}{10}$ on the tenths strip, so $\frac{1}{2}$ is equivalent to 0.5.

On Labsheet 5.2, label each mark on the nine fraction strips with an approximate decimal. Be prepared to explain your answers.

The students had 24 boxes for packing the food they collected. They wanted to share the supplies equally among the families who would receive the boxes. They had small bags and plastic containers to use to repack items for the individual boxes.

The students collected the following items:

48 tins of cocoa mix	6 pounds of Swiss cheese
72 boxes of powdered milk	3 pounds of hot pepper cheese
264 boxes of juice	7 pounds of peanuts
120 boxes of granola bars	5 pounds of popcorn kernels
36 pounds of wheat crackers	475 apples
18 pounds of peanut butter	195 oranges
12 pounds of cheddar cheese	

A. How much of each item should the students include in each box? Explain your reasoning.

B. What operation ($+$, $-$, $\times$, $\div$) did you use to find your answers? Why did this operation work?

C. How can your calculator help you decide how to distribute the food items?

Using the database and Labsheet 6.1, mark all the cats that are female on one chart and all the cats that are kittens on another chart. When you are finished, answer the following questions.

A. What fraction of the cats are female? Write the fraction as a decimal and a percent.

B. What fraction of the cats are male? Write the fraction as a decimal and a percent.

C. What do you notice about the combined percentage of female and male cats?

D. What fraction of the cats are kittens? Write the fraction as a decimal and a percent.

E. What fraction of the cats are adults? Write the fraction as a decimal and a percent.

F. What do you notice about the combined percentage of kittens and adult cats?

Cat	Gender	Age (yrs)	Weight (lbs)	Eye color	Pad color
Alex	m	18	11	green	black
Amanda	f	4.5	9.75	blue	gray
Augustus	m	2	10	yellow/green/blue	pink/black
Baguera	m	0.17	13	yellow	brown
Black Foot	m	0.33	1.5	yellow	gray
Blacky	f	1	5	yellow	gray/black
Blue	f	0.25	2	green	gray
Bob	f	4	12	green	black
Boggie	m	3	10	green	pink
Boo	m	3.5	10.75	yellow/green	brown
Boots	m	0.25	3	brown	black
Bosley	m	0.33	1.5	yellow/brown	pink
Bradley	m	0.6	11	yellow	pink/gray
Buffy	m	0.75	8	blue/green	pink
Charcoal	m	11	12	yellow	black
Chelsea	f	2	9	yellow	black
Chessis	f	1.5	6	green	brown
Chubbs	m	1	7	green	pink
Cookie	f	4	9	gold	black
Dana	f	10	8	green	black
Diva	f	3.5	11	green	pink
Duffy	m	1	9	yellow/green	black
Ebony Kahlua	m	1.5	15	blue	brown
Elizabeth	f	10	9	green	pink
Emma	f	4	9.25	gold	pink
Emmie	f	4	7	green	black
Ethel	f	5	8	green	black
Feather	m	2.5	13	green	pink
Fire Smoke	f	0.25	2.5	green/brown	pink
Fluffy	f	5	10	green	pink
Fuzzy	f	1.25	2	green	pink

You may want to use fraction strips or hundredths squares to help you to think about these questions.

A. 1. Rewrite the text on the sign for leashes so that the discount is shown as a *fraction off* the original price of the leashes.

    2. What will a $10.00 leash cost after the discount?

B. 1. Rewrite the text on the sign for pet carriers so that the discount is shown as a *percent off* the original price of the carriers.

    2. What will a $10.00 pet carrier cost after the discount?

C. 1. Rewrite the text on the pet food sign so that the discount is shown as a *percent off* the original price of pet food.

    2. Now, write the discount as a *percent* of the original price customers will pay.

    3. Rewrite the discount as a *fraction* of the original price customers will pay.

    4. Rewrite the discount as a *fraction off* the original price customers will pay.

    5. What will $10.00 worth of pet food cost after the discount?

D. 1. Rewrite the text on the pet treats sign so that the discount is shown as a *decimal.*

    2. What will $10.00 worth of pet treats cost after the discount?

Labsheet 6.3 contains the table below and a hundredths grid.

A. Fill in the missing information in your table.

B. Shade in the hundredths grid with different colors or shading styles to show the percent responding to each of the six choices. Add a key to your grid to show what each color or type of shading represents. When you finish, the grid should be completely shaded. Explain why.

	Percent	Decimal	Fraction
$2000 and up	18%		
From $1500 to $1999		0.03	
From $1000 to $1499			$\frac{3}{100}$
From $500 to $999	25%		
From $1 to $499		0.31	
Nothing			$\frac{1}{5}$

Preference	Out of 100 dog owners	Out of 100 cat owners
Human food only	50	27
Pet food only	30	58
Human and pet food	20	15

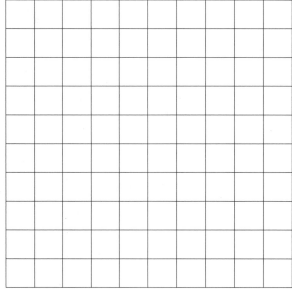

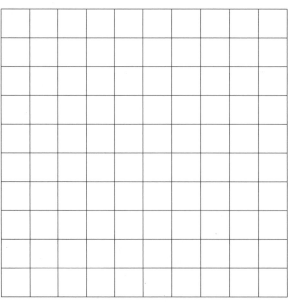

Consider the results of the survey.

Preference	Out of 150 dog owners	Out of 200 cat owners
Human food only	75	36
Pet food only	45	116
Human and pet food	30	48

A. What kind of food is favored by the greatest number of dogs, according to their owners? Write this number as a fraction, a decimal, and a percent of the 150 dog owners surveyed.

B. What choice is favored by the greatest number of cats, according to their owners? Write this number as a fraction, a decimal, and a percent of the 200 cat owners surveyed.

C. What percent of dog owners reported that their dogs liked either human food only or pet food only? Write this percent as a fraction and a decimal.

D. What percent of cat owners reported that their cats liked either human food only or pet food only? Write this percent as a decimal and a fraction.

Dear Family,

The next unit in your child's course of study in mathematics class this year is *Bits and Pieces I*. It is the first of two units to develop understanding of fractions, decimals, and percents—the ideas that are at the heart of the middle-grades experience with number concepts.

Bits and Pieces I focuses on developing a deep understanding of rational numbers, rather than on rules and formulas for computation. Computations with fractions, decimals, and percents will be the focus of the second fraction unit, *Bits and Pieces II*. In this unit, your child will learn the meanings of fractions, decimals, and percents, and will become comfortable moving among these three representations of rational numbers. Your child will work on problems that reflect real-world situations and that involve writing, comparing, and ordering fractions and decimals.

This unit makes use of concrete models, such as fraction strips, number lines, and grids to help students reason about fractions. Skill with estimating and comparing fractions is developed through a set of benchmark fractions and their decimal and percent equivalents. These benchmark fractions are those that occur often in real-world situations.

Fraction	$\frac{1}{10}$	$\frac{1}{8}$	$\frac{1}{5}$	$\frac{1}{4}$	$\frac{1}{3}$	$\frac{1}{2}$	$\frac{2}{3}$	$\frac{3}{4}$
Decimal	0.10	0.125	0.2	0.25	0.33	0.5	0.67	0.75
Percent	10%	12.5%	20%	25%	33%	50%	$66\frac{2}{3}\%$	75%

It is important that you do not show your child rules or formulas for working with fractions. This unit helps students to discover these rules for themselves and to develop a firm understanding of why these rules work. You can help your child with his or her work for this unit in several ways:

- Talk to your child about the ways you use fractions, decimals, and percents.

- Point out examples of how fractions, decimals, and percents are used in newspapers, magazines, radio, and television.

- Look over your child's homework and make sure all questions are answered and that explanations are clear.

As always, if you have any questions or concerns about this unit or your child's progress in class, please feel free to call. All of us here are interested in your child and want to be sure that this year's mathematics experiences are enjoyable and promote a firm understanding of mathematics.

Sincerely,

Estimada familia,

La próxima unidad del programa de matematicas de su hijo o hija para este curso se llama *Bits and Pieces I* (*Trocitos y pedacitos I*). Es la primera de dos unidades que intentan ampliar sus conocimientos sobre las fracciones, los decimales y los porcentajes, es decir, las ideas que constituyen lo esencial de las experiencias que los alumnos de los grados intermedios tienen con los conceptos numéricos.

Bits and Pieces I tiene por objetivo desarrollar una profunda comprensión de los números racionales en lugar de las reglas y las fórmulas para hacer cálculos. La segunda unidad sobre fracciones, *Bits and Pieces II*, trata principalmente sobre los cálculos realizados con fracciones, decimales y porcentajes. En esta unidad su hijo o hija aprenderá el significado de las fracciones, los decimales y los porcentajes y llegará a manejar con facilidad estas tres representaciones de los números racionales. Además, trabajará con problemas que reflejan situaciones del mundo real en los que se escriben, comparan y ordenan fracciones y decimales.

En esta unidad los alumnos usarán modelos concretos como, por ejemplo, tiras de fracciones, rectas numéricas y cuadrículas para así facilitar sus razonamientos sobre las fracciones. Perfeccionarán su capacidad para estimar y comparar fracciones mediante una serie de fracciones de referencia y de decimales y porcentajes equivalentes. Las fracciones de referencia son aquellas que se dan con frecuencia en situaciones del mundo real.

Fraction	$\frac{1}{10}$	$\frac{1}{8}$	$\frac{1}{5}$	$\frac{1}{4}$	$\frac{1}{3}$	$\frac{1}{2}$	$\frac{2}{3}$	$\frac{3}{4}$
Decimal	0.10	0.125	0.2	0.25	0.33	0.5	0.67	0.75
Percent	10%	12.5%	20%	25%	33%	50%	$66\frac{2}{3}\%$	75%

Es importante que ustedes no muestren a su hijo o hija las reglas o fórmulas relativas a las fracciones. Esta unidad ayuda a los alumnos a descubrir por sí solos las reglas y a desarrollar una sólida comprensión del funcionamiento de las mismas. Para ayudar a su hijo o hija con el trabajo de la unidad, ustedes pueden hacer lo siguiente:

- Háblenle sobre las maneras en que se utilizan las fracciones, los decimales y los porcentajes.

- Señalen ejemplos de los periódicos, las revistas, la radio y la televisión que traten sobre el uso de fracciones, decimales y porcentajes.

- Repasen su tarea para asegurarse de que conteste todas las preguntas y escriba con claridad las explicaciones.

Y como de costumbre, si ustedes necesitan más detalles o aclaraciones respecto a esta unidad o sobre los progresos de su hijo o hija en esta clase, no duden en llamarnos. A todos nos interesa su hijo o hija y queremos asegurarnos de que las experiencias matemáticas que tenga este año sean lo más amenas posibles y ayuden a fomentar en él o ella una sólida comprensión de las matemáticas.

Atentamente,

Mystery Number

_ _ _ _

Problem 1

Clue

The number has no repeated digits.

Problem 2

Clue

The number has no repeated digits.

Problem 1

Clue

All of the digits in the number are odd.

Problem 2

Clue

All of the digits in the number are even.

Problem 1

Clue

The digit in the ones place is greater than the digit in the tens place.

Problem 2

Clue

The digit in the hundreds place is 2 times the digit in the tens place.

Problem 1

Clue

The digit in the ones place is less than the digit in the hundreds place.

Problem 2

Clue

The digit in the tens place is 2 times the digit in the ones place.

Problem 1

Clue

The sum of the digits is 9.

Problem 2

Mystery Number

_ _ _

Problem 2

Mystery Number

_ _ _ , _ _ _

Problem 3

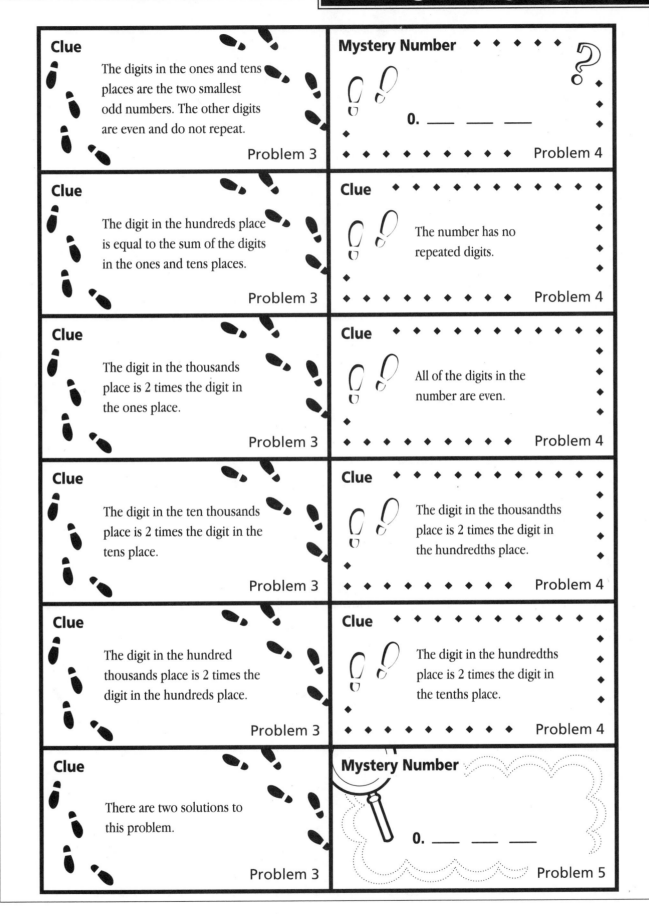

Clue

The digits in the ones and tens places are the two smallest odd numbers. The other digits are even and do not repeat.

Problem 3

Mystery Number

0. ___ ___ ___

Problem 4

Clue

The digit in the hundreds place is equal to the sum of the digits in the ones and tens places.

Problem 3

Clue

The number has no repeated digits.

Problem 4

Clue

The digit in the thousands place is 2 times the digit in the ones place.

Problem 3

Clue

All of the digits in the number are even.

Problem 4

Clue

The digit in the ten thousands place is 2 times the digit in the tens place.

Problem 3

Clue

The digit in the thousandths place is 2 times the digit in the hundredths place.

Problem 4

Clue

The digit in the hundred thousands place is 2 times the digit in the hundreds place.

Problem 3

Clue

The digit in the hundredths place is 2 times the digit in the tenths place.

Problem 4

Clue

There are two solutions to this problem.

Problem 3

Mystery Number

0. ___ ___ ___

Problem 5

Distinguishing Digit Cards

Clue The number has no repeated digits. Problem 5	Clue The number has no repeated digits. Problem 6
Clue Two of the digits are odd. Problem 5	Clue All of the digits are even and positive. Problem 6
Clue The digit in the hundredths place is 3 times the digit in the tenths place. Problem 5	Clue The digit in the tenths place is less than the digit in the thousandths place. Problem 6
Clue The digit in the thousandths place is 2 times the digit in the tenths place. Problem 5	Clue The sum of all the digits is greater than 16. Problem 6
Clue There are two possible solutions to this problem. Can you find them both? Problem 5	Clue There are two possible solutions to this problem. Can you find them all? Problem 6
Mystery Number 0. ___ ___ ___ Problem 6	Mystery Number 0. ___ ___ ___ ___ Problem 7

Clue

? ? ? ?

The digit in the tenths place is odd.

Problem 7

Mystery Number

___ ___ ___ . ___ ___

Problem 8

Clue

The digit in the ten thousandths place is the sum of the digits in the tenths, hundredths, and thousandths place.

Problem 7

Clue

The digits in the tens and tenths places are the same, odd digit.

Problem 8

Clue

The number has no repeated digits.

Problem 7

Clue

The digit in the ones place is the sum of the digits in the hundreds, tens, tenths, and hundredths place.

Problem 8

Clue

The digit in the ten thousandths place is 3 times the digit in the tenths place.

Problem 7

Clue

The digit in the hundreds place is 2 times the digit in the tens place.

Problem 8

Clue

The digit in the hundredths place is a multiple of the digit in the tenths place.

Problem 7

Clue

The digits to the right of the decimal point are consecutive (like 3 and 4 or 8 and 9).

Problem 8

Clue

All of the digits are greater than 1, except for the digit in the thousandths place.

Problem 7

Clue

The digits in the hundreds and hundredths places are the same, even digits.

Problem 8

Clue

The digit in the ones place is 5 more than the digit in the tenths place.

Problem 8

Clue

The digit in the hundreds place has consecutive factors whose sum equals the digit in the thousands place.

Problem 9

Mystery Number

— — , — — — . — — —

Problem 9

Mystery Number

— — , — — — . — — — —

Problem 10

Clue

The number has no repeated digits.

Problem 9

Clue

None of the odd digits repeats.

Problem 10

Clue

The digit in the hundreds place is 1 more than the digit in the thousands place.

Problem 9

Clue

The digits in the ten thousands, thousands, and tenths places are the same.

Problem 10

Clue

The digits in the tens, ones, hundredths, and thousandths places are in order, beginning with 1 in the tens place.

Problem 9

Clue

The hundreds digit is 1 more than the thousands digit.

Problem 10

Clue

The sum of the digits in the tens and tenths places is 1.

Problem 9

Clue

The digit in the ten thousandths place is the sum of the digits in the thousands and ten thousands places.

Problem 10

Clue

The digit in the hundred thousandths place is the sum of the digits in the tenths and hundredths places.

Problem 10

Clue

The part of the number to the right of the decimal has no repeated digits.

Problem 10

Clue

The only odd digits appear in the thousandths, hundreds, and ones places.

Problem 10

Clue

The digit in the ones place is the sum of the digits in the tens and hundreds places.

Problem 10

Clue

The digits in the tens and hundredths places are the same and are half of the digit in the tenths place.

Problem 10

Clue

The digits in the tenths and thousandths places have exactly 3 factors.

Problem 10

Grid Paper

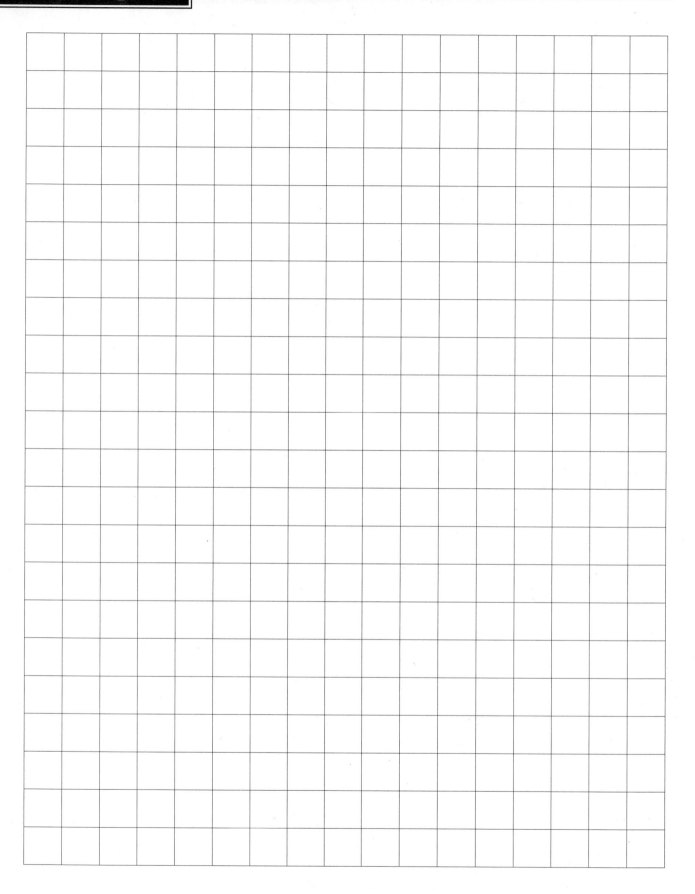

Additional Practice

Investigation 1

1. **a.** For each of the fraction strips below, write a fraction that expresses how much of the strip is shaded.

    i.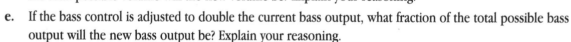

    ii.

    iii.

    iv.

    v.

    vi.

    b. For each of the six fraction strips above, write a fraction that expresses how much of the strip is *not* shaded.

    c. What is the relationship between the fraction you wrote for the shaded part and the fraction you wrote for the unshaded part for each of the six fraction strips?

2. The drawing below shows the controls on a portable stereo system. Use the drawing to answer the following questions. Record all of your answers as fractions.

    a. At what fraction of the total possible volume is the stereo playing?

    b. At what fraction of the total possible bass output is the stereo playing?

    c. At what fraction of the total possible treble output is the stereo playing?

    d. If the volume is turned down to half the current volume, what fraction of the total possible volume will the new volume be? Explain your reasoning.

    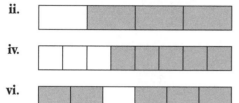

    e. If the bass control is adjusted to double the current bass output, what fraction of the total possible bass output will the new bass output be? Explain your reasoning.

3. A bag contains 24 marbles (Note: You may want to use 24 cubes or chips to help you solve this problem).

    a. If 16 of the marbles are removed from the bag, what fraction of the marbles are left in the bag?

    b. Of the 16 marbles taken from the bag, one-fourth are put back in the bag. Now how many marbles are in the bag? Explain your reasoning.

    c. Based on your answer to part b, what fraction of the original 24 marbles are *not* in the bag?

4. Joey's father stops at the gas station to buy gas. His car has a 16-gallon tank, and the fuel gauge says that there is $\frac{3}{8}$ of a tank left. (Note: You may want to use 16 cubes or chips to help solve this problem.)

    a. How many gallons of gas are left in the tank?

    b. If Joey's father buys 6 gallons of gas, what fraction of the tank will be full?

    c. Based on your answer to part b, what fraction of the gas tank is empty after Joey's father puts 6 gallons of gas in the tank?

Investigation 2

1. Use the fraction strips below to compare each pair of fractions. Insert a less-than symbol (<), a greater-than symbol (>), or an equals symbol (=) between the fractions to make a true statement.

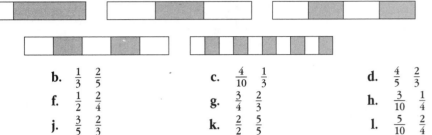

   a. $\frac{1}{2}$ $\frac{5}{10}$ b. $\frac{1}{3}$ $\frac{2}{5}$ c. $\frac{4}{10}$ $\frac{1}{3}$ d. $\frac{4}{5}$ $\frac{2}{3}$

   e. $\frac{3}{4}$ $\frac{8}{10}$ f. $\frac{1}{2}$ $\frac{2}{4}$ g. $\frac{3}{4}$ $\frac{2}{3}$ h. $\frac{3}{10}$ $\frac{1}{4}$

   i. $\frac{8}{10}$ $\frac{4}{5}$ j. $\frac{3}{5}$ $\frac{2}{3}$ k. $\frac{2}{2}$ $\frac{5}{5}$ l. $\frac{5}{10}$ $\frac{2}{4}$

2. For each group of fractions, rewrite the fractions in order from least to greatest.

   a. $\frac{2}{3}, \frac{1}{2}, \frac{3}{4}, \frac{2}{6}$ b. $\frac{24}{4}, \frac{1}{3}, \frac{11}{12}, \frac{1}{7}$ c. $\frac{1}{2}, \frac{1}{5}, \frac{1}{3}, \frac{1}{9}, \frac{1}{6}$ d. $\frac{11}{16}, \frac{3}{4}, \frac{3}{8}, \frac{1}{2}, \frac{3}{16}$

3. For each of the six fraction strips below, write two fractions that express the portion of the strip that is shaded.

   a.   b.

   c.   d.

   e.   f.

4. a. Write a fraction that is greater than $\frac{1}{2}$ and less than $\frac{3}{4}$.

   b. Write a fraction that is greater than $\frac{1}{4}$ and less than $\frac{1}{2}$.

   c. Find two other names for each of the fractions you wrote in parts a and b.

5. a. For each pair of fractions, insert a less-than symbol (<), a greater-than symbol (>), or an equals symbol (=) between the fractions to make a true statement.

      i. $\frac{2}{3}$ $\frac{2}{5}$ ii. $\frac{4}{6}$ $\frac{4}{5}$ iii. $\frac{3}{4}$ $\frac{3}{8}$

   b. Describe a way to compare two fractions whose numerators are the same.

6. a. For each pair of fractions, insert a less-than symbol (<), a greater-than symbol (>), or an equals symbol (=) between the fractions to make a true statement.

      i. $\frac{2}{5}$ $\frac{4}{5}$ ii. $\frac{4}{9}$ $\frac{7}{9}$ iii. $\frac{5}{11}$ $\frac{3}{11}$

   b. Describe a way to compare two fractions whose denominators are the same.

7. a. Write a fraction that is greater than $1\frac{1}{2}$ and less than 2.

   b. Write a fraction that is less than the fraction you wrote for part a and greater than 1.

   c. Compare each of the fractions you wrote in parts a and b with the fraction $1\frac{3}{4}$. Express each comparison using a less-than symbol (<), a greater-than symbol (>), or an equals symbol (=).

Investigation 3

1. For each shape below, write a fraction to express the portion of the entire shape that is shaded.

   a. 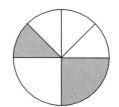   b. 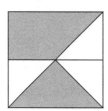   c. 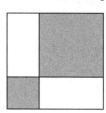   d.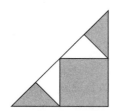

2. Tony is driving from Alma, Michigan, to Elizabeth City, North Carolina. The drive covers a total distance of 1100 miles. Tony's car can travel 400 miles on a tank of gas. How many tanks of gas will Tony's car need for the entire trip? Explain your reasoning.

3. For each of the following problems, trace the grids on your paper, and then shade each grid to represent the given fraction.

   a. Represent the fraction $\frac{4}{5}$ on each grid:

         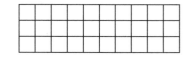

   b. Represent the fraction $\frac{3}{7}$ on each grid:

   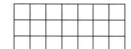   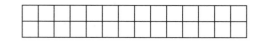

   c. Represent the fraction $\frac{1}{6}$ on each grid:

   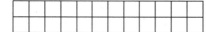   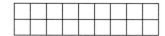

Investigation 4

1. Use the grid to answer each of the following questions. Write each answer in both decimal and fraction form.

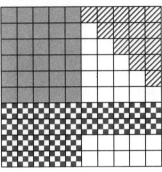

    a. What portion of the grid is grey?

    b. What portion of the grid is striped?

    c. What portion of the grid is checkered?

    d. What portion of the grid is blank?

2. Chris has 70 cents in his pocket and Kristy has three-fourths of a dollar. Who has more change, Chris or Kristy? Explain your reasoning.

3. Helen has three quarters and five dimes in her pocket.

    a. What fraction of a dollar does Helen have? Explain your reasoning.

    b. Write your answer to part a in decimal form.

4. Insert a less-than symbol (<), a greater-than symbol (>), or an equals symbol (=) between each pair of numbers to make a true statement.

    a. $2.5 \quad 2\frac{2}{5}$ b. $0.65 \quad \frac{2}{3}$ c. $0.8 \quad \frac{4}{5}$

    d. $0.625 \quad \frac{5}{8}$ e. $0.3 \quad \frac{3}{7}$ f. $2.1 \quad 1\frac{9}{10}$

    g. $\frac{11}{12} \quad \frac{11}{11}$ h. $\frac{3}{6} \quad 0.5$ i. $9 \quad 8\frac{8}{10}$

Investigation 5

1. Name three fractions that are equivalent to each decimal below. Explain your reasoning. Draw a picture if it helps you explain your thinking.

   a. 0.60   b. 1.7   c. 0.05

   d. 2.3   e. 0.15   f. 0.625

2. Name a decimal that is equivalent to each fraction below. Explain your reasoning. Draw a picture if it helps you explain your thinking.

   a. $\frac{1}{2}$ b. $\frac{3}{15}$ c. $\frac{7}{4}$

   d. $\frac{3}{8}$ e. $\frac{111}{20}$ f. $\frac{18}{24}$

3. Sarah can jog at a steady pace of 4.75 miles per hour, and Tony can jog at a steady pace of 4.25 miles per hour.

   a. How many miles can Sarah jog in 30 minutes? Explain your reasoning.

   b. How many miles can Tony jog in 30 minutes?

   c. If Sarah and Tony jog for 45 minutes, how much farther will Sarah go than Tony? Explain your reasoning.

4. Each small square on the grid represents $\frac{1}{5}$.

   a. What whole number is represented by the whole grid?

   b. What decimal is represented by the shaded region of the grid?

5. Each small square on the grid represents 0.25.

   a. What whole number is represented by the whole grid?

   b. What fraction is represented by the shaded region of the grid?

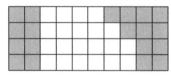

6. Paul claims that the fraction $\frac{1}{3}$ is a good estimate for the decimal 0.3.

   a. Do you agree or disagree with Paul's claim? Explain your reasoning.

   b. Is Paul's estimate less than, greater than, or equal to 0.3? Explain your reasoning.

7a. In the English system of measurement, a mile is equal to 5280 feet. A furlong is equal to one-eighth of a mile. How many feet are in a furlong? Explain your reasoning.

   b. A hand is an English system unit equal to 4 inches. How many hands are in $1\frac{1}{3}$ feet? Explain your reasoning.

Investigation 6

1. For each of the grids below, express the area of the shaded region as a fraction, a decimal, and a percent of the whole grid.

    a.   b.   c.

    d.   e.   f.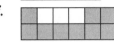

2. Angie and Jim conducted a survey of the students in their mathematics class. They found the following information:
    - 70% of the students in the class do homework three or more nights each week.
    - Of the students who do homework three or more nights each week, half do homework five nights each week.

    a. What percent of the students do homework two nights or less each week? Explain your reasoning.

    b. What fraction of the students do homework five nights each week? Explain your reasoning.

    c. What percent of students in the class do homework three or four nights a week?

    d. From the information provided, can you tell how many students are the class? Explain why or why not.

3. In a class of 24 sixth-graders, 25% walk to school, $\frac{1}{8}$ ride bicycles to school, $\frac{1}{3}$ take the bus, and the remainder commute by car.

    a. How many students in the class walk to school? Explain your reasoning.

    b. How many students in the class ride bicycles to school? Explain your reasoning.

    c. How many students in the class take the school bus?

    d. What fraction of the class commute by car? Explain your reasoning.

    e. What percent of the students in the class walk, ride bicycles, take the bus, or come by car? Explain your reasoning.

4. Express the area of the shaded region of each drawing as a fraction, a decimal, and a percent of the whole drawing.

    a. 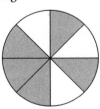   b. 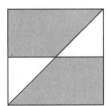   c.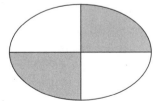

    d.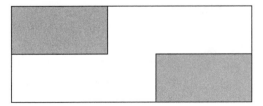

Answer Keys

Investigation 1

1. a. i. $\frac{5}{12}$ ii. $\frac{3}{4}$ iii. $\frac{1}{3}$

    iv. $\frac{5}{8}$ v. $\frac{11}{12}$ vi. $\frac{5}{6}$

    b. i. $\frac{7}{12}$ ii. $\frac{1}{4}$ iii. $\frac{2}{3}$

    iv. $\frac{3}{8}$ v. $\frac{1}{12}$ vi. $\frac{1}{6}$

    c. The sum of the fractions is 1 in each case.

2. a. $\frac{1}{2}$ b. $\frac{3}{8}$ c. $\frac{3}{4}$

    d. $\frac{1}{4}$; half of $\frac{1}{2}$ is $\frac{1}{4}$.   e. $\frac{3}{4}$; twice $\frac{3}{8}$ is $\frac{6}{8} = \frac{3}{4}$.

3. a. $\frac{1}{3}$ b. 12   c. $\frac{12}{24} = \frac{1}{2}$

4. a. 6   b. $\frac{3}{4}$ c. $\frac{1}{4}$

Investigation 2

1. a. $\frac{1}{2} = \frac{5}{10}$ b. $\frac{1}{3} < \frac{2}{5}$ c. $\frac{4}{10} > \frac{1}{3}$ d. $\frac{4}{5} > \frac{2}{3}$

    e. $\frac{3}{4} < \frac{8}{10}$ f. $\frac{1}{2} = \frac{2}{4}$ g. $\frac{3}{4} > \frac{2}{3}$ h. $\frac{3}{10} > \frac{1}{4}$

    i. $\frac{8}{10} = \frac{4}{5}$ j. $\frac{3}{5} < \frac{2}{3}$ k. $\frac{2}{2} = \frac{5}{5}$ l. $\frac{5}{10} = \frac{2}{4}$

2. a. $\frac{2}{6} < \frac{1}{2} < \frac{2}{3} < \frac{3}{4}$ b. $\frac{1}{7} < \frac{1}{3} < \frac{11}{12} < \frac{24}{4}$ c. $\frac{1}{9} < \frac{1}{6} < \frac{1}{5} < \frac{1}{3} < \frac{1}{2}$ d. $\frac{3}{16} < \frac{3}{8} < \frac{1}{2} < \frac{11}{16} < \frac{3}{4}$

3. Students' answers will vary. Any fraction equivalent to these sample responses is correct.

    a. $\frac{1}{3} = \frac{2}{6}$ b. $\frac{3}{5} = \frac{6}{10}$ c. $\frac{7}{8} = \frac{14}{16}$

    d. $\frac{3}{4} = \frac{6}{8}$ e. $\frac{3}{6} = \frac{1}{2}$ f. $\frac{9}{10} = \frac{18}{20}$

4. a. Possible answers: $\frac{2}{3}$ and $\frac{3}{5}$

    b. Possible answers: $\frac{1}{3}$ and $\frac{2}{5}$

    c. Answers will vary, but the answers must be equivalent fractions.

5. a. i. $\frac{2}{3} > \frac{2}{5}$ ii. $\frac{4}{6} < \frac{4}{5}$ iii. $\frac{3}{4} > \frac{3}{8}$

    b. When the numerators are the same, consider the denominators. The larger denominator means the whole is divided in more pieces and each piece is smaller than the pieces of the whole for the smaller denominator. Thus, the fraction with the smaller denominator is the larger fraction.

6. a. i. $\frac{2}{5} < \frac{4}{5}$ ii. $\frac{4}{9} < \frac{7}{9}$ iii. $\frac{5}{11} > \frac{3}{11}$

    b. When the denominators are the same, the fraction with the larger numerator is greater because it represents more of the same size pieces.

7. a. Answers will vary.   b. Answers will vary.   c. Answers will vary.

Answer Keys

Investigation 3

1. **a.** $\frac{3}{8}$ **b.** $\frac{5}{8}$ **c.** $\frac{5}{9}$ **d.** $\frac{3}{4}$

2. $2\frac{3}{4}$ tanks of gas will be needed for the trip.

3. **a.** Shade 8, 16, and 24 squares, respectively, on the three grids.

   b. Shade 9 and 12 squares, respectively, on the two grids.

   c. Shade 4 and 3 squares, respectively, on the two grids.

Investigation 4

1. **a.** 0.3 or $\frac{3}{10}$ **b.** 0.15 or $\frac{3}{20}$ **c.** 0.3 or $\frac{3}{10}$ **d.** 0.25 or $\frac{1}{4}$

2. $\frac{3}{4}$ of one dollar is 75 cents, so Kristy has more change.

3. **a.** $\frac{5}{4}$ **b.** 1.25

4. **a.** $2.5 > 2\frac{2}{5}$ **b.** $0.65 < \frac{2}{3}$ **c.** $0.8 = \frac{4}{5}$

   d. $0.625 = \frac{5}{8}$ **e.** $0.3 < \frac{3}{7}$ **f.** $2.1 > 1\frac{9}{10}$

   g. $\frac{11}{12} < \frac{11}{11}$ **h.** $\frac{3}{6} = 0.5$ **i.** $9 > 8\frac{8}{10}$

Investigation 5

1. Answers will vary. All fractions equivalent to the sample responses are correct.

   a. $\frac{6}{10} = \frac{3}{5} = \frac{9}{15}$ **b.** $1\frac{7}{10} = 1\frac{14}{20} = 1\frac{21}{30}$ **c.** $\frac{5}{100} = \frac{1}{20} = \frac{10}{200}$

   d. $2\frac{3}{10} = 2\frac{6}{20} = 2\frac{12}{40}$ **e.** $\frac{15}{100} = \frac{3}{20} = \frac{30}{200}$ **f.** $\frac{5}{8} = \frac{10}{16} = \frac{15}{24}$

2. **a.** 0.5   **b.** 0.2   **c.** 1.75

   d. 0.375   **e.** 5.55   **f.** 0.75

3. **a.** $2\frac{3}{8} = 2.375$ miles   **b.** $2\frac{1}{8} = 2.125$ miles   **c.** $\frac{3}{8}$ or 0.375 mile.

4. **a.** 4   **b.** 2.6

5. **a.** 10   **b.** 4.75

6. **a.** Possible answer: I agree because $0.3 = \frac{3}{10}$ is close to $\frac{1}{3} = \frac{3}{9}$.

   b. Paul's estimate is greater than 0.3 because $\frac{1}{3}$ is about 0.33, and 0.33 > 0.3.

7. **a.** $\frac{5280}{8} = 660$ feet   **b.** $1\frac{1}{3}$ feet = 16 inches; $\frac{16}{4} = 4$ hands

Investigation 6

1. a. $\frac{2}{5} = 0.4 = 40\%$ b. $\frac{11}{20} = 0.55 = 55\%$ c. $\frac{9}{25} = 0.36 = 36\%$

    d. $\frac{3}{8} = 0.375 = 37.5\%$ e. $\frac{1}{2} = 0.5 = 50\%$ f. $\frac{3}{4} = 0.75 = 75\%$

2. a. 30%   b. Half of 70% = 35% = $\frac{35}{100} = \frac{7}{20}$ of the class does homework 5 nights each week.

    c. 35%   d. No, because fractions are comparisons, not exact quantities.

3. a. 6   b. 3   c. 8   d. $\frac{7}{24}$

    e. 100%, because each student takes one of the four means of getting to school.

4. a. $\frac{5}{8} = 0.625 = 62.5\%$ b. $\frac{3}{4} = 0.75 = 75\%$ c. $\frac{1}{2} = 0.5 = 50\%$ d. $\frac{2}{5} = 0.4 = 40\%$

base ten number system The common number system we use. Our number system is based on the number 10 because we have ten fingers with which to group. With the common understanding that each group represents ten of the previous groups, we can write numbers efficiently. By extending the place-value system to include places that represent fractions with 10 or powers of 10 in the denominator, we can easily represent very large and very small quantities. Below is a graphic representation of counting in the base ten number system.

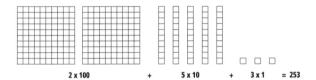

2×100 + 5×10 + 3×1 $= 253$

benchmark A "nice" number that can be used to estimate the size of other numbers. For work with fractions, 0, $\frac{1}{2}$, and 1 are good benchmarks. We often estimate fractions or decimals with benchmarks because it is easier to do arithmetic with them, and estimates often give enough accuracy for the situation. For example, many fractions and decimals—such as $\frac{37}{50}$, $\frac{5}{8}$, 0.43, and 0.55—can be thought of as being close to $\frac{1}{2}$. You might say $\frac{5}{8}$ is between $\frac{1}{2}$ and 1 but closer to $\frac{1}{2}$, so you can estimate $\frac{5}{8}$ to be about $\frac{1}{2}$. We also use benchmarks to help compare fractions. For example, we could say that $\frac{5}{8}$ is larger than 0.43 because $\frac{5}{8}$ is larger than $\frac{1}{2}$ and 0.43 is smaller than $\frac{1}{2}$.

decimal A special form of a fraction. Decimals, or decimal fractions, are based on the base ten place-value system. To write numbers as decimals, we use only 10 and powers of 10 as denominators. Writing fractions in this way saves us from writing the denominators because they are understood. When we write $\frac{375}{1000}$ as a decimal—0.375—the denominator of 1000 is understood. The digits to

the left of the decimal point show whole units, and the digits to the right of the decimal point show a portions of a whole unit. The diagram below shows the place value for each digit of the number 5620.301.

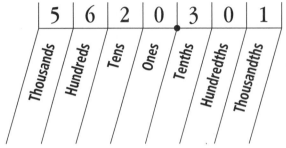

denominator The number written below the line in a fraction. In the fraction $\frac{3}{4}$, 4 is the denominator. In the part-whole interpretation of fractions, the denominator shows the number of equal-size parts into which the whole has been split.

equivalent fractions Fractions that are equal in value but have different numerators and denominators. For example, $\frac{2}{3}$ and $\frac{14}{21}$ are equivalent fractions. The shaded part of this rectangle represents both $\frac{2}{3}$ and $\frac{14}{21}$.

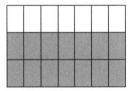

fraction A number (quantity) of the form $\frac{a}{b}$ where a and b are whole numbers. A fraction can indicate a part of a whole object or set, a ratio of two quantities, or a division. For the picture below, the fraction $\frac{3}{4}$ shows the part of the rectangle that is shaded: the denominator indicates the number of equal-size pieces, and the numerator indicates the number of pieces that are shaded.

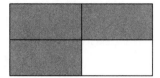

The fraction $\frac{3}{4}$ could also represent three of a group of four items meeting a particular criteria; the ratio 3 to 4 (for example, when 12 students enjoyed a particular activity and 16 students did not); or the amount of pizza each person receives when three pizzas are shared equally among four people, which would be $3 \div 4$ or $\frac{3}{4}$ of a pizza.

numerator The number written above the line in a fraction. In the fraction $\frac{5}{8}$, 5 is the numerator. When you interpret the fraction $\frac{5}{8}$ as a part of a whole, the numerator 5 tells that the fraction refers to 5 of 8 equal parts.

percent "Out of 100." A percent is a special decimal fraction in which the denominator is 100. When we write 68%, we mean 68 out of 100, $\frac{68}{100}$, or 0.68. We write the percent sign (%) after a number to indicate percent. (Some say that the percent sign % is what was left after people were writing a denominator of 100 many times and got sloppy.) The shaded part of this square is 68%.

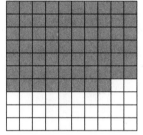

unit fraction A fraction with a numerator of 1. For example, in the unit fraction $\frac{1}{13}$, the part-whole interpretation of fractions tells us that the whole has been split into 13 equal-size parts and that the fraction represents 1 of those parts.

Index

Time
Passages

AMERICAN CULTURE

Edited by Stanley Aronowitz, Sandra M. Gilbert, and George Lipsitz

George Lipsitz

Time
Passages

Collective Memory and American Popular Culture

University of Minnesota Press • Minneapolis

Part or all of the following articles have been reprinted in this book with
permission: "This Ain't No Sideshow: Historians and Media Studies," from *Critical
Studies in Mass Communication*, v. 5, n. 2 (June) 1988. Reprinted by permission of
the Speech Communication Association. "The Meaning of Memory: Family, Class,
and Ethnicity in Early Network Television Programs," reproduced by permission of
the American Anthropological Association from *Cultural Anthropology* 1:4, 1986.
"Against the Wind: The Class Composition of Rock and Roll Music," from
Knowledge and Society, v. 5 (1985), JAI Press Inc., Greenwich, Connecticut.
"Cruising Around the Historical Bloc: Postmodernism and Popular Music in East
Los Angeles," from *Cultural Critique*, n. 5 (1986). "Mardi Gras Indians: Carnival
and Counter-Narrative in Black New Orleans," from *Cultural Critique*, n. 10 (1988).
"Myth, History, and Counter-Memory," from Adam Sorkin, ed., *Politics and the
Muse: Studies in the Politics of Recent American Literature*. 1989, Bowling Green
State University Popular Press. "Land of a Thousand Dances: Youth, Minorities, and
the Rise of Rock and Roll," from Lary May, ed., *Recasting America*. University of
Chicago Press, 1989.

Cover photo of Mardi Gras Indians courtesy of Gayle Plummer.

Published by the University of Minnesota Press
2037 University Avenue Southeast, Minneapolis, MN 55414.
Printed in the United States of America.

Library of Congress Cataloging-in-Publication Data

Lipsitz, George.
    Time passages : collective memory and American popular culture /
George Lipsitz.
        p.   cm. — (American culture)
    Includes bibliographical references.
    ISBN 0-8166-1805-4
    ISBN 0-8166-1806-2 (pbk.)
    1. United States—Popular culture—History—20th century.   2. Mass
media—United States—Social aspects.   3. Memory—Social aspects—
United States—History—20th century.   I. Title.   II. Series :
American culture (Minneapolis, Minnesota)
E169.12.L55   1990   89-5209
973.9—dc20   CIP

Contents

Contents

Preface

This is a book about collective memory and popular culture in the United States since 1945. It does not survey or analyze the aesthetics of popular culture itself, nor does it chronicle direct references to "historical" issues within popular culture texts. Rather, I wish to explore the ways in which collective memory and popular culture are peculiarly linked — how the infinitely renewable present of electronic mass media creates a crisis for collective memory, and how collective memory decisively frames the production and reception of commercial culture. This is not an uncritical celebration of mass-mediated imagery. I believe that the ever expanding influence, reach, and scope of the mass media has worked insidiously to legitimate exploitative social hierarchies, to colonize the body as a site of capital accumulation, and to inculcate within us the idea that consumer desire is the logical center of human existence. But neither is this a jeremiad against popular culture and the individuals who create and receive it. People act in the arenas open to them; there is nothing intrinsically better or worse about the generation and circulation of ideas through electronic mass media than through the printed word. Our time has more than its share of barbarism, but that barbarism is more the product of very old patterns of social organization than it is the product of new communications technology. New technologies do lend themselves to new forms of exploitation and oppression, but they also have possible uses for fundamentally new forms of resistance and revolution.

In the first section of this book I present discussions of history and popular culture. My intention is to show how forms of popular culture emerging over the past two centuries have helped make a crisis of historical memory the constitutive problem of our time. Rather than signaling the death knell for historical inquiry, electronic mass media make collective memory a crucial constituent of individual and group identity in the modern world. In section two I examine the relationship between commercial network television and popular memory, first by examining the "meaning of memory" in a series of early network programs on American commercial television in the 1950s, and second by exploring the dynamics of remembering and forgetting surrounding one representative show of that era, *Mama*. In section three I turn my attention to popular music, starting with a general inquiry into the "dialogic" nature of rock-and-roll music, and then concluding with a detailed case study about the relationship between past and present in rock music made by Mexican-Americans in Los Angeles since World War II. Section four outlines an approach to motion pictures and collective memory, emphasizing the ways in which Hollywood films do more to reveal social contradictions than to provide political solutions to them. I conclude section four with a detailed examination of two Hollywood auteurs, Samuel Fuller and Edgar Ulmer, for whom questions of past, present, and future offered a guiding aesthetic and a recurrent source of dramatic tension. In section five I turn my inquiry to popular narrative, first examining the sense of "counter-memory" pervading novels by women and "minority" authors, and then exploring the "open closures" of a subcultural oppositional narrative, that of the Mardi Gras Indians in New Orleans. Finally in "Buscando America" (looking for America), I try to survey the cumulative effects of the struggle for collective memory within popular culture over the past five decades.

This ordered framework obscures the tortuous struggle that brought this book into existence. A conceptual revolution in the humanities and social sciences has given new vigor to inquiries about cultural studies in a variety of fields over the past twenty years, but that ongoing revolution leaves investigators with no stable ground on which to stand. A dizzying succession of new methods and theories has shattered traditional disciplinary paradigms, forcing scholars to engage in bold departures from their own training, to become "specialists" in fields with few acknowledged experts and few firm standards of evidence and argument. My own inquiries have often left me between fields—too historical for the sociologists, too socio-

logical for the linguists, and too linguistic and too sociological for the
historians. Under those circumstances, speaking to readers and audiences outside of academic circles becomes even more difficult, because one must explain or at least neutralize the special vocabularies
and concerns of many disciplines, not just one. But this book is not a
product of some abstract revolution in scholarly methods; rather, it is
a manifestation of the more general social crisis that brought that
scholarly revolution into being in the first place. That social crisis is
not something I learned about solely in libraries and classrooms; it
has been the determinant experience of my life, and I would not be
telling the whole truth about this book if I failed to relate it to the
personal life struggles of which it is a part.

Over the past ten years I have been teaching American history and
culture courses in colleges under conditions that have demanded a
series of detours. I went to school in the politically charged 1960s
and 1970s, and made myself the kind of teacher I wished that I had
encountered in those years. But when I started to teach, I faced students who came of age in more quiescent and apolitical environments. My graduate research focused on labor history at precisely the
time when deindustrialization and political reaction devastated the
constituencies most interested in that subject. My deepest personal
and professional commitments connected me to scholarship and social change at a moment when anti-intellectualism and materialism
dominated American culture and politics. In my teaching and writing, I too often seemed to be delivering the wrong message to the
wrong audience at the wrong time.

My career and professional development took place in the context
of extraordinary changes in American society. The painful after-
shocks of the Vietnam War, the startling misuses of power revealed
by the Watergate investigations, and the deindustrialization of the
American economy added elements of uncertainty and instability to
the lives of all Americans in the 1970s. I found myself facing some of
the contrasts of that era directly. The economic crises engendered by
deindustrialization wreaked havoc on American higher education in
those years; I moved from St. Louis to Houston to Minneapolis in
pursuit of secure employment. In St. Louis, I rode to work everyday
on the City Limits bus through a devastated inner-city ghetto, and at
the University of Missouri-St. Louis I taught working-class students
who were afraid that for the first time in generations higher educa-

tion would not result in upward mobility. In Houston, I routinely saw homeless people scavenging food from garbage bins as I drove off to teach at a campus in the middle of one of the most affluent suburban areas in the country. In Minneapolis, my students directed my attention to the ways in which the concurrent demise of blue-collar manufacturing jobs and the family farm undercut the political, moral, and economic foundations of their lives. Through all of this turmoil, my students and I attempted to study "American culture" from books that, for the most part, treated America as a secure stable repository of timeless truths.

Popular culture texts provided me with one means of understanding and enduring the circumstances I found myself in. Popular music and films seemed to resonate with the tensions of the time in a way that more formal academic texts did not. Even older works of popular culture seemed to speak to my personal crises and anxieties in important ways. For example, in the 1958 film "Wind Across the Everglades," Burl Ives advises Christopher Plummer that "sometimes the long way around is the shortest way through." In the context of that motion picture, Ives's counsel concerns the best way to cross a swamp, but his phrase also encapsulates the devotion to detour characteristic of the film's director, Nicholas Ray. For Ray, film making itself was the long way around, an ostensibly escapist medium that afforded him an opportunity for serious social criticism. A one-time architecture student at the University of Chicago and a former director for John Houseman's Group Theatre, Ray made his mark on the world in Hollywood as the creative force behind such eminently commercial ventures as *They Live by Night* (1949), *Johnny Guitar* (1954), and *Rebel without a Cause* (1955). A disillusioned 1930s radical working in 1950s Hollywood, Ray found no easy venue for expressing the political and social views closest to his heart. But denied "the shortest way through," he took "the long way around," negotiating the swampy ground of commercial culture by injecting subtle critiques of capitalism, McCarthyism, and suburbanization into "escapist" films. I feel a deep affinity for Nicholas Ray's work, in part because I know what it is like to take the long way around. For me, too, popular culture has been a way of expressing indirectly values and beliefs about which I had no direct means of expression.

I have spent the better part of a decade struggling to remain in the profession and to keep my voice alive. I do not want this to sound like whining. I know that I was better off than most: better off than my fellow graduate students who never got jobs, better off than my colleagues who got fired through no fault of their own when enrollments declined, and certainly better off than the urban underclass and dispossessed industrial workers who have suffered so brutally from the radical restructuring of American society in this age of neo-conservatism.

I know as well that my own choices had something to do with my difficult working conditions. I chose to write about the powerless rather than the powerful. I knew full well that the types of experiences and issues that I wished to chronicle would not bring grants from corporate foundations or rewards from politically timid college administrators. I knew that my work would make powerful enemies and that the friends it made would rarely have any resources with which to support it. In addition, I have to acknowledge that I sometimes created unnecessary difficulties for myself. Too often I was too proud to ask for help, too arrogant to understand that nearly everyone had something to teach me, and too frightened for my own future to see each petty battle along the way as anything other than a microcosm of the larger social crisis that had marginalized me and the people I cared about most. But I have to be honest. Attempting to teach and learn under these conditions has been excruciatingly painful. Nothing came easy, nothing came directly. Always there were the detours.

I taught colonial America and recent America, pre-industrial China and post-industrial Europe. My courses ranged from film theory to American slavery, from popular music and television to the European Enlightenment. Most of my students showed up in these courses by accident; they were pursuing degrees in other subjects and wound up in my classroom to fill a requirement or to fill an empty hour in their schedules. Some had come back to school in the mistaken belief that a degree would automatically entitle them to higher wages, while others found themselves in school because they had no jobs and nothing else to do with their time. They were a detour for me, but I was a detour for them too.

Yet sometimes, the long way around *is* the shortest way through. Everywhere I found more than a detour; I found people with something to teach me. My students ranged from prison inmates to Catholic nuns, from working-class evening school adults to young undergraduates at an exclusive women's college, from profoundly anti-intellectual technocrats seeking credentials in business to passionately committed graduate students with astounding gifts for intellectual work. Their knowledge was not always in the form I expected (and maybe not in the form I would have preferred), but it was real and compelling and significant. They came to me with stories in their heads—stories about their lives that exposed me to both the diversity and the unity of the American experience.

The stories my students told me resonated with the hurts of history. They exposed the unhealed wounds of decades of political turmoil and cultural change. They revealed the frustrations of Americans conditioned to expect happiness and security only to face disappointments and instability. Every area of human endeavor emerged as problematic in their stories—sexuality, romance, family, careers, race relations, ecology, and global politics all provoked uncertain and self-doubting stories. Sometimes their stories displayed a sadistic rage directed against groups identified as "others"—homosexuals, Iranians, Afro-Americans, intellectuals, and Asians. Sometimes their stories saw through that process of scapegoating and faced up to the hard facts about the American mainstream itself. But in all cases, these stories reflected the hurts of history.

Most compelling to me about the stories students brought to my classes was how sharply they differed from the dominant narrative then being fashioned within politics and popular culture. I began teaching at the end of the Carter presidency and the beginning of the Reagan years, a time when neo-conservatism clearly captured the dominant narrative about American culture. It was a time when Ronald Reagan's rhetoric turned the Vietnam War into America's "most heroic moment" rather than the "unjust and immoral war" that Dr. Martin Luther King, Jr. and others had described fifteen years earlier. It was a time when television programs like "Dallas," "Dynasty," and "Lifestyles of the Rich and Famous" stoked the fires of material desire, eclipsing the 1970s depictions of urban working-class life in "Kojak," "Good Times," and "All in the Family." It was a time when James Watt declared environmentalists the main threat to the environment while William Bradford Reynolds presented the preservation of white male rights as the main task of civil-rights law enforcement. Yet this dominant story was not what I heard from my students, even those whose political affiliations and career ambitions hinged on the success of the neo-conservative agenda.

Inside my classes and in discussions with students outside of them, I came to see that the dominant neo-conservative narrative of the 1980s conflicted with the experiences and memories of even those Americans who desperately wanted neo-conservatism to succeed. The Vietnam War caused too much pain to be reframed as a singularly heroic moment; such a story immediately summoned up its opposite—the collective recollection of the division and disillusion engendered by the war's terrible destruction of American and Vietnamese lives. In the context of the worst depression in America in forty years, glittering displays of wealth on television programs raised anxieties about the morality of the rich and the fate of the poor. The consciousnesses raised by the 1960s struggles for equality could not easily accept the protection of white male privilege as America's most important civil-rights task, especially given the context of the consequences of economic deindustrialization for female and ethnic minority wage earners and their children. Even those students who clearly benefited from the neo-conservatism of the 1970s and 1980s expressed deep doubts about the emerging world and their place in it.

But if my students would not buy the dominant narrative, neither did they accept the oppositional narratives one might have expected them to embrace. My students were not right-wing, they were not left-wing. They believed deeply in their own powerlessness. They never objected to my left-wing politics; what troubled them was that I had any politics at all, that I seemed to believe that humans operated out of any but the basest self-centered motivations. Their cynicism made them intensely critical of the dominant narratives, but left them unwilling to fashion alternatives, at least in discussions about politics and economics. But popular culture texts provoked a different response from them. They identified with television programs, films, and popular music in a way that they would not even consider about politics. These texts unleashed the memories and experiences suppressed by the dominant rhetoric of their private and public lives. Here hope was still an issue, and happiness was still possible. The gap between dominant political rhetoric and their lived experiences left them with enormous tensions and anxieties with no outlet for expression save in their responses to popular culture texts. Here was a sphere they saw as their own, a presentation of choices about the world that mattered to them, and in discussing these texts they brought forth the full passion and anger and hope that they repressed elsewhere. For them, too, the long way around was the shortest way through: a detour was the way to confront emotions very close to home.

As my students and I used popular culture texts from the past to gain insight into the complex stories defining our present identities, we found terrains of conflict and struggle in the most unexpected places and allies in the most improbable individuals. Not because these films, songs, and shows reflected our lives directly, but, rather, because they reflected the core contradictions of our lives indirectly enough to make discussion of them bearable.

It was not that any of these texts told our stories directly; rather, they enabled us to see the resemblances between our own stories and those of others, calling ever more attention to the structural unities that underlay seemingly diverse experiences. For example, the film *Flaming Star* (1960) featuring Elvis Presley as a young (and blue-eyed) American Indian growing up in a mixed-white and Indian family on the 1870s Texas frontier provoked a vigorous discussion. An older Chicano male remembered the film as a favorite in his neighborhood when it first came out because it detailed the anguish of having an ethnic identity that left one caught in the middle between warring ethnic groups. A middle-class housewife read the inter-racial family in the film as the kind of Aquarian voluntary community that the hippie communes of the 1960s tried to build. A working-class white woman identified with Presley himself and his character as an emblem of upward mobility for her class, a sign of the right to dream of something better in the face of all the rejections and disappointments around her. A young black male found the justifications of Indian resistance in the film as evocative of the black militant rhetoric he had grown up with in the 1960s. A radical lesbian viewed Presley as an androgynous image, a heroic subject that was neither completely male nor female, but that enabled one to choose the best of both identities. A young Chinese-American woman felt that the film demonstrated the immutable power of American racism and its determination to destroy any identities that do not fit the dominant image. A middle-class male attorney found the film dangerously tragic in its obliviousness to women's wishes and its celebration of reckless male heroism. The plurality of views provoked by this text left no one correct reading, but, instead, provided a locus of meanings intersecting around the content of the film and the lived experiences of its viewers.

Discussions about popular culture in my classes always seemed to become discussions about the relationship between the past and the present in American life and culture. The stories on the screen clashed with dominant political and historical stories, and the stories my students and I told often clashed with each other. But the very diversity of these stories helped map out the contours of what we had and did not have in common, and taken collectively they explained a lot about the American past and present. Provoked by these discussions, I found myself increasingly investigating the concrete contexts of popular culture production and reception. These investigations caused me to reframe my understanding of the roles played by discourse and ideology in social change; they led me to rethink the labor and social history I had been trained to do, while they provided me with tools for inquiries for which I had no training. Everywhere I found others engaged in the same kinds of inquiries, both professionally and avocationally. Eventually I found myself part of a field, part of "cultural studies" in a variety of disciplines. I discovered colleagues in anthropology, literature, sociology, music, and speech communication whose experiences with their disciplines and with scholarship in the 1980s led them to projects similar to my own. Our enterprise is still fragile and always imperiled, but it has an institutional existence now that we would have thought impossible a decade ago. Whether we make appropriate use of this institutional space will depend in large measure upon our ability to keep faith with all the students and colleagues who led us to this kind of inquiry in the first place, on our success in relating media texts to the social crises in which they are produced and received.

Exploring any part of the American past has its built-in risks. No amount of contextualization can obscure the grim realities of slavery, conquest, and genocide; no amount of mythologizing the "American way" can erase how hard life has been on this continent for so many people. On the other hand, the hard facts about America are not the only facts, the perpetrators of American aggression are not the only Americans. I am quite prepared to say that the ruling elites in America have committed quiet and systematic crimes and that they have been supported in those crimes by many ordinary citizens. But I am unwilling to let the history of monopoly, imperialism, racism, and sexism stand for the totality of American experience. When one examines American culture, one inevitably finds all the hard facts, but one also sees the earnest longings and heroic struggles for something different that have characterized the American past. This book is not one of those exercises that finds only the debased and distorted in American history and culture. For all its crimes, this is too good a country, its cultures too rich and varied and inspiring to justify that kind of pessimism, a pessimism that masquerades as critique but which is so one-dimensional that it ultimately serves as a form of collaboration with the oppressors.

* * * * *

I cannot possibly acknowledge all of the individuals who have contributed so much to my understanding of the issues outlined in this book, but I would like to thank my mother, Paulette Lipsitz, for all the support she has given me, as well as for the moral vision that forms the core of her own world view. At the University of Missouri-St. Louis I received the benefit of wisdom and friendship from Neal Primm, George Rawick, Peter Fuss, Charles Korr, Dick Miller, Gary Burns, Beth Kizer, Linda Kulla, Neda Hardin, Deland Edwards, Gerald Hall, Sister Anita Louise Frantz, and Katharine Corbett.

At the University of Houston-Clear Lake I had the privilege of team teaching and sharing an office with Edward Hugetz, whose intellectual power and cultural vision have left an indelible mark on me. At that same institution I also had the benefit of counsel and criticism from many good friends including Mitchell Aboulafia, Barbara Ellman, Don and Jean Quataert, Sandy Gabin, Bruce Palmer, Curt Smith, and Debbie Arnold. At Mount Holyoke College I had the opportunity to learn from wonderful colleagues including Daniel Czitrom, Don Weber, Edward Royce, William McFeely, and Fi Herbert.

In the summer of 1984 I attended a National Endowment for the Humanities seminar about television studies conducted by Nick Browne at UCLA. That summer changed my life; it provided me with the tools for cultural analysis that have become essential to my scholarship. I will always feel grateful to Professor Browne and to members of that seminar including Robert Deming, Mary Beth Haralovich, Phil Lane, John Leo, Beverly O'Neill, and Tom Zynda. In 1985 I attended my first meeting of the International Association for the Study of Popular Music and wish to express my appreciation for all that I have learned within that organization, especially from Reebee Garofalo, Charles Keil, Leslie Roman, Cameron McCarthy, Francois Gougeon, David Horn, Herman Gray, Josee Destrempes, and Line Grenier.

Ever since I started work at the University of Minnesota in 1986, I have felt that I have been in the right place at the right time. One could not ask for better colleagues in cultural studies than Susan Mc-Clary, Richard Leppert, David W. Noble, Lary May, Elaine May, John Mowitt, Bruce Lincoln, Rey Chow, and Maria Damon. Nor could one ask for better students than Wendy Kozol, Rob Walser, Csaba Toth, Joe Austin, and Betty Bergland. I would also like to acknowledge the help and criticism I have received from scholars across the country including Janice Radway, Michael M. J. Fischer, Horace Newcomb, Dana Polan, Mari Jo Buhle, Paul Buhle, Stanley Aronowitz, Elizabeth Long, Tom Dumm, Brenda Bright, Sharon O'Brien, Adam Sorkin and Lynn Spigel. Barbara Tomlinson has been generous with her time as a critic and editor; my work always benefits from her help.

With so many debts to pay for this kind of work, it is difficult to single out any individuals from among the rest. But Aaron Neville, Johnny Otis, Billy Peek, and Irma Thomas have not only taught me indispensable truths about American culture, they have also enabled me to live with the consequences of those truths. With deep respect and admiration, this book is dedicated to each of them.

Culture and History

(Cincinnati, 1846)

1

Popular Culture: This Ain't No Sideshow

In this great future, you can't forget your past.
Bob Marley

The late jazz musician Rahsaan Roland Kirk used to preface his performances with an unusual word of advice for the audience. A burly black man who often wore a stovepipe hat with a feather in it, and who frequently carried two saxophones (which he sometimes played simultaneously), Kirk would peer out at the crowd through dark sunglasses and growl, "This ain't no sideshow." Invariably people would laugh at the incongruity of this consummately theatrical individual denying his theatricality. Yet once Kirk began to play, discerning listeners grasped his point.

There was a show going on when Roland Kirk played music, but it was not a sideshow. Nearly everything that Kirk did and said, nearly everything that he played and sang called attention to his role as a black musician in a society controlled by whites. With bitingly satiric renditions of hymns like "The Old Rugged Cross," Kirk related the forms and conventions of popular music to their origins within the historical struggles of the Afro-American past. With mischievous wordplay his song "Blacknuss" called attention to the unequal relationship between the black keys and the white keys on the piano. Kirk's attire and stage behavior subverted conventional expectations about performance, and his aggressive humor exposed the tension between music as a commodity and music as an expression of lived experience.

What distinguished Rahsaan Roland Kirk's "show" from a "sideshow" was history. All his eccentricities called attention to his identity as a historical subject, a descendant of slaves and a victim of white racism, a human being forced to disguise his pain and anger within the outward appearances of a sideshow. In songs like "The Old Rugged Cross" and "Blacknuss," Kirk translated his experiences and aspirations into art, just as his ancestors had done when they fashioned spirituals, blues, and jazz out of the clash between Afro-American values and Euro-American racism. His stage antics played against the expectations of the audience because they revealed a sedimented layer of historical knowledge and historical critique beneath the surface appearance of novelty and performance. Within the commercial context of commodified mass culture, Rahsaan Roland Kirk created a history that could be hummed, a story of the past that relied on sharps and flats instead of on footnotes, and one that testified to the historicity of experience even while avoiding the linearity and teleology generally associated with historical narratives.

The elements of historical inquiry and explanation encapsulated in Rahsaan Roland Kirk's stage performance present both possibilities and problems. They testify to the importance of historical thinking as an organic and necessary way of understanding human experience, a mode of organizing ideas and interpretations that is as indispensable in everyday life as it is in scholarly research. Yet its location within popular culture gives Kirk's "history" an impressionistic, interpretive, and allegorical aspect. His art contained multilayered and heavily coded covert messages about the past, but for a large part of his audience, Kirk's music inevitably appeared as just another novelty and diversion within the seemingly autonomous realms of commercialized leisure.

Kirk's problem is our problem. The powerful apparatuses of contemporary commercial electronic mass communications dominate discourse in the modern world. They supply us with endless diversion and distraction mobilized to direct our minds toward advertising messages. They colonize the most intimate and personal aspects of our lives, seizing upon every possible flaw in our bodies, minds, and psyches to increase our anxieties and augment our appetites for consumer goods. Culture itself comes to us as a commodity. The artistry and historical consciousness of a Rahsaan Roland Kirk becomes obscured by our contexts of reception. We buy records and attend concerts, watch films and television commercials as a matter of course. Rarely do we ask about the origins and intentions of the messages we encounter through the mass media; sometimes we forget that artists have origins or intentions at all, so pervasive are the stimuli around us.

Yet mass communications also embody some of our deepest hopes and engage some of our most profound sympathies. People ingeniously enter those discourses to which they have access; the saxophone or the guitar, the stage or the camera can offer precious and unique opportunities for expression. For some populations at some times, commercialized leisure is history—a repository of collective memory that places immediate experience in the context of change over time. The very same media that trivialize and distort culture, that turn art into commodities, and that obscure the origins and intentions of artists also provide meaningful connection to our own pasts and to the pasts of others. But they do so only indirectly, constrained by the nonlinear biases of the electronic media as well as by a commercial matrix hostile to the kinds of empathy, inquiry, and analysis basic to historical thinking.

The presence of sedimented historical currents within popular culture illumines the paradoxical relationship between history and commercialized leisure. Time, history, and memory become qualitatively different concepts in a world where electronic mass communication is possible. Instead of relating to the past through a shared sense of place or ancestry, consumers of electronic mass media can experience a common heritage with people they have never seen; they can acquire memories of a past to which they have no geographic or biological connection. This capacity of electronic mass communication to transcend time and space creates instability by disconnecting people from past traditions, but it also liberates people by making the past less determinate of experiences in the present.

History and commercialized leisure appear to be polar opposites—the former concerned with continuities that unite the totality of human experience, the latter with immediate sense gratifications that divide society into atomized consumers. But both the variants of history and the forms of commercialized leisure familiar to us originated at the same time and for the same reasons. Both developed in the nineteenth century in response to extraordinary technological and social changes. Recognition of the common origins of history and commercialized leisure can explain the seemingly paradoxical tensions within Roland Kirk's music, while also helping to explain how the "remembering" of history and the "forgetting" of commercialized leisure form parts of a dialectical totality.

Commercialized Leisure and the Crisis of History

As literary critic Richard Terdiman has demonstrated, nineteenth-century industrialization and state-building entailed a massive disruption of traditional forms of memory. The instrumental mentality capable of building the political and industrial machines of that century had to countenance the destruction of tradition—the enclosure of farm lands, massive migrations to industrial cities, the construction of an interchangeable work force, and a consumer market free from the constraints of tradition. A sense of disconnection from the past united an otherwise fragmented and stratified polity, and consequently the study of the past took on new meaning. Terdiman notes that "history became the discipline of memory," whose task was to uncover "the crisis which inevitably entailed disconnection with the past as a referent."[1] Michelet, Dilthey, Bancroft, and the other great historians of the nineteenth century emerged to provide a sense of continuity and connection with the past in societies riddled with the ruptures and dislocations of modernity.

The beginnings of the electronic mass media in the form of the telegraph exacerbated the nineteenth-century crisis of memory. The telegraph enabled simultaneous communication for the first time, dissolving previous barriers of time and space. But that very simultaneity favored the agenda of ascendant industrial capitalism. The telegraph innately privileged the transmission of isolated facts like prices or recent events; it did little to convey context or continuity. Newspapers took on a new role with the stimulus of the telegraph, but it was a role geared toward commerce and change rather than to the preservation of cultural memory. The daily newspaper naturalized a kind of confusion in which the world seemed structured by isolated and discrete events; news became synonymous with change and more important than tradition.

A new kind of commercialized leisure emerged as a corollary to the telegraph in the United States during the late nineteenth century. Previously, churches, lodge halls, and community centers had served as sites for theatrical productions designed to mark festive occasions like weddings and holidays. But urban taverns, dance halls, amusement parks, and theaters brought new meanings to culture. The new commercial theaters, and later variety, vaudeville, and motion-picture halls, needed no special occasions and no association with ritualized activities to justify plays, skits, and music. They carved away a new kind of social space for working-class people—buildings devoted exclusively to leisure activities. Theatrical performances became commodities sold to strangers for an agreed-upon price rather than collective creations by communities enacting rituals essential to group identity and solidarity.[2]

Of course, commercialized theater had existed since the sixteenth century in Europe. Jean-Christophe Agnew, among others, has delineated the complicated connections between the assumptions of theater and the values central to the capitalist marketplace, but in nineteenth-century America, theater, medicine shows, circuses, taverns, dance halls, amusement parks, and vaudeville-variety houses intervened in culture and society in especially important ways. They helped Americans make a decisive break with Victorian restraints, while at the same time blending an ethnically diverse working class into an "audience" with a unified language and sign-system.

The success of popular theater in nineteenth-century America aggravated the crisis of historical memory by further detaching culture from tradition. It institutionalized a kind of dissembling, one feared by philosophers as far back as Plato. To speak someone else's words or to wear someone else's clothes meant hiding one's own identity. In a world where ancestry, locality, and vocation determined social status and identity, the inherent disguise of acting threatened core values. Role playing in the theater suggested that identities could be changed, that one was not bound by bloodlines, nationality, or occupation. This contained the essence of egalitarian and utopian thought by challenging the legitimacy of static identities inherited from the past, but it also threatened a sense of authentic self-knowledge and created the psychic preconditions for the needy narcissism of consumer desire. On stage, actors deliberately speak and act inauthentically, off stage everyone learns to act, because everyone needs to take on ever-changing roles as a consumer and worker. As literary scholar Michael Bristol points out about the cultural crises posed by theater in Elizabethan England, "An actor is not just someone whose speech is 'dissembling'; the deeper problem is that he is most valued for his ability to dissemble convincingly."[3] As commercialized theaters in nineteenth-century America helped destroy connections to the past, historical tableaux and dramas became common features within them, offering a fictive representation of what was being destroyed in reality. Thus the contents of theatrical productions sometimes ministered to the very wounds that their forms had helped to open.

Along with the telegraph and the daily newspaper, the theater helped reshape cultural memory and consciousness. Its role on behalf of the emergent industrial order helped mold a diverse population into a unified working and consuming force, but it also raised anxieties about the moral costs of disconnection from the past. To many critics, the "dissembling" of theater presented a challenge to established order and morality. These critics feared that nothing genuine or refined could come from a sphere of activity devoted to false representations and masked identities. Furthermore, they recognized that theatrical "time" presented an alternative to work time, pitting the pleasures of leisure against the responsibilities of labor. Theater attendance enabled individuals to play out fictive scenarios of changed identities, to escape from the surveillance and supervision of moral authorities and institutions. The fantasy world of the theatrical stage encouraged audiences to pursue personal desires and passions at the expense of their socially prescribed responsibilities.

Yet audiences embraced the new possibilities presented by commercial theater with enthusiasm. Unlike the wedding celebration or the community festival, the theater assembled an audience with no shared history, with no reciprocal responsibilities and obligations. Theatergoers in nineteenth-century America shared intimate and personal cultural moments with strangers. The unfamiliarity of the crowd with each other provided a kind of protective cover—a "privacy in public" whereby personal feelings and emotions could be aired without explanation or apology.[4] Women especially utilized the new popular culture as a way of escaping parental surveillance and patriarchal domination.[5] Using the borrowed legitimacy of theater's status as a form of cultural refinement, audiences flocked to the melodramas, vaudeville and variety shows, and later to motion pictures for decidedly unrefined productions and performances. In the theater, they encountered a world momentarily liberated from the

8

sexual and emotional repressions of the nineteenth century. Theatrical performances provided an outlet for expression of the needs and desires for pleasure long suppressed by the normative constraints of Victorian America.[6]

The sexual repressions of the Victorian era created powerful anxieties and tensions that could not be confronted directly by "respectable" citizens. But theater productions offered audiences an opportunity to view the forbidden and to contemplate the unthinkable. This "freedom" came less in the form of true sexual emancipation, however, than through a redirection of frustrations. The unfilled desires and unconsummated lusts of theater audiences made them good customers for sexually suggestive images, no matter how coded, coy, or indirect. The theater offered immediate but transitory gratification. It turned sexual impulses and desires into symbolic commodities to be purchased from others. One bought a theater ticket to see a performance that depicted happiness and pleasures missing from one's own life. Pleasure itself could not be purchased as a commodity—at least not legally—but the image of pleasure represented in the theater could be obtained for a small price. Similarly, theatrical productions evoked other desires—for intimacy, for recognition, for connection to the past. But the very forms of commercial theater aggravated rather than salved the wounds they pretended to heal.

Yet the theater did encompass a kind of free space for the imagination—an arena liberated from old restraints and repressions, a place where desire did not have to be justified or explained. By establishing commodity purchases as symbolic answers to real problems, the theater also helped lay the groundwork for the consumer-commodity culture of our own day wherein advertisers and entrepreneurs offer products that promise to bring pleasure and fulfillment. The nineteenth-century theater may have emerged in part as a rebellion against sexual repression, but its greatest long-term significance lay in shaping the psychic and material preconditions for Americans to shift from a Victorian industrial economy to a hedonistic consumer-commodity economy. It would not be the last time that the commercial matrix in which popular culture was embedded worked to undermine its potential for educational or social transcendence.

Melodramas, vaudeville and variety shows, and motion pictures taught Americans to make a break with the discipline, sobriety, thrift, and sexual repression that formed the core of Victorian culture. Appropriate to an industrializing economy, Victorian values provided necessary preconditions for economic growth during the nineteenth century. They stressed the work ethic, personal responsibility, punctuality, and willingness to defer gratification necessary for life as an industrial worker. But by the 1890s, it appeared that Victorian culture had done its work all too well. The hard-working Americans who internalized Victorian values helped build a powerful industrial economy that produced more products than the domestic market could consume. Overproduction and underconsumption threatened the very survival of industrial capitalism in the 1880s and 1890s, as business failures led to massive unemployment and repeated financial panics. The "false promise" of the Victorian code, that sober self-management would lead to upward mobility, helped provoke general strikes and other forms of "aggressive festivity" among workers. To solve their many problems, business leaders had to move away from the production of capital goods like railroads and locomotives and start producing consumer goods for the domestic market. But as long as Victorian repressions inhibited desires for immediate gratification, consumers lacked the psychological makeup necessary for an economy oriented around ever-increasing purchases of commodities by individuals.

Commercialized leisure evolved out of the contradictions in late nineteenth-century capitalism. As I. C. Jarvie notes, motion pictures not only served as renewable commodities in themselves, but they also helped legitimate the consciousness necessary for purchasing other renewable commodities. The specialization of industrial capitalism requires individuals "detachable from tradition, family, and ascription." Jarvie argues that motion pictures encouraged people to see themselves as detached and autonomous consumers by replacing ritualistic community celebrations with leisure that could be purchased as a commodity and shared with strangers.[7] Between 1890 and 1930 American society underwent extraordinary changes, from a Victorian culture of thrift to a consumer-oriented culture of spending. By the 1920s, production of renewable commodities like automobiles and appliances played a more important role in the U.S. economy than production of nonrenewable capital goods like heavy equipment and machinery. Economic historians have long understood the logic of this change for the interests of capital; building factories and locomotive engines brought enormous immediate profits, but the market for them became saturated rather quickly. Consumer goods did not need to last—indeed advertisers worked very diligently to see to it that considerations of fashion and style would render old goods obsolete and engender a demand for new ones.

Scholars examining the transition from Victorianism to consumerism in the U.S. have concentrated on the idea of leisure as contested terrain. Drawing upon the research of E. P. Thompson and Herbert Gutman, they have emphasized the ways in which the transition from agrarian to industrial life gave new meanings to work and play. In pre-industrial society, agrarian labor could be done at one's own pace and for one's own benefit. In the industrial workplace, factory time replaced natural time, and unremitting labor measured by the time-clock replaced the task-oriented work of the farm. No longer could leisure be mixed in with work, and work itself became a more prominent and a more alienating part of human existence. Just as the centralized industrial work site replaced home labor, so commercial establishments devoted to leisure-time pursuits replicated in the arena of play the capitalist division of labor. Intense resistance against these practices fueled strikes, sabotage, and other forms of working-class self-activity throughout the era of industrialization, but religious, medical, and legal authorities attempted to prevent revolt by inculcating Victorian values within the character structure of the work force, values championing repression, denial, thrift, chastity, sobriety, and hard work. But like most forms of ideological legitimation, they contained severe internal contradictions. When workers *internalized* Victorian norms, their labor produced a surplus of goods that could not be consumed by a domestic market filled with poorly paid thrifty self-denying individuals like themselves. When workers *resisted* Victorian norms, their repressions and anger drove them toward the only available source of pleasure—the illicit vices offered for sale by the underworld.

Thus commercialized leisure both facilitated the triumphs of industrial capitalism and focused attention on their psychic and emotional costs. Commercial culture sought credibility with its audiences by promising at least the illusion of connection with the past. But the gap between lived experience and the false promises of popular culture always created the possibility for counter-memories, for ethnic, class, and regional music, art, speech, and theater. Culture itself contributed to retraining and reshaping the masses to serve the interests of capital, but also to articulating unfilled desires and expressing disconnection from the past. British cultural studies theorist Stuart Hall notes the contradictions in this process as well as the centrality of tradition as a contested category in the nineteenth century,

> Capital had a stake in the culture of the popular classes because the constitution of a whole new social order around capital required a more or less continuous, if intermittent, process of re-education. And one of the principal sites of resistance to the forms through which this 'reformation' of the people was pursued lay in popular tradition. That is why popular culture is linked, for so long, to questions of tradition, of traditional forms of life—and why its 'traditionalism' has been so often misinterpreted as a product of a merely conservative impulse, backward looking and anachronistic.[8]

The transformations in behavior and collective memory fueled by the contradictions of the nineteenth century have passed through three major stages in the United States. The first involved the establishment and codification of commercialized leisure from the invention of the telegraph to the 1890s. The second involved the transition from Victorian to consumer-hedonist values between 1890 and 1945. The third and most important stage, from World War II to the present, involved extraordinary expansion in both the distribution of consumer purchasing power and in the reach and scope of the electronic mass media. The dislocations of urban renewal, suburbanization, and deindustrialization accelerated the demise of tradition in America, while the worldwide pace of change undermined stability elsewhere. The period from World War II to the present marks the final triumph of commercialized leisure, and with it an augmented crisis over the loss of connection to the past. Popular culture has played an important role in creating this crisis of memory, but it has also been one of the main vehicles for the expression of loss and the projection of hopes for reconnection to the past.

What Is Popular Culture?

As historian Ramon Gutierrez observes, the term "popular culture" is a description crafted exclusively from the outside. The creators of popular culture do not think of themselves as operating within an endeavor called "popular culture"; they see themselves merely creating signs and symbols appropriate to their audiences and to themselves. It is only from the vantage point of Enlightenment ideals of "high culture" that something called popular culture can be seen to exist. In recent years, scholars have increasingly challenged the divisions between "high" and popular culture, and rightly so. Yet it is also clear that what we call popular culture differs markedly in its aims and intentions from the Enlightenment culture of "beauty and truth" idealized in the nineteenth century by Matthew Arnold, as well as from the isolated "folk" cultures studied by anthropologists and folklorists. In general, we have a better idea of what commercial culture *is not* (high art and folklore) than what it is. But we can identify some aspects of commercialized leisure that have come to define its conditions of possibility.[9]

Popular culture has no fixed forms: the historical circumstances of reception and appropriation determine whether novels or motion pictures or videos belong to a sphere called popular culture. Similarly, individual artifacts of popular culture have no fixed meanings: it is impossible to say whether any one combination of sounds or set of images or grouping of words innately expresses one unified political position. Images and icons compete for dominance within a multiplicity of discourses; consumers of popular culture move in and out of subject positions in a way that allows the same message to have widely varying meanings at the point of reception. Although cultural products generally reflect the dominant ideology of any given period, no cultural moment exists within a hermetically sealed cultural present; all cultural expressions speak to both residual memories of the past and emergent hopes for the future.

Rather than looking for innately emancipatory or hegemonic forms and meanings within popular culture, we would do better to study its "transformations," which Stuart Hall defines as

> "the active work on existing traditions and activities, their active re-working so that they come out a different way: they appear to 'persist'—yet, from one period to another, they come to stand in a different relation to the ways working people live and the ways they define their relations to each other, to 'the others' and to the conditions of life."[10]

In the United States since World War II, these transformations have coalesced around identifiable conditions of possibility. These conditions are not an "aesthetic," or a finite set of rules guiding artistic production and reception; they are not inherently "progressive" practices guaranteed to advance struggles against exploitation and hierarchy wherever they appear; they are not pure, authentic, or transcendent by themselves. They are historically specific elements within commercial culture that allow for the expression of collective popular memory and the reworking of tradition. Participation and investment, carnival, and a struggle for hegemony have provided significant conditions of possibility within American commercial culture since World War II. At times, all of these have created frames of reception consistent with dominant ideology, but they have also worked to hone and sharpen collective popular memory.

Sociologist Pierre Bourdieu's categories of participation and investment accurately characterize audience expectations from American popular culture since World War II.[11] Unlike "high culture" where a dogmatic formalism privileges abstraction over experience, the effectiveness of popular culture depends on its ability to engage audiences in active and familiar processes. Tania Modleski has demonstrated how television soap operas and game shows win credibility with viewers by turning into play the everyday work of nurturing families and making purchases, much as rodeo events or car customizing do for cowboys and mechanics.[12] Fredric Jameson describes popular songs as copies for which there exist no originals, texts whose popularity depends less on innovation or imagination than upon a sense of familiarity conducive to immediate audience appropriation.[13]

Traditions of participation and investment, combined with the internal biases of electronic mass media, tend to privilege forms of communication emanating from aggrieved and marginal communities. Sociolinguists Basil Bernstein, Leonard Schatzman, and Anselm Strauss have identified empathy, immediacy, and emotion as core components of working-class speech, and they have demonstrated how working-class speakers subordinate linear, individualistic, and analytic ways of speaking to stress nonlinear effects and collective emotions.[14] Rhetorician Kathleen Hall Jamieson points out that television favors a style of speaking that historically has been associated with women—an unself-conscious sense of self-disclosure about one's private self and an ability to integrate others into one's discussions—and that, conversely, the medium works against speech styles traditionally associated with men, which favor projection of the self against the environment.[15] The ever changing meanings and deliberate indeterminacies of subcultural slang undercut the authority of the word, replacing it with an appreciation of the inevitable metaphoricity of language. Such usage entails a break with the logocentric world of the Enlightenment in which univocal utterances and precise descriptions serve to fix final meanings and identities; at the same time it foregrounds a sense of language so new that it resembles postmodern poetry and so old that it echoes the ancient Nahuatl poet who insisted that "no one among us truly and finally speaks here."[16]

Melodrama presents a particularly significant form of participation and investment within American commercial culture since World War II. Melodrama emerged out of the same nineteenth-century dislocations responsible for the problem of historical memory and the rise of popular culture itself. It emerged as an expression of the inadequacies of Enlightenment language and art, displacing conventional narratives and reasoned discourse with broad physical gestures, tableaux, simple binary oppositions between good and evil, and plots resolved more by fate and sudden reverses than by human action. A precursor to film noir, the gothic romance, and the television night-time serial, melodrama established important subtexts within American popular culture. Television critic Jane Feuer points out that melodrama's unsatisfying endings resist the unproblematic closures of dominant narratives, while cinema scholar Laura Mulvey demonstrates how melodrama contains a critique of the cinematic apparatus itself by subjecting its protagonists to "the curious and prurient gaze of intrusive community, neighbors, friends, and family so that the spectator's own look becomes self-conscious and awkward."[17]

Carnival traditions have provided another important frame of reception for American popular culture since World War II. Bourdieu speaks of popular forms that "satisfy the taste for and sense of revelry, the free speaking and hearty laughter which liberate by setting the social world head over heels, overturning conventions and proprieties."[18] Literary critic Mikhail Bakhtin identifies these sensibilities as the essence of carnival—ritualized celebrations oriented around the passions of plenitude, inversions of the social order, and mocking laughter designed to "uncrown power." The dangerous "dissembling" that so troubled nineteenth-century opponents of popular theater, the anarchic anti-authoritarianism of the Marx Brothers, and the sense of entitlement to the good life enshrined in popular music and television all build upon the oppositional possibilities of carnival. Practices within popular culture like constituting the body as a site for decoration and style, valorizing the street as a locus of sociality and creativity, and inverting dominant icons to affirm a prestige from below also resonate with the legacy of carnival.[19] For Bakhtin, retentions of carnival laughter and display evidence a "materials memory," by which words themselves contain ideological traces from the past that take on renewed significance when they are appropriated in the present.[20]

Like participation and investment, carnival privileges certain social dispositions, but it has no intrinsic political meaning. Only in the context of a struggle for hegemony can the latent possibilities of collective memory be activated. The idea of "a struggle for hegemony" originates with the Italian Marxist Antonio Gramsci, who maintains that elites rule not merely by force but by "managed consent" as well, that they form "historical blocs" with other groups that make existing power relations appear natural and just. Some scholars emphasize the ways in which Gramsci's formulations explain how elites impose their will on society and turn potential rebels into unwitting accomplices in their own victimization. But hegemony is not just imposed on society from the top; it is struggled for from below, and no terrain is a more important part of that struggle than popular culture.

Cultural forms create conditions of possibility, they expand the present by informing it with memories of the past and hopes for the future; but they also engender accommodation with prevailing power realities, separating art from life, and internalizing the dominant culture's norms and values as necessary and inevitable. Politics and culture maintain a paradoxical relationship in which only effective political action can win breathing room for a new culture, but only a revolution in culture can make people capable of political action. Culture can seem like a substitute for politics, a way of posing only imaginary solutions to real problems, but under other circumstances culture can become a rehearsal for politics, trying out values and beliefs permissible in art but forbidden in social life. Most often, however, culture exists as a form of politics, as a means of reshaping individual and collective practice for specified interests, and as long as individuals perceive their interests as unfilled, culture retains an oppositional potential. Fredric Jameson argues that the dominant culture can only presume to ease anxieties like disconnection from the past by calling attention to them in the first place, thereby running the risk of re-opening the very ruptures it seeks to close.[21] For Jameson, the best cultural creations present contemporary social contradictions in such a way as to suggest eventual resolutions of them, but even works that fall short of that goal retain the potential to play a role in the struggle for hegemony.[22]

The complicated relationship between historical memory and commercial culture, between the texts of popular culture and their contexts of creation and reception, resist conventional forms of cultural criticism. The coded, indirect, and allegorical aspects of popular culture, its inversions of speech and ideology, and its refusal to isolate art from lived experience (a source of corruption as well as social connection) baffle and frustrate critics trained in traditional Western aesthetics and criticism. Neil Postman indicts television as a force debasing public discourse in America because its claims are made with images rather than language. For Postman, the eclipse of language renders empirical tests and logical analysis "impotent."[23]

In a similar vein, Allan Bloom assures us that rock and roll music's entire meaning rests in its rhythm (as if there were only one), which he confidently explains is the "rhythm of sexual intercourse" (as if here, too, there were only one).[24] The equally uninformed Robert Pattison contends that rock music represents the "triumph of vulgarity," through mindless celebration of a debased primitivism. The nadir of Pattison's slipshod argument comes in his dismissal of the Silhouettes' 1958 hit record "Get a Job" as solipsism rejoicing "in the conclusion that language is meaningless." In actuality, the record became a hit during the recession of 1958, and the song's lyrics described the anxieties of looking for work when there are no jobs available. The scat singing of "nonsense" syllables that leads Pattison to see the song as meaningless plays upon well understood conventions within black music of imitating musical instruments with the human voice, a tactic that Louis Armstrong (to use just one example) employed brilliantly to punctuate some of the lyrics in his songs. In fact, Afro-American poets and writers including Bob Kaufman and Ishmael Reed have long drawn on the creative wordplay of scat singing as a vital source for their poetry and prose.[25] Like the anthropologist some years back who decided that the *penitente* cults of New Mexico were "mired in webs of iconographic confusion" because their iconography made no sense to her, Pattison assumes that "Get a Job" has no meaning because it is not expressed in language that he understands. But like the many other errors of fact and interpretation in Pattison's and Bloom's criticisms, these are beside the point because they stem from a larger conceptual error. Like Postman, Pattison and Bloom are so eager to tell us what popular culture does *not* do (advance the agenda of the Enlightenment) that they fail to tell us what popular culture actually *does* or how it is shaped by the economic and social matrix in which it is embedded.

Television provides an important test case for critics of popular culture. As David Marc quips, the number of people who condemn television are exceeded only by the number of people who watch it, but it is difficult to understand or evaluate television's popularity from most of the critical literature about the medium. This is not to call for uncritical approval of everything or anything within popular culture; it is merely to say that questions of connoisseurship and aesthetics need to follow rather than precede an understanding of how the medium does its work within larger social contexts. Even if we could safely dismiss every program on television as artistically worthless, we would still need to understand the ways in which television presents the illusion of intimacy, how it intervenes in family relations, how it serves the consumer economy, and how its hold on the viewing audience relates to the disintegration of public resources, the aggravations of work, and the fragility of interpersonal relations that characterize our lives. Furthermore, to function as a mechanism of escape, television and other forms of popular culture often recuperate the very history that their content appears to erase. Certainly the reach and content of commercial television provide ample grounds for criticism. Television is both an advertising mechanism and the primary discursive medium of our culture; it irreparably inscribes consumer desire and commercialism into the fabric of entertainment, news, and sports. Television colonizes intimate areas of human sexuality and personality, exacerbating anxieties and fears to sell more products. Its penetration into the home helps order domestic space, leisure time, and family identity, while its seemingly endless flow reduces complex ideas and images to a melange of distraction and trivilization. By addressing viewers as atomized consumers, the medium obscures experiences of race, region, class, and gender. By turning politics into entertainment, television transforms citizens into spectators and turns politicians into performers. Television critic Arthur Kroker may be unique in describing Ronald Reagan's State of the Union addresses as more like "Presidential holograms," than political speeches, but Kroker is hardly alone in noticing the ways in which artistic "representation" defined as the depiction of images has superseded political "representation" defined in relation to the distribution of power and resources.

Yet responding to television's popularity with blanket condemnation of its content misses the point; questions of connoisseurship focus too much on how television fails to meet critical expectations at the expense of understanding how television succeeds at intervening in the everyday life of the society it addresses. Like many popular music critics, television's detractors condemn the medium because they feel it debases an otherwise successfully functioning society. Without discounting the shallow vulgarity of the medium, it is important to note that television also reflects an already ongoing unraveling of social relations in society; its needy narcissism serves as a salve for the wounds of everyday life.

Guided by emotion and empathy, working through ritual and repetition, television's core vocabulary reflects its role as a therapeutic voice ministering to the open wounds of the psyche. As a "close-up" medium whose dramatic and social locus is the home, television addresses the inner life by minimizing the heroic while maximizing the private and personal aspects of existence. Where motion pictures favor the panoramic shot, television privileges the zoom shot, looking *in* rather than out. To represent conversation, film directors use the "shot-counter-shot" effect while television directors employ the tightly constructed "two faces east." Thus motion-picture conversation emphasizes the separations between people, while television depicts people as closely linked to one another. This vocabulary of television lends itself to certain kinds of representation — the empathetic nurturing of others that viewers feel while watching a soap opera or a game show, the nonlinear quick cuts and distractions of action/adventure and comedy programs, and the situation comedy's fixation on stars mugging for the camera which stresses individual moments rather than teleological closure. These all focus attention inward and undermine the psychic prerequisites for a public life, but they also reflect a society already turned inward by the rise of consumerism and the demise of a healthy public life.

For all of their triviality and frivolity, the messages of popular culture circulate in a network of production and reception that is quite serious. At their worst, they perform the dirty work of the economy and the state. At their best, they retain memories of the past and contain hopes for the future that rebuke the injustices and inequities of the present. It might be thought a measure of the inescapable irony of our time that the most profound intellectual questions emerge out of what seem to be ordinary and commonplace objects of study. It may well be that such a paradox exposes the decline of intellectual work and the eclipse of historical reason. But there is another possibility. Perhaps the most important facts about people and about societies have always been encoded within the ordinary and the commonplace. Rahsaan Roland Kirk had an eminently serious agenda, but little access to the arenas in which "serious" decisions about power and resources are contested. However, every time he picked up the saxophone (or saxophones), he made a statement about the past, present, and future. By examining the relationship between collective popular memory and commercial culture, we may be on the threshhold of a new kind of knowledge, one sensitive to contestations over meaning and capable of teaching us that a sideshow can sometimes be the main event.

2

Precious and Communicable: History in an Age of Popular Culture

At the end of her wonderful novel *My Antonia*, Willa Cather speaks about "the precious and incommunicable past."[1] Her formulation identifies historical work as necessary and indispensable, but always incomplete. We need to understand the past in order to make informed moral choices about the present, to connect our personal histories to a larger collective history. But that larger history can never be fully comprehended; the complexities and pluralities of the past always resist definitive evaluation and summary. Reconstructing the infinitely complex experiences of the past through the paltry bits of evidence about it available to historians inevitably renders some aspects of the past as incommunicable.

Those of us who teach history rarely think about history as "precious and incommunicable" in the sense that Cather means. Perhaps we walk into the classroom believing that history is precious, but find our students' disinterest in the subject so thorough that we despairingly conclude that it is incommunicable. Too often, we think of history as neither precious nor incommunicable, but rather as an inert body of facts to be retrieved by diligent scholarship and to be learned by rote memorization. Even historical methodologies that try to do justice to the pluralities of the past, that hone the necessary skills of empathy, imagination, and analysis basic to historical thinking confront resistant audiences. History as an academic subject and as a way of understanding the world appears increasingly in jeopardy, regarded inside and outside academia as exceedingly "incommunicable" but scarcely "precious."

In accepting the 1980 Nobel Prize for literature, Czelaw Milosz identified a "refusal to remember" as the characteristic vice of our time.[2] For Milosz, the horrors of history, of Nazi barbarism and Stalinist totalitarianism, loom so monstrously over the present that people find it easier to forget than to take on the burdens and responsibilities of remembering. Intellectual historian Russell Jacoby sees a similar erasure in the eclipse of historical memory. Totalitarianisms thrive on "social amnesia" in Jacoby's view, because people who have lost the ability to "think back" have lost the ability to think at all. "Society has lost its memory," Jacoby writes, "and with it, its mind."[3]

The rapid pace of change itself helps explain the crisis of historical understanding for some. Lawrence Grossberg describes the post-World War II era as an age of "postmodernity" where "change increasingly appears to be all that there is," where "there is no sense of progress which can provide meaning or depth and a sense of inheritance," and where "both the future and the past appear increasingly irrelevant; history has collapsed into the present."[4] John Berger — artist, novelist, and critic — makes a similar argument, contending: "Today what surrounds the individual life can change more quickly than the brief sequence of that life itself. The timeless has been abolished and history has become ephemerality. History no longer pays respect to the dead: the dead are simply what has passed through."[5] Whether due to the suppression of hard and unpalatable facts about the brutalities of the past (and present), or to the debilitating effects of incessant change, historians and history teachers today confront intellectual trends that include what the social historian Warren Susman characterizes as "a fundamentally antihistorical view of the world."[6]

The Neo-Conservative Critique of History

The contemporary crisis of historical thinking extends across the globe, and represents only a part of a larger crisis in the humanities and the social sciences about the uneasy relationship between "truth" and our accounts of it. But the most publicized efforts to address this crisis in the United States have posed the problem in parochial and technical terms. Lynne Cheney, Ronald Reagan's director of the National Endowment for the Humanities, issued a 1987 report

blaming history teachers and textbooks for shortcomings in student
knowledge about the American past. Drawing upon a study commis-
sioned by the Department of Education, *What Do Our Seventeen
Year Olds Know?* by Diane Ravitch and Chester Finn, Cheney blasted
"a system of education that fails to nurture memory of the past."[7]
Cheney's well publicized remarks came in the wake of the substantial
sales garnered by books by Allan Bloom and E. D. Hirsch, which also
cite alleged deficiencies in student knowledge about literature and
history that they blamed on the bad values and poor teaching strategies of instructors.

What unites these pronouncements by Cheney, Ravitch, Finn,
Bloom, and Hirsch is their failure to connect arguments to evidence
and their inability to address issues of context and power. Most of
them presume (without proof) a previous golden age when students
possessed mastery of historical facts and methods. All presume that
the crisis of historical thinking begins in the classroom, not in the
world outside, and that teachers can solve the problem merely by
compelling children to memorize and recite the proper phrases.
They ignore the suppressions of memory fostered by the public relations arms of totalitarian states East and West, the dizzying pace of
change engendered by technological change and social dislocation,
and the "crisis of representation" affecting not just history, but all of
the humanities and social sciences. They find no fundamental difference between teaching the children of yesterday (at least those who
could afford to stay in school)—who lived in homes where class, ethnicity, religion, neighborhood, and region all contained visible
markers of the past—and children of today—who live in a world of
electronic mass media, corporate transfers, and social pressures to
obsess about contemporary fashions and styles so as not to be identified with any personal or collective past. In short, these "defenders"
of historical thinking are themselves abysmal historians, unable to
ground either their own analyses or their proposed solutions in the
world of power relations, personal subjectivity, and change over
time in which we all live.

It is not surprising that the Reagan administration and wealthy
foundations representing corporate interests would sponsor such research. The very same Department of Education that tried to eliminate school-lunch programs and reduce loans to college students
paid for Ravitch and Finn's study; the Olin Foundation supported

Bloom's writing, while Hirsch received funds from the Exxon Foundation. The resulting research makes no mention of the ways in which the deindustrialization of America in the 1980s undermines people's ties to the past and threatens their hopes about the future. It makes no mention of the ways in which the tax cuts of this decade that fuel merger manias and luxury spending sprees mandate a diversion of resources away from schools and universities, devastating support for new scholarship, library resources, and graduate programs in history. Even the technical educational recommendations emerging from these reports serve to narrow rather than broaden the scope of historical knowledge. They do not call for a reinvigoration of historical writing and teaching so much as they mandate censorship of the most interesting and most effective research methods developed within the historical profession over the past two decades.

Given the depth of their dissatisfaction with students and teachers, the neo-conservative critics make surprisingly few affirmative suggestions about how to improve the discipline. Ravitch and Finn offer a few common-sense "proposals" that merely codify the way history is already being taught. Cheney calls for textbooks like those "in the early decades of this century," which she characterizes as "filled with stories—the magic of myths, fables, and tales of heroes."[8] Hirsch offers a list of disconnected nouns for students to memorize on the dubious premise that the ability to recognize the items on his list constitutes "cultural literacy." These "remedies" might possibly encourage religious revivals, frenzies of uncritical nationalism, or unthinking acceptance of the dictates of authority figures, but they do nothing to solve the crisis of historical thinking. Indeed, they undermine the very cornerstones of historical research—appreciation of difference, understanding of context, and ability to make critical comparative judgments on the basis of empathy and evidence.

The neo-conservative educational critics champion heroic stories told from one point of view that make the power hierarchies of the present appear natural and inevitable. Bloom argues that "the contempt for the heroic is only an extension of the perversion of the democratic principle that denies greatness and wants everyone to feel comfortable in his [sic] skin [sic] without having to suffer unpleasant comparisons."[9] Cheney argues that "our history and literature give us symbols to share; they help us all, no matter how diverse

24

our backgrounds, feel part of a common undertaking."[10] Hirsch claims that an agentless "history" has determined what we need to know about the past, and that no value judgments or ideologies have shaped the "common elements" available to us.[11] These assertions seek closure on the very possibilities that history opens up. For in historical research the "heroic" is a matter of context and perspective, what people have in common can be studied empirically rather than mandated from above, and it is understood that all information available to historians has been shaped by the ideological conditions of its origins and preservation. In addition, the true neo-conservative agenda becomes clear when these authors expound on the kinds of historical scholarship they wish to eliminate. Cheney claims that textbooks have become vacuous because they are preoccupied with concepts like "expanding environments" and "recognizing the interdependence among people."[12] In a 1988 report on the state of the humanities in America, Cheney airs her agenda more fully. While paying lipservice to the necessity of historical inquiry, Cheney defends her emphasis on the great books and great works in the Western tradition by asserting in decidedly ahistorical fashion that these works and the concepts of "truth," "beauty," and "excellence" that they embody are "timeless." Of course, because historical inquiry emphasizes how time and place are crucial determinants in the origins and uses of these works, to call them "timeless" is to ignore the insights historical study can provide. Cheney takes on the critics of Western tradition by quoting them out of context and misrepresenting their views—hardly a tribute to the effects of classical learning— and then she asserts, without benefit of comparative study, that we need to focus on Western civilization because it really is *better* than all other civilizations, past and present.[13] Bloom asserts that "the problem of getting along with outsiders is secondary to, and sometimes in conflict with, having an inside, a people, a culture, a way of life. A very great narrowness is not incompatible with the health of an individual or a people, whereas with great openness it is hard to avoid decomposition."[14] Hirsch contends that national cultures are contrived by intellectuals, and have no innate moral value, but they must be taught to the young because the modern nation state depends upon them.[15] Ravitch and Finn argue, "It is not coincidental that general knowledge of history and literature in the schools appears to be imperiled at the same moment that specialists in the uni-

versities devote themselves to arcane debates among deconstructionists, structuralists, neo-Marxists, and other specialized schools
and esoteric interpretations."[16] What is really no coincidence is that
Ravitch and Finn choose to ally themselves with mythical constructs
of history while venting their anti-intellectualism against methods
that seek true and useful accounts of the past by subjecting the forms
and contents of historical narratives to rigorous analysis.

What can we learn from a history like Cheney's, one that considers
concepts like "expanding environments" and "interdependence
among people" as vacuous compared to "myths, fables and tales of
heroes"? From a history like Bloom's that cultivates "a very great narrowness" to avoid the "decomposition" of openness? From Hirsch
who wants us to memorize stories and disembodied facts about the
past without worrying about whether or not they are true? From Ravitch and Finn who seek to silence discussion about the ways in
which every story about the past has been told from someone to
someone else in keeping with the interests of the speaker and the
listener? We certainly will not learn very much about the history of
the United States with its many conflicts and disagreements. The
"heroism" of westward expansion from the settlers' perspective may
have seemed like genocide to the Native American Indians. The
"progress" of American agriculture and industry might have appeared as naked exploitation to slaves and industrial laborers. The
inclusive story about immigrants coming to find freedom in America
excludes many blacks, Chicanos, and Native Americans who did not
come to America, but instead had America come to them. The icons
and images of our culture—that appear value-free to Hirsch—might
bear traces of oppression from the perspectives of women and ethnic minorities. Much recent scholarship has worked to open up these
differences, eschewing univocal heroic narratives for a multi-vocal
story more reflective of the experience of the American people as a
whole. The impetus for this recent scholarship has not been to divide
a unified society, but to understand existing divisions by tracing their
historical roots. Nor has the goal of this scholarship been what
Bloom calls "moral relativism" where the multiplicity of stories
means that no value judgments can be made. On the contrary, it assumes that value judgments can be made only on the basis of knowledge and evidence, that moral or political synthesis can be accom-

plished only by honest acknowledgment of what is being synthesized.

Thus the neo-conservatives are not so much against the way history is taught and written, as they are against the complex realities of American history itself. Their desire to elevate a few heroes from the past above their contemporaries, to suppress difference and disagreement, to accept uncritically the past and present as "givens" independent of human agency, rejects the complicated and plural history that has actually happened in favor of a mythical construct invented to impose cultural unity and obedience to the present government. Even worse, they profess to "save" historical inquiry by returning it to an uncritical glorification of the past and present, to an institutionalized cheerleading for the victors of the past, no matter how villainous or immoral they may have been. They laud history while fearing historical inquiry, because that inquiry might lead to critical reappropriation of the past by aggrieved groups. One might call this history a kind of ancestor worship, but its bias toward a certain kind of experience—white male upper-class experience—means that most of us are being called upon to worship not our own, but someone else's ancestors. We are being asked to imagine the past as a succession of military, political, and economic struggles beginning in antiquity and culminating in the "progress" manifested by the nation state in our own day. But at the same time we are being ordered to forget the hurts of history, the complicated struggles and deadly rivalries out of which real history is made.

Although their standards of evidence and argument tend to undercut their claims, neo-conservative critics often profess to ground their views on history within the traditions of the European "Enlightenment." This "project of man," beginning in the Renaissance, combined diverse developments in art and in the natural and human "sciences." Through a variety of intellectual devices ranging from the scientific method to perspectival painting to historical narrative, the Enlightenment created a subjectivity or point of view that has become synonymous to its adherents with the human subject. Thus the scientific advancements and artistic expressions of Europe are considered the best that humanity has ever achieved, and the story of the world told from the European point of view is presented as total world history.

All contemporary scholars and every reader of these pages has benefited from the Enlightenment in an extraordinary number of ways, but it is also apparent that this tradition has done a lot of harm. The instrumental view of nature behind the natural and physical sciences has led to exploitation of the environment and to an instrumentality inevitably directed against other human beings. The bourgeois perspective in painting constituted European males as the viewers and relegated females and non-Western people to the status of objects for viewing. Every day this power of the bourgeois "look," with its capacity for racial differentiation and sexual objectification, serves to humiliate and oppress human beings who suffer from the ideals of body image and the metaphors for activity and passivity (male vs. female) encoded within European visual traditions. The idea of history as synonymous with European "progress" has elevated a minute part of global experience to the center stage of history, while lumping all the rest into a kind of contextless "other," worthy of mention only when it impinges on the European consciousness. The popular and academic attack on history in recent years, especially by the very "structuralists" and "deconstructionists" that Finn and Ravitch wish to silence, has largely focused on the shortcomings of the Enlightenment and its legacy. It is to these perspectives that we now turn in our search for a precious and communicable past.

Textual Criticism and Historical Thinking

Post-structuralist and deconstructionist critiques of history revolve around the textual nature of historical narratives. Enlightenment standards of "objectivity" compelled traditional historians to remove their own voice from the text, to present evidence as if the facts "spoke for themselves." But instead of eliminating subjectivity, this method only disguised it. It tended to favor the written word over all other forms of human expression. It privileged the experiences of those with the power and position to leave behind documentary evidence about themselves, and it silenced those without access to the printed word. Post-structuralist and deconstructionist critics recognize that the "crisis of representation" stems from the "inevitability of representation," from the ways in which all facts are also interpretations singled out for notice because of some subjective judgment. They elect to analyze all texts, including historical narratives, to expose the hidden ideological biases built into any mode of representation.

Hayden White began leveling particularly effective critiques of history in the 1960s and 1970s. White wonders "why so much of modern fiction turns on the attempt to liberate Western man from the tyranny of the historical consciousness."[17] He concludes that writers understand history as just another text, one presuming to stand for collective world experience, but which in reality fabricates a chronological and teleological frame upon an infinitely plural and decidedly non-teleological reality. White echoes Nietzsche in his view that history prevents rather than permits informed action because it makes people feel "that they were latecomers to a world in which everything worth doing had already been done."[18]

Jacques Derrida's explorations into the inevitability of representation in language and the ways in which centralized perspectives silence difference provide linguistic reinforcement for textually oriented criticisms like White's. Derrida sees destructive binary oppositions as the core of the historical method, which in his view always counterposes continuity to rupture, the universal to the specific, without seeing ways in which they might overlap. In place of the traditional historical notions of time as chronological and teleological, Derrida offers temporality as "repetition with change." In this way, events do not just happen, but they are articulated and rearticulated in ways that illumine rather than suppress multiple differences.[19]

Michel Foucault's path-breaking research in the late 1970s and early 1980s brought the critique of history to a new level; Foucault demonstrates the ways in which the presumption of a common human history allows centralized structures of power to extend their reach into every level of human experience. Foucault sees historical narratives as irrevocably tainted with the language of power and control. He argues,

> The history which bears and determines us has the form of a war rather than that of language: relations of power, not relations of meaning. History has no "meaning," though this is not to say that it is absurd or incoherent. On the contrary, it is intelligible and should be susceptible to analysis down to the smallest detail—but this in

accordance with the intelligibility of struggles, of strategies and tactics.[20]

White, Derrida, and Foucault have influenced some post-structuralists to reject history altogether, to see it as simply another repressive vestigial remnant of the Enlightenment.[21] But it is possible to read White, Derrida, and Foucault in a different fashion; to see in their critiques a means of passing from one historical paradigm to another. Derrida himself concedes that "if the word 'history' did not entail in itself the motif of a final repression of difference, one could say that only differences can be from the outset and thoroughly historical." Richard Terdiman outlines how this might be established in his exemplary work on nineteenth-century French literature.[22] Terdiman supports Derrida's claim that language always involves metaphorical comparisons that should not be confused with the object under description. But Terdiman points out that historical accounts do not have to presume final and fixed meanings, that they can become important mechanisms for opening up and understanding the multiple possibilities contained in any one account. "The diachronic" claims Terdiman, "is the experience of time over difference," and consequently change over time offers a fundamental model for the study of difference. Precisely because the truth about the past is created by inquiry in the present, history is not just an inert body of facts from the past constraining the present. Instead, history can be a way of opening up the present, of seeing its multiple possibilities by exploring the "roads not taken" from the past.

Hayden White's more recent work acknowledges this power of historical narratives to open up rather than to constrain possibilities. White views the work of Fredric Jameson as particularly significant in this regard, because for Jameson "every present is at once a realization of projects performed by past human agents and a determination of a field of possible projects to be realized by living human agents in their future."[23] Thus Jameson holds on to the necessity of historical narratives without imposing on them the kinds of closure condemned by Derrida and Foucault. Jameson argues that even conventional narratives (historical and otherwise) with their "strategies of containment" which eliminate all but one resolution and which make that conclusion appear inevitable and necessary can be opened for investigation of the ideological possibilities they constrain. The implications of Jameson's work for historical scholarship are neatly summarized by Dana Polan, who points out that "we don't so much write *the* meaning of the period as a history of some possible meanings: we study what was able to emerge within, and against, what seems at first glance at least, to be a dominant field of social perception."[24]

Defenders of history like Polan, Jameson, and Terdiman are not simply calling for more stories. Each believes that the past imposes constraints on the present that cannot be wished away or imagined out of existence. To them, historical truth is neither subjective nor objective; rather, it consists of a dialectical interaction between the two. Knowing subjects (themselves shaped by historical contingencies beyond their control) construct the periodizations and cause-effect relationships characteristic of historical narratives, but they do so with a commitment to come as close as possible to an inclusive and collective truth. They do not presume the disinterested objectivity that blinds traditional historians to their own ideologies, nor do they let the fact that history appears in story form convince them that history is just stories. Instead, they accept retrospective narratives as useful tools, as ways of organizing and understanding evidence about experiences with change over time.

It may be impossible to bridge fully the gap between the post-structuralists and deconstructionists on the one hand and the historically grounded literary critics on the other. Textually oriented critics distrust the idea of a total human history, while the historically oriented critics insist on it. For the textualists, history is one of many texts that order and interpret experience; for the historians history can only be comprehended as a text, but it possesses an independent identity as "necessity," "absent cause," and the cumulative collective legacy of human ideas and actions. But even if no final reconciliation between the two camps is possible, the dialogue between them has enriched our understanding of history and enabled us to explore new methods of expressing historical consciousness. It suggests ways of teaching and learning history that avoid neo-conservative myth-making, Enlightenment pseudo-objectivity, and post-structuralist resignation.

History in an Age of Popular Culture

In his acceptance speeches at the 1980 and 1984 Republican National Conventions, and in his inaugural addresses in 1981 and 1985, President Ronald Reagan frequently invoked the American past. He located the origins of the American story in 1620 when the Pilgrims landed at Plymouth Rock. He talked about how "we" came to North America from Europe, how "we" tamed the wilderness and the frontier until settlement reached California, and how "we" fought two world wars and conquered space.[25] In his second inaugural address, the President compressed American history into a series of vignettes where

> a general falls to his knees in the hard snow of Valley Forge; a lonely President paces the darkened halls and powers, [sic] ponders his struggles to preserve the union; the men of the Alamo call out encouragement to each other; a settler pushes west and sings a song, and the song echoes out forever and fills the unknowing air.[26]

The President's speeches constructed the audience as historical subjects with a common past. They were asked to begin their story in Europe in 1620 and to see westward expansion, military triumphs, and space exploration as their common heritage. In so doing, the speeches reflected the "truths" of the popularly understood history of the United States.

But there were other truths that Reagan's address omitted. It denied the memory and perspectives of those Americans who traveled to this country from Asia or Latin America. It erased the experiences of those Americans who came in chains from Africa, or whose Chicano and Native American ancestors had their land stolen from them by "westward expansion." As many histories have done, his address presented the history of the American state as if it were the history of the American people. In so doing, it neglected the plurality of personal stories that shaped the American past.

In contrast, Jesse Jackson's speech to the Democratic National Convention in 1988 constructed the audience in a different fashion. Jackson spoke of his childhood experiences, growing up poor in South Carolina. He recalled how his grandmother could not afford to buy a blanket, so she sewed together a quilt out of all the patches of leftover and discarded fabric in the house. Jackson then used the construction of that quilt as his organizing metaphor about political power. The many groups who make up the American electorate, in Jackson's view, had only piecemeal resources. But joined together on "common ground," they could survive and prosper. Just as his grandmother had pieced together a quilt from different patches, Jackson urged workers, women, blacks, Chicanos, Native Americans, Asian-Americans, homosexuals and lesbians, senior citizens, and the handicapped to piece together a coalition that could encompass them all.

Jackson's speech constructed his audience on both the margins of society and at the center. His narrative about the past neglected the history of the state and claims about "the inevitable trajectory of progress" in favor of the ingenuity and effort of his grandmother. Rather than uniting his listeners in fictive identification with a unified past that they did not share, he contended that their very historical diversity and fragmentation united them in mutual interdependence.

At first glance it may appear as if Reagan's speech drew upon history while Jackson's relied on myth. After all, the president listed specific events and facts in chronological order, while the civil-rights leader recited a private story about a person unknown outside of her own immediate family. But on closer examination, it becomes clear that both speakers mixed myth and history in ways that dramatically illustrate the contested nature of historical memory in our time. While the text of Reagan's speech dealt with historical events, his credibility with the audience did not depend upon his skill as a historian. Rather, the images he invoked of westward expansion, world war, and space exploration activated deep layers of sentiment and emotion shaped by endless narratives—dime novels, motion pictures, television programs. The nature of "heroic" action, the inevitability of conflict, and the march of progress have been portrayed in popular culture over and over again; Reagan's skill as a politician rests in no small measure with his ability to understand and tap these structures of consciousness among Americans. Similarly, Jackson's seemingly innocent family narrative scarcely rested upon the superiority of quilts to blankets or on any actual shared memory of the process of quiltmaking. Rather, it rested on the audience's understanding of history, on its identification with experiences of deprivation and adaptation, and on a perception of difference and fragmentation. Jackson's metaphor would not have seemed credible to his audience if his grandmother's perseverance in the face of suffering did not embody the collective historical experience of the groups he was addressing. Nor would Reagan's "historical" allusions have worked with an audience that was not already conditioned to accept the triumphs of the state as their own.

When confronted with competing versions of reality like Reagan's and Jackson's, we have to rely on our understanding of evidence and our understanding of our own interests. Historical research can determine whose story is more in keeping with the facts: which does a better job of connecting the present with the past? Political analysis can determine whose interests are served by each story: which legitimates decisions likely to help or harm us as individuals or as a society? But competing narratives are not just fights about the past, they also serve to transform cultural identity and political dialogue in the present. Both Reagan and Jackson wish to tap collective popular memory and imagination, to make their political stances express the values of America. But these values are not static, not bequeathed to us willy-nilly by the accidents of history, as E. D. Hirsch would have us believe. Rather, they are struggled over and contested every day on innumerable fronts and in countless arenas. What we choose to remember about the past, where we begin and end our retrospective accounts, and who we include and exclude from them—these do a lot to determine how we live and what decisions we make in the present. Political speeches and history books provide two important sites for that contestation; the texts and practices of popular culture encompass the battle as well.

James Brown, the great black rhythm and blues singer, has made millions of dollars in show business, has owned airplanes, motels, and radio stations. Yet when asked to describe his career he points to the scars on his pock-marked and discolored knees, damaged from repeated full impact landings during his wild stage shows. "They made my daddy crawl," Brown relates, "crawl under cars, behind mules. Crawl all kinds of ways. Four years ago they made me go down on my knees—my comeback they call it to prove that I could still do it."[27] Brown's comparing his own suffering with his father's adds historical, class, and racial dimensions to grievances that could just as easily be discussed without reference to history, class, or race. Yet the connection is real. Brown's suffering and mistreatment as a performer have everything to do with who he is, with what class he comes from, and with his racial identity. Even though his financial success and popular acclaim separate him from his father's particular crises, he is too self-aware to ignore the ways in which history shapes his present-day experiences and subjects him to the same kinds of demeaning power realities that his father faced.

Bruce Springsteen is younger and wealthier than James Brown, an object of adulation, and a white male hero in a symbolic order that privileges white men. But he, too, finds remnants of history shaping his stance toward the world. "I grew up in this house where there was never any books or I guess anything that was considered art," he told a concert audience one night. Continuing, he explained that he had ignored most of what his teachers were trying to teach him in school, either because of the way they were teaching it or because he just wasn't interested. But then, Springsteen told the crowd

> when I got older I looked back and I saw that my father, he quit high school and went in the Army and he got married real young and picked up jobs where he could, workin' in a factory, driving a truck. And I look back at my grandfather and he worked in a rug mill in the town that I grew up in. And it seemed like we all had one thing in common and that was that we didn't know enough, we didn't know enough about what was happening to us. Like I'm thirty-one now and I just started to read the history of the United States. And the thing about it is, I started to learn about how things· got to be the way they are today, how you end up a victim without even knowing it. And how people get old and just die after not having hardly a day's satisfaction or peace of mind in their lives.[28]

Pat Benatar's 1982 music video "Shadows of the Night" offered one of the first heroic narratives about women in the notoriously sexist music video field. Benatar fashioned a story about a 1940s woman war worker who sheds her daytime "Rosie the Riveter" work clothes to be airlifted behind Nazi lines for night-time commando raids and acts of sabotage. From all the icons and images of women in popular culture, Benatar chose to periodize her story in the 1940s, a time of importance to 1980s feminists because in that decade women worked outside the home for wages with societal and government approval. Positioning herself as a woman entering a male-dominated field in the 1980s, Benatar legitimated and explained her struggle by reference to the repressed self-activity of the last great opportunity for women workers.

This is not to suggest that James Brown, Bruce Springsteen, and Pat Benatar hold the answers to the contemporary crisis of historical thinking. Certainly quotations from other entertainers might lead in opposite directions, and even Brown, Springsteen, and Benatar are not always consistent about their relationships to the past. But the desire to connect to history, the impulse to pose present problems in historical terms, and the assertion of a temporal and social reality beyond one's immediate experience pervade popular culture in significant ways. I want to argue that the ruminations on the past reflected in the films of John Sayles, in television programs like *Crime Story*, in the novels of Eudora Welty and Toni Morrison, or in the music of John Cougar Mellencamp equal or exceed the quality of historical acumen represented in most political speeches or history textbooks. If by themselves they do not hold an answer to the crisis in historical thinking, they go a long way toward showing us where answers might be found.

The crisis in historical thinking is certainly real. The dislocations of the past two centuries, the propaganda apparatuses of totalitarian powers, disillusionment with the paradigms of the Enlightenment, and popular culture itself have all served to make the search for a precious and communicable past one of the most pressing problems of our time. But simply because historical inquiry has been reframed, it does not necessarily follow that it has been diluted. It is just that historical memories and historical evidence can no longer be found solely in archives and libraries; they pervade popular culture and public discourse as well. As Eudora Welty wrote about Willa Cather's own sense of the precious and incommunicable,

> In the world of her novels, history lies in persistence in the memory, in lost hidden places that wait to be found and to be known for what they are. Such history is barely accessible, the shell of it is only frailly held together, it will be loseable again. But the continuity is *there*.[29]

Popular Television

3

The Meaning of Memory: Family, Class, and Ethnicity in Early Network Television

In 1949, one of the first episodes of the nationally televised CBS network comedy *The Goldbergs* featured a rent strike by disgruntled tenants against a landlord who refused to make repairs. The premise of a rent strike grew logically from the show's setting. Molly and Jake Goldberg, their children Rosalie and Sammy, and Molly's Uncle David all lived together in a crowded Bronx apartment building filled with working-class Jews like themselves. During every episode, neighbors and relatives passed through the Goldberg apartment. They carried on conversations by shouting through windows and yelling into dumbwaiter shafts. The Goldbergs met their friends on the streets, they shared night-school classrooms and Lewisohn Stadium concerts with the extended kinship network of their neighborhood, and problems like a leaking roof or a defective elevator immediately became group concerns.

Seven years later, *The Goldbergs* became *Molly*. The Goldberg family moved away from Tremont Avenue in the Bronx and bought a house in the Long Island suburb of "Haverville." (City of "the haves" as David Marc points out, the opposite of "Hooverville.")[1] In Haverville, neighbors did not walk through the Goldberg apartment or converse with them through windows and airshafts. The streets became a locus of danger, the threatening alternative to the centrality of the suburban home. Instead of rent strikes and collective action, comic premises in "Molly" emerged from the relative isolation and alienation of the suburban setting. Consumer purchases and fears of installment credit took center stage. Adjustments to the expectations of strangers through dieting or home decorating provided major sources of comic tension. Even though the Goldberg family seemed more autonomous in Haverville than it had been in the Bronx, it now seemed strangely in jeopardy. New products made family keepsakes and memorabilia obsolete. New patterns of social acceptance made children the tutors to their inflexible and backward-looking parents. The new standard of living and opportunity for upward mobility secured by the Goldbergs for their children only served to push the children into a different world, one that mocked the foreign accents and archaic customs of the family.

The journey from the Bronx to Haverville, from an ethnic, urban, working-class, extended family and kinship network to a detached, single-family, suburban home was a journey from the past to the present. It relied upon the language, icons, and images of the ethnic immigrant past to explain the suburban consumer present. Between 1949 and 1956 millions of American families made the same journey, and they looked to programs like *The Goldbergs* for a reflection of their own circumstances. Television not only recorded migration to the suburbs, but it provided important economic stimuli and significant ideological justifications for that move. By looking at television programs like *The Goldbergs*, we can understand something of the dimensions of that transformation in American life, and we can gain important insight into how Americans explained drastic changes to themselves and to others.

The popularity of *The Goldbergs* coincided with that of other television situation comedies between 1949 and 1957 based on ethnic working-class family life. *Mama* depicted the experiences of turn-of-the-century Norwegian immigrants to San Francisco; *Amos 'n' Andy* portrayed blacks in Harlem. *The Honeymooners* and *Hey, Jeannie* showed Irish working-class families in Brooklyn. *Life With Luigi* concerned Italian immigrants in Chicago, and *Life of Riley* presented the adventures of working-class migrants to Los Angeles during and after World War II.[2]

The presence of this subgenre of urban, ethnic, working-class situation comedies on television network schedules seems to run contrary to the commercial and artistic properties of the medium. Television delivers audiences to advertisers by glorifying consumption, not only during commercial breaks, but in the programs themselves.[3] The relative economic deprivation of ethnic working-class households would seem to provide an inappropriate setting for the display and promotion of commodities as desired by the networks and their commercial sponsors. Furthermore, the mass audience required to repay the expense of network programming encourages the depiction of a homogenized mass society, rather than the particularities and peculiarities of working-class communities. Finally, as an artistic medium, television's capacity for simultaneity conveys a sense of living in an infinitely renewable present—a quality inimical to the sense of memory permeating shows about working-class life. Yet whether set in the distant past like *Mama*, or located in the contemporaneous present, the subgenre of ethnic, working-class, situation comedies in early network television evoked concrete historical associations and memories in their audiences.[4]

Anomalous to the commercial and artistic propensities of television, these programs also ran counter to the dominant social trends in the era in which they were made. They presented ethnic families in working-class, urban neighborhoods at the precise historical moment when a rising standard of living, urban renewal, and suburbanization contributed to declines in ethnic and class identity.[5] They showed working-class families struggling for material satisfaction and advancement under conditions far removed from the *embourgeoisement* of the working class celebrated in popular literature about the postwar era. They displayed value conflicts about family identity, consumer spending, ethnicity, class, and gender roles that would appear to be disruptive and dysfunctional within a communications medium primarily devoted to stimulating commodity purchases.

The dissonance between urban, ethnic, working-class situation comedies and their artistic, commercial, and historical surroundings might be explained by the persistence of artistic clichés and the conservatism of the entertainment business. Yet while four of these seven television programs previously existed as radio serials, radio popularity did not guarantee adaptation to television: many successful radio series never made that transition, and television networks actually made more profit from productions specially created for the new medium.[6] Even when radio programs did become television shows, they underwent significant changes of plot and premise. Television versions of urban, ethnic, working-class situation comedies placed more emphasis on nuclear families and less on extended kinship and ethnic relations than did their radio predecessors.[7] These changes reflect more than the differences between television and ra-dio as media; they illuminate as well significant transformations in U.S. society during the 1950s, and they underscore the important role played by television in explaining and legitimizing those transi-tions to a mass audience.

More than their shared history in radio or their reliance on a col-lective theatrical tradition from vaudeville and ethnic theater unites the subgenre of urban, ethnic, working-class situation comedies. Through indirect but powerful demonstration, all of these shows ar-bitrated complex tensions caused by economic and social change in postwar America. They evoked the experiences of the past to lend legitimacy to the dominant ideology of the present. In the process, they served important social and cultural functions, not just in return-ing profits to investors or by attracting audiences for advertisers, but most significantly as a vehicle for ideological legitimation of a funda-mental revolution in economic, social, and cultural life.

The Meaning of Memory

In the midst of extraordinary social change, television emerged as the most important discursive medium in American culture. As such, it was charged with special responsibilities for making new eco-nomic and social relations credible and legitimate to audiences haunted by ghosts from the past. Urban, ethnic, working-class com-edies provided one means of addressing the anxieties and contradic-tions emanating from the clash between the consumer present of the 1950s and collective memory about the 1930s and 1940s.

The consumer consciousness generated by economic and social change in postwar America conflicted with the lessons of historical experience for many middle-and working-class American families. The Great Depression of the 1930s had not only damaged the econ-omy, it had also undercut the political and cultural legitimacy of American capitalism. Herbert Hoover had been a national hero in the 1920s, with his credo of "rugged individualism" forming the basis for a widely shared cultural ideal. But the Depression discredited Hoo-ver's philosophy and made him a symbol of yesterday's blasted hopes to millions of Americans. In the 1930s, cultural ideals based on mutuality and collectivity eclipsed the previous decade's individualism, and helped propel massive union organizing drives, anti-eviction movements, and general strikes. President Roosevelt's New Deal attempted to harness and co-opt that grass-roots mass activity in its efforts to restore social order and recapture credibility and legitimacy for the capitalist system.[8] The social welfare legislation of the "Second New Deal" in 1935 went far beyond any measures previously favored by Roosevelt and most of his advisors, but radical action proved necessary if the administration was to contain the upsurge of activism that characterized the decade. Even in the private sector, industrial corporations conceded more to workers than naked power realities necessitated because they feared the political consequences of mass disillusionment with the system.[9]

World War II ended the Depression and brought prosperity, but it did so on a basis even more collective than the New Deal of the 1930s. Government intervention in the wartime economy reached unprecedented levels, bringing material reward and shared purpose to a generation raised on the deprivation and sacrifice of the Depression. In the postwar years, the largest and most disruptive strike wave in American history won major improvements in the standard of living for the average worker, through both wage increases and government commitments to support full employment, decent housing, and expanded educational opportunities. Grass-roots militancy and working-class direct action wrested concessions from a reluctant business and government elite—mostly because the public at large viewed workers' demands as more legitimate than the desires of capital.[10]

Yet the collective nature of working-class mass activity in the postwar era posed severe problems for capital. In sympathy strikes and secondary boycotts, workers placed the interests of their class ahead of their own individual material aspirations. Strikes over safety and job control far outnumbered wage strikes, revealing aspirations to control the process of production that conflicted with the imperatives of capitalist labor-management relations. Mass demonstrations demanding government employment and housing programs indicated a collective political response to problems previously adjudicated on a personal level. Radical challenges to the authority of capital (like the United Auto Workers' 1946 demand during the General Motors strike that wage increases come out of corporate profits rather than from price hikes passed on to consumers) demonstrated

The Meaning of Memory

a social responsibility and a commitment toward redistributing wealth rare in the history of American labor.[11]

Capital attempted to regain the initiative in the postwar years by making qualified concessions to working-class pressures for redistribution of wealth and power. Rather than paying wage increases out of corporate profits, business leaders instead worked to expand the economy through increases in government spending, foreign trade, and consumer debt. Such expansion could meet the demands of workers and consumers without undermining capital's dominant role in the economy. On the presumption that "a rising tide lifts all boats," business leaders sought to connect working-class aspirations for a better life to policies that ensured a commensurate rise in corporate profits, thereby leaving the distribution of wealth unaffected. Federal defense spending, highway construction programs, and home-loan policies expanded the economy at home in a manner conducive to the interests of capital, while the Truman Doctrine and Marshall Plan provided models for enhanced access to foreign markets and raw materials for American corporations. The Taft-Hartley Act of 1947 banned the class-conscious collective activities most threatening to capital (mass strikes, sympathy strikes, secondary boycotts): the leaders of labor, government, and business accepted as necessary the practice of paying wage hikes for organized workers out of the pockets of consumers and unorganized workers in the form of higher prices.[12]

Commercial network television played an important role in this emerging economy, functioning as a significant new object of consumer purchases as well as an important marketing medium. Sales of sets jumped from three million during the entire decade of the 1940s to over five million *a year* during the 1950s.[13] But television's most important economic function came from its role as an instrument of legitimation for transformations in values initiated by the new economic imperatives of postwar America. For Americans to accept the new world of 1950s consumerism, they had to make a break with the past. The Depression years had helped generate fears about installment buying and excessive materialism, while the New Deal and wartime mobilization had provoked suspicions about individual acquisitiveness and upward mobility. Depression era and wartime scarcities of consumer goods had led workers to internalize discipline and frugality while nurturing networks of mutual support through family, ethnic, and class associations. Government policies after the war encouraged an atomized acquisitive consumerism at odds with the lessons of the past. At the same time, federal home-loan policies stimulated migrations to the suburbs from urban, ethnic, working-class neighborhoods. The entry of television into the American home disrupted previous patterns of family life and encouraged fragmentation of the family into separate segments of the consumer market.[14] The priority of consumerism in the economy at large and on television may have seemed organic and unplanned, but conscious policy decisions by officials from both private and public sectors shaped the contours of the consumer economy and television's role within it.

Commercial Television and Economic Change

Government policies during and after World War II shaped the basic contours of home television as an advertising medium. Government-sponsored research and development during the war perfected the technology of home television while federal tax policies solidified its economic base. The government allowed corporations to deduct the costs of advertising from their taxable incomes during the war, despite the fact that rationing and defense production left business with few products to market. Consequently, manufacturers kept the names of their products before the public while lowering their tax obligations on high wartime profits. Their advertising expenditures supplied radio networks and advertising agencies with the capital reserves and business infrastructure that enabled them to dominate the television industry in the postwar era. After the war, federal antitrust action against the motion-picture studios broke up the "network" system in movies, while the FCC sanctioned the network system in television. In addition, FCC decisions to allocate stations on the narrow VHF band, to grant the networks ownership and operation rights over stations in prime markets, and to place a freeze on the licensing of new stations during the important years between 1948 and 1952 all combined to guarantee that advertising-oriented programming based on the model of radio would triumph over theater TV, educational TV, or any other form.[15] Government decisions, not market forces, established the dominance of commercial television, but these decisions reflected a view of the American economy and its needs which had become so well accepted at the top levels of business and government that it had virtually become the official state economic policy.

Fearing both renewed Depression and awakened militancy among workers, influential corporate and business leaders considered increases in consumer spending—of 30% to 50%—to be necessary to perpetuate prosperity in the postwar era.[16] Defense spending for the Cold War and the Korean conflict had complemented an aggressive trade policy to improve the state of the economy, but it appeared that the hope for an ever-expanding economy rested on increased consumer spending fueled by an expansion of credit.[17] Here, too, government policies led the way, especially with regard to stimulating credit purchases of homes and automobiles. During World War II, the marginal tax rate for most wage earners jumped from 4% to 25%, making the home ownership deduction more desirable. Federal housing-loan policies favored construction of new single-family, detached suburban houses over renovation or construction of central-city multi-family units. Debt-encumbered home ownership in accord with these policies stimulated construction of 30 million new housing units in just twenty years, bringing the percentage of home-owning Americans from below 40% in 1940 to more than 60% by 1960. Mortgage policies encouraging long-term debt and low down payments freed capital for other consumer purchases, while government highway building policies undermined mass-transit systems and contributed to increased demand for automobiles. Partly as a result of these policies, consumer spending on private cars averaged $7.5 billion per year in the 1930s and 1940s, but grew to $22 billion per year in 1950 and almost $30 billion by 1955.[18]

Business leaders understood the connection between suburban growth and increased consumer spending. A 1953 article in *Fortune* celebrated the "lush new suburban market" which "has centered its customs and conventions on the needs of children and geared its buying habits to them."[19] For the first time in U.S. history, middle-class and working-class families could routinely expect to own homes or buy new cars every few years. Between 1946 and 1965, residential mortgage debt rose three times as fast as the gross national product and disposable income. Mortgage debt accounted for just under 18% of disposable income in 1946, but it grew to almost

55% by 1965.[20] To ensure the eventual payment of current debts, the economy had to generate tremendous growth and expansion, further stimulating the need to increase consumer spending. Manufacturers had to find ways of motivating consumers to buy ever increasing amounts of commodities. Television provided an important means of accomplishing that end.

Television advertised individual products, but it also provided a relentless flow of information and persuasion that placed acts of consumption at the core of everyday life. The physical fragmentation of suburban growth and subsequent declines in motion-picture attendance created an audience more likely to stay at home and to receive entertainment there than ever before. But television also provided a forum for redefining American ethnic, class, and family identities into consumer identities. To accomplish this task effectively, television programs had to address some of the psychic, moral, and political obstacles to consumption among the public at large.

The television and advertising industries knew they had to overcome consumer resistance. Marketing expert and motivational specialist Ernest Dichter observed that "one of the basic problems of this prosperity is to give people that sanction and justification to enjoy it and to demonstrate that the hedonistic approach to life is a moral one, not an immoral one."[21] Dichter later noted the many barriers inhibiting consumer acceptance of unrestrained hedonism, and he called on advertisers "to train the average citizen to accept growth of his country and its economy as *his* growth rather than as a strange and frightening event."[22] One method of encouraging that acceptance, according to Dichter, consisted of identifying new products and styles of consumption with traditional, historically sanctioned practices and behaviors. He noted that such an approach held particular relevance in addressing consumers who had only recently acquired the means to spend freely and who might harbor a lingering conservatism about spending based on their previous experiences.[23]

Insecurities and anxieties among consumers compelled network television to address the complex legacies of the 1930s and 1940s in order to promote consumption in the 1950s. In the middle of its appeals to change the world in the present through purchase of the appropriate commodities, commercial network television in its early years also presented programs rooted in the historical experiences and aspirations of diverse working-class traditions. From the evocations of the Depression era that permeated the world of *The Honey-mooners*, to the recycled minstrel show stereotypes of *Amos 'n' Andy*, from the textured layers of immigrant experience underpinning the drama and charm of *The Goldbergs* and *Mama*, to the reenactment of immigrant histories in contemporaneous circumstances in *Life of Riley, Life With Luigi,* and *Hey, Jeannie*, the medium of the infinitely renewable present turned to past traditions and practices in order to explain and legitimate fundamentally new social relations in the present.

Family Formation and the Economy—The Television View

Advertisers incorporated their messages into urban, ethnic, working-class comedies through direct and indirect means. Tensions developed in the programs often found indirect resolutions in commercials. Thus Jeannie MacClennan's search for an American sweetheart in one episode of *Hey Jeannie* set up commercials proclaiming the virtues of Drene shampoo for keeping one prepared to accept last-minute dates and of Crest toothpaste for producing an attractive smile.[24] Conversations about shopping for new furniture in an episode of *The Goldbergs* directed viewers' attention to furnishings in the Goldberg home provided for the show by Macy's department store in exchange for a commercial acknowledgment.[25]

The content of the shows themselves offered even more direct emphasis on consumer spending. In one episode of *The Goldbergs*, Molly expresses disapproval of her future daughter-in-law's plan to buy a washing machine on the installment plan. "I know Papa and me never bought anything unless we had the money to pay for it," she intones with logic familiar to a generation with memories of the Great Depression. Her son, Sammy, confronts this "deviance" by saying "Listen, Ma, almost everybody in this country lives above their means—and everybody enjoys it." Doubtful at first, Molly eventually learns from her children and announces her conversion to the legitimacy of installment buying, proposing that the family buy two cars in order to "live above our means—the American way."[26] In a subsequent episode, Molly's daughter, Rosalie, assumes the role of ideological tutor to her mother. When planning a move out of their Bronx apartment to a new house in the suburbs, Molly ruminates about where to place her old furniture in her new home. "You don't mean we're going to take all this junk with us into a brand new house?" asks an exasperated Rosalie. With traditionalist sentiment Molly answers, "Junk? My furniture's junk? My furniture that I lived with and loved for twenty years is junk?" But by the end of the episode she accepts Rosalie's argument—even selling off all her old furniture to help meet the down payment on the new house and deciding to buy all new furniture on the installment plan.[27]

Chester A. Riley confronts similar choices about family and commodities in *The Life of Riley*. His wife complains that he only takes her out to the neighborhood bowling alley and restaurant, not to "interesting places." Riley searches for ways to impress her and discovers from a friend that a waiter at the fancy Club Morambo will let them eat first and pay later, for a cost of a dollar per week plus 10% interest. "Ain't that dishonest?" asks Riley. "No, it's usury," his friend replies. Riley does not borrow the money, but he impresses his wife anyway by taking the family out to dinner on the proceeds of a prize that he receives for being the one thousandth customer in a local flower shop. Though we eventually learn that Peg Riley only wanted attention and not an expensive meal, the happy ending of the episode hinges on Riley's restored prestige once he demonstrates his ability to provide a luxury outing for the family.[28]

The same episode of *The Life of Riley* reveals another consumerist element common to this subgenre. When Riley protests that he lacks the money needed to fulfill Peg's desires, she answers that he would have plenty of cash if he didn't spend so much on "needless gadgets." His shortage of funds becomes personal failure caused by incompetent behavior as a consumer. Nowhere do we hear about the size of his paycheck, relations between his union and his employer, or, for that matter, of the relationship between the value of his labor and the wages paid to him by the Stevenson Aircraft Company. Like Uncle David in *The Goldbergs* (who buys a statue of Hamlet shaking hands with Shakespeare and an elk's tooth with the Gettysburg address carved on it), Riley's comic character stems in part from a flaw which might be more justly applied to the entire consumer economy: a preoccupation with "needless gadgets." By contrast, Peg Riley's desire for an evening out is portrayed as reasonable and modest, as reparations due her for the inevitable tedium of housework. The solution to her unhappiness comes from an evening out, rather than from a change in her work circumstance. Even within the home, television elevates consumption over production: production is assumed to be a constant, only consumption can be varied. But more than enjoyment is at stake. Unless Riley can provide Peg with the desired night on the town, he will fail in his obligations as a husband and father.[29]

A similar theme provides the crisis in an episode of *Mama*. The youngest daughter, Dagmar, "innocently" expresses envy of a friend whose father received a promotion and consequently put up new wallpaper in his house. "Why doesn't Papa get promoted?" Dagmar chirps, "Everyone else does." When Mama explains that a carpenter makes less money than other fathers, Dagmar asks if it wouldn't be smarter for Papa to work in a bank. Overhearing this dialogue, Papa decides to accept his boss's offer to promote him to foreman, even though he knows it will ruin his friendship with the other workers. The logic of the episode instructs us that fathers will lose their standing if they disappoint their children's desires for new commodities.[30] Shows exploring tensions between family obligations and commodity purchases routinely assert that money cannot *buy* love, but they seem less clear about whether one can *trade* material wealth for affection. Even the usually self-absorbed Kingfish on *Amos 'n' Andy* gives in to his nephew Stanley's wish for "a birthday party with lots of expensive presents," while Jeannie MacClennan's search for romance suffers a setback when a prospective suitor sees her shabby apartment with its antiquated furniture.[31] On *The Goldbergs*, a young woman is forbidden to marry the man she loves by her mother because her mother says "I didn't raise my daughter to be a butcher's wife."[32] Alice Kramden in *The Honeymooners* can always gain the upper hand in arguments with her husband by pointing to his inadequacies as a provider. In each of these programs, consumer choices close the ruptures in personal relations, allowing episodes to reach narrative and ideological closure.

One episode of *Mama* typifies the confusion between consumer purchases and family happiness pervading urban, ethnic, working-class situation comedies in early network television. "Mama's Birthday," broadcast in 1954, delineated the tensions between family loyalty and consumer desire endemic to modern capitalist society. The show begins with Mama teaching Katrin to make Norwegian meatballs, which she used long ago to "catch" Papa. Unimpressed by that accomplishment, Katrin changes the subject and asks Mama what she wants for her birthday. In an answer that locates Mama within the gender roles of the 1950s, she replies, "Well, I think a fine new job for your Papa. You and Dagmar to marry nice young men and have a lot of wonderful children—just like I have. And Nels, well, Nels to become president of the United States."[33] In one sentence Mama sums up the dominant culture's version of legitimate female expectations: success at work for her husband, marriage and childrearing for her daughters, the presidency for her son—and nothing for herself.

But we learn that Mama does have some needs, although we do not hear it from her lips. Her sister, Jenny, asks Mama to attend a fashion show, but Mama cannot leave the house because she has to cook a roast for a guest whom Papa has invited to dinner. Jenny comments that Mama never seems to get out of the kitchen, adding that "it's a shame that a married woman can't have some time to herself." The complaint is a valid one, and we can imagine how it might have resonated for women in the 1950s. The increased availability of household appliances and the use of synthetic fibers and commercially processed food should have decreased the amount of time women spent in housework, but surveys showed that homemakers spent the same number of hours per week (between 51 and 56) doing housework as had been the norm in the 1920s. Advertising and marketing strategies undermined the labor-saving potential of technological changes because they upgraded standards of cleanliness in the home and expanded desires for more varied wardrobes and menus for the average family.[34] In that context, Aunt Jenny would have been justified in launching into a tirade about the division of labor within the Hansen household or about the possibilities for cooperative housework, but network television specializes in less social and more commodified dialogues about problems like housework. Aunt Jenny suggests that her sister's family buy Mama a "fireless cooker," a cast-iron stove, for her birthday. "They're wonderful," she tells them in language borrowed from the rhetoric of advertising. "You just put your dinner inside them, close 'em up, and go wherever you please. When you come back your dinner is all cooked." Papa protests that Mama likes to cook on her woodburning stove, but Jenny dismisses that objection with an insinuation about his motives when she replies,

"Well I suppose it *would* cost a little more than you could afford, Hansen."[35]

By identifying a commodity as the solution to Mama's problem, Aunt Jenny unites the inner voice of Mama with the outer voice of the television sponsor. Mama's utility as an icon of material selflessness would be compromised if she asked for the stove herself, but Aunt Jenny's role in suggesting the gift removes any taint of selfishness while adding the authority of an outside expert. Aunt Jenny's accusation of stinginess when Papa expresses reluctance to buy the stove encourages the audience to resent him for not making enough money and even to see his poverty as a form of selfishness—it denies his wife the comforts due her. In reality, we know that Aunt Jenny's advice probably contains the usual distortions of advertising claims, that even if the fireless cooker enabled Mama to go where she pleased while dinner cooked, it would bring with it a hidden set of tasks and demands like keeping the stove clean or having to prepare a wider variety of meals. But in the fantasy world of television, such considerations do not intervene. Prodded by their aunt, the Hansen children go shopping and purchase the fireless cooker from a storekeeper who calls the product "the new Emancipation Proclamation—setting housewives free from their old kitchen range."[36] Our exposure to advertising hyperbole should not lead us to miss the analogy here: housework is compared to slavery and the commercial product takes on the aura of Abraham Lincoln. The shopkeeper's appeal convinces the children to pool their resources and buy the stove for Mama. But we soon learn that Papa plans to make a fireless cooker for Mama with his tools. When Mama discovers Papa's intentions, she persuades the children to buy her another gift. Even Papa admits that his stove will not be as efficient as one made in a factory, but Mama nobly affirms that she will like his better because he made it himself. The children use their money to buy dishes for Mama (a gift hardly likely to leave her with less work), and Katrin remembers the episode as Mama's happiest birthday ever.

The stated resolution of "Mama's Birthday" favors traditional values. Mama prefers to protect Papa's pride instead of having a better stove. The product built by a family member has more value than the one sold as a commodity. Yet as was so often the case in these urban, ethnic, working-class comedies, the entire development of the plot leads in the opposite direction. The "fireless cooker" is the star of the

episode, setting in motion all the other characters, and it has an unquestioned value, even in the face of Jenny's meddlesome brashness,
Papa's insensitivity, and Mama's old-fashioned ideals. Buying a product appears as the true means of changing the unpleasant realities
and low status of women's work in the home.

This resolution of the conflict between consumer desires and family roles reflected television's social role as mediator between the
family and the economy. Surveys of set ownership showed no pro-
nounced stratification by class, but a clear correlation between family
size and television purchases. Households with three to five people
were most likely to own television sets, while those with only one
person were least likely to own them.[37] The television industry recognized and promoted its privileged place within families in advertisements like the one in *The New York Times* in 1950 that claimed,
"Youngsters today need television for their morale as much as they
need fresh air and sunshine for their health."[38] Like previous communications media, television sets occupied honored places in family living rooms and helped structure family time; but unlike other
previous communications media, television displayed available commodities in a way that transformed home entertainment into a glorified shopping catalog.

Publicity about television programs stressed the interconnections
between family and economy as well. Viewers took the portrayals of
motherhood on these shows so seriously that when Peggy Wood of
Mama appeared on the *Garry Moore Show* and invited questions
from the audience, women asked her for advice about raising their
families as if she were actually Mama, rather than an actress playing
that role.[39] *The Ladies Home Journal* printed an article containing
"Mama's Recipes," featuring photographs of Peggy Wood, while Gertrude Berg wrote an article as Molly Goldberg for *TV Guide* that contained her recipes for borscht and blintzes. "Your meal should suit
the mood of your husband," Berg explained. "If he's nervous give
him a heavy meal. If he's happy, a salad will do."[40] Actors on the
shows also ignored the contradictions between their on-stage and
off-stage roles. Marjorie Reynolds told *TV Guide* that she enjoyed
playing Mrs. Chester A. Riley because, "I've done just about everything in films from westerns to no-voice musicals, and now with the
Riley show, I'm back in the kitchen. Where every wife belongs."[41]

The focus on the family in early network-television situation comedies involved a special emphasis on motherhood. Images of long-suffering but loving mothers pervaded these programs and publicity about them. Ostensibly representations of "tradition," these images actually spoke to a radical rupture with the past: the establishment of the isolated nuclear family of the 1950s with its attendant changes in family gender roles. The wartime economic mobilization that ended the Depression stimulated an extraordinary period of family formation that was in sharp contrast to the experience of preceding decades. Americans married more frequently, formed families at younger ages, and had more children in the 1940s than they had had in the 1920s and 1930s.[42] The combination of recommendations for permissive childrearing and social changes attendant to increases in consumer spending isolated mothers as never before. Work previously shared with extended kinship and neighborhood networks now had to be done at home in isolation by machines. Childrearing took up more time and responsibility, but inflation and expanded consumer desires encouraged women to work outside the home for pay. When the conflicting demands of permissivism created guilt and feelings of inadequacy, outside authorities—from child psychologists to television programs—stood ready to provide "therapeutic" images of desired maternal behavior.

While placing special burdens on women, changes in family identity in the postwar era transformed the roles of all family members. As psychoanalyst Joel Kovel demonstrates, the decomposition of extended kinship networks made the nuclear family the center of the personal world, "a location of desire and intimacy not previously conceptualized."[43] Kovel argues that contemporary society encourages a kind of "needy narcissism" in individuals, structuring them as ideal consumers. In his view, participation in civil society can keep individuals from sliding back into total narcissism, but the separation of family from society in modern capitalism blocks access to the public realm. The family becomes the locus of all social demands, an institution lauded all the more in theory as its traditional social functions disappear in practice. The family appears to be private and voluntary, yet its isolation from neighborhood and class networks leaves it subject to extraordinary regulation and manipulation by outside authorities like psychologists and advertisers. The family appears to be the repository of mutuality and affection, but commodity society has truncated its traditional functions into the egoism of possession. The family appears to maintain the privileges and authority of patriarchy, but "like a house nibbled by termites," the outwardly strong appearance of patriarchy masks a collapsing infrastructure no longer capable of wielding authority in an increasingly administered and institutionalized society. According to Kovel, the demise of the traditional family creates a need for authority that becomes filled by the "administrative mode"—the structure of domination that offers commodities as the key to solving personal problems.[44] Sociologist Nancy Chodorow draws a similar conclusion in her observation that "the decline of the oedipal father creates an orientation to external authority and behavioral obedience."[45] Chodorow also points out that the idealization of masculinity inherent in the "distant father" role in the nuclear family gives ideological priority to men, while channeling resentment and rebellion against the power wielded by the accessible and proximate mother. Kovel and Chodorow both stress that these patterns are neither natural nor inevitable: they emerge in concrete social circumstances where the nuclear family serves as the main base of support for consumer society.[46]

Commercial network television emerged as the primary discursive medium in American society at the precise historical moment when the isolated nuclear family and its concerns eclipsed previous ethnic, class, and political forces as the crucible of personal identity. Television programs both reflected and shaped that transition, defining the good life in family-centric, asocial, and commodity-oriented ways. As Todd Gitlin argues, "What is hegemonic in consumer capitalist ideology is precisely the notion that happiness, or liberty, or equality, or fraternity can be affirmed through existing private commodity forms, under the benign protective eye of the national security state."[47] Yet the denigration of public issues and the resulting overemphasis on the home contained contradictions of their own. If the harmonious and mutually supportive family of the past granted moral legitimacy to the consumer dilemmas of urban, ethnic, working-class families, the tensions of the modern nuclear household revealed the emerging nuclear family to be a contested terrain of competing needs and desires.

The structural tensions inherent in the "father-absent/mother-present" family identified by Chodorow pervaded television portrayals of urban, ethnic, working-class life in the 1950s. Peg Riley, Alice

Kramden, and Sapphire Stevens heroically endure their husbands' failures to deliver on promises of upward mobility, and they earn the sympathy of the audience by smoothing over the consequences of the inefficiency of their spouses. Yet their nagging insistence on practicality also marks them as "shrews," out to undercut male authority. Male insensitivity to female needs forms the focal point of humor and sardonic commentary in these programs, as in the episode of *The Life of Riley* where Riley can't understand Peg's complaints about staying home all the time. "I can't figure her out," he tells his son. "She's got a home to clean, meals to cook, dishes to wash, you two kids to look after, floors to scrub—what more does she want?"[48] Few shows displayed hostility between husbands and wives as openly as *The Honeymooners*. (Even the title functioned as bitter irony.) When Alice employs sarcasm in response to Ralph's "get rich quick" schemes and his neglect of her needs, Ralph invariably clenches his fist and says, "One of these days, Alice, one of these days, pow! right in the kisser!" Coupled with his threats to send her "to the moon," the intimation of wife-beating remains a recurring "comic" premise in the show. Jackie Gleason told one interviewer that he thought many husbands felt the way Ralph did about their wives. And an article in *TV Guide* quoted an unnamed "famous" psychiatrist who contended that the program's popularity rested on male perceptions that women had too much power, and on female perceptions that male immaturity demonstrated the superiority of women."[49] *The Honeymooners* might end with a humbled Ralph telling Alice, "Baby, you're the greatest," but the show clearly "worked" because tensions between men and women spoke to the experiences and fears of the audience.

Structural tensions within families, women betrayed by irresponsible and incompetent husbands, and men chafing under the domination of their wives: hardly an ideal portrait of family life. These depictions reflected the fissures in a fundamentally new form of family, a form which increasingly dominated the world of television viewers. One might expect commercial television programs to ignore the problems of the nuclear family, to present an idyllic view of the commodity-centered life. But the industry's imperial ambition—the desire to have all households watching at all times—encouraged exploitation of real fears and problems confronting viewers. Censorship eliminated many possible topics, but family tensions and resentments offered legitimate and fertile ground for television programs. Individuals cut off from previous forms of self-definition and assaulted by media images encouraging narcissistic anxieties had insatiable needs to survey the terrain of family problems, to seek relief from current tensions and reassurance about the legitimacy of current social relations.

In order to create subjects receptive to the appeals of advertisers and to achieve ideological and narrative closure for their own stories, the creators of television programs had to touch on real issues, albeit in truncated and idealized forms. While they unfailingly offered only individual solutions to problems, the mere act of exposing the contradictions of the nuclear family created the structural potential for oppositional readings by viewers. Representations of generational and gender tensions undercut the legitimating authority of the televised traditional working-class family by demonstrating the chasm between the memories of yesterday and the realities of today. If the programs remained true to the past, they lost their relevance to current tensions. Yet when they successfully addressed contemporary problems, they forfeited the legitimacy offered by the past, making it easier for viewers to escape the pull of parochialism and parental authority embedded in the traditional family form. This clash between the legitimizing promise of urban, ethnic, working-class shows and their propensity for exposing the shortcomings of both past and present social relations extended beyond family issues and affected portrayals of work, class, and ethnicity as well.

Work, Class, and Ethnicity

Changes in the nature of working-class identity accompanied the changing roles of family and consumer in the 1950s. The decade of the 1940s had not only witnessed an unprecedented transformation in the nature of the American family, but it also encompassed an extraordinary social upheaval among workers, which labor historian Stanley Aronowitz has characterized as a period of "incipient class formation."[50] War mobilization reindustrialized the sagging U.S. economy and it reconstituted the working class. Migrations to defense production centers and breakthroughs by women and blacks in securing industrial employment changed the composition of the work force. Traditional parochial loyalties waned as mass production and full employment created new work groups on the shop floor and new working-class communities outside the factory gates. Mass strikes and demonstrations united workers from diverse backgrounds into a polity capable of sustained collective action. Of course, racism and sexism remained pervasive on both institutional and grass-roots levels, but the mass activity of the postwar era represented the stirrings of a class consciousness previously unknown in a proletariat deeply divided by ethnicity, race, and gender. By the 1950s, expanded consumer opportunities, suburbanization, and access to education offered positive inducements away from that class consciousness, while anti-Communism, purges of dissidents, and restrictions on rank-and-file activism acted negatively to undermine trade unions as crucibles of class consciousness. Yet retentions of the incipient class formation of the 1940s percolated throughout the urban, ethnic, working-class situation comedies of the 1950s.

Jeannie Carson, the star of *Hey, Jeannie*, began her career as a performer by singing to Welsh miners as they came out of the pits. Appropriately enough, her U.S. television series adopted a working-class locale—the home of Al Murray, a Brooklyn cab driver, and his sister, Liz.[51] The setting imposed certain structural directions on the program's humor, directions that gave voice to sharp class resentments. One episode contains Al Murray's efforts to hide his cab in a neighbor's garage so that he can take the day off from work to watch his beloved Dodgers play baseball at Ebbetts Field. Sensing Murray's dereliction of duty, the cab company president delivers a self-righteous harangue about the evils of such behavior to his secretary. Pontificating about the social responsibilities of a taxi-cab company, a "public utility," he asks his secretary if she knows what happens when one of his cabs is not operating. "No, what?" she inquires. "It cuts into my profits," he responds.[52] Humor based on such hypocrisy by employers has a long history in working-class culture, but it is rarely the subject of mass-media comedy. As the episode continues, the boss's secretary (in an act of solidarity) calls Liz and Jeannie to warn them that the boss is out on the streets looking for Al's cab. Jeannie takes the taxi out of the garage to prevent Al's boss from finding it there, but accustomed to driving in her native Scotland, she drives on the left side of the street and gets stopped by a police officer. The policeman discovers that she is an immigrant and remembering his own days as an immigrant from Ireland, lets her off with a warning. The resolution of the episode finds Jeannie getting to the ballpark in time to get Al back to the cab where his boss finds him and apologizes for even suspecting his employee of misconduct. The episode resonates with class consciousness, from the many acts of solidarity that get Al off the hook to the final victory over the boss—a victory gained by turning work time into play time and getting away with it. That kind of collective activity in pursuit of common goals appears frequently in the urban, ethnic, working-class situation comedies of the 1950s, in incidents ranging from the rent strike by tenants in *The Goldbergs* to community protests against a utility company's destruction of a favorite neighborhood tree in *Life With Luigi*.[53]

The workplace rarely appears in television comedies about working-class life; when it does, it usually signals seething class resentments. On one episode of *Mama*, Lars Hansen tells another worker that he prefers working for Mr. Jenkins to working for Mr. Kingsley because "Mr. Jenkins doesn't lose his temper so much." Mr. Kingsley also demands work speed-ups from his employees and he tries to pressure Papa into making the other workers produce at a faster pace.[54] In this episode, the workplace is a site where workers with common interests experience fragmentation. In *The Goldbergs*, even after Jake Goldberg graduates from his job as a tailor to become owner of a small dressmaking firm, work prevents him from enjoying life. Business pressures take him away from his family and prevent him from developing any recreational interests. When Molly's Uncle David starts playing pool, Jake confides that he never learned to play because "pool is a game that requires leisure." However, his business sense causes him to lean over the table, touch it, and murmur with admiration, "nice quality felt, though."[55] Jake's work brings in a bigger financial reward than Al Murray's cab driving or Lars Hansen's carpentry, but it still compels him to trade the precious minutes and hours of his life for commodities that he hardly has time to enjoy. Work as a noble end in itself is almost entirely absent from these shows. No work ethic or pride in labor motivates these workers. In fact, Ed Norton's pride in his job as a sewer worker provides a recurrent comic premise in *The Honeymooners*. The object of work in these programs consists of material reward to enhance one's standing within the family or to obtain some leisure-time commodity.

Not only does work appear infrequently in 1950s comedies about working-class life, but blue-collar labor often appears as a stigma, a condition that retards the acquisition of desired goods. The Kramdens' barren apartment in *The Honeymooners* underscores their barrenness as a childless couple; Ralph's circular bus route symbolizes the dead-end nature of his job and of his life which is going nowhere.[56] But even demeaning portrayals of working-class people sometimes contain contradictions, allowing for negotiated or oppositional readings. Advertisers and network officials lauded Chester A. Riley's "magnificent stupidity" as the key to the big ratings garnered by *The Life of Riley*. But that "stupidity" sometimes masked other sensibilities. At a fancy dinner where the Rileys are clearly out of place, they meet a blue-blood named Cecil Spencer Kendrick III. "You mean there's two more of you inside?" Riley asks. The audience laughter at his gaffe comes in part from resentment against the antidemocratic pretensions of Kendrick and his associates.[57] Similarly, when Riley's neighbor Jim Gillis tries to impress him with tales about the fancy food at an expensive restaurant, Riley gets Gillis to admit that crepes suzette are nothing more than "pancakes soaked in kerosene and then set on fire."[58] That capacity for unintentional insight also propels the malaprop-laden humor of Molly Goldberg. Who could dispute her self-sacrificing virtue when Molly vows to save money by purchasing old furniture: "I don't care how old, even antique furniture would be fine." She complains that her cousin has been gone for two weeks and that she hasn't seen "hide nor seek of him," and she warns her uncle that she will give him only one word of advice, and that word is "be sure." When Molly says that "patience is a vulture," or that "it never rains until it pours," her misstatements carry unexpected wisdom.[59]

Resentments about work, refusals to acknowledge the legitimacy of the upper classes, and creative word play abound in these programs, transmitting the texture of decades of working-class experience. Similarly, fraternal orders and ethnic lodges appear in television shows of the 1950s as a reflection of real historical experience. Historically, fraternal orders and mutual-aid societies offered essential resources to working-class people, often providing insurance, burial expenses, recreational facilities, and adult education at a time when neither the private sector nor the state accepted any of those responsibilities. Yet, in the urban, ethnic, working-class situation comedies of the early 1950s, the fraternal lodge appears as an archaic and anachronistic institution, a remnant of the past at odds with the needs of the contemporary family. Thus Lars Hansen's dinner guests from the Sons of Norway only produce more work for Mama.[60] Chester A. Riley wastes his time and money on the Brooklyn Patriots of Los Angeles, an organization set up to revere the world he left behind when he moved to the west coast. The Mystic Knights of the Sea provide Kingfish with a theater of operations for bilking his "brothers" out of their money, and for indulging his inflated sense of self-importance. The Royal Order of Raccoons keeps Ralph Kramden from spending time with Alice, and lodge dues eat away at his paycheck at the expense of his household. In one show Alice asks Ralph what benefit she derives from his lodge activities. With much bombast he informs her proudly that his membership entitles both of them to free burial in the Raccoon National Cemetery in Bismarck, North Dakota. With appropriate sarcasm, Alice replies that the prospect of burial in North Dakota makes her wonder why she should go on living.[61]

In organic popular memory, lodges may have retained legitimacy as sources of mutuality and friendship, but they represented an ideological threat to the consumer-and family-centered world of early network television. In an age when suburban tract housing replaced the urban ethnic neighborhood, when the state took on welfare functions previously carried out by voluntary associations, and when the home sphere became increasingly isolated from the community around it, the lodge hall became a premise for comic ridicule. The interests of television families took precedence over those of the lodge hall, and a binary opposition between the two seemed inevitable. Yet the very inclusion of the lodges in these programs demonstrates the power of the past in discourse about the present. Television programs validated the atomized nuclear family at the expense of the extended kin and class networks manifested in the fraternal order. When successful, these shows undercut the ability of the past to provide legitimacy for contemporary social relations. When unsuccessful, these shows called attention to the possibilities of other forms of community and culture than those that dominated the present.

Cultural specificity about working-class life provided credibility for early network television programs, but at the same time created problems for advertisers. Erik Barnouw points out that sponsors hardly relished the prospect of shows situated in lower-class environments (like the enormously successful teleplay *Marty*), because "Sponsors were meanwhile trying to 'upgrade' the consumer and persuade him to 'move up to a Chrysler,' and 'live better electrically' in a suburban home, with 'help from a friend at Chase Manhattan.' The sponsors preferred beautiful people in mouth-watering decor to convey what it meant to climb the socioeconomic ladder. The commercials looked out of place in Bronx settings."[62]

The working class depicted in urban, ethnic, working-class situation comedies of the 1950s bore only a superficial resemblance to the historical American working class. Stripped of essential icons of ethnicity and class, interpreted through perspectives most relevant to a consuming middle class, and pictured in isolation from the social connections that gave purpose and meaning to working-class lives, the televised blue-collar family summoned up only the vaguest contours of its historical counterpart. Even in comparison to depictions of class in other forms of communication like folklore, theater, music, literature, or radio, television presented a desiccated and eviscerated version of working-class life. Yet the legitimizing functions served by locating programs in working-class environments caused some attempts at authenticity that brought sedimented class tensions to the surface. While the producers of these shows hardly intended to direct viewers' attentions toward real ethnic and class conflicts, the social location of the writers and actors most knowledgeable about working-class life served to make some of these programs focal points for controversy. When producers took on the task of replicating working-class settings as a form of local color, they also burdened themselves with the contradictions of the communities that provided the color, as evidenced by the public controversies provoked by *The Goldbergs* and *Amos 'n' Andy*.

Part of the convincing authenticity of *The Goldbergs* came from actors and writers who developed their skills within the Yiddish theater and the culture that supported it. An organic part of that culture included political activists, among them Communists, socialists, and antifascists whose concerns found expression in a variety of community activities including the theater. Philip Loeb, who played Jake Goldberg, became the center of controversy when a right-wing anti-Communist publication accused him of subversive connections be-

cause of his appearances at antifascist rallies and his having signed a
petition calling for the admission of Negroes into professional baseball. Afraid of threatened boycotts by anti-Communist groups, nervous sponsors and advertising representatives dropped their support
of *The Goldbergs* and demanded that Gertrude Berg use her position
as producer and star to fire Loeb. At first she refused, pointing out
that Loeb had never been a Communist, but ultimately Berg gave in
to the pressure and fired her co-star in order to keep her show on
the air. Sponsors resumed their support after Loeb left the program
in 1952, and *The Goldbergs* ran for four more years. Loeb received a
$45,000 settlement in exchange for a promise not to sue the show for
firing him, but he never worked again as an actor because producers
viewed him as controversial. In 1956, Loeb committed suicide.[63]

Similarly, Mady Christians played Mama in the Broadway play *I Remember Mama*, but could not get the role on television. Anti-
Communist pressure groups harassed Christians because she had
worked on behalf of refugees from fascism in the 1930s and 1940s
along with individuals accused of subversive associations. Blacklisted
from her profession, Christians sank into a severe depression that
friends felt sapped her strength and made her unable to overcome
health problems that led to her death in 1951. Loeb and Christians
dismayed advertisers, not because of their political views, but because their presence provoked political controversy and interfered
with the illusions of a world without politics created by their programs. Like the real-life Goldbergs and Hansens of America, Philip
Loeb and Mady Christians lived in a world made up of more than
consumer purchases, a world where ethnicity connected people to
important political issues. The controversy over their histories and
the public attention directed toward them threatened to unmask the
world of *Mama* and *The Goldbergs* as a created artifact, polarizing the
audience and depriving television of its legitimating power.

Amos 'n' Andy contained similar, but more culturally explosive,
connections. Stereotyped and demeaning portrayals of Afro-
Americans have long constituted an obsessive theme in American
theater (and, for that matter, in American life). Historian Nathan Irvin
Huggins points out that the minstrel-show stereotypes enabled white
society at the turn of the twentieth century to attribute to black people the very characteristics it feared most in itself. At a time when
industrialization demanded a revolutionary transformation in behav-

ior, compelling Americans to accept Victorian values of thrift, sobriety, discipline, and abstinence, the minstrel show emerged to identify greed, gluttony, laziness, and licentiousness as singular traits of black people. These images worked to legitimate the emerging Victorian code by associating opposition to dominant ideology with the despised and taboo culture of Afro-Americans. The minstrel show "Negro" presented white society with a representation of the natural self at odds with the normative self of industrial culture. Uninhibited behavior could be savored by the id during the minstrel performance, but overruled afterward by the superego. The viewer could release tension by pointing to the minstrel show "darkie" and saying "It's him, not me." But the viewer came back, again and again. The desire to subjugate and degrade black people had political and economic imperatives of its own, but emotional and psychic reinforcement for that exploitation came from the ways in which racist stereotypes enabled whites to accept the suppression of their natural selves.

The centrality of racist images to white culture presented peculiar problems for Afro-Americans. Entry into white society meant entry into its values, and those values included hatred of blacks. To participate in the white world, blacks had to make concessions to white America's fantasy images. As Huggins notes, black people found it dangerous to step out of character, either on or off stage. The great black vaudeville entertainer Bert Williams embodied the absurd contradictions of this process: he donned blackface makeup to perform on stage—a black man imitating white men imitating black men. Williams' artistic genius and stubborn self-respect led him to inject subtle elements of social criticism into his act, but for most spectators, he merely reinforced their *a priori* conclusions about the stage Negro.[64]

The black cast of *Amos 'n' Andy* came out of the theatrical traditions that spawned Bert Williams, and they perpetuated many of his contradictions. As a successful radio program, the all-black world of *Amos 'n' Andy* had been performed mostly by its white creators (Freeman Gosden and Charles Correll). With the move to television, Gosden and Correll hired an all-black cast, but they faced protests from community groups. The National Association for the Advancement of Colored People and black actor James Edwards campaigned to have the program taken off the air because they felt it made the only televised presentation of Afro-American life an insulting one. The NAACP complained in federal court that black citizens routinely suffered abuse from whites addressing them as "Amos" or "Andy," and that the program defamed black professionals by presenting them as liars and cheats. In response, black actors employed on the program and a few black intellectuals defended *Amos 'n' Andy* as a harmless satire and an important vehicle for bring much needed exposure to black actors.[65] But Nick Stewart, who played the demeaningly stereotypical character "Lightnin' " on the television program, hated his role. Years later he told a reporter, "I saw it as an opportunity. I couldn't have learned without an opportunity to play these roles, but I saw how this was poisoning the black community."[66] Stewart used his earnings from *Amos 'n' Andy* to build the Ebony Showcase Theatre, an Afro-American community repertory group, but he felt that the kinds of racist imagery perpetuated by the program continued to make it difficult for black actors.

Placed in historical context, *Amos 'n' Andy* did for the values of the 1950s what the minstrel show accomplished for previous generations. Everything considered precious but contested in white society—like the family or the work ethic—became violated in the world of Kingfish. Ambition for upward mobility drew ridicule only when pursued by blacks. In a society nurtured on Horatio Alger stories about rising from rags to riches, this lampooning of a black man's aspirations served to release tensions about the fear of failure. It could redirect hostility away from the elite toward those on the bottom of society. When Kingfish pretends to be educated and uses grandiose language, the audience can howl derisively at his pretensions. But the same audience could glow with warm recognition when Mama Hansen uses her broken English to express her dreams for her son to grow up to be president. Ambition viewed as worthy and realistic for the Hansens becomes a symbol of vanity and weak character when voiced by Kingfish.

Consistent with the values of the 1950s as mediated through popular culture, family responsibilities—or neglect of them—define Kingfish even more than work or ethnicity. The glorification of motherhood pervading psychological and popular literature of the 1950s becomes comedy in *Amos 'n' Andy*. Wives named for precious stones (Ruby and Sapphire) appear anything but precious, and "Mama" in this show appears as a nagging harpy screaming invective at the cowering—and emasculated—black man. Kingfish shares Ralph Kramden's dreams of overnight success, but his transgressions against bourgeois morality are more serious. Kingfish has no job, his late-night revelries and lascivious grins hint at marital infidelity, and he resorts to criminal behavior to avoid what he calls "the horrors of employment." He betrays his family and cheats his lodge brothers (and by implication the "brothers" of his race) with no remorse. But his most serious flaws stem from neglect of the proper roles of husband and father. In one episode, Kingfish's late-night excursions cause his wife, Sapphire, to leave home and live with her mother. Kingfish misses her and orders one of his lackeys to find out where she has gone. When the report comes back that Sapphire has been seen entering an obstetrician's office, Kingfish assumes that he is about to become a father. In reality, Sapphire has simply taken a job as the doctor's receptionist, but the misunderstanding leads Kingfish to tell Amos how much fun he plans to have as a father. When Amos warns him that fatherhood involves serious responsibilities, Kingfish replies, "What you mean serious? All you gotta do is keep 'em filled up wid milk an' pablum and keep chuckin' em under de chin."[67] Kingfish's ignorance plays out the worst fears of people in a society with a burgeoning obsession with family. By representing the possibility of incompetent parenting, Kingfish provides the audience with a sense of superiority, but one that can be maintained only by embracing parental responsibilities. Lest we miss the point of the show, Kingfish and his friend Andy go to a clinic for prospective fathers where they learn to bathe a baby by practicing with a doll. Kingfish lets his slip under the water and "drown."[68]

Black protests made *Amos 'n' Andy* a much debated phenomenon, unmasking the calculation that went into its creation. In the context of the 1950s, when migration to industrial cities created greater concentrations of black political and economic power, these protests could not be dismissed casually by advertisers or the networks. Blatz Beer decided to drop its sponsorship of *Amos 'n' Andy* in 1954, knocking the show off prime-time schedules and into syndication until 1966 when another wave of protests made it untenable even in reruns. As the program most thoroughly grounded in ideologically charged historical material, *Amos 'n' Andy* lent itself most easily to critical historical interpretation and action. That capacity conflicted with the needs and desires of advertisers. But just with shows rooted in white working-class histories, structural contradictions in black working-class life also allowed for oppositional readings of the program's content. Black activist and author Julius Lester recalls his own formative experiences with *Amos 'n' Andy* in his autobiography in a quintessential example of reinterpreting hierarchically prepared and distributed mass culture. Ruminating on the seeming paradox of a home life that installed black pride into him, but that also encouraged him to listen to the antics of the Kingfish, Lester recalls

> In the character of the Kingfish, the creators of Amos and Andy may have thought they were ridiculing blacks as lazy, shiftless, scheming and conniving, but to us Kingfish was a paradigm of virtue, an alternative to the work ethic. Kingfish lived: Amos made a living. It did not matter that my parents lived by and indoctrinated me with the Puritan work ethic. Kingfish had a *joie de vivre* no white person could poison, and we knew that whites ridiculed us because they were incapable of such élan. I was proud to belong to the same race as Kingfish.[69]

Whether through the careful decoding exemplified by Julius Lester, or through the politicization of *Amos 'n' Andy* by mass protest, audience response to the program in some cases focused on the show's artifice and distortions of history. As was the case with *The Goldbergs*, the traditions needed to provide legitimacy for advertising messages surrounding *Amos 'n' Andy* contained sedimented contestation that undermined their effectiveness, and instead provoked negotiated or oppositional readings. Dominant ideology triumphed on television in the 1950s, just as it did in political and social life. But historically grounded opposition remained possible and necessary for at least part of the audience.

The realism that made urban, ethnic, working-class situation comedies convincing conduits for consumer ideology also compelled them to present alienations and aspirations subversive to the legitimacy of consumer capitalism. As Antonio Gramsci insists, ideological hegemony stems from the ability of those in power to make their own interests appear to be synonymous with the interests of society at large. But appeals for legitimacy always take place within concrete historical circumstances, in contested societies with competing interests. In a consumer capitalist economy, where unmet needs and individual isolation provide the impetus for commodity desires, legitimation is always incomplete. Even while establishing dominance, those in power must borrow from the ideas, actions, and experience of the past, all of which contain potential for informing a radical critique of the present.

Dialogue, Negotiation, and Legitimation: Method and Theory

Recent scholarship in literary criticism, cultural studies, and sociology offers investigative methods and theoretical frameworks essential to understanding the historical dialogue about family, class, and ethnicity in early network television. The literary criticism and "dialogic imagination" proposed by Mikhail Bakhtin demonstrates how all texts inherit part of the historical consciousness of their authors and audiences.[70] Cultural studies theorist Stuart Hall notes that commercial mass media seek legitimacy with audiences by effectively representing diverse aspects of social life including memories of past experiences, current contradictions, and potential sources of division and opposition.[71] Sociologist Jürgen Habermas observes that contemporary capitalist culture destroys the very motivations that it requires for the smooth functioning of the system, such as the work ethic or the willingness to defer gratification. Consequently, capitalist societies draw upon the borrowed legitimacy of cultural values and beliefs from the past, like religion or the patriarchal family, to provide the appearance of moral grounding for contemporary forces inimical to the interests of tradition.[72] Taken collectively, these approaches to culture provide a useful context for understanding the persistence of seemingly outdated and dysfunctional themes in early network television.

Bakhtin's analysis of text construction argued that communication does not begin in the present with a speaker or story, but, rather, that both speech and narrative come from a social matrix that is (at least in part) historical. Each speaker enters a dialogue already in progress; every work of art contains within it past, present, and future struggles over culture and power. Forms of communication from the past not only make current discourse comprehensible and legitimate, but they also imbed within the present a collective historical experience rich with contradictions. The producers of early network television worked in a new medium, but they addressed an audience acclimated to specific forms of comedy and drama that reflected, however indirectly, the real texture of past struggles and present hopes.

Structural unities underlie the seemingly divergent stories of different ethnic, working-class situation comedies. Viewers rarely saw Ralph Kramden's bus or Jake Goldberg's dressmaking shop, but the cameras introduced them to every detail of furnishing in the Kramden and Goldberg households. Difficulties encountered in the aircraft factory assembly line by Chester A. Riley or at the construction site by Lars Hansen paled in significance in contrast to the dilemmas of consumption faced in the Riley and Hansen families. The texture and tone of *Life with Luigi* and *Amos 'n' Andy* came from the ethnic worlds they depicted, but the plots of those shows dealt with the aspirations of individuals as if ethnic rivalries and discrimination did not exist. Instead, ethnics attain a false unity through consumption of commodities: Jeannie MacClennan learns to "be an American" by dressing fashionably and wearing the right makeup; Luigi Basco hopes to prove himself a worthy candidate for citizenship by opening a checking account and purchasing an insurance policy; Molly Goldberg overcomes her fears of installment buying and vows to live above her means, "the American way."[73] Comedies in this subgenre reflect Stuart Hall's contention that the commercial mass media tend to direct popular consciousness toward consumption and away from production. They present social actions and experiences as atomized individual events, fragmenting social groups into isolated consumers. They resolve the tensions confronting their audiences by binding them together in false collectivities defined for the convenience of capital accumulation.[74]

But Hall also shows that the imperial aspirations of the mass media lead to a disclosure of contradictions, allowing cultural consumers to fashion oppositional or negotiated readings of mass culture. To make their dramas compelling and their narrative resolutions dynamic, the media also reflect the plurality of consumer experiences. A system that seeks to enlist everyone in the role of consumer must appear to be addressing all possible circumstances; a system that proclaims consensus and unanimity must acknowledge and explain obvious differences within the polity, if for no other reason than to co-opt or trivialize potential opposition. Television, and other forms of electronic mass media, so effectively recapitulate the ideology of the historical bloc in which they operate that they touch on all aspects of social life—even its antagonistic contradictions. While the media serve to displace, fragment, and atomize real experiences, they also generate and circulate a critical dialogue as one unintended consequence of their efforts to expose the inventory of social practice.

Of course, mere disclosure of opposition does not guarantee emancipatory practice; ruling elites routinely call attention to "deviant" subcultures to draw a distinction between permitted and forbidden behavior. In urban, ethnic, working-class situation comedies in the 1950s, "deviant" traits, like Kingfish's aversion to work in *Amos 'n' Andy* and Lars Hansen's lack of ambition in *Mama*, taught object lessons about the perils of unconventional behavior. Yet the operative premises and enduring tensions in each of these shows revolved around the "otherness" of the lead characters. The "old-world" attitudes of newly arrived immigrants in *Hey, Jeannie* and *Life with Luigi* or the proletarian cultural innocence manifested in *The Life of Riley* or *The Honeymooners* led to comedic clashes that exposed the inadequacies and deficiencies of those on the margins of society. But at the same time, these clashes counterposed the conformity and materialism of the mainstream to the narratively privileged moral superiority of those with connections to the past. Traditional values and beliefs prevented protagonists in these shows from achieving success or happiness as defined by society, but those values and beliefs also facilitated a critical distance from the false premises of the present. As Gertrude Berg noted in an explanation of the popularity of her character Molly Goldberg, Molly "lived in the world of today but kept many of the values of yesterday."[75]

The complicated dialogue between the past and present embodied in Molly Goldberg underscores the complex role played by historical referents in early network television. The past that brought credibility and reassurance to family dramas also contained the potential for undermining the commodified social relations of the present. The Goldberg family interested advertisers because audiences identified their story as part of a precious collective memory resonating with actual experiences and lessons from the past. The Goldbergs could not be credible representatives of that past if they appeared to live amid the plethora of consumer goods that dominated commercials, or if they appeared uncritical of the consumer world of the present that made such a sharp break with the values of the past. Yet the Goldberg family had little value to advertisers unless their experiences sanctioned pursuit of commodities in the present. The creators of the program resolved this potential contradiction by putting the borrowed moral capital from the past at the service of the material values of the present. They acknowledged the critiques of materialism and upward mobility sedimented within the experiences of working-class families, but they demonstrated over and over again how wise choices enabled consumers to have *both* moral and material rewards. By positing the nuclear family as a transhistorical and "natural" locus for the arbitration of consumer desires, television portrayed the specific value crises of the 1950s as eternal and recurrent. By collapsing the distinction between family as consumer unit and family as part of neighborhood, ethnic, and class associations, television programs in the early 1950s connected the most personal and intimate needs of individuals to commodity purchases. They implied that the past sanctioned rather than contradicted the ever-increasing orientation toward shopping as the cornerstone of social life, an orientation characteristic of most media discourse in the postwar era.

The reliance on the past to justify controversial changes in present behavior forms the core of Jürgen Habermas's analysis of contemporary capitalism's "legitimation crisis." According to Habermas, the consumer consciousness required by modern capitalism revolves around "civil and familial-vocational privatism," a syndrome that elevates private consumer decisions over social relations and public responsibility. Individuals view their families as primarily centers of consumption and leisure, while they regard employment as primarily a means of engaging in status competition. Instead of the rooted independence demanded by traditional family and community life, contemporary capitalist society encourages an atomized dependence on outside authorities—on advertisers, self-help experts, psychiatric, educational, and political authorities. Clearly useful for purposes of capital accumulation, this process undermines traditional motivations for work, patriotism, and social relations, causing real crises for society. In addition, the infantile narcissism nurtured by this consumer consciousness requires validation by outside authorities, requires assurance that the impoverishment of work, family, and political life characteristic of late capitalism constitutes a legitimate and necessary part of progress toward a better life.[76]

For Habermas, the mass media play a crucial role in legitimation, but they do so imperfectly. The new forms of family and vocational consciousness cannot be justified on their own, but can be validated by invoking the moral authority of past forms of family and community. Thus the "work ethic" is summoned to justify a system based on commodified leisure. Mutual love and affection are called upon to sanction families that exist primarily as consumer units. The social relations of the past are used to legitimate a system that in reality works to destroy the world that created those historical relations in the first place. Consequently, the invocation of the past in the service of the present is a precarious undertaking. Tradition used to legitimate untraditional behavior may instead call attention to the disparity between the past and the present. Collective popular memory may see the manipulative use of tradition by advertisers as a conscious strategy, as an attempt to create artifacts that conflict with actual memory and experience. As Habermas cautions, "traditions can retain legitimizing force only as long as they are not torn out of interpretive systems that guarantee continuity and identity."[77]

Habermas provides us with a framework capable of explaining both the presence of historical elements in early network television shows and their limitations. In conjunction with Bakhtin's emphasis on dialogue and Hall's delineation of negotiation, Habermas's analysis explains how portrayals of traditional, ethnic, working-class families might have been essential for legitimizing social forces that undermined the very values that made those kinds of families respected icons in popular consciousness. At the same time, Habermas directs our attention to the fundamental instability of this legitimation process, to the ways in which audiences might come to see manipulative uses of the past as created artifacts at war with the lessons of history as preserved in collective popular memory.

After 1958, network television eliminated urban ethnic working-class programs from the schedule. Marc Daniels, who directed *The Goldbergs*, recalls that a changing society less tied to class and ethnicity demanded different kinds of entertainment, and certainly the emergence of ethnically neutral, middle-class situation comedies between 1958 and 1970 lends credence to his interpretation.[78] The entry of major film studios into television production in the mid-1950s also had an impact, since the working-class shows tended to be produced by small companies like Hal Roach studios. Major studio involvement in television production increased the proportion of action/adventure shows with production values ill-suited to the realism of urban, ethnic, working-class programs. In action and adventure shows, no embarrassing retentions of class-consciousness compromise the sponsors' messages and no social connections to ethnic history bring up disturbing issues that might make programs susceptible to protests and boycotts.

One might conclude that television and American society had no more need for urban, ethnic, working-class programs after 1958 because tensions between consumerist pressures and historical memories had been resolved. But the re-appearance of race, class, and ethnicity in 1970s situation comedies like *All in the Family, Chico and the Man, Barney Miller*, and *Sanford and Son* testifies to the ongoing relevance of such tensions to subsequent mass-media discourse. Michael Morris, who produced *Chico and the Man*, had spent eight years with Gertrude Berg as a writer, story editor, and director of *The Goldbergs* in the 1940s and 1950s. The programs of the 1970s reprised both aspects of the 1950s shows—legitimation through representations of working-class life and commodification through product-centered plot lines and portrayals of families divided by market interests. Like their predecessors, urban, ethnic, working-class shows of the 1970s mixed their commercial messages with visions of connections to others that transcended the limits of civil and familial vocational privatism. They held open possibilities for transcending the parochialisms of traditional ethnicity and for challenging the patriarchal assumptions of both extended and nuclear families. The same communications apparatus that presented consumerism as the heir to the moral legacy of the working-class past also legitimized aspirations for happiness and community too grand to be satisfied by the lame realities of the commodity-centered world.

In the early 1950s, an advertising instrument under the control of powerful monopolists established itself as the central discursive medium in American culture. With its penetration of the family and its incessant propaganda for commodity purchases, television helped erode the social base for challenges to authority manifest in the mass political activity among American workers in the 1940s. Yet television did not so much ensure the supremacy of new values as it transformed the terms of social contestation. As mass culture gained in importance as an instrument of legitimation, oppositional messages filtered into even hierarchically controlled media constructions like network television programs. The internal contradictions of capitalism fueled this process by generating anxieties in need of legitimation, and by turning for legitimation to the very beliefs and practices most threatened by emerging social relations. Thus every victory for the ideology of civil and familial vocational privatism can also constitute a defeat. Every search for legitimacy can end in the dilution of legitimacy by unmasking media messages as prepared and fabricated ideological artifices. Even successful legitimation fails to a degree, because the new social relations destroy their own source of legitimacy.

This is not to assume that the final outcome of television's ideological imperatives must be emancipatory. Inculcation of narcissistic desire coupled with destruction of traditional sources of moral restraint might well suit the needs of capital and produce a population eager for fascist authority. But structural conditions exist to make an alternative future possible. As Joel Kovel argues, "The point is not that people desire the administrative mode, it is rather that administration protects them against the desires they can not stand, while it serves out, in the form of diluted rationalization, a hint of the desire and power lost to them."[79] The separation of individuals from political and community life, combined with the destruction of cultural traditions that previously gave direction and purpose to individuals, might make status competition and "possession" of a secure family role all that much more attractive. Certainly the neo-conservatism of the 1980s seems to revolve around "protecting" the family from the increasing barbarism of society and upon shifting the blame for the social disintegration caused by civil and familial vocational privatism onto the opposition movements formed to combat it.[80] But the sleight-of-hand inherent in the neo-conservative position allows for other possibilities. Reconnection to history and to motivational structures rooted within it is both desirable and possible. More than ever before communication and criticism can help determine whether people accept the commodity-mediated desires that turn others into instruments and objects, or whether they build affirmative communities in dialogue with the needs and desires of others. By identifying the historical reality behind the construction of television texts in the

74

early 1950s, we demystify their "organic" character and reveal their implications as created artifacts. We uncover sedimented critiques from the past and potential forms of opposition for the present and future.

The historical specificity of early network television programs led their creators onto dangerous ideological terrain. By examining them as part of our own history, we learn about both the world we have lost and the one we have yet to gain. Fredric Jameson claims that "history is what hurts, what sets inexorable limits to individual as well as collective praxis."[81] But the unfinished dialogue of history can also be what helps, what takes us back into the past to break its hold on the present. By addressing the hurt, and finding out how it came to be, we begin to grasp ways of understanding the past and ending its pain.

4

Why Remember Mama?
The Changing Face
of a Woman's Narrative

Almost every Friday night between 1949 and 1956, millions of Americans watched Rosemary Rice turn the pages of an old photograph album. With music from Edvard Grieg's "Holverg Suite" playing in the background, and with pictures of turn-of-the-century San Francisco displayed on the album pages, Rice assumed the identity of her television character, Katrin Hansen, on the CBS network program *Mama*. She told the audience about her memories of her girlhood, her family's house on Steiner Street, and her experiences there with her big brother Nels, her little sister Dagmar, her Papa, and her Mama—"most of all," she said, "when I remember that San Francisco of so long ago, I remember Mama."[1] Katrin Hansen's memories of her Norwegian immigrant, working-class family had powerful appeal for viewers in the early years of commercial network broadcasting. *Mama* established itself as one of CBS's most popular programs during its first season on the air, and it retained high ratings for the duration of its prime-time run.[2]

In December 1985, the Museum of Broadcasting in New York City presented a retrospective tribute to *Mama*, featuring a reunion with four members of the cast and crew. In the thirty years since the show had been broadcast, each of the featured guests had gone on to interesting and important careers. Rosemary Rice, who played Katrin, became a featured voice on many popular cartoons and children's records. Dick Van Patten, who played the Hansens' son Nels, went on to establish himself as one of America's best known father figures, through his acting role on the popular television show *Eight Is Enough*, and, as well, through his real-life role as father when his children achieved fame as actors and professional tennis players. Robin Morgan, who played Dagmar, became the author of several highly acclaimed books on feminism that established her as a leading thinker and spokesperson for the radical wing of the feminist movement. Ralph Nelson, the show's director, became one of the leading liberals in Hollywood as well as the creative genius behind magnificent motion pictures including *Lilies of the Field, Soldier Blue*, and *Charlie*. Despite their busy schedules and varied fields of endeavor, Rice, Van Patten, Morgan, and Nelson came together at the Museum of Broadcasting to pay tribute to their memories of *Mama*.

"Every show had a tear and a laugh, and every show taught you something," Rice remembered, adding that working on that series "Christmas didn't come just once a year, it came every Friday night." Van Patten talked about *Mama*'s enormous effect on his life: he named his first son Nels after his character on the show, and he secured his role on *Eight Is Enough* largely because producer Fred Silverman had watched *Mama* as a child and admired Nels. Morgan said that she had learned discipline, professionalism, and team play on *Mama*, and that those skills had been crucial to her success as a political activist. In addition, she discerned a connection between the show's content and her evolution into a feminist. "After all, this was *I Remember Mama*, not *Father Knows Best*," she quipped, explaining that the scripts showed girls to be as important as boys, and that Judson Laire's characterization of Papa presented a strong, loving, but gentle male.[3] Ralph Nelson discussed how *Mama* prepared him for Hollywood by giving him the opportunity to direct both the regular cast and skilled guest performers including Paul Newman, Inger Stevens, Jack Lemmon, and Cliff Robertson. "When I did *Lilies of the Field* I followed the same structure as *Mama*, and I was quite conscious of it at the time."[4]

Through sympathetic laughter and applause, the audience at the Museum of Broadcasting symposium registered approval of all the praise for *Mama*. But the discussion took a bizarre turn when the audience began to question the speakers. One woman expressed her appreciation to the cast both for their remarks that evening and for their performances thirty years ago. She explained that while growing up she felt very alienated and unhappy with her own family, so she "adopted" the television Hansen family and pretended that they were her own mother and father, brother and sisters. Rosemary Rice responded, "We really were a family, we grew up together—we became a real family." Rice added that she attended classes at New York University while starring in the show and that she always showed her term papers to Judson Laire, who played Papa, because "I thought I should show my father my homework."[5] Robin Morgan indicated that the show helped provide a surrogate family for her as well. Her father had deserted her mother shortly after Morgan was born, providing her with a bitter early lesson about the family. But Judson Laire became a parental role model on and off camera for the young Morgan, and Peggy Wood encouraged her in her desire to become a writer, encouragement that she said, "meant a great deal to me."[6] Ralph Nelson recalled that *Mama* had helped reconcile him to his own family. As a teen-ager Nelson had argued constantly with his Swedish-American father, especially over the latter's racism and anti-Semitism. When his father tried to send him to a reform school, Nelson ran away from home and wandered all across the country. Not until he began directing *Mama* could he muster any affection or nostalgia for his background, but weekly contact with the fictional Norwegian Hansen family reconnected Nelson to his past. Then Nelson made a startling connection between his own negotiations with ethnic memory and those of Kathryn Forbes, the author of the original stories on which *Mama* was based. Nelson said that he had read somewhere that Forbes had fashioned a similar relationship to her own past through the Hansen family. Forbes was ethnically Norwegian, but she had spent much of her childhood in foster homes and felt deserted by her family. In her fiction, she "re-invented" her mother on the basis of the few stories she had heard about her grandmother and presented experiences that she wished had actually happened to her.

This projection of the Hansen family as part of the real family experiences of the woman from the audience, Rice, Morgan, Nelson, and Forbes turned the symposium into an exercise in a different kind of nostalgia from what had been planned. For one of the commonplace assumptions about *Mama* among contemporaneous critics and media historians has been that the show succeeded because it reflected the "real" family experiences precious to Americans. But the comments at the Museum of Broadcasting indicate that it played to another frame of reception as well—the past as people wish it had been rather than the past as they actually experienced it. The fact that so many of the speakers at the symposium treasured vicarious memories of a family life that none of them actually had, one that in fact ran directly counter to their own experience, illumines an important function of memory within popular culture in general—memory as managed *misappropriation*.

The popularity of *Mama* among people with unhappy family experiences might be seen as a quintessential example of the media's power to naturalize oppression. No one at the symposium expressed outrage at the program for presenting family life as sweeter and more loving than it actually was for them; instead they treasured a picture of the Hansens as normal and typical. One can well imagine the problems that might follow from this process—unrealistically high expectations about family relations, inability to anticipate problems that cannot be resolved by the final commercial, and the likelihood of blaming individual choices and behaviors for what in fact might be systemic problems between men and women or between children and adults. Indeed, as David Marc points out, much critical anger at the content of television programs revolves around these possibilities: critics understandably enough become alienated from a televised world in which nearly everyone is white and heterosexual, where no one sleeps on a mattress on the floor instead of a bed, where no one drives a used car, and where physical bravery and force always outperform moral courage and intellect.

But memory as misappropriation can have positive as well as negative consequences. It enables us to see beyond our own experience, rendering the oppressions of the past as contingent and unnecessary while modeling an alternate past, one as responsive to human wishes and desires as to the accidents of history. It says that biology is not destiny, that family and ethnicity can be sources of self-affirmation and connection to others, but only if they meet certain conditions of humane behavior. If our own personal pasts cannot be venerated as moral guides for the present, we must choose another from history or art and embrace it as our own. But such leaps cannot be fashioned purely from the imagination; the past has more informative power and more relevance to the present if we believe that it is what actually happened, because what people have done before they can do again, while what they imagine may never be realized. Even when misappropriated, memory has to appear credible, to resonate with lessons of some real past. *Mama* succeeded in that role because even its misappropriations resonated with the lessons of history. Because its core tensions exuded the truths of lived experience and memory, *Mama* enabled audiences to arbitrate the tensions facing them and to negotiate utopian endings.

It was not just the audience, cast, and crew of the television show *Mama* who made creative use of the Hansen family. From its inception in the Kathryn Forbes stories of the early 1940s, the narrative about the Hansen family has provided a particularly fertile field for misappropriation. As stories, a book, a broadway play, a radio special, a film, and finally as a television program, remembering Mama has engaged the revisionist energies of both artists and audiences. At each stage, alterations in narrative as well as in media responded as much to the larger political and ideological context as to dramatic necessities. Though they appear on the surface to be an uncontrollable obscuring of the historical record, the various versions of *Mama* represent in reality a creative adaptation of memory to arbitrate the indignities and alienations of everyday life. These changes were not always positive; some were obviously steps backward— regressive adaptations that precluded rather than promoted possibilities. But they demonstrate the indispensable dialogue with the past that accompanies any present, and they reflect the enduring potential of the past to help us see beyond the present even while speaking to its psychic and ideological preoccupations. The many incarnations of *I Remember Mama* reflected a continuing dialogue about the family and its proper social roles—a dialogue necessitated by extraordinary social changes between the early 1940s and the mid-1950s. Changes in the succeeding versions of these stories offer a significant index to the transformations in family life and family images in that period, as well as to the ways in which social pressures altered the forms and purposes of families.

This is not to argue that the many individuals involved in shaping the short stories, book, play, film, radio show, and television program about the Hansen family decided consciously to make their efforts relevant to contemporary affairs. Rather, it is to claim that commercial mass culture seeks credibility with its audience, at least in part, by arbitrating the ideological tensions created by disparities between cultural promises and lived experiences. As the core tensions facing families in society changed, intellectuals working in the culture industry participated in bending discursive practices to social realities, shaping their art to speak to current issues. Commerical pressures certainly contributed to their decisions: investors, editors, and advertisers had obvious stakes in supporting the status quo, and no doubt made their preferences known to those on the creative side of the enterprise. But more interesting than the conclusions and plot resolutions of these cultural artifacts are the oppositions that precede the conclusions, oppositions indicative of extraordinary contestation and confusion in society about family identity.

Operative Tensions in a Changing Narrative

As short stories, a book, and a Broadway play, the experiences of the Hansen family revolve around the legacy of the Depression. The operative tensions in the stories come from the mother's struggle to protect her family from hard times and from ethnic rivalries and hatreds. In the motion picture, the focus shifts to the differences between Mama and her daughters, to a story of a traditional mother raising independent daughters. The television program rescinds the independence enjoyed by the daughters in the film, presenting instead a narrative about threats to the family posed (or solved) by consumer goods. These three frames of reference responded to changes in American society at large—the remnants of the Depression in the early 1940s, the entry of large numbers of women into the workforce during World War II, and the rise of suburbs and increases in consumer spending in the early 1950s.

Kathryn Forbes published her first story about the Hansen family, "Mama's Bank Account," in the *Toronto Star Weekly* early in 1941. The *Reader's Digest* printed two excerpts from the story almost immediately upon publication, and Harcourt published an extended collection as a book titled *Mama's Bank Account*. The book received a warm welcome from reviewers and from the reading public; even the War Department deemed it worthwile and wholesome reading, purchasing 50,000 copies for soldiers overseas. The success of *Mama's Bank Account* inspired the play "I Remember Mama" by John Van Druten, which opened in 1944 and ran for 713 performances. Both the book and the play depict Mama as an effective manager of the family's finances, successfully maneuvering around illness, unemployment, and the demands of the children so that she does not have to "go to the bank" and withdraw their savings. When Katrin's success as a writer eventually brings in some surplus cash, Mama can finally admit that there is no bank account, that she talked about one so that the children would be shielded from how desperate their financial circumstances actually were. Now they can go to the bank, but to open an account for Katrin's money, not to use up their "savings."

Forbes's book tells about a battle between family and the economy; it delineates the ways in which poverty threatens love. Mama's resolute courage in the face of deprivation connects her to the "Madonnas of the Fields"—the strong and courageous farm women made into icons by 1930s FSA photographers. In this ethos, women attain beatific status by keeping families together in the face of the Depression. *Mama's Bank Account* also revolves around ethnicity: retracing the steps taken by immigrants to find common cause in a new land filled with not-so-friendly strangers. Mama draws upon her special knowledge and skills rooted in the old country to help her children succeed in America.

The story of the bank account forms the core of the Hansen family narrative, touching effectively on historical memories about the Depression—especially its threats to the survival of families and the new roles demanded of women by changing economic circumstances. In the book, Papa turns to carpentry only after failing as a farmer; in the play he responds to Katrin's desire to be a writer by asking how much writers earn. But a subtext of ethnicity in the book and play also addresses the collective memory of the audience. Trade-union organizing drives and new political coalitions ranging from the New Deal to the Communist Party's popular front transformed the meaning of ethnicity in the 1930s, and the unity of the war effort eclipsed some internal ethnic rivalries. In Forbes's book, Katrin enrolls in a school where anti-foreign prejudice makes her sensitive about her Scandinavian background. At one point the principal complains about the immigrant children enrolling in his school, fulminating "Italians, Jews, what next? Negroes or even Orientals?" Katrin feels like an outsider—her only friend is an Italian-American girl—and she fears total humiliation when Mama is asked to take her turn with the other mothers and cook a meal for the class. Katrin worries that Mama's Norwegian meatballs will draw more anti-foreign ridicule, but when her classmates and teachers love Mama's cooking, Katrin sees that she can be accepted in American society by offering it her ethnic gifts instead of hiding them.[7]

The ethnic component of *Mama's Bank Account* appealed to actress Mady Christians. Born in Vienna in 1900, Christians first acted in her father's German-American theater productions in New York and spent much of the '30s as both an actress and an activist on behalf of refugees from Nazi persecution. When she heard that Rodgers and Hammerstein were thinking of basing a Broadway play on the book, Christians asked for the part. They eventually decided not to do the play, but they mentioned her interest to John Van Druten, who wrote his adaptation to the stage with her in mind and made sure that she got the part (along with a young Marlon Brando cast as Nels).[8] But even in its first incarnations, sharp contradictions divided the fictional representations of the Hansen family and the lives of the artists responsible for it. Forbes wrote what most critics and viewers considered "realistic" accounts of Norwegian-Americans, even though she had no real first-hand knowledge of them, and she fashioned a touching portrayal of family life despite herself having a fragile marriage that ended in divorce in 1946 on the grounds of her husband's "extreme mental cruelty."[9] Similarly, for all Christians' conviction about *I Remember Mama* as testimony to the immigrant presence in America, she was passed over for the film and television roles as Mama because as the Cold War deepened, her work with the American Committee for the Protection of the Foreign Born drew the ire of xenophobic anti-communists. A parade of "investigators" harassed Christians about her political affiliations, and both the film and television industries blacklisted her even though no evidence of "disloyalty" ever surfaced.[10]

If the story, book, and play versions of the Hansen family's adventures coalesced around New Deal mutuality, director George Stevens's 1948 film *I Remember Mama* focused on the rooted independence of immigrant daughters raised by traditional mothers.[11] Dewitt Bodeen's screenplay retained the emphases on gender, class, and ethnicity pervading previous versions of the Hansen story, but adapted them to the dominant social tensions of the war and postwar periods. As film scholar Andrea Walsh points out, the film reflected the "pressure to grow up" facing young girls in the 1940s, at a time when millions of men served overseas and millions of women embraced new roles as war workers. Within the discourse of the day, *I*

Remember Mama steered a middle way between hysterical anti-feminist tirades (like Philip Wylie's *Generation of Vipers*) that charged domineering mothers with destroying the independence of American children, and the emerging war and postwar feminist consciousness stimulated by women's success in securing and maintaining war production jobs. The film featured Mama as a source for reconciliation, as a means of proving that threatening changes could be resisted while one accommodated to progress.

Indeed the entire film *I Remember Mama* presents threatening contradictions and then shows that they are not contradictions at all. For example, an opposition between family and money pervades the narrative. Mama has to supervise the budget to see that her family survives, with financial crises popping up at every turn — her daughter Christine needs an operation, a boarder pays his rent with a bad check, her sister Trina has no dowry, her Uncle Chris leaves them nothing in his will. But love proves superior to money. Mama mediates in an argument between her Uncle Chris who has the money and a doctor who has the expertise to secure the operation for her daughter. She teaches her children that the works of literature left behind by their deadbeat boarder are worth more than money. Along with Uncle Chris she neutralizes issues of pride and honor to enable her sister to marry a man who does not insist on a dowry. She finds that Uncle Chris spent all his money on charities for crippled children, and she uses that fact to encourage her son Nels to be a doctor and carry on his uncle's good works. Although Mama works within the home for her family, the narrative suggests that her work has great economic value even though she does not succumb to the self-centered greed of the work world.

Lessons about greed dominate one particularly important exchange between Katrin and Mama. Shortly after Mama makes her only consumer purchase in the film, a bouquet of violets, Katrin promises her "When I'm rich and famous . . . I'll buy you just lovely clothes: white satin gowns with long trains on them and jewelry. I'll buy you a pearl necklace."[12] Mama replies that she prefers her *solje*, her brooch, to a pearl necklace. Her immigrant loyalties confuse the American daughter who protests that Mama must want to be rich. When Mama replies that being rich is like being ten feet tall, "good for some things — bad for others," Katrin asks why she came to America if not to be rich. Mama tells us, "We came to America because they are all here—all the others. Is good for families to be together."[13] The exchange about the superiority of a *solje* to a pearl necklace and the pre-eminence of family over wealth prefigures a crucial scene which marks Katrin's maturation into an adult. Katrin admires a dresser set in a store window, even though Mama warns her that what Katrin takes to be ivory is probably just plastic. But Katrin persists, hinting about the dresser set for her high-school graduation present. Mama and Papa had intended to give her the *solje*, but pressured by their daughter's consumer desire they pawn the brooch to buy her the dresser set. At this point younger sister Christine intervenes, scolding Katrin for her selfishness and reminding her that with Papa on strike their parents could hardly afford the present she wanted. "Why I don't believe you even know what they're striking for. Do you? All you and your friends can talk about is the presents you're going to get. You make me ashamed of being a girl."[14] Humbled by Christine's priorities, Katrin pawns the dresser set and returns the *solje* to Mama and Papa who reward her passage to adult responsibility by letting her drink coffee with them.

Yet for all its privileging of love over money, *I Remember Mama* ultimately validates love as one way of securing happiness *and* money. Mama's old-fashioned female identity provides the key breakthrough for Katrin's aspirations to become a professional writer. When Katrin despairs because her stories have been rejected and complains that she needs the critiques of an expert, Mama uses her traditional skills to launch her daughter's career. Seeing a picture of "famous author" Florence Dana Moorhead in the paper, Mama decides that Moorhead looks like a woman "who likes to eat." Mama visits the author's hotel, and at first appears to be totally out of her element in its magnificent lobby. But she bravely locates Moorhead and explains that her daughter needs criticism from a writer. Initially, Moorhead refuses, but when Mama offers to share her recipe for delicious Norwegian meatballs, Moorhead relents and provides the advice that proves decisive to Katrin's later success. When Katrin sells her first story, she buys Mama a new coat with her earnings. Katrin may reject plastic consumer goods in favor of a family heirloom, but her mother's skills become validated only when they demonstrate their ability to open doors in the outside world.

The ambiguous resolution of the tension between family and money in *I Remember Mama* resonates with the value crises about female identity in the 1940s. Confronted with unprecedented opportunities in the job market and fundamentally new definitions of social responsibilities, women of the 1940s could turn to *I Remember Mama* and see that they did not have to disown the past to participate in the present, nor did they have to surrender opportunities in the present out of a misplaced fidelity to the past. Their mothers' traditional skills paved the way for the independence of the present; the moral dilemmas of the present could be kept under control by seeing their continuities with the past. Thus Katrin can have a career, but it is one composed of writing about her family, thereby maintaining her female identity. Katrin works at home, writes for love (of her mother) rather than for money, and measures her success by assisting her mother's work within the family rather than by any narcissistic gratification. On the other hand, Mama encourages Katrin, Christine, and Dagmar to have careers rather than talking to them about marriage; she provides an example of sisterly solidarity when she defends Uncle Chris's wife from accusations of promiscuity; and she comes to the aid of Aunt Trina, scorned for taking so long to marry. Mama pays lip service to the authority of Papa and Uncle Chris, but she takes action as an independent woman centering her concerns on the welfare of others. She rejects the false lures of consumer goods and gossip, while revering education, creativity, and mutuality. Yet that very identity was a construct of the possibilities of the 1940s, and when women's roles underwent serious alterations in the late 1940s and early 1950s, the next incarnation of the Hansen narrative reflected those drastic changes.

A successful special performance of *I Remember Mama* on the Lux Radio Theater helped convince CBS and General Foods to make a television version for the 1949–1950 season. An instant success, the program often appeared among the ten "most-watched" shows, enjoying an eight-year run before its cancellation in 1957. While retaining the main contours of previous versions, the televised *Mama* shifted focus from ethnicity, class, and gender, using those categories largely as a foil for a more pressing social problem—the family as unit of consumption. Just as economic realities during the war encouraged an emphasis on the gender-centered aspects of Forbes's stories, expansion of the consumer market in the 1950s made commodity purchases the core dramatic and narrative issue of the program.

Structural changes in cast and setting reflected external social changes each time *I Remember Mama* reached a new medium. In the stories and book, the Hansen family lived in a large house with seven boarders. The play and film whittled down the size of the house and featured only one boarder. The television program showed the Hansens as a modern nuclear family, owning their own house, without boarders. Forbes's original stories mentioned four aunts for the family to contend with; the play and the film showed three; the television program mentioned two, but tended to show only one. The Hansen family had four children in the stories, book, play, and film, but only three on television. In the print versions of the family's saga, Papa Hansen had failed as a farmer before becoming a carpenter. In the play and film his decision to participate in a strike represents an important chapter in the family's history. But the television show made no mention of failed business ventures and trivialized its few references to strikes. Ethnic rivalries provided significant tensions and taught important lessons in the book and the short stories, but they tended to disappear from the stage, screen, and television versions.

Changes in casting and plot no doubt owed something to the demands of different media and their attendant time constraints. Yet most of these changes also represent clear ideological and social changes as well. Over two decades and five forms of media, the Hansens changed from an ethnic working-class family deeply enmeshed in family, class, and ethnic associations, to a modern nuclear family confronting consumption decisions as the key to group and individual identity. Similarly, the spheres of action reserved for women change considerably from one version to another. In the stories and book, Mama uses her culinary skills to help her daughter win acceptance from classmates who made fun of her Scandinavian heritage. In the 1940s film, Mama uses those same cooking skills to advance her daughter's aspirations to become a writer. But in the 1950s television show, Mama's skill at cooking only provides hints to Katrin about how to get a husband. As the possibilities of the l940s became transformed into the gender prison of the 1950s, Mama directed her daughter away from a career and toward a husband. Predictably, the child dropped from the family when it shrank for the television version was Christine, an independent, intelligent, and ambitious adolescent whose sisterhood, class loyalties, and integrity had provided important guidance for Katrin.

Not that career ambitions totally disappeared from the television program. But they changed. Katrin voices ambitions to become an actress instead of a writer. She actually becomes a secretary, and in the last episode of the program, becomes a full-time wife. She then receives Mama's *solje* as a gift, a reward for choosing her proper female role, unlike the film which rewarded her choice of history over consumer goods. Similarly, in the book and film, Katrin's brother Nels seeks to become a doctor because he wants to follow in the footsteps of his Uncle Chris who helped people by giving away all of his money to lame children in need of operations. In the television program, Nels's ambition to become a physician stems from a desire to own consumer goods and to socialize with "better" people.

The changing role of coffee as an icon in both the film *I Remember Mama* and the television program *Mama* maps the ideological difference between the two versions. In the motion picture, Katrin is allowed to drink coffee when she rejects the dresser set in favor of the *solje*, proving her maturation into adulthood by rejecting consumer goods in favor of tradition. In the television program, tradition serves only to legitimate consumer goods; the entire Hansen family story serves as a lure to bring the audience commercial messages by the program's sponsor, Maxwell House coffee. The narrative sequence that framed every episode of *Mama* demonstrates the centrality of advertising messages and their importance in establishing narrative and ideological closure. As soon as Katrin Hansen introduced the show with the words "I remember Mama," a male narrator announced, "Yes, here's Mama, brought to you by Maxwell House coffee." The camera then panned away from the photograph album to show Mama (played by Peggy Wood) making coffee for the Hansen family in their turn-of-the-century kitchen. The authority of the male narrator's voice established a connection between the continuity of family experiences and the sponsor's product, between warm memories of the past and Mama making coffee in the kitchen. In this progression, the product becomes a member of the Hansen family, while tradition and emotional support become commodities to be secured through the purchase of Maxwell House coffee. The sponsor's introduction announces ownership of the television show *Mama*, but it also lays claim to the moral authority and warmth of motherhood itself.

Coffee drinking also appeared in the dramatic narratives of the show with amazing regularity. In the very first episode, Katrin opens the program with a reminiscence about Mama and Papa drinking coffee in the family kitchen, and subsequent episodes feature the beverage as a means of calming down upset children, as a catalyst for conversations among women, as a requirement for receiving company, as a break from housework, and as an aid to clear thinking and problem solving.[15]

The magical attributes of coffee prepare viewers for equally respectful treatment of other commodities. In keeping with the economic imperatives of commercial television, *Mama* touted not only its sponsors' products, but an entire attitude about consumption as well. In one episode the children make home-made presents for Mama's birthday—a bread box, a pen wiper, and a bookmark. But Katrin tells them "those things don't count," and she argues instead for "a bought present." When Nels needs a new suit for his Sunday School graduation, Mama wants to alter one of Papa's, but her son insists on a "bought" suit. The children demand the purchase of goods that are "necessities" to them, but seem foolish to their parents—a telephone, a victrola, a magic-lantern slide projector, a pedigreed dog. But in these matters, the children are always right: a telephone that the family cannot really afford proves instrumental in securing a job for Papa; a victrola purchased to mollify the children shows Papa's boss that he is a music lover and worthy of promotion; a picture in the newspaper of Dagmar with her dog motivates yet another employer to offer work to Papa.[16] Unlike the film in which Katrin's own creativity (nurtured by Mama) enabled her to contribute to the family economy, on television consumer goods themselves mysteriously add to rather than subtract from the family's wealth. The lessons from the film about the false lure of consumer goods become inverted. On television products have no false glitter; instead they establish the necessary preconditions for continued familial ties.

Commodities not only help the family's financial status on *Mama*, they also minister to emotional needs. When an elderly neighborhood woman dies, Mama's social club delegates her to buy flowers for the deceased. But Mama learns that the woman's grandson is heartbroken because his grandmother had promised to buy him a tricycle before she died. Mama uses the flower money to buy the boy his gift and signs the birthday card from his grandmother. "Tricycles are better than flowers," she tells the club, "they last."[17] Grandmothers with the audacity to die before delivering desired toys to their grandchildren share the problem confronting all parents in *Mama*: the loss of face precipitated by inadequate performance as a consumer. In one episode Nels works as a toy salesman in a department store and confronts a bricklayer who cannot afford the expensive electric train that his son desires. Nels suggests a less expensive model, but the father bristles at the idea that he cannot provide the best for his child. Nels buys a raffle ticket for the train in question, and when he wins he gives it to the young boy because he remembers how he never got over his own disappointment at not receiving a pony when he was younger.[18] When Mama is not asked to join an elite social club, Papa fears it is because of his lowly job as a carpenter, and he wonders if his failures do not also explain Dagmar's exclusion from a prestigious dancing school the year before.[19] Papa's self-doubts receive reinforcement from his children. When Nels cannot afford to make long-distance calls to his girlfriend, he decides to start a business, cautioning his partner that they must be serious about upward mobility. "We can't be like my father. I don't even know what he ever came to this country for."[20] The blurred distinction between dramatic content and advertising messages in *Mama* did not just depend upon indirect ideological influences; sometimes the connection was intentional. Gordon Webber of the advertising agency that handled the show's accounts wrote several scripts for the show, and a 1954 memo from assistant producer Doris Quinlan to the producer, head writer, and director of the program reveals a sometimes conscious connection to product-plugging as Quinlan reminds her co-workers

> *Good Housekeeping Magazine* is coming out next month with a spread on "Mama." As you know, we have told them for some time we would make use of the magazine on the program. Could we please try to keep this in mind. It does not have to be anything elaborate. For example, the next time Katrin or Dagmar is looking at a pattern or a new dress, can they not use *Good Housekeeping* and mention it by name? We have a period copy of the magazine.[21]

Yet for all its embrace of consumer-commodity society, *Mama* still depended upon its ability to evoke the moral legitimacy of the past for its success in the present. Katrin Hansen's retrospective narrative and the pictures from the family album reassured viewers by depicting events that had already happened in the emotionally secure confines of the audience's collective childhood memories and imaginations. This false authenticity encouraged viewers to think of the program as the kind of history that might be created about their own homes. A CBS press release during the program's first broadcast season proclaimed, "On *Mama*, we try to give the impression that nobody is acting," and went on to claim success for that effort, quoting an unnamed viewer's contention that the show depicted a real family because "nobody but members of a real family could talk like that."[22] Free from the real history of ethnic, class, and gender experience, the history presented on *Mama* located its action within the personal spheres of family and consumer choices. Within these areas, realism could be put to the service of commodity purchases, as when the narrator followed his opening introduction with a discussion about how Mama in her day "had none of the conveniences of today's modern products" like Minute Rice, Jello, or Maxwell House instant coffee.[23] Thus the morally sanctioned traditions of hearth and home could be put to the service of products that revolutionized those very traditions—all in keeping with Ernest Dichter's advice to his fellow advertising executives: "Do not assert that the new product breaks with traditional values, but on the contrary, that it fulfills its traditional functions better than any of its predecessors.[24]

Stability and Rupture in a Women's Narrative

In the 1970s, literary and film critics began to stress the conservative functions of narrative. They charged that narrative closure worked to forestall social change, to inculcate a distrust for contradiction and conflict in readers and viewers. These critics argued that some narratives, especially in popular literature, film, and television, posed imaginary solutions to real social problems, gave the appearance of openness but allowed only one possible solution, in fact teaching inevitability. In some ways, the Hansen family narrative, even in its many incarnations, could serve as evidence for that line of argument. Its inscribed ideological content taught tolerance and self-help as solutions to the ethnic and class divisions of the Great Depression, favored a rooted independence as an arbitration of changes in women's roles in the 1940s, and presented consumer purchases as the key to family happiness in the 1950s. But narrative closure is not so easy to achieve. It is difficult to soothe anxieties without first aggravating them, and impossible to predict in any given case whether the emotional appeal of closure will silence the questions and criticisms provoked by narrative's evocation of the real hurts of history.

One significant failure to ensure narrative closure in the television program *Mama* may illumine more general principles. The single strongest ideological element in the transfer of the Hansen story to television came from the focus on the home. Television shifted the site of popular culture reception away from the public theater to the home, and both commercial and creative personnel thought of it as a medium where "families watched families." Yet as feminist literary critics have observed, the notion of the home as a safe haven from society encompasses some dramatic contradictions, for the glorification of domesticity traditionally draws legitimacy from the idea of the home as the moral center of society, as a social institution whose influence extends outward.[25] On *Mama* the narrative need to reaffirm the Hansen home as such a center of morality opens up rather than contains social contradictions. In one Halloween episode, delinquent street toughs harass the Hansens, throwing stones at their house. When Papa captures two of the youths, Mama serves them cider as they wait for the police to arrive. One asks her, "How do you think we feel when we look in windows and see kids eating ice cream and ducking for apples and stuff like that?" Mama says, "Like throwing stones ... I would too."[26] Mama tells Katrin to invite her friends over, and instead of turning the youths over to the police she invites them to join the party. Even Mama can feel the pain of economic deprivation, her class loyalties connecting her to the youths despite their decidedly unfamilial behavior.

Even the pursuit of consumer goods takes on some odd wrinkles because of the role of the home as the moral center of society. When the Hansens purchase a telephone that they cannot afford, Papa's boss fires him, claiming that a man who could afford such luxuries does not need work as badly as the other men. But Mama does not believe him. She says (in her accented television Swedish-English), "No, Lars, he do it because he do not like you to have same things that he has. That is not nice thing to say about Mr. O'Hara or any man, but is true. That is why we keep telephone, because I do not ever want anyone in this house to be afraid of men like Mr. O'Hara."[27] In this context, acquisition of consumer goods is no longer posed as a universal private need, but, rather, it becomes part of a class-conscious sense of entitlement to the good things in life. Awareness of a larger world outside the home also produces criticism of the home itself. In one episode Katrin bristles at the constant surveillance of her close-knit extended family and expresses a desire to move to Los Angeles to enjoy some freedom. Even though the plot reaches narrative closure by showing Katrin that her gossipy family protects her from malevolent strangers, the suffocating confinement of family identity leaves a bitter residue to the episode.

Similarly, *Mama* could glorify domesticity only by "containing" the allure of work outside the home. A parade of glamorous opera singers, cultured heiresses, and famous female actresses and writers tempt Katrin and her sister in ways that make Mama appear uninteresting, at least temporarily. Mama herself discloses the negative side of her life. She is jealous of women with public roles and fearful that they will attract Papa's interest. "I am someone who cooks and sews and makes the beds and takes care of the children, but when Lars sits and smokes his pipe and thinks thoughts they are not always of me."[28] Another time she complains after a frustrating day of housework, "Sometimes I wish I was an old maid. What does a family mean? Work. And who appreciates it?" Again, the resolution of these shows reassures us that Mama is loved and valued for her work, but for any given viewer the ruptures opened by the show might carry as much impact as the narrative resolution.

Frankfurt School Marxist T. W. Adorno claims that the culture industry opens such ruptures only to close them, that it disciplines all potential opposition by showing the possibility and then the futility of criticism. But as long as ruptures and closures accompany each other within media texts, at least the possibility of oppositional readings remains alive. One reason for that possibility comes from the contradictions of those fashioning the narratives. The tension between the ideological imperatives of commercialized leisure and the need for making the narratives credible creates a space for the airing of historical memories and contradictions. The sources of "authenticity" for these artists often belie the narrative closures and preferred readings demanded from their work. Earlier we saw how Rice, Morgan, Forbes, and Christians created parts of the Hansen narrative both with and against the grain of their own experiences; some of the contradictions about social reality and family roles evident within *Mama* resonate with the tension between life and art for its two main creators, writer Frank Gabrielson and director Ralph Nelson.

As the chief writer for *Mama*, Frank Gabrielson created some of the warmest and most touching images of family harmony in the history of television. But his own behavior often conflicted with the values that he projected onto the screen. His wife sacrificed her own career in radio to allow him to move to Hollywood and work as a writer for Twentieth Century Fox, and she supported him with her earnings when he could not find paying work. But Gabrielson abandoned his wife and young daughter in 1947, shortly before securing his position on *Mama*. As head writer he often took the entire cast out to dinner at expensive restaurants while neglecting to send alimony checks to his own family. His writings beautifully portrayed a kind of family loyalty and responsibility that had nothing to do with his own life. "He created the ideal family out of what we were not," observes his daughter, Hale Lamont Havers.[29] But however reprehensible his behavior, Gabrielson obviously drew upon his unhappy family experiences in his scripts. "Audiences are willing to accept the idea that good things are not the only things that happen in families," he told one interviewer, citing in particular an episode where Mama fears she will lose Papa's interest if she wears the eyeglasses that have been prescribed for her.[30]

Gabrielson's writing not only disclosed the contradictions of domesticity, with Ralph Nelson's encouragement it also used the moral concerns of the Hansen household to critique society. An episode about Halley's comet provided a pretext for airing concerns about nuclear war metaphorically; the presence of a Chinese laundryman provoked a lesson about the evils of racial prejudice, and an episode set during World War I gave Mama an opportunity to question the "glories" of war and the enthusiasms of uncritical nationalism. Nelson viewed his own liberal politics and his commitment to acting as part and parcel of a rebellion against his father's values, and he welcomed opportunities to combine the two. Censorship pressures within the industry only redoubled his resolve. Executives from a company that bought large amounts of commercial time on television once warned Nelson that he was to hire "no communists, no socialists, and we're even thinking of eliminating Democrats."[31] But he did not give in to that pressure, joining Martin Ritt in refusing to sign a loyalty oath. Nelson told the network, "There's nothing in my background that's subversive, and the loyalty oath is unconstitutional."[32] Like the creators of earlier incarnations of the Hansen family narrative, Nelson and Gabrielson developed the contradictions within *Mama* because those contradictions formed an important part of their lives. Their work both resisted and reinforced dominant ideology by highlighting operative ideological tensions in the social context in which their art appeared.

The serial nature of television situation comedies and the recombinant nature of popular culture texts inhibit premature closures. Narrative devices that fix meanings in other media leave them unstable and subject to revision on television. When combined with the continual changes in social life characteristic of our era, they contain the possiblity for opening up previously closed discussions. It is certainly possible that the Hansen family narrative served the interests of patriarchy, capitalism, and the state, but it is also possible that it exposed contradictions conducive to resistance to those institutions. As long as people's needs and desires remain unsatisfied, the prospects for narrative and ideological closure are always incomplete. As the old people used to say in the days of slavery, "You can hide the fire, but what you gonna do with the smoke?"

Popular Music

5
Against the Wind: Dialogic Aspects of Rock and Roll

Nothing is absolutely dead: every meaning will have its homecoming festival.

Mikhail Bakhtin

All music is derivative. It's built on what people did before.
Joe Perry of Aerosmith

Literary critic Bakhtin's observation has special significance for popular music.[1] As much as any other art form, popular music depends upon the recovery and re-accentuation of previous works. Bakhtin developed his concept of "dialogic" criticism to explain how popular carnival traditions influenced the content of writings by Rabelais, Pushkin, and Dostoevsky; his theories have been most often applied to the written word. Dana Polan and Horace Newcomb have applied dialogic criticism to cinema and television, respectively, but music critics have been strangely unresponsive to the implications of Bakhtin's work for their own discipline. Popular music is nothing if not dialogic, the product of an ongoing historical conversation in which no one has the first or the last word. The traces of the past that pervade the popular music of the present amount to more than mere chance: they are not simply juxtapositions of incompatible realities. They reflect a dialogic process, one embedded in collective history and nurtured by the ingenuity of artists interested in fashioning icons of opposition.

According to Bakhtin, culture is cumulative, a barrier reef constructed out of the choices and negotiations of everyday speech. Everyone enters a dialogue already in progress; all speech carries within it part of the social context by which it has been shaped. The dialogic model sees artistic creation as innately social and innately historical. As Richard Terdiman observes

> Dialogism in other words, is a memory model. It seeks to recall the semantic and social history carried by a culture's language, but which tends to be forgotten, to be blanked, in the characteristic form of cultural mystification since the revolutions of the nineteenth century.[2]

The novel drew Bakhtin's particular attention because of its "polysemic" nature—filled with contradictory voices representing the contradictions of social life. Popular music contains many of the features that attracted Bakhtin to the novel. Its "voices" resonate with the vernacular and sacred traditions of the past, incorporating musical and linguistic figures into readily understood icons and images. Bakhtin saw characters in a novel as representing different ideological responses to European culture; lyrical and musical elements in American popular music can be seen as standing for attitudes and "character zones" in the present. Bakhtin's novelists drew upon popular traditions of carnival laughter as a way of mocking and uncrowning power, of crying out for a just world; contemporary musicians draw upon the language and traditions of the postwar, urban, working-class subcultures that gave birth to rock and roll. Just as the European novel never lost touch with the popular traditions it seemed to eclipse, popular music has never been totally severed from the energy and imagination of the postwar American industrial communities in which it originated.

Four contentions form the core of my argument about the dialogic nature of rock and roll music. First, the presence of the past in rock and roll music has meaning beyond the lure of nostalgia and the persistence of artistic clichés. Second, the experiences of the past help shape both the structure of music and the intentions of artists. Third, the origins of rock and roll music in the postwar American industrial city infuse the music with certain democratic and egalitarian propensities. Finally, while no cultural form has a fixed political meaning, rock and roll music has been and continues to be a dialogic space, an arena where memories of the past serve to critique and change the present.

The Dialogic Challenge to Anthropological and Semiotic Criticism

Explaining exactly how musical notes create their powerful affect is one of the most daunting problems facing cultural critics. Musicologists tend to take a formalistic approach, transposing musical creations into mathematical schemas and evaluating them on the basis of their complexity and originality. This approach tends to present the critic as the maximally competent listener, and it tends to portray the relationship between audiences and musical pieces as abstract, detached, and technical. Even with European classical music for which this method was devised, the traditional musicological approach has serious deficiencies, but it is a disaster when applied to popular music. The aesthetic intentions of popular-music composers and their relationship to their audiences are completely different from what confronts a classical-music composer. A popular-music audience expects entry and engagement with the work of art in a way that classical audiences do not (or at least do not any longer, although they once did). What might seem technically competent or original within classical music might seem dangerously unfamiliar or offputting to a popular-music audience. Finally, the interpellation of popular music into everyday life through dancing, repetition, and background noise makes engagement with it fundamentally different from music composed for the concert hall or refined stereo system.

Anthropological and semiotic criticism have emerged among popular-music critics as the two primary alternatives to musicological formalism. The anthropological approach focuses on the uses and effects of popular music in the everyday lives of listeners, while the semiotic approach identifies the underlying structural unities that determine the ideological consequences of popular music's production and reception. Anthropological and semiotic critiques offer indispensable insights about popular music, but they tend to obscure both affect and agency. They obscure affect either by ignoring the music entirely and focusing on the social processes it fosters, or by accounting for affect with a formalism of their own which assigns static social meanings to musical figures regardless of their context of creation or reception. Such critiques obscure agency by reifying the complex social interactions that create popular music into abstract structures like "the rock and roll apparatus" or "the sociology of youth." Disturbing elements of Parsonian sociology and Geertzian anthropology in anthropological and semiotic criticism further elide human agency by presenting culture as a way for societies to stabilize themselves as total systems. Thus all oppositional practice becomes a way of letting off steam and of reconciling potential dissidents back into a total social structure that remains unified by virtue of the stories it tells itself. At any given moment societies may secure stability through culture, but over time we can see that some features of culture are ascendant and others descendant, that some serve the interests of dominant groups while others serve to educate and agitate aggrieved populations. Without an adequate sense of culture as conversation and contestation, without an adequate understanding of historical change, anthropological and semiotic critiques of popular music tend to degenerate into recycled formalism in their appraisals of music, and into recycled "consensus" social science in their judgments about society.

Dialogic criticism offers a means of transcending some of the limits of musicological, anthropological, and semiotic approaches to popular music. It connects affect to agency, and grounds social and ideological choices within the life worlds and collective memories of actual historical subjects. It shows how part of "what popular music is" can be found in "how popular music came to be," but it also avoids the twin pitfalls of formalism and essentialism. Dialogic criticism eschews formalism by finding meaning not in forms themselves, but in how forms are put into play at any given moment to re-articulate or dis-articulate dominant ideology. It avoids essentialism by evaluating cultural practice as an ongoing dialogue responsive to the demands of both past and present, rather than as a fixed inventory of practices to be approved or disapproved. Thus the problem for dialogic criticism is not whether rock music is oppositional or co-optive, but rather how it arbitrates tensions between opposition and co-optation at any given historical moment. Similarly, the dialogic evaluation of music forms like heavy metal, country music, reggae, or punk depends less on an identification of their core structures than upon the ways in which they mediate between past and present for their audiences.

The importance of the dialogic approach can best be demonstrated by what happens to even the best anthropological and semiotic criticism when it fails to account adequately for history, affect, and agency. Lawrence Grossberg, E. Ann Kaplan, and Simon Frith have written eloquent and intelligent works on rock music that have established them as the pre-eminent academic critics in the field. Yet all three have also been led to incomplete or erroneous judgments about rock and roll because their methods do not allow for sufficient consideration of music-making as a dialogic process.

Grossberg locates the reception of rock music within a historical time frame, but one that signals the end of history. He explains, "As history becomes mere change—discontinuous, directionless and meaningless—it is replaced by a sense of fragmentation and rupture, of oppressive materiality, of powerlessness and relativism."[3] Kaplan describes the MTV television channel as "part of a contemporary discourse that has written out history as a possible discourse," and she claims that the channel's teen-age audience "is constituted by the station as one decentered mass that absorbs all the types indiscriminately—without noting or knowing their historical origins."[4] Certainly the disorientation and fragmentation that Grossberg and Kaplan describe are part of the consciousness of our time. But the crisis of memory to which they allude is not new; indeed, it has been the constitutive problem of bourgeois society since the nineteenth century.[5] As Fredric Jameson points out, historical epochs like our own do not reflect one sense of history or one sense of values, but instead reflect many simultaneous ways of living and many simultaneous stories explaining life from the vantage point of competing interests.[6]

Compare the ahistoricity of rock critics Grossberg and Kaplan with the perspectives of rock artists Chuck D of the rap group Public Enemy and David Bowie, rock's "great chameleon." Chuck D says, "You have people saying, 'But the problems of the past are over, let's not even think about it.' But the problems growing out of hundreds of years of slavery remain for millions of black people and the only way I see them overcoming the problems is through education and networking."[7] David Bowie points out, "In our music, rock 'n' roll, the blues are our mentor, our godfather, everything. We'll never lose that, however diversified and modernistic and cliché ridden with synthesizers it becomes. We'll never ever, be able to renounce the initial heritage."[8] A rapper like Chuck D and a spectacular performance artist like David Bowie juxtapose seemingly incompatible forms from the past and present in their art in a way that would satisfy the most demanding postmodern appetites. But their art also remains connected to the social formations in which they first developed. Chuck D's deployment of the past is expressly political, while Bowie's relates specifically to music. But both serve to illustrate the pervasive presence of the past in and around popular music, even in an age of postmodernism. Of course, Grossberg and Kaplan would be correct to contend that at any given moment audiences of Chuck D and David Bowie might have no meaningful knowledge of the past, but that is a far different matter from saying that audiences are positioned outside history, or that maximally competent listeners could not discover meaningful historical connections in their work.

Simon Frith sees historical traces in popular music, but finds them completely reactionary and defeatist. Citing Greil Marcus, Frith presents rock music's core tension as a battle between ambition, style, adventure, risk-taking, and a refusal to be satisfied on one hand, and a feeling for roots, history, "a dependence on community and tradition, the acceptance of one's lot" on the other. Frith's equation of roots, history, community, tradition, and "acceptance of one's lot" neglects the ways in which the past often serves as a critique of the present, as a refusal of one's lot and an assertion of entitlement to something better. Bruce Springsteen, John Cougar Mellancamp, and Bob Seger often use the past in that way, but Frith dismisses the meaning of such works simply because they are rooted in the past. "By the end of the 1970s," Frith explains, "there was no music a rock musician (however young) could make that did not refer back, primarily, to previous rock readings; the music was about itself now, whether it liked it or not—this was obvious even (perhaps especially) in the work of a skilled rock naturalist like Bruce Springsteen."

Thus for Frith, references to the past are innately conservative, but if they are not conservative then they are to be dismissed because they are really about music, not about society. Yet one reason for popular music's powerful affect is its ability to conflate music and lived experience, to make both the past and present zones of choice that serve distinct social and political interests. Frith's one dimensional view of the past becomes most evident in his dismissal of country music as "a conservative form carrying a conservative message," the music of people whose "dignity derives from their passivity," with only one lyrical message "We're a loser." Aside from the anti-working class and anti-intellectual prejudices shaping such a description, it suffers from a lack of historical knowledge about the traditions of the white working class, of populism, Evangelical Protestantism, and the labor movement, and their impact on the historical imagination of country music. This is not to take the opposite view and say that there is nothing conservative about country music, but, rather, to assert that progressive and conservative elements interact in any memory of the past, and that the specific contexts in which these elements are deployed, rather than their focus on the past or present, determines their social meaning.

The same kind of one-dimensional either/or approach that enables Frith to reduce a reverence for tradition to "acceptance of one's lot," and which finds only a single message of defeatism and conservatism in country music, leads him to misunderstand rock and roll texts as well. Challenging what he terms "an unproblematic relationship between social experience and musical expression," Frith points out that under conditions of commodified mass culture "the sounds that fill our lives are always made *for* us," and that consequently "we hear music as natural and think nothing about how it came to be made that way." An unproblematic relationship between musical expression and social experience should be challenged, but Frith opposes it with an equally unproblematic assumption of rupture between cultural expression and history. For example, he claims that the materiality of human voices comprises an essential element in rock and roll music, and that "the only way" we can explain Elvis Presley's appeal is "not in terms of what he 'stood for,' socially or personally, but by reference to the *grain* of his voice." Obviously, we need more than one explanation to account for Presley's popularity, but to claim that the primary factor is the pitch and timbre of his voice is to totally overlook the context in which that voice was received. As I have argued, social context is the matrix of production and reception of popular music. For example, Bruce Springsteen remembers the voices he heard on the radio while growing up, but was struck by their social claims as well as by their "grain." Dave Marsh recounts Springsteen's words to a concert audience,

> I started reading this book, *The History of the United States*, and it
> seemed that things weren't the way they were meant to be—like the

way my old man was living, and his old man, and the life that was
waiting for me—that wasn't the original idea. . . . But even if you find
those things out, it's so hard to change those things. And it wasn't
until I started listening to the radio, and I heard something in those
singers' voices that said there was more to life than what my old man
was doing and the life that I was living. And they held out a promise,
and it was a promise that every man has a right to live his life with
some decency and some dignity. And it's a promise that gets broken
every day, and in the most violent way. But it's a promise that never,
ever dies, and it's always inside of you.[9]

This is not to argue that grain of voice is an irrelevant category, but
rather to demand that any formal musical device be studied to understand how it produces its desired affect for concrete historical
subjects. Frith's neglect of the historical contexts of musical creation
and reception leaves him with largely formalistic criteria for musical
analysis and interpretation. He attributes the appeal of reggae music
to "the music itself—its lack of a hierarchy of sounds, its depth of
pulse," contending that "it didn't express anything else, some prior
reality, but was the structure of experience, for musician and audience alike."[10] Frith contends that British punk music of the 1970s "no
more reflected directly back on conditions in the dole queue than it
emerged spontaneously from them," claiming that "punk was an effect of formal conventions, a particular combination of sounds."[11] According to Frith, black music's popularity depends on its "immediate
and democratic" nature which he claims means that listeners "need
no special training or knowledge to appreciate it," because "the qualities that are valued in spontaneous music making are emotional
rather than technical."[12] Frith is to be commended for his interest in
the music itself; indeed it is a tribute to his integrity as a scholar and
his acumen as a critic that he writes so sensitively of the ways in
which music affects the senses. But his laudable desire to avoid crude
reductionism, to resist the temptation of treating music as *merely* a
direct reflection of social and historical tensions leads him too far in
the opposite direction. Frith understates the importance of musical
and historical traditions in the construction of rock and roll. For example, black musicians need great technical skill and knowledge to
make emotional contact with discerning audiences. The raw energy
of punk music draws at least part of its power from a very real social
crisis of the 1970s that threatened the futures of the young, and the

hypnotic depth that Frith celebrates within reggae music owes a great deal to its functional role within aggrieved communities. It is one thing to assume an unproblematic relationship between musical expression and social experience, and quite another to see music as social, as a part of collective historical memory and continuing social dialogue.

It is not just the music that becomes one dimensional when anthropological and semiotic critics neglect dialogic and historical evidence. The complex interactions of the pop music world, their competing agents and ideologies, become flattened into a stable and seemingly monolithic system. True to his Parsonian methdology, Frith states the case most baldly: "The music doesn't challenge the system, but reflects and illuminates it."[13] Grossberg and Kaplan find more oppositional practice and potential within rock and roll than does Frith, but they see ideological incorporation into commodity society as the ultimate effect of popular-music consumption. Grossberg argues that rock and roll provides a diversion from the meaninglessness and boredom of contemporary adolescence by positioning "insiders" (white music listeners) as "outsiders" (rebels, hedonists, undifferentiated "others") "even while they exist within the hegemony."[14] For Kaplan, MTV is "symptomatic of Reagan's America in its unquestioning materialism," and the very structures of music video calls up a "desire for plenitude" that can only be filled by the consumer economy.[15]

Frith, Grossberg, and Kaplan also seem united in their views about the persistence of racism and the superficiality of black-white interchanges within rock and roll. Frith notes, "One of the most obvious features of rock'n'roll and street life, is how poorly racially integrated it is, how much it still reflects the problems of white leisure and white youth."[16] Grossberg claims that "the production and reception" of rock and roll by white youths severed the music from its country and blues origins, and made it the locus of a boundary within social reality "marked only by its otherness."[17] Kaplan argues that "the largely white middle-American audience to which MTV gears itself are uninterested in black bands, and this we must attribute to cultural codes that shape this group in Reagan's America."[18] Critics who attribute all the power in the world to the rock-and-roll apparatus, to its ability to construct comprehending and obedient subjects, strangely enough blame the audience rather than the commercial apparatus for the appearance of sexism, racism, and class hierarchies in popular music.

The portrayal of popular music as an enclave of conservatism, as a stimulus for consumer desire, and an agent of white racism is not incorrect, but it is incomplete. Popular culture is indeed a site for the iteration and reiteration of dominant values, commercialized leisure does provide distraction and diversion rather than fulfillment. But the very sites where ruling ideologies can be articulated are also the places where they can be disarticulated. As Stuart Hall writes

> Popular culture is neither, in a "pure" sense, the popular traditions of resistance to these processes; nor is it the forms which are superimposed on and over them. It is the ground on which the transformations are worked.[19]

Dialogic criticism insists that we understand "the ground on which the transformations are worked" by locating them within their proper historical context. Messages about commodity desire or racism within popular music enter a dialogue already in process. On the one hand, systematic exercises of power throughout society encourage expressions in popular culture reflective of economic, racist, and sexist hierarchies. On the other hand, oppositional traditions deeply embedded within the past and present lives of concrete historical subjects work to undermine dominant ideologies and to stimulate real and imagined alternatives. Thus racism in popular music needs to be seen in the context of other social institutions—of the systematic re-segregation of schools, neighborhoods, and recreation areas that has accompanied the assault on "public" space during the neoconservative ascendancy of the 1970s and 1980s. Similarly, the pervasiveness of commodity form and materialism in popular music needs to be assessed within the context of older traditions about plenitude and the good life—for example, the luxuriant boasting of blues and country-music songs that stake a claim on the good life for ordinary people. No articulation has meaning by itself: we need to see the ways in which it mediates between lived experience and desire, between the realities of the present and the blasted hopes of the past. Most important, we need to learn the language, to detect the exact nature of the dialogue that we have all entered.

Perhaps the best test case of the dialogic method concerns the persistence of working-class forms and images within rock and roll music. The anthropological and semiotic critics are also in accord about the class content—or lack of it—in rock and roll music. Grossberg argues, "The fact that particular forms of rock and roll, and even perhaps rock and roll in general, have specific class roots does not necessarily say anything about its reception and social effects in particular contexts."[20] Frith minimizes the working-class origins of rock-and-roll music and musicians, claiming that "to be a rock musician is, indeed, to be detached from a class background."[21] Kaplan acknowledges the significance of rock-music videos stressing social commentary in working-class settings, but insists that "the placement of the videos within the 24-hour televisual flow often eliminates any possible effectiveness."[22] Yet having specific class roots means that rock and roll contains specific class imagery, with biases toward specific class ideologies. Artists themselves may no longer be part of the working class when they achieve success as musicians, but the dialogue from which they emerge, and the one they maintain with their fans, prevents them from becoming completely detached from their class backgrounds. To credit the "24-hour" visual flow with totally suppressing the class content of popular music is to present capitalism's most grandiose self-inflated image of itself as reality and to underestimate greatly the guile and skill of artists who come from a tradition that has repeatedly placed oppositional messages in media unreceptive to popular control.

The creation of musical affect always takes place within a historical context. Musical forms have meaning only as they can be interpreted by knowing subjects. An inventory of the basic vocabulary of rock and roll reveals something about the triumphs of class hierarchies, of racism, sexism, materialism, and individualism, but it also identifies an unfinished dialogue about the potential of oppositional traditions. By looking at the music itself, we can find dialogic traces of the past and discern their enduring utility in the present.

What the Notes Mean: The Core Vocabulary of Rock and Roll in Social and Historical Perspective

Little Richard's "Good Golly Miss Molly" provides the quickest introduction to the vocabulary of rock-and-roll music. It employs a three-line, twelve-bar blues structure with an AAB rhyme scheme, uses call and response between instruments and voice, displays falsettos and similar "impure" tones, relies on blues chord progressions and blue notes, utilizes a rolling bass line in 8/8 time, and expresses a playful wit and joyous hedonism in its lyrics. These forms have displayed tremendous affective power; they undergird a music that has attained popularity around the globe. But they come from concrete historical circumstances; they emerged to express specific ideological positions; and they retain a bias toward those positions as they are played and interpreted today.

The three-line, twelve-bar blues echo the dominant forms of traditional West African poetry with their characteristic AAB rhymes. Little Richard sings "Good Golly Miss Molly, you sure like to ball" two times, and then completes the verse with a third line that comments on the first two—"when you're rockin' and a rollin,' you can't hear your mama call." Throughout the song, instrumental bursts "answer" and "respond" to the vocalist's "call." This antiphony, or "call and response," also originated in Africa and survived in North America in work songs and in responsive singing in churches. Rather than striving for "pure" tones as defined by the Western measured scale, Little Richard's singing involves leaps of register into high-pitched falsettos as well as an assortment of slides and growls down the scale. African languages characteristically vary meaning by changing tone register and that continent's musics draw upon the entire range of sounds open to the human ear, rather than merely upon the precisely measured vibrations that count as notes in the West. Part of the dynamic tension felt by listeners to "Good Golly Miss Molly" comes from the presence of "blue" notes—flatted thirds, fifths, and sevenths on the Western scale and by the I-IV-V blues chord progressions. These forms evolved within American popular music as a result of the efforts by Afro-Americans to "bend" the notes of western instruments to conform to the harmonies of African traditions. "Good Golly Miss Molly" also displays rhythmic properties of African derivation. Underneath the vocals, the band plays a rhythmic 8/8 time featuring the "rolling bass" notes popularized by "boogie woogie" piano players in the 1930s. The drummer complements this basic rhythm with accents and afterbeats that give the song a polyrhythmic quality reminiscent of African music.

Obviously, the Africanisms in "Good Golly Miss Molly" contain traces of America's most oppressive labor system—chattel slavery.

But more than origins are at stake here. The musical figures and lyrical choices represented by those song forms testify to ongoing beliefs about music and society that form an important subtext of rock-and-roll music. Historically, Afro-Americans have treasured African retentions in speech, music, and art both as a means of preserving collective memory about a continent where they were free and as a way of shielding themselves against the hegemony of white racism. As long as Africa existed, as long as African forms contrasted with Euro-American forms, white racism was a particular and contingent American reality, not an inevitable or necessary feature of human existence. But music with retentions of African culture have long held enormous appeal for American whites as well. Pre-industrial values endured longer in Afro-American culture than among more privileged groups because slavery and racism prevented black assimilation. White workers, whose own ancestors had been farmers or peasants, made a painful break with the past as they journeyed from field to factory. Industrial culture demanded regular disciplined work, competition, thrift, individualism, and delayed gratification. Residual elements of opposition to industrial values had to be purged from most Euro-American workers, but Afro-Americans maintained a closer connection to the pre-industrial world. Thus working-class whites could find a consistent and eloquent critique of individualism and competition in Afro-American culture which also displayed a humane and human alternative to industrial values in its music.

Dialogic criticism draws out the world view of Afro-American music and explains how musical devices use affect to create ideological coherence. Critical methods that ignore history can obscure the subjectivity of black music and grossly misrepresent white audience reception. For example, Robert Pattison's analysis of selected song lyrics leads him to claim

> White rockers adopted black bluesmen as their primitive ideals
> because there were no Navahos or Samoans available for the role.
> Most Americans have never met an Indian, but the black man is a
> ubiquitous American presence—thought to be primitive in his dark
> skin, his poverty, his strange dialect, his mysterious African origins. In
> the white man's imagination, he is only a few generations from the
> jungle and therefore the perfect candidate to be the realization of the
> Romantic idea of the primitive.[23]

Native American Indians and viewers of western films might wonder what kind of evidence leads Pattison to assume Americans incapable of turning Indians into popular culture icons. Those who study the various stereotypes of blacks in American popular culture might wonder how Pattison has decided that only *one* of them—the primitive—influences reception of black music. But to make these valid objections is to draw attention away from Pattison's central, and certainly false, presumption—that black music has nothing to say, that its entire creative meaning comes from the twisted imagination of white listeners who do not hear the music, but instead project on it a frame of reception designed for nineteenth-century European poetry. Pattison's conclusion is based solely on his investigations into song lyrics. He does not consider the music or its audiences. He projects himself as the ideal, maximally competent listener (actually reader), capable of articulating a "truth" unknown to the artists and audiences themselves.

In historical practice, black music has emphasized community, creativity, and criticism. Constant repetition of familiar forms like call and response encourages a close relationship between artists and audiences in collaborative cultural creation. Music that explores the entire range of possible sounds open to voice and instruments stresses individual creation and emotion in contrast to the mechanical system of notation in Western music that demands replication of standardized "pure" notes. The rhythmic complexity of Afro-American music encourages listeners to think of time as a flexible human creation rather than as an immutable outside force.

The glorification of pleasure and play in song lyrics serves as implicit and sometimes explicit criticism of a society that places primary emphasis on the duty of labor. The sense of time conveyed within Afro-American music directly contradicts one of the main disciplining forces of industrial culture. Before the rise of the factory, people generally worked at their own pace for their own purposes, disciplined by necessity or desire, but not by the time clock. Industrial labor brought the clock and its incessant demands into the workplace and into the home; days became divided into units of working time and individuals lost control over the nature, purpose, and duration of their labor. Controlling workers accustomed to preindustrial values was the primary focus of management for over one hundred years. Despite rewards of high wages and punishments including the threat of starvation, workers never wholeheartedly embraced time-work discipline, and their culture reflected that refusal. Instead of the regular beat that measured time by the clock, working-class musics embraced polyrhythms and irregular time signatures as a way of realizing in culture the mastery over time denied workers in the workplace. Prison songs like "The Cryderville Jail" were changed to "Hard Times in the Mill," where every hour marked another indignity. Rock-and-roll musicians built on that tradition, rhythmically and lyrically. If nineteenth century workers marked every hour with mention of another indignity at work, rock and roll songs offered fantasies about partying or making love around the clock. Bill Haley's "Rock Around the Clock" and Chuck Berry's "Reelin' and Rockin' " became rock anthems by inverting the icon of the clock and using it to measure out doses of pleasure instead of units of labor.

Incorporating elements of Afro-American music into their own cultures enabled white working-class musicians to taste in culture what they missed in life. Incorporating elements of Afro-American music into rock and roll enabled middle-class people to draw upon their own sedimented traditions and receive a working model of "the good life" at odds with the hegemonic norms of industrial society. At least in music, harmony with others could replace competition, work and art could be united in creative labor, and the repressions of the industrial workplace could be challenged by the uninhibited passions of love and play.

The historical revolt against hierarchy and exploitation that gave voice to the Afro-American devices at the heart of rock-and-roll music also account for the many other retentions in popular music of vernacular working-class cultures. Rock-and-roll songs stressed continuity and community by reworking familiar melodies. Bill Haley and His Comets reached the middle class with "Rock Around the Clock" when the film *Blackboard Jungle* used it as its opening theme, but the song had a long history in the collective memory of the audience in that its basic structure appeared in country music ("Move It On Over" by Hank Williams, 1953), in rhythm and blues ("Cornbread" by Hal Singer, 1948), and in New Orleans parade music of indeterminate age ("Second Line"). The basic pattern of the Bo Diddley beat pervading so many songs from "Bo Diddley" (Bo Diddley, 1955), to "Not Fade Away" (Buddy Holly, 1957; Rolling Stones, 1964), "Willie and the Hand Jive" (Johnny Otis, 1958), "Marie's the Name" (Elvis

Presley, 1961), "Mickey's Monkey" (Miracles, 1963), and the Strange-loves' "I Want Candy" (1965) originated even earlier in a traditional children's clapping and rhyming game, "Shave and a Haircut."

One of the most frequently imitated rhythm-and-blues songs, Johnny Ace's 1955 "Pledging My Love," came straight out of country music through "Down in the Valley," "Send Me Some Loving," and "Birmingham Jail." The Rivieras' 1964 "California Sun" remade Chuck Berry's 1959 "Broken Arrow," but "Broken Arrow" essentially copied "Old MacDonald." Children's rhyming games provided the lyrics for Lee Dorsey's 1961 "Ya Ya" and Shirley Ellis's 1964 "The Name Game" and 1965 "Rubber Dolly." Cheerleaders at a football game in Florida yelling "Our team is red hot, your team ain't doodley squat" gave Billie Emerson the inspiration for his 1955 hit "Red Hot," a song covered a year later by rockabilly artist Billy Lee Riley.[24] Bo Diddley's 1959 "Say Man" and "Say Man, Back Again" drew upon the street-corner insult game, the dozens. The "bragging tale" of black folklore found expression in the music of blues singer Muddy Waters's 1954 "Hootchie Cootchie Man" as well as in white artist Johnny Rivers's 1965 "Seventh Son."

Songs with references to familiar folk tales and sagas or to everyday speech or street-corner games tended to include listeners in a community of improvisation and elaboration. The songs came from life and easily blended back into it. As the members of the audience remembered and repeated, they ritualistically confirmed the commonality of everyday experience. Direct references to working-class legend and folklore framed the dialogue within rock and roll. Afro-American street singers in St. Louis's rough Chestnut Valley district in the 1890s sang a tale of romance and revenge titled "Frankie and Johnny." White country-music singer Jimmie Rodgers recorded a version of "Frankie and Johnnie" in the 1930s, and it appeared in rock-and-roll songs by Brook Benton (1961), Sam Cooke (1963), and Elvis Presley (1966). Another Afro-American ballad of the same era told about the "bad man" Stacker Lee, who emerged as a staple of black folklore and as the hero of rock-and-roll songs by Lloyd Price (1958), Wilson Pickett (1971), and Tommy Roe (1971). The traditions of southern storytellers like Brother Dave Gardner and Jimmie Driftwood infused the lyrics of hit songs by Ray Stevens and Johnny Horton, while black folktales, legends, and word games permeated records by Louis Jordan, Screamin' Jay Hawkins, Chuck Berry, and

Huey Smith and the Clowns. These folk retentions survived because of their appeal as narratives, but also because they marshaled the resources of the past as part of defining identity in the present.

Very few rock-and-roll songs addressed social issues directly, but their roots in working-class folklore traditions enabled them to encode social messages in metaphorical form. The definitive folk song of American working-class history has more likely been "John Henry" than "Solidarity Forever," but there is a lot of solidarity in workers singing about John Henry, the man who was better than a machine and who died trying to prove it. Social protest in rock and roll grew from that tradition. Gospel singer Bessie Griffin illumines this protest sensibility in a story about her childhood. Griffin explains that she used to sing hymns and spirituals as a way of challenging authority in her family. When scolded, she never talked back but would start singing "I Been 'Buked and I Been Scorned" or "Sometimes I Feel Like a Motherless Child," until one day her grandmother said "I know what you doing."[25] Griffin learned covert resistance from a culture that had developed it into a fine art under circumstances that prevented them from posing more direct challenges to power. Griffin's community may have paid a terrible price for their inability to confront oppression directly, but they also preserved their dignity and self-worth by asserting faith in some kind of ultimate justice. The same spirit pervaded rock-and-roll songs that celebrated the triumphs of clever tricksters over more powerful foes, from the De John Sisters' 1958 "Straighten Up and Fly Right" to Chuck Berry's 1958 "Jo Jo Gunne" to the Coasters' 1959 "Run Red Run."

Another form of encoding protest came in a series of songs with special meaning for particular reception communities. Chuck Berry's 1956 "Brown Eyed Handsome Man" enjoyed great popularity among blacks who knew that he meant brown *skinned* handsome man. The Five Keys' 1954 "Ling Ting Tong" (and its many cover versions) employed the slang of marijuana users, while seemingly mysterious references in the Jaynetts' 1963 "Sally Go 'Round the Roses" described a lesbian relationship to maximally competent listeners. Oppressions of class, age, and gender also provoked indirect forms of protest. Chuck Berry's 1956 "Too Much Monkey Business" equated frustrations at work, school, home, and in the army—attributing them all to the "monkey business" imposed on individuals by outside authority. Eddie Cochran's 1958 "Summertime Blues" drew a connection between youth, dependency, sexual repression, poverty, and the political impotence of youth. Three songs from 1956 illustrate resistance to alienated labor by contrasting it with leisure: Little Richard's "Rip It Up" boasts about spending Friday's paycheck on a wild Saturday night rather than saving it; Carl Perkins's "Blue Suede Shoes" invites the listener to take any of the singer's other material goods but to leave him his treasured subcultural symbols, his shoes; and Fats Domino's "Blue Monday" justifies the weekend spree by comparing it to having "to work like a slave all day" during the week. Women singers in the early 1960s highlighted the unfair constraints and double standards applied to females in a number of songs ranging from Jan Bradley's 1963 "Mama Didn't Lie," Sandy Posey's 1966 "Born a Woman," and Leslie Gore's dialectical 1963 trilogy "It's My Party," "Judy's Turn to Cry," and "You Don't Own Me."

From its tradition of social criticism to its sense of time, from its cultivation of community to its elevation of emotion, rock-and-roll music embodies a dialogic process of active remembering. It derives its comedic and dramatic tensions from working-class vernacular traditions, and it carries on a prejudice in favor of community, collectivity, and creativity in its very forms and constructs.

History and Rock-and-Roll Criticism

Literary critics Richard Terdiman and Allon White have emphasized the degree to which the dialogic approach is "a memory model," and therefore innately historical. The formal properties of rock-and-roll songs developed in response to concrete historical conditions rather than to a pre-established aesthetic agenda. To understand such songs in context, it is necessary to see how they shaped and reflected historical changes, particularly in regard to the rapid growth and immediate decline of the American industrial city in the 1940s and 1950s.

In essence, I argue that industrial labor created the preconditions for rock and roll, and the first rock-and-roll artists, entrepreneurs, and audiences came out of wartime working-class communities. Defense production for World War II attracted millions of rural whites and blacks to industrial cities, and the interactions between their cultures in the urban setting created rock-and-roll music. On the factory floor, at the neighborhood tavern, and on the radio, workers heard music previously restricted to limited audiences. Country music and blues interacted with jazz, pop, and ethnic music to form a new synthesis. Defense production centers like Los Angeles, Detroit, and St. Louis experienced enormous increases in population during World War II. Blacks left the South in large numbers during the 1940s, and during the war years alone 750,000 whites moved to Los Angeles and more than 200,000 moved to Detroit. Overcrowding created new realities in defense production centers. In Beaumont, Texas the housing shortages reached such levels that workers rented beds for eight-hour shifts, and the mounting piles of garbage in the streets led city officials to send hogs through the alleys in the hope that they would eat garbage and lessen dangers to public health. Crowded neighborhoods and buses created face-to-face contacts among previously separated groups. The new urban realities of the 1940s sometimes led to violence, but they also allowed for new cultural exchanges that would have been impossible in prewar America.

Black migrations to industrial cities during and after the war had profound cultural implications. Middle-class American popular music, dance, and dress reflected Afro-American influences as never before, and previously marginalized aspects of black and white southern culture influenced the national culture as never before. Following the most convenient railroad routes, black workers from the Southeast tended to migrate to the Baltimore, Philadelphia, New York corridor. Those from the Mississippi Delta and mid-South took the Illinois Central to Memphis, St. Louis, and Chicago, or took the Louisville and Nashville line to Cincinnati, Indianapolis, and Detroit. Blacks from Texas and Louisiana went to Los Angeles and San Francisco. As a result, east-coast music owed its structure to the music of the Southeast, Chicago's music encompassed the music of the Delta, and California music during and after the war contained a heavy dose of Texas blues.

Many of the black blues artists whose music prefigured rock and roll participated in these migrations and developed their music while employed as defense workers. John Lee Hooker moved from Mississippi to St. Louis and then to Detroit where he worked as a janitor in one of Chrysler's defense plants. Fellow Mississippians Muddy Waters and B. B. King followed the same pattern of rural-urban migration; Waters worked as a truck driver in Chicago, while King labored at construction jobs in Memphis. Lowell Fulson grew up in Oklahoma and Texas, but journeyed to Oakland, California to work in the wartime shipyards. Texas musicians Charles Brown, T-Bone Walker, and Amos Milburn all moved to the west coast to find factory jobs during the war.[26]

The white country-music artists who played crucial roles in creating rock-and-roll music also took part in those wartime migrations. Hank Williams came from rural Alabama to work in the Mobile shipyards. Elvis Presley's family left Tupelo, Mississippi after the war when his father found employment in Memphis's expanded industrial plant. Bob Wills brought his band from Texas to southern California to play for the transplanted "okies" and Texans drawn west by that region's burgeoning war production factories.[27]

When country music and blues mixed to form rock and roll, industrial cities became centers of the new music, and black and white workers became its leading performers. Fats Domino worked in a Louisiana factory making bedsprings. Chuck Berry worked on the General Motors assembly line in St. Louis. Little Richard washed dishes in the Greyhound Bus Station in Macon, Georgia. Bill Haley learned country music and blues in industrial Detroit, and worked as a disc jockey in Chester, Pennsylvania, a shipyard production center. Elvis Presley drove a truck for the Crown Electric Company in Memphis, and Buddy Holly pursued a career in music as an alternative to his part-time jobs in high school as a bricklayer and steel-manufacturing worker in Lubbock, Texas.[28]

Why did young workers from all over the country participate in the creation of rock and roll music? One strong motivation came from the desire to leave behind the alienations and indignities of work; a career in music could be the alternative to a career washing dishes. Working-class people have long pursued upward mobility through careers in show business that required disassociation from ethnic and class roots. This process involved something different. Raised in the newly desegregated environments of industrial cities, these artists represented a synthesis of historical traditions that had previously been kept apart. Rather than embracing the existing alignments within American popular culture, they sought recognition as part of something new—something infinitely more democratic and pluralistic than existing popular music.

The major recording companies dominating the music industry in the 1940s and 1950s largely ignored the earliest expressions of rock and roll. Secure with their rosters of famous artists and their connections to radio stations and promoters, they detected no demand for a new music. But small entrepreneurs in working-class communities noticed that their customers wanted to hear country music and blues, and so they began to establish small recording companies as sidelines to their regular businesses. More than four hundred new record labels came into existence in the years immediately following World War II, and these labels pioneered the recording of rock and roll music.[29]

Syd Nathan started King Records in Cincinnati because he observed the demand for music by war workers shopping at his department store. Another store owner, Herman Lubinsky of Newark, New Jersey, established Savoy Records to produce music for "the man with the dinner pail and the lady over the washtub."[30] Bob Geddins owned a music store in Oakland, and decided to create his own product by recording Johnny Fuller (a mechanic at Sears) and Lowell Fulson (a shipyard worker). Phil and Leonard Chess operated a night club in a working-class area of Chicago, and the title of their first release on their Chess label — Andrew Tibbs's "Union Man Blues" — gave some indication of the intended audience for their records. Saul Bihari, who operated juke boxes in Los Angeles, formed Modern and RPM Records along with his brothers because the major labels failed to keep him supplied with the kinds of music his customers wanted to hear. Sam Phillips in Memphis had been a radio engineer and owned a small recording studio where he produced records by black and white workers and sharecroppers. Phillips initially leased songs by Ike Turner, Junior Parker, and Howlin' Wolf to other labels, but he eventually started his own Sun Records featuring the music of Elvis Presley, Jerry Lee Lewis, and Carl Perkins.[31]

These small firms succeeded because they identified the cultural preferences of working-class audiences. New recording techniques (magnetic tape, 45 rpm and long-playing records) lessened the capital requirements for entry into the business and made it possible to record without a big studio. The newly acquired purchasing power and cultural interests of the working class, both products of wartime prosperity, created a demand that was invisible to the established firms in the music business. During the late 1940s, five companies essentially dominated the industry; but cut off as they were from working-class audiences and their tastes, these companies failed to anticipate the tremendous appeal of rock and roll. They regained control of the record industry by 1959, but only after a bitter battle with the independent companies making rock-and-roll records.

The Middle Class Encounters Rock and Roll

Because rock-and-roll music developed in highly concentrated urban markets, it became accessible to the middle class in a way that had not been true of blues and country music. The radio stations and record stores that specialized in rock and roll reached audiences previously unaware of working-class cultures. Young whites especially requested music by black artists as well as the blues/country fusions evident in "rockabilly" performances. Less tied to the history of racist norms than their parents, witness to a hybrid black/white culture all around them, and profoundly alienated by the oppressive conformity of 1950s popular culture, they embraced working-class music as their own.

That generation of teen-agers occupied a pivotal position in U.S. history. As the first generation of young people with money of their own to spend without necessarily having to work, they had the freedom to reject the values of their parents and to seek out cultural alternatives. Raised in times of unprecedented consumer affluence, they found more meaning and value in working-class culture than in the signs and symbols of their own emerging middle class. In part, they simply sought escape from the stifling blandness of 1950s popular music, but they also developed their preferences as people anticipating life in an increasingly bureaucratic and conformist society. In a culture that recommended obedience to all authority and lauded the "organization man," they sought autonomy, emotion, and authentic connection to others in the cultures of the working class.[32]

The process of "prestige from below" that infused middle-class fascination with rock and roll had been prefigured during World War II with subcultures that developed around "zoot suits" and "bop talk."[33] The zoot suit (draped coats, pants wide at the knee and narrow at the ankle, wide lapels, pleats and cuffs in the pants) originated in black and Chicano communities, but became a symbol of rebellion that spread to middle-and working-class whites. By wearing zoot suits, young people identified with the dress of the poor rather than the rich, and flaunted their alienation from the surrounding culture.[34]

Closely allied with the zoot-suit culture, bop talk originated among black jazz musicians. Their slang favored internal rhymes (a zoot suit with a drape shape and a reet pleat might impress a slick chick), inverted meanings (something "crazy" really made sense, "cool" people used an aloof posture to hide great passion), and relied on African retentions (a hip cat had the requisite knowledge about life—as one would expect from a term derived from the Wolof word "hipicat," meaning one who has his eyes open).[35] The popularity of bop talk as American slang severed its organic connection to black nationalism, but it remained identified with drugs, hostility to work, and a vaguely un-Christian attitude—a perfect expression of opposition to middle-class norms.

Rock-and-roll musicians often utilized the legacy of bop talk. Elvis Presley billed himself as "The Hillbilly Cat" early in his career, and Buddy Holly and his first singing partner, Bob Montgomery, advertised themselves as "Buddy and Bob—Western and Bop." Berry Gordy's first song-writing success for Jackie Wilson bore the title "Reet Petite," and Jerry Lee Lewis remembers the jazz anthem "Hey Ba-ba Re-Bop" as one of the formative influences on his music. From Carl Perkins's hit "Boppin' the Blues" to Alvadean Coker's "We're Gonna Bop," the word had a magic power for rock-and-roll pioneers. In addition, they made full use of the internal rhymes of bop talk in titles like "See You Later Alligator," "Tutti Frutti," "Ready Teddy," "Money Honey," "Boney Moronie," "Lean Jean," and "Skinny Minnie." These variations of bop talk may have misunderstood its original connotations, but they maintained its rebellious posture, its playfulness with words, and its capacity to create an oppositional in-group.[36]

By pursuing black music, working-class whites explored forbidden ground as did middle-class whites pursuing working-class music. The lure proved greater than the risks to people like Elvis Presley, who listened to Big Bill Broonzy and Big Boy Crudup at home, even though his parents scolded him for listening to that "sinful" music. Buddy Holly also embraced a music and a culture not designed for him. After he toured with a rock-and-roll caravan of stars, Holly's mother asked him if he got along with the Negroes in the other bands. "Oh we're Negroes too," he responded, "we get to feeling like that's what we are."[37]

People who made their living from rock and roll in the early 1950s recognized the ways in which the music helped break down barriers of race and class. Jerry Wexler, a producer for Atlantic Records, described the culture of rock and roll as neither black nor white, but as "southern proletarian." Yet many of the audiences that Wexler observed consisted of college students at elite southern schools; if their culture could be termed proletarian, it was by deliberate identification, not by birth.[38] In St. Louis, Chuck Berry found himself popular with middle-class, white audiences even though he had lived his whole life within a segregated ghetto and even though his music drew mainly upon the blues. At his first, paying musical jobs with the Johnnie Johnson trio in 1953, he noticed many young whites in the audience which struck him as odd "since a lot of white people were afraid to enter a black community."[39]

Consumption of mass popular culture always involves varied motivations and complex choices, and it is difficult to account fully for any specific consumer choice. But at least part of the motivation for the middle-class white youth adoption of Afro-American and working-class music as their own in the 1950s stemmed from a collective judgment about the demise of the urban industrial city and the rise of the suburb. At the very moment that residential suburbs increased class and racial segregation, young people found "prestige from below" by celebrating the ethnic and class interactions of the urban street. Visible markers of class and ethnic identity disappeared as the single-family, detached suburban home replaced the multi-family dwellings of ethnic neighborhoods, as network television eclipsed the neighborhood movie theater, and as a culture of consumption and conformity encouraged standardization of dress and behavior as the entrance requirements into the burgeoning, corporate white-collar world. Mass communications, upward mobility, and the anti-foreign atmosphere fueled by hysterical anti-communism and exaggerated "patriotic" Americanism left many middle-class youths without tangible ties to their own pasts. Facing a choice between the sterile and homogeneous suburban cultures of their parents or the dynamic street cultures alive among groups excluded from the middle-class consensus, a large body of youths found themselves captivated and persuaded by the voices of difference. Mass consumer culture had become so hegemonic that middle-class young people flocked to the cultures of the dying industrial city for connection to the past, for emotional expression, and for a set of values that explained and justified rebellion.

Defenders of middle-class morality and spokespersons for the major record companies recognized the ideological and economic threats to the status quo embodied in the new music. The Artist and Repertoire Director at Columbia Records, Mitch Miller, predicted the rapid demise of rock and roll, damning it as "the comic books of music." A Catholic Church official in Boston claimed that "the suggestive lyrics of rock'n'roll records are a matter for law enforcement agencies." Frank Sinatra told a Congressional investigating committee that rock and roll constituted "the most brutal, ugly, desperate, vicious form of expression it has been my misfortune to hear," adding that the "lewd" lyrics of rock and roll made it "the martial music of every sideburned delinquent on the face of the earth."[40] The actual musical selections that aroused the ire of these businessmen, clergy, and performers might seem quite tame by today's standards, but the musical censors of the 1950s (like their New Right counterparts in the 1980s) raised the specter of sexuality and its threat to youth as a cover for their real concerns — the "transgressions" perpetrated by middle-class white youths when they embraced "prestige from below" and undercut the ideological hegemony of their own race, class, and family. The anti-rock critics were (and are) no doubt sincere in their revulsion at rock and roll's refusal to separate romantic love from sexual pleasure, but this refusal to separate mind and body is merely one manifestation of an even more "menacing" refusal, that of a symbolic system which insists on "naturalizing" the socially constructed divisions and hierarchies between black and white, rich and poor, male and female. For in choosing truck drivers, dishwashers, and sharecroppers as cultural heroes, middle-class white youths challenged the legitimacy of the emerging corporate-suburban culture and validated the pluralities and ambiguities of the dying industrial city.

Thus the 1950s brought a revolution in popular music, but also provoked a counter-revolution. The major record labels and their allies attempted to regain control over the content of popular music, while business and government leaders continued their assault on the social formations that gave rise to working-class leadership in popular culture. By 1959, both groups had succeeded. At first, the major labels ignored rock and roll, but when independent producers reaped the benefits of the increased sales generated by the new music, the big companies began issuing "cover" versions of rock songs performed by pop artists. The cover system made money: with their advertising and distribution powers, the big labels could see to it that their versions enjoyed broader exposure than the originals. But royalties and publication rights went to outsiders under the cover system, and an unpredictable network of artists and small entrepreneurs remained the driving force in the music industry. The popularity of independent artists like Sam Cooke, Jerry Lee Lewis, Little Richard, and Chuck Berry on small labels persisted despite efforts by the majors to "invent" new white and middle-class rock stars like Tommy Sands, Tab Hunter, and Pat Boone. RCA signed Elvis Presley and smoothed off the rough edges of his style for mass distribution, but even then it was specifically Presley the star under contract to RCA that they pushed, not the broader musical culture which had produced him.

Failing to "cover" rock and roll, the music companies then tried to destroy it. Working in tandem with radio-station chains, they encouraged smaller radio playlists (top 40 radio) which had built-in advantages for the big companies with their established connections to station managers. With fewer records on the air, marginal, innovative, or controversial music tended to be squeezed out. This practice rationalized production and minimized risks of new styles by saturating the air with the blandest common denominators of mass taste. When top 40 radio came in, much of the rougher, wilder, blacker, and more working-class music disappeared from the radio.

Limited playlists also encouraged "payola," bribes to disc jockeys for playing certain records. Although the big companies engaged in payola, their resources made them less dependent on it than were the smaller labels. Big companies could count on their contacts and interlocking business relations with radio networks, their influence with advertisers, their ability to supply or withhold future products, and their economy of scale to get their records played. Congressional investigators looking into payola virtually ignored the big firms; their targets were the independent labels likely to feature the harder-edged rock and roll. Government investigators harassed disc

jockey Alan Freed and drove him out of the business for his acceptance of $30,000 in exchange for playing some of the wild rock-and-
roll music that made his show popular, but the Congressional committee had only words of praise for clean-cut and middle-class Dick
Clark, with his heavily white and pop playlists. Clark owned stock in
record companies and publishing houses whose songs he played on
his own shows, yet investigators saw nothing suspicious in the
$500,000 in salary and stock or the estimated $25 million in free advertising that Clark derived from his dual role as nationally televised
disc jockey and record-company impressario.[41]

Censorship and monopoly within the music industry pervade the
history of rock and roll, but critics lacking a historical perspective too
often miss their significance. For example, Steve Chapple and Reebee Garofalo, in their *Rock'n'Roll Is Here To Pay*, provide extensive
documentation of malicious corporate distortion of rock-and-roll
music. But Simon Frith misunderstands their argument, accusing
them of objecting to commercial culture itself because of an unrealistic devotion to music as "art" or "folk culture." Despite Chapple
and Garofalo's evidence (and that available from other sources),
Frith contends, "There is, in fact, less conflict between art and commerce in rock than in any other mass medium," and "commerce is
then a serious constraint only at this lower level, for musicians getting into the business."[42] Knowledge of the history of rock and roll
indicates otherwise. One thinks of John Fogerty cheated of his royalties and left without a record contract for nearly a decade, of Boston
unable to release new records at the peak of its popularity because of
contract disputes with its label, or of Irma Thomas, the "soul queen
of New Orleans," who records for the tiny Rounder label, despite
more than twenty years of exquisite performances. Thomas says, "I
know that unless you're on a major label that's spending megabucks
for promotion, you haven't got a snowball's chance in hell of getting
a record played on radio."[43] These examples from the 1980s underscore the pernicious effects of commercialism on rock-and-roll music, effects that are the rule rather than the exception in a business
where more performers *lose* money than make money, but where
publishing houses and recording conglomerates almost always increase their wealth. This pattern emerges from the historical record,
and it validates rather than disproves the allegations of anti-corporate
rock critics.

One need only look at the fate of the 1950s rockers caught up in the whitewashing of popular music that propelled Clark to prominence. In addition to the Congressional committee that lauded Clark, other government agencies also participated in cleaning up rock and roll. The army drafted Elvis Presley at the peak of his popularity, cut his hair, and took him out of circulation for two years. Presley's willingness to let the state borrow his prestige and turn him into a symbol of "patriotism," and his affiliation with RCA enabled him to withstand further harassment. Other artists were not as fortunate. Local prosecutors, the Federal Bureau of Investigation, and the Department of Justice persecuted Chuck Berry for acts that would have been overlooked if they had been committed by a mainstream entertainer. Berry eventually served twenty months in federal prison for allegedly engaging in voluntary sexual relations with a prostitute that who he met while on tour. Jerry Lee Lewis faced a media blackout after marrying his fourteen-year-old cousin. But Elvis Presley faced no legal consequences when upon meeting fourteen-year-old Priscilla Beaulieu in Germany, he had her come live with him in Memphis at the age of sixteen.

Record companies and the government exaggerated rock and roll's threat to middle-class morality in the 1950s, but they did not invent it. Unquestionably, the performers and their music did violate middle-class norms. Elvis Presley's gyrations on television (copied from Bo Diddley's stage show) brought a defiant sensuality and unbridled hedonism into American living rooms. Chuck Berry drove big pink Cadillacs and Lincolns, and appeared in public in the company of white women. Little Richard's screeching falsetto, exuberant stage antics, and sexual ambiguities drew upon historical antecedents among black entertainers, but appeared shocking to much of the white middle class. Whether by active conspiracy or enlightened self-interest, the system struck back effectively at the rock-and-roll threat, using the protection of the family as justification to reinforce sexual repression, racial separation, and class divisions—elements that characterized most of the emerging corporate culture.

During the heyday of rock and roll, the percentage of best-selling records by black artists increased from 3 in 1954 to 29 in 1957. After 1959, the percentage declined every year. Sales of all records increased by as much as 36 percent each year between 1955 and 1959, but sales leveled off until 1964. As the industry became whiter and more middle class, its sales declined. But the major companies destroyed their independent competitors and regained their share of the record market.[44]

Yet rock and roll remained alive in working-class neighborhoods of industrial cities. In New Orleans it reached great artistic heights in the early 1960s on the strength of records by Lee Dorsey, an automobile-body repairman; Irma Thomas, a waitress and department store clerk; and the Neville Brothers—Art, an elevator operator; Aaron, a longshoreman; and Cyril, who cleaned box cars and grave yards.[45] Lee Dorsey later remembered his days in New Orleans as marked by a healthy confusion about whether he wanted to be an auto-body repairman who sang, or a singer who did auto-body work.[46]

In New York, young, middle-class and working-class, white songwriters like Carol King, Neil Sedaka, Cynthia Weil, Barry Mann, Doc Pomus, and Mort Shuman drew upon the changing nature of the working class to reinvigorate rock and roll. Inspired by the influx of Hispanic workers in that city and the attendant popularity of musicians Tito Puente, Ray Barretto, and Mongo Santamaria, such songwriters fashioned a series of Latin-tinged rock-and-roll songs for black singers such as the Drifters, Shirelles, and Isely Brothers. Pomus and Shuman even deliberately inverted the words of "Save the Last Dance for Me," making it sound like the English of a nonnative speaker.

Despite this enduring working-class urban presence, and despite the occasional entry onto the best-seller charts of rockabilly survivors like Dorsey Burnette or blues veterans like Lloyd Price, popular music between 1959 and 1964 became whiter, blander, and less working class each year.[47] It took the stimulus of the "British Invasion," spearheaded by the Beatles and Rolling Stones, to restore the viability and profitability of the record industry—by reviving the very same American urban, working-class sounds that had been gradually purged from American popular music over the previous five years.

British groups acknowledged their lineage to urban working-class rock and roll. The Beatles "covered" and remade the Isley Brothers' "Twist and Shout," Chuck Berry's "Roll Over Beethoven" and "Rock and Roll Music," Carl Perkins's "Match Box" and "Honey Don't," and Larry Williams's "Slow Down." The Rolling Stones remade Chuck Berry's "Come On" and "You Can't Catch Me," Irma Thomas's "Time

Is On My Side," Marvin Gaye's "Hitch Hike," and Sam Cooke's "Little Red Rooster." The Stones took their name from a Muddy Waters song on Chess Records, and their song "2120 S. Michigan Avenue" paid tribute to the records made at the Chess Studios located at that address in Chicago in the 1950s. John Lennon directly quoted Chuck Berry's "You Can't Catch Me" in his "Come Together," and early Beatles records contained an encyclopedia of Chuck Berry guitar licks, Buddy Holly harmonies, and Little Richard falsettos.

The British invasion of 1964 won a new middle-class audience for rock and roll. Working-class forms seemed less threatening to middle-class morality when interpreted by cute, middle-class, white, British males whose good humor always left open the possibility that they might be joking. Of course, the music lost something in this transformation, but it retained much of importance as well. The collective memory of the audience located these sounds in a context of powerful social associations with rebellion, emotion, and sensuality. Just as zoot suits and bop talk lost some of their original meaning but nonetheless remained valuable as icons of opposition to middle-class subcultures, the recycled rock and roll of the 1950s proved important to the consciousness of middle-class youths of the 1960s. For artists and audiences alike, the starting point of self-identity came from identification with the working-class cultures that created rock and roll.

By the late 1960s, a hippie counterculture coalesced around rock-and-roll music and around a group of values inimical to the traditional concerns of the middle class. Hippies glorified pleasure while resisting work, championed the supportive community over the rugged individual, and responded to a nation at war with proclamations of faith in peace and love. Men adopted long hair, jewelry, and a level of ornamentation and display in dress previously associated with women; women wore comfortable clothing that conformed to the natural contours of the human body rather than to the fashion world's idealized female shape. Middle-class and affluent young whites moved to poor neighborhoods and imitated Afro-American hairstyles and the political rhetoric of the black community. All of these acts of rebellion had severe limits, and in its own way the hippie counter-culture mirrored many of the consumerist values of the society at large. But in attempting to reclaim the physical space of the abandoned inner city and to champion the cause of urban prestige from below, it represented a real rebellion in dialogue with the traces of previous working-class cultures and urban life.

Nothing better illustrates the sedimented, urban working-class traces in 1960s counter-culture better than the personal histories of its two leading symbols, Jimi Hendrix and Janis Joplin. Hendrix grew up in Seattle where his father worked on aircraft assembly lines, as a gardener, and as a steel worker. While still a teen-ager, Hendrix toured with black rock acts like Little Richard and the Isley Brothers and with white and mixed groups including Joey Dee and the Starlighters and Bobby Taylor and the Vancouvers. Hendrix derived his musical vocabulary from the blues which he learned while a foster child living with a family of transplanted Texans in Berkeley, California, and while touring with Ike Turner and Albert King. Like Elvis Presley Hendrix grew up in a public housing project, part of a working-class family, and became famous for fusing black and white music. He adapted traditional blues techniques to contemporary technology with his use of feedback, wah-wah pedal, and simulation of the human voice on guitar. His virtuosity and apocalyptic sensuality had powerful appeal for middle-class youths eager to blot out the ugly realities of everyday life.

Like Hendrix, Janis Joplin became popular both for her music and for her ability to symbolize new values. As a white child in industrial Port Arthur, Texas, she listened to records by blues singers Odetta and Leadbelly to vent her feelings of alienation from the society in which she lived. Unpopular in high school and unwilling to conform to the standards of dress and behavior deemed appropriate for girls her age, Joplin struck out on her own in search of new possibilities. She began her singing career performing Jimmie Rodgers-styled country songs in an Austin night club, but she also imitated Bessie Smith, the "Empress of the Blues." After moving to the west coast (an old Texas tradition) she wound up working as a secretary in San Francisco. An impromptu singing session at a party there led to the formation of the band Big Brother and the Holding Company, and their free concerts in Golden Gate Park made Joplin one of the focal points of the Haight-Ashbury counter-culture.

In every detail, Joplin personified the ideals of the counter-culture. Her untrained but powerful voice and her accidental "stardom" reinforced the belief that everyone could become an artist. Her emergence as a sex symbol elevated sensuality and emotion over conventional standards of beauty. Like Hendrix, her absorption in her art, indulgence in drugs and alcohol, and intense passion reflected the values of young people living for the moment and anticipating little future. But Hendrix and Joplin also shared a profound sense of the past, of the emancipatory cultures of early rock-and-roll music forged in urban industrial settings in their childhoods. Joplin's music relied on techniques originating in country music and blues, but honed and refined by the rock and roll of her youth—three line, twelve bar blues, falsettos, call and response, and bending notes for effect. For both artists and audiences, historical working-class music offered an appropriate grammar and vocabulary for the oppressions and alienations of a new cultural moment.

The hippie counter-culture confronted its own demise most dramatically in the deaths of Hendrix and Joplin. With the break-up of the Beatles, the murder of a participant in the 1969 Altamont Rock festival while the Rolling Stones played onstage, and the degeneration into drug-ravaged slums of hippie "liberated zones" like Haight-Ashbury and New York's East Village, it became clear even to its adherents that "the dream" was over. But that very recognition spread most powerfully through a popular song that placed hippie aspirations within the historical context of 1950s rock and roll—Don McLean's "American Pie." The nation's best-selling song during the winter of 1971–1972, "American Pie" located the death of the counter-culture within a historical cycle of death and rebirth, beginning with the plane crash that killed Buddy Holly and Ritchie Valens and ending with the death of Janis Joplin. McLean's song paid tribute to the erotic and life-affirming currents in rock music, drawing a direct connection between the teen-age passion of the 1950s and the cultural and political dissent of the 1960s. It interchanged references to musicians Bob Dylan, the Beatles, and the Rolling Stones with references to historical figures like the Kennedys and Martin Luther King. By citing a long history of struggle, the song attempted to cushion the blow of current failures and hold open the possibility of future victories.

Against the Wind, the 1970s and 1980s

Much of 1970s and 1980s rock and roll shows the traces of the impact of working-class culture on the industrial cities of the 1940s and 1950s. Bruce Springsteen's automobile metaphors and musical structures borrow freely from Chuck Berry, and Springsteen's characteristic sound—devoid of either high or low tones—echoes the "wall of sound" pioneered by Phil Spector's productions for the "girl groups" of the early 1960s. Springsteen's ties to the past are exemplified by his work as a co-producer with his friend Little Steven Van Zandt for 1960s star Gary Bonds's comeback album "Dedication" (1981). Buddy Holly's first work as a producer brought together country singer Waylon Jennings and rhythm and blues saxophone player King Curtis to do the Cajun song "Jole Blon"; in a gesture of recognition Springsteen and Van Zandt placed the same song on Bonds's album. Van Zandt's co-production of Artists Against Apartheid's "Sun City" album and video in 1985 (which featured Springsteen and a pantheon of rock-and-roll heroes), displayed the same ability to draw upon the rock-and-roll past to reinforce its capacity for mixing races and cultures in progressive unity in the present.

Yet for all his talents as a collaborator with Van Zandt, Springsteen's working-class past informs the present most profoundly on his own records. Whether making autobiographical references to the factory that took his father's time and labor, or defining the American condition through the working people of his "Nebraska" album, Springsteen contrasts the pains of alienated labor to the utopian aspirations for emancipation that have always occupied center stage within rock-and-roll performances. As he explains in "My Home Town," the roots of the malaise confronting men and women "born in the U.S.A." in the 1980s lie in the de-industrialization that has killed off so much of the heterogeneous culture of industrial urban communities.

From Bob Seger's self-conscious anthems about "that old time rock and roll" to the stylistic and lyrical tributes to Chuck Berry and Bo Diddley by Dave Edmunds and George Thorogood, rock and roll in the 1980s carries an extraordinary awareness of its own history. Bo Diddley toured with the Clash, appeared on a George Thorogood video, and found his famous Bo Diddley beat revived in hit records by Bow Wow Wow ("I Want Candy," 1982) and Joan Jett ("Bad Reputation," 1981). Brian Setzer of the Stray Cats pays tribute to Eddie Cochran in interviews, and members of The Look wear Buddy Holly shirts. Even Jim Morrison and the Doors have become favorites among young people who were born years after Morrison's death.

Values and beliefs rooted in working-class experiences set the standards of criticism and the parameters of debate about American life within popular music. Just as previous generations of middle-class listeners nurtured memories and values of working-class pasts, today's "middle class" turns to images from working-class life to express its own discontents as in Billy Joel's 1982 "Allentown" and John Cougar Mellancamp's 1987 "Empty Hands." The working class in the U.S. exists as an empirical fact in the lives of those trading their labor power for wages, but it also lives in the collective historical memory of the middle class. Oppositional thought denied expression by the monopolies who market culture survives in the subtle nuances of cultural moments too small for co-optation or censorship. The working class may not be the agency of emancipation envisioned by Karl Marx, but whatever form emancipation eventually takes, it will be that much easier because there is and has been an American working class. As a class, American workers are "older now, but still running against the wind," nurtured and sustained by a dialogue within popular music that enables them to remember the past and to imagine the future.

6

Cruising Around the Historical Bloc:
Postmodernism and Popular Music
in East Los Angeles

During his first visit to Los Angeles, Octavio Paz searched in vain for visible evidence of Mexican influence on that city's life and culture. The great Mexican writer found streets with Spanish names and subdivisions filled with Spanish Revival architecture, but to his surprise and dismay he perceived only a superficial Hispanic gloss on an essentially Anglo-American metropolis. Mexican culture seemed to have evaporated into little more than local color, even in a city that had belonged to Spain and Mexico long before it became part of the United States, a city where one-third of the population traced its lineage to Olmec, Maya, Toltec, Aztec, Spanish, and Mexican ancestors, and a city which had more Mexican residents than all but two of Mexico's own cities. Paz detected a "vague atmosphere" of Mexicanism in Los Angeles, manifesting itself through "delight in decorations, carelessness and pomp, negligence, passion and reserve." But he felt that this "ragged but beautiful" ghost of Mexican identity only rarely interacted with "the North American world based on precision and efficiency." Instead, this Mexicanism floated above the city, "never quite existing, never quite vanishing."[1]

As both the oldest and the newest immigrants to Los Angeles, Mexican-Americans have faced unique problems of cultural identity and assimilation. But the anguish of invisibility that Paz identified among them is all too familiar to minority ethnic communities around the globe. Everywhere, cultural domination by metropolitan elites eviscerates and obliterates traditional cultures rooted in centuries of shared experience. For ethnic minorities, failure to assimilate into dominant cultures can bring exclusion from vital economic and political resources, but successful assimilation can annihilate prized traditions and customs essential to individual and collective identity. Cultural institutions and the mass media alike depict dominant cultures as "natural" and "normal," while never representing the world from the vantage point of ethnic communities. Active discrimination and economic exploitation reinforce a sense of marginality among aggrieved peoples, but mass-media images rarely grant legitimacy to marginal perspectives. Traditional forms of cultural expression within ethnic communities lose their power to order and interpret experience, yet they persist as important icons of alienated identity. Surrounded by images that exclude them, included in images that seem to have no real social power, ethnic communities come to feel that they never quite exist and never quite vanish.

But the transformation of real historical traditions and cultures into superficial icons and images touches more than ethnic communities. A sharp division between life and culture provides an essential characteristic of life in all modern industrialized societies, affecting dominant as well as subordinated groups. As Walter Benjamin points out, the production and distribution of art under conditions of mechanical reproduction and commodity form lead to an alienated world in which cultural objects are received outside of the communities and traditions that initially gave them shape and meaning.[2] Created artifacts from diverse cultures blend together into a seeming contextless homogenized mass, encountered independently from the communities that gave birth to them. Mass communications and culture rely on an ever-expanding supply of free-floating symbols only loosely connected to social life. Experience and traditions seem to have no binding claims on the present. Ours is a world in which "all that is solid melts into air" as Marshall Berman asserts in a phrase appropriated from the *Communist Manifesto*.[3]

Members of dominant social groups might not feel quite the same anguish of invisibility that oppresses cultural minorities, but cultural identity for them has become no less an exercise in alienation. The seeming collapse of tradition and the tensions between cultural commodities and social life make mass cultural discourse a locus of confusion and conflict. A proliferation of composite cultural creations and marginal subcultures claim the same "authority" wielded by traditions rooted in centuries of common experience. The revered "master narratives" of the past—religion, liberal humanism, Marxism, psychoanalysis—survive in truncated form, influencing but not dominating social discourse. Instead, a multivocal and contradictory culture that delights in difference and disunity seems to be at the core of contemporary cultural consciousness. This "postmodern" culture allows the residues of many historical cultures to float above us, "ragged but beautiful," "never quite existing and never quite vanishing."[4]

Postmodern culture places ethnic minorities in an important role. Their exclusion from political power and cultural recognition has allowed aggrieved populations to cultivate sophisticated capacities for ambiguity, juxtaposition, and irony—all key qualities in the postmodern aesthetic. The imperatives of adapting to dominant cultures while not being allowed full entry into them leads to complex and creative cultural negotiations that foreground marginal and alienated states of consciousness. Unable to experience either simple assimilation or complete separation from dominant groups, ethnic cultures accustom themselves to a bifocality reflective of both the ways that they view themselves and the ways that they are viewed by others. In a world that constantly undermines the importance and influence of traditions, ethnic cultures remain tied to their pasts in order to explain and arbitrate the problems of the present. Because their marginality involves the pains of exclusion and exploitation, racial and ethnic cultures speak eloquently about the fissures and frictions of society. Because their experience demands bifocality, minority-group culture reflects the decentered and fragmented nature of contemporary human experience. Because their history identifies the sources of marginality, racial and ethnic cultures have an ongoing legitimate connection to the past that distinguishes them from more assimilated groups. Masters of irony in an ironic world, they often understand that their marginalized status makes them more appropriate spokespersons for society than mainstream groups unable to fathom or address the causes of their alienations.

Discussions about postmodern sensibilities in contemporary culture often revolve around trends and tendencies in painting, architecture, and literature, but they have even greater relevance to analyses of commercialized leisure. It is on the level of commodified mass culture that the most popular, and often the most profound, acts of cultural *bricolage* take place.[5] The destruction of established canons and the juxtaposition of seemingly inappropriate items characteristic of the self-conscious postmodernism in "high culture," have long been staples of commodified popular culture. With their facility for cultural fusion and their resistance to univocal master narratives, expressions of popular culture contain important lessons about the problems and promises of culture in a world in which "all that is solid melts into air."

The Mexican-American community of Los Angeles that so disappointed Octavio Paz provides an instructive example of how ethnic minority groups can fashion forms of cultural expression appropriate to postmodern realities. Paz's static and one-dimensional view of Mexican identity prevented him from seeing the rich culture of opposition embedded within the Los Angeles Chicano community. What seemed to him an ephemeral cloud "hovering and floating" above the city in actuality represented a complicated cultural strategy designed to preserve the resources of the past by adapting them to the needs of the present. In many areas of cultural production, but especially in popular music, organic intellectuals within Mexican-American Los Angeles pursued a strategy of self-presentation that brought their unique and distinctive cultural traditions into the mainstream of mass popular culture. Neither assimilationist nor separatist, they drew upon "families of resemblance" — similarities to the experiences and cultures of other groups — to fashion a "unity of disunity."[6] In that way, they sought to make alliances with other groups by cultivating the ways in which their particular experiences spoke with special authority about the ideas and alienations felt by others. They used the techniques and sensibilities of postmodernism to build a "historical bloc" of oppositional groups united in ideas and intentions, if not experience.[7]

Popular Music in Mexican-American Los Angeles

During the 1940s, defense spending and war mobilization changed the face of Los Angeles, stimulating a massive in-migration of whites, blacks, and Chicanos. Traditional residential segregation confined Afro-Americans to the south-central area, while limiting Chicanos largely to housing in downtown East Side neighborhoods.[8] Private bankers and government planners encouraged housing segregation by class and race, viewing ethnic heterogeneity in Los Angeles (as in other cities) as a defect of urban life rather than as one of its advantages. In this way vicious prejudice became written into federal loan policies and private commercial practices. For example, the Home Owners Loan Corporation City Survey File on Los Angeles for 1939 contained a confidential memorandum that argued against the feasibility of loans to Mexican-Americans because

> While many of the Mexican race are of high caliber and descended from the Spanish grandees who formerly owned all of the territory in Southern California, the large majority of Mexican peoples are a definite problem locally and their importation in the years gone by to work the agricultural crops has now been recognized as a mistake.[9]

Translated into public policy, that perception of Mexican-Americans meant that Chicano neighborhoods would not be eligible for housing loans, thereby ensuring residential segregation in the region. Federal appraisers rated the eligibility of each Los Angeles neighborhood for home loans, giving the highest rating to areas reserved for the exclusive use of white Christians, while assigning the lowest rating to black, Chicano, and mixed neighborhoods. The Federal Housing Authority gave its lowest possible rating to Boyle Heights in East Los Angeles because its mixture of Chicano, Jewish, and Eastern European residents convinced the appraisers that

> This is a "melting pot" area and is literally honeycombed with diverse and subversive racial elements. It is seriously doubted whether there is a single block in the area which does not contain detrimental racial elements and there are very few districts which are not hopelessly heterogeneous.[10]

Yet the opening of new shipyards and aircraft assembly plants combined with Los Angeles's severe housing shortage produced unprecedented inter-ethnic mixing in the city. Official segregation gave way bit by bit as Chicanos and European ethnics lived and worked together in Boyle Heights and Lincoln Park, while blacks and Chicanos lived in close proximity to each other in Watts and in the San Fernando Valley suburb of Pacoima.[11] On the factory floor, on public transportation, and on the streets of thriving commercial districts, diverse groups mixed with each other as never before. Wherever one traveled in the city's *barrios*, ghettos, and mixed neighborhoods, one could easily find the potential for inter-group conflicts and rivalries;

sometimes they took the form of actual racial and ethnic violence. But there also existed a vibrant street life built upon communication and cooperation in community organizations and in neighborhood life.

In this milieu, small entrepreneurs catering to the local market sensed a demand for cultural commodities that reflected the social life of the new urban environment. Before RCA's purchase of Elvis Presley's contract from Sun Records in 1955, the major studios ignored the music emanating from working-class neighborhoods, leaving the field to the more than four hundred independent labels that came into existence after the war. Existing outside corporate channels, the smaller firms in working-class areas produced records geared to local audiences, especially in minority communities. The invention of magnetic recording tape made it possible to enter the record business with relatively little capital, while concentrations of transplanted war workers provided a ready market for music based on country music and blues.[12] (See Chapter 5)

Recruiting performers from the communities they knew best, small-scale local record producers responded to trends in the streets. In addition, the proliferation of local radio stations in the postwar years offered exposure to new audiences. Juke box operators, furniture-store owners, and musicians responded to the consumer demand for a popular music that reflected the folk roots and multiracial ethos of the new urban streets. For example, a 1948 hit record by Los Angeles's Don Tosti Band titled "Pachuco Boogie" went on to sell more than two million copies, an extraordinary total for any Spanish-language record in the U.S., but especially for one that glorified one of the *barrio*'s more reviled subcultures—the Pachucos.[13]

In many ways, Pachucos embodied the defiance of conventional authority that came to symbolize the appeal of rock and roll. Pachucos were teen-aged gang members sporting zoot suits, ducktail haircuts, and distinctive tattoos; they had attracted public attention during the war years when newspaper stories blamed them for much of the youth crime in Los Angeles. Tensions peaked in June 1943 when hundreds of sailors invaded the East Los Angeles community to beat up Mexican-American youths who wore zoot suits. The police, prosecutors, and city council joined forces to praise this criminal attack, lauding the sailors for the efforts to "clean up" the city. But the racism manifest in the attacks caused many Mexican-Americans to start looking at the Pachucos as defenders of the community against outside encroachments and as symbols of Chicano victimization and marginality.[14]

The Don Tosti Band's "Pachuco Boogie" captured the spirit of that new-found admiration for street rebels. The song's lyrics employed *calo*, the street slang associated with Pachucos but considered vulgar by "respectable" Mexican-Americans. "Pachuco Boogie" blended Mexican speech and rhythms with Afro-American scat-singing and blues harmonies to form a provocative musical synthesis. Some Spanish-language radio stations refused to play the song, but Anglo disc jockeys programming black rhythm-and-blues shows aimed at white teen-agers put it on their playlists, to the delight of their listeners. Band member Raul Diaz remembers what it was like before that record became a hit, how Mexican-American musicians like himself often had to wear sombreros and tropical outfits to get work playing music during intermissions at motion-picture theaters. "We wanted to play Chicano music, not come on like some clowns," Diaz recalls, "but at the time the scene was dominated by people like Desi Arnaz and Xavier Cugat and the music was really bland."[15] The Don Tosti Band changed that when "Pachuco Boogie" sold more than two million copies. Itself a blend of Chicano, Anglo, and Afro-American musical forms, "Pachuco Boogie" garnered commercial success by uniting a diverse audience into a new synthesis—a "unity of disunity."[16]

"Pachuco Boogie" signaled the start of creative new links among previously divided groups. Anglo youths especially imitated the distinctive dress of Mexican-American "cholos" with their khaki pants and long-sleeved Pendleton shirts over sleeveless white undershirts, and "cholo" became a hip slang word with larger meanings. The word "cholo" probably derives from an Aztec word meaning servant, and it connotes someone with low status, usually a recent immigrant from a rural area. Cholos spoke a bilingual slang, displayed elaborate tattoos, and staked their claims to urban neighborhoods by covering walls with stylized graffiti. The studied disinterest and cultivated detachment affected by cholos echoed the oppositional postures of other postwar subcultures including bop musicians and beat poets. But in Los Angeles the cholo relationship to rock and roll made that subculture the most accessible model of "otherness" for middle-class white youths. When Anglo, black, or even Chicano youths embraced the cholo image, they flaunted their alienation by openly identifying with one of society's most despised groups.[17]

The ability of musicians to learn from other cultures played a key role in their success as rock-and-roll artists. For example, in 1952, black saxophonist Chuck Higgins had a hit recording with "Pachuko Hop"—a song he wrote as a tribute to the dancing, style, and slang of the Mexican-American youths he encountered while playing dances at East Los Angeles union halls.[18] White songwriter Jerry Leiber's widowed mother operated a grocery store near a black neighborhood in Baltimore in the early 1940s where he was first exposed to black music. The family moved to Los Angeles in 1945, and as a teen-ager he resumed his infatuation with the blues while working in a record store with a largely black clientele. A high-school classmate introduced Leiber to another middle-class white fan of black music, Mike Stoller, who had grown up on Long Island but had taken piano lessons in Harlem as an eleven-year-old student of the great jazz and blues pianist James P. Johnson. As a teen-ager, Stoller joined a Harlem "social club" before moving to Los Angeles with his family in 1949. "I learned the pachuco dances and joined a pachuco social club," Stoller later explained when asked how he got his start as a musician.[19] He played piano with the Blas Vasquez band which exposed him to Chicano appropriations of Afro-American and Euro-American forms and styles as well as to indigenous Mexican music. Within a year after joining the Vasquez band, Stoller began writing rhythm-and-blues songs for black vocal groups along with his writing partner Jerry Leiber. "We found ourselves writing for black artists," recalls Leiber, "because those were the voices and rhythms that we loved. By the Fall of 1950, when both Mike and I were in City College, we had black girlfriends and were into a black lifestyle."[20] Leiber and Stoller went on to write the original "Hound Dog" for Big Mama Thornton, and they fashioned dozens of best-selling songs for black artists that celebrated the speech, folklore, and subcultures of Afro-American city life.

Perhaps the artist who best exemplified the new cultural fusions engendered by Chicano rock-and-roll music was Johnny Otis. The son of a Greek immigrant grocer and shipyard worker from Northern California, Otis first came to Los Angeles in 1943 as the white drummer in a black band playing at the Club Alabam on Central Avenue in Watts. Otis had developed his interest in black music while growing up in a mixed but mostly black neighborhood in Berkeley. He accompanied his playmates to "sanctified" churches to listen to the gospel preachers, singers, and choirs, and they made a lasting impression on him. "This society says no white kid can stay in black culture," Otis observes, "but see, that culture had captured me. I loved it and it was richer and more fulfilling and more natural. I thought it was mine."[21] When a high-school teacher suggested that he spend less time with blacks and associate more with whites, Otis capped a long battle with his teachers and principals by dropping out of school in disgust. He became a drummer with Count Otis Matthews's West Oakland House Rockers and then went on the road to tour with a variety of Afro-American bands including Lloyd Hunter's Territory Jazz Band.

In Los Angeles, Otis worked with black musicians, married his high-school sweetheart, a black woman, and thought of himself as "black by persuasion." But part of the consciousness of the black community he joined there involved staking a claim for full participation in American life and culture, and that claim led to interactions with other groups and other cultures. "I got here in '43 and at that time the Avenue [Central] was just swinging. It was like a transplanted Harlem Renaissance," Otis remembers.[22] One night at the Lincoln Theater he saw the blues singer and piano player Charles Brown win a talent contest by playing "Clair de Lune." Otis recalls,

He kind of apologized for what he played, but they loved him, they made him do an encore—"Rhapsody in Blue"—he just broke it up. And it was a good lesson for me, because in later years people would tell me that 'You can't take Big Mama Thornton to New York because she's too rough and bluesy, and you can't take Sally Blair to the Apollo because she's not bluesy enough,' well, bullshit on both counts. The people just liked it. If it's really strong and it has artistry, they like it.[23]

Otis began promoting rhythm-and-blues shows for mixed audiences, offering Chicano and white youths a chance to hear the music of the black community. He promoted and starred in weekly rhythm-and-blues shows at Angeles Hall on the East Side that demonstrated the powerful appeal of black music for Mexican-American audiences and which helped stimulate the growth of rock-and-roll music within the *barrio*.[24] Otis had rock-and-roll television programs on three Los

Angeles television stations in the early 1950s and promoted dances all over the city, despite harassment from local authorities upset about a music that crossed racial and class lines. "The cops would come and hassle the kids standing in line to get into the television show," Otis recalls. "They see black kids and Hispanic kids and Asian kids and they don't like it. They just didn't want to see that. If it were all Asian and Hispanic and black they wouldn't care, but there were whites there and they're mixing with the blacks and what not."[25] Despite the official harassment, the teen-agers kept coming out to Otis's shows, and despite rumors of gang violence and racial incidents about to happen Otis remembers "We never had any trouble, the people got along great."[26]

Exemplifying the fusion of small entrepreneur and musician that often brought rock and roll to the public, Otis started a small record label and recording studio in the mid-fifties featuring many of Los Angeles's leading rhythm-and-blues singers including L'il Julian Herrera, the city's first commercially successful Chicano rock and roller. Otis produced Herrera's 1956 local hit "Lonely, Lonely Nights," a classic do-wop ballad, and featured him in his stage shows as part of a special effort to attract Chicano audiences. As Otis tells it,

> L'il Julian came to me as a kid, a young Mexican-American guy and sang. He wasn't great, but he could sing and he was charming and it was nice and real. I put him on stage and the little Mexican girls loved him and our Chicano audience was a big part of our audience in those days. I put him in the band and then he lived in my house.[27]

Herrera's relationship with Johnny Otis illustrates the ways in which rock-and-roll music became a common ground for people from diverse backgrounds in Los Angeles in the early 1950s. After all, "Lonely, Lonely Nights" presented a Chicano's rendition of a black vocal style on a record produced by a white man who thought of himself as black. But Otis found out that the story of L'il Julian Herrera was even more complicated than he knew. One day a juvenile officer walked into Otis's record company in search of Ron Gregory, a run-away youth from the east. When the officer showed Otis a picture, he realized that Ron Gregory was L'il Julian Herrera. "He ran away from home, hitchhiked out here, and this Mexican lady in Boyle Heights takes him in and raises him as her son," Otis relates.[28] It turned out that Los Angeles's first Chicano rock-and-roll star was born a Hungarian Jew and became "a Chicano by persuasion," just as Johnny Otis had become "black by persuasion."[29]

The pinnacle of this brown-white-black mixing in rock-and-roll music in Los Angeles came with the enormous popularity of Ritchie Valens, East Los Angeles's best-selling and most significant rock-and-roll artist. Independent record producer Bob Keane discovered Valens when he noticed that the car-club cholos of East Los Angeles and of the San Fernando Valley responded to a band called the Silhouettes and their lead singer, Richard Valenzuela. Shortening (and Anglicizing) the youth's last name to Valens, Keane signed him to a contract and recorded the singer with the same back-up musicians that Keane used on sessions by the black gospel and rock singer Sam Cooke. These session musicians brought a wealth of musical experience to Valens's recordings—bass player Red Callendar had played with jazz great Art Tatum, and drummer Earl Palmer had recorded with rhythm-and-blues artists in New Orleans, including Roy Brown, Fats Domino, and Little Richard.[30] But Ritchie Valens did not have to learn his cultural pluralism in a studio; life in postwar Los Angeles prepared him well for the mixing of forms and styles that would come to characterize his recorded music.

More than any other artist, Valens brought the folk traditions of Mexican music to a mass audience via rock and roll, but his music also reflected an extraordinary blending of traditions and styles from other cultures. Valens's father, Steve, and his mother, Concepcion, met while both were employed at a munitions factory in Saugus, California, north of the city of San Fernando. He was born in 1941 in the San Fernando Valley suburb of Pacoima, where he learned music by listening to his relatives sing Mexican songs as they gathered at each others' homes in the evenings. At the age of five Valens made a toy guitar out of a cigar box and learned to fret it with the help of an uncle who taught him how to play his first song—the traditional Mexican *huapango* "La Bamba." In Pacoima, Valens met William Jones, a black musician who lived across the street from the youth's Aunt Ernestine. Jones taught Valens how to tune a guitar and play chords. After building a green and white electric guitar for himself in his junior-high-school wood-shop class, Valens began to experiment with the Afro-American rhythm and blues songs he heard on the radio. But he liked country music as well, idolizing Roy Rogers and

Gene Autry, and delighting his classmates in school with a parody of the theme song to the Walt Disney television program "Davy Crockett."[31] The very plurality of the industrial city excited Valens, he drew his friends from diverse communities. As classmate Manny Sandoval recalls, "They used to put Ritchie down, especially the Mexican kids. They used to call him *falso* and call me that, too, because we liked to be with everybody—Blacks, Mexicans, whites, whatever. So they [Chicanos] wouldn't come around that much to group into the music thing with us. It would be the Blacks, some of the whites, and a few Chicanos."[32] In 1957 he joined the Silhouettes, a mostly Chicano but multi-racial band put together by vibraphonist Gil Rocha that included Valens on guitar, William Jones's Afro-American sons Conrad and Bill on drums and woodwinds, Italian-Americans Dave Torreta and Sal Barragan on trumpet and alto saxophone, and Japanese-American Walter Takaki on tenor saxophone. Although primarily a rock-and-roll band, the Silhouettes' Chicano members were well schooled in traditional music; when the occasion called for it, they could break into Mexican *corridos* as easily as they played "Shake, Rattle, and Roll."[33] Valens became the featured vocalist with the band, and his tributes to the black rhythm-and-blues singer Little Richard motivated his admirers to start calling him "Little Ritchie."[34]

In the brief period between Valens's emergence on the best-selling record charts and his death in a plane crash early in 1959, he brought an extraordinary range of music before pop audiences. He borrowed from white rockabilly, black blues, and Mexican folk musicians because they all made up parts of his cultural environment in postwar Los Angeles. "La Bamba" and "Come On, Let's Go" featured variations on melodies and harmonies common to Mexican fiesta music, while "Ooh My Head" employed the boogie-woogie form and vocal mannerisms common to Afro-American music. One of Valens's unfinished records included an attempt to lay the rhythm popularized by blues guitarist Bo Diddley underneath the melody of "Malagueña," a song originally written by Cuban bandleader Ernesto Lecuona, but blended by Valens with the Mexican march "Espani Cani." Radio programs and phonograph records made Eddie Cochran's rockabilly and Bo Diddley's rhythm-and-blues songs an organic part of Valens's life, while the limited but nonetheless real cultural mixing in working-class neighborhoods enabled young people to explore the culture of their neighbors. Valens wrote his big hit song "Donna" about a failed romance with an Anglo classmate whose father ordered her to stop going out with "that Mexican," and he recorded a version of his favorite rhythm-and-blues song "Framed," which had originally been recorded by a Los Angeles rhythm-and-blues group, The Robins, but which had been written by Mike Stoller and Jerry Leiber.[35]

Valens's tragic death at age seventeen deprived the Los Angeles Chicano community of its biggest star, and it cut short the career of one of rock and roll's most eclectic synthesizers. But other artists carried on his propensity for blending the folk music of the *barrio* with the styles and forms circulated within popular music. In the late 1950s and early 1960s, groups including the Salas Brothers, Carlos Brothers, Rene and Ray, and the Romancers had regional and national hit songs that reflected the *barrio*'s dialogue with mainstream rock-and-roll music. Just as Ritchie Valens established himself as a commercial performer by playing rhythm-and-blues-styled versions of Anglo and Mexican songs for a mixed audience, later Chicano musicians played a mix of different kinds of music for a combination of audiences. In concerts at East Los Angeles College and at El Monte Legion Stadium, at dances held in youth centers and union halls, and in popular nightclubs like the Rhythm Room and Rainbow Gardens, Chicano rock and rollers learned to blend Mexican and rock music into a synthesis that won them admirers both inside and outside the *barrio*.[36]

In 1965 Frankie "Cannibal" Garcia and his group, the "Headhunters," brought Los Angeles Chicano rock music to new audiences when their "Land of a Thousand Dances" entered the national bestseller charts. Garcia got his start as a rock singer when the lead vocalist for the Royal Jesters (another East Los Angeles rock group) got sick, and the band recruited Garcia to take his place "because I sang in school with a mariachi band, doing traditional Mexican music."[37] Garcia later joined with some friends from the Ramona Gardens Housing Project to form Cannibal and the Headhunters, taking their name from Garcia's "street" (gang) name of "Cannibal" gained when he bit an opponent in a fight. One of their most effective songs in live performances had been Chris Kenner's "Land of a Thousand Dances," but at one show Garcia forgot the words at the beginning of the song and ad-libbed "na-na-na-nana" to the delight of the crowd. In the studio they retained Cannibal's accidental improvisation to give the record a captivating introduction. They also borrowed the double drum sound prominent in Stevie Wonder records to forge a synthesis that attracted the attention of audiences all over the country.

Yet however much they might influence popular culture, Chicano rock musicians could not be completely assimilated. Frankie "Cannibal" Garcia feels that his group's Chicano identity prevented them from attaining greater success after they reached the Billboard Top Forty with "Land of a Thousand Dances" in 1965. Garcia remembers, "They didn't know how to market us, for one. There were basically only black or white groups in the early 1960s, not even many mixed groups. The people didn't even know what we were half of the time; a lot of people thought we were Hawaiian or something. And with the name Cannibal and the Headhunters, most people just assumed we'd be black."[38]

Whether the audience knew what they were or not, Cannibal and the Headhunters found that *they* could not forget who they were. Remembering a tour through the southern states with the Rolling Stones, Garcia relates, "It was a shock to us to go somewhere and see restrooms that would say 'white only' or 'black only.' I'd say 'Where do *we* go? We would get kicked out of restaurants, no Latins allowed. There was a big billboard in Jacksonville, Florida that said 'No niggers, no spics, no Mexicans allowed.' I wrote home and said 'You know what Mom? There's this big marquee that says they don't like us here.' "[39]

Other Chicano musicians in the 1960s combined a fusion of popular and Mexican music with lyrics that evoked the complex pluralities of the city streets. Thee Midnighters scored a national hit in 1965 with "Whittier Boulevard," a song honoring the main traffic artery of the East Los Angeles *barrio*. Drawing inspiration from the energy and imagination of the car customizers and cruisers who claimed the boulevard as their own territory on weekend nights, Thee Midnighters presented the activities of the car-club cholos to the outside world, while at the same time elevating the self-image of the cruisers by inserting their subculture into the discourse of mainstream popular culture. As Thee Midnighters' lead singer Little Willie G (for Garcia) once explained, "A lot of people say you guys made Whittier Boulevard famous, but we just took the action off the boulevard and made it into a song."[40]

The car culture's quest for fun and good times expressed a desire for the good life of material success, but it also provided a means for satirizing and subverting ruling icons of consumer society. Just as Chicano car customizers "improved" upon the mass-produced vehicles from Detroit, Chicano rock songs like "Whittier Boulevard" celebrated Mexican-American appropriations of automobiles as part of a community ritual. By the late 1960s, that dialogue between the images of mass culture and the realities of *barrio* life increasingly took on an expressly political cast. At that time, changes in urban economics and politics threatened to destroy the social basis for the cultural pluralism of Los Angeles rock and roll by undermining the social and economic infrastructure of the central city. The cumulative effects of postwar highway and housing policies had subsidized suburban growth at the expense of the inner city, had exacerbated racial and class polarizations, and had encouraged residential segregation. For Chicanos, increased migration from Mexico, inadequate access to decent housing, and discrimination within a segmented labor market all combined to help create a new consciousness.[41]

The failures of 1960s social programs including the War on Poverty, the effects of the Vietnam War on poor and working-class youths, and the repressive policies of the Los Angeles Police Department all contributed to a growing political activism and cultural nationalism. On August 29, 1970, the Chicano community mobilized for a massive anti-war demonstration that expressed anger over many pent-up grievances and complaints. Taking their opposition to the war and their growing nationalism to the streets, demonstrators relied on their cultural traditions to give form to their protest activity. As one participant chronicled the start of that day's events,

> The boulevard was filled with *gente*, doing Latino chants and playing *música* right in the streets. It started taking on the atmosphere of a carnival. Some even danced.[42]

This demonstration involved an attempt to reclaim city streets as a terrain for culture, politics, and celebration. But its aggressive festivity provoked a violent reaction from the authorities. Los Angeles police officers used force against the demonstrators; one officer shot and killed *Los Angeles Times* columnist Ruben Salazar. The Salazar killing outraged many people within the Mexican-American community and helped mobilize subsequent activism and demonstrations.[43]

The political ferment surrounding the 1970 demonstration found its way into Mexican-American rock-and-roll music in significant ways. Thee Midnighters (who had recorded "Whittier Boulevard") recorded a song titled "Chicano Power" in 1970, and the V.I.P.'s changed their name that same year to El Chicano. In the early 1970s, East Los Angeles musicians began to feature Latin musical forms and Spanish-language lyrics more prominently in their songs, and they attached themselves to a variety of community icons and subcultures. A series of outdoor music festivals, known popularly as "Chicano Woodstocks," showcased the community's musicians and provided an arena for displaying and celebrating diverse images of Chicano identity. The band Tierra emerged as a favorite of the "low rider" car customizers in the early 1970s, while Los Lobos got their start with an album recorded under the aegis of Cesar Chavez's United Farm Workers union. Mixing images from the past of pachucos and cholos with contemporary ones like low riders, these bands and their audiences placed current struggles in historical perspective, preserving a measure of continuity in a period of extraordinary change.[44]

Yet the music of East Los Angeles still had a significant influence on artists and audiences outside the *barrio*. In 1975, for example, a mostly Afro-American jazz/funk ensemble from Long Beach calling themselves War recorded "Low Rider," a tribute to Chicano car customizers, cruisers, and musicians.[45] One of the year's best-selling records, "Low Rider," expressed War's own experiences playing dances and concerts for Mexican-American audiences throughout southern California, but the song also reflected demographic trends in Los Angeles that encouraged black-Chicano cultural interaction. In 1970 more than 50,000 Hispanics lived in the traditionally black south-central area of Los Angeles; by 1980 that figure had doubled, with Chicanos making up 21% of the total population of the south-central area.[46] The clear Latin influence on the subject and style of "Low Rider" testifies to the importance of Chicano music to American popular music, even when Chicano artists themselves might not enjoy access to a mass audience.

Popular Music and Postmodernism

The rock-and-roll music created by Mexican-American musicians in

Los Angeles since World War II bears particular relevance to the issues of ethnicity, identity, and culture raised in Octavio Paz's lament. From the Don Tosti Band of the 1940s through Los Lobos in the 1980s, Los Angeles's Chicano musicians have made commercially successful records by blending the folk music of Mexico with the cultural fusions of the modern day *barrio*. [47] Their proclivities for mixing eclectic styles, for making references to their community and its history, and for acknowledging the diverse influences on their art display a conscious or intuitive postmodernism—delighting in difference, undermining univocal master narratives, and celebrating the decentered and polyglot nature of popular culture. In its most successful commercial forms, Chicano rock-and-roll music from Los Angeles transformed a specific ethnic culture rooted in common experiences into more than just a novelty to be appropriated by uncomprehending outsiders. Confronted with media monopolies and public sentiments blind to the unique circumstances of Mexican-Americans, Chicano musicians drew upon both residual and emergent elements in their community to win some measure of participation in the creation and dissemination of mass popular culture. Musical forms and social attitudes emanating from the isolation and marginality of *barrio* life took on new meaning when appropriated as "youth" music by consumers with little knowledge or concern about the ethnicity of the musicians.

In his superb work on ethnic autobiographies, anthropologist Michael M. J. Fischer identifies the core components of the postmodern sensibility as bifocality or reciprocity of perspectives, juxtaposition of multiple realities, intertextuality, inter-referentiality, and comparisons through families of resemblance. [48] Fischer's categories encompass the central practices of Los Angeles Mexican-American rock-and-roll musicians since World War II. Caught between the realities of life in their community and the hegemony of Anglo-capitalist culture, Chicano artists fashioned a bifocal music accessible from both inside and outside their community. They juxtaposed multiple realities, blending Mexican folk music with Afro-American rhythm and blues, playing English-language songs in a Mexican style for audiences filled with Spanish speakers, and answering requests for both Mexican and rock music with the same song—"La Bamba." They practiced particularly intricate forms of intertextuality by connecting their music to community subcultures and institutions ori-

ented around speech, dress, car customizing, art, theater, and politics. References to shared historical and cultural experiences
permeated Mexican-American rock-and-roll songs, but these references extended beyond the immediate Chicano community as songs
featured rockabilly and soul influences borrowed from white and
black working-class music. That inter-referentiality complemented
an equally adept facility for making comparisons through families of
resemblance. Chicano musicians and artists could incorporate white
rockabilly or black rhythm-and-blues music into their songs because
they recognized similarities in form and content that transcended
surface differences. Yet even while drawing upon families of resemblance, Mexican-American musicians in Los Angeles never lost sight
of the singular historical realities shaping them and their community.

The emergence of Los Lobos as a significant commercial rock-and-
roll band in the 1980s provides an illustration of the persistent bifocality, juxtaposition of multiple realities, intertextuality, inter-referentiality, and comparisons through families of resemblance in Los
Angeles Chicano music. Mixing Mexican *Norteno* accordions and
guitarrons with Afro-American and Anglo rockabilly drums and electric guitars, Los Lobos stand between Chicano culture and mass culture, playing to audiences in both camps. The five members of the
group first learned to play their instruments in response to the popularity of the Beatles, but they secured their first employment as musicians playing Mexican folk music for neighborhood gatherings. In
response to critics who charge that the band's forays into rock and
roll betray their roots in folk music, drummer Louis Perez replies,
"We always aspired to play to everybody, but there was no place to
expose it. We haven't gone back on the basic philosophy of this band,
which was to play cultural music. It's a music that's as much Mexican
culture as it is American, and that's what we are."[49]

Rock-and-roll audiences first discovered Los Lobos when they
served as the opening act for a U.S. tour by the punk/new wave band
the Clash. A white band from England playing new-wave music with
strong reggae and rhythm-and-blues influences, the Clash recognized the families of resemblance that tied their music to that of Los
Lobos, and sought to give the Chicano band greater commercial exposure. Subsequently, the Blasters, a Los Angeles Anglo band
steeped in rhythm and blues and rockabilly, arranged to have Los
Lobos open live shows for them. Conrad Lozano of Los Lobos ac-

knowledged his group's debt to the Blasters in a 1984 interview when he told a reporter, "Musically it gave us someone to look at and reinforced our commitment to our style. We met them and had a lot in common. We became friends and they liked our music so much that they had us open some gigs for them. That really allowed many more people to see and hear us."[50]

Anglo saxophonist Steve Berlin left the Blasters to join Los Lobos, a transition that seemed logical to him because of his own commitment to juxtaposing multiple musical realities. Born in Philadelphia and nurtured on that city's rhythm-and-blues music, Berlin introduced Los Lobos to some old rhythm-and-blues songs, while they taught him to play their traditional polkas and *corridos*. Describing his connections with Los Lobos and other artists on Los Angeles's Slash Records label, Berlin observes, "A lot of us have similar record collections, and a shared appreciation for people like Hank Williams and George Jones. The Del Fuegos' heroes are the Blasters' heroes and they're our heroes too. If you went to everybody's house, there would be the same bunch of records they consider important."[51]

When similar record collections enable Steve Berlin, a white musician influenced by black rhythm and blues, to join a Chicano rock band on the basis of a mutual affinity for country and western singers Hank Williams and George Jones, we have gone a long way toward a world in which "all that is solid melts into air." Cultures appear interchangeable and works of art seem divorced from real historical experience. But the fusions that characterize Chicano rock-and-roll music reflect more than the confusions and ambiguities of postmodern society. Their definitive contours come from the conscious choices made by organic intellectuals attempting to address the anguish of invisibility by bringing their own cultural traditions into the mainstream of mass culture. Mexican-American musicians could stay with traditional Chicano musical forms like *ranchera* or *cumbia* musics and find recognition and reward within their own community. Or they could master Anglo styles and assimilate into the mainstream without anyone being aware of their Chicano identity. But Los Angeles Chicano rock-and-roll artists have generally selected another path. They have tried to straddle the line between the two cultures, creating a fusion music that resonates with the chaos and costs of cultural collision. Their choices arbitrate particularly complex tensions emanating from ethnicity and oppression for Chicanos, while holding open to other groups a vision of cultural fusion based on families of resemblance and similarities of emotion and experience.

As members of an aggrieved community, and as artists involved in the generation and circulation of ideas reflecting the needs of that community, Mexican-American rock musicians from Los Angeles have functioned as what Antonio Gramsci referred to as "organic intellectuals."[52] Gramsci felt that dominant social groups wield power as much through ideological hegemony as through physical force, and he charged that traditional intellectuals reinforce social hierarchies by serving as "experts in legitimation."[53] But Gramsci pointed out that subordinated groups have their own intellectuals who attempt to pose a "counter-hegemony" by presenting images subversive of existing power relations. The elite try to "manage consent" by making domination appear natural, voluntary, and inevitable. Organic intellectuals, on the other hand, attempt to build a "historical bloc"—a coalition of oppositional groups united around counter-hegemonic ideas. The efforts by Chicano rock musicians in Los Angeles to enter the mainstream by linking up with other oppositional cultures reflect their struggle to assemble a "historical bloc" capable of challenging the ideological hegemony of Anglo cultural domination. In the struggle, they found that their primary weapons included bifocality, juxtaposition of multiple realities, intertextuality, inter-referentiality, and comparison through families of resemblance.

Juxtaposition of multiple realities in Chicano life allowed for juxtaposition of multiple realities in Mexican-American music. In a culture that drew sharp lines among black, white, and brown music and audiences, Chicano rock-and-roll artists worked to break down barriers. To a commercial marketing structure that imposed rigid categories on rock, popular, folk, and ethnic music, they offered songs that fit no simple description. The dominant culture and its popular culture industry often treated ethnicity as a discrete and finite entity, but Chicano musicians treated it as plastic and open-ended. For them, ethnicity seemed as much a dynamic construct as an inherited fact, as much a strategic response to the present as an immutable series of practices and beliefs derived from the past. Consequently, they brought a sense of play and whimsy to the arts of *bricolage*. Just as Ritchie Valens experimented with a Bo Diddley-style rhythm-and-blues bass line beneath the Latin guitar standard "La Malaguena," Los

Lobos brought the accordion and *guitarron* into use as rock-and-roll instruments.

The same forces that encourage Los Angeles's Chicano rock-and-roll musicians to roll back the boundaries of ethnic identity also compel them to incorporate ideas from nonmusical sources into their work. As organic intellectuals chronicling the cultural life of their community, they draw upon street slang, car customizing, clothing styles, and wall murals for inspiration and ideas, as well as upon more traditional cultural creations such as literature, plays, and poems. Their work is intertextual, constantly in dialogue with other forms of cultural expression, and most fully appreciated when located in context.

The commercially successful Chicano band Tierra got its start in the early 1970s as a favorite band of the low-rider subculture in Los Angeles. As anthropologist Brenda Bright demonstrates in her fine work on Mexican-American car customizers, low riders are themselves masters of postmodern cultural manipulation. They juxtapose seemingly inappropriate realities—fast cars designed to go slowly, "improvements" that flaunt their impracticality, like chandeliers instead of inside overhead lights. They encourage a bifocal perspective—they are made to be watched but only after adjustments have been made to provide ironic and playful commentary on prevailing standards of automobile design. They are intertextual—cars are named after songs or incidents in Mexican history, zoot-suited *pachucos* appear in car paintings. Low-rider "happenings" incorporate elements of popular fashion, dance, and music in a community ritual celebrating the utility and beauty of automobiles that the dominant culture would deem impractical, tasteless, and garish. Tierra incorporated low-rider intertextuality in its music, using fragments of *barrio* memories in song lyrics that celebrate zoot suits and rhythms that approximate the jitterbug dancing of the 1940s and 1950s. In a similar fashion Thee Midnighters wrote and recorded "Whittier Boulevard" in 1965 to celebrate the culture of car customizers and cruisers along East Los Angeles's main thoroughfare in the 1960s. In 1982 Ruben Guevara's "c/s" explored Chicano history through the "writing on the walls"—the distinctive graffiti of the *barrio*.[54]

Chicano musicians had to assume a bifocal perspective as a matter of self-respect. The dominant culture imposed an identity on them. Regardless of their characteristics as individuals, Anglo stereotypes about Mexicans and their culture influenced the ways in which Chicanos were perceived outside the *barrio*, and they had to be aware of the limits imposed on them by that cultural domination. But to accept the stereotypes would mean denying one's own vision. Prevented from defining themselves because of pervasive discrimination and prejudice, but unwilling to leave the work of definition to others, they adopted a bifocal perspective that acknowledged but did not accept the majority culture's images of Chicanos.

A conscious inter-referentiality accompanies the pervasive intertextuality of Los Angeles's Chicano rock-and-roll music. Even though they seek success in commercial popular culture, these musicians employ repeated references to individual and collective histories in the manner of folk artists. Mexican-American rock-and-roll artists acknowledge their roots; Ritchie Valens hit the best-seller charts with "La Bamba," a song that he learned from his family when he was five. Los Lobos won a Grammy Award for folk music with a faithful rendition of "Anselma," a hundred-year-old Mexican song. But they also connect the musical past to social and political history. "I grew up listening to the folk groups and balladeers," Ruben Guevara explains in tracing the origins of his music, but he plays little traditional music himself. Instead, Guevara adapts the music of today to collective popular memory. He founded Zyanya Records in 1982 ("zyanya" is a Mexican-Indian word meaning "always") to provide an outlet for Chicano musicians and a forum for addressing the community's youth. "The younger Chicanos who did not experience the Chicano movement of the 60s and 70s lost a cultural awareness, and through this music I would like to make them aware of social issues," Guevara insists. Groups on the Zyanya label including Con Safos, Los Perros, and Califas use overtly political lyrics and a self-conscious ethnic nationalism to address the problems of contemporary *barrio* life. But even those groups that shun direct political or historical references in their lyrics still evoke the past through references to *pachucos, cholos*, zoot suits, and community heroes like Ritchie Valens.[55] Willie Herron, a Chicano punk/rock musician, mural painter, and poet, sees the fate of *barrio* musicians directly wrapped up in the fate of the community itself. Explaining why Chicano rock-and-roll music has failed to achieve greater commercial acceptance, Herron points out, "We had setbacks all along—the death of Ritchie Valens in '59 being one of the biggest. In the 70s the reasons became more political—the Chicano moratorium [an anti-war demonstration that ended in a police riot], the death of Ruben Salazar [a newspaper columnist killed by police officers during the Chicano moratorium], many of the people in the Hispanic community just dropped out."[56]

Decisions by Chicano rock-and-roll musicians to blend cultural and political history echo the stance taken by artists in other media in their community. John Valdez, an artist who grew up in the Estrada Courts Housing Project in East Los Angeles, gained critical recognition in the 1980s for paintings that featured *pachucos* and other *barrio* symbols. "I like to show the Pachuco image," Valdez relates, "even if some Chicanos who are trying to assimilate think they left this in the past. It's still something that is very much with us." For Valdez, *pachuco* imagery retains meaning because it displays "the beauty of a people we have been told are not beautiful."[57] Similar tensions inform the writing of Mary Helen Ponce from East Los Angeles. In one of her short stories she recalls a childhood in which, "We really lived in two worlds. The secure *barrio* that comforted and accepted us, and the 'other,' the institutions such as the school that were out to acculturate us, sanitize us, Americanize us, and de-lice us at least once a year."[58] Ponce describes her feelings of solidarity with a classmate found to have lice in her hair, because Ponce resented the smug sense of superiority that enabled Anglo school officials to make Chicano children feel ashamed of their homes. The same bifocality that makes Ponce want to describe the world as divided in two, and that makes her side with the despised ethnic world, induces Willie Herron to claim that he formed his punk rock group Los Illegals "to talk about the experience of being a *cholo*, a low rider, of being in gangs, all of it."[59] The same stubborn inter-referentiality that leads John Valdez to celebrate the *pachuco*, compels Ruben Guevara to explain his song "c/s" with a motto—"The present day Pachuco refuses to die."[60] Inter-referentiality, intertextuality, juxtaposition of multiple realities, and bifocality characterize the music of Los Angeles's Chicano rock-and-roll musicians, and they explain much of its aesthetic. As part of mass popular culture that aesthetic appealed to people from other communities, building alliances on the basis of comparisons through families of resemblance. In Los Angeles, Anglo rock-and-roll musicians Frank Zappa and Captain Beefheart (Don Van Vleit) included references to *pachucos* in their 1970s albums, and Zappa invented a mythical Chicano band, Ruben and the Jets, to embody the pure spirit of rock and roll. He persuaded Ruben Guevara to form an actual group called Ruben and the Jets during a backstage conversation after Zappa had attended Guevara's cultural nationalist play, "Who Are the People?" Guevara's recollection of that meeting testifies to the power of families of resemblance; he recalled that he and Zappa "rapped from Bo Diddley to Beethoven. We found that we had the same musical roots."[61] Of course, neither Zappa nor Guevara made music that actually sounded very much like Beethoven's or Bo Diddley's, but the commodity culture of the postmodern world made them feel they were on common ground because they shared appreciation of those two musicians.

Families of resemblance also brought together suburban Los Angeles punk and new-wave audiences and artists with rock bands from East Los Angeles in the late 1970s and early 1980s. Chicano bands including the Brat, Odd Squad, and the Plugz blended the urgency and emotionalism of 1950s rock and roll (the Plugz even recorded a version of Ritchie Valens's "La Bamba") with lyrics speaking to the alienation and frustration of contemporary youth. Relatively affluent suburban teen-agers could identify with the music of a band like Los Illegals, not because they really knew what it was like to be a *cholo*, but because the real historical experiences of the Chicano community gave its artists a well-developed vocabulary for talking about alienation and oppression. Neither the punk-rock musicians nor their audiences were actually *cholos*, but the subjective act of identification with *cholismo* created a family of resemblance—a mutual desire to draw upon real historical experiences to proclaim distance from the dominant culture and its values.

The commercial popularity of Los Lobos in the 1980s provides another example of the capacity for Los Angeles's Chicano rock-and-roll musicians to form a historical bloc with other groups based on families of resemblance. Los Lobos proudly affirm their cultural heritage, but they reject separatism. They insist on acceptance as "legitimate contributors to contemporary music" without having to hide their ethnic identity. Aware of the ways in which they might be perceived as a novelty by a mass audience, they attempt to use their marginality to find families of resemblance connecting themselves to other groups. Drummer Louis Perez explains the group's philosophy by talking about the title song from their 1984 album, "How Will the Wolf Survive?" Perez recalls that he read a *National Geographic* article about wolves as an endangered species and that he compared their plight to those of people he knew. As he describes writing the song

> It started out being about the wolf and the next verse turned into a message of hope for the middle class. And the last verse is about how bands all over the country are trying to preserve something close to the heart of America. So yeah, it's about whether or not Los Lobos will survive. Not only us . . . [62]

Perez's lyrics talk about a wolf "running scared now forced to hide, in a land where he once stood with pride"—a clear reference to the Chicano people and to Los Lobos ("the wolves" in Spanish) themselves. The narrator predicts that the hunted creature will somehow find its way and concludes with a tribute to the "young hearts and minds" in bands whose "songs of passion" keep alive the wolf's hope for survival. For Perez, the world of rock-and-roll music does not obliterate local cultures by rendering them invisible; rather, it is an arena where diverse groups find common ground while still acknowledging important differences. The prefigurative counter-hegemony fashioned by Los Lobos has succeeded in winning the allegiance of musicians from other marginalized cultures. Their songs have been recorded by polka artist Frankie Yankovic as well as by country and western star Waylon Jennings. The southern "swamp rocker" Tony Joe White introduced Jennings to "Will the Wolf Survive." At first, Jennings could not make out all the lyrics in the song, but he loved the record's sound, so he decided to record it himself. He recalls,

> The funny thing is, we couldn't understand all the words on the record, and that often means the lyrics are bad and they are trying to cover them up. Still, I loved the feel of the record and we decided to record it—even without knowing what it said completely. When we got the words from the publisher, I was knocked out. The words were great. I think everyone can relate to that song.[63]

The Cajun accordion player and singer Jo-El Sonnier views Los Lobos as artists whose cultural struggles parallel his own. As he explains

> I've sold myself as French, as R&B, as country, and as rock. But I want to do it all if I can; I think we could open doors for this music. Look at what Los Lobos has done for ethnic music, and they got

signed without really changing. It can't just be that all people want is Madonna and punk music! All I've ever wanted to do is bring my music and my culture to the people. I have a message about the preservation of it. I feel like if I let my culture die, I die with it.[64]

Sonnier's strategy of using the plasticity of popular music as a means of preserving his ethnic culture echoes the efforts by Chicano musicians like Los Lobos to build a historical bloc; his acknowledgment of their importance as a model reveals a self-conscious understanding of the families of resemblance that they nurture and cultivate. With their bifocality, juxtaposition of multiple realities, intertextuality, inter-referentiality, and families of resemblance, Chicano rock-and-roll musicians from Los Angeles explore all the main axes of postmodern art. Jean-François Lyotard has celebrated this postmodern condition as a logical and healthy response to the totalitarian imperatives of technology and capital. Lyotard and other postmodernists see the proliferation of marginal subcultures and the confusing display of remnants from past eras in contemporary culture as a break with oppressive master narratives. To postmodernists, improvised cultural forms and free-floating signs and symbols appropriated out of context can open up a world of play and desire previously constrained by the tyranny of master narratives.[65]

Scholars uneasy about the open-ended implications of some postmodernist theory nonetheless concede its central point—that contemporary society entails a fragmentation and decentering that radically alters the nature and function of cultural creation and reception. Fredric Jameson attempts to steer Lyotard's discussion toward a re-emphasis on the importance of history and historical consciousness, arguing that a world view with no sense of the past or expectation for the future only degenerates into schizophrenia, trapping individuals within the bounds of their own immediate sense perceptions. Jameson maintains that the emancipatory possibilities in contemporary cultural forms come from a "political unconscious"—from "buried" master narratives that carry on the historical traditions of opposition sedimented within the collective experience and memory of aggrieved populations. In a similar vein, Jürgen Habermas argues that the plasticity of contemporary culture reveals a "legitimation crisis" brought on by the failure of capitalist society to fulfill the promises of Enlightenment and revolutionary traditions. Thus the decentered and fragmented culture of the contemporary world is not an end in itself for Habermas, but, rather, an indication of popular desire for an eventual consensus, for a practice that closes the ruptures and disruptions of capitalism.[66] Marshall Berman shares the sentiment voiced by Jameson and Habermas that modernity is "an incomplete project" rather than a totalitarian master narrative, and like them he champions the "unity of disunity" by which modern culture represents a collective struggle to feel at home in the world.[67]

What Jameson, Habermas, and Berman champion on the plane of criticism, Mexican-American rock-and-roll musicians have created in art. The marginality of Chicano rock-and-roll musicians has provided them with a constant source of inspiration and a constant spur toward innovation that gained them the attention of mainstream audiences. But this marginal sensibility amounts to more than novelty or personal eccentricity; it holds legitimacy and power as the product of a real historical community's struggle with oppression. The "buried" narratives in this music—narratives about group identity, oppositional subcultures, and a desire for unity—amount to more than a "political unconscious." As Chicano musicians demonstrate in their comments about their work, their music reflects a quite conscious cultural politics that seeks inclusion in the American mainstream by transforming it.

Almost forty years after Octavio Paz's visit to Los Angeles, Mexican-Americans in that city still suffer from the anguish of invisibility. Their numbers have increased, but discrimination and exploitation leave them under-represented and under-rewarded. The expanded reach and scope of the mass media over the past four decades has exacerbated the cultural crisis facing Mexican-Americans; rarely do they see their world presented sympathetically or even accurately in the communications media that reinforce and legitimate Anglo cultural hegemony. But the "vague atmosphere" of Mexicanism perceived by Paz persists in the present. In community subcultures and styles, in the prefigurative counter-hegemony of organic intellectuals, it continues to inform the struggles of the present with the perceptions and values of the past. Conscious of the fragmentation of the modern world, this constantly changing "Mexicanism" cultivates its own marginality even as it reaches out to other groups. It is not a buried master narrative, but, rather, a conscious cultural politics that survives by "floating and hovering," never quite existing and never quite vanishing. Invisibility has its psychic and political costs, but for

Chicano musicians in Los Angeles, it provides the ultimate camouflage for the difficult but necessary work of building a historical bloc.

Popular Film

7

No Way Out:
Dialogue and Negotiation
in Reel America

Commercial motion pictures generally do not claim to present historical truth. Even when films are set in the past, artists and audiences understand that the function of the movies is to entertain. Few would consider subjecting movies to the kinds of tests about evidence and logic that we routinely apply to printed historical narratives. Yet Hollywood pictures need to engage the attention and the emotion of individuals who live within historical time and who construct their identities, at least in part, in dialogue with the past. If film-makers have our permission to tell fanciful lies, we nonetheless insist that they make those lies moderately credible. We require "true" lies, depictions of the past and present that are comprehensible to us and that locate our own private stories within a larger collective narrative.

It may seem strange to assert an important connection between lived experience and film viewing. We have come to think of the movies as an "escape" from the world. Inside theaters, motion pictures occupy their own space and time, and even on home video they command a level of attention that distinguishes our reception of them from our viewing of television or our listening to popular music. Camera angles and film editing fragment vision and time as much in film as in as any other art, and the effective spectacles of cinema — its giant screen, lush colors, powerful soundtracks, and special effects — overwhelm us as no other medium does. In addition, film seems more resistant to popular influence than almost any other popular culture form, because the high capital costs required to enter the film industry discourage new entrants and vest control of film contents in an infinitesimal segment of society.

Yet motion pictures could not function as an "escape" if they were merely distraction. An escape must take us from one place to another, specifically from confinement or peril to a locus of freedom. If films show us a world too little like our own, they fail to address and neutralize our feelings of confinement and peril. If they show us a world too much like our own, they deprive us of the freedom to recast the past and present in keeping with the preferences of imagination and desire. Hollywood films highlight the tensions between confinement and peril, on the one hand, and freedom and imagination, on the other. They depict battles between necessity and desire, between inherited objective circumstances and subjective human will. In that respect they resemble historical narratives. Whether situated in the past, present, or future, commercial motion pictures invariably resonate with the value crises of the times in which they appear. Thus they are historical in the sense of being cultural artifacts and social-history evidence about the times in which they were made. But films are historical in another way as well: they reposition us for the future by reshaping our memories of the past.

An exceptional body of research by historians and film scholars in recent years has highlighted the historicity of the motion picture experience. Social historians Roy Rosenzweig and Kathy Peiss explain how the very existence of motion-picture theaters served to alter the consciousness of urban industrial workers in the late nineteenth and early twentieth centuries. In his study of Worcester, Massachusetts, Rosenzweig contends that a search for "free spaces"—capable of posing alternatives to the time-work discipline of the factory—led workers to saloons, parks, and picnic grounds before they found refuge in the motion-picture theater. Peiss shows how early commercial cinema helped unmarried working women in New York break the constraints of family, ethnicity, and class that tied them to a restricted "women's world," giving them new access to public space and new control over personal relationships.[1] Similarly, Lary May explains how both the content of motion pictures and the process of watching them taught audiences in the 1920s ways to break with the Victorian past and to embrace the leisure-oriented hedonism of the emerging consumer commodity-oriented society. In addition, recent detailed studies of motion-picture content and its relationship to specific time periods by Dana Polan (1940s), Peter Biskind (1950s), and Michael Ryan and Douglas Kellner (1967-1987) have clearly established the importance of film as evidence about social and cultural history.[2] Social historians Rosenzweig, Peiss, and May locate the process of viewing motion pictures within larger historical contexts, while film critics Polan, Biskind, Ryan, and Kellner concentrate on the texts of films themselves for general trends and tendencies in the periods they have elected to examine. But their fine work leaves one important aspect of the relationship between films and history under-examined—the congruence between the "escape" mechanisms of movies and the necessary practices of historical thinking. Hollywood films may get all the details wrong, they may perpetuate misinformation and ignorance about everything from the frontier to the family, yet they still might encourage ways of asking and answering questions conducive to historical investigation.

However, when we look for broad categories capable of creating coherence out of the many kinds of stories told by Hollywood in the years since World War II, the five main themes that emerge do not seem sensitive to issues of change over time. These themes—the family in jeopardy, agonies of empire, corruption at the top, personal autonomy, and what literary critic Nina Baym (in another context) calls "melodramas of beset manhood"—encompass an extraordinary number of Hollywood productions during this period. The groupings may seem more structural than historical, evidence of recurrent myths reworking the same ground over and over. But what changes over time in these representations is often more important than what stays the same.

Two Hollywood films from 1946 illumine the complex contradictions of the historical context in which they were made. Robert Montgomery's *Ride the Pink Horse* and Edward Dmytryk's *Till The End of Time* addressed the anxieties of postwar America by emphasizing antagonistic aspects of collective memory. *Ride the Pink Horse* spoke to the accumulated anger and bitterness produced by wartime suffering and sacrifice, while *Till The End of Time* played upon the satisfactions of solidarity, upon the mutuality and sense of connection to others attendant to the war effort. The two films reveal widely divergent possibilities within the same historical moment, and the differences between them underscore the uncertain relation between objective social conditions and subjective popular perceptions.

Ride the Pink Horse frames the postwar experience from the perspective of "Gagan," a returning veteran whose lack of a first name reflects the anonymity of his social standing. The film opens with Gagan stepping off an interstate bus that had brought him to Taos, New Mexico during festival time, but he has not come to celebrate. Gagan wants "to finish a job," to exact revenge on a former war profiteer responsible for the murder of Gagan's wartime pal "Shorty." Everything about Gagan emphasizes his marginality. Unable to get a seat on the bus, he had been forced to stand for most of the trip. He made no room reservation and cannot get into any of the hotels booked to capacity for the festival crowd. There is no place for him on the bus or in the hotels of Taos; he is a returning veteran who feels crowded out of the society that he left behind when he went to war.

As Gagan walks the streets, his determination to avenge the past sets him apart from the fiesta crowds who are absorbed in their celebration at the moment. His alienations stem from his memories of the war. He feels that he and Shorty endured unbearable hardships with no real reward, while people like the war profiteer got all the benefits without doing any of the sacrificing. Yet Gagan's anger does not quite take the form of class consciousness: his resentments are personal, not systemic, and his experiences have made him suspicious of all people, not just war profiteers. These anti-social feelings come out in racist contempt for the Chicanos in Taos as easily as in resentment of the rich. When Pila, a young Indian girl, tries to help him "because he looks in danger," he accuses her of soliciting him for prostitution. When an elderly Chicano man lets Gagan sleep under the protective cover of the little carousel he runs, Gagan initially dismisses the man's offers of help with condescending racial epithets.

Gagan discovers that he is not alone in pursuit of his prey. An FBI agent has been following him and warns Gagan that private revenge may endanger the government's case against the murderer. But Gagan wants no alliance with the government, bitterly reminding the agent that the last "errand" he ran for Uncle Sam (the war) got him nothing but made the profiteer wealthy. But the profiteer is too strong for Gagan to handle alone. After a series of beatings that he survives only because the Indian girl and the Mexican-American man help him, Gagan corners his enemy and reluctantly turns him over to the FBI. In a final twist, the carousel operator reminds Gagan that he should express his gratitude to Pila. They encounter her by accident, but as Gagan fumbles with his words, unable to acknowledge his debt to a woman and an Indian, she informs him that no thanks are necessary. Pila then turns to her friends and recounts for them, in Spanish, the entire story, obviously placing herself and her own heroism at the center. We realize that she has her own story to tell and that Gagan's narrative is only part of it.

Till The End of Time also focuses on a returning veteran, middle-class Cliff Harper. The war years have helped Harper mature; he is no longer the callow college youth who went to war. But he feels that the war has robbed him of time and direction, and he finds it hard to reconnect with the world he left behind. His old clothes no longer fit, his parents do not acknowledge that the dreadful things he has seen have changed him, and he feels no desire to get a job or resume his education. Unlike Gagan, Harper feels a nostalgia for the war, horrible as it was. The war gave him purposeful work, it revealed the sheltered nature of his previous experiences, and it bonded him closely to his fellow soldiers from diverse class, ethnic, and regional backgrounds. Harper and his friends miss the camaraderie of military life, their failure to fit into civilian life stems from a critique of its individualism and materialism.

Harper solves his problems with the help of a woman. Pat Ruscomb lost her husband in combat during the war, but she has made a new life for herself as a worker in a defense plant. She dates Cliff, but feels impatient with his lack of direction and purpose. It becomes clear that Cliff will have to display some responsibility and maturity to secure a relationship with Pat as well as to solve his own problems. But in this film, individual action is not enough—institutional and collective solutions must be found. While *Ride the Pink Horse* demonstrates a distrust of all institutions and authority figures as pawns of the elite, *Till The End of Time* presents business, army, and government as the salvation of the common man. From the lengthy "mustering out" Marine Corps ceremony to the careful counseling of the Veterans Administration to the kindly guidance of a factory foreman (certainly the most understanding foreman in the history of American industry) the big institutions in *Till The End of Time* are looking out for the little man. As one would expect from this benign picture of socialization, the film's characters solve their many problems in one heroic effort when they join together to beat up neo-Fascists harassing one of their buddies in a bar. They discover that they can translate wartime collectivity and solidarity to their civilian lives, and they resolve to face the future together.

On the surface, *Ride the Pink Horse* and *Till The End of Time* seem to represent diametrically opposite viewpoints. With its cynicism about wealth and power, its identification of corporate greed as the source of all evil, and its acceptance of broadened perspectives on ethnicity, gender, and class, *Ride the Pink Horse* seems to embody a cultural direction that we can term "democratic culture." Contrastingly, the middle-class perspective and the glorification of authority and collectivity in *Till The End of Time* marks it as emblematic of what we can call "corporate culture." But democratic culture and corporate culture, rather than being polar opposites, sometimes are in complicated dialectical relationships. Both *Ride the Pink Horse* and *Till The End of Time* address residual popular memories of the war, they also re-enact it. Gagan becomes a soldier fighting one more battle, but this time he identifies the "right" enemy—the war profiteer—and the "right" allies—an impoverished elderly Mexican-American, a young Native American Indian girl, and, more hesitantly, an agent of the government. Similarly, the wartime buddies in *Till The End of Time* suffer from their new status as "rugged individuals," until they join together to take violent action against the fascist threat once again. While the two films differ about the interests of authority vs. the interests of individuals, for Hollywood productions they both give extraordinary moral power to women, to workers, and to non-WASP characters. The ultimate meaning of the war may remain contested, but some of its attendant social consequences seem deeply embedded in the discursive world of these films.

The ironic personal histories of the creators of *Ride the Pink Horse* and *Till The End of Time* underscore the films' identities as products of their historical moment. Robert Montgomery, who made the more radical and anti-establishment film of the two, went on to become President Eisenhower's television coach after appearing as a friendly witness before the House Un-American Activities Committee. Edward Dmytryk, whose film expressed supreme faith in the government, became one of the "Hollywood Ten," the film artists called before the HUAC for suspected communist affiliations and sent to jail for refusing to testify as the committee required. Alone among the ten, Dmytryk renounced his former political ideas when he got out of prison. In 1954 he directed *The Caine Mutiny*, a film which exposed the "dangers" posed by people who question and belittle authority, and which argued that even paranoid and incompetent authority had to be obeyed and supported. There are many reasons for the evolution of Montgomery's and Dmytryk's views. One might even argue that the films contained contradictions that made the later political transformations consistent with earlier tendencies. But it also seems clear that the visions projected in *Ride the Pink Horse* and *Till The End of Time* reflected a social discourse about the past and present that set boundaries for the individual artists. That discourse, and its contradictions, illumines the ways in which Hollywood motion pictures can be important artifacts for historical research.

For example, both *Picnic* (1955) and *Kramer vs. Kramer* (1979) depict the family in jeopardy. But in *Picnic*, female dependence on men—mandated by unequal economic opportunities and by the power of the male gaze—leaves women vulnerable to the irresponsibility of individual males. In *Kramer vs. Kramer*, female independence and entry into the job market threatens the family and forces the man to take on new domestic burdens. The connections between these films and their historical contexts are far from simple: we know too much about the 1950s and the 1970s to to be convinced that *Picnic* and *Kramer vs. Kramer* reflect a direct linear progression or regression, that feminism influenced films of the 1950s more than films of the 1970s, or that the 1970s were a less progressive decade for women than were the 1950s. But what are we to make of the contradictions that these films expose? On the one hand, *Kramer vs. Kramer* shows none of the sympathy for women's confinement that resonates so powerfully in *Picnic*. On the other hand, *Picnic* cannot even suggest some of the possibilities for female autonomy that are accepted as a matter of course in *Kramer vs. Kramer*, even when the latter film argues that things have gone too far.

Each of these films responds to tensions exposed by the social moment of its creation, but each also enters a dialogue already in progress, repositioning the audience in regard to dominant myths. *Picnic* responds to arguments evident in preceding anti-feminist (*Our Very Own* 1950, *I Want You* 1951) and proto-feminist films (*Adam's Rib* 1949, *The Marrying Kind* 1952) as well as to the social contradictions that spawned them. Similarly, *Kramer vs. Kramer* makes its statements about the family in a context that included both conservative critiques (*An Unmarried Woman* 1978) and feminist critiques (*Girlfriends* 1978) of patriarchy and male privilege. Each of these films contains inscribed preferred readings: their conclusions imply one true source of conflict and one viable method of resolution. Yet those endings do not fully resolve the contradictions they raise. To engage our interests as viewers they need to make us fight against ourselves, to see opposite interpretations as plausible and desirable, making any closure somewhat unsatisfying. Both *Picnic* and *Kramer vs. Kramer* end by asserting that one can have both marriage and independence, obligations and freedom. Yet the emotional impact of the preceding narratives undercuts those closures; we know that the family might be in jeopardy again tomorrow, no matter how hopeful we find the happy endings of the films.

The complex and contradictory arbitrations of social tensions in *Picnic* and *Kramer vs. Kramer* preclude some kinds of historical conclusions. We cannot argue from this limited evidence that the history of the family has one clear trajectory from patriarchy to feminism or vice versa. But we can see that change over time depends on arguments, actions, and ideologies that are constantly being constructed and reconstructed even in periods of seeming stasis. In addition, we can learn that arguments have to change with circumstances, that generalized myths draw their social power from the ways in which they are articulated or disarticulated in any given social circumstance. Finally, diachronic narratives depend on revisionism. Present problems force us to redesign our psychic and intellectual maps of the past.

Similar historical processes underlie two films that combine "melodramas of beset manhood" with the "agonies of empire," *The Man Who Shot Liberty Valance* (1962) and *An Officer and a Gentleman* (1983). In both films men learn to make themselves strong enough to act in a brutal world, and their victories are not merely personal. In these films the "manly" capacity for violence wins the approval of women and makes possible the survival of the nation. In *The Man Who Shot Liberty Valance*, young Ransom Stoddard suffers from an idealistic devotion to law and the social contract that makes him seem too weak to combat the evil deeds of outlaw Liberty Valance. Only when rugged frontiersman Tom Doniphon arms Stoddard with some of Valance's brutality does the young man emerge victorious. He destroys Valance, makes the west safe for civilization, and acquires the respect he needs to win Doniphon's girl away from him. By contrast, in *An Officer and a Gentleman*, Zack Mayo's problem is the opposite of Stoddard's: he is too anti-authoritarian and anti-social to accept discipline and become a successful soldier. But just as Stoddard had Doniphon to guide him, the intervention of Drill Instructor Foley channels Mayo's rage and capacity for brutality into a form that enables him to become a credit to society—an officer and a gentleman. In both films, the young men initially see their tutors as enemies, while Doniphon and Foley display open contempt for the men they eventually transform. In each case, the voices of experience (Doniphon and Foley) triumph by transferring some of their own brutality to the novices to make them more like the enemies they must combat. For both tutors, the process entails an ultimate sacrifice—they must allow their charges to surpass them and receive the glory that should properly belong to them.

In *The Man Who Shot Liberty Valance*, both Doniphon and Stoddard wind up disgraced. Doniphon "helps" Stoddard by hiding in the dark and shooting Liberty Valance in the back when the outlaw and Stoddard appear to be dueling each other. On the surface this act enables Doniphon to get rid of Liberty Valance, and, therefore, a threat to civilization while making Stoddard a hero. But Doniphon has stooped to Valance's level; he cannot enjoy the fruits of civilization because he has violated its codes. Even worse, Doniphon could kill Valance only because he was so much like him. Valance's death and the triumph of civilization make Doniphon useless; he is not needed to deal with Valance any longer, nor can he fit into the civilized world. Stoddard becomes a hero because of Doniphon's act, but a false hero. He knows that he did not, in fact, shoot Liberty Valance, and the triumphs of civilization rest neither on his own beloved legal code or on Doniphon's code of honor. Instead, the moral basis of civilization rests upon the very barbarism it supplants. Stoddard "wins": he marries Doniphon's girl and becomes a senator, but his marriage is childless and his place in history has been secured by what he knows to be a lie. The inscribed reading of *The Man Who Shot Liberty Valance* implies that corruption is inevitable and maybe even necessary, but neither the "manhood" of Ransom Stoddard nor the "triumph" of civilization hold any real glory or merit.

In contrast with *The Man Who Shot Liberty Valance* and its serious self-reflection and criticism, *An Officer and a Gentleman* presents its closures as unproblematic. The sadistic brutality of Sgt. Foley and his power to humiliate Mayo put into play the main oppositions of the film: on the one side, an angry, white, working-class male who hates authority and commitment; on the other side, a military bureaucracy that makes him dependent upon a group of fellow officer candidates whom he hates, under the command of a black sergeant who seems determined to prevent his advancement. The inscribed reading of the plot encourages the audience to identify with Mayo's anger and resentments, and to share his sense of self-empowerment through aggression. To succeed, he must take on the identity of Sgt. Foley, channeling his brutality within the disciplined confines of the military. Just as Ransom Stoddard and Tom Doniphon "save" civilization by becoming like their enemy Liberty Valance, Mayo emerges as a hero to his fellow officers and girlfriend when he becomes like Foley.

The similarities between *The Man Who Shot Liberty Valance* and *An Officer and a Gentleman* suggest some underlying structural unities endemic to "melodramas of beset manhood" and the agonies of empire in Hollywood films. But important differences between the two films illumine significant historical traces as well. Made at a time when both U.S. military hegemony and patriarchal authority within the nuclear family appeared stronger than ever before, *The Man Who Shot Liberty Valance* betrayed serious doubts about the efficacy and legitimacy of these hierarchies. *An Officer and a Gentleman*, on the other hand, emerged after the American defeat in Vietnam and the Iranian hostage crisis, and after more than a decade of feminist criticism of patriarchy. *An Officer and a Gentleman* reaffirmed values that seemed to many to have been discredited and abandoned, while *The Man Who Shot Liberty Valance* questioned dominant values—or apparently dominant values. The inverse relationship between these films and their historical contexts illustrates the point made so effectively by Kellner and Ryan about a lag between historical experience and cultural expression. To Kellner and Ryan, Hollywood films often express the pent-up frustrations of an era, not reflecting dominant views as much as prefiguring the next swing of the pendulum.[3]

Just as *Picnic* could anticipate feminist critiques of female dependency during an era of seeming patriarchal hegemony, *Kramer vs. Kramer* anticipated the popularity of New Right anti-feminism by airing the resentments percolating against ascendant feminism. *Picnic* asked its audiences to question the legacy of the recent past, to reassess the 1950s gender roles that had reversed some of the gains made by women in the 1940s. *Kramer vs. Kramer* didn't celebrate the successes of ascendant feminism in creating opportunities for women, but, rather, blamed these women for broken homes and unhappy children. *Kramer vs. Kramer* ignores the historical and social fact that in our society men abandon women and children routinely; ideologically the film succeeded in putting the onus for broken families on women and on feminism. In the same way, a seemingly conservative film like *The Man Who Shot Liberty Valance* contained all the doubts about national legends and patriarchy that would soon emerge in 1960s social movements, while *An Officer and A Gentleman*, apparently liberal in its showing people from different races and classes becoming a unified group, actually played out the narcissistic grandiosity essential to the patriarchal family and the militaristic state.

This contrast between the criticisms of patriarchy and nationalism in *Picnic* and *The Man Who Shot Liberty Valance* and the antifeminism and authoritarian nationalism of *Kramer vs. Kramer* and *An Officer and a Gentlemen* of course is not to suggest that the 1950s and 1960s were more liberal than the 1970s and 1980s. It shows, rather, how films can be dissonant with their own time, asking and answering historical questions that might push discourse and political behavior in another direction.

Sometimes reversals in a genre can be directly emblematic of the context in which a film is made, as in two films organized around "corruption at the top," *The President's Analyst* (1967) and *Rambo* (1985). Consistent with its 1960s surroundings, *The President's Analyst* depicts a psychiatrist, Dr. Sidney Stone, chosen as therapist for the president of the United States. At first he is in awe of power, dazzled by his patient and the enormous responsibilities he wields. But exposure to the centers of power makes Stone a target for a tug of war between the FBI and the CIA, between the secret operatives of friendly and hostile nations. He comes to see them all as interchangeable, committed to power rather than to values or ideology. When his inquiries eventually lead him to the conspiratorial force behind all of the pointless chicanery he has witnessed, the psychiatrist discovers it to be corporate capitalism—in the form of the telephone company. Although satirical and light-hearted in its barbs, *The President's Analyst* expresses a cynical distrust of corporate and national power which it contrasts with the good instincts of ordinary citizens who for the most part would do fine if they were just left alone.

Rambo also discovers malefactors in high places, but their identity and the putative solutions to their wrongdoing are distinctly different. For John Rambo, the conspirators are Washington bureaucrats whose incompetence "lost" the War in Vietnam despite the gallant efforts of soldiers like Rambo. Even after the war they attempt to sabotage his efforts to rescue U.S. prisoners left behind in order to neutralize the war as a political issue. Rambo uses physical bravery and rather unbelievable fire power to escape their "no-win" philosophy and to kill and maim the Vietnamese enemies responsible for his memories of suffering.

Both *The President's Analyst* and *Rambo* use individualism as the focal point for historical revisionism. Iconoclast and rebel Sidney Stone battles the FBI and the CIA, understands the working relationship and mutual respect manifest between KGB and CIA operatives, takes refuge with hippies and other social outcasts while fleeing from a middle-class suburban family, and eventually takes up arms against the "real enemy," corporate monopoly capitalism. In contrast, working-class John Rambo gives the appearance of 1960s rebellion (he has long hair and eats natural foods), but finds his enemy in the government bureaucracy and his solution in a "rescue mission" that serves as a surrogate replay of the war in Vietnam. *The President's Analyst* questioned the entire legacy of the cold war at a time when Americans were being asked to fight in Vietnam; *Rambo* sought to control the historical verdict on Vietnam by arguing for renewed war in a time of peace. In the 1960s film, individual distrust of government served liberal ends; by the 1980s that same sentiment had become the foundation for an ultra-conservative critique.

Two motion pictures about personal autonomy evidence a similar reversal in themes. In *Rebel Without a Cause* (1955) teen-ager Jim Stark resists the conformist pressures of his affluent suburban community. His parents live for appearances. They tell him to choose his friends carefully and to be seen with the right crowd, but he is more concerned with proving himself to a gang of delinquents when they tease him about being "chicken." The world of his parents suffocates Jim. His domineering grandmother, hen-pecked father, and embittered mother provide him with inadequate adult role models. The surveillance at school is even more intense. Peer pressure drives him to participate in a dangerous and foolish automobile race simply because he would lose face by declining a challenge. Home and school worlds converge when Jim's opponent dies in the race. In the pivotal scene in the film, he tells his parents he wants to inform the police about his involvement in the race, but in typical 1950s fashion they tell him not to get involved. "You can't be idealistic all the time," his father tells him. But Jim insists that a human life has been taken, that he has responsibility for it, and that he cannot choose to turn his back on that responsibility to society. Through a complicated series of circumstances, his nonconformity enables him to form an egalitarian relationship with a girlfriend, a relationship that becomes a model even to the adults around him. Although Jim's sense of responsibility ultimately cannot save the life of a young friend who idolizes him, Stark's decision to connect his life to others eventually puts nonconformity to the service of social advancement.

Director Nicholas Ray once commented about Jim in his *Rebel Without a Cause* saying a hero is not someone who is better than you; a hero is someone just like you who for a little while does something better than you.[4] That kind of egalitarian populism provided the informative moral power behind *Rebel Without a Cause*; the film championed nonconformity as a way of unleashing the nobility and heroism of the ordinary person. A different notion of nonconformity was presented in *Amadeus* (1984), a notion that reflected the neoconservatism of the 1980s. The Wolfgang Amadeus Mozart in *Amadeus* rebels because he believes that he really is better than other people: he is a genius who produces great art without labor, while they are mediocrities who conspire against his superior talents. Mozart's nonconformity is vicious, anti-social, and contemptuous of others, but the film implies that it is all validated by his music. Whereas society seemed oppressive in *Rebel Without a Cause* because its materialism and conformity constrained the potential of an ordinary citizen, in *Amadeus* society's oppressions served the common people by cheating the exceptional ones. As was the case with *Rambo* and *The President's Analyst*, anti-authoritarian individualism in the 1980s served the purposes of hierarchy and conservatism in *Amadeus* whereas it had been a feature of liberalism in *Rebel Without a Cause*.

Yet it would not be accurate to say that liberalism captured the concept of individualism in the 1950s and conservatism captured it in the 1980s. Instead, both liberalism and conservatism have jockeyed for position throughout the postwar era by appropriating overt and latent structures of feeling capable of legitimating and sustaining their positions. No fixed inventory of character traits marks a film as belonging to corporate culture or to democratic culture; rather, it is the way character traits are put in place in any given historical moment. Furthermore, effective ideological argument often anticipates hostile reactions, if only to co-opt them. For example, the 1941 film *Sergeant York* succeeds as pro-war interventionist propaganda largely because it presents the pacifist position so movingly, then disposes with it so effectively. Director Dorothy Arzner's *Craig's Wife* (1937) advances a persuasive feminist critique of marriage as an institution by misdirecting audience resentments against the heroine and then showing us how the built-in power relations of patriarchal marriage turned her into the person we have come to dislike. Sometimes these oppositions appear so compelling that we do not know which side to choose. Film scholar Peter Biskind argues that *Rebel Without a Cause* works to reconcile a rebel to the nuclear family, teasing us with the possibilities of opposition but eventually disciplining the hero into submission. Yet other critics offer a directly opposite interpretation: they argue that Jim Stark's position wins out, that the family and society change because of his actions rather than vice versa. Effective presentation of both options widens the potential audience for a film, but it leaves questions about any film's ideological and political effectiveness. In the case of *Rebel Without a Cause*, reception may depend upon the historical consciousness of viewers—whether they read the rise of suburbia as an advance for American society or as a moral and social disaster.

The contradictory readings inscribed in most Hollywood motion pictures may seem like craven opportunism, examples of how commercial culture compromises the moral authority of art. For commercial and ideological reasons, producers do want to "have it both ways," and they do not want to polarize the audience unduly. But this two-sided nature of ideology in films also illumines the innately dialogic nature of political discourse itself. Part of persuading others involves understanding their points of view. Constructing alliances around unifying ideals and images necessitates concessions and compromise, and a recognition of what we might call a "unity of opposites." Only someone frightened by the temptations of democratic culture would submit to the repressions of corporate culture. Only someone capable of submitting to the oppressions of corporate culture would endure the risks of fighting for a democratic culture.

These polar positions do not represent fixed dramatic forms, or even fixed segments of society. They reflect battles that take place inside each of us as we negotiate our relationships to other people, past and present.

In their studies of "black rage," psychiatrists William Grier and Price Cobbs identify a peculiar phenomenon among Afro-American males that they term "tears without emotion." They observe a tendency among black men to break into tears while watching popular-culture representations of celebration. The sight of a halfback exulting after scoring a touchdown or an actress bowing to the applause of an adoring audience might start tears streaming down the cheeks of a black male viewer. Grier and Cobbs attribute these "tears without emotion" to an unlocking of repressed hopes. These men cry for "all that might have been," for all the desires and ideals crushed by historical power relations, for all the celebrations they will never have.[5] Popular culture often works very much as these "tears without emotion" do. It resists univocal interpretations and inscribed ideological closures because of the hurts of history. The deep emotional investment with the fictions of popular culture amounts to more than brain-washing or a stupefied numbness engendered by the power of the media apparatus. Rather, it stems from the gap between lived experiences and human hopes in a world with too many broken promises and too many unrealized dreams.

8

The New York Intellectuals: Samuel Fuller and Edgar Ulmer

In his trenchant analysis of the gangster film, Robert Warshow noted that "a dark city of the imagination" pervades the crime genre. In his view, the city menaced the American imagination because it represented a psychic landscape on which desires for upward mobility turned into cut-throat competition, a place where rugged individualism expressed itself through brutalization and humiliation of others. By contrast, traditions of American pastoralism represented the frontier and the farm as places of freedom, opportunity, and mutuality.

Anyone familiar with American history might object that the frontier and the plantation have been sites of extraordinary brutality and sadism, while the city has been the place where compromise and mutual accommodation enabled diverse populations to live together. But the pastoral myth does not rest on historical facts and cannot be refuted by evidence. In addition, historical understanding in America has become so entwined with the pastoral myth that a historical critique of pastoralism seems a contradiction in terms. For the frontier and the farm seem innately historical; they seem to be places where a future is still possible and where individual narratives of success can unite the past and present. The city, on the other hand, seems to be the place where the freight train of history jumped the track. The city enjoys the latest technologies and conveniences, but its very collectivity seems to rebuke the tradition of individual narratives that Americans have come to understand as history.

The city became a cultural and intellectual problem in the nineteenth century, at the very moment when anxieties about history emerged as the constitutive problem of modern society. As Laura Mulvey writes

> Over and over again, the mysterious, fascinating and frightening image of the city recurs throughout the nineteenth century. It represents an outside to the rule of order. To the individual swallowed up in the crowd, to the law in the refuge given to the criminal, to morality faced with a profusion of bars and prostitutes, the city at night epitomises chaos and uncertainty.[1]

Chaos and uncertainty were the problems history was expected to solve. The serious dislocations and distortions of industrialization disoriented individuals from their pasts and led to what E. J. Hobsbawm calls "the invention of tradition." Much of the public imagery and ceremony celebrating "history" in the nineteenth century had in fact been invented and fabricated in the present simply to ease anxieties about disconnection from the past. In this context, historical narratives tended to stress the inevitability of progress, the heroism of isolated individuals, and the narrative closures that brought reassurance or fatalism to people suffering amid chaos and uncertainty.

Thus the city became an enemy of history, or at least of historical narratives. Its energies and pluralities suggested many stories not just one. Its injustices and exploitations called into question the inevitability (or even the reality) of progress. Finally, the real city of mutuality and accommodation rebuked both the dark city of the imagination and the unrealistically bright countryside of pastoralism. As Warshow's critique suggests, dominant culture continued to contrast the dark city with the bright frontier, but in the art of organic intellectuals the city and its relationship to history became a focal point for a plethora of oppositional narratives.

Two film-makers exemplify the recovery of the city as a terrain for a new kind of historical thinking. Samuel Fuller and Edgar Ulmer are not the kind of people usually included in discussions about "New York intellectuals," but their love for that city and their recognition of the possibilities within it mark them as profound contributors to debates about the city and history. Operating on the fringes of the film industry, they were far removed from the world of traditional intellectuals and the institutions that support them. But as artists committed to their communities and to the still unrealized potential within them, they served as organic intellectuals, as agents of agitation and education for hopes that had not yet taken organized political identity. Because they were engaged in making low-budget products for a commercial medium, they often found themselves constrained by the tools at their disposal. Both the form and content of their professional work resonated with a sensationalism and an intentional vulgarity that deflected critical attention from the reflective, contemplative, and critical core of their films. But life as organic intellectuals also gave them access to the rough energy of the city, to the democratic pluralism of its communities, and there they found a vision capable of critiquing the seemingly unquestioned myths of their day.

Samuel Fuller: A Post-Industrial Prophet

Samuel Fuller is very much a New Yorker and very much an intellectual. His childhood in the city and his experiences as a copy boy and crime reporter for its tabloid newspapers gave determinate shape to the artistic and social vision that permeates all of his professional work. Many of Fuller's books and films use New York for local color and dramatic tensions, but they also use the complexities and contradictions of the twentieth-century metropolis as a stimulus for a unique kind of intellectual work. For Fuller, the textures of urban experience challenge the preoccupations of traditional intellectuals by privileging human interaction and inter-subjectivity over abstract standards of refinement and performance.

Critics have rarely appreciated the complexity and integrity of Samuel Fuller's world view. In fairness it must be conceded that he has made it difficult for them. A director who gives a goofy smile and waves to the camera while wearing a silly hat and gaudy flower-print shirt as Fuller did during the closing credits of *Dead Pigeon on Beethoven Street* is not likely to be revered as a serious artist. Nor is an auteur who insists on writing, directing, and producing films about mental illness (*Shock Corridor*), child molesting (*The Naked Kiss*), safecracking, teen-age drug addiction and school-girl prostitution (*Underworld U.S.A.*) likely to be understood as a sensitive interpreter of the moral dilemmas of modern life. And someone who celebrates violence as enthusiastically as Fuller did in his description of a scene from *Pickup on South Street* ("I liked the idea of Widmark pulling Kiley down by the ankles, and that the heavy's chin hits every step. Dat-dat-dat-dat-dat: It's musical.") can hardly expect intellectuals to look to him for moral guidance. Given these choices on Fuller's part, it is not surprising that even his admirers have frequently qualified their praise by describing him as "an intelligent primitive," a "master of shock realism," and "the maker of a few brilliant movies and a few more awful ones."[2]

Yet part of Fuller's flamboyant quirkiness comes from his seriousness as an interpreter of urban life. The low budgets that sometimes make his feature films look like glorified home movies also enabled Fuller to make films free from interference by producers and studio executives. As he once explained, for most of the seventeen "B" pictures he made between 1948 and 1963 "the budget was so little that they [producers and financial backers] never gave a damn about my premise, my content, and that's what interested me."[3] Despite their lurid and melodramatic content, most Fuller films raise serious issues in serious ways. "Every film must have a message," Fuller declares. "Maybe I'm too didactic. If so, too bad. That's just the way I write. Even if people don't agree with me, I like to make them think a bit. I'd like them to learn something. I'm not what you would strictly call an educator, but all the same I think the cinema must be used in this way."[4]

Those critics who have been able to look beyond Fuller's excesses and eccentricities have discovered profound meaning in his work. Frank McConnell hails Fuller's film *Pickup on South Street* for its sensitive representation of the crises in American popular mythology and American political aesthetics generated by anti-communism in the McCarthy era.[5] Luc Moullet praises Fuller for the ways in which his films challenge the unrealistic glamour of Hollywood conventions, choosing instead to explore life at the margins of society by raising difficult issues and presenting unpleasant images.[6] Jim Hoberman celebrates Fuller's "shock realism," locating the film-maker within a tradition of urban-influenced artists that include the cartoonist Chester Gould and the photographer Weegee.[7] As these critics discern, Fuller has more to offer us than his questionable taste and his uneven professional history. Yet his ideas about culture, ideology, and society are more significant than even his most sympathetic critics have thus far acknowledged. McConnell's emphasis on Fuller's historical location, Moullet's understanding of Fuller's aesthetics, and Hoberman's appreciation of Fuller's ties to the city all present part of the picture. But it is necessary to integrate these three frames of analysis into one unified totality to grasp the full import of Fuller's artistic and social vision.

In all of his films, but especially those set in New York City (*Pickup on South Street, Park Row,* and *Underworld U.S.A.*), Fuller uses urban life as a vehicle for examining key questions about culture and ideology in the modern world. In his films and books, he shuns the noble and the heroic to concentrate on the ordinary and the mundane. He distrusts institutions and ideologies, but displays great faith in the instincts and intuitions of ordinary people. Working in a cinematic tradition generally dominated by simple binary oppositions, Fuller depicts his protagonists as disturbingly similar to the enemies they go out to confront.

The cultural positions articulated within Samuel Fuller's films should be easily understood by intellectuals in the 1980s; indeed they resonate with the concerns of much contemporary cultural criticism. The "new social history" of the past decade has used the everyday life experiences of ordinary people as a basis for generalizations about entire societies, past and present. Poststructuralists have challenged the dominance of "master narratives" and the legitimacy of cultural institutions in order to illumine and savor localized practices of subjectivity and resistance. My purpose in this presentation will be to examine how Fuller's engagement with late industrial New York City enabled him to formulate these distinctly postmodern principles in an era of seemingly unchallenged and ascendant modernism.

In formulating his artistic vision, Fuller drew upon his personal history and upon the history of the society in which he lived. His focus on the underside of urban life was partially autobiography and partially social commentary. Fuller spent his earliest years in Worcester, Massachusetts, but his mother brought the family to New York when his father died in 1922. Fuller attended elementary school in Manhattan and explored the city's complex urban textures selling papers on street corners after school. Fascinated by tabloid newspapers, he dropped out of high school to secure employment as a copy boy for the *Daily Graphic*, and soon found himself running errands for William Randolph Hearst's prize columnist Arthur Brisbane. While still a teen-ager, Fuller worked his way onto the crime beat, and he soon familiarized himself with the lives of gamblers, street hustlers, thieves, and pickpockets in the underworld of his beloved city. He found himself horrified by the brutality, aggression, and systematic corruption of the city, but at the same time attracted to the peculiar moral codes and social loyalties that he encountered on the streets of poverty-stricken ethnic neighborhoods. In the city he found the worst manifestations of selfishness and competition, but he also discovered there a sense of community and mutuality that enabled people to survive in a hostile environment.

Fuller worked as a crime and waterfront reporter for the *San Diego Sun* in the 1930s. He published four novels between 1935 and 1944, including one about a criminal sentenced to execution in the electric chair and one about the newspaper industry. Fuller started work as a screen writer in Hollywood in 1937, where scripts like *Federal Man-Hunt*, *Gangs of New York*, *Bowery Boy*, *Power of the Press*, and *Gangs of the Waterfront* reflected his interests in crime and urban life. During World War II, Fuller served with distinction as an infantryman in Europe, and after his return from the war began to produce, direct, and write his own films.

Critics have often observed that every Fuller film is a "war" film, focused on violent conflict, the solidarity of comrades in arms, and the unfair burdens placed on individuals who find themselves caught up in other people's battles. Certainly, Fuller's wartime experiences left a lasting impression on him, and his films resonate with the lessons he learned in combat. But every Fuller film is also an "urban" film, even his westerns and war movies. His motion pictures characteristically explore the difficulties of uniting diverse populations and reconciling competing interests. They examine the tensions generated by ethnic rivalries, and they investigate the dangers of unbridled individualism in an interdependent world. No matter what their setting or ostensible genre, his films again and again return to the core tensions of the urban communities that Fuller encountered in his years as a journalist for tabloid newspapers.

Just as they did for him as a reporter, murders initiate the action in many Fuller films, drawing him out into some kind of city on a quest for information and understanding. In *The Steel Helmet*, a 1951 film about the Korean War, the massacre of the rest of his company leads Sgt. Zack into a "city" composed of misfits and undesirables from other units. The dramatic tension within *The Steel Helmet* comes from efforts by this multi-racial group of stragglers to get along with one another in order to successfully resist assaults by their common enemy. The shooting of a stripper in *Crimson Kimono* leads two Los Angeles detectives (one Japanese-American and one Anglo) into the mysterious world of that city's "Little Tokyo," which in turn makes them examine the ways in which their ethnicity has shaped their identities and their relations with each other. *Crimson Kimono* uses the city of Los Angeles as a "supporting character" much as John Ford used the wide-open spaces of the Monument Valley to symbolize pastoral freedom. Aerial views of the city stress its density, but as the camera focuses on individuals the viewer begins to make sense out of the chaos. Young Tolly Devlin in *Underworld, U.S.A.* sees a group of thugs beat his father to death on New Year's Eve, and he embarks on a life of crime to avenge that slaying. The murder of a mental patient attracts the attention of an ambitious reporter in *Shock Corridor* and leads him into another kind of city—a mental hospital where the main hall corridor is called "the street." In *Dead Pigeon on Beethoven Street*, the murder of a private detective's partner brings him out into the streets of Bonn, Germany and into alliances with unreliable and dishonest accomplices.

Yet while Fuller's city suffers from violence and disorder, it also contains important sources of sociability and mutual aid. Ultimately, the city educates and eventually offers salvation to Fuller's protagonists. In his films, the people on the margins of urban life, especially women excluded from the centers of power, give the city its moral capacity. From the derelict bag lady in *Pickup on South Street* to the alcoholic artist in *Crimson Kimono* to the café owner in *Underworld, U.S.A.*, unmarried, aging, androgynous female characters offer moral instruction to confused male "heros." These women exude moral authority without being mothers or grandmothers or wives; they act on the world even though they hold no positions of authority within it. But Fuller does not need to divorce women from sexuality in order to take them seriously. A series of sensuous young women engaged in amorous relationships also play key roles in his films. A prostitute in *Pickup on South Street* risks death to help the pickpocket hero who clearly does not deserve her loyalty, while another prostitute in *Underworld U.S.A.* testifies against the mob to help her gangster boyfriend. A stripper in *Crimson Kimono* displays intellectual curiosity about another culture when she tries to incorporate an authentic Japanese dance into her act, and another stripper in *Shock*

Corridor provides the only voice of reason in the film when she argues that her journalist boyfriend's unbridled ambition is dangerous because it isolates him from meaningful connection to other people. These women represent the residue of the urban past. They function as part of mutual-aid networks (Sandy is not related to Tolly in *Underworld U.S.A.* but raises him in her home when his parents cannot), as conduits of working-class solidarity (Moe protects Skip from the police in *Pickup on South Street* and takes a bullet in the heart rather than sell his address to the communists even though she needs the money), and as moral witnesses testifying to the necessity of forming meaningful attachments to people rather than to ideas or possessions (Mac tells Charlie she doesn't want to be called "a pearl" in *Crimson Kimono* because she prefers anything made by man to something made by an oyster). Fuller trusts these women because they have their feet on the ground—figuratively, in the sense that they make rational and practical choices without being beguiled by money, position, or power, but literally as well, in the sense that their feet touch the pavement of city streets and their choices are grounded in the moral imperatives of their sphere of the city.

Jim Hoberman correctly identifies Fuller's ruling aesthetic as the product of "sensibilities so keyed to the routine textures of urban life that they hardly seem to be sensibilities at all."[8] He compares Fuller's cinematic New York to the 1940s photography of Weegee, but the film maker's work also bears a striking resemblance to those other great New York photographers, Helen Leavitt and Berenice Abbott. As Max Kozloff points out, Leavitt saw the city as "a jumble of diverse sensations," not as a unified set of images signaling the triumph of progress. Her photographs of the 1940s counterposed a "humbling, problematic, and apparently deflating modernity" to the self-congratulatory appeals to "history" in public art.[9] Abbott studied with the Parisian photographer Atget in the 1920s, and absorbed her mentor's notion of depicting "history" through the everyday activities of ordinary people.[10] In her 1939 collection, *Changing New York*, Abbott concentrated on city streets and small businesses, on the neglected corners of New York life. Her depiction of New York displayed little enthusiasm for "progress," neglecting the city's great skyscrapers and famous landmarks to lovingly detail activities and enterprises that might be exhausted or obsolete. For Abbott, images of the waterfront formed the core icons of urban life in New York, images that underscored the city's economic dependence upon the movement of products and people, but which also emphasized the interdependence of Manhattan Island's inhabitants.[11] Fuller's depictions of urban life echo Abbott's sensibilities in significant ways. For example, in *Pickup on South Street* we encounter New York City from the perspectives of the major characters—a pickpocket, a prostitute, and a professional informer. Much of the film's action takes place in slum apartments, on the subway, under the Brooklyn Bridge, and in the pickpocket's dwelling which is constructed on pylons above the East River. In *Underworld U.S.A.*, Fuller acknowledges the existence of another New York—one which boasts modern skyscrapers and "hip" coffee houses. But we soon learn that the skyscrapers conceal the business activities of a crime syndicate responsible for gambling, prostitution, and racketeering, while the coffee houses are fronts for drug pushers. Like Abbott and Weegee, Fuller distrusts big institutions, but finds redeeming value in the immediate, local, and personal networks created by even the shadiest characters in the city.

Yet while Fuller's urban films of the 1950s and 1960s resonated with the sensibilities pioneered by Weegee and Abbott, they also responded to fundamentally changed historical circumstances. Abbott's photographs from the 1930s, and Leavitt's and Weegee's pictures of street life in the 1940s portrayed the fears and tensions of New York City life during the Depression and World War II. It is not difficult to understand Abbott's perception of New York as an aging and exhausted city during a decade when economic hardships precluded the construction of new buildings or the renovation of old ones. Her skepticism about large institutions and her curiosity about small-scale communities (and the people in them) echoed the dominant cultural preoccupations of her time.[12] Similarly, Weegee's emphasis on urban violence and instability reflected the frenzied pace of urban life during the war years as well as the threat posed to traditional values by violent behavior on all sides during that conflict. In that respect, Weegee's photography reflected the dominant cultural aesthetic of the 1940s, an aesthetic pervading many forms of popular culture from film noir to crime fiction.[13] But Samuel Fuller presented his dark vision of New York City during a decade of prosperity and growth, in an era of urban renewal and upward mobility. Instead of reinforcing the dominant cultural vision of the 1950s and 1960s, Fuller challenged it. He swam against the current by expressing both his fondness for the gritty residues of the urban past and his skepticism about the promises of the urban future.

Fuller championed the dying industrial city at a time when surburbanization and superhighways emerged as the putative cure to "urban blight." He focused his cameras on aging inner-city neighborhoods at a time when popular magazines and commercial network television glorified the residential suburb. He continued to make films in black and white at a time when most producers and directors insisted on using color. Yet Fuller was no stubborn reactionary, clinging to an idyllic past. In his westerns and historical films, Fuller goes to great lengths to show that the triumphs of "civilization" in the past rested on the same kinds of barbarism that plague humanity in the present. For Fuller, the past offered no escape from the difficult realities of the present. But rather enduring remnants of the past seemed to him a repository of moral guidance for understanding and acting within the historical present.

In his extraordinary critique of *Pickup on South Street*, Frank McConnell argues for the historicity of Fuller's work, demonstrating the degree to which the film-maker responded to the imperatives of post-World War II America. McConnell argues that the repressions and paranoia attendant to cold war anti-communism provided the crucial historical subtext for the issues aired in Fuller's film. In *Pickup on South Street* a pickpocket accidentally intercepts the delivery of microfilmed defense secrets to Russian spies. At first he resists pressures from his old enemies—police officers and the FBI—to turn over the film and help them track down the spies, but eventually comes to the aid of the authorities, albeit for personal rather than for political or patriotic reasons. McConnell argues that the convoluted nature of the film's plot helps it succeed in articulating the full complexities and contradictions of American anti-communism. He notes that the film eschews the binary oppositions characteristic of the "spy thriller," instead infusing the "spy thriller" genre with the sensibilities of "film noir" where the lines between good and evil are often indistinct. In McConnell's view, Fuller's genius in this film rests on the film-maker's understanding that anti-communism functioned in part as a means of channeling uneasiness about life in America into hatred of an outside enemy that could be blamed for the very qualities Americans most feared in themselves. As McConnell explains, "Our fear of the alien political machine, in other words, was in many ways a psychological projection of postwar fears of the economic machine, the Detroit which had beat the Germans but could provide only Levittowns for the families of the victors."[14] For McConnell, *Pickup on South Street* uses the outward devices of a spy thriller to cloak its real message — the elevation of personal responsibility and desire over the commands of ideologies and authorities.

McConnell is quite correct in his identification of McCarthyism as a relevant historical subtext for *Pickup on South Street*. Just as he does in *The Steel Helmet* (1951) and *China Gate* (1957), Fuller views the American struggle against communism in *Pickup on South Street* as pre-eminently a confrontation with itself. Fuller recognized a serious threat to individual citizens by government mobilization for World War II and by postwar anti-communism. Even while affirming pride in his own tour of combat duty, to this day Fuller refuses to call World War II a just war. After conceding the necessity to act against Hitler, Fuller once told an interviewer: "But even for such a reason, and I personally feel it was the right reason and the right move we made against [Hitler], it was wrong because the bottom line of living is that it is wrong to kill a human. It is abnormal, it is immoral."[15] Similarly, Fuller directed the full force of his cynicism and sarcasm against anti-communism in another interview in which he said: "One day I'd like to make a film on McCarthy the great Witch Hunter or Martin Dies, and on that shifty Parnell Thomas, and show them as they were: racketeers sleeping with the flag for a toga and ripping off a nation for loot and position."[16]

Yet while making a plausible and persuasive case for a political/historical reading of *Pickup on South Street*, McConnell neglects the distinctly urban character of the film and the urban sociology of its creator. Postwar disillusionment and the cold war provided one historical frame for Fuller, but urban history also figured prominently in shaping both the content and the form of *Pickup on South Street* and his other urban films. Fuller once bragged, "I did a film, *Pickup on South Street* set in New York but I shot it all in Los Angeles and the backlot at 20th Century Fox. *The New York Times* gave it an immense review: said it was tremendous and how for the first time in a long time a Hollywood movie had captured the spirit of New York, the smell of the metropolis."[17] Urban life itself provides the core dramatic tensions confronting Fuller's urban heros, and their quests end only when they find ways to draw upon the resources of the city for solutions to their problems. But it is not just any city that commands Fuller's attentions in these films; he directly addresses the urban crisis of the 1950s and 1960s by locating his films in the forgotten corners of exhausted industrial cities.

A sense of living in a "post" period pervades Fuller's urban imagery. Skip McCoy in *Pickup on South Street* literally lives on the margins of the city in a lean-to fabricated on top of a pier in the East River, connected to others by only a tiny wooden bridge. His "home" was built to sell bait to fishermen, and the word "bait" on the outside reinforces Skip's marginality—he is a way for police officers to trap "bigger fish." The person who cares most about him, an elderly female derelict, talks constantly of her fear of being buried in an unmarked pauper's grave and, consequently, sells his name to the police in order to buy herself a burial plot. In *The Crimson Kimono* Fuller presents Los Angeles's "Little Tokyo" as a no longer vital neighborhood, a place where young Nisei disown their heritage. The person with the most knowledge about the community is a forlorn and isolated figure, the sole remaining worshiper at the sole remaining Shinto shrine. Tolly Devlin in *Underworld U.S.A.* moves through the modern city blind to both its dangers and its rewards because he remains rooted in the past through his desire to avenge the murder of his father which he witnessed as a child. In *Shock Corridor*, the mental hospital's "street" numbers among its inhabitants three men unable to escape the tragic consequences of their pasts. Even the community inside the Buddhist Temple in *The Steel Helmet* consists of undisciplined and battered survivors from diverse units who remain divided by class and racial hatreds even when under attack by the enemy.

The seedy corners of the exhausted industrial city trap Fuller's characters in the past, leaving them to sift through the rubble of blasted hopes and unfulfilled aspirations. History has not been kind to them, and their dilapidated dwelling places and their worn clothing symbolize the stigma of their connection to the past. Moe, in *Pickup on South Street*, is living just to die, hoping to earn enough money to be buried in a cemetery. The scene that introduces her murder begins at a construction site, the modern powers of urban renewal mean death for the marginal inhabitants of the city. But Fuller invests his street people with a certain moral power, a certain dignity. As he explains,

> I am only concerned that these people, whom I call "Gutter People," have their own code of honor. Even though I may not agree with them, they have a code that interests me. I met quite a few when I was a reporter. I found out that their way of thinking and living, ironically enough, had more solidity, as far as the unity of their camaraderie, than the saintly people. They are thieves, pimps, and whores, and are very "low" people, but they stick together in a way that the churches would like to have people in their congregations unite, though they never do. They do not secretly try to outlive each other or live on lies—and we do.[18]

Once Fuller begins contrasting the shabby remnants of the urban past with the relentless processes of the urban present, he finds that the appearance of decay masks the enduring moral resources at the margins of the city, while the pretense of progress obscures the festering corruption at the center.

In *Pickup on South Street*, the police and the FBI use the same tactics as the communists, while the Russian spies themselves look like successful businessmen. Organized crime and an anti-crime strike force in *Underworld U.S.A.* occupy similar looking buildings and function through similar chains of command. Fuller presumes that his audience will share the dominant culture's uncritical faith in progress and modernity. He plays to these prejudices with his evocations of the ugliness of the urban underworld at the beginning of his New York City motion pictures, but by the end of the films, Fuller inverts the icons of morality to expose ugliness at the center and beauty at the margins. Implicit in that process is a revisionist interpretation of urban history, one that questions the assumptions of more than one hundred years of urban development. Rather than celebrating the world being created by the forces of progress, Fuller looks back wistfully to the world being lost because it provides a profound critique of the present. Nowhere is this process more evident than in his critique of the atomized nuclear family of the 1950s in *Underworld U.S.A.*

This is one of the few Fuller films in which blood ties to relatives meaningfully affect the identity of the characters. Released in 1961 at a time when the postwar baby boom, the growth of single-family, detached suburban housing, and the saturation of the market for commercial network television all contributed to a largely uncritical celebration of the family in popular discourse, *Underworld U.S.A.*

presents the glorification of families as a cruel hoax. In the film, a crime syndicate that sells drugs to teen-agers and recruits schoolgirls for prostitution wins awards from the Chamber of Commerce for youth work because it admits underprivileged children to its swimming pool in the summer. A hit man for the mob tells how much he enjoys serving as a lifeguard for the children at that pool, then calmly drives his car over a little girl because her father gave information about the syndicate to the police. The police chief himself takes bribes and allows the syndicate free rein in their corruption of youth because he wants to protect his own wife and daughter from retaliation by the gangsters. The lead character in the film embarks on a life of crime to avenge his father's murder. After killing two of the syndicate's "soldiers" as part of his revenge, he asks to join the syndicate, explaining that he killed their henchmen out of loyalty to his father. "I wish I had a son that felt that way about me," says the mob boss tenderly. Throughout the film, the concept of family appears as an empty slogan, an invocation of natural and noble sanction for vile and violent ends. Like other abstractions and grand narratives—from patriotism to progress—family represents an empty promise to Fuller. But he takes quite seriously the mutuality and affection imputed to family ties. His investigations of life in the late industrial city coalesce around a quest for networks and associations that can genuinely provide to people what progress and modernity only promise them.

Fuller's solutions to the problems posed by modernity come directly from the enduring practices of the urban past. Unlike urban reformers who promise to "clean up the mess" and ensure an orderly reorganization of city life, Fuller revels in the diversity and difference of the industrial city. He accepts the inevitability of conflict and expresses skepticism about the chances for grandiose reforms. But he does insist on an active subjectivity and a recognition of the needs of others. In many small ways, his characters save themselves by helping others; they acquire an ability to live with contradictions by rooting themselves in concrete ties to the people around them. As Fuller explained in one interview, "Listen, we're living in a world where you have to belong to something, even if you're a loner."[19]

Yet that something to which Fuller wants us to belong is not an institution, a political movement, or an ideology. His blueprint does not come from any projected utopia purporting to represent universal truth. Rather, he seeks to draw upon the resources of the past to solve the problems of the present. He finds his model in a world that actually exists, but which is fast disappearing. The late industrial city with its deep divisions, its incorrigible characters, and its disturbing disorder nonetheless contains an enduring relevance for Fuller. In it, he finds an appreciation of difference, a delight in diversity, and an obligation to engage oneself in the problems of others. The late industrial city provides Fuller with a vision which is both political and artistic, a vision encapsulated in one of his formulaic proclamations,

> You cannot force people to love one another, to think in the same way. You cannot make them, and I'm delighted. I love confusion, I love conflict. I love argument.[20]

Fuller's artistic choices flow naturally from his politics. His uneasiness about the oppressions of modernist rationality lead him to value interruption, incongruity, and difference. Luc Moullet writes, "In Fuller we see everything that other directors deliberately excise from their films: disorder, filth, the unexplainable, the stubbly chin, and a kind of fascinating ugliness in a man's face."[21] This is not personal perversity or unintentional artlessness on Fuller's part. The inclusion of what has generally been excluded provides an essential part of his intellectual perspective. Rather than rubbing our noses in the dirt of everyday life, Fuller seeks to make us suspicious of the "prettiness" of the Hollywood and Madison Avenue images that dominate our lives and to rediscover the unconventional beauty that we might find all around us. It is not enough for Fuller to make this argument merely on the level of dialogue and plot; like all good artists, he helps us experience for ourselves the sensibilities that his art and politics seek to advance.

By drawing on his own experiences with the city, Samuel Fuller formulated a critique of modernity in his urban films that anticipated subsequent arguments by cultural critics of many political perspectives. Precisely because he remained so rooted in the modern industrial city and its contradictions, he created a body of work with tremendous import for our postmodern postindustrial present. In his films we find a way of savoring the legacies of the past without resorting to reactionary self-deception, and we find as well a means of actively contesting the present and the future without succumbing to the allure of grand narratives that account for everything but the lives of ordinary people like ourselves. Fuller's cultural practice might not fit into our conventional definitions of intellectual work, but perhaps that only underscores the necessity of changing those definitions to fit our current circumstances.

Beyond a Boundary: Edgar G. Ulmer

In the face of low budgets, hurried production schedules, and inferior supporting personnel, Edgar Ulmer made films stunning in their simplicity and awesome in their aspiration. In a medium that involves visual, aural, and narrative elements as a matter of course, Ulmer's films stand out for their ability to make us see, hear, and think about the world in new ways. Behind his aesthetic commitments lies a powerful social vision insisting that loneliness and alienation are neither necessary nor inevitable.

Samuel Fuller once told an interviewer that anyone could make a great film with millions of dollars, great actors, and a strong dramatic premise, but that real talent lay in making a work of art out of more limited resources. Most film-makers simply coast on the strengths of their medium, but directors like Fuller and Ulmer plumb the depths of cinema to come up with something new. It is the integrity of their inquiry as much as the ingenuity of their answers that touches us when we watch their films. Like all of the best cultural creators, they concentrate on process rather than on conclusions. They explore the ambiguities of life instead of reducing complicated experiences to simple formulas.

To contemporary film-viewers accustomed to elaborate special effects, sophisticated camera work, and extensive editing, Ulmer's films may appear appallingly unsophisticated and primitive. He made 128 films, many in less than six days, most with budgets that permitted no wasted footage and allowed no opportunities for alternate takes. In fact, what little critical reputation Ulmer currently enjoys comes in large part from tongue-in-cheek cultists who see his films as subjects for "camp" humor. One critic described *Detour*, probably Ulmer's greatest film, as "an exercise in sustained perversity." Another gave an annual award to the best low-budget film capturing the aesthetic of Edgar Ulmer, whom he portrayed as "the most tattered *auteur* ever to emerge from the Hollywood underground" and whose work he described as defined by "gratuitous artistic fortitude in the face of infinitesimal budgets, utter disregard for prevailing standards of good taste, complete commercial failure, and instant critical obscurity."[22]

Ulmer's own sense of humor encourages a sense of playfulness in his audience; we can never be sure that he is not putting us on. In *Detour*, a musician gets a $10 tip, but calls it "a piece of paper with germs crawling on it," and a dying woman's cough in the same film invites jokes about *Camille*. In *Bluebeard*, Ulmer responds to the limitations of a small budget by staging a musical production number performed by puppets "lip-synching" to a record. He uses low-key lighting, smoke pots, and dream sequences to create moods and effects that directors with larger budgets establish through scenery, editing, and dialogue in more deliberate, and perhaps more believable, fashion.

There is nothing wrong with our sharing in this fun — indeed, one suspects that Ulmer would be flattered to see the minute attention paid to his money-saving schemes. But it would be quite foolish to assume that Ulmer took those steps unknowingly or to believe that in making his tough little films he tried to make *Gone With The Wind* and failed. Ulmer chose to make small films on low budgets because they gave him an opportunity to explore ideas and techniques that would not have been tolerated by the big studios. His entire life history in theater and films testifies to a self-conscious struggle to pursue artistic and social truths at the risk of commercial failure. That the finished products appear more laughable than laudable to some critics tells us more about the distorted values of our culture than about the unworthiness of Ulmer as an artist. For by any fair standard of evaluation, Ulmer's films display the consummate skill of a master craftsman absorbed in a personal (albeit somewhat odd) agenda.

Born in Vienna in 1904, Ulmer studied architecture in preparation for employment as a set director in Max Reinhardt's famous Josefstadt Theater. Like other film directors who came to cinema from architecture study (Nicholas Ray and Orson Welles), Ulmer maintained a commitment to complex visual imagery throughout his career. His minimalist but carefully designed sets exude atmosphere, and he uses pictures to convey what other directors might have to belabor through complications of plot and dialogue. Ulmer came to the United States in 1923 to work on the set of the play "The Miracle," and while there he started designing sets for Universal Studios. The great director F. W. Murnau, a colleague from theater productions in Berlin, introduced Ulmer to Hollywood and used his sets in early silent films including *Tabu* and *Sunrise*.

Returning to Europe in 1929, Ulmer gained his first experience as a film director collaborating with Robert Siodmak on *Menschen Am Sonntag* (People on Sunday). Less than an hour long, the film employs a documentary style in its fictional treatment of a typical Sunday in the lives of five people. In its effort to peer into the everyday lives of ordinary people, *Menschen Am Sonntag* prefigured the concerns that would dominate most of Ulmer's later work, just as it also influenced the subsequent cinematic efforts of Siodmak and of scriptwriters Billy Wilder and Fred Zinneman.

With the release of *Menschen Am Sonntag*, Ulmer moved back to the United States. He worked as an art director at MGM Studios and directed films there for overseas release. At the same time, he pursued a career in music, teaching music history and designing opera sets in Philadelphia. Ulmer's life-long love of music assumed an important role in his films as well. In many of them he played out his childhood dream of becoming an orchestra conductor through innovative uses of music as part of the cinema experience. Ulmer used a classical music score in *The Black Cat* in 1934, possibly the first such use of classical music by Hollywood. In *Detour*, the lead character plays the piano. The villain in *Bluebeard* acts out his sinister desires by putting on puppet shows with operatic themes. *Carnegie Hall* revolves around a woman who works as a janitor in that concert hall to assist her son's musical education. It would be difficult to identify a film director more interested in music than Ulmer; the entire corpus of his work engages in serious and profound exploration of the relationship between life and art, and he consistently selects musicians, actors, and painters as protagonists.

After making *Mr. Broadway* in 1932 (a film starring Ed Sullivan), Ulmer's second American film provoked controversy because of its theme—the treatment of venereal disease. Sponsored by the American Social Hygiene Association and advised by health-care professionals, *Damaged Lives* used a fictive scenario about a young couple seeking treatment for syphilis to relay correct clinical information in an effective manner. But it touched on too delicate a subject for its time (1933) and encountered fierce opposition from censors who tried to stop its distribution. After a successful battle with the New York State Board of Censors, the film won high praise for both its social and cinematic accomplishments. Ulmer made the film in eight days; it earned $1.4 million in box-office revenues.

One year later, Ulmer made *The Black Cat* with Boris Karloff and Bela Lugosi. Produced by Carl Laemmle for Universal Pictures, it remains the one Ulmer film remembered by the casual moviegoer, probably Ulmer's greatest commercial success. Ostensibly based on an Edgar Allen Poe story, it features a conflict between old adversaries in a strange castle built on a World War I battlefield. Ulmer took advantage of Laemmle's absence from the studio to experiment with sets, camera movement, and music. But even though the producer hated the final version of the film, Laemmle had to respect its box-office appeal. *The Black Cat* rode the crest of popular interest in previous horror films like *Frankenstein*, but it succeeded on its own largely because of the performances Ulmer elicited from its stars. Ulmer thought of *The Black Cat* as a satire about the stupidity of war, but audiences more likely came away from it with memories of the rich characterizations by Karloff and Lugosi, which they repeated over and over again in subsequent pictures. Ulmer enjoyed particularly fine rapport with Karloff, who amused the director and crew by habitually staring into the camera upon entering a scene and intoning "Here comes the heavy . . . ," although, of course, they always had to reshoot those scenes.[23]

Ulmer's skill with actors in *The Black Cat* revealed a talent that characterized his entire directing career. We might not know to this day that Hedy Lamarr could act were it not for her riveting performance under Ulmer's direction in *The Strange Woman*. John Carradine created one of the most memorable characterizations of his career in *Bluebeard*, as did Arthur Kennedy in *The Naked Dawn*. For a film-maker whose reputation rests on *mise en scène* and visual effects, Ulmer succeeded magnificently with the actors under his direction. That skill would serve him well in the mid-1930s when he began making motion pictures outside of Hollywood, largely with amateur casts from diverse ethnic communities.

After a brief stint directing westerns under the name John Warner, Ulmer left Hollywood to make films with amateurs. A trade union of Ukranian window-washers hired him to make *Natalka Poltavka* in 1936, a self-financed film celebrating the culture and language of their homeland. Ulmer threw himself into the project with enthusiasm, even though he personally knew nothing about Ukranian culture. He believed that cinema as a medium had a responsibility to educate and communicate, that it belonged as much to people striving to define their ethnic identity as it did to investors seeking profits from whatever product Hollywood could convince the public to buy. Volunteer carpenters built the sets for *Natalka Poltavka*, and Ukranian cultural groups from Canada provided singers and dancers who worked under the tutelage of the famous Ukranian dancer Avromenkov, who also served as the film's producer. The picture opened at the Roosevelt Theater in New York City on Christmas Day 1936 with strong patronage from Ukranian-Americans. *The New York Times* film reviewer praised the picture's music and dancing, lauded its amateur cast, and gave special mention to the fine camera work and dance sequences designed by Edgar Ulmer.[24]

Success with *Natalka Poltavka* led to a series of Yiddish films beginning with *Green Fields* in 1937. Drawing on the stories of S. J. Abramowitz and the plays of Peretz Hirschbein, Ulmer's Yiddish films featured the talents of the Jewish Art Theater and other New York ensembles. Although Ulmer had been born a Jew, he had no formal religious training and no cultural familiarity with Yiddish literature, theater, or speech. But thanks to the sensitive tutelage of Peretz Hirschbein, who asked Ulmer to make these films, Ulmer's pictures beautifully reflected the subtle nuances of Yiddish culture, especially its delicate balance between humorous satire and serious ethical commentary.

Green Fields, The Singing Blacksmith (1938), and *The Light Ahead* (1939) featured wonderful performances by Michael Goldstein, Helen Beverly, Izidore Casher, David Opatashu, and a very young Herschel Bernardi. Financed by community organizations including the International Ladies Garment Workers Union, these films dramatized life in eastern European *shtetls* in the nineteenth century for 1930s audiences made up of immigrants and their children. Traditional themes from literature and folklore reminded American Jewish audiences of their roots and helped preserve ties to their European cultural heritage. In *Green Fields*, a bashful young man leaves the serenity of religious studies and encounters a farmer with an interest in learning and the farmer's daughter who may or may not have an interest in marriage. *The Singing Blacksmith* recruited its cast from the Jewish Art Theater and relates a David Pinski tale of a poverty-stricken apprentice blacksmith who gives himself over to the pleasures of wine, women, and song until the prospect of marriage presents him with a conflict of desires and loyalties.

Ulmer received critical and commercial acclaim for his Yiddish films. *Green Fields* won an award as the "Best Foreign Picture" of 1938, and it earned Ulmer an offer from Darryl Zanuck to make pictures in Hollywood with Shirley Temple. But Ulmer declined that opportunity, because, as he confided later to an interviewer, "I did not want to be ground up in the Hollywood hash machine."[25] In fact, he prided himself on having become the kind of film-maker whom the Hollywood establishment would not hire. Instead, he directed his energy toward making additional ethnic films, including the beautiful *The Light Ahead*.

Of all his Yiddish motion pictures, *The Light Ahead* best demonstrates Ulmer's extraordinary skill at combining personal problems with social circumstances. The film details the slow evolution of a love affair between a blind girl and a crippled youth in a poor Polish village in the 1880s. When a cholera epidemic strikes, the villagers squabble over whom to blame for provoking the wrath of God. To placate evil spirits, they concoct a "good deed" and arrange for a marriage between the blind girl and the crippled boy. Faced with an outside calamity, the villagers respond selfishly, trying to ingratiate themselves with heaven by patronizing the outcasts they have scorned in the past. Yet for all their hypocrisy, the villagers inadvertently bring happiness to the young couple. Released in 1939 as the Nazi war machine advanced its conquest of Europe, *The Light Ahead* presented its knowing audiences with a parable about the horrifying tragedy confronting European Jewry at that very moment. The past and present of the Jewish people became linked in this motion picture, with its ruminations about the dangerous weaknesses and enduring strengths of the Jewish community in the face of outside enemies. Rooted in a collective past and present, *The Light Ahead* enabled its audience to address fears about the future that empowered it for the difficult tasks ahead.

Ever curious about the ethnic mosaic of American culture, Ulmer also made two films in 1938 about Afro-American life and culture, *Let My People Live* and *Moon over Harlem*. Financed by the Department of the Interior and filmed at Tuskeegee Institute, *Let My People Live* used a dramatic story as the vehicle for delivering an educational message about the dangers of tuberculosis. Starring Rex Ingram, *Let My People Live* won a prize at the 1939 New York World's Fair. A black producer saw *Let My People Live* and asked Ulmer to join him in making a motion picture about the Harlem underworld. Ulmer entered production of the film with the script already completed and the main actors already cast, but he soon found they could afford no full reels of film, only short ends left over from other productions. He had to stop and reload the cameras whenever they ran out of film, sometimes in as little as one hundred feet. Ulmer hired extras off the streets of Harlem and directed the all-black cast and crew with skill and efficiency. Consequently, for all its quick cuts and cheap sets, *Moon over Harlem* comes across as an effective film, representative of political trends and social conditions in the community that gave it determinate shape. It broke the monopoly of light-skinned actors in Afro-American films, and its complicated story line included an attempt by Harlem gangsters to free their community from domination by the white mob.

Ulmer spent the first years of World War II making educational films for the Ford Motor Company, as well as for the Health Education division of the Department of the Interior. He returned to fiction films with the low-budget Producers Releasing Corporation in 1943, where he made some of the films for which he is best known and most reviled—*Girls in Chains, Isle of Forgotten Sins*, and *Jive Junction*. But operating with the low budgets and concomitant artistic freedom offered at PRC, Ulmer created some fine moments in small films, and he did much to shape the genre with which he would be most closely identified—film noir.

Identified as a genre by admiring French film-makers and critics including François Truffaut, André Bazin, and Luc Moullet, "film noir" refers to the dark, claustrophobic, and paranoid films made in the U.S. during the 1940s and 1950s. Ulmer's old colleague from Berlin, Robert Siodmak, had a hand in shaping the genre, but it was Ulmer as much as any other film-maker who provided its characteristic techniques. He used low-key lighting to emphasize shadows that made it difficult to distinguish friend from foe. Tightly framed shots of people in doorways and windows accentuated the psychological traps and social constraints ensnaring the characters. Most typically relating stories about isolated male heroes adrift in a hostile world, film noir played out anxieties about alienation and persecution in the years after the second World War.

Bluebeard and *Strange Illusion* employ film noir techniques, but *Detour* remains the quintessential expression of the genre. In less than one hour, its fatalistic narrative draws the viewer into a world of overpowering hopelessness shaped by the random blows of fate. Its hero bitterly recounts the story of his attempt to hitch-hike to the west coast to be reunited with his girlfriend, only to run into detours that draw him first into the appearance, and then into the actuality of murder. His innocent intentions and actions cannot save him from the fact that everyone would likely think him guilty of one murder; his panic over his appearance of guilt then leads him to accidentally commit a second. Fate, he tells us, can stick out its foot and trip any one of us at any time.

Like many of Ulmer's other films, *Detour* calls upon all of Ulmer's resources as a master of minimalism. He shot the film in six days and was forced to rely on a few stock sets for background. Most Hollywood film-makers of that time shot twenty to fifty feet of film for every foot used, but low budgets forced Ulmer to shoot *Detour* with a ratio of one and a half to one. Yet those technical limitations forced him to make more imaginative use of lighting, music, and camera angles to fashion an absorbing and convincing film.

In their incisive critiques, Tania Modleski and Dana Polan have demonstrated how *Detour* signals a radical break with dominant narratives. Ulmer had always been a rebel, but even films like *The Black Cat* or *Damaged Lives* or *Natalka Poltavka* had been content to argue that films should include the excluded, that their glorifications of war should be balanced by accounts of its destructiveness, that their focus on glamour should be balanced by insights into illness, and that their univocal story of white Anglo-Saxon America should be balanced with narratives about other ethnic and racial groups. But in *Detour*, Ulmer identified an emptiness in the heart of America, and it caused him to question his previous optimism about history, cities, and culture itself.

Polan notes how the image of a detour appeared prominently in '40s films as an appropriate metaphor for individuals whose lives and hopes had been interrupted (or shattered) by the war. In *Detour*, Ulmer shows us a world out of control, as Polan writes, "where coffee cups are visually enormous, where the opening of a car door can kill, where temporal progression dilates and becomes a nightmare of coincidence and alogical repetition."[26] This sense of rupture pervades the film's narrative, as hero Al Roberts's very American journey to Hollywood in search of his girl leads him to the shabbiest recesses of inner-city Los Angeles. Modleski shows how Ulmer's disillusionment with the heroic narratives of culture extends to a disillusionment with the very terms and conditions of social activity itself. Modleski sees the unsettling confusion of *Detour* (all plans go awry) as an expression of both a refusal by the hero to make an oedipal break and his refusal to remain at the pre-oedipal stage. Beginning with Al's meeting with Sue at the "Break of Dawn Club" (an appropriate name in a film exploring a return to origins), Al acts like a child abandoned by his mother. Instead of following the normal narrative trajectory from outlaw to husband and father, Al slides from being Sue's fiance into a series of identities that disconnect him completely from identity and responsibility. In Modleski's view, it is no accident that the villain in *Detour* is a woman whose insatiable greed "forces" Roberts into his retreat from identity.[27]

Detour reveals a dark side of human experience, one rarely portrayed in Hollywood films. The bitter resentments of lead character Al Roberts, and the predatory viciousness of Vera, the woman whom he accidentally kills, make us uneasy because they convey a tone rarely hinted at on screen, but all too present in life. In a culture where happiness preoccupies mass-media representations and where all popular art appears to have enlisted in the army of positive thinking, the existential despair of *Detour* stands out with stunning clarity. Yet, it is a despair with a social context. The amoral, frightening universe faced by Al Roberts is the world of postwar America in Ulmer's view. Film noir techniques pervaded the movies of the postwar era because they spoke to popular fears about the demoralizing influences of war and the proliferation of conflicts that followed it. Coming from Edgar Ulmer, the man who celebrated the joyful creativity and energizing diversity of prewar America, the radical pessimism of *Detour* bears powerful witness to the latent consequences of World War II.

In a series of minor masterpieces, Ulmer further developed his critical vision of postwar America. *The Strange Woman* (1946) shows the ruinous consequences of a beautiful woman's lust for power and wealth. Its most memorable scene presents a frontier preacher delivering a lengthy jeremiad against the vanity and destructiveness of materialism. Similar themes inform Ulmer's 1948 film *Ruthless*, secretly scripted by blacklisted writer Alvah Bessie. In that picture, an ambitious young man rises to the top of the business world by betraying friends, victimizing everyone in his path. Ulmer depicts capitalism as innately exploitive, a system in which one can make gains only at the expense of others. In the climactic final scene, two rival millionaires grapple for a gun at the edge of pier. They tumble into the water and thrash about fruitlessly until they both drown in a deadly stalemate. Observing how the lead character's greed brought this end upon himself, a woman who had appeared to be falling under his spell comments, "He wasn't just a man, he was a way of life."[28]

Although best known for his 1940s films, Ulmer went on to make significant motion pictures in succeeding decades. His science-fiction films especially revolved around social issues. In *The Man from Planet X* (1951), an explorer from a dying planet visits earth to assess its suitability as a resettlement center for his own people. An American pilot travels into the future in *Beyond the Time Barrier* (1960), and a mad scientist uses his powers for criminal purposes on his path to worldwide domination in *The Amazing Transparent Man* (1960). The fantasies of science fiction offered Ulmer the opportunity in the 1950s and 1960s to raise some of the same questions about society that informed his psychological dramas of the 1940s and his examinations of ethnic cultures in the 1930s. He produced significant works in other genres as well. *Naked Dawn* (1955) explored corruption in rural Mexico in a taut drama that won the Venice Film Festival award for best picture and served as the inspiration for Truffaut's *Jules and Jim*. In *Murder Is My Beat* (1955) Ulmer updated some film noir elements to present a complex study of delusion and paranoia, while he displayed a fine gift for comedy in *St. Benny the Dip* (1951) and *Babes in Bagdad* (1952).

In 1965 Ulmer made *The Cavern*, a war picture about six men and one woman trapped in an Italian cave during World War II. That would be his last picture. He spent the years until his death in 1971 battling the effects of a series of serious strokes. He received belated critical recognition for his work from film-makers Jean-Luc Goddard, François Truffaut, and Peter Bogdanovich as well as from sympathetic film critics Myron Meisel and John Belton. In the years since his death, the prescience of Edgar Ulmer's vision and the emancipatory implications of his world view have begun to take hold among audiences and artists alike.

To what can we attribute the growing reputation of Ulmer's films? One answer lies in the way that the compulsive cheerleading of the mass-culture industry wears thin as Americans confront the disappointments of deindustrialization and the agonies of imperial decline. An artist like Ulmer who detailed impotence, rage, and claustrophobia has much to say about our world. While cynical and pessimistic about authority figures and elites, Ulmer's films explore the realities of ordinary people in a compassionate, yet critical manner. Unlike John Ford's films, Ulmer's heroes do not rise above the masses. They like everybody else are trapped in mass insanity. In contrast to Alfred Hitchcock's films, the obsessions of Ulmer's villains contain a melancholy allure rather than an abhorrent terror. Unlike Frank Capra's characters, Ulmer's suffer the burdens of societal corruption without recourse to easy individualistic solutions. By remaining on the margins of the film industry, and by focusing on the social and psychological frontiers of American culture, Ulmer left a legacy of pictures that seem to penetrate the internal logic of everyday life. He respected film audiences and felt he could entertain and educate them at the same time. He made serious and significant statements about life and art under the most preposterous pretexts in an intensely commercial and notoriously unreflective medium.

How can we explain why a refined and cultured European artist would choose to make low-budget films about a homicidal puppeteer (*Bluebeard*), a deranged architect (*The Black Cat*), and a paranoid night-club pianist (*Detour*)? Why does an associate of F. W. Murnau and Max Reinhardt choose to make "B" movies shot in six days on topics ranging from venereal disease to time travel? Why would a perfectionist trained in set design and legitimate theater turn his back on the major studios and choose to make motion pictures dependent upon the uncertain financing and amateur acting of ethnic Americans during the hard years of the Great Depression?

Ulmer hinted at the answer to these questions in an interview with Peter Bogdanovich during which he confided, "I really am looking for absolution for all the things I had to do for money's sake."[29] In most of Ulmer's films, art and money are bitter enemies; for him, money corrupts all it touches, and it forces everything to conform to its needs. Ulmer's real sympathies lie with artists — the piano player whose music expresses his passion for his lover, the puppeteer who plays out obsessive fantasies in his shows, and even the deranged architect who builds his dream house on a former battlefield. These men at least have real feelings and passions. They may be tragic, but their tragedies come from real struggles between their own aesthetic visions and the mercenary logic of the outside world.

Ulmer's disdain for materialism helps explain his fascination with ethnic subcultures. In the music of *Natalka Poltavka* and *Moon over Harlem* he found a cultural creativity and eloquence of articulation unrepresented in commercial popular music. The Ukranian-Americans and Afro-Americans in those films had organic cultures tied to everyday life experiences. Their art celebrated and interpreted life, it brought them closer together as a group. They created art collectively, drawing upon common traditions to be shared with a knowing audience. In contrast, film-makers in Hollywood sought the lowest common denominator of mass taste to fulfill their profit-making responsibilities to the monopolists who employed them. Hollywood directors censored the contents of their pictures, they surrendered control over editing decisions to producers, and they participated in pandering to whatever weaknesses might motivate film-goers to part with the price of admission. Instead of using their powerful medium to expand experience and break down barriers, Hollywood film-makers created artificial commodities designed to overwhelm and paralyze viewers rather than to connect them to other peoples and cultures.

Edgar Ulmer had an alternative vision. In ethnic films and "B" movies, he found small spaces for representations of life that could not be co-opted by the culture industry. He found that he could work in those small spaces and carve away niches of independence that allowed him more artistic integrity than he would have had in the heart of the industry. Precisely because the "B" film did not appear to be serious art, it escaped the censorship imposed on other films. Of course, the section of Hollywood's "poverty row" in which Ulmer worked had its own set of limitations — low production values, frantic shooting schedules, bad scripts, and preposterous plots. But all in all, the "cheap" film allowed auteurs like Ulmer a freedom for artistic exploration and social dialogue unavailable at the major studios.

Perhaps the most enduring contribution to cinema by Edgar Ulmer lies in the breakthroughs made possible by his film aesthetics. His long takes, inventive uses of music, and "noir" sensibilities now form a basic vocabulary for film artists and audiences alike. In the long take, film time approximates real time, and scenes seem to have a life of their own. The extended dialogue in *The Black Cat, Detour*, and *Ruthless* provides emblematic examples of this technique, one of Ulmer's favorite devices for disguising the limitations of his budgets. Musical backgrounds provide another important element in Ulmer's aesthetic. Whether relying on the beautiful scores of Erdody, the folk music of his ethnic films, or classical musical selections, Ulmer's choices about melody and rhythm expand his arsenal of devices for determining mood and pace in his films. The sardonic use of an idyllic love song, "I Can't Believe You're in Love with Me," throughout the most bitter moments in *Detour* provides an unnerving musical/ social counterpoint, setting an example for later uses of the same technique, like Carl Foreman's "Merry Little Christmas" in *The Victors* and Woody Allen's "You Make Me Feel So Young" in *The Front*. But even more than the long take and inventive uses of music, it is the "noir sensibility" that endures as Ulmer's lasting contribution to cinematic language.

"Noir" sensibilities pervade the aura of persecution that consumes Ulmer's lead characters, but those thematic elements depend to a great degree upon technical manipulations. Ulmer uses lighting to suggest a dark world with danger lurking in the shadows. The inner world of psychological torment finds external expression in the cramped quarters of rooms without windows, closed automobiles, and underground caves and passageways. The conflicts that initiate his dramas pit the frailties of ordinary people against frightening and evil external realities threatening to overwhelm them.

In *Ruthless* and *Strange Illusion*, the good people triumph; in *Detour* and *Bluebeard* evil wins. But in all of Ulmer's films, the outcomes are uncertain and the prospects for tragedy ever present. By comparison with almost any other film-maker, his is a dark vision. But not by comparison with history. After Auschwitz and Afghanistan, after Saigon and San Salvador, can we afford to dismiss a film-maker who insists that the world is a frightening and threatening place, who worries about the alienated individuals in mass society, and who fears that the emancipatory potential of art may be obliterated by the machinations of materialism? The ugliness in Edgar Ulmer's films reflects the pain and horror of history. We do not act honorably if we condemn him for showing us a world that we know exists. By directly addressing the dark sides of life, Ulmer reminds us that other people see the evils around us and still dream of something better.

In the end, it may all be futile. It just may be that it is not darkest before dawn. Rather, as David Wagner puts it, it is darkest just before real, real, real dark. But in the art of Edgar Ulmer we find the hopes of one artist who tried to buck the tide, who tried to assert his independence from money worship and its attendant moral corruption. His little films with their low production values and silly titles may seem like unusual vehicles for conveying profound thoughts, but his messages have much to teach us.

In *The Black Cat*, one of Ulmer's characters explains to a young husband that his wife's sleep-walking has been caused by a variety of medical, psychological, and mystical factors, that in fact she has become a conduit for the intangible forces of evil around her. The husband snorts that this explanation sounds to him like "superstitious baloney." Like the young husband, we may find Ulmer's allegations about society and its evils to be just so much superstitious baloney. But we would do well to remember the film's next line, and to offer it to all who scoff at Ulmer's seemingly paranoid vision of society. The older man leans forward and says to the young husband, "Superstitious perhaps. Baloney, perhaps not. There are many things under the sun."

Popular Narrative

9

History, Myth, and Counter-Memory: Narrative and Desire in Popular Novels

> I will tell you something about stories,
> [he said]
>
> They aren't just entertainment.
> Don't be fooled.
> They are all we have, you see,
> all we have to fight off
> illness and death.
>
> Leslie Marmon Silko[1]

In the opening paragraph of *Their Eyes Were Watching God*, the novelist Zora Neale Hurston draws a distinction between men and women. According to Hurston, men watch the far horizon where ships at a distance carry their wishes on board. Some men, whose ships come in with the tide, see their dreams realized. Others, whose ships stay out at sea, find their dreams "mocked to death by Time." But women's lives, in Hurston's view, proceed by another process. "Now, women," she writes, "forget all those things they don't want to remember and remember everything they don't want to forget. The dream is the truth. Then they act and do things accordingly."[2]

The world of men in Hurston's account is a world of objectivity and action. It is the world of history, of events and of progress. The world of women, as she describes it, is contrastingly a world of subjectivity and sentiment. It is a world of myth, of stories, and of cycles. Men confront their dreams as entities outside themselves, as stories with clear resolutions knowable to all. Women experience their dreams as created constructs, as stories subject to revision under the pressures of conflict between desire and opportunity.

Literary critic Barbara Johnson detects a clear pattern in Hurston's imagery. The progression from "every man" to "men," and from "women" into a story about one woman signals to Johnson a refusal of totality, an insistence that every individual story belies a generalization. Yet Johnson also recognizes the ways in which individual stories take on added meaning to the extent that they symbolize generalizable experiences. "The task of the writer, then," Johnson argues, "would seem to be to narrate both the appeal and the injustice of universalization."[3] Real social experiences and injustices divide men and women; stories that elide that division compound injustice by rendering it invisible. Yet socially created divisions appear natural and inevitable unless we can tell stories that illustrate the possibility of overcoming unjust divisions. Thus, the point of Hurston's distinction between men and women was not so much to promote invidious comparisons between the genders as it was to foreground a strategy of story-telling appropriate to her experience as an Afro-American woman. Women and blacks, as subjugated groups, often find themselves relegated to the margins of the narratives fashioned by members of dominant groups. Excluded from a legitimate share of public power and victimized by male privilege in private life, women learn from both historical and fictional narratives that only men may look out to sea for their dreams. Similarly, Afro-Americans know all too well that historical narratives relating stories of "human" progress all too often conceal the inhuman oppressions of race and class upon which the triumphs of "civilization" rest. Women, Afro-Americans, and other groups relegated to the margins of dominant discourse learn that the "truths" of society obscure unconscionable lies, while the lies of myth and folklore offer opportunities for voicing long suppressed truths.

But myth and folklore are not enough. It is the oppressions of history—of gender, of race, and of class—that make aggrieved populations suspicious of dominant narratives. The radical subjectivity that Hurston describes, where the dream is the truth and where people act and do things accordingly, can only provide momentary refuge from the consequences of history. Story-telling that leaves history to the oppressor, that imagines a world of desire detached from the world of necessity, cannot challenge the hegemony of dominant discourse. But story-telling that combines subjectivity and objectivity, that employs the insights and passions of myth and folklore in the service of revising history, can be a powerful tool of contestation. Zora Neal Hurston advanced just such a strategy of story-telling in *Their Eyes Were Watching God*, and subsequent writers from marginalized communities have frequently followed her lead. Seizing upon the adaptive strategies of story-tellers from diverse oral traditions, these writers have advanced a consistent body of principles about communication and action in their battles against dominant narratives. These principles have privileged empathy over individualism, emotion over analysis, and effects over intentions. Their efforts to transcend the boundaries of dominant narratives have led them beyond history and myth to explore the sometimes dangerous terrain of counter-memory.

Counter-memory is a way of remembering and forgetting that starts with the local, the immediate, and the personal. Unlike historical narratives that begin with the totality of human existence and then locate specific actions and events within that totality, counter-memory starts with the particular and the specific and then builds outward toward a total story. Counter-memory looks to the past for the hidden histories excluded from dominant narratives. But unlike myths that seek to detach events and actions from the fabric of any larger history, counter-memory forces revision of existing histories by supplying new perspectives about the past. Counter-memory embodies aspects of myth and aspects of history, but it retains an enduring suspicion of both categories. Counter-memory focuses on localized experiences with oppression, using them to reframe and refocus dominant narratives purporting to represent universal experience.

My definition of counter-memory differs sharply from that used by Michel Foucault. In his view, counter-memory "must record the singularity of events outside of any monotonous finality." It must "cultivate the details and accidents that accompany every beginning," and it must describe "the endlessly repeated play of dominations."[4] Foucault's perspective offers an important critique of dominant ideology about myth and history, and it contains a healthy suspicion of totalizing narratives. Like Jean-François Lyotard, Foucault worries that historical writing tends to celebrate the oppressions of the past and present as necessary and inevitable. In addition, he fears that teleological thinking demands closure, that it requires disciplining the uncertainties of the present to conform to some *a priori* vision of the future. Yet in a world where dialogue, curiosity, and conflict create webs of interdependency, no single story can be understood except in relation to other stories. A "monotonous finality" could do violence to the "singularity of events," but refusal of all totality could just as easily obscure real connections, causes, and relationships—atomizing common experiences into accidents and endlessly repeated play. We may never succeed in creating a truly total story inclusive of the plurality of experiences on our planet, but the pursuit of such totality is essential. Only by recognizing the collective legacy of accumulated human actions and ideas can we judge the claims to truth and justice of any one story. We may never succeed in finding out all that has happened in history, but events matter and describing them as accurately as possible (although never with certain finality) can, at the very least, show us whose foot has been on whose neck.

Ever since the nineteenth century, the novel has been a crucial vehicle for intellectual exploration of the tensions between the past and present. The novel tends to question the appearances of everyday life, it presents conflicts between individual values and social reality, while reliance on speech and dialogue open it to traces of influences by many sectors of society. Counter-memory's delicate negotiation between local, immediate, and personal experiences and global, indirect, and social realities can be illustrated in five popular novels written since World War II by authors from marginalized communities. *Song of Solomon* by the Afro-American female writer Toni Morrison, *Losing Battles* by the southern, white female writer Eudora Welty, *Ceremony* by the Native American Indian female writer Leslie Marmon Silko, *No-No Boy* by the Japanese-American male writer John Okada, and *Bless Me Ultima* by the Chicano male writer Rudolfo Anaya all evidence the sense of counter-memory invoked in Hurston's introduction to *Their Eyes Were Watching God*.

These books speak to the needs of oppressed groups grappling with the hegemony of dominant narratives, but they also address the general contradictions and confusions of our time with unrivaled clarity and coherence. In the contemporary world, the bifocal and ironic sensibilities of marginalized groups take on new meaning because of their power in expressing the increasingly decentered and fragmented consciousness characteristic of the current era. The declining legitimacy of grand ideologies in both capitalist and communist countries, the role of the mass media in transcending time and space to fragment experience, and the loss of intimacy and identity engendered by bureaucratic mass societies have all contributed to a sense of alienation and displacement that in prior times primarily affected groups on the margins of society. But in our time, sensibilities nourished in the oral traditions of oppositional ethnic and racial communities, in the spheres of activity dominated by women, and in the subcultures of working-class life contain extraordinary significance. Thus, in recuperating strategies of story-telling from the past, Morrison, Welty, Silko, Okada, and Anaya not only tell the stories of particular oppressions, but they identify as well a use of the past that speaks to present day intellectual concerns with time, history, subjectivity, and fragmentation.

Beyond History and Myth

Contemporary novelists from marginalized cultures grapple with issues of consequence to everyone when they address the tensions between grand historical narratives and lived experience. Jean-François Lyotard identifies "an incredulity toward meta-narratives" as the operative principle of intellectual life in the world today. That incredulity poses particularly serious challenges to the legitimacy of both history and myth.[5] History is nothing if not a master narrative, a grand story that includes everyone whether they know it or not. Historians believe that time and chronology have meaning, that knowledge of the past enables people to place their "common sense" impressions of the world in a larger and truer context. As social historian Warren Susman explains in a formulaic statement

> It is history that can more reasonably explain the origin, the nature, and the function of various institutions and their interaction. Further, history seems able to point the direction in which a dynamic society is moving. It brings order out of the disordered array that is the consequence of change itself. As a result, history is often used as the basis for a philosophy that while explaining the past offers also a way to change the future.[6]

Susman realizes that his description undercuts any claim for history as trans-subjective or universal. For it is only in Western industrialized societies since the Enlightenment that this concept of history as an instrument of progress has taken root. Traditional societies often blur the distinction between the past and present, emphasizing the cyclical and repetitive aspects of human experience rather than its linear or teleological dimensions. On the other hand, what Susman calls "contract" societies—a short-hand term for Western capitalist countries—produce historical narratives that posit active and atomized individuals detachable from tradition, family identity, and ascribed roles.[7] Susman assumes that contract societies are superior to traditional ones; therefore he sees the decline of historical narratives in the West as a blow to progress and a barrier against positive future change. Yet Susman fails to acknowledge that the declining legitimacy of Western historical narratives is not just a reversion to a pre-modern consciousness; rather, it reflects an emerging critique of the inadequacies of contract societies and of the kinds of consciousness they nurture.

Unlike Susman, Hayden White, especially in his early writings on history, applauds the declining legitimacy of historical narratives. In White's view, history is an insidious fiction, a fabricated text passing for reality. White argues that historians impose a linear narrative on what is essentially a plural and nonlinear experience. He takes issue with formulations like Susman's that present history as a means of solving problems. To the contrary, White sees the thrall of history as a major barrier against action on immediate problems because the master narrative of history makes individual and local consciousness so insignificant. In addition, he sees in historical narratives a totalizing tendency, a compulsion to judge all actions by a single standard that in White's view can only encourage the powerful to impose their own self-interest on others in the name of "humanity."[8]

Yet for all its sensitivity to the totalitarian effects of historical narratives, White's critique does little to fashion a true and useful means of accounting for the accumulated legacy of human actions from the past that historical narratives generally encompass. The logical alternative to history is myth, a form of story-telling that goes beyond verifiable evidence to providing unifying symbols and rituals that enable people to interpret common experiences. Although often associated with pre-industrial peoples, myths flourish in modern societies as well, as even Warren Susman reluctantly concedes. In many ways, myths supersede history in contemporary popular consciousness.

Will Wright offers a useful explanation for this enduring power of myth in his exegesis of the Hollywood western film as one form of modern myth. Wright argues that

> For us the past is history; it is necessarily different from the present.
> ... But for this very reason, history is not enough: it can explain the
> present in terms of the past, but it cannot provide an indication of
> how to act in the present based on the past, since by definition the
> past is categorically different from the present. Myths use the past to
> tell us how to act in the present.[9]

Thus Wright reverses Susman's argument about utility and problem solving, claiming that it is myth rather than history which enables us to act in the present. But Wright also acknowledges the conservative nature of this kind of mythology. Because myth emphasizes the eternal and the cyclical, it speaks more to reconciliation with existing power realities than to challenges against them. Myth provides legitimation for the world as it is; it reconciles people to the disparity between their desires and their opportunities. Roland Barthes contends that myth functions primarily as a means for rendering "natural" and consequently inevitable that which is social and subject to revision. In this way, myth can explain the past and order the present, but it does so only by accepting the inevitability of the status quo.[10] History, on the other hand, involves a search for hidden truths and a look beyond surface appearances. History explores how things came to be, and it inevitably confronts all the roads not taken and all the blasted hopes of the past. It enables us to judge competing myths by a single standard, that of factual investigation into the accumulated consequences of past actions. If myth enables us to live with our pain by naturalizing it, history encourages us to ease our pain by understanding it intellectually and analytically.

In an age of incredulity toward meta-narratives, neither myth nor history can adequately order or explain experience. History's connection to contract societies with their instrumental and utilitarian philosophies prevents it from fully airing the continuities of human striving masked by narratives of progress. But mythical constructs with their emphasis on repetition and cycles tend to account for rupture, conflict, and change inadequately. The sense of change over time employed in the five novels that form the object of this study is neither historical nor mythical. Rather, they draw upon oral traditions and historical experiences to fashion the time of counter-memory. They challenge traditional Western historical narratives, but not out of an unwillingness to solve problems or a denial of the connections that bind all human beings together. On the contrary, they seek to expand the scope of history by reconnecting with experiences and emotions rendered invisible by the ideology of individualism and by the privileging of power common to historical stories as they are told within contract societies.

The Burden of History

In *The Song of Solomon*, Toni Morrison takes aim at the nature of historical evidence by means of a story about the giving of names. Her protagonist suffers from the embarrassing name "Macon Dead III." When the young man inquires how his grandfather acquired such an unflattering appellation, his father explains that it came from a drunken white man representing the U.S. government. The father relates

> He asked Papa where he was born. Papa said Macon. Then he asked
> him who his father was, Papa said, "He's dead." Asked him who
> owned him, Papa said "I'm free." Well, the Yankee wrote it all down,
> but in the wrong spaces. Had him born in Dunfrie, wherever the hell
> that is, and in the space for his name the fool wrote "Dead" comma
> Macon.[11]

In this instance, the written tradition of historical evidence obscures total confusion by turning it into a seemingly immutable fact, while the oral tradition of myth explains what really happened. Of course, Macon has no particular reason to trust his father's version of the story which comes from an oral tradition with a fanciful sense of invention of its own. But his contemporary experiences as an Afro-American encourage Macon Dead III to distrust authority and the written word on which it relies, while vital information about his identity comes to him through the oral tradition throughout the novel.

In *Song of Solomon*, people and objects have meaning only as they bridge the past and the present. Milkman Dead has access to his father's money and property, but they only deepen his anomie by hiding knowledge of his history. Only when Milkman embarks on a quest to find out the truth about the past can he live effectively in the present. By deciphering what critic Susan Willis calls "the twin texts of history: song and genealogy," Milkman manages to "unlearn" both false family narratives and malicious untruths of history. He discovers an Afro-American history that predates slavery and in it, a capacity to flee from oppression by recognizing it as such.

Traditional historical evidence also emerges as unreliable in Eudora Welty's *Losing Battles*. Faced with Enlightenment rationality as personified in the local school teacher and the local judge, a rural Mississippi family clings to the subjectivity of their oral tradition. When the judge tries to read them a letter, they protest the primacy he gives to the written word. "I can't understand it when he reads it to us," one of them complains. "Can't he just tell it?"[12] Similarly, the family constructs a young woman's identity out of speculation and memory in defiance of the "evidence" presented to them by the judge. He complains that they cannot possibly know her true identity because there are no birth certificates or marriage licenses to confirm the family's claim. He ridicules their interpretation of a scrawled message on a postcard which they interpret as evidence of her patrimony. The judge says, "But a postcard isn't the same evidence as a license to marry, or a marriage certificate; and even that—," but one of the relatives interrupts him, saying "It's better! There's a whole lot more . . . in that postcard if you know how to read it."[13]

The argument in *Losing Battles* is less about the nature of evidence than it is about the necessity of interpreting it. Welty presents both oral and written sources as valid and invalid; each has strengths and weaknesses. Problems arise when individuals privilege one kind of evidence over the other, when they refuse to interpret information actively and creatively. Thus the rural family immerses itself in lies and rationalizations because their desires conflict with the known facts of linear history. But, on the other hand, the school teacher and the judge devote themselves so thoroughly to the primacy of written evidence that they cut themselves off from other people and their desires.

Welty encapsulates the battle between linear history and nonlinear myth in a conversation among members of the family circle concerning the teacher, Miss Julia Mortimer. In that exchange, Gloria Short tells Jack that the teacher wanted "everything brought out in the wide open, to see and be known. She wanted people to spread out their minds and their hearts to other people so they could be read like books." Jack Renfro says that Miss Mortimer must have been wise like Solomon, but Gloria replies "No, people don't want to be read like books."[14] For to be read like books is to acquire a static and impersonal identity.

The kind of history that gives each individual a separate and autonomous story that can be validated in marriage licenses and birth certificates is a history that denies intersubjectivity—the ways in which people shape and transform each other through collectively authored stories. Yet Welty insists that nonlinear histories preserved through oral traditions also distort and demean the human condition. The myths and mappings of the Beacham family produce a localized tyranny of misunderstanding and misreading. Political allegiances become matters of kinship. Individuals become defined by their places in family narratives rather than by what they actually do and think. Life and death issues of survival become clouded by paralyzing myths rooted in ignorance and deliberate misreadings of evidence. As Jennifer Randisi shows in her extraordinary critique of Welty, there is no winner in the battle between myth and history in *Losing Battles*. But there is something to be gleaned from the strengths of each form and something to be salvaged from the clash between them. That something, a blend of myth and history, belongs to the category of counter-memory.

A similar conflict between myth and history provides the operative tension in Native American Indian author Leslie Marmon Silko's *Ceremony*. In her story, a half-breed part Laguna Pueblo Indian works through his alienation from linear history and the scientific Enlightenment world view behind it. Much of Tayo's personal pain comes from experiences that we might consider historical—combat during World War II, captivity as a prisoner of war, incarceration in a mental hospital after his service as he attempts to accept the death of his brother in battle and to readjust to civilian life. His identity as a Native American forces Tayo to confront one other monstrous historical crime—the conquest and settlement of his native land by Americans of European ancestry.

Tayo's cultural clash with Anglo society revolves around questions of citizenship, property, and self-respect, but he experiences the con-

flict most directly as a battle about *which* stories are to be believed—
the mystical, mythical, and spiritual stories that order experience
along empathetic lines, or the linear, scientific, and historical "facts"
that keep the world divided. Tayo remembers being told that anything could be accomplished if one knew the stories from the past—
"If a person wanted to get to the moon, there was a way; it all depended on whether you knew the story of how others before you
had gone. He had believed in the stories for a long time, until the
teachers at the Indian School taught him not to believe."[15] By teaching him not to believe in superstition, the school authorities take
away Tayo's belief that his problems can be solved; they tell him that
the stories of the past must yield to the hegemony of historical and
scientific facts. In the world of the school, as well as in the world of
the army and the mental hospital, Tayo encounters the forces of division: dividing the past from the present, animals from people, people from the land, and people from one another. As he recalls when
thinking about school,

> The science books explained the causes and effects. But old
> Grandma always used to say, "Back in time immemorial, things were
> different, the animals could talk to human beings and many magical
> things still happened." He never lost the feeling he had in his chest
> when she spoke those words, as she did each time she told them the
> stories; and he still felt it was true, despite all they had taught him in
> school—that long ago things had been different.[16]

Yet while linear history and scientific thought provide barriers to
true understanding for Tayo, they are not irrelevant to his search for
truth and empowerment. The consequences of history cannot be ignored; the conquest of the Southwest, the war with Japan, and the
enduring racism of postwar America offer specific historical oppressions in need of historical understanding. To retreat into a localized
world of magic and tradition offers no solution to Tayo, because that
retreat would not explain or even address the root causes of his pain.
In addition, even the Indian "ceremonies" he tries have lost much of
their power because they have not been changed to fit new circumstances. Only a medicine man outside his own tribe can lead him to
the truth, a truth which involves a critical stance toward both Indian
myth and Anglo-European history. As Tayo realizes, "The liars had

fooled everyone, white people and Indians alike; as long as people believed the lies, they would never be able to see what had been done to them or what they were doing to each other."[17]

Only by combining myth and history can Tayo create a useful synthesis for understanding and action. The very forces of science and rationality responsible for division in his world also provide the possibility for ending division. Tayo understands that science has created a peculiar kind of unity in the modern world, because everyone is united in fear of a nuclear holocaust. The ancient minerals of his native New Mexico provide the elements for the epitome of scientific rationality, the atom bomb. Yet in creating a device with sufficient destructive power to destroy the whole world, the scientists have also restored ancient unities. Silko explains Tayo's perception of these unities by telling us

> There was no end to it; it knew no boundaries; and he had arrived at the point of convergence where the fate of all living things, and even the earth had been laid. From the jungles of his dreaming he recognized why the Japanese voices had merged with Laguna voices, with Josiah's voice and Rocky's voice: the lines of cultures and worlds were drawn in flat dark lines on fine light sand, converging in the middle of witchery's final ceremonial sand painting. From that time on, human beings were one clan again, united by the fate the destroyers planned for all of them, for all living things; united by a circle of death that devoured people in cities twelve thousand miles away, victims who had never seen the delicate colors of the rocks which boiled up their slaughter.[18]

The horrible power of the atomic bomb undermines the legitimacy of Enlightenment rationality, enabling Tayo to understand his own history for the first time. Because his story has been ostracized from or trivialized within the master narratives, he understands the evils of exclusion and trivialization as basic flaws in the system of Western thought. Yet rather than accepting or celebrating his marginality through a "delight in difference" as the postmodernists might advise, he struggles for a unity capable of overcoming centuries of division. In the mental hospital the white doctors try to cure Tayo by urging him to accept divisions, to adjust to his differences. But he comes to the realization that "medicine didn't work that way" and instead insists that "his cure could be found only in something great and inclusive of everything."[19]

A history that built its synthesis from the plural and diverse experiences of people like Tayo would be that "something great and inclusive of everything." Tayo's desire to understand both his personal crises and the oppression of his people through the interaction of grand and small narratives embodies the essence of counter-memory. His way of thinking recaptures the totalizing imperatives of historical thought, but grounds them in the plurality of particular oppressions. Counter-memory in this sense is not a denial of history, only a rejection of its false priorities and hierarchical divisions. In the modern world, marginal and excluded people like Tayo take on particularly important roles in reclaiming historical thought because their experiences make them uniquely sensitive to the diversities upon which a new unity might be built.

Marginalized and excluded groups also understand the shortcomings of the categories and labels employed within dominant narratives. Just as Macon Dead could not trust the name he had been given by the historical record in *Song of Solomon*, Tayo cannot accept the narrow range of identities open to him as a Native American Indian stereotyped and defined by the conquerors of his people. Barbara Christian points out that Afro-American female writers like herself must see beyond existing categories because their lives are more complex than the available descriptions and definitions applied to them. Christian writes, "Our expression of our lives cannot be narrowly conceived, for we cannot change our condition through a single minded banner."[20] Learning the truths of history for marginalized groups demands a complex negotiation between the legacy of historical events that affect everyone and the partial and limited accounts of those events that make up the historical record as authored by dominant groups. But women writers and authors from other aggrieved populations often have specific resources for managing that negotiation. "Such complexity," Christian contends, "is not confusion. It is that feeling awareness which June Jordan expresses in her 'Declaration,' the interconnectedness of supposed opposites, of mental knowledge and feeling knowledge, of the self and of the other."[21]

The sense of counter-memory that informs the work of women writers like Hurston, Morrison, Welty, and Silko also pervades the writings of male authors from ethnic communities. Japanese-American writer John Okada and Chicano novelist Rudolfo Anaya provide particularly strong presentations of counter-memory as a means of reclaiming historical thinking from contexts created by dominant narratives. In their writings, a complex search for identity includes explorations into history that require more information than the written record can supply. For Okada as a Japanese-American and Anaya as a Mexican-American, ethnicity is a story filled with ambiguities and contradictions, not a static fact. To be an ethnic American for these authors is to be involved in a delicate set of relationships among multiple identities, to sort through the many competing stories that make up any one individual's story.

In Okada's *No-No Boy*, a son of Japanese immigrants finds himself torn between two cultures. The outbreak of war between the U.S. and Japan presents Ichiro Yamada with difficult choices, and underscores his uncertain relationship to both countries. The American government sends him and his family to an internment camp, where his mother prays for Japan to win the war. In an exercise of filial piety, Ichiro defers to his mother's wishes and refuses the army's offer to release him from the camp if he will accept service in the military. Thus he is a "No-No Boy," one who refuses to serve in the army. But still, he cannot accept his mother's view of Japan as a sacred homeland. Ichiro believes himself to be an American, even when his ethnicity and his own actions prevent him from being accepted as one.

The consequences of historical events — migrations from Asia to North America, war between America and Japan, and the anti-Japanese racism of the war and postwar years — combine to pose difficult questions of personal identity for Ichiro. Where does he fit into these quarrels not of his own making? He cannot attribute his problems simply to Japanese ancestry; he knows that his refusal to serve in the military brings him scorn from many other Japanese-Americans. Yet he knows that his people face suffering no matter what their choices. Like Tayo's brother Rocky in *Ceremony*, all the Japanese-Americans in *No-No Boy* who volunteer for army service are destroyed. Ichiro's friend Bob Kumasaka goes into the army and gets killed in combat. His friend Kenji serves gallantly only to die of war wounds on his return home. Kenji even tells Ichiro that refusing induction was the right choice, but Ichiro wishes in some ways that he could change places with Kenji. The reality for all of them is that there are no uniformly good choices, because they are all subject to forces beyond their control. But like Tayo in *Ceremony*, Ichiro survives only when he realizes that his pain and his marginality help him acquire wisdom about the nature of American identity.

Okada presents some kind of larger unity as the solution to the pain of marginality and division. But he does not call for assimilation into the dominant society or for an acceptance of dominant historical narratives. Rather, he demands that society and history acknowledge the truths found in experiences deemed marginal. Ichiro Yamada sees that the monolithic appearance of America is a lie; his own exclusion is merely symptomatic of all who have been left out. At one point Ichiro asks

> Where is that place they talk of and paint nice pictures of and describe in all the homey magazines? Where is that place with the clean white cottages surrounding the new, red-brick church with the clean white steeple, where the families all have two children, one boy and one girl, and a shiny new car in the garage and a dog and a cat and life is like living in the land of the happily ever after.

He the answers his own question with a suggestion,

> Maybe the answer is that there is no in. Maybe the whole damned country is pushing and shoving and screaming to get into someplace that doesn't exist, because they don't know that the outside would be the inside if only they would stop all this pushing and shoving and screaming, and they haven't got enough sense to realize that.[22]

But acting upon that answer proves more difficult than Ichiro anticipates. By the end of the novel he remains convinced that "the margins are at the center" as Derrida might put it, but that it is dangerous to pretend that the established center no longer exists. Ichiro seeks to reconstruct the center, to build a new consensus based on the utility and wisdom of marginalized perspectives. Using his own history of exclusion as a guide, he begins to understand other excluded individuals and groups. He cannot accept the "history" that relegates him to marginal status, but neither can he escape its consequences. Instead, Ichiro mixes his subjective understandings of his own oppression with objective evidence about the pain suffered by others. In this way, memories are not barriers to understanding; rather, they make it possible for Ichiro to understand his immediate experience and to move beyond it.

Like Okada, Rudolfo Anaya tells a story about ethnic American counter-memory in his novel *Bless Me Ultima*. Anaya's Antonio Marez confronts the same kinds of competing stories that confound the identity of the protagonists in *Ceremony* and *No-No Boy*. Antonio is Mexican and American, Catholic and pagan, Indian and Spaniard, promising student to his teachers and potential priest to his mother. The narratives surrounding Antonio's life force him to choose between languages, flags, religions, philosophies, and histories. Antonio's journey toward self-awareness revolves around his growing recognition that these choices are false, that he cannot give up any of them. Instead, he learns to step in and out of identities in order to fabricate a multi-layered consciousness reflective of his true history as the product of many cultures.

Given the sensitivity to these issues of multiple identity among female novelists, it seems particularly significant that a male author like Anaya chooses to embody wisdom in Ultima, the oldest female character in the book and the person who teaches Antonio that the highest truths involve connections to others. Ultima sees the unity of opposites and reconciles magic and science, paganism and Catholicism, and even men and women. Unlike Antonio's mother and father who want him to obliterate contradictions by choosing one side or the other, Ultima teaches Antonio to embrace contradictions, to use the divisions created by history without succumbing to their oppressions.

Yet Ultima also encourages Antonio to fashion a new synthesis by drawing on the past. As Antonio relates

> Ultima told me the stories and legends of my ancestors. From her I learned the glory and the tragedy of the history of my people, and I came to understand that history stirred in my blood.[23]

But like Tayo and Ichiro, Antonio cannot find the answer in difference and division. Ultima comes to him in a dream and explains, "You have been seeing only parts, . . . and not looking beyond into the great cycle that binds us all."[24] It is in looking at the great cycle that binds us all that counter-memory surpasses history and myth, that it transcends the false closures of linear history and the destructive ruptures and divisions of myth to create an active memory which draws upon the pluralities of the past and present to illumine the opportunities of the future.

Counter-Memory and History

Thus counter-memory is not a rejection of history, but a reconstitution of it. As Barbara Christian says on behalf of black women writers,

> It is the resonance of history that lets us know we are here. Memory not only reproduces the past, it gives us guides by which to evaluate the present, and helps to create the future, which is an illusionary concept unless we know that yesterday we saw the present as the future. It is not surprising then that contemporary Afro-American women writers have spent so much energy on reclaiming their history, so disrupted and ignored by both black and white scholarship.[25]

The truths of history that mean so much to Afro-American women also compel the attentions of white Southern women, Native American Indian women, and men from marginalized ethnic communities. By dwelling on difference and disunity, by playing myth against history, writers like Morrison, Welty, Silko, Okada, and Anaya have pointed the way toward a new synthesis, one that offers dignity interchangeably to all peoples without first forcing them into an imaginary identity constructed from a top-down perspective on human experience.

In his extraordinary book on modernism and postmodernism, *All That Is Solid Melts Into Air*, Marshall Berman argues

> Modern environments and experiences cut across all boundaries of geography and ethnicity, of class and nationality, of religion and ideology; in this sense modernity can be said to unite all mankind. But it is a paradoxical unity, a unity of disunity: it pours us all into a maelstrom of perpetual disintegration and renewal, of struggle and contradiction, of ambiguity and anguish. To be modern is to be part of a universe in which, as Marx said, "all that is solid melts into air."[26]

Cultural conservatives like Christopher Lasch bemoan the declining authority of traditional history in the modern world; they see the rise of counter-memory as a threat to knowledge and order, as a kind of contamination originating among the underclass and spreading to the rest of the population. As Lasch writes, "The poor have always had to live for the present, but now a desperate concern for personal survival, sometimes disguised as hedonism, engulfs the middle class as well. Today everyone lives in a dangerous world from which there is little escape."[27] Lasch's fear is that the middle and upper classes have sunk to the intellectual and cultural levels traditionally reserved for the poor and exploited. There is some truth in his assessment, but his pejorative description of the poor and their cultures prevents him from seeing the positive things they have to offer to displaced elites. The modern world described by Berman and Lasch does place a priority on the consciousness and perspectives developed over centuries by oppressed groups. They are the people who have had to develop dual and triple consciousnesses, who have had to live with the consequences of history, and who have had to find their identities in stories that never mentioned them. Out of necessity they have learned about both the pain and pleasure of division. But rather than impoverishing knowledge about the past as Lasch fears, the traditions of counter-memory provide for the first time an accounting of some of the complexities of collective experience.

By combining linear history and orally transmitted popular history, counter-memory combines the best of both modes. If counter-memory lacks the traditional truth tests of evidence basic to linear histories, it also subjects itself to an even more rigorous test—the standard of collective memory and desire. For these narratives to succeed, they must resonate with the experiences and feelings of their audiences. For them to succeed completely, they must address the part of audience memory in touch with real historical oppressions and memories. Authors take great risks when they draw upon oral traditions; they surrender some of their individual control over the text to the contours and demands of collective memory. But that very surrender of authority brings them closer to truth. As anthropologist James Clifford asks, "If we are condemned to tell stories we cannot control, may we not, at least, tell stories we believe to be true?"[28]

Women's Time and Counter-Memory

When Zora Neale Hurston wrote about men finding their dreams mocked to death by Time (using the upper case), she implied that women confront another kind of time. Julia Kristeva in her essay "Women's Time" offers a contemporary reformulation of the uses of time propounded by Hurston. Kristeva asserts that women find themselves torn between two kinds of time—cursive time and monumental time. Cursive time, the time of linear history, is important to women because it is there that sexism and discrimination become inscribed in state policies. In Kristeva's view, the first stage of the women's movement battled for inclusion in cursive time by demanding public political action against juridical and economic discrimination. Monumental time, the time of life cycles and private rituals, is important to women because it is there that private and personal spheres of autonomy are carved away within the constraints of male hegemony. Kristeva sees the second stage of the women's movement as oriented toward monumental time through demands for recognition of "the specificity of female psychology and its symbolic realizations" and through its efforts to "give a language to the intrasubjective and corporeal experiences left mute by culture in the past."[29] Thus Kristeva argues that women must understand both the time of men and the time of women, a parallel to the efforts by novelists using counter-memory to understand both the linear history of contract societies and the oral traditions of aggrieved populations.

But this dual consciousness is not enough. Left separate, these two spheres cancel each other out. Exclusive focus on cursive time obscures the resources and institutions nurtured by ritual and myth. Exclusive focus on monumental time obscures the institutional and structural forces of oppression that constrain local subjectivities. What Kristeva calls "women's time" is also the time of other oppressed and marginalized groups. It is the essence of counter-memory. Counter-memory understands the limits of historical time, but still tries to act within it. Counter-memory celebrates the subversive visions and stubborn *jouissance* of monumental time while still insisting on relating local oppositional practices to macro-social causes and consequences.

Literature plays a special role in the articulation of counter-memory. As public texts touching audiences with historical memories, popular novels have some responsibility for historical accuracy in order to be perceived as credible. At the very least, they cannot disregard collective historical memory. On the other hand, as works of art and imagination, they are not bound by the constraints of public records and verifiable evidence as would be the case for historical scholarship. They belong to a realm between myth and history, and they present a world view that mediates between the two. It is literature that brings out the hidden resources of collective historical memory. As Kristeva asks

> Is it because, faced with social norms, literature reveals a certain knowledge and sometimes the truth itself about an otherwise repressed, nocturnal, secret, and unconscious universe? Because it thus redoubles the social contract by exposing the unsaid, the uncanny? And because it makes a game, a space of fantasy and pleasure, out of the abstract, and frustrating order of social signs, the world of everyday communication?[30]

Kristeva's implied answer to her own rhetorical questions is an affirmative one, and her insights apply not only to popular literature but to the entire concept of popular culture.

In what sense are the novels by Morrison, Welty, Silko, Okada, and Anaya "popular?" They each appear in mass-market paperback editions, although Okada's and Anaya's are published by small presses. None of them have been commercially successful enough to make the top of the best-seller lists, and all have received critical acclaim from scholars and critics. Yet they do not fall into the realm of "high" culture; they do not attempt to live up to the codes of transcendent truth, of embodying the best and highest that civilization might imagine, as was true of elite culture in the nineteenth century. These novels, like so much else in popular culture, seem to lie in a sphere with no name. They are not folklore or disposable mass commercial art, but neither are they works clamoring for admission to the rarified canon of great art. In that sense, they are like their protagonists; composed of multiple and contradictory identities, hailed and classified by categories with real social power but which also obscure their own intentions and aims.

Traditional categories of classification cannot encompass the structure and aims of novels employing counter-memory, just as they cannot encompass other forms of popular culture from the romance novel to the rock-and-roll song to the "B" movie. All these forms share aspects of counter-memory; they can be considered "popular" not because of the sheer numbers of people who consume them, but, rather, because of certain sensibilities that occupy a central place within them. They all draw upon oral traditions, vernacular speech, and a focus on the immediate and ordinary concerns of everyday life.

Most important, they tap sources of collective popular memory to identify the repressed and suppressed traditions of resistance to oppression. While originating in local, particular, and specific experiences, they use modern means of communication to reach out to other groups and individuals with similar, though perhaps not identical oppressions and aspirations.

Cultural conservatives who bemoan the loss of historical consciousness in the modern world seriously misread the texts of popular culture. Certainly, dominant historical narratives have lost much of their legitimacy. But within the interstices of popular culture, a rich collective counter-memory carries on the tasks of historical thinking in new and significant ways.

Fredric Jameson understands the presence of this sedimented historical tradition when he argues that all works of popular culture have utopian dimensions that enable them to critique contemporary power relations. But even Jameson relegates the historical work of popular culture to a "political unconscious," an uncomprehending desire to give concrete form to the absent cause that might make sense out of the incoherence of a world without believable historical narratives. But the "empty chair" that Jameson believes to be waiting for a future history and politics is already occupied. The qualities that Kristeva attributes solely to literature exist within many forms of popular culture. They contain many limitations, shortcomings, and contradictions. But in their focus on counter-memory, they draw upon an oppositional cultural practice deeply rooted in art, in history, and in popular collective consciousness. In the midst of division and disunity, they dare to imagine a world in which everyone's wishes may come in with the tide.

10

Mardi Gras Indians:
Carnival and Counter-Narrative
in Black New Orleans

"It cannot be easy to move from oppression and its mythologies to resistance in history; a detour through a no-man's land or threshold area of counter-myth and symbolisation is necessary."

Laura Mulvey[1]

More than fifty years ago, alarmed by the rise of commercial culture and the attendant eclipse of literature and folklore, the great cultural critic Walter Benjamin envisioned a world without stories. Benjamin complained that in such a world, "It is as if something that seemed inalienable to us, the securest of our possessions, were taken from us; the ability to exchange experiences." Certainly, subsequent events have more than justified Benjamin's pessimism.[2] Social and economic changes have undermined the ascribed roles and inherited customs historically responsible for most story-telling traditions. A commodified mass-culture industry covers the globe, replacing traditional narratives with mass-produced spectacles, while the "ability to exchange experiences" often degenerates into the necessity to consume the same cultural commodities.

Yet story-telling persists, even inside the apparatuses of commerical mass culture. Indeed, commerical culture expressly depends upon the residues of local popular narratives for its determinate forms and themes. Blues and reggae music form the unacknowledged subtext of most contemporary popular music. Suppressed ethnic, class, and gender rage undergirds much of the comedy displayed on motion-picture screens around the world, while vernacular art and popular oral traditions provide the raw materials for much of mass culture's visual and aural stimuli.[3] Outside of popular culture, personal and collective memories of region, race, class, gender, and ethnicity continue to provide the raw materials for shared stories. But the pervasiveness of popular narrative forms and themes is not just a matter of the sedimented residue of historical communities and cultures. Mass society and commercial culture provoke a new popular narrative response, one that draws upon both old and new forms of cultural creation. By circulating the stories of particular communities and cultures to a mass audience, the culture industry invites comparison, interpretation, and elaboration. Culture consumers find profound meaning in stories fashioned outside their own communities, and they inevitably re-examine their own traditions in light of what they discover about other cultures.

Sensitive and sympathetic cultural critics have vested great hopes in the enduring emancipatory potential of popular narratives. In his extraordinary review essay, "Western Marxism and Folklore," José Limon argues that popular self-generating cultural expressions and performances can challenge the hegemony of the dominant commercial culture by presenting cultural creations as having an organic "use" value, rather than just a commercial "exchange" value. Limon quotes with approval Michel de Certeau's contentions that these kinds of cultural performances contain political meaning, and that they exist not just in the fading memories of marginalized groups, but "in the strongholds of the contemporary economy."[4] Fredric Jameson's germinal article "Reification and Utopia in Mass Culture" insists that all popular-culture texts contain a radical utopian kernel that contrasts the indignities of the present social order with the possibilities for happiness conjured up by collective and individual imagination.[5] Similarly, in his persuasive discussion of "Folklore and Fakelore," William Fox contends that even with a decline in identification with the traditional sources of popular narratives — region, occupation, race, ethnicity, and religion — contemporary society offers new possibilities for sources of identity, possibilities likely to produce stories underscoring the tensions between lived experience and the self-congratulatory propaganda for the status quo that is generated from within the culture industry.[6]

The Mardi Gras Indians of New Orleans offer an important illustration of the persistence of popular narratives in the modern world, providing a useful case study about the emancipatory potential of grass-roots cultural creation. Every Mardi Gras day, "tribes" of anywhere from fifteen to thirty working-class, black males dress as Plains Indians and take to the streets of New Orleans. They parade through black neighborhoods, displaying their costumes and flags, singing and chanting in a specialized argot, while treating themselves to the hospitality offered in neighborhood bars and private homes. The Indians work all year designing and sewing their costumes, but generally they show them in public only on Mardi Gras Day and St.Joseph's Day. Organized into a rigid status hierarchy of official positions (spy boy, flag boy, wild man, third chief, second chief, big chief, and council chief), the tribes celebrate their own worthiness in chants and songs, while remaining vigilant for competing tribes who might challenge them with aggressive word play to compare costumes, dances, or singing and rhyming ability.[7] Although tribe members must be chosen directly by the group leader, the organizations represent entire neighborhoods. They practice all year in neighborhood bars, and they draw a group of neighborhood residents into the streets behind them as a "second line" of supportive singers and dancers.[8]

On the surface, the core practices of the Mardi Gras Indians resemble quite conventional behaviors by other groups. Under the aegis of carnival, they form secret societies, wear flamboyant costumes, speak a specialized language, and celebrate a fictive past. Carnival revelers all around the world engage in the same practices to release tension from the repressions and frustrations of everyday life. But what distinguishes the Mardi Gras Indians is their use of conventional forms for unconventional purposes. Drawing upon dominant icons and images, they invert them and subvert them. What for other groups might be a symbolic and temporary release from deep-seated repressions functions very differently for the Indian tribes. Rather than merely expressing utopian desires, the Indian spectacle gives coded expression to values and beliefs that operate every day in the lives of black workers in New Orleans. Although it takes place in response to the rituals and timetables of European carnival traditions, the Indian spectacle is not primarily European. It presents visual and narrative references to Native American Indians, but it bears little resemblance to genuine Indian celebrations and ceremonies. It draws its determinate modes of expression from African culture and philosophy, but it is not a purely African ritual. Instead, it projects a cultural indeterminacy, picking and choosing from many traditions to fashion performances and narratives suitable for arbitrating an extraordinarily complex identity.

The working-class blacks who create the Mardi Gras Indian tribes collectively author an important narrative about their own past, present, and future. Drawing upon the tools available to them—music, costumes, speech, and dance—they fashion a fictive identity that gives voice to their deepest values and beliefs. They replicate many traditional folk practices such as the aggressive festivity of carnival, the ritualistic observance of holidays, and the celebration of a heroic lineage. They tap literary and oral traditions of story-telling through song lyrics, chants, word games, and names. But their collective narrative goes beyond literature and folklore. It draws upon a myriad of contradictory images and icons to fashion a syncretic unity. In the aesthetics of their performance, the Mardi Gras Indians balance the competing claims of commerical culture and folk culture, of America and Africa, of resistance and accommodation, and of spontaneity and calculation. Their art stems less from ancient story-telling traditions or aesthetic intentions than from the necessity imposed upon them by oppressive social conditions. Their utopian projections originate less from abstract images of an ideal future than from a determination to read the lessons of solidarity and struggle from the past and present into the future. If the practices of story-telling, and the qualities of criticism and creativity embedded with them, are to survive in the modern world, it will likely be through the multidimensional practices of artists and individuals like the Mardi Gras Indians.

The Mardi Gras Indian narrative does not always take the form of pure narrative—of a sequence of events taking place over time in a cause-and-effect relationship—but its central recurring theme is a story of heroic warriors resisting domination. The Indians tell about past Mardi Gras days when challenges from other groups forced them to bring to the surface the bravery and solidarity they must repress in everyday life. Song lyrics, chants, and costumes celebrate brave tribes who "won't kneel, won't bow, and don't know how."[9] This Indian imagery draws upon many sources. In slavery times, Indian communities offered blacks a potential alternative to a society in which to be black was to be a slave and to be white was to be free. In New Orleans, black slaves mingled with Indians in local markets, and interactions between Native American Indians and blacks gave many

Louisiana blacks a historical claim to a joint Indian and Afro-American heritage. In addition, more than twenty black spiritualist churches in New Orleans venerate the Native American Indian Chief Black Hawk as a martyr, in keeping with the teachings of Leith Anderson, a half Mohawk woman who preached the doctrine of "spirit returning." But the evidence tying the Mardi Gras Indians to direct Indian ancestry is slight.[10] New Orleans "tribes" wear the headresses and costumes of Plains Indians, not of Southeastern Indians, and with the exception of some styles of bead work, few of their practices replicate the crafts of local Native American Indian tribes. South American and Caribbean carnival traditions feature Indians prominently, and some of the New Orleans chants more closely resemble French and Spanish carnival phrases than they do any known Native American Indian tongue.[11] As one Mardi Gras Indian told a researcher

> We're not real Indians, we just masquerade as Indians really, and we
> just give our tribe a name, and different positions and things like
> that. But as for real Indians, like you'd have to go to Arizona or Texas
> or something like that to talk to a real Indian, and on a reservation
> or something like that, but he wouldn't tell you the things I'm telling
> you because what we're doing is just something that we copies
> behind the Indians really.[12]

In fact, the touring "Wild West" shows of Buffalo Bill Cody and other late nineteenth-century popular culture entrepreneurs were probably the real impetus for the creation of these mock Indian tribes. Carnival parades in New Orleans began in 1827, but blacks did not generally dress up as Indians until Becate Batiste formed the Creole Wild West tribe in the early 1880s.[13] Donning headdresses and face paint enabled Afro-Americans to circumvent the local laws that made it illegal for blacks to wear masks, but the Indian imagery held important symbolic meaning for them as well. One former Chief of the Golden Blades tribe suggests that *both* blood ties and consumer tastes played a role in the formation of an early Indian tribe, telling a reporter, "In 1895, Robert Sam Tillman got the idea to mask Injun by seeing a Wild West show that came through N'Awlins. Brother Tillman came from Indians himself, and in 1897 he started the [Yellow] Pocahontas tribe."[14] But to see the identification with Indian culture as more a matter of choice than a matter of blood lines hardly lessens its significance. While carnival masking for all groups proclaims a generalized "right to be other" (as Bakhtin asserts), the Mardi Gras Indians adopt a very specific sense of otherness. Most other carnival celebrants might dress as pirates or crows or cowboys in any given year to escape from their everyday identities, but the Indians are always Indians. Furthermore, the Indian image calls attention to the initial genocide upon which American "civilization" rests. It challenges the core dualism of American racism that defines people as either white or black. To perpetuate collective consciousness about Indians in this context is to perpetuate memories about runaway slaves seeking shelter. Other revelers may use carnival masking to escape the repressions of their everyday existence, but the Indian tribes' disguise brings out into the open dimensions of repression that the dominant culture generally tries to render invisible. Of course, this kind of inversion runs the risk of being captured by the very forms it seeks to satirize. Native American viewers might not appreciate the Mardi Gras Indian appropriation of demeaning stereotypes; too many groups in American history have used the image of the Indian for their own purposes, and what comprises symbolic emancipation for one group might consequently oppress another. But images in negotiation with power are often ambiguous, complicated, and implicated in the crimes they seek to address.

In both content and form of presentation, the Mardi Gras Indian narratives and imagery revolve around self-affirmation and solidarity. Members of Indian tribes might be construction workers, dock hands, bakers, or porters oppressed by both their race and their class in everyday life, but in their rehearsals and performances as Indians they become part of a community of resistance and self-affirmation. They treat life as precious, celebrating its joys and pleasures, even while mourning the dead. Their song lyrics, costumes, speech, and dances all reinforce the same values—grace, strength, elegance, precision, happiness, composure, and dignity.[15] But the key to their collective story rests in more than specific words and images; it comes from the aesthetics of their performance. The Mardi Gras Indian narrative is eloquent and compelling because the forms used to convey it correspond to its basic message, and because the daily lived experience of its adherents reinforces its core values.

In its aesthetics, the Mardi Gras Indian narrative resonates with the culture and philosophy of African music. Of course, they are Afro-

Americans and make distinctly Afro-American music, but the Africanisms within Mardi Gras Indian music raise important ideological and
artistic issues. Ethnomusicologist John Miller Chernoff identifies the
definitive feature of the African musical sensibility as a "functional
integration" of music and culture. In African communities, audience
handclapping is seen as a vital part of a musical performance, not
merely a response by the spectators. Similarly, during African rituals,
music is joined with dance, drama, and visual representation to form
a fused art made up of interdependent elements. These musical performances blend with lived experiences, accompanying day-to-day
events rather than providing a break from them as a self-conscious
form of leisure or enlightenment. Finally, music-making in Africa is a
functional group activity—a means for organizing and communicating tradition by giving different social groups rights and privileges
connected to specific songs.[16]

The Mardi Gras Indian ritual draws upon these African sensibilities
in significant ways. The neighborhood residents who attend weekly
practice sessions and who follow the tribes into the streets as their
"second line" function as active participants in the performance, not
just as passive spectators. Second liners beat on bottles with sticks,
shake tambourines attached to long poles, and dance to rhythmic
chants in an interactive call and response with the singers and dancers in the tribe. Years ago, the second line had an additional
function—to protect the costumes and persons of the Indians when
the parade entered hostile neighborhoods.[17] In addition, the tribes
function as more than musical aggregations. While they do offer opportunities for leisure, recreation, and creative expression, they also
serve as mutual-aid societies providing burial insurance, bail money,
or other forms of assistance.[18] Most important, the Indians use artistic expression as a means of reinforcing desired behaviors within
their community. As Chernoff says about African music,

> the practice of art is an explicitly moral activity because African art
> functions dynamically to create a context of values where criticism is
> translated into social action. The meaning of the music is
> externalized through an event in which participation parallels the
> musician's artistic purpose: an artist's coolness lends security to
> intimacy, and the rhythms of an ensemble become the movement of
> an event when people dance.[19]

In New Orleans, as in Africa, this translation of criticism to action takes place through a fusion of music, dress, speech, and dance.

Fewer than twenty songs make up the basic corpus of Mardi Gras Indian music, although each song has many variants. New songs have become popular and old songs have disappeared, but year in and year out, on Mardi Gras Day and in rehearsals throughout the year, the Indians rework familiar words and melodies.[20] All the tribes sing all of the songs, changing the words to insert the distinctive histories and features of their own group. Musical traditions from around the globe appear in Mardi Gras Indian music. Songs like "Handa Wanda" and "Get Out the Way" involve an interaction between leader and chorus by means of antiphony, or "call and response," a form which originated in West Africa, but which has become a basic feature of Afro-American and Euro-American popular music. In "Don't Like That Song," the leader and chorus exchange groups of phrases in the manner of Anglo-American Protestant hymns. "Indian Red," the song used to end all rehearsals and to begin the Mardi Gras Day procession, contains Caribbean phrases and styles.[21]

The structural forms of Mardi Gras Indian songs relate directly to their functions. The limited corpus of songs ensures a great deal of repetition, but it also places a premium on subtlety and improvisation. As Chernoff points out about African music

> People can hear the music for years and always find it fresh and lively because of the extent to which an African musical performance is integrated into its specific social situation. In traditional African music-making situations, the music is basically familiar, and people can follow with informed interest the efforts of the musicians to add an additional dimension of excitement or depth to a performance. Relatively minor variations stand out clearly and assume increased importance in making the occasion successful.[22]

These musical principles reflect philosophical and moral stances. Unlike the Euro-American musical tradition which places a premium on individual authorship of finite texts, the African tradition manifest in Mardi Gras Indian music values dialogue and conversation between artists and audiences to adapt old texts to new situations. The "audience" participates in the creation of this music by singing responses to the leader, by handclapping, and by dancing or chanting in a way that acknowledges the creativity of the musicians. As Chernoff exlains, "The music works more by encouraging social interaction and participation at each performance than by affirming a fixed set of sanctioned concepts or beliefs."[23]

But it is not merely an abstract philosophy that emerges from the Indian music; the musical forms employed by the tribes reflect concrete social relations. Thus the "call and response" between the leader and the tribe in "Handa Wanda" represents the symbiotic relationship between the individual and the group. The chiefs have certain concrete responsibilities—in life and in songs—and when appropriate they take the lead both musically and socially. But each individual plays an important role in the tribe, replete with occasions to show off individual skills and attributes for the benefit of the entire group. Similarly, the form of "Indian Red" mirrors the social organization of Indian tribes. Only the chief can sing lead on this song, but his responsibility is to call forth the other members of the tribe by naming their roles—spy boy, flag boy, trail chief, etc. In most tribes, each "rank" has three people in it, and appropriately enough, "Indian Red" employs a triple meter.[24] The song "Big Chief Wants Plenty of Fire Water" tells a story about a chief who likes to drink, but the Indian tribes and the audiences know that it is used to take up a collection to buy wine for the Indians.[25] Obviously reflective of Anglo and mass-media stereotypes about Indians and alcohol, this song is one of the places where the metaphor employed undermines the culture of anti-racism intended by the Mardi Gras Indian ritual. Yet the act that accompanies it—hospitality and treating within the community—affirms self-worth and solidarity at the same time.

Like their music, the Mardi Gras Indians' costumes and insignia serve both expressive and functional purposes. Most generally, their beads, feathers, designs, and colors celebrate the bounty of life. Plumes and feathers extend outward magnificently, laying claim to dominion over all the space around them, just as bright colors and rhinestones command spectators' fields of vision. This sartorial display draws upon both the Euro-American sensibility of carnival as a time of pleasure before the deprivations of Lent, as well as on the celebration of life's pleasures ritualized in Afro-American funerals in New Orleans. But it is impossible to understand the full meaning of the Indian suits from their appearances alone. To the Indians, these costumes have meaning only as coded reflections of a complex social process.

Designing and sewing Indian suits is a year-round endeavor; as soon as one carnival ends, the Indians begin to prepare for the next. No one wears the same suit two years in a row; indeed no one wears the same *color* suit two years in a row. Each member of the tribe selects his own colors and designs his own suit, although tribes generally adopt at least one theme color that appears in all of the costumes.[26] Although specialized craftspersons may be asked to assist others with drawing or other particular tasks, Indians are responsible for all their own beading and sewing. The sense of craft is so strong among them that using sewing machines risks unqualified disapproval. Individual expression is encouraged and prized, but most of the sewing takes place in collective work sessions involving the sharing of skills, advice, and opinions.[27] Like music rehearsals, these sewing sessions bring the group closer together and provide an opportunity for passing along skills, attitudes,and traditions.

The costumes and insignia also serve as part of the tribe's communications system. Flags display the names of treasured symbols of each group, but they are also used by the flag boys to signal directions along the line of march, to warn of the approach of other tribes, and even to encourage changes in rhythms for the chants, songs, and dances.[28] The Indians also send a message to the community via the costume of their chief, whose prestige rests largely on the beauty of his suit. One of the stock songs of the Indians boasts "My big chief got a golden crown." The entire tribe takes pride in the chief's appearance as well as responsibility for his protection. Many tribes have body guards in plain clothes accompanying the line of march, and most have a "wild man" whose sole job is to clear the path for the chief and to make sure that no one attacks his costume.[29]

The same calculated playfulness that informs Mardi Gras Indian music and dress makes itself felt in its language as well. Les Blank captures the logic of this speech beautifully in his 1978 documentary film *Always for Pleasure*, in which he has an informant reel off a dazzling set of rhymes in "Indian talk." When asked how he knows what to say, the man replies, "It's no script, no set language; you say what you feel."[30] Of course, most viewers of Blank's film (like most readers of this book) could say what they feel all day and never come up with "Wild Tchoupitoula, uptown ruler, blood shiff ahoona, won't kneel, won't bow, don't know how." Such words come "spontaneously" only to those whose preparation is so thorough that the language has become completely internalized. But the seeming inaccessibility of "Indian talk" plays an important role within the subculture, drawing lines between insiders and outsiders, and cultivating an active sense of ambiguity capable of serving many purposes.

For years, ethnomusicologists have attempted to decode the language of the Mardi Gras Indians. Some phrases contain a direct meaning when chanted or sung during parades. For example, "Two Way Pockaway" conveys a warning to get out of the way, while "on tendais" means approval of the previous phrase.[31] Folklorist Alan Lomax believed that the phrase "Two Way Pockaway" came from Louisiana dialect French *t'ouwais bas q'ouwais*, which he surmised came either from *tu n'as pas couilles* (you don't have testicles) or from *tuez bas qu'ou est* (kill who is over there). Lomax believed that "on tendais" also came from the French *entendez* (understand) or *attendez* (wait up or listen).[32] Similarly, the song "Indian Red" has been traced by Andrew Pearse to a carnival song from Trinidad, "Indurubi," which he felt came from the Spanish *Indo Rubi* (Indian Red). In New Orleans, "Indian Red" is generally preceded by the chant "Ma Day Cootie Fiyo." Jason Berry, Jonathan Foose, and Tad Jones point out that *matar* in Spanish means "to kill," while *qui tu est fijo* can mean "who is immobile to you," giving "Ma Day Cootie Fiyo" the possible meaning of "kill who is in your way."[33]

But to search for a static and literal meaning for each Mardi Gras Indian phrase is to gravely misread their playful and deliberately ambiguous language. Word play provides an important facet of many expressions of Indian identity. As one former chief explained, "The idea of singing a Indian song is rhyming something, thinking fast to rhyme it."[34] When tribes meet on the streets, part of their competition involves "talking" by the chiefs who rhyme praise for themselves and insults for their enemies in the manner of the popular Afro-American folk game "playing the dozens."[35]

Just as the Mardi Gras Indian music features variation and improvisation on traditional forms, tribal speech reflects a similarly creative dynamism. For example, The Golden Blades tribe used to be known as Creole Wild West, but changed their name because of a verbal interchange between one of their singers and someone from their "second line." In 1935, during a rehearsal at a bar near Third and Rocheblave streets, this tribe member started singing about his big chief's "diamond crown." When a woman in the crowd responded, "Give it to the boys from Third and Rocheblave," the singer picked up on her phrase but soon changed "Third and Rocheblave" to "give it to the gang from the Golden Blades."[36] Similarly, the 1930s chant by the Wild Squatoolas, "Somebody got to sew, sew, sew," became transformed in the l960s by the Wild Magnolias to "Everybody's got soul, soul, soul."[37]

The imprecision of "Indian talk" might not engender confidence in the idea of language as a central feature of the Mardi Gras Indian ritual. After all, if the origins of words remain obscure, and if the words themselves change over time, how can we be sure that speakers know the significance of what they are saying? It is likely that the tribes and their followers are not always exactly aware of the denotative meaning of every word they use. But in another sense, the use of this language in collective rituals conveys a greater meaning than can be found in the individual words themselves. Another African example might help illumine the consciousness behind this approach to language. Chernoff interviewed a famous Ghanaian musician known as "The Entertainer" about the meaning of his songs,

> When I asked him what the songs he sang were about, he said that he did not really understand some of them, that he would have to go ask the old men who had given him the proverbs which he had set to music. People from various walks of life told me that The Entertainer's songs were in "deep Dagbani," which they could not "hear." They did not have to understand the songs to be moved, but nevertheless, they valued the songs' expression of their deepest traditional sentiments. What was important to them was that the songs had a depth which they enjoyed trying to interpret even while they acknowledged that the songs were often beyond them. In effect, the music does and does not rely on a specific traditional meaning.[38]

Just as African audiences value the traditions conveyed by The Entertainer, Mardi Gras Indians and their audiences profit from the cultural legacies of the past, even while adapting them to the present. Mardi Indian traditions are not a matter of establishing precise origins or maintaining authentic folk forms; rather, they seek to unite the present with the past in a dynamic, yet continuous process. Words and names often play key roles in building that unity. When new tribes form, they often connect themselves to the past by using the name of a disbanded group. Yet they only do so if they can locate the disbanded tribe's chief and secure his permission.[39]

Mardi Gras Indians

Song lyrics also connect contemporary heroism to traditional figures. Thus the Wild Tchoupitoulas' "Brother John," pays tribute to John "Scarface" Williams (a rhythm-and-blues singer and Mardi Gras Indian who died from a knifing shortly after carnival in 1972) by comparing him to "Cora" who "died on the battlefield." An earlier song by Willie Turbinton of the Wild Magnolias (based on a chant by the Magnolias' chief Bo Dollis), told the story of a rebellious slave named Corey. In the 1920s jazz musician Danny Barker recorded a song "Corrine Died on the Battlefield," a song which Paul Longpre of the Golden Blades claims told the story of a woman named Cora Anne who masked as queen of the Battlefield Hunters, but who died of gunshot wounds incurred when she got caught in a crossfire between the Hunters and the Wild Squatoolas.[40] Cora thus refers to at least four people living more than a hundred years apart, three of them male and one female. The story touches on the histories of at least five tribes and appeared in four separate songs. There is no one authentic Corey; the purpose of all this borrowing is precisely to fashion a collective narrative embracing a wide range of actual events and individuals. No one lyricist or story-teller can control the narrative about Corey; it filters through the community, undergoing significant changes, yet retaining important continuities.

Language, costumes, and music combine to shape the fused art of Mardi Gras Indian pageantry, but it is largely through dancing that each of these separate forms becomes part of a larger totality. Indians who chant "two way pockaway" ("get out of the way") will dance differently from those chanting "handa wanda" ("we're not looking for trouble"). Dancing offers an opportunity to display the beauty of one's costume; conversely, costume design anticipates the movements of street dancing. Musical selections not only have their own lyrics, melodies, and rhythms, but they also have specific dance steps that accentuate their other meanings.

In recent years, dancing has taken on even greater importance among the Mardi Gras Indian tribes as a symbolic form of combat. At one time the tribes carried real hatchets and spears and used the aggressive festivity of carnival as a cover for gang warfare. After a day of drinking and marching they would meet to settle grudges and rivalries on the "battlefield"—an empty lot at the intersection of Claiborne and Poydras streets. But when urban renewal destroyed the basis for neighborhood competitions, and when police vigilance made violent acts on carnival day more difficult, a new spirit began to emerge. Aesthetic rivalries took the place of street fighting, and dancing became a key way of demonstrating one's superiority over others. When Indians challenge each other in the streets, they draw an imaginary line between them and compete by dancing as close as possible to it without crossing. Their dance enacts a mock fight replete with attacks on territory and each other's bodies. The dancers capable of giving the appearance of fighting without resorting to actual combat win the highest esteem from their tribe and from other spectators.[41]

The transformation of actual violence into symbolic aesthetic competition has many precedents and parallels in Afro-American communities all across the nation, but it has a special history in New Orleans. Art Neville, a rhythm-and-blues musician who has played with the Hawketts, the Meters, and the Neville Brothers (and whose "Uncle Jolly" formed the Wild Tchoupitoulas tribe in 1972), remembers music as a viable alternative to gang fighting in the public housing project where he grew up in the 1940s and 1950s. "We used to do the doo-wop thing," Neville recalls, referring to the close harmonies and scat singing favored by his friends and relatives at that time. "There were gangs from different neighborhoods and some would fight. I was with a gang that did the singing, so I didn't have nothing to worry about."[42]

Yet dancing means much more to the Indian tribes than the mere displacement of aggressive tendencies. Dancing is a communications system in its own right. In parade situations, certain steps by the spy boys and flag boys alert the rest of the tribe to the presence of hostility ahead.[43] Second liners and tribe members create the rhythms for chants and songs with their dancing, every bit as much as the beating of tambourines and sticks conveys a beat for the dancers. Willie Turbinton of the Wild Magnolias remembers that it was the dancing of the Indians that attracted him to them in the first place. When he was eleven years old Turbinton saw his first Indian tribe and remembers, "It just always intrigued me. There were certain steps and certain moves they'd make that were synonymous with the kind of rhythm they played."[44] Turbinton liked the Indian costumes and language, and he was fascinated by the rituals that gave each member of the tribe a particular significance. But he felt drawn into the spectacle most strongly by the ways that the rhythms made him want to dance. "It was the kind of groove that you couldn't resist," he recalls. "The pulse affected you. You find yourself patting your foot, and if you're shy, you just feel it inside yourself."[45]

The centrality of dancing to the Mardi Gras Indian ritual reveals yet another layer of African cultural retentions among New Orleans blacks. Chernoff's research on African music discovered villagers who identified pieces of music by the dances that accompanied them, and he found over and over again that musicians expected their audiences and dancers to demonstrate active involvement with the music by providing a beat for the musicians to follow. Unlike the concert and dance traditions of Euro-American popular music, the audience in Africa is part of the performance through their dancing, handclapping, and singing. In addition, dancing in African cultures is a form of public worship, a visual demonstration of belief, just as the dance itself is a visual expression of the music.[46] Like their African counterparts (and forebears), Mardi Gras Indians in New Orleans manifest their values about art and life through performance of a "danced faith."[47] Certainly, Chernoff's analysis of public dancing by African village chiefs applies equally to the chiefs of Mardi Gras Indian tribes:

> In his dance, the chief combines aesthetic command and moral command, and the satisfying beauty of his dance is a visible display of his closeness to his ancestors and his fitness for authority. The chief asserts the community through a dance in which gracefulness implies the tranquility of mature strength, elegance implies the bounty of life, precision implies dedication of purpose, happiness implies the accessibility of compassion, composure implies the discretion of power, and dignity implies destiny.[48]

Much of the power of the Mardi Gras Indian ritual stems from its force as a counter-narrative challenging the hegemony of New Orleans' social elite. During Mardi Gras, New Orleans "high society" celebrates its blood lines and mythologizes itself as the heir to a powerful tradition of mysticism and magic. The elite mask themselves in expensive costumes and ride motorized floats along the city's main thoroughfares, throwing beaded necklaces and souvenir doubloons to crowds of spectators. The Indians subvert this spectacle by declaring a powerful lineage of their own, one which challenges the legitimacy of Anglo-European domination. Their costumes are made, not bought. They avoid the main thoroughfares and walk through black neighborhoods. They define the crowds along their route as participants, not just as spectators. Their fusion of music, costumes, speech, and dance undermines the atomized European view of each of those activities as distinct and autonomous endeavors, while it foregrounds an African sensibility about the interconnectedness of art and the interconnectedness of human beings.

Yet the degree to which this counter-narrative actually threatens the hegemony of the dominant culture is open to dispute. One can well imagine how easily those in power might dismiss black workers in outlandish costumes drinking and dancing in the streets on Mardi Gras Day. Certainly within the black community, the ambiguities and multi-layered symbolism of the Indian ritual might well obscure the historical and social power realities behind its genesis, as the traditional internal rivalries it has provoked have demonstrated. The dominance of males and the peripheral role allotted to females within the Indian ritual reinforces the sexist hierarchies of the dominant culture. Furthermore, even if one were to claim that the Indian ritual served an oppositional purpose within black New Orleans, there would be no guarantee that this particular counter-narrative could transcend specific experiences of race, region, and class to speak to people with different values and histories. The forms and styles fashioned by the Indians seem so rooted in the specific history and culture of New Orleans that it is difficult to imagine how their practice could be representative of counter-narratives generated under different conditions.

Indeed, even the cultural critics most sympathetic to the emancipatory potential of popular narratives express reservations about them that are relevant to an evaluation of the ultimate significance of the practices of the Mardi Gras Indians. Limon warns that ostensibly oppositional behaviors sometimes simply reflect unequal opportunities and resources. Thus, rather than parodying or undermining dominant narratives, these behaviors might instead be imitating them, albeit with inadequate resources. Limon emphasizes that traditional folklore best retains a critical edge in the modern world when it represents self-generated and relatively autonomous cultural practices that contrast radically with the "largely imposed character of mass media culture."[49] In a similar vein, Fox points to the ways in which modern society undermines the kinds of communities and cultures traditionally oriented toward the creation and preservation of folklore. Fox notes that folk practices often draw their critical content from an essentially conservative function—preserving group cohesion and conformity in traditional societies under attack by modernization. He points out that such societies are increasingly rare and increasingly anomalous in the modern world, and that they constitute an inadequate basis for cultural and political contestation.[50] Jameson contends that truly "popular" art has all but disappeared under the assault of commercial mass culture, surviving only in isolated pockets removed from the main channels of communication and commerce.[51]

The concerns raised by Limon, Fox, and Jameson offer useful cautions about analyzing the Mardi Gras Indian ritual as an example of counter-narrative. Like all subordinated groups, the Indians lack access to significant power and resources, and their organizations do serve purposes of mutual aid and self-affirmation denied them in other spheres. Their ritual may have started in relative isolation from the "largely imposed character of mass media culture," but their present-day and future audiences have been saturated with competing images and sounds from other cultures through the mass media. They seem to exemplify Jameson's contention that truly "popular" art exists only in specialized and marginalized circumstances, far removed from the centers of mainstream commerce and culture.

Yet the same forms of commercial culture that destroy the organic basis for traditional folklore enable people to escape the prejudices and parochialisms of their own communities. The same forces that relegate ethnic, linguistic, and subcultural minorities to the margins of contemporary culture, also transmit the oppositional sensibilities of marginal groups to a mass audience. The same feelings that motivate people to fashion autonomous signs and symbols within folkloric traditions impel them to put the stamp of their own experience on the ideas and images circulated within commercial culture. Most important, the internal properties of the electronic mass media favor precisely the kinds of dynamic cultural creation basic to the entire Mardi Gras Indian activity. Commercial culture destroys the sense of "origins" and "authenticity" prized by Euro-American music and folklore, but its biases toward repetition, nonlinear reasoning, and immediacy make it a viable conduit for oppositional narratives like those created by the Mardi Gras Indians. Nothing illustrates this tendency more convincingly than the way in which New Orleans musicians have inserted Mardi Gras Indian music into American and international popular music.

As early as the 1920s, jazz musicians from New Orleans recorded Mardi Gras Indian songs. Danny Barker and his Creole Cats did "My Indian Red" and "Chocko Mo Fendo Hando" on the King Zulu label, while Louis Dumaine and his Jazzola Eight performed "To Wa Bac a Wa" for Vic Records.[52] In 1954, Sugar Boy Crawford inserted Indian music into mainstream popular culture when his song "Jock-A-Mo" became a big regional hit. Although not an Indian himself, Crawford created "Jock-A-Mo" by combining two songs he remembered hearing them sing when he was growing up near the "battlefield" on Claiborne and Poydras streets.[53] Dave Bartholomew's 1957 "Can't Take It No More" begins with chanting evocative of Indian call and response.[54] In 1965, the Dixie Cups, a female trio from New Orleans, reached the national top-twenty list with "Iko Iko"—which like "Jock-A-Mo" originated with the Mardi Gras Indians. In a story that illustrates how commercial and folk cultures can intersect, Barbara Hawkins of the Dixie Cups relates how "Iko Iko" became a record:

> We were clowning around the studio while the musicians were on break, it was just the three of us using drumsticks on ashtrays and glasses singing "Iko Iko." We didn't realize that [producers] Jerry and Mike (Leiber and Stoller) were in the control room with the tape rolling. They came out and said that's great, they had never heard it before, all they added was a calypso box. We had never planned on recording it.[55]

Hawkins described the song as "the type of thing the Indians have always used, inventing new words as they march along."[56] In the late 1970s, Hawkins herself came full circle with the Indians, marching as Queen of the Wild Magnolias on Mardi Gras Day.

Other Indian songs which have been recorded successfully include versions of "Iko Iko" by Doctor John and by the Neville Brothers, "Handa Wanda" by the Wild Magnolias, and compilations of carnival songs by the Wild Tchoupitoulas and the Wild Magnolias.[57] In addition, songs about parts of the Mardi Gras Indian ritual have been recorded by Professor Longhair, Huey Smith and the Clowns, and Earl King. Some of the influence of the Indians on New Orleans pop music has been indirect. Cyril Neville of the Neville Brothers attributes his skill on percussion instruments to the lessons he learned from the tambourine playing of his "Uncle Jolly" (George Landry) who founded the Wild Tchoupitoulas tribe in 1972.[58] Those lessons involved the kind of interactions with African music characteristic of the Mardi Gras Indian aesthetic. As Neville explains:

> The drum comes to me as a symbol of what I, or we, used to be. I can't speak on the drums, but I try to convey my feelings. . . . I think about Africa when I play. To me, right now, my Africa is the drums 'cause when I feel like going back to Africa, I play my drums."[59]

Evidently, Cyril Neville learned his lessons well; when the Neville Brothers played on the bill in Chicago with the Nigerian JuJu band, King Sunny Ade and His African Beats, a reporter for the *Chicago Sun Times* noted, "Many of the African players were enchanted with the funk and soul of the Neville Brothers, most notably the West African persuasions of percussionist Cyril Neville."[60]

But to trace only the direct links between the Indians and popular artists and songs underestimates their true influence on New Orleans, American, and world popular music. An amazing variety of recorded music from New Orleans resonates with the values, aesthetics, and musical traditions of the Indians. Their jubilant celebration of the bounty of life informs Shirley and Lee's 1956 "Let the Good Times Roll," Aaron Neville's 1966 "Tell It Like It Is," and The Meters' 1972 "They All Axed for You." Indian-style call and response dominated Huey Smith and the Clowns' 1958 "Don't You Just Know It," while "second line" rhythms permeated The Meters 1970 "Handclapping Song."

The great New Orleans rhythm and blues pianist Professor Longhair replicated Mardi Gras Indian music in his polyrhythmic compositions, demonstrating a philosophical commitment to the unity among percussion, dance, and melody by refusing to play grand pianos and insisting on uprights so that he could kick the base boards rhythmically at appropriate moments. Alfred Roberts, who played conga drums behind Professor Longhair, once described what the two of them tried to do musically in words that serve as a capsule introduction to African musical sensibilities:

> I try and answer whatever he's doin' and try and lay out a basic pattern that he could listen to and build off. Cause this is what he made me think of the role he wanted me to play. If the drummer is

> playing a certain rhythm with his foot, and Fess [Professor Longhair]
> got somethin' happenin' with his hands, syncopatin,' it's best for you
> to play in a space where nothin' is happenin' and kind of blend in
> with the drummer and the bass player. It's just backwards and
> forwards your hands and your brain, your eyes, your ears, and it's
> just flowin' like that into a rhythm.[61]

Just as Alfred Roberts and Professor Longhair reproduced African
musical forms in New Orleans, musicians from all over the world
knowingly and unknowingly absorbed Mardi Gras Indian music into
the basic vocabulary of rock and roll. New Orleans drummer Earl
Palmer laid a solid "parade beat" beneath the rhythm-and-blues hits
of Little Richard and Sam Cooke, while the melody and chord progressions from the parade song "Second Line" predate their appearance in Bill Haley and His Comets' "Rock Around the Clock."[62] New
Orleans rhythm-and-blues artist Ernie K-Doe exaggerated only
slightly when he said in 1979, "I'm not sure, but I'm almost positive,
that all music came from New Orleans."[63]

In 1986, rock singer Cyndi Lauper delayed the release of her "True
Colors" album in order to include "Iko Iko" on it. Lauper had been
listening to playbacks of her rendition of Marvin Gaye's 1960s anti-
war, anti-racist "What's Going On," and she began to be reminded of
another song. Eventually, she realized that the rhythms she had been
using in "What's Going On" fit perfectly into "Iko Iko," which came
to Lauper through listening to the Neville Brothers, Doctor John, and
the Dixie Cups.[64] On the surface, her connection might seem absurd.
The profound political lyrics of "What's Going On" bear little resemblance to the nonsense rhymes of "Iko Iko." The life experience of a
white woman rock star from New York seems to have little in common with the historical struggle against racial and class domination
waged by the Mardi Gras Indians. Yet Lauper's intuition led her to the
right place. "What's Going On" and "Iko Iko" *are* both about fighting
racism and exploitation. The magnificent plumes and bright colors
of the Mardi Gras Indians express in their way what the multi-
colored hair and self-parodying costumes of Cyndi Lauper represent
in another way. The proto-feminist blend of adolescent female voices
and adult sexual desires in the Dixie Cups' "Iko Iko" serves as a legitimate progenitor to Lauper's own breakthrough hit in 1985, "Girls
Just Want to Have Fun."

That Lauper came to "Iko Iko" through the apparatuses of commercial culture raises intriguing questions about the supposedly diminishing power of popular narratives. It illustrates how marginalized cultures can insinuate their oppositional values into the texts of popular culture and create allies among people with similar though not identical experiences. It is no more ridiculous for Cyndi Lauper to appropriate "Iko Iko," than it was for nineteenth-century, working-class blacks to use the Wild West Show, Mardi Gras, and gang-fighting as a basis for an oppositional subculture. As part of the history of rock and roll, as part of the historic opposition to hierarchy and exploitation in America, "Iko Iko" offered a logical source of inspiration and celebration for Lauper. The critics may be right when they talk about the decline of traditional narratives, the marginalization of "popular" art, and the "largely imposed character of mass media culture." But people fight with the resources at their disposal, and frequently their pain leads them to quite innovative means of struggle. They do not all have the same story, and they often fail to understand the stories of others. They often suffer terrible oppression and anguish as they search for a narrative capable of making sense out of their existence. But story-telling survives, even when the story-tellers develop coded and secret ways of communicating with one another, inside and outside of commercial culture. For all of his pessimism, even Walter Benjamin understood this. In the same essay in which he fretted about the demise of story-telling, Benjamin offered a phrase which he meant figuratively, but which has a literal meaning as well. "Indeed," Benjamin observed, "each sphere of life has, as it were, produced its own tribe of storytellers."[65]

History and the Future

11

Buscando America (Looking for America): Collective Memory in an Age of Amnesia

"Tomorrow people, where is your past?"
Ziggy Marley

In his elegantly crafted *All That Is Solid Melts into Air*, Marshall Berman identifies Goethe's *Faust* as a narrative emblematic of modernity. Suffocated by the parochialisms and prejudices of his little village, Faust arms himself with instrumental knowledge and becomes a builder. But a builder of the new is also a destroyer of the old, and when the adult Faust returns to the village of his youth, he finds an exquisite beauty in the world he has labored so hard to destroy. For Berman, the dilemma facing Faust confronts us all. In a world devoted to progress and change, the past becomes ever more precious the more it disappears. Human beings act to change and "improve" the world, but as a result, many feel the sting of disconnection from the past, seeing the villages of our childhoods turn into what Berman calls "little worlds emptied out."[1]

Within much of American commercial culture after World War II, the "little world emptied out" became the industrial city. During the war production boom and the vast migrations that accompanied it, Americans formed a new pluralist culture in urban industrial centers. Mass strikes and political mobilizations expressed popular desires for material advancement in the postwar era, while new cultural and social formations reshaped race, class, ethnicity, and gender in lasting ways. The possibilities generated within wartime industrial cities have had enduring consequences, influencing everything from suburban growth to race relations, from foreign policy to gender identity.[2]

But for some the dream died almost as soon as it began. As a white man living within a black community, Johnny Otis thrived on the energy and imagination of wartime Los Angeles. He thought that the social changes he witnessed there signaled the birth of a new pluralism in America, the realization of long suppressed hopes and dreams. He found his previous cynicism about America giving way to a hopeful optimism. "I saw the whole community lifting," he recalls, "I thought we were going to realize the American dream. We'd say 'It's a bitch, there's still a lot of racism, but it's going to be OK because our kids will realize a fresh new democratic America!"[3] But this optimism did not last, as Otis saw returning white soldiers claim jobs held during the war by female and black workers, federal urban renewal and home loan policies subsidizing white flight from central cities to the suburbs, military spending and corporate investment overseas redirecting funds that might have been use to bolster the American industrial infrastructure or to invest in the nation's social capital through expenditures on education, health, and housing. Otis watched his hopes crumble. "Things were grim, and I realized my original appraisal was accurate and that my enthusiasm and my happiness were not well-founded—that the majority did not give a shit about black folk and in fact despised them."[4] The curtailment of the emerging pluralistic and democratic urban culture that held Otis's allegiance did real harm to Afro-American communities, but it also devastated a variety of urban, ethnic working-class cultures and subcultures on behalf of the suburb-centered consumer mentality of the 1950s. Urban renewal enabled large corporations to build new downtown corporate headquarters at bargain rates. Federally subsidized loans for segregated suburban housing brought millions of dollars in mortgages to financial institutions, while federal highway projects dispersed populations for the enrichment of building firms, not to mention their indirect subsidy to the automobile and gasoline industries. All of these policies had a devastating impact on the pluralistic democratic culture that emerged in American cities during World War II.

Throughout the 1950s and 1960s individuals like Johnny Otis fought to retain the legacies of 1940s urban industrial life. In terrains as diverse as civil-rights activism and popular music they won many important victories, wresting concessions from their enemies and keeping alive an active opposition between corporate culture and democratic culture. But by the late 1970s, corporate culture had won decisive victories: Cutbacks in government spending on social programs reversed previous commitments to education, housing, and health. Plant shutdowns and capital flight undermined the common ground that had given both the poor and the middle class a meaningful stake in society, while tax policies fueled a spending spree by the rich. Some of the distance between blacks and whites, between rich and poor, which had started to close in the 1960s re-opened in the 1970s and 1980s.

During the postwar era, commercial popular culture has functioned largely to fashion a symbolic order conducive to the interests of corporate America. The same investors who redirect capital away from urban industrial areas control the form and content of the commercial mass media. They determine the monopoly structure of commercial network television as well as its identity as an advertising mechanism. They skew the content of mass communications toward the wealthy by making advertising demographics the prime determinant of what appears on radio or television. They ensure that our society devotes superior resources to advertising than to education, and that its central discursive media "naturalize" private commodity consumption while presenting social commitments as unnatural intrusions on private lives. Their marketing research reinforces existing prejudices and retards innovation by silencing images and ideas not already acceptable to broad segments of the population. They suppress knowledge about cultural and historical differences to unite the audience as a homogeneous buying public; then they create and exaggerate petty divisions—based on brand loyalty, fashion, style—to divide the audience into market segments.

Media scholar Ben Bagdikian demonstrates how the commercial imperatives of corporate America undermine local knowledge and a sense of history. His studies of print and electronic journalism reveal a pernicious relationship between the monopolistic tendencies of commercial enterprises and the free flow of information required for informed political judgments. For example, urban renewal not only dispersed central-city populations to the suburbs, it also destroyed the densities favorable to "impulse" buying of newspapers. Fewer street sales made newspapers more dependent upon advertising revenues which in turn mandated less space devoted to news. In addition, the newly dispersed reading audience cost more to reach (by deliveries) and had a more fragmented sense of locality. To appeal to the broadest possible suburban audience, newspapers geared their content toward more general features rather than specific local stories, and they followed the demographic tyrannies that made the appeal of fewer wealthier readers more desirable to newspapers (and their advertisers) than a larger but less wealthy clientele. Bagdikian attributes the drastic demise in the number of daily newspapers since World War II to these changes in format and content, and he shows how television merely extends this process by dispersing its news to an even larger and more diffuse audience.[5]

Commercial mass media fragment and dilute entertainment in much the same way that they do news. In the early 1980s, the Federal Communications Commission restricted the three commercial television networks from initiating programming during the early evening hours on the grounds that this time period should be devoted to local programming needed to ensure diversity and community responsibility. But the reach and scope of television draw such exorbitant support from advertisers that local producers cannot possibly compete with the slick appeal and advanced technologies of national syndicators and distributors. Local stations make the most money when they show programs that bring the highest advertising ratings and that cost the least to obtain. Rather than suffer the expenses of local production or the uncertainty of audience response, they prefer to buy syndicated shows from national producers. Consequently, during the "local access" hours all across the nation, viewers see exactly the same syndicated comedies and game shows which reinforce a mediated national consciousness rather than any kind of local knowledge or memory.

Yet the mercenary aims of media conglomerates and the commercial and ideological imperatives of corporate culture have not quite succeeded in erasing desires for connection to the urban past. As Stuart Hall quips, "hegemonizing is hard work": obliterating suppressed memories and desires requires constant vigilance, especially when the dislocations and fragmentations of the media nurture a longing for reconnection. To be sure, representations of both the past and the industrial city often appear on television and film as warnings against sociability and public space. These portrayals of the

city as so ominous and social difference so threatening invite a retreat into a consumer world bounded by cul-de-sacs and subdivisions. Nonetheless, ideological predilections often conflict with commercial opportunities; cultural portrayals laced with traces of the
urban industrial past can make money, both as novelties within and
as alternatives to a commodity-consumer society. The very forms
most responsible for the erosion of historical and local knowledge
can sometimes be the sources of reconnection in the hands of inge-
nious artists and audiences. By these processes they remember their
own actual pasts, but they also use the powers of electronic mass media to transcend time and space, connecting themselves to the pasts
of others, pasts that bear moral and political lessons. Instead of serving as an instrument of division, commercial culture in these instances
serves as a way for bridging barriers of time, class, race, region, ethnicity, gender, and even nationality. This "return of the repressed"
within the media creates one of its conditions of possibility.

A few examples from popular music and television may help illustrate the persistence and ingenuity of popular memory within the
mass media. In 1982 British rock singer Kevin Rowland recorded an
album titled *Celtic Soul Brother*, exploring his musical and cultural
roots. He wrote a series of songs for himself and his band—Dexy's
Midnight Runners—that foregrounded acoustic instruments and folk
melodies. Raised in working-class Coventry by Irish parents, Rowland mapped his own musical past as a dialogue between the rock-
and-roll music that he heard on the radio and the Irish folk music
that he heard at home. One of the songs on the album, "Come On
Eileen," became a hit single in England and in the U.S., and *Celtic
Soul Brother* became one of the best-selling albums of 1983.

One song on *Celtic Soul Brother* did not seem to fit in an album
from 1982–1983. "Jackie Wilson Said" paid tribute to the American
rhythm-and-blues singer Jackie Wilson, who since 1975 had been in
a coma and who was all but forgotten by the recording industry until
his death in 1984. Kevin Rowland's "folk" memories did not include
Jackie Wilson directly, but the story of how a song about the American singer became included on *Celtic Soul Brother* reveals sedimented networks and associations beneath the surfaces of the seemingly
disconnected world of commodified musical production.

Kevin Rowland sang "Jackie Wilson said it was 'reet petite' . . . " because in 1971 Rowland's fellow Irishman Van Morrison wrote and re-

corded the original "Jackie Wilson Said." Morrison grew up in Belfast enamored of American popular music, and in a moment of reflection about his own musical roots he penned a tribute to Jackie Wilson. This affinity between Irish and Afro-Americans should not be surprising. Wilson himself recorded a magnificent version of the Irish ballad "Danny Boy" in 1965, and Irish-American rock singer Michael McDonald claims that his childhood exposure to Irish ballads enabled him to make a "natural progression" to the music of Ray Charles and Marvin Gaye. "I was attracted to black music for the same reason that I loved those old Irish ballads," McDonald asserts. "Both were social statements of sorts and both were indigenous to their respective cultures: Ireland, where my father had grown up, and towns like St. Louis along the Mississippi River, where I was growing up."[6] But Morrison's memory of Jackie Wilson saying "Reet Petite" held meaning beyond the general families of resemblance tying Afro-American to Irish music.

Jackie Wilson's "Reet Petite" was his first hit as a solo artist in 1957. The song was written for him by aspiring writer and producer Berry Gordy, Jr., who would go on to success as the founding and guiding force behind Motown Records. But in 1957 Gordy was just a former assembly-line worker and failed music-store owner trying to break into the business. He drew the expression "Reet Petite" from the "bop" language of jazz musicians in the 1940s whose music, dress, and speech held an enduring fascination for Gordy. When Jackie Wilson found a mass audience (including Van Morrison) for "Reet Petite," he brought to them a piece of a subculture that was already ten years out of date. "Bop" talkers of the 1940s cultivated an in-group mentality to distance themselves from the homogenizing power of popular culture. They favored a music built on blues chord progressions and abstract improvisations to break with the simple formulas of Tin Pan Alley. They peppered their speech with internal rhymes about exotic clothes. The bop talkers wearing clothes with a draped shape and a reat pleat or a stuffed cuff might catch the eye of a slick chick. The bop talkers and zoot suiters of the 1940s manifested one of the first instances of "prestige from below" in postwar Western societies. Previously, fashion, dress, and speech popular among the middle class started with the wealthy and trickled down. In the postwar period, "bop" talk, zoot suits, and rock music originating in black and Chicano working-class communities filtered up to set the pace for middle-class groups, especially youth.

The complicated genealogy that ties Kevin Rowland to oppositional subcultures of the 1940s via "Jackie Wilson Said" reflects more than the serendipitous confusion of mass mediated culture and art. Because in his own way, Rowland found what he was looking for. Like him, the "bop" talkers and zoot suiters who coined the phrase "reet petite" sought to assert their historical identity and flaunt their social marginality while at the same time staking a claim for participation in global popular culture. Not only did Rowland find an appropriate role model in Van Morrison, but Morrison's discovery of Wilson (and Wilson's use of Gordy, and Gordy's appropriation of the 1940s "bop" talkers) united all of them in an oppositional quest, a search for inclusion in the mainstream of popular music without losing sight of the differences mandated by ethnic and racial history. When he adopted Irish acoustic instruments and melodies, Kevin Rowland aired some roots that he knew about consciously and clearly. But when he chose to record "Jackie Wilson Said," he also connected with some roots that he may have sensed only obliquely and second-hand.

The presence of sedimented networks and associations within rock-and-roll music illumine a career-turn in the life of another musician, the American rock guitarist Billy Peek. Late one night in 1975 Rod Stewart and his band, including Ron Wood, sat in a Colorado motel room watching Chuck Berry performing on "Rock Concert" on television. Stewart found his attention drawn to Berry's lead guitarist, Billy Peek. Stewart wanted to start a new band at the time and Ron Wood suggested that Peek had the talent and the sound that Stewart wanted. It took Stewart and his manager several months to locate Peek, but they set up an audition by the end of the year.

Billy Peek had grown up in the 1940s and 1950s in a white, working-class St. Louis neighborhood known as "The Grove." Peek's father worked in a nearby tobacco warehouse, and his mother was employed by a meatpacking firm; eventually they opened up a neighborhood bar featuring live country-and-western music, the Peek-A-Boo Inn. Although he heard only country music at home, when he was thirteen a friend introduced Peek to Chuck Berry's "Maybelline" on a neighborhood juke box. From that moment on, Peek vowed to make his living playing rock and roll. He practiced for hours in his room, trying to emulate the sounds he heard on records and the radio. As a teen-ager, he went to black night clubs to hear performances by local musicians including Ike Turner, Albert King, and Chuck Berry. He began to play for school dances and was featured on a local television program. One night while playing a string of Chuck Berry songs at a local club, he noticed Berry sitting in the audience. Fearful of offending his idol, Peek steered clear of any more of Berry's compositions that evening, but at the end of the show Berry came up, congratulated him on his playing, and invited him to perform at Berry's club, Berry Park. Their subsequent long-term association culminated in Peek's appearance with Berry on "Rock Concert" in 1975.

Peek auditioned for Stewart a few months later. At the session, Stewart stayed in the control booth with head phones on, and he asked Peek to listen to one track and to play whatever came to mind. The song, which had been giving the rest of the band difficulty, turned out to be "The Wild Side of Life," originally a Hank Thompson country song from 1952. Peek remembered the song as a favorite of his father's, one that he had heard around the house incessantly when he was growing up. In addition, years of playing with Chuck Berry had schooled him in playing a hard-driving St. Louis boogie-woogie riff "that told a story and told it in overdrive."[7] What Peek produced at the audition was his cultural history translated into music, a fusion of white, working-class country music and Afro-American rhythm and blues, but also the organic musical language of the industrial city in which he was raised. Peek knew he had gotten the job when he saw Stewart jump in the air and practically hit the ceiling of the control booth yelling, "That's it! That's it!"

With Billy Peek's guitar helping to set the pace, the Rod Stewart band became one of the best-selling musical aggregations in the world over the next five years. Peek's guitar solos on "Better Off Dead," "Blondes Have More Fun," "Ball Trap," "Hot Legs," and "Wild Side of Life" anchored the band in a traditional rock-and-roll style that provided an effective contrast to Stewart's pop vocalizing. But Peek secured his place in that band through more than technique alone; his entire life history had prepared him for that role. Other musicians could play the same notes, but Peek "had the feel" of the music, a feel he acquired through hard experience in the 1950s.

When Stewart's band dissolved in 1980, Peek returned to St. Louis where he became a local favorite at clubs and dances. His skills at Chuck Berry songs and his connection to the shared pasts of many of his listeners drew Peek into repeated conversations about the origins of St. Louis rock and roll. Eventually he worked those conversations into a song that recalled his desire to learn the blues at East Side night clubs. The song, "Can a White Boy Sing the Blues?" led to a blues album which attracted some attention in the U.S. and England, and which led to Peek's emergence in the late 1980s as a performer on the midwestern blues circuit and as a recording artist with records like "The Hammer" played on blues radio stations.[8]

The sedimented layers of cultural history underlying the music of Kevin Rowland and Billy Peek testify to the dialogic nature of popular music, and they also offer evidence about the capacity of popular culture to serve as a conduit for connection to meaningful possibilities in the urban industrial past. Yet such uses of memory are not always progressive. In the late 1980s, radio stations across the country have adopted another strategy in relation to the past—adult-oriented "oldies" programming, sometimes referred to without a trace of irony as "Big Chill" programming (in "honor" of the popularity of that film's soundtrack). "Oldies" programming in the late 1950s filled an oppositional role; it maintained collective memory and resisted the manipulations of an industry trying to purge itself of its black and white working-class resonances. But in the 1980s, such programming stems from demographic tyranny (the large number of listeners with high disposable incomes who developed their musical tastes in the 1960s) and cultural conservatism (an alternative to new music). At a time when the most creative music—rap and Latin dance mix—come from the pluralities of the postindustrial city, this particular nostalgia for the urban industrial past can be quite racist and regressive, a way of precluding rather than promoting new possibilities. Yet the artists responsible for rap and hip hop musics are masters at appropriating the tools used against them to inject themselves into venues from which they have been excluded. Recent rap artists have colonized the "oldies" format for their own purposes as Run-DMC collaborated with Aerosmith's Steve Tyler to do a rap remake of that group's "Walk This Way," while the Fat Boys teamed up with Chubby Checker to do a rap version of his hit, "The Twist." In a further twist, James Brown laid claim to having originated rap with his "I'm Real" recorded with

Full Force. These collaborative works secure new commercial spaces for the artists involved, defy the record industry's established codes about the inviolability of genres, and reveal an organic cultural memory at the same time: Run-DMC did listen to Aerosmith, the Fat Boys do know about Chubby Checker, and James Brown does hear traces of his old records in every rap and hip hop selection.

If popular music has been a vehicle for artists and audiences to reconnect with the disappearing textures of urban life, commercial network television has done its best to present city life in a negative light. Between 1958 and 1970, American commercial network television largely "abandoned" the city, placing most of its situation comedies in suburbs or rural areas while mainly locating action adventure shows on the western plains or in exotic postindustrial sunbelt or resort settings.[9] But after 1970, American television "remembered" the city and once again adopted it as a location for comedy and drama. Humor no longer remained confined to places like "Mayberry" (*The Andy Griffith Show*) and "Springfield" (*Father Knows Best*) but cropped up in working-class Queens (*All in the Family*), Watts (*Sanford and Son*), and Chicago's south side (*Good Times*). Even middle-class comedies celebrated formerly unprestigious urban locales—Minneapolis (*The Mary Tyler Moore Show*), Indianapolis (*One Day at a Time*) and Cincinnati (*WKRP*). Action adventure shows rediscovered the city as well, but largely to reveal it as a dangerous and threatening place (*Kojak, Starsky and Hutch, SWAT*, and *Streets of San Francisco*). Even if its portrayals made no direct reference to the past, the recovery of forgotten images amounted to a recasting of collective memory about a social formation that had been rendered obsolete by previous television programs.

None of the new urban television programs of the 1970s evoked the historical knowledge or progressive sentiments found in the music of Kevin Rowland or Billy Peek, but these shows did display an interest in the city and a continuum of attitudes about it. Even though set in the present, they inevitably had to work with or against the grain of popular understanding of the historical legacy of the industrial city. The situation comedies tended to take place indoors, revalidating the home (and its consumer purchases) as the center of the psychic world. But these comedies also made a break with the homogeneous nuclear family of 1960s television comedies by emphasizing differences with neighbors (Julio on *Sanford and Son*, Lionel on *All in the Family*), or by remapping the family onto the workplace (*The Bob Newhart Show, The Mary Tyler Moore Show*).[10] The middle-class city dwellers enjoyed the variety of urban experiences even without necessarily being in show business as had been true of previous such shows (*I Love Lucy, The Danny Thomas Show, The Dick Van Dyke Show*), while the mismatched neighbors of the shows about poorer people still managed to maintain some sociability and mutuality despite their differences. Even an action adventure show like *Rockford Files* could finally show the city as an arena of mutuality and affectionate humor among an extended family and work network. What tied these shows to the urban past was not just their use of older dwellings (*All in the Family, Chico and the Man, Good Times*) or urban institutions (radio stations, office buildings, junkyards), but also their liberal politics. Some viewers might side with conservative foils Archie Bunker, Ted Knight, or Les Nessman, but the inscribed preferred readings of these shows encouraged reconnection with urban liberalism. More conservative readings were encouraged by the action adventure shows where paternalistic, male police officers took command over diverse underlings to make them effective in containing the vicious criminals capable at any moment of reducing the city to barbarism. Rather than celebrating the diversity of the city, these shows tended to pose difference as a problem to be solved by authority and discipline. Veteran police officers in *Mod Squad, Starsky and Hutch, Police Woman*, and *Streets of San Francisco* constrain their multi-racial and multi-gendered (and vaguely counter-cultural) subordinates from any real rebellion by convincing them that they are needed in a struggle to control the vicious and threatening "differences" of the city.

The tension between corporate and democratic readings of the urban legacy extend into the 1980s, most notably in the differences between *Hill Street Blues* and *Miami Vice*. Both programs depict an uphill battle by police officers against urban corruption, yet both emphasize the city (or at least its police force) as an arena where people from different backgrounds learn to work together for the common good. Yet their sensibilities head in opposite directions. *Hill Street Blues* emphasizes the decay of the urban industrial city. The defective wiring and plumbing of the station house mirrors the dark terrors and social pollution of the adjacent neighborhood. Like the 1970s action adventure shows, diversity within the police force provides a challenge to management, while diversity outside poses savagery as the alternative to effective hierarchical leadership. Although the show has multiple story lines and no narrator, each episode ends with a summary from the white male managerial hero, Captain Furillo. Alone among the characters, he sees the big picture; he is sensitive enough to work with other races and genders without a hint of prejudice, but seasoned enough to realize that the rules don't work, that the system has failed, and that people like him are asked to do too much. Furillo's liberalism has a residue of self-pity in it; the decline of the industrial city has left him in charge of a lesser entity than he really deserves.

By contrast, *Miami Vice* exposes the corruption of postindustrial society, rooting its critique in the residual morality of the industrial past. For all the avant-garde music video interludes in their show, the fashionable postmodern clothes, and the fancy cars, the officers in *Miami Vice* seem closer to the democratic culture of the industrial city than their counterparts in *Hill Street Blues*. Citizens become victims in *Miami Vice* because wealthy and powerful people control too much and act too viciously. The poor are more likely to be victims than perpetrators here, and while not necessarily better than anyone else, neither are they necessarily any worse. In fact, their dialects, dress, and music add a dignified texture to the urban mosaic, providing a backdrop for drama as well as for crime. The officers in *Miami Vice* routinely fail to hold back evil pressing in on their city, but they insist on trying without resorting to cynicism. Their problems are social rather than individual; the demise of the urban community is a historical rather than a personal problem, one caused by the evils of the kind of city that has supplanted it—a city of indecent gaps between rich and poor, and one with little to offer its remaining middle class.

Televised portrayals of the city inevitably convey the vitality and ingenuity of urban popular music; yet they present city life as far more violent and far less viable than it actually us. But the fact that they have to present it all, that the city remains an important icon for both conservative and liberal politics indicates its enduring fascination. More important than the inscribed biases or resolution of any particular television show are the possibilities still embedded within an urban context. As Marshall Berman writes,

The contemporary desire for a city that is openly troubled but intensely alive is a desire to open up old but distinctively modern wounds once more. It is a desire to live openly with the split and unreconciled character of our lives, and to draw energy from our inner struggles, wherever they may lead us in the end.[11]

This desire to open up wounds seems strangely out of place. In a society given over to suburban subdivisions, where franchised fast-food restaurants guard against surprises, and where cities rebuild their unique and distinctive historical districts by hiring the same developers to build the same kinds of malls all over the country, the fascination with risk may seem like either masochism or madness. To critics like Jean Baudrillard it represents the final triumph of electronic media, an acceptance of total disorientation and fragmentation in a world of totally artificial experience. Baudrillard sees a world composed of signs without referents, of cultural symbols unhinged from any organic social experience.[12] But as Berman makes clear, the mixture of sensations and images in a world excite us not so much because they are fundamentally new, but because they remind us of something familiar but threatened by forgetting.

In some cases, remembering our own pasts links us to people quite different from ourselves. When musician Michael Tempo of the Los Angeles group the Bonedaddys talks about the African influences in his music, he tells people, "I play music indigenous to the natives of Western Kentucky. I could find African records when I grew up in Paducah. That was as much a part of my culture as the country music coming over the radio and through the kitchen window."[13] But one reason why Tempo could absorb the African music that he heard was because African musicians like Nigeria's King Sunny Ade grew up listening to American country-and-western, steel-guitar players like Ralph Mooney and singers like Jim Reeves.[14] Jerry Harrison of the Talking Heads describes his explorations into African music by referring to the Africanisms already present in American rhythm and blues and vice versa. Harrison explains,

I really consider there to be a clear link between African music and R&B and rock'n'roll, and it had not been elucidated clearly before. There are definite connections between Fela and James Brown. That's why we could learn about African music because we had heard about that, and read about that, and we loved James Brown, and we went and looked at it. Once we saw how great Fela was, we started looking at some of the other stuff. It wasn't because we were interested in Pygmy music or something like that. It came up from things that had already developed. It was as if we worked back from our culture, and then we realized things that people had said about these connections.

Harrison and the Talking Heads found their way to Africa the same way that Kevin Rowland found his way to the zoot suiters, the same way that Billy Peek found Rod Stewart—through commercial culture as it reflected and resonated with historical traces relevant to their lives. Commercial culture enabled these musicians, and their audiences, to understand more about their own memory and experience by connecting with the memories and experiences of others.

*   *   *   *   *

As much as any single individual, Johnny Otis has devoted his life to appreciating what Albert Murray calls the "incontestably mulatto nature of American culture."[15] He speaks bitterly about what he calls the "predatory capitalism" that enables the culture industry "to grab people from almost the cradle and to cater to the most juvenile tastes."[16] What angers Otis most is not so much what popular culture has produced, but, rather, what it has suppressed. "That's been the big question in my life, " he says, "I've got to figure that one out. Instead of thanking God for the African presence, cause they've been a great gift to this country . . . and they constantly attempted to share this gift. But they were always rebuffed and always used and abused, not accepted."[17] Johnny Otis has always struggled to call attention to that precious resource for America, to use his own life as an example of the kind of culture that could be built on imagination and desire as well as on tradition—the kind of culture that began to emerge in those postwar industrial cities. That quest links Johnny Otis to other Americans, to Herman Melville and Mark Twain and Willa Cather and Scott Joplin, who reveled in America's exuberant pluralities. It links him as well to representatives of other marginalized and suppressed groups—gays and lesbians, Native Americans, Chicanos, Asian Americans, women, workers, and the myriad other voices that find their realities at best distorted and at worst erased from popular culture. But they continue to create, they continue to speak their minds, they continue to learn from each other.

These quests open up wounds, and they take place under conditions of communications distorted by commerce, racism, state power, and sexism. But they persist, even against the grain of economic and cultural matrices, because they keep alive cherished possibilities. In defiance of concentrated economic and political power unprecedented in world history, they continue to look for an America that is a realization of its own best hopes—a chorus of many voices and a land of a thousand dances.

Notes

Notes

CHAPTER 1.

1. Richard Terdiman, "Deconstructing Memory: On Representing the Past and Theorizing Culture in France Since the Revolution," *Diacritics* (Winter), 1985, 14, 19.

2. I am indebted to Bruce Lincoln for pointing out to me that itinerant actors, lecturers, medicine salesmen, and circus performers lacked direct ties of kinship, propinquity, business, or history with their audiences, thus gaining special privileges to perform, but losing certain protections from the consequences of their performances.

3. Michael Bristol, *Carnival and Theater* (New York: Methuen, 1985), 113.

4. For a discussion of the concept of "privacy in public" see John F. Kasson's social history of Coney Island, *Amusing the Million* (New York: Hill and Wang, 1978).

5. See Kathy Peiss, *Cheap Amusements* (Philadelphia: Temple University Press, 1986).

6. Of course, temporary liberation from sexual repression often mandated a re-problematization of sexuality as well in, for example, the melodrama.

7. I. C. Jarvie, *Thinking about Society: Theory and Practice* (Norwell, MA: Kluwer Academic Press, 1986), 372.

8. Stuart Hall, "Notes on Deconstructing 'the Popular,' " in Raphael Samuel, ed., *People's History and Socialist Theory* (London: Routledge and Kegan Paul, 1981), 227.

9. Here I wish to avoid the debates about "popular" vs. "mass" culture, in which popular describes voluntary bottom-up creation and mass refers to top-down, mass-marketed commercial culture. These polarities obscure the important grass-roots creation that takes place within "mass culture," as well as the manipulated "mass" aspects of "popular culture."

10. Stuart Hall, "Notes on Deconstructing 'the Popular,' " 228.

11. Pierre Bourdieu, "The Aristocracy of Culture," *Media, Culture, and Society* n. 2 (1980), 237.

12. Tania Modleski, "The Rhythms of Reception: Daytime Television and Women's Work," in E. Ann Kaplan, ed., *Regarding Television* (Los Angeles: University Publications of America, 1983), 67–75.

13. Fredric Jameson, "Reification and Utopia in Mass Culture," *Social Text* v. 1, 1979.

14. See George Lipsitz, *Class and Culture in Cold War America: A Rainbow at Midnight* (South Hadley, MA: Bergin and Garvey, 1982), 187–88.

15. Kathleen Hall Jamieson, *Eloquence in an Electronic Age* (New York: Oxford University Press, 1988), 81.

16. Quoted by Willard Gingerich, "Heidegger and the Aztecs: The Poetics of Knowing in Pre-Hispanic Nahuatl Poetry," in Brian Swann and Arnold Krupat, *Recovering the Word* (Berkeley: University of California Press, 1987), 100–101.

17. Jane Feuer, "Narrative Form in American Network Television," in Colin McCabe, ed., *High Theory/Low Culture* (New York: St. Martin's, 1986), 112. Laura Mulvey, "Melodrama in and out of the Home," in Colin McCabe, ed., *High Theory/Low Culture*, 96.

18. Pierre Bourdieu, "The Aristocracy of Culture," 239.

19. Stuart Hall,"The Economy of Prestige," Minneapolis, Minnesota, April 9, 1988, author's notes.

20. See Richard Terdiman, "Deconstructing Memory."

21. Fredric Jameson, "Reification and Utopia in Mass Culture."

22. See Hayden White, *The Content of the Form* (Baltimore and London: Johns Hopkins University Press, 1987), 157.

23. Neil Postman, *Amusing Ourselves to Death* (New York: Penguin, 1985), 127.

24. Allan Bloom, *The Closing of the American Mind* (New York: Simon and Schuster, l987).

25. Maria Damon, " 'Unmeaning Jargon'/Uncanonized Beatitude: Bob Kaufman, Poet," *The South Atlantic Quarterly* 87:4 (Fall) 1988, 708–9.

CHAPTER 2

1. Willa Cather, *My Antonia* (New York: Random House, 1918), 254.

2. Quoted in Neil Postman, *Amusing Ourselves to Death* (New York: Penguin, 1985), 137.

3. Russell Jacoby, *Social Amnesia* (Boston: Beacon Press, 1975), 3–4.

4. Lawrence Grossberg, "Another Boring Day in Paradise: Rock and Roll and the Empowerment of Everyday Life," *Popular Music* 5, 1985.

5. John Berger, "In Opposition to History, In Defiance of Time," *Village Voice*, October 8–14, 1984, 89–90.

6. Warren I. Susman, *Culture as History* (New York: Pantheon, 1984), 25–26.

7. Quoted in *On Campus* (November) 1987, v. 7, n. 3, 2.

8. Quoted in *On Campus*. Cheney's contradictory attitude about "history" is revealed most fully in her 1988 "Report to the President, the Congress, and the American People," where she laments students' lack of historical aptitude yet asserts that the value of the humanities lies in its "timeless" truths. Scholars who attempt to locate those "timeless" truths within historical time draw Cheney's derision for "politicizing" the curriculum. See *The Chronicle of Higher Education*, September 21, 1988, v. 35, n. 4.

9. Allan Bloom, *The Closing of the American Mind* (New York: Simon and Schuster, 1987), 58.

10. Quoted in *On Campus* (November), 1987, v. 7, n. 3, 2.

11. E. D. Hirsch, Jr., *Cultural Literacy* (Boston: Houghton-Mifflin, 1987), 107.

12. Quoted in *On Campus*.

13. Lynne Cheney, "Report to the President, the Congress, and the American People," esp. A18–A19.

14. Allan Bloom, *The Closing of the American Mind*, 37.

15. E. D. Hirsch, Jr., *Cultural Literacy*, 84, 107.

16. Diane Ravitch and Chester Finn, "What Do Our 17 Year Olds Know?" *Chronicle of Higher Education* October 7, 1987, B4. *What Do Our 17 Year Olds Know?* (New York: Harper and Row, 1987) especially pp. 205–14.

17. Hayden White, *Tropics of Discourse: Essays in Cultural Criticism* (Baltimore: Johns Hopkins University Press, 1978), 39.

18. Hayden White, *Tropics of Discourse*, 32.

19. See Dominick La Capra, *History and Criticism* (Ithaca, New York: Cornell University Press, 1985), 106.

20. Michel Foucault, "Two Lectures," p. 108, quoted in Thomas Dumm, *Democracy and Punishment* (Madison: University of Wisconsin Press, 1987), 151.

21. For example, Sande Cohen, *Historical Culture* (Berkeley and Los Angeles: University of California Press, 1986).

22. Quoted in Richard Terdiman, "Deconstructing Memory: On Representing the Past and Theorizing Culture in France Since the Revolution," *Diacritics* (Winter), 1985.

23. Hayden White, *The Content of the Form* (Baltimore and London: Johns Hopkins University Press, 1987), 149.

24. Dana Polan, *Power and Paranoia* (New York: Columbia University Press, 1986), 10.

25. *New York Times*, July 18, 1980, p. A8; July 21, 1981, p. 1; January 22, 1985, p. A17. I am indebted to Ron Takaki for calling this to my attention.

26. *New York Times*, January 22, 1985, p. A17.

27. Gerri Hirshey, *Nowhere to Run* (New York: Times Books, 1984), 266–67). I thank Adam Levy for calling this quote to my attention.

28. Dave Marsh, *Glory Days* (New York: Pantheon, 1986), 35–36.

29. Eudora Welty, "The House of Willa Cather," in Bernice Slote and Virginia Faulkner, ed., *The Art of Willa Cather* (Lincoln: University of Nebraska Press, 1974), 20.

CHAPTER 3

1. David Marc, *Comic Visions* (Boston: Unwin Hyman, 1989) 51.

2. Stuart Ewen condemns these shows for their hostility to immigrant life and their insistence on imposing a consumerist frame upon it in his *Captains of Consciousness: Advertising and the Social Roots of the Consumer Culture* (New York: McGraw Hill, 1976), 208–10. Marty Jezer takes a more favorable view in *The Dark Ages*, (Boston: South End, 1982), 191–94.

3. Erik Barnouw, *The Sponsor* (New York: Oxford University Press, 1979).

4. For a discussion of the "infinitely renewable present" see Daniel Boorstin, *The Americans: The Democratic Experience*, (New York: Vintage, 1973), 392–97.

5. Of course, class, ethnicity, and race remained important, but their relationship to individual identity changed radically at this time. Elsewhere I have argued that the bureaucratization of trade unions and xenophobic anti-communism also contributed to declining identification with ethnicity and class, see my *Class and Culture in Cold War America: A Rainbow at Midnight*, (South Hadley, MA: Bergin and Garvey, 1982).

6. Robert Allen, *Speaking of Soap Operas* (Chapel Hill: University of North Carolina Press, 1985), 126, 164. Richard de Cordova, "The Transition from Radio to Television," unpublished paper presented at the Society for Cinema Studies meetings, New York, New York, June 12, 1985.

7. Note the discussions in this chapter on *The Goldbergs* and *Amos 'n' Andy*, and the evolution of *I Remember Mama* as presented in the next chapter.

8. See Albert U. Romasco, *The Poverty of Abundance* (New York: Oxford University Press, 1965) and Barton Bernstein, "The Conservative Achievements of New Deal Reform," in Barton Bernstein, ed., *Towards a New Past* (New York: Vintage, 1968).

9. Henry Berger, "Social Protest in St. Louis," unpublished paper presented at a Missouri Committee for the Humanities Forum, St. Louis, Missouri. March 12, 1982.

10. George Lipsitz, *Class and Culture in Cold War America*.

11. Ibid.

12. Ibid.

13. *TV Facts* (New York: Facts on File, 1980), 141.

14. Neilsen ratings epitomize television's view of the family as separate market segments to be addressed independently.

15. William Boddy, "The Studios Move into Prime Time: Hollywood and the Television Industry in the 1950s," *Cinema Journal* 12 (4), 1986, 23–37. Jeanne Allen, "The Social Matrix of Television: Invention in the United States," in E. Ann Kaplan, ed., *Regarding Television* (Los Angeles: University Publications of America, 1983), 109–19.

16. George Lipsitz, *Class and Culture in Cold War America*. 120–21.

17. Geoffrey Moore and Phillip Klein, *The Quality of Consumer Installment Credit* (Washington, D.C.: National Bureau of Economic Research, 1967). Marty Jezer, *The Dark Ages* (Boston: South End, 1982).

18. Susan Hartmann, *The Home Front and Beyond* (Boston: Twayne, 1982), 165–68. John Mollenkopf, *The Contested City* (Princeton: Princeton University Press, 1983), 111.

19. "The Lush New Suburban Market," *Fortune* (November) 1953, 128.

20. Michael Stone, "Housing: The Economic Crisis," in Chester Hartman, ed., *America's Housing Crisis: What is to be Done?* (London and New York: Routledge and Kegan Paul, 1983), 122.

21. Quoted in Marty Jezer, *The Dark Ages*, 127.

22. Ernest Dichter, *The Strategy of Desire* (Garden City, NY: Doubleday, 1960), 210.

23. Ernest Dichter, *The Strategy of Desire*, 209.

24. "The Rock and Roll Kid," *Hey, Jeannie*. Academy of Television Arts Collection, University of California, Los Angeles.

25. "The In-laws," *The Goldbergs (Molly)*, Academy of Television Arts Collection, University of California, Los Angeles.

26. "The In-laws," *The Goldbergs (Molly)*.

27. "Moving Day," *The Goldbergs (Molly)* Academy of Television Arts Collection, University of California, Los Angeles.

28. "R228," *Life of Riley*, Academy of Television Arts Collection, University of California, Los Angeles.

29. "R228," *Life of Riley*. "Bad Companions," *The Goldbergs (Molly)*, Academy of Television Arts Collection, University of California, Los Angeles.

30. "Mama and the Carpenter," *Mama*, Academy of Television Arts Collection, University of California, Los Angeles.

31. "Andy the Godfather," *Amos 'n' Andy*, Academy of Television Arts Collection, University of California, Los Angeles. "The Rock and Roll Kid," *Hey, Jeannie*, Academy of Television Arts Collection, University of California, Los Angeles.

32. "Der Fledermaus," *The Goldbergs (Molly)*, Academy of Television Arts Collection, University of California, Los Angeles.

33. Elizabeth Meehan and Bradford Ropes, "Mama's Birthday," Theater Arts Collection. University Research Library. University of California, Los Angeles.

34. Susan Hartmann, *The Home Front and Beyond* (Boston: Twayne, 1982), 168.

35. Elizabeth Meehan and Bradford Ropes, "Mama's Birthday."

36. Elizabeth Meehan and Bradford Ropes, "Mama's Birthday."

37. Charles E. Swanson and Robert L. Jones, "Television Ownership and Its Correlates," *Journal of Applied Psychology* v. 35, 1951, 352–57.

38. Martha Wolfenstein, "The Emergence of Fun Morality," *Journal of Social Issues* v. 7, n. 4. 1951, 15–25.

39. *TV Guide*, May 7, 1954, p. 11.

40. *Ladies Home Journal*, September, 1956. pp. 130–31. *TV Guide*, August 7, 1953, 7.

41. *TV Guide*, November 2, 1953, 17.

42. Susan Hartmann, *The Home Front and Beyond*, 164–65.

43. Joel Kovel, "Rationalization and the Family," *Telos* (37),13–14.

44. Kovel, "Rationalization and the Family."

45. Nancy Chodorow, *Reproduction of Mothering* (Berkeley: University of California Press, 1978), 189.

46. Nancy Chodorow, *Reproduction of Mothering*, 181. Joel Kovel, "Rationalization and the Family," 14.

47. Quoted in Horace Newcomb, *TV: The Critical View* (New York: Oxford University Press, 1978).

48. "R228," *The Life of Riley*.

49. *TV Guide*, October 1, 1955, 14.

50. Stanley Aronowitz, *Working Class Hero* (New York: Pilgrim, 1983).

51. *TV Guide*, December 29, 1956, 17.

52. "Jeannie the Cabdriver," *Hey, Jeannie*. Academy of Television Arts Collection, University of California, Los Angeles.

53. "The Rent Strike," *The Goldbergs*, Museum of Broadcasting, New York, New York. "The Power Line," *Life With Luigi*, Script 10. Norman Tokar Papers, Special Collections Room, Doheny Library. University of Southern California. Los Angeles.

54. "Mama and the Carpenter," *Mama*, Academy of Television Arts Collection, University of California, Los Angeles.

55. "Bad Companions," *The Goldbergs (Molly)*.

56. I want to thank Ruth Wood of the English Department of the University of Minnesota for calling my attention to these symbols in *The Honeymooners*.

57. "R228," *The Life of Riley*.

58. Ibid.

59. "Is There a Doctor in the House," "Boogie Comes Homes," "Moving Day," *The Goldbergs (Molly)*, Academy of Television Arts Collection, University of California, Los Angeles.

60. Yet the *Mama* show still sought credibility with its audience by relying on the Bay Ridge, Brooklyn chapter of the Sons of Norway order for advice on authentic Nor-

wegian folk customs and stories. Remarks by Dick Van Patten and Ralph Nelson, Museum of Broadcasting, New York, New York. December 17, 1985.

61. "The Loud Speaker," *The Honeymooners*, Academy of Television Arts Collection, University of California, Los Angeles.

62. Erik Barnouw, *The Sponsor* (New York: Oxford University Press, 1979), 106.

63. Erik Barnouw, *Tube of Plenty* (New York: Oxford University Press, 1982), 126. Marty Jezer, *The Dark Ages* (Boston: South End, 1982), 193–94. Stefan Kanfer, *A Journal of the Plague Years* (New York: Atheneum, 1973), 154. *New Republic* January 21, 1952, 8. February 18, 1952, 22.

64. See Nathan Irvin Huggins, *Harlem Renaissance* (New York: Oxford University Press, 1978).

65. Thomas Cripps, "The Amos 'n' Andy Controversy," in John O'Connor, ed., *American History and American Television* (New York: Ungar, 1983), 33–54. J. Fred Macdonald, *Blacks and White TV* (Chicago: Nelson Hall, 1983), 27–28. *Newsweek*, July 9, 1951, 56.

66. *Los Angeles Times* Calendar Section, February 29, 1984, 1.

67. "Kingfish Has a Baby," *Amos 'n' Andy*, Theater Arts Collection, University Research Library, University of California, Los Angeles.

68. Ibid.

69. Julius Lester, *All Is Well* (New York: Morrow, 1976), 14.

70. For an application of Bakhtin's work to television, see Horace Newcomb, "On the Dialogic Aspects of Mass Communication," *Critical Studies in Mass Communication* v. 1, n. 1. (1984), 34–50.

71. Stuart Hall, "Culture, Media, and the 'Ideological' Effect," in James Curran, Michael Gurevitch, and Janet Woollacott, eds., *Mass Communication and Society* (Beverly Hills: Sage, 1979).

72. Jürgen Habermas, *Legitimation Crisis* (Boston: Beacon Press, 1975).

73. "The Rock and Roll Kid," *Hey, Jeannie*. "The Insurance Policy," *Life With Luigi*, Script 2. "The In-laws," *The Goldbergs (Molly)*.

74. Stuart Hall, "Culture, Media, and the 'Ideological' Effect."

75. Gertrude Berg, *Molly and Me* (New York: McGraw Hill, 1961), 167.

76. Jürgen Habermas, *Legitimation Crisis*, 71–75.

77. Jürgen Habermas, *Legitimation Crisis*, 71.

78. Marc Daniels, Presentation at the Directors Guild of America, Los Angeles, California. July 11, 1984.

79. Joel Kovel, "Rationalization and the Family," *Telos* (37), 1978, 19.

80. Protection of the family represents an old theme for conservatives, and it has been a traditional device for creating dramatic tension. But never before have these two traditions been as thoroughly unified as dramatic and political themes, and never before have they dominated conservative thought as they have in the last decade.

81. Fredric Jameson, *The Political Unconscious* (Ithaca: Cornell University Press, 1981), 101.

CHAPTER 4

1. Elizabeth Meehan and Bradford Ropes, "Mama's Birthday," Theater Arts Collection. University Research Library. University of California, Los Angeles.

2. Rick Mitz, *The Great TV Sitcom Book*, (New York: Perigree, 1983), 458.

3. Rosemary Rice, Dick Van Patten, and Robin Morgan, *I Remember Mama* Symposium, Museum of Broadcasting, New York City, December 17, 1985, author's notes. Ralph Nelson, private conversation with author, December 17, 1985, repeated during interview with author on January 11, 1986, Monteceito, California.

4. *Interview with Ralph Nelson*, Monteceito, California, January 11, 1986

5. Rosemary Rice, *I Remember Mama* Symposium.

6. Robin Morgan, *I Remember Mama*.

7. Kathryn Forbes, *Mama's Bank Account* (New York: Harcourt, 1943).

8. *Current Biography*, 1945, 102. John Van Druten, *I Remember Mama* (New York: Dramatists Play Service Incorporated, 1944).

9. *New York Times*, May 17, 1966.

10. Stefan Kanfer, *A Journal of the Plague Years*, (New York: Atheneum, 1973), 154.

11. Andrea Walsh, *Women's Film and Female Experience* (New York: Praeger, 1984), 104.

12. Quoted in Andrea Walsh, *Women's Film and Female Experience*, 106–7.

13. DeWitt Bodeen screenplay, "I Remember Mama," Fred Guiol Collection, California State University at Fullerton, #4–87.

14. De Witt Bodeen screenplay, "I Remember Mama."

15. Ralph Nelson Papers, University of California, Los Angeles. Box 78. Scripts #1, 13, 20, 6. "T.R.'s New Home" and "Mama's Bad Day," Academy of Television Arts Collection, University of California, Los Angeles.

16. Ralph Nelson Papers, Special Collection 875, University Research Library, University of California at Los Angeles. Box 78. Scripts # 9, 2. Frank Gabrielson Papers, Sudbury, Massachusetts, "Mama and the Magic Lantern," "The Pet Show," "Nels and the Girl with the Lively Eyes."

17. "Tricycles Last," T86 1142, Museum of Broadcasting, New York.

18. "Nels and the Train Set," T86 0092, Museum of Broadcasting, New York.

19. "The Hansens Rise in the World," T86 1128, Museum of Broadcasting, New York.

20. Ralph Nelson Papers, Special Collection 875, Box 45, University Research Library, University of California, Los Angeles.

21. Ralph Nelson Papers, Special Collection 875, Box 44. Memo from Doris Quinlan to Carol Irwin, Frank Gabrielson, and Ralph Nelson, December 8, 1954.

22. CBS Press Release, 1949, Ralph Nelson Papers, Special Collection 875, Box 44, University Research Library, University of California, Los Angeles.

23. "T.R.'s New Home," *Mama*.

24. Ernest Dichter, *The Strategy of Desire* (Garden City, NY: Doubleday, 1960), 209.

25. Tania Modleski, "Femininity as Mas(s)querade: A Feminist Approach to Mass Culture," in Colin McCabe, ed., *High Theory/Low Culture* (New York: St. Martin's, 1986), 42.

26. Script #13, Ralph Nelson Papers, Special Collection 875, Box 78, University Research Library, University of California, Los Angeles.

27. Script #2, Ralph Nelson Papers, Special Collection 875, Box 78.

28. Script #15, Ralph Nelson Papers, Special Collection 875, Box 78.

29. *Interview with Hale Lamont Havers*, Sudbury, Massachusetts, May 15, 1987.

30. Murray Schumach, "Writing for Video," *New York Times*, February 18, 1951, x9.

31. *Interview with Ralph Nelson*, Monteceito, California, January 11, 1986.

32. *Interview with Ralph Nelson*.

CHAPTER 5

1. M. M. Bakhtin, *Speech Genres & Other Late Essays* (Austin: University of Texas Press, 1986), 170.

2. Richard Terdiman, "Deconstructing Memory: On Representing the Past and Theorizing Culture in France Since the Revolution," *Diacritics* (Winter), 1985, 23.

3. Lawrence Grossberg, "Another Boring Day in Paradise: Rock and Roll and the Empowerment of Everyday Life," *Popular Music* 5 (1985).

4. E. Ann Kaplan, *Rocking Around the Clock* (New York and London: Methuen, 1987, 145–46), 29.

5. See Richard Terdiman, "Deconstructing Memory," 20. Also see chapter 2.

6. Hayden White, *The Content of the Form* (Baltimore and London: Johns Hopkins University Press, 1987), 156.

7. Robert Hilburn, "Public Enemy's Chuck D: Puttin' on the Rap," *Los Angeles Times* calendar section, February 7, 1988, 63.

8. "David Bowie," *Musician* (May) 1983.

9. Dave Marsh, *Glory Days* (New York: Pantheon, 1986), 36.

10. Simon Frith, *Sound Effects* (New York: Pantheon, 1981), 163.

11. Simon Frith, *Sound Effects*, 158.

12. Simon Frith, *Sound Effects*, 16–17.

13. Simon Frith, *Sound Effects*, 272.

14. Lawrence Grossberg, "Another Boring Day in Paradise."

15. E. Ann Kaplan, *Rocking Around the Clock* (New York and London: Methuen, 1987), 30, 44.

16. Simon Frith, *Sound Effects*, 88.

17. Lawrence Grossberg, "Another Boring Day in Paradise."

18. E. Ann Kaplan, *Rocking Around the Clock*, 31.

19. Stuart Hall, "Notes on Deconstructing 'the Popular,' " in Raphael Samuel, ed., *People's History and Socialist Theory* (London: Routledge, Kegan Paul, 1981), 228.

20. Lawrence Grossberg, "Another Boring Day in Paradise," 229.

21. Simon Frith *Sound Effects*, 75.

22. E. Ann Kaplan, *Rocking Around the Clock*, 31.

23. Robert Pattison, *The Triumph of Vulgarity* (New York: Oxford, 1987), 39.

24. *Living Blues* n. 45/46, 1982.

25. *Wave Length* (January), 1982, 27.

26. Arnold Shaw, *The Rockin' 50s* (New York: Dutton, 1974), 89–92.

27. Jerry Hopkins, *Elvis* (New York: Warner, 1972), 37. *Time*, February 11, 1946.

28. Arnold Shaw, *The Rockin' 50s*, 89–92. George Lipsitz, *Class and Culture in Cold War America: A Rainbow at Midnight* (South Hadley, MA: Bergin and Garvey, 1982), 204–21. John Goldrosen, *The Buddy Holly Story* (New York: Music Sales, 1979).

29. Steve Chapple and Reebee Garofalo, *Rock'n'Roll Is Here to Pay* (Chicago: Nelson Hall, 1978), 29.

30. Arnold Shaw, *The Rockin' 50s*, 247–56. Anthony Heilbut, *The Gospel Sound* (New York: Simon and Schuster, 1971), 297.

31. George Lipsitz, *Class and Culture in Cold War America*, 206–7.

32. See William H. Whyte, *The Organization Man* (New York: Simon and Schuster, 1957), and Herman L. Wouk, *The Caine Mutiny* (New York: Doubleday, 1954).

33. The phrase "prestige from below" is from a talk by Stuart Hall at the Economy of Prestige Conference, University of Minnesota, April 9, 1988, Minneapolis, Minne-·sota.

34. Octavio Paz, *Labyrinth of Solitude* (New York: Grove, 1962), ch. 1. George Lipsitz, *Class and Culture in Cold War America*, 25–28.

35. Dizzy (John Birks) Gillespie, *To Be or Not to Bop* (New York: Doubleday, 1979).

36. Arnold Shaw, *The Rockin' 50s*, 190–93. John Goldrosen, *The Buddy Holly Story* (New York: Music Sales, 1979), 37.

37. Steve Chapple and Reebee Garofalo, *Rock'n'Roll Is Here To Pay*, 41. John Goldrosen, *The Buddy Holly Story* 97.

38. Arnold Shaw, *The Rockin' 50s* 79.

39. "Interview with Chuck Berry," *Jet Lag* (September) 1980, 10.

40. Steve Chapple and Reebee Garofalo, *Rock'n'Roll Is Here to Pay*, 46–47.

41. Steve Chapple and Reebee Garofalo, *Rock'n'Roll Is Here to Pay*, 60–64.

42. Simon Frith, *Sound Effects*, 83, 84.

43. Ted Drozdowski, "Irma Thomas: Radio or Not, She's Still Queen," *Musician* n. 119 (September) 1988, 11.

44. Steve Chapple and Reebee Garofalo, *Rock'n'Roll Is Here to Pay*, 69.

45. *Wave Length* (May) 1982, 21–28, (August) 1982, 12–15. *New Orleans Times-Picayune*, May 3, 1981, 41. Charles Neville was in New York at this time.

46. *Interview with Billy Peek*, August 5, 1982. *Wave Length* (August) 1982, 14.

47. Charlie Gillett, *The Sound of the City* (New York: Dutton, 1970). Steve Chapple and Reebee Garofalo, *Rock'n'Roll Is Here to Pay*, 246–48.

CHAPTER 6

1. Octavio Paz, *The Labyrinth of Solitude* (New York: Grove Press, 1961), 13.

2. Walter Benjamin, *Illuminations* (New York: Harcourt, Brace, and World, 1968), 255.

3. Marshall Berman, *All That Is Solid Melts into Air* (New York: Simon and Schuster, 1982).

4. Paz, *The Labyrinth of Solitude*, 13.

5. The term *bricolage* is from Claude Lévi-Strauss, who uses it to propose a universal description of innate human characteristics, but it is used here simply as a description of cultural amalgamation processes.

6. Berman, *All That Is Solid*, 1982, 15.

7. Antonio Gramsci, *Selections from the Prison Notebooks*, eds., Quintin Hoare and Geoffrey Nowell Smith (New York: International Publishers, l971).

8. Eshref Shevky and Marilyn Williams, *The Social Areas of Los Angeles*. (Berkeley: University of California Press, 1949). Ricardo Romo, *East Los Angeles*. (Austin: University of Texas Press, 1983). Romo also reveals some long-standing ethnic interaction between blacks and Chicanos.

9. *Home Owners Loan Corporation City Survey Files*, Los Angeles 1939. National Archives, Washington, D.C., p. 7.

10. *Home Owners Loan Corporation City Survey Files*, Area D-53.

11. Gilbert G. Gonzales, "Factors Relating to Property Ownership of Chicanos in Lincoln Heights, Los Angeles," *Aztlan*, 2, Fall 1981. pp. 111–14.

Notes to Chapter 6

12. George Lipsitz, " 'Against the Wind': The Class Composition of Rock and Roll Music," *Knowledge and Society*, v. 5. 1984.

13. Lindsey Haley, "Pachuco Boogie," *Low Rider*, June 1985, 34. *Los Angeles Times* Calendar Section, October 12, 1980, 6. Roberto Caballero-Robledo, "The Return of Pachuco Boogie," *Nuestro*, November 1979, 14–17.

14. Mauricio Mazon, *Zoot Suit Riots*. (Austin: University of Texas Press, 1984). George Lipsitz, *Class and Culture in Cold War America*, 26–28.

15. *Los Angeles Times*, October 12, 1980; *Nuestro*, November 17, 1979.

16. Marshall Berman, *All That Is Solid Melts into Air*, 15.

17. Ruben Guevara, "The View from the Sixth Street Bridge: The History of Chicano Rock," in Dave Marsh, ed., *Rock'n'Roll Confidential Report*. (New York: Pantheon. 1985), 118. Marjorie Miller, "Cholos Return to Their Roots and Find They Bloom," *Los Angeles Times*, September 9, 1984, part I, 3.

18. Ray Topping, "Chuck Higgins Pachuko Hop," liner notes, Ace Records. Ch 81, 1983.

19. Robert Palmer, *Baby That Was Rock and Roll* (New York: Harvest/HBJ, 1978), 19.

20. Robert Palmer, *Baby That Was Rock and Roll*, 16.

21. *Interview with Johnny Otis*, Altadena, California. December 14, 1986.

22. *Interview with Johnny Otis*.

23. *Interview with Johnny Otis*.

24. *Interview with Johnny Otis*. Steven Loza, "The Musical Life of the Mexican-Chicano People in Los Angeles, 1945– 1985," Ph.D. Dissertation, University of California, Los Angeles. 1985, 124.

25. *Interview with Johnny Otis*.

26. *Interview with Johnny Otis*.

27. *Interview with Johnny Otis*. Ruben Guevara, "The View from the Sixth Street Bridge," 118.

28. *Interview with Johnny Otis*.

29. Johnny Otis, *Listen to the Lambs*. (New York: W. W. Norton, 1968). *Los Angeles Times* Calendar Section, April 3, 1985. Joe Sasfy, "Johnny Otis' Fifth Decade," *Washington Post*, June 24, 1985. Section B. 7.

30. Jim Dawson and Bob Keane, "Ritchie Valens—His Life Story," Rhino Records insert. 1981, 10.

31. Beverly Mendheim, *Ritchie Valens: The First Latino Rocker* (Tempe, AZ: Bilingual Press, 1987), 18, 21.

32. Beverly Mendheim, *Ritchie Valens: The First Latino Rocker*, 23.

33. Beverly Mendheim, *Ritchie Valens: The First Latino Rocker*, 34.

34. Jim Dawson, "Valens, the Forgotten Story," *Los Angeles Times*, February 3, 1980, 100. Jim Dawson and Bob Keane, "Ritchie Valens—His Life Story," Rhino Records insert. 1981, 5.

35. Jim Dawson and Bob Keane, "Ritchie Valens—His Life Story," 3–5. Jim Dawson, "Valens, the Forgotten Story," 100.

36. Don Snowden, "The Sound of East L.A., 1964," *Los Angeles* Times Calendar Section. October 28, 1984, 6.

37. Ethlie Ann Vare, "Cannibal and the Headhunters," *Goldmine*, November 1983, 26, 53. Don Snowden, "The Sounds of East L.A., 1964," *Los Angeles Times* Calendar Section, October 28, 1984, 7.

Notes to Chapter 6

38. Ethlie Ann Vare, "Cannibal and the Headhunters," 26.

39. Ibid. 53.

40. Don Snowden, "The Sound of East L.A., 1964," 6–7.

41. For a detailed explanation of the urban crisis of the 1960s and 1970s see John Mollenkopf, *The Contested City* (Princeton: Princeton University Press, 1983).

42. Luis Rodriguez, "La Veintineuve," in L.A. Latino Writers Workshop, 201 — *Latino Experience in Literature and Art*, n.d. 9.

43. Ruben Guevara, "The View From the Sixth Street Bridge," 120. 44. Ruben Guevara, "The View From the Sixth Street Bridge," 120. *Los Angeles Times* Calendar Section, November 9, 1980, 69. El Larry, "Los Lobos," *Low Rider*, Mar–Apr. 1984, 34.

45. Joel Whitburn, *The Billboard Book of Top 40 Hits*. (New York: Billboard, 1984).

46. Melvin Oliver and James Johnson, Jr., "Inter-Ethnic Conflict in an Urban Ghetto," *Research in Social Movements: Conflict and Change*, v. 6, JAI Sage, 57–94.

47. Ruben Guevara, "The View from the Sixth Street Bridge."

48. Michael M. J. Fischer, "Ethnicity and the Post-Modern Arts of Memory," in James Clifford and George Marcus, ed,. *Writing Culture* (Berkeley: University of California Press, 1986), 194–233.

49. *Los Angeles Times*, December 28, 1982.

50. El Larry, "Los Lobos," *Low Rider* (March-April) 1984, 34.

51. Rob Tannenbaum, "Los Lobos," *Musician* 77 (March) 1985, 19.

52. Antonio Gramsci, *Selections from the Prison Notebooks*, eds., Quintin Hoare and Geoffrey Nowell Smith (New York: International Publishers, 1971), 9–10.

53. Ibid. 9-10.

54. Brenda Bright, "The Meaning of Roles and the Role of Showing: Houston Low Riders," unpublished, 1984. Luis F. B. Plascencia, "Low Riding in the Southwest: Cultural Symbols in the Mexican Community," paper for the Center for Mexican-American Studies: University of Texas, Austin, 1984. Don Snowden, "The Sounds of East Los Angeles," *Los Angeles Times*, October 28, 1984.

55. Don Snowden, "The Sound of East Los Angeles," *Los Angeles Times*, October 28, 1984. Lindsey Haley-Alemon, "Zyanya," *Low Rider* (March–April) 1984, 24–25.

56. *Los Angeles Times*, October 12, 1980.

57. Victor Valle, "Chicano Art: An Emerging Generation," *Los Angeles Times*, August 7, 1983.

58. Mary Helen Ponce, "Los Piojos," in *201 — Latino Experience in Literature and Art* (Los Angeles: Los Angeles Latino Writers Workshop, n.d.).

59. *Los Angeles Times*, October 8, 1980; November 9, 1980.

60. *Los Angelinos — The Eastside Renaissance*, (Zyanya Records), liner notes.

61. *Los Angeles Times*, October 12, 1980.

62. Rob Tannenbaum, "Los Lobos," 19.

63. Robert Hilburn, "Willie Packs 'Em In, Down on the Farm," *Los Angeles Times* Calendar Section, July 13, 1986, 63.

64. Judy Raphael, "Ragin' Cajun: Jo-El Sonnier's Last Stand," *L.A. Weekly*, August 8–15, 1985, 57.

65. Jean-François Lyotard, *The Postmodern Condition* (Minneapolis: University of Minnesota Press, 1984), 71–82.

66. Jürgen Habermas, *Legitimation Crisis* (Boston: Beacon Press, 1975).

67. Berman, *All That Is Solid*, 15.

285

CHAPTER 7

1. Roy Rosenzweig, *Eight Hours for What We Will* (Cambridge: Cambridge University Press, 1985). Kathy Peiss, *Cheap Amusements: Working Women and Leisure in Turn-of-the-Century New York* (Philadelphia: Temple University Press, 1985).

2. Dana Polan, *Power and Paranoia* (New York: Columbia University Press, 1986). Peter Biskind, *Seeing Is Believing: How Hollywood Taught Us to Stop Worrying and Love the Fifties* (New York: Pantheon, 1983). Michael Ryan and Douglas Kellner, *Camera Politica* (Bloomington: University of Indiana Press, 1988).

3. William Simon, "Liberty Valance Lives," *Southwest Media Review*. n. 3. 1985.

4. Charles Bitsch, "Interview with Nicholas Ray," in Jim Hillier, ed., *Cahiers du Cinema: The 1950s: Neo-Realism, Hollywood, New Wave* (Cambridge: Harvard University Press. 1985), 120.

5. William Grier and Price Cobbs, *Black Rage*. (New York: Basic, 1986), 72–73.

CHAPTER 8

1. Laura Mulvey, "Melodrama in and out of the Home," in Colin McCabe, ed., *High Theory/Low Culture* (New York: St. Martin's, 1986), 90.

2. Luc Moullet, "Sam Fuller: In Marlowe's Footsteps," in Jim Hillier, ed., *Cahiers du Cinema: The 1950s: Neo-Realism, Hollywood, New Wave* (Cambridge: Harvard University Press, 1985), 149. J. Hoberman, "American Abstract Sensationalism," *Art Forum* (February) 1981, 42. Frank McConnell, "Pickup on South Street and the Metamorphosis of the Thriller," *Film Heritage* v. 8, n. 3 (Spring) 1973, 9.

3. "Samuel Fuller Rises from Oblivion," *Drama-Logue* v. 11, n. 31, July 31–August 6, 1980, 1.

4. Phil Hardy, *Samuel Fuller* (London: Studio Vista Ltd, 1970), 372.

5. McConnell, "Pickup," 10.

6. Moullet, "Sam Fuller," 149.

7. Hoberman, "American Abstract Sensationalism," *Art Forum*, 45–46.

8. Hoberman, "American Abstract Sensationalism," 42.

9. Max Kozloff, "A Way of Seeing and the Act of Touching: Helen Leavitt's Photographs of the Forties," in David Featherstone, ed., *Observations*, 1984, 72.

10. John Raeburn, " 'Culture Morphology' and Cultural History in Berenice Abbott's *Changing New York*," in Jack Salzman, ed., *Prospects* v. 9 (New York: Cambridge University Press, 1984), 256, 263.

11. Raeburn, " 'Culture Morphology,' " 258.

12. See Warren I. Susman, *Culture as History* (New York: Pantheon, 1984) and David P.Peeler, *Hope Among Us Yet* (Athens and London: University of Georgia Press, 1987).

13. See, for example, Edgar Ulmer's *Detour* (1945) or Elia Kazan's *Boomerang* (1947) for representative films, or read fiction from the 1940s ranging from Mickey Spillane to Chester Himes.

14. McConnell, "Pickup," 15.

15. Tom Milne, "Sam Fuller," *Sight and Sound*, n. 49, 1980, 257. Quoted from *Monthly Film Bulletin*, July 1980, 168.

16. Richard Thompson, "Interview with Samuel Fuller," *Film Comment*, v. 13, n. 1 (Jan–Feb), 1977, 25.

17. Alan Hunter, "Sam Fuller," *Films and Filming*, n. 350 (November), 1983, 99–100.

18. Tom Ryan, "Samuel Fuller: Survivor," *Cinema Papers* n. 30 (Dec.–Jan.), 1980–1981, 424.

19. Ginger Varney, "The Fundamental Sam Fuller," *L.A. Weekly*, August 1–7, 1980, 7.

20. Nicholas Garnham, *Samuel Fuller* (London: BFI, 1971), 117.

21. Luc Moullet, "Samuel Fuller," 149.

22. Dave Kehr, "Cinema in 79: The Year's Top Ten Movies," *Chicago Reader*, January 4, 1980, 22.

23. Peter Bogdanovich, "Interview With Edgar G. Ulmer," *Film Culture*, n. 58–60 (1970), 206.

24. *New York Times*, December 25, 1936, 19.

25. Peter Bogdanovich, "Interview With Edgar Ulmer," *Film Culture* n. 58–60 (1970), 222.

26. Dana Polan, *Power and Paranoia* (New York: Columbia University Press, 1986), 194.

27. Tania Modleski, "Film Theory's Detour," *Screen* 23 (5), November–December, 1982, 74–75.

28. See interview with Shirley Castle Ulmer, *San Francisco Chronicle*, November 21, 1982, 33.

29. Todd McCarthy and Charles Flynn, *Kings of the B's* (New York: E. P. Dutton, 1975), 409.

CHAPTER 9

1. Leslie Marmon Silko, *Ceremony* (New York: American Library, 1977) 2.

2. Zora Neale Hurston, *Their Eyes Were Watching God* (Champaign, Illinois: University of Illinois, 1979), 1.

3. Barbara Johnson, "Metaphor, Metonymy and Voice in *Their Eyes Were Watching God*," in Henry Louis Gates, ed., *Black Literature and Literary Theory* (New York and London: Methuen, 1984), 218.

4. Donald F. Bouchard, ed., Sherry Simon, tr., Michel Foucault, *Language, Counter-Memory, Practice: Selected Essays and Interviews* (Ithaca: Cornell University Press, 1980), 139, 144, 150.

5. Jean-François Lyotard, *The Postmodern Condition* (Minneapolis: University of Minnesota Press, 1984).

6. Warren I. Susman, *Culture as History* (New York: Pantheon, 1984), 8.

7. Warren I. Susman, *Culture as History*, 12.

8. Hayden White, *Tropics of Discourse* (Baltimore: Johns Hopkins University Press, 1978), esp. chapter 1.

9. Will Wright, *Sixguns and Society* (Berkeley: University of California Press, 1975), 187.

10. Roland Barthes, *Mythologies* (New York: Hill and Wang, 1972), 129.

11. Toni Morrison, *Song of Solomon* (New York: New American Library, 1977), 53.

12. Eudora Welty, *Losing Battles* (New York: Random House, 1970), 298.

13. Ibid. 432.

14. Ibid. 432.

15. Leslie Marmon Silko, *Ceremony* (New York: New American Library, 1977), 19.

16. Ibid. 99.

17. Ibid. 199.

18. Ibid. 257.

19. Ibid. 132.

20. Barbara T. Christian, *From the Inside Out: Afro-American Women's Literary Tradition and the State* (Minneapolis: Center for Humanistic Studies, 1987), 4.

21. Ibid. 16.

22. John Okada, *No-No Boy* (Seattle: University of Washington Press, 1976), 159.

23. Rudolfo Anaya, *Bless Me Ultima* (Berkeley: Tonatiuh International, 1986), 115.

24. Ibid. 113.

25. Barbara T. Christian, *From the Inside Out*, 4.

26. Marshall Berman, *All That Is Solid Melts into Air*, 15.

27. Quoted in Elizabeth Long, *The American Dream and the Popular Novel* (London: Routledge, Kegan Paul, 1986),191.

28. James Clifford, "On Ethnographic Allegory," in James Clifford and George Marcus, ed., *Writing Culture* (Berkeley: University of California Press, 1986), 121.

29. Julia Kristeva, "Women's Time," in Toril Moi, ed., *The Kristeva Reader* (New York: Columbia University Press, 1986), 193–94.

30. Ibid. 207.

CHAPTER 10

1. Laura Mulvey, "Myth, Narrative, and Historical Experience," *History Workshop* (Spring) 1987.

2. Walter Benjamin, *Illuminations* (New York: Shocken Books, 1969), 83.

3. See Paul Buhle, *Popular Culture in America* (Minneapolis: University of Minnesota Press, 1987).

4. José E. Limon, "Western Marxism and Folklore," *Journal of American Folklore*, v. 96, n. 379, 1983, 49.

5. Fredric Jameson, "Reification and Utopia in Mass Culture," *Social Text*, v. 1, n. 1, 1979.

6. William Fox, "Folklore and Fakelore: Some Sociological Considerations," *Journal of the Folklore Institute*, v. 17, n. 2–3, May–December, 1980, 249.

7. David Elliott Draper, "The Mardi Gras Indians: The Ethnomusicology of Black Associations in New Orleans," (Ph.D. dissertation, Tulane University, 1973), 7, 27, 38, 40.

8. Draper, "The Mardi Gras Indians," 35, 54.

9. Les Blank, *Always for Pleasure*, Flower Films, 1978.

10. See Jason Berry, "Controversy Swirls Around Mardi Gras Indian Origins," *New Orleans Times-Picayune*, February 17, 1984. sec. 1, 6.

11. Jason Berry, Jonathan Foose, and Tad Jones, *Up from the Cradle of Jazz* (Athens and London: University of Georgia Press,1986) 210, 218.

12. Helen Joy Mayhew, "New Orleans Black Musical Culture: Tradition and the Individual Talent" (M.A. Thesis, University of Exeter, 1986), 187–88.

13. Jason Berry, Jonathan Foose, and Tad Jones, *Up from the Cradle of Jazz*, 210.

14. Jason Berry, "Pomp and Circumstance of the Mardi Gras Indians," *Dynamic Years*. n. 16. March 1981.

15. Draper, "The Mardi Gras Indians," 42. John Miller Chernoff identifies grace, strength, elegance, precision, happiness, composure,and dignity as key elements in performances by African chiefs on p. 150 of his wonderful book *African Rhythms and African Sensibility* (Chicago and London: University of Chicago Press,1979).

16. Chernoff, *African Rhythm and African Sensibility*, 33–34.

17. Draper, "The Mardi Gras Indians," 54. See also Alan Lomax, *Mr. Jelly Roll* (Berkeley: University of California Press, 1950, 1973), 12.

18. Draper, "The Mardi Gras Indians," 23. See also John Blassingame, *Black New Orleans, 1860–1880* (Chicago and London: University of Chicago Press, 1973).

19. Chernoff, *African Rhythms and African Sensibility*, 143.

20. Draper, "The Mardi Gras Indians," 218, 360.

21. Draper, "The Mardi Gras Indians," 227, 276, 286. Jason Berry, Jonathan Foose, and Tad Jones, *Up from the Cradle of Jazz*, 213.

22. Chernoff, *African Rhythm and African Sensibility*, 61.

23. Chernoff, *African Rhythm and African Sensibility*, 125.

24. Draper, "The Mardi Gras Indians," 362, 363.

25. Finn Wilhelmsen, "Creativity in the Songs of the Mardi Gras Indians of New Orleans, Louisiana," *Louisiana Folklore Miscellany*, v. 3, l973, 58.

26. Draper, "The Mardi Gras Indians," 130, 166, 167.

27. Draper, "The Mardi Gras Indians," 122, 166, 167.

28. Draper, "The Mardi Gras Indians," 103.

29. Draper, "The Mardi Gras Indians," 51, 53, 54.

30. Les Blank, *Always for Pleasure*, Flower Films, 1978.

31. Draper, "The Mardi Gras Indians," 115. Jason Berry, Jonathan Foose, and Tad Jones, *Up from the Cradle of Jazz*, 221.

32. Jason Berry, Jonathan Foose, Tad Jones, *Up from the Cradle of Jazz*, 218.

33. Ibid. 213.

34. Ibid. 218.

35. Draper, "The Mardi Gras Indians," 117, 118.

36. Jason Berry, Jonathan Foose, Tad Jones, *Up from the Cradle of Jazz*, 218.

37. Ibid.

38. John Miller Chernoff, *African Rhythm and African Sensibility*, 124, 125.

39. Draper, "The Mardi Gras Indians," 69, 70.

40. Jason Berry, Jonathan Foose, Tad Jones, *Up from the Cradle of Jazz*, 224, 235.

41. Ibid. 216. David Elliott Draper, "The Mardi Gras Indians," 36, 38.

42. Don Palmer, "Gumbo Variations," *The Soho News*, August 11, 1981, 23.

43. Draper, "The Mardi Gras Indians," 103.

44. Jason Berry, Jonathan Foose, Tad Jones, *Up from the Cradle of Jazz*, 220.

45. Ibid.

46. John Miller Chernoff, *African Rhythm and African Sensibility*, 50, 144, 150.

47. The phrase "danced faith" is Robert F. Thompson's. See Chernoff, *African Rhythm and African Sensibility*, 144.

48. Chernoff, *African Rhythm and African Sensibility*, 150.

49. José E. Limon, "Western Marxism and Folklore," *Journal of American Folklore*, v. 96, n. 379, 1983, 39.

50. William Fox, "Folklore and Fakelore: Some Sociological Considerations," *Journal of the Folklore Institute*, v. 17, n. 2–3, May–December 1980, 249, 255, 256.

51. Fredric Jameson, "Reification and Utopia in Mass Culture," *Social Text*, v. 1, n. 1, 1979, 134, 137, 138.

52. Draper, "The Mardi Gras Indians," 389.

53. Jeff Hannusch, *I Hear You Knockin'* (Ville Platte: Swallow Publications, 1985), 262.

54. Helen Joy Mayhew, "New Orleans Black Musical Culture: Tradition and the Individual Talent" (M.A. thesis, University of Exeter, 1986), 215.

55. Shepard Samuels, "The Dixie Cups," *Wavelength*, May 1982, 18. For a description of Leiber and Stoller's role in disseminating other popular narratives, see George Lipsitz, "Land of a Thousand Dances, Youth, Minorities, and Rock and Roll," in Lary May, ed., *Recasting America* (Chicago and London: University of Chicago Press, 1988).

56. Shepard Samuels, "The Dixie Cups," *Wavelength*. May 1982, l8.

57. See Jeff Hannusch, *I Hear You Knockin'*, 359–73.

58. Jason Berry, "Pomp and Circumstance of the Mardi Gras Indians," *Dynamic Years*, n. 16, March 1981.

59. Jason Berry, Jonathan Foose, and Tad Jones, *Up from the Cradle of Jazz*, 232.

60. Dave Hoekstra, "King Sunny Brightens Sound of Juju Music," *Chicago Sun-Times*, May 10, 1987, 10.

61. Jason Berry, "The Caribbean Connection," *New Orleans*, v. 19, May 1985, 67.

62. See also Hal Singer's song "Cornbread," and Hank Williams's "Move It On Over."

63. Quoted in *Wavelength*, n. 19, May 1982, 3.

64. Jon Bream, "Cyndi Lauper," *Minneapolis Star and Tribune*, December 7, 1986. 1G. A 1982 recording of "Iko Iko" by the Belle Stars appeared in the 1988 film *Rain Man* and subsequently made the best-seller charts in 1989.

65. Walter Benjamin, *Illuminations* (New York: Shocken, 1969) 85.

CHAPTER 11

1. Marshall Berman, *All That Is Solid Melts into Air* (New York: Simon and Schuster, 1982).

2. George Lipsitz, *Class and Culture in Cold War America: A Rainbow at Midnight* (South Hadley, MA: Bergin and Garvey, 1982).

3. *Interview with Johnny Otis*, December 14, 1986, Altadena, California.

4. *Interview with Johnny Otis*.

5. Ben Bagdikian, *The Media Monopoly* (Boston: Beacon Press, 1987).

6. Thomas K. Arnold, "Yes, There Is Life after the Doobie Brothers," *L.A. Times*, March 24, 1988, Sec VI, 1–6.

7. *Interview with Billy Peek*, August 5, 1982, St. Louis, Missouri.

8. *Interview with Billy Peek*, March 19, 1988, St. Louis, Missouri.

9. Action adventure show *Naked City* and dramatic series *East Side, West Side* were exceptions to these trends; they resonated with the sensibilities of an earlier era.

10. See Jane Feuer, "Narrative Form in American Network Television," in Colin McCabe, ed., *High Theory/Low Culture* (New York: St. Martin's, 1986), 106. Ella Taylor, *All in the (Work) Family* (Berkeley: University of California Press, forthcoming).

11. Marshall Berman, *All That Is Solid Melts into Air* (New York: Simon and Schuster, 1982), 171.

12. Jean Baudrillard, "The Ecstasy of Communication," in Hal Foster, *The Anti-Aesthetic* (Seattle: Bay Press), 1983.

13. Don Snowden, "Global Music with a Single Heart," *Los Angeles Times* Calendar section, August 7, 1988, 3.

14. "King Sunny Ade," *Musician* (May), 1983.

15. Albert Murray, *The Omni-Americans* (New York: Vintage Books, 1983), 22.

16. *Interview with Johnny Otis*, December 14, 1986, Altadena, California.

17. *Interview with Johnny Otis.*

Index

Index

Index

Beefheart, Captain, 155. *See also* Van Vleit

Belton, John, 203

Benatar, Pat, 35, 36

Benjamin, Walter, 134, 233, 253, 283n, 288n, 290n

Benton, Brook, 114

Berg, Gertrude, 53, 70, 73

Berger, Henry, 278n

Berger, John, 22, 276n

Berkeley (CA), 129, 141

Berlin, Steve, 151

Berman, Marshall, 134, 159, 227, 228, 257, 268–69, 283n, 284n, 285n, 288n, 290n

Bernardi, Herschel, 198

Bernstein, Barton, 278n

Bernstein, Basil, 14

Berry, Chuck, 113, 114, 115, 118, 122, 124, 126, 127, 128, 131, 263, 264, 265, 283n

Berry, Jason, 243, 288n, 289n, 290n

Bessie, Alvah, 203

Beverly, Helen, 198

Beyond the Time Barrier, 203

Big Brother and the Holding Company, 129

Big Chief Wants Plenty of Fire Water, 241

Big Chill, The, 265

Bihari, Saul, 119

Birmingham Jail, 114

Biskind, Peter, 164, 165, 176, 286n

Bismarck, North Dakota, 61

Black Cat, 196, 197, 201, 204, 206, 207

Blackboard Jungle, 113

Blair, Sally, 141

Blank, Les, 242, 288n, 289n

Blasters, The, 150–51

Bless Me Ultima, 225–26, 288n

Bloom, Allan, 17, 18, 23, 24, 25, 26, 276n, 277n

Blue Monday, 116

Blue Suede Shoes, 116

Bluebeard, 195, 196, 201, 204, 206

Bob Newhart Show, The, 267

Boddy, William, 278n

Bodeen, Dewitt, 84, 281n

Bogdanovich, Peter, 203, 204, 287n

Bonds, Gary U.S., 131

Bonedaddys, The, 262, 269

Boorstin, Daniel, 277n

Bop talk, 121

Born a Woman, 116

Boston, 125

Bouchard, Donald, 287n

Bourdieu, Pierre, 14, 275n, 276n

Bow Wow Wow, 131

Bowie, David, 103–4, 282n

Bradley, Jan, 116

Brando, Marlon, 84

Bream, Jon, 290n

Bright, Brenda, 153, 285n

Bristol, Michael, 7, 275n

Broken Arrow, 114

Bronx (NY), 40, 48, 62

Brooklyn (NY), 40, 58, 279n

Brother John, 245

Brown Eyed Handsome Man, 115

Brown, Charles, 118, 141

Brown, James, 34, 35, 36, 265–66

Brown, Roy, 143

Burnette, Dorsey, 127

Caballero-Robledo, Roberto, 284n

California Sun, 114

Callendar, Red, 143

Camille, 195

Can a White Boy Sing the Blues?, 265

Cannibal and the Headhunters, 145–46. *See also* Garcia

Can't Take It No More, 250

Capitalism, 6

Capra, Frank, 204

Carlos Brothers, The, 145

Carnegie Hall, 196

Carnival, 14, 15–16, 235, 245

Carradine, John, 197

Carson, Jeannie, 58

Carter, Jimmy, xii

Casher, Izidore, 198

Cather, Willa, 21, 36, 270, 276n, 277n

Cavern, The, 203

Celtic Soul Brother, 261

Ceremony, 214, 220–23, 224, 226, 287n

Changing New York, 186

Index

Index

Index

Griffin, Bessie, 115
Grossberg, Lawrence, 22, 103, 107, 109, 276n, 282n
Group Theatre, x
Guevara, Ruben, 153, 154, 155, 156, 284n, 286n
Guiol, Fred, 281n
Gurevitch, Michael, 280n
Gutierrez, Ramon, 12
Gutman, Herbert, 11

Habermas, Jürgen, 68, 71–72, 158–59, 280n, 285n
Haley, Bill (and his Comets), 113, 118, 252
Haley, Lindsay, 284n, 285n
Hall, Stuart, 12, 13, 68, 69, 72, 108, 260, 275n, 276n, 280n, 282n, 283n
Handa Wanda, 241, 250
Handclapping Song, 251
Hannusch, Jeff, 289n, 290n
Hard Times in the Mill, 113
Hardy, Phil, 286n
Harlem, 40, 140
Harrison, Jerry, 269–70
Hartman, Chester, 278n
Hartmann, Susan, 278n, 279n
Havers, Hale Lamont, 95, 281n
Hawketts, The, 246
Hawkins, Barbara, 250
Hawkins, Screamin' Jay, 114
Hearst, William Randolph, 183
Hegemony, 16, 212–13, 247
Hendrix, Jimi, 129–30
Herrera, L'il Julian, 142–43
Herron, Willie, 154–55
Hey Ba-ba Re-bop, 121
Hey, Jeannie, 40, 48, 50, 58–59, 69, 70, 278n, 279n, 280n
Higgins, Chuck, 140, 284n
Hilburn, Robert, 282n, 285n
Hill Street Blues, 267–68
Hillier, Jim, 286n
Hirsch, E. D., 23, 24, 25, 26, 34, 276n, 277n
Hirschbein, Peretz, 198
Hirshey, Gerri, 277n
History, vii–viii, 6–12, 21

Hitch Hike, 128
Hitchcock, Alfred, 204
Hoare, Quintin, 283n, 285n
Hoberman, Jim, 182, 186, 286n
Hobsbawm, Eric, 180
Hoekstra, Dave, 290n
Holly, Buddy, 113, 118, 121, 122, 128, 130, 131, 282n, 283n
Home ownership: loan policies, 46, 137; mortgage debt, 46
Honey Don't, 127
Honeymooners, 40, 48, 50, 55, 56, 59–60, 61, 66, 69, 280n
Hooker, John Lee, 117
Hootchie Cootchie Man, 114
Hoover, Herbert, 42–43
Hopkins, Jerry, 282n
Horton, Johnny, 114
Hound Dog, 140
Houston (TX), ix, x
Huggins, Nathan Irvin, 63–64, 280n
Hunter, Alan, 286n
Hunter, Lloyd, 141
Hunter, Tab, 124
Hurston, Zora Neale, 211–12, 213, 214, 223, 228–29, 287n

I Can't Believe That You're in Love with Me, 206
I Love Lucy, 267
I Remember Mama, 82, 84–87, 278n, 281n. *See also Mama*
I Want Candy, 114, 131
I Want You, 169
Iko Iko, 250, 252–53
I'm Real, 265
Indian Red, 241, 243
Indianapolis (IN), 117, 266
Ingram, Rex, 200
Installment buying, 48, 49
International Ladies Garment Workers Union, 198
Irish-Americans, 262
Irwin, Carol, 281n
Isle of Forgotten Sins, 200
Isley Brothers, The, 127, 129
It's My Party, 116

Index

Index

Index

George Lipsitz is an associate professor of American studies and history at the University of Minnesota. He received his master's degree from the University of Missouri-St. Louis and his doctorate from the University of Wisconsin-Madison. Lipsitz has been an assistant professor of historical studies at the University of Houston and a visiting professor at Mount Holyoke College and the University of Missouri-St. Louis. He is author of *Class and Culture in Cold War America: A Rainbow at Midnight* (1985) and *A Life in the Struggle: Ivory Perry and the Culture of Opposition* (1989), and a contributor to *Critical Studies in Mass Communication*, the *Journal of American History, Cultural Critique, Cultural Anthropology*, and *Society*.